EVIDENCE

Text and Materials

AUSTRALIA
LBC Information Services
Sydney

CANADA AND USA
Carswell,
Toronto, Ontario

NEW ZEALAND
Brooker's
Auckland

SINGAPORE AND MALAYSIA
Thomson Information (S.E. Asia)
Singapore

EVIDENCE:
Text and Materials

Steve Uglow
Reader in Criminal Justice,
Kent Law School, University of Kent

London
Sweet & Maxwell
1997

Published in 1997 by
Sweet & Maxwell Limited
100 Avenue Road
London NW3 3PF

Typeset by LBJ Enterprises Ltd,
Aldermaston and Chilcompton
Printed and bound in Great Britain by
Clays Ltd, of St Ives plc

No natural forests were destroyed to make this product;
only farmed timber was used and re-planted.

ISBN 0 421 571306

A CIP catalogue record for this book is available from the British Library

IN THE MEMORY OF EMMA SMITH WHO DIED OF
EPILEPSY IN JULY 1995 AGED 25

PREFACE

The rules of evidence are often given a bad name — as I write this, I have just read a discussion on an e-mail list of evidence teachers. The case involved a stolen cockatoo who the thief alleged was known as Billy but who, on meeting its true owner, squawked "Hallo, I'm Primrose". Could the owner testify as to the bird's statement as evidence of its identity or should such testimony be excluded as hearsay! It is not surprising that the public (and more vocally the police) are often amazed (and sometimes angered) that what they see as relevant information, such as the accused's previous convictions, is not allowed to be given in evidence. Acquittals which are on the basis of excluded evidence are often referred to as an acquittal on a "technicality".

Some 25 years ago, I listened, somewhat bemused, to Rupert Cross patiently explaining the law of evidence. At that time, it appeared to me as a mass of ancient cases with arcane names with some, deeply obscure, statutes occasionally intervening.

Undoubtedly it was my own shortcomings that led me to the conclusion that evidence was rather like a ball of wool that was no longer capable of being unravelled. It was woolly as well in its apparent absence of underlying structure and basic principles.

But like a good student, I took my notes and passed the exams. Nowadays I concede that this early judgment on the coherence of the subject was probably (but only probably) wrong. To treat the field simply as a matter of technicalities is also (probably) unfair.

Like football, evidence can be a simple game if the key concepts of relevance, probative value and fairness are adhered to. It is only too easy to lose sight of those basic precepts and the principles of procedural justice that underlie them. Certainly the rules are complex, but that is the result of putting those principles into practice. Returning to my lecture notes over a decade later as a prelude to teaching the subject, I was struck by how well Cross achieved that balance between simplicity and sophistication. His lectures were still fresh, clear and brimming with intellectual curiosity and insight. At the time I may not have understood, but my notes reveal that at least I knew what passages to write down! Rupert Cross is still the modern collossus in the field, with his work ably carried on by Colin Tapper. His book is both bible and goldmine for any researcher in the subject. But opening the volume is a daunting prospect even for the final year law student; the book is an essential reference tool but perhaps not the starting point for one's first steps into the subject. It is here that I find the justification for this book. Despite the erudition and scholarship of modern evidence scholars such as Zuckerman, Birch, Twining, Choo, Pattenden, John Smith and Keane among many others, in teaching evidence I have felt the lack of a book which is accessible to and easily digested by law students. Primarily aimed at students, the "text and materials" format was pioneered, in the criminal law area, by Heather Keating and Chris Clarkson and I have, unashamedly, copied their approach and objectives, namely to produce a book which has the "flow and coherence" of a textbook but which seeks to expose students to a variety of material from a diversity of sources. It is a format which lends itself to exploring evidence from a range of perspectives. It is not a topic, unlike criminal law, that lends itself naturally to a contextual approach. But wherever possible, I have sought to achieve this, especially in sections on the nature of adversarial trial, on the reliability of witnesses, on confession and identification evidence. It has been much harder to achieve when discussing estoppel! I owe a great deal to my long term colleagues at Kent Law School — Wade Mansell, Richard de Friend, Ian Grigg-Spall, Alan Thomson and Peter Fitzpatrick among others — who have created an ethos of openness towards the study of law which is occasionally (although not enough) reflected in this text. I also would like to record the considerable help of the Kent Law School Office team, headed by Liz Cable. Jenny, Tom, Hannah, Jamie and Luke showed their normal and admirable forbearance during the long months of preparation and writing. But most of all, I owe a huge debt of gratitude to Venous Telford, who, despite claims of family and bar school, worked so hard gathering material, reading drafts, checking references and making constructive suggestions. Without her, the book would contain less of value and more errors. She deserves credit for the former but I alone am responsible for any mistakes that remain.

October 1996
Steve Uglow

CONTENTS

6. IMMUNITIES FROM TESTIFYING: PUBLIC INTEREST IMMUNITY 175

7. IMMUNITIES FROM TESTIFYING: PRIVATE PRIVILEGES AND CONFIDENTIAL INFORMATION 203

8. THE TESTIMONY OF WITNESSES: THEIR RELIABILITY, COMPETENCE AND COMPELLABILITY 241

9. THE TESTIMONY OF WITNESSES: THE NEED FOR SUPPORTIVE EVIDENCE 275

10. THE TESTIMONY OF WITNESSES: PRE-TRIAL DISCLOSURE AND EXAMINATION-IN-CHIEF 313

17. COMMON LAW EXCEPTIONS TO HEARSAY 521

18. STATUTORY EXCEPTIONS TO HEARSAY IN CRIMINAL PROCEEDINGS: THE CRIMINAL JUSTICE ACT 1988 AND OTHER ANIMALS 557

ACKNOWLEDGEMENTS

Grateful acknowledgement is made for permission to reproduce from the undermentioned works:

BLACKSTONE PRESS LTD:
Spencer and Flin, *The Evidence of Children* (1993)

BLACKWELL PUBLISHERS:
Stephenson, *The Psychology of Criminal Justice* (1992)

BUTTERWORTHS LAW PUBLISHERS LTD:
The All England Law Reports
Sanders and Young, *Criminal Justice* (1994)
Cross and Tapper, *Cross on Evidence* (7th & 8th ed.)
Anderson and Twining, *Analysis of Evidence* (1991)
Eggleston, *Evidence, Proof and Probability* (1983)

THE INCORPORATED COUNCIL OF LAW REPORTING FOR ENGLAND AND WALES:
Various extracts from the *Law Reports*

MACMILLAN PRESS LTD:
Atkinson and Drew, *Order in Court* (1979)
McBarrett, *Conviction* (1983)

OXFORD UNIVERSITY PRESS:
Zuckerman, *The Principles of Criminal Evidence* (1989)

Acknowledgement is made for extracts from the following works:

CAVENDISH PUBLISHING LTD:
Mansell, Meteyard and Thomson, *A Critical Introduction to Law* (1995)

TIMES NEWSPAPERS LTD:
The Times, leader comment, August 23, 1996

UNIVERSITY OF CHICAGO PUBLISHING:
Waddle and Potts, "Rape Trauma Syndrome", *University of Chicago Legal Forum* (1989)

WILEY AND SONS LTD:
Lloyd-Bostock and Clifford, *Evaluating Witness Evidence* (1983)

While every care has been taken to establish and acknowledge copyright, and contact the copyright owners, the publishers tender their apologies for any accidental infringement. They would be pleased to come to a suitable arrangement with the rightful owners in each case.

TABLE OF CASES

TABLE OF STATUTES

[*Page references in* **bold** *type indicate extracts of the statute*]

TABLE OF STATUTORY INSTRUMENTS

1

THE ADVERSARIAL, THE LOGICAL AND THE LEGAL

Introduction

The law relating to evidence is a strange and unruly beast. It is unruly because, first, it refuses to fit into any easy structure for analysis and exposition and, second, it often adopts the characteristics of an uncharted minefield, by which is meant that any set of facts has the potential of throwing up evidential problems, not just of one but of several types, often unforeseen. It is strange because it fulfils different functions than the familiar areas of substantive law. It is in such areas that we see legal rules at their most visible, dealing with the *consequences* of facts — if a contract is broken, damages are paid; if a theft is committed, punishment is imposed. Damages, imprisonment and other civil and criminal remedies are the sanctions accompanying rules which require or prohibit certain types of conduct or which lay down conditions under which that conduct can take place. These rules are often referred to as the substantive law. Within most contested trials, such rules form the background to the case but play little part since there is no conflict over the substance of the rule. We know what the rule says and what the consequences of a breach will be: if there has been a road accident and a driver has been negligent, damages for personal injuries will be paid to any plaintiff; if a sane defendant intentionally kills another person, he or she will be prosecuted and generally receive a life sentence.

But the real conflict in a court, before any substantive rule is brought to bear, is about establishing the facts: was the driver negligent? did the defendant cause the victim's death? what happened? The law of evidence is not about determining the consequences of facts but about *establishing those facts*. In a contested trial, under the common law system of justice, the opposing parties will present differing, sometimes diametrically opposed, views of the same event. Having listened to these accounts, the trier of fact[1] must decide what the facts are. It is this problem as to how "facts" are established with which the law of evidence is concerned: what

[1] This means the magistrates in summary trials, juries in Crown Court cases and, normally, the judge in the county court or High Court.

information can be presented to the court; through what means; how does a court decide whether that information proves whether an event happened in a particular way or not? Such rules, alongside the rules of civil and criminal procedure, can be described, not as *substantive*, but as *adjectival* law. This means that these rules attach themselves to and qualify the operation of a substantive rule but never, by themselves, directly decide the rights and wrongs of any issue. The law of evidence qualifies the operation of a substantive rule because it controls the flow and nature of the information which can be presented to the court. Indirectly, of course, the law of evidence can be decisive since the outcome of a case can depend on whether a particular item of evidence is allowed to be presented to the court or not. For example, a guilty verdict or an acquittal can hang on whether the prosecution can meet the preconditions for the admissibility of a confession in a criminal trial; in a civil case where the weight of the evidence is evenly balanced, the decision may hinge on the question as to where the burden of proof rests.

Many of these evidential issues seem very technical to a layperson and, especially in criminal trials, to exclude relevant and important information from the proceedings. Examples might be given of the rule against the admission of hearsay evidence — a witness would be usually prevented from testifying that the victim, now dead, had identified the accused as the assailant; similarly the jury would rarely be allowed to hear about any previous convictions of the defendant. But these are not technicalities for their own sake and reflect the nature and characteristics of the common law trial.

The Common Law Trial

An understanding of the modern rules of evidence cannot be divorced from a knowledge of the common law system of trial, especially its adversarial nature. The common law gives predominance to the day in court, with oral testimony by witnesses physically present in court with the opportunities for cross-examination of opposing witnesses and for argument on both sides. An example of the potential effects of this emerged in an episode of *The Bill* when, at the start of a drugs trial, an important police witness was discovered to be on his honeymoon in Thailand![2] His written statement was not admissible and the whole prosecution foundered, an outcome that would not happen in, for example, France where the trial is less pivotal — the judge in a criminal trial will have a full *dossier* prepared by the *juge d'instruction*, who may well have conducted several hearings, taken relevant witness statements and interrogated the defendant. The trial will be on the basis of these documents and is merely the final stage of a *judicial* process.

In both England and France, our trials are presented as formally rational proceedings. But dispute resolution can take different forms. The Eskimos, for example, use several, apparently ludicrous, techniques:

[2] Compare the facts in *R. v. Bray* (1988) 88 Cr.App.R. 354.

Mansell W., Meteyard B. and Thomson A., *A Critical Introduction to Law* (1995) 54–55

The song-duel is an important form of dispute resolution but it is not the only form. It stands alongside boxing and head-butting contests as a means of resolving disputes not involving homicide. Clearly in both boxing and head-butting competitions the facts which have led to the dispute are completely irrelevant. Like trial by battle there is no concern with issues of justice but only with a resolution, whatever that might be. He who wins acquires vindication and esteem, he who loses, loses standing in the eyes of the community. Song-duels are altogether more subtle in their operation . . . a typical song-duel will take place in a public gathering with each of the disputants (or his representative) singing in turn a song of contempt and abuse directed at the opponent. Like the boxing or buffeting contest the song need have no relevance to the dispute in hand or its facts. Rather it is concerned to score points through ridicule and it is said that singing skill may equal or outrank gross physical prowess. . . .

There are a number of features of the song-duels which are relevant to our consideration of law. . . . Even more significantly the winner of the song-duel wins the dispute even though neither the case itself nor the facts of the case are ever alluded to. The rights and wrongs of the social dispute are determined not by a discussion of the merits of the case but by talking about something which *can* be decided.

The great advantage of this process is that a social dispute to which there is simply no ready or obvious solution which would be accepted as correct by both parties is translated into a form which is amenable to decision. It is because of the very insolubility of the social problem that the problem is not faced but rather sidestepped. . . .

Admittedly at first sight this bizarre process for resolving disputes seems to be of little relevance to our perception of our way of dealing with disputes but several points need to be made. The most obvious is that in our experience most law students on first visiting the courts, and particularly courts hearing appeals are immediately impressed (as often are the litigants themselves) by the fact that the court does not seem to be hearing argument 'about the real issue'. Rather what they experience is a debate over what seems to be a technical point of law. It is of course just such legal points that determine cases.

Similarly in Anglo-Norman and Angevin England, disputes were settled through trial by battle[3] or by the ordeal, the '*judgment of god*'. But do modern legal systems, which seem so obvious and sensible, differ that fundamentally? Western European courts translate the events in dispute into substantive legal concepts that, only too often, do not appear to the participants to be about 'the real issue'. Having transformed social disputes into legal terms, we deal with these by court techniques, especially the rules of evidence, which aspire to reconstruct the past, by definition an impossible task. The Inuit anthropologist may be as bemused at observing this as his Western European counterparts are when they watch a song-duel.

This preliminary point is that we should not take our legal systems or techniques as self-evident. However, for our purposes, the most common

[3] Availability of wager by battle was discussed in *Ashford v. Thornton* (1818) 106 E.R. 149.

comparison is between common law and civilian jurisdictions. The former, such as England and the USA, employ the *adversarial* mode of trial and possess a sophisticated jurisprudence on the rules of evidence. The latter jurisdictions, such as France and Germany, adopt an *investigative or inquisitorial* mode of trial and as a result place much less emphasis on *formal* rules of proof which are so significant in common law proceedings.

In England, the adversarial form still dominates criminal proceedings and, to a lesser extent, civil actions. In this section the emphasis will be on the criminal case as the paradigm of the common law trial. In brief, the presentation of information (evidence), the argument and the decision all take place within a trial which is separated, geographically, chronologically and formally, from all the previous events such as the police investigation, the review of the evidence by the prosecution, or any preliminary hearings before magistrates.[4] It is only the information which is given in evidence at the trial itself which can form the basis of any decision. The judge, in common with the jury and the spectators in the public gallery, will be hearing the evidence for the first time. Common law judges have no investigative functions, such as instructing the police to undertake specific inquiries or calling and examining witnesses on their own initiative.[5] The judge plays a formally passive role, listening to evidence which is advanced by the prosecution and the defence.[6] This is a major difference between common law countries and other European jurisdictions.[7] The common law trial is a partisan system: both parties only call those witnesses likely to advance their cause and both are permitted to attack the credibility and reliability of the witnesses testifying for the other side. The criminal case is prepared for trial by the Crown Prosecution Service (CPS) or defence lawyers and in court, the lawyers decide which evidence is to be produced and which witnesses are to be called.

The rules of evidence draw their significance from this process since it is solely on the evidence retailed in court, usually by formal oral testimony, that the decision is based. This autonomy of the trial verges on quarantine: the court's decision is not allowed to be infected by information that derives from any source other than through the formal rules of evidence,

[4] The Criminal Procedure and Investigations Act 1996, Pt. 3 now allows for preparatory hearings before a judge in criminal cases.

[5] A judge does have discretion to call and question a witness but the power should only be used sparingly in the interests of justice: *R. v. Oliva* [1965] 3 All E.R. 116; *R. v. Roberts* (1984) 80 Cr.App.R. 89.

[6] See Chap. 2 on the functions of the judge in a trial.

[7] Ploscowe M., "Development of Inquisitorial and Accusatorial Elements in French Procedure" 23 *Journal of Criminal Law, Criminology and Police Science* 372; Tomlinson A., "Non-adversarial Justice: The French Experience" 42 *Maryland Law Review* (1983) 131 at 146 ff.; Brouwer G., "Inquisitorial and Adversary Procedures — a Comparative Analysis" 55 A.L.J. (1981) 207 at 212ff. In Europe, several jurisdictions are considering reforms which would allow the defence lawyer to question prosecution witnesses directly — at present questions have to be asked indirectly through the presiding judge. This was one of the reforms in Italy's new Code of Criminal Procedure in 1989 — Zander M., "From Inquisitorial to Adversarial — the Italian Experiment" 141 New L.J. (1991) 678.

except the assistance that the court can obtain in interpreting the law from appellate court decisions; once the jury has retired, they remain together[8] and incommunicado and their discussions are absolutely privileged.[9]

Cooper J., "Criminal Investigations in France" 141 New L.J. (1991) 381

A serious criminal trial in England has been likened by one commentator to the "clash of gladiatorial armies in the night". The jury does not participate in the battle but as passive observers. Its members are asked to adjudicate over the conflict while being kept "in the dark" on a host of factors which a detached observer might consider highly relevant to the issue of the defendant's guilt or innocence. Evidence of the defendant's past convictions for similar offences, social welfare reports on the defendant and psychological profiles of witnesses are considered too prejudicial to be presented, for the time honoured reason that the jury is simply being asked to consider the evidence of the crime before it. Legal argument on the admissibility of evidence is similarly considered to be something to which the jury should not be privy.

The evidence that members of the jury are permitted to hear is presented to them under the direction of opposing legal warriors with cross-examination as the principal weapon of combat. Barristers involved in the case describe themselves as "opponents". To make things worse, the jury is asked to carry out its adjudication, with no previous knowledge of any aspect of the case or the characters involved, in the artificial and stress-laden tension of a courtroom.

In contrast civilian jurisdictions do not distinguish between the gathering of information and its presentation. There is judicial supervision of the process from the beginning of the investigation so that, for example, in France the trial judge will have a full dossier prepared by the *juge d'instruction*, including witness statements and the interrogation of the defendant. The examination of witnesses will be on the basis of these documents. In contrast, the English trial judge will usually know nothing about the case before the trial, will not have been engaged in supervising any investigation, in taking statements from witnesses or the accused or in making bail decisions.

Cooper J., *op. cit.*

Although there are significant differences between the way that a criminal trial is conducted in France and in England and Wales, at the heart of the distinction between the two systems lies the method of criminal investigation before a case comes to trial. The French system of investigation of serious criminal charges differs from our system in two fundamental respects: in the person who has control over the investigation, and in the way in which the evidence collected in the course of investigation is made available to the ultimate adjudicator, the *Cour d'Assises*.

. . . The police investigative powers are . . . far more limited in France than in this country, and it is normal for the police to relinquish control of an investigation within one or two days of arrest, even in the most serious cases. At this stage, the

[8] *R. v. Alexander* [1974] 1 All E.R. 539.
[9] *R. v. Thompson* [1962] 1 All E.R. 65.

investigation of the case can be taken over by . . . an examining magistrate, the *juge d'instruction*. It is when we examine both the training and the powers of the *juge d'instruction* that it immediately becomes apparent why the French process of criminal investigation and adjudication of serious criminal charges is so fundamentally different from our own.

Juges d'instruction are young judges recruited on graduation from the National School of the Magistracy . . . All French judges are career judges who have passed through the same route, though not all serve as examining magistrates before taking higher judicial offices. They are not recruited from the senior ranks of practising advocates as in the United Kingdom, and have not themselves been advocates. Their training is in the art of interrogation, criminal investigation, forensic analysis, the sifting and preparation of evidence, psychology and the conduct of a trial. They are attached to a particular court with the sole purpose of investigating serious crimes that have been assigned to them by the police or the *Procureur* . . .

It is important when evaluating the role, value and effect of the *juge d'instruction* in the criminal justice process to be clear as to what he or she is setting out to do. Contrary to popular mythology, it is a profoundly held axiom of the French system, rooted in French constitutional law, that a person cannot be guilty of a crime unless the state can establish guilt at a level that would create an "inner certainty" in the minds of any jury member. This is more than mere rhetoric. Guilty pleas are not permitted in the French criminal justice system. A confession of guilt is no more than another piece of the jigsaw through which the *juge d'instruction* sets out to complete a picture of the crime.

All civil law systems are grounded in a philosophy of state responsibility and the French system is no exception. Thus, with an infallible Cartesian logic, it is axiomatic to the French system that the *juge d'instruction*, who is charged by the state with establishing the truth, should suffer no procedural or technical hindrance in investigating any matter that may be relevant to establishing guilt or innocence. In this respect individuals' right to a high level of freedom from state intrusion upon their civil liberties can be said to be less important in France than in the United Kingdom. At the same time, it is felt by many observers that fewer guilty people are acquitted in France and more significantly, fewer innocent people are convicted. The investigative powers are so wide, that few stones can be left unturned.

A list of the powers of the *juge d'instruction* illustrates this point. They are very substantial. They include the power to interrogate the defendant anywhere, at any time; to interrogate any witness; to visit the scene of the crime with the defendant and any witness; to arrange identifications, or confrontations between accused and victim; to set up reconstructions of the crime to test evidence; and to investigate the social, economic and — if relevant — criminal background of the defendant and witnesses, and to draw inferences from such evidence. The investigation is not limited by time. And most significant of all, if the *juge* thinks there is a case to answer, he or she is obliged to pass on to the subsequent trial court a dossier which will contain all the relevant evidence on which this belief is grounded.

The powers seem awesome, and to the civil libertarian brought up in the British system, oppressive, but there are safeguards. First, the suspect is entitled to be represented by a lawyer at all stages of the investigation. Second, the relatively informal and extended nature of the investigation paradoxically allows the defendant far more scope for establishing his or her innocence than under the tightly regulated, formalistic, controlled contact that exists in England or Wales in the investigation of crime, limited as it is to the period before charge, and the occasion of the trial.

Third, the *juge d'instruction* is not partie prise. He or she is neither prosecutor (police/CPS) nor defence solicitor. The task of the *juge* is to establish whether the state can satisfactorily perform its constitutional function of establishing guilt at a level of "inner certainty". The fact that a *juge d'instruction* does not appear in court and has not been trained in the adversarial process cannot be overemphasised. The independence of the office of the *juge* from the trial process is quite genuine.

. . . It is not, of course, the *juge d'instruction* who determines the guilt of the accused in the French system, nor is it the accused themselves, by pleading guilty. It is the court. Because of the extensive nature of the investigation, however, and the availability to the court of all the findings of that investigation, court hearings in France are relatively short. The only court that sits with a jury is the *Cour d'Assises*, the lower courts being presided over exclusively by professional judges. As it is a principle of the French system that the adjudicators should have access to all the available evidence, as sifted and analysed by the *juge d'instruction*, the rules of evidence in the Cour d'Assises are scant. The procedure is formal, and very much under the direction of the presiding judge (who sits with two assessors). But it lacks the drama and tension of an English criminal trial as there is scant scope for cross-examination or surprise at such an advanced stage of the investigation. There is little eloquent advocacy, and it is normally only the judge who asks questions. It is clear that as only five per cent of defendants are acquitted in hearings in the *Cour d'Assises*, the trial process is largely concluded in advance of the hearing. The final decision as to guilt or innocence is, however, made formally by the jury and judges, sitting as an equal panel, on a majority of at least eight to four. . . .

. . . Much is (rightly) made of the quality of advocacy available to those accused of grave crimes in this country at the expense of the state. But this argument is also as an uncritical defence of the status quo, which, it is said, protects vulnerable people from miscarriages of justice. The argument should perhaps be turned around by those who defend it. For if the quality of investigation of crime could be improved to a level where a near certainty of guilt or innocence can be achieved by the investigation process, there can be little justification for maintaining the criminal court system in its current overblown and grossly expensive form.

Adversarialism — origins and characteristics

The adversarial trial is one of the major constitutional institutions of the common law and the modern composition, jurisdiction and procedures are significantly the product of its history. In its origins, a central question of any hearing lay in discovering the truth of an accusation.[10] Truth was not a matter of witnesses and evidence but instead might be found through ordeal, trial by battle[11] or by compurgation.[12] But in 1166, the Assize of Clarendon provided for a "jury of presentment"[13] which was a group of local people put on their oath to tell the truth about local crimes. This was not a trial jury but one of accusation. The allegations were tested through the ordeal of water[14] which was the only means of proof for those indicted by the presenting jury.

[10] Milsom S., *Historical Foundations of the Common Law* (1981) Chap. 14; Plucknett T., *A Concise History of the Common Law* (5th ed., 1956).

[11] Initially introduced after the Conquest for appeals of felony where a Norman was the accused.

[12] Suspicion was often the basis of accusation and proof by compurgation involved the accused producing a set number of neighbours to swear to his or her overall good character.

[13] This was later known as the grand jury which was not abolished in England until 1933 to be replaced by committal proceedings but still survives in the USA.

[14] The accused was bound and lowered by a rope into a deep pool — if he or she sank to the level of a knot tied in the rope at the distance of his or her hair, he or she was declared innocent but if he or she floated, the water would not receive him or her and he or she was judged guilty. Warren W., *The Governance of Norman and Angevin England 1086–1272* (1987) 109.

The ordeal was the *judicium dei*, the legitimacy of which came from God and as such the proceeding required the presence of a priest. But at the Lateran Council in 1215 the Church declared the ordeal to be mere superstition.[15] Without the religious imprimatur, other methods of proof had to be found. Continental Europe turned to the Roman-canonical law of proof[16] with its calculus of evidence ranging from the full confession to eye-witnesses down to mere circumstantial evidence or *indicia*. There was a formal, objective logic to this approach which sought to assess the weight of each item of evidence and to aggregate these to judge whether there was a "full proof". This approach still has its modern adherents, not least in Scotland. But this logical calculus did not take hold in England which turned instead to the jury of trial. This was known as a petty jury, distinguishable from the "grand jury" of accusation. The petty jury who could decide on the truth of the allegations was initially apparently the choice of the accused. But it slowly became the custom of the royal courts and after the Statute of Westminster in 1275, those who refused to "put themselves upon the country" could be imprisoned. The trial was still not a fact-finding forum, however, since the jurors were people who already knew the circumstances of the accusation.[17]

In small, rural, homogenous communities, juries may well have been an effective means for the determination of the truth, let alone the resolution of quarrels and disputes amongst members of the community. For centuries, the initiation of criminal prosecution was a matter for local grand juries or private individuals with little involvement by the State. How the accused was to confront or refute accusations (except through the knowledge of the local jury) remains shrouded in mystery:

> Of the actual conduct of a trial we know almost nothing before the sixteenth century, not nearly enough until the eighteenth. How the jury informed itself or was informed, how rules of evidence emerged, when and in what detail directions were given by the justices, these are things we do not know.[18]

The embryonic roots of the adversarial system were challenged during the absolutist monarchies of the Tudors and Stuarts which developed "inquisitorial" courts such as Star Chamber, which operated without juries, on a basis of unidentified accusation and with the defendant interrogated by the judges under oath and perhaps under torture.[19] Political and popular reaction in the seventeenth century to such courts was to delineate the conditions under which the monarch or state has the power to restrict a

[15] Warren: *ibid.* 213.
[16] Langbein J., *Torture and the Law of Proof* (1977).
[17] Milsom, *op. cit.* 411. It is not until after the 17th century that personal knowledge of the case becomes a disqualification for a juror. Lord Justice Coke still talked of trial being by jury and not by evidence.
[18] Milsom, *op. cit.* 412.
[19] Radcliffe and Cross, *The English Legal System* (5th ed., 1971) 107; Milsom, *op. cit.* 418–9; Holdsworth W., *History of English Law* (1936–72) Vol. 5, 155 *et seq.*

person's freedom and to inflict punishment. The common law trial was a significant element of this and adversarialism was the technique which emerged. The two basic building blocks were the two principles of natural justice: *nemo iudex in suam causam*, a man should not be a judge in his own cause, and *audi alteram partem*, the court should hear both sides of a case. Progress was slow. The neutrality of the court was embedded in Chief Justice Coke's declaration in 1610 that a man should not be judge in his own cause.[20] The second cardinal principle was recognised by the early eighteenth century.[21] But the criminal defendant had no means of getting his or her story heard since it was not possible to compel witnesses to testify (although they might do so voluntarily) nor was there professional assistance to examine witnesses or to speak on the accused's behalf until 1836. Furthermore the defendant could not give sworn testimony until 1898.[22] Even the "bulwark of freedom", the jury, could not be relied on to be impartial.[23] The central elements of the adversarial trial were not in place by the end of the nineteenth century. These may be summarised:

(1) the court (judge and jury) in making decisions, does not act as an investigative body, calling and examining witnesses on its own initiative. It plays a passive role, listening to evidence which is advanced by the prosecution and the defence.

(2) both parties only call those witnesses likely to advance their cause and both parties are permitted to attack the credibility and reliability of the witnesses testifying for the other side. In court, the lawyers decide which evidence is to be produced and which witnesses are to be called. The judge should not interfere or act as an investigator.

(3) the issues between the parties will be decided by the "day-in-court" and, in criminal cases, mainly by oral testimony. This derives from perhaps the main rationale underlying adversarialism, namely that any party has the right to confront their accuser and the evidence against him or her. Confrontation implies that the witness should be there in person in order that the reliability of the evidence and the credibility of the witness can be tested. This can lengthen trials because, even where the evidence to be given is uncontroversial, the witness is normally present. Criminal trials still do not use pre-trial written pleadings, although this occurs in civil cases. Such a process would reduce trial length by concentrating on those matters in dispute.

[20] *Dr. Bonham's Case* (1610) 8 Co. Rep. 113b.

[21] *The King v. University of Cambridge* (1723), 1 St. Tr. 557; see Wade H., *Administrative Law* (1961) Chap. V "Natural Justice".

[22] The accused was not a competent witness until Criminal Evidence Act 1898, s.1 — see 263.

[23] After the trial of the Quakers, Penn and Mead, in 1670, for a "conspiratorial gathering", the jury were fined and imprisoned until eventually released by the Chief Justice who declared "the right of juries to give their verdict by their conscience". Harman H. and Griffith J., *Justice Deserted* (1979) 11.

(4) the judge acts as umpire, ensuring that the rules on procedure and evidence are followed, directing the jury on the law to be applied and reminding them of the evidence that they have heard.
(5) the jury's role is firstly to decide questions of fact — that is, to make up their minds between conflicting accounts as to what happened — and then to decide on the guilt or innocence of the defendant.

The common law trial is regarded as the single, public proceeding, both the beginning and end of the affair. It is difficult to explain why the adversarial process rather than the investigative process should have emerged in England: the relatively short period of absolutist monarchy and the impact of the puritan revolution in reaction to that experience of undiluted state power is one factor; the historical dominance of the local state over the national may be another. It is undoubtedly linked to the retention of private prosecution and the image of a society that was the product of the actions of its more powerful members and not of an interventionist government. But the existence of the adversarial form and of the jury system has always meant that judges have needed to exercise considerable caution and control over the information that could be properly placed before a court.

Fairness

As well as adversarialism, the other major characteristic of the common law trial which dictates many aspects of the law of evidence is the priority given to procedural fairness. A fight model requires rules of engagement which are essentially based on the idea of fairness. There are three types of fairness: of the rule, of the procedure or of the decision. With regard to the first, the doctrine of sovereignty of Parliament has meant that the courts do not interfere in the substance of a statute. Nor, in relation to the last, is there intervention of any kind with jury deliberations or verdict.[24] Consequently, to talk about fairness in the courtroom is to discuss procedural justice with its assumption that truth is more likely to emerge from confrontation mediated through due process of law. This attitude is also reflected in the appeal system which is not a review of the decision but rather of the process by which the decision is reached. If the decision is one which could reasonably have been reached, the Court of Appeal will not interfere.

The root values of procedural justice are encapsulated in the House of Lords' decision in *Woolmington v. DPP*[25] when Lord Sankey said:

[24] But see the criticisms by the Royal Commission on Criminal Justice that the Court of Appeal has been too heavily influenced by the jury decision in its reconsideration of cases, especially those alleging miscarriages of justice: *Report* Cm. 2263 (1993) Chap. 10.
[25] [1935] A.C. 462.

Throughout the web of English criminal law one golden thread is always to be seen that it is the duty of the prosecution to prove the prisoner's guilt . . . If, at the end of and on the whole of the case, there is a reasonable doubt, created by the evidence given by either the prosecution or the prisoner, as to whether the prisoner killed the deceased with a malicious intention, the prosecution has not made out the case and the prisoner is entitled to an acquittal. No matter what the charge or where the trial, the principle that the prosecution must prove the guilt of the prisoner is part of the common law of England and no attempt to whittle it down can be entertained.[26]

Lord Sankey's "golden thread" of justice is that the prosecution have to prove every element in a criminal charge beyond reasonable doubt. In civil proceedings the burden of proof is normally on the plaintiff. The defendant has to prove nothing. More specifically the elements of fairness in criminal proceedings are:

- the right to know the nature of the charges and evidence
- the right to be represented by a lawyer
- the presumption of innocence which incorporates both the right to silence and the burden of proof on the prosecution
- the standard of proof to be applied is proof beyond reasonable doubt
- the right to a public trial in a neutral forum
- the right to cross-examine and test the prosecution evidence
- the right to call evidence and give evidence on the accused's behalf
- the right to appeal.

These also relate, *mutatis mutandis,* to civil proceedings. Such procedural rights underpin our perception of a "fair trial". These take precedence over the justice of the decision itself and over more pragmatic aims such as the determination of truth or law enforcement.

Frank J., *Courts on Trial* (1973) 103–104

[Substantive] rules, it is said, state what a man may or may not lawfully do out of court, before any litigation occurs. The orthodox theory holds that, from those rules, grow 'substantive legal rights', such as the right not to have others trespass on one's land or the right to have a contract performed . . .

But if one of a man's 'substantive' rights has been invaded, or threatened with invasion, and he does bring a law-suit, the suit is supposed to be governed by another kind of rules, rules of 'procedure', which relate to what must be done in court. Those conduct-in-court rules cover such subjects as the way a suit must be commenced, the way in which a party must state ('plead') his claim or defence, the

[26] *ibid.* at 481.

sort of evidence the courts will receive or reject. These 'procedural' rules are customarily designated as 'adjective', or 'remedial', or 'dependent' or 'subordinate'. These labels indicate that these rules are really subordinate, are mere means or 'machinery', used in vindicating the rights given by the 'substantive' rules, rules which supposedly pre-exist and are independent of what any court may do about them.

That notion of the 'subordinate' character of 'procedure' may easily mislead. For the failure of a lawyer to comply with a procedural rule . . . may spell a litigant's defeat in a law-suit, completely frustrating his 'substantive' right. Such a defeat, for 'procedural' errors, is fully as disastrous to him as if the court held that he had no such right.

Instead, then, of saying, 'If certain facts occur, a court will attach to them certain legal consequences,' we might say, 'If certain facts occur, and if the procedural rules are complied with, a court will attach these consequences.' A more accurate way of stating the matter is this: 'If certain facts are 'proved', in accordance with the requirements and within the limits allowed by the procedural rules, then a favourable decision should result.' Which is to say that, practically, 'procedure' shows up as fully as important as the 'substantive' rules. Indeed, the differentiation between the 'substantive' and 'procedural' rules, although useful for some purposes, is artificial from at least one viewpoint: All the rules, including the 'substantive' may be looked at as 'procedural' in the sense that they are all merely weapons in the courtroom fight.

Some[27] attack the ritual formality of the trial, arguing that priority is not given to truth determination and the substantive justice of the decision itself. For such commentators, the most sacred of cows is not immune: where is the logic in the presumption of innocence, even, when an accused's very appearance before a court makes it more likely than not (as most defendants plead guilty) that he or she committed the offence?[28] It is suggested that the Anglo-American criminal procedure detracts from the discovery of the truth. Were we to invent a mechanism to find out facts and allocate blame, the solution would not be an adversarial system, with partisan advocates, untrained judges, heavily reliant on cross-examination and where the final decision is left to 12 people plucked arbitrarily off the street. The goal of discovering the truth and making a reliable decision might require a trained chairperson with investigative powers, sitting with assessors expert in the relevant field and with the parties' representatives having a much lower profile. Lord Woolf's review[29] of the impact of adversarialism in civil process is equally critical:

Woolf, Lord, *Access to Justice: Interim Report* (June 1995)

3. By tradition the conduct of civil litigation in England and Wales, as in other common law jurisdictions, is adversarial. Within a framework of substantive and procedural law established by the state for the resolution of civil disputes, the main

[27] Mark R., *Minority Verdict* (BBC, Dimbleby Lecture 1973).
[28] Cross R., "The Right to Silence and the Presumption of Innocence — Sacred Cows or Safeguards of Liberty" (1970) 11 J.S.P.T.L. 66.
[29] Woolf, Lord, *Access to Justice: Interim Report* (June 1995); the final report was published in July 1996.

responsibility for the initiation and conduct of proceedings rests with the parties to each individual case, and it is normally the plaintiff who sets the pace. The role of the judge is to adjudicate on issues selected by the parties when they choose to present them to the court.

4. Without effective judicial control, however, the adversarial process is likely to encourage an adversarial culture and to degenerate into an environment in which the litigation process is too often seen as a battlefield where no rules apply. In this environment, questions of expense, delay, compromise and fairness may have only low priority. The consequence is that expense is often excessive, disproportionate and unpredictable; and delay is frequently unreasonable.

5. This situation arises precisely because the conduct, pace and extent of litigation are left almost completely to the parties. There is no effective control of their worst excesses. Indeed, the complexity of the present rules facilitates the use of adversarial tactics and is considered by many to require it. As Lord Williams, a former Chairman of the Bar Council, said in responding to the announcement of this Inquiry, the process of law has moved from being "servant to master, due to cost, length and uncertainty".

6. It is often said that the existing rules and practice directions contain the solution to the present problems, if only litigation were to be conducted in accordance with them. But the present system does not ensure this. Instead the rules are flouted on a vast scale. The timetables they contain are generally ignored and their other requirements are complied with when convenient to the interests of one of the parties and not otherwise.

7. The powers of the courts have fallen behind the more sophisticated and aggressive tactics of some litigators. The orders for costs which are made are an ineffective sanction applied after the damage is done. The delay in being able to obtain effective intervention by the court both encourages rule-breaking and discourages the party who would be prejudiced from applying for preventive measures.

8. It is significant that the main procedural tools for conducting litigation efficiently have each become subverted from their proper purpose. Whether through incompetence or deliberation, pleadings often fail to state the facts as the rules require. This leads to a fundamental deficiency, namely the failure to establish the issues in the case at a reasonably early stage, from which many problems result.

9. Witness statements, a sensible innovation aimed at a "cards on the table" approach, have in a very short time begun to follow the same route as pleadings, with the draftsman's skill often used to obscure the original words of the witness.

10. The scale of discovery, at least in the larger cases, is completely out of control. The principle of full, candid disclosure in the interests of justice has been devalued because discovery is pursued without sufficient regard to economy and efficiency in terms of the usefulness of the information which is likely to be obtained from the documents disclosed.

11. The approach to expert evidence also shows the characteristic range of difficulties: instead of the expert assisting the court to resolve technical problems, delay is caused by the unreasonable insistence on going to unduly eminent members of the profession and evidence is undermined by the partisan pressure to which party experts are subjected.

But do such arguments, especially in relation to criminal proceedings, ignore the symbolic force which lies in a trial's procedural justice? The rules of evidence and procedure emphasise the distinction between the trial as a logical function and the trial as a symbol. In its outward form, the trial is about the determination of truth and the application of that truth to legal rules. Were we to compare the courtroom with a police station, what would be the public reaction if a court were to interrogate a defendant over days and nights with limited rest, no legal assistance, perhaps using the threat of violence or the inducement of release to obtain responses to questions? In the court, the accused's rights are paramount because the covert function of the trial is its concrete illustration of a fair and just society:

Arnold T., *The Symbols of Government* (1962) 141–143

. . . If the Alabama court in the Scottsboro case dared to say as a matter of principle negroes were not entitled to sit on juries and that negroes who had intercourse with white women were to be treated as white men who had committed rape, we would find a calm atmosphere about the trial which is now completely lacking. The negroes might be convicted but the trial would have been fair. The Southern court, however, did not have that confidence in the reasonableness of its conduct which permitted it to spread frankly on the record. Therefore the trial became a maze of attempts to keep relevant material out of the record. Blunders occurred so obviously against the accepted form of a trial that the Supreme Court of the United States reversed the case.[30]

Yet the cultural value of the ideal of a fair trial is advanced as much by its failure as it is by its success. Any violation of the symbol of a ceremonial trial rouses persons who would be left unmoved by an ordinary non-ceremonial injustice. Thus the Scottsboro Case gained nationwide attention. The defendants may finally be hanged, but the cause of tolerance has been dramatised in a way no one will quite forget. Harmless anarchists may be shot by the police in a strike. Liberals will be sorry and forget. But let them be unfairly treated by a court . . . and, before the dissatisfaction has died away, the prejudice or phobia which created the unfair atmosphere of the trial will receive a public analysis and examination which otherwise it would not get . . .

It is of course true that all the machinery surrounding the ideal of a fair trial has its social cost in delays, technicalities and injustices in the judicial process. It is equally true that in times of public fear and intolerance this machinery is seldom strong enough to prevent the conviction of weak and harmless persons. Yet the cultural effect of these failures on mass psychology is probably worth everything it costs because of its contribution to the ultimate survival of a great humanitarian ideal.

Evidence and Proof — Preliminary Matters

The rules of evidence are a central feature of a fair trial. As we shall see, the rules are supported by certain principles of fairness, especially the ideas of relevance, reliability, probative worth and absence of prejudice. But first it is necessary to define some of the terms which will constantly occur:

(a) evidence: at its most general level, this term means those items of information which are presented to the court by the parties as a means of persuading the court that their argument is correct — in other words, information advanced to prove their case. The court does not permit all

[30] *Powell v. Alabama* 278 U.S. 45 (1932), *Patterson v. Alabama* 294 U.S. 600 (1934).

information to be placed before it — it must be relevant, have probative weight, be non-prejudicial and not subject to any rule of exclusion. If the information possesses these characteristics, it is *admissible evidence*, often known as judicial evidence.

The information placed before the court can be of different types: oral testimony by witnesses, normally of their perceptions, especially what they have seen or heard, but perhaps also the opinions of expert witnesses; documents, often written but now frequently containing visual or sound recordings or electronic data; real evidence, namely material objects such as fingerprints, automatic recordings or a witness's demeanour.

(b) direct and circumstantial: evidence can also be divided into *direct* and *circumstantial* evidence. Direct evidence is evidence which, if believed, establishes a *fact in issue*. For example, an eyewitness to a stabbing testifies to the fact of the wounding, an element of the offence. Such testimony, if believed, would constitute direct evidence, as would the accused's confession. Circumstantial evidence, on the other hand, consists of evidence of circumstances, none of which speak directly to the facts in issue but from which those facts may be inferred. Feelings of animosity towards the victim, presence in the area of the attack, the victim's blood on the accused's clothing — all of these can build up into a strong but inferential case.

(c) collateral: collateral evidence is information which does not in itself seek to prove any of the facts in issue in a case. In any trial there is the question of credibility, namely whether the direct or circumstantial evidence which has been adduced is to be believed. This depends on several factors, such as the testimony's consistency with the other evidence in the case. But very significantly we weigh the probative value of evidence by the credibility that we attach to its source. The word of a priest is treated with greater weight than that of a convicted confidence trickster. In cross-examining witnesses, a party is entitled to question on such collateral issues such as character, not because it bears on any fact in issue but because it affects the weight which the trier of fact will attach to the testimony.

(d) facts in issue: facts in issue are as much legal concepts as they are are facts and are normally to be found in the substantive law, in the statute or precedent which creates the offence or the cause of action. Sometimes the facts in issue are to be found in the pleadings in civil proceedings or in the defences raised by the accused in a criminal case: was the defendant acting in self-defence, under duress or under a mental handicap?

For example, on a theft charge, the prosecution must prove five elements: that the defendant appropriated property belonging to another, dishonestly and with the intention to permanently deprive. These are the facts in issue.[31] In a simple theft case, if the prosecution can show that the

[31] Often known as the *facta probanda*, the facts that need to be proved.

accused walked out of a shop with goods which were not paid for, the court is likely to conclude from these, intermediate, facts that all the elements of the offence, the facts in issue, are satisfied. In a civil action, there may be an issue as to whether there was a contract in existence and the court would have to be satisfied that there had been an offer, an acceptance, consideration and any necessary intention. The party bearing the burden of proof must persuade the court of the existence of these if he or she wishes to have a favourable finding.

(e) facts: it is necessary to distinguish these legal "facts in issue" from the more mundane information provided by witnesses. Who was where when? and with whom? what did they do? But such testimony is not (yet) facts or proof (although many police witnesses have been known to start their testimony with, "*The facts in this case are . . .*"). What the witness provides for the court is simply items of information, data, which the trier of fact has to assess. The trier may or may not believe the testimony, may draw inferences from it but must decide what the facts in the case are, in other words, "What happened".

At this stage it is useful to recognise that the term "fact" is being used in three different senses:

- the information provided by witnesses and other evidence
- the conclusions drawn by the trier of fact from the information presented in court as to what actually happened
- the legal concepts, facts in issue, that must be established if a particular party to legal proceedings is to succeed.

In the shoplifting example, the jury can hear a store detective's information about a shoplifter taking whisky from the shelf, concealing it under a coat and leaving the shop. They may hear the defendant explain how she had simply forgotten the bottle when she paid for other items. This is straightforwardly evidence, some of which may be believed by the jury, some of which may be disbelieved. From the evidence, the jury may conclude that she did take the bottle and that she never intended to pay for it. These are now the facts as found by the court and both are clearly important and relevant, but logically they are intermediary facts since there is a further step to be taken since the jury must use these facts to determine whether they establish the facts in issue. The taking of the bottle and the intent not to pay are not themselves the facts in issue but are facts which are relevant to the facts in issue.[32] The jury must now use those facts to consider whether there was a dishonest appropriation contrary to section 1 of the Theft Act 1968.

[32] They are referred to as *facta probantes* — facts from which we derive other facts in issue.

(f) admissibility: litigants are not free to place whatever information they wish before the court to establish the facts. The information must be admissible evidence, often referred to as judicial evidence. Evidence is not admissible if it is not relevant, if it is of insufficient weight, if its prejudicial effect is greater than its probative value, if its admission would have an adverse effect on the fairness of the proceedings or if it is excluded by any specific rule of evidence.

(g) relevance: this is a central concept. Relevant evidence is prima facie admissible unless excluded for some other reason whereas irrelevant evidence is not admissible. The probative value of evidence depends on its relevance allied to the weight accorded to it. We define relevant information as information which tends to make the existence or non-existence of another relevant fact or fact in issue more or less probable. Under the U.S. Federal Rules of Evidence:

401.—'Relevant evidence' means evidence having any tendency to make the existence of any fact that is of consequence to the determination of the action more probable or less probable than it would be without the evidence.[33]

Several recent cases on possession of drugs with intent to supply have centred on the problem of relevance. In *R. v. Batt*[34] the accused was charged with possession of cannabis resin with intent to supply. The drugs were found in a rabbit hutch in the garden and in an egg cup; there were a set of scales with traces of cannabis resin on them and £150 was found in an ornamental kettle. The appellant denied any knowledge of the drugs in the garden and said that the drugs in the egg cup belonged to her husband. She appealed on the basis that the evidence of the money should not have been admitted. The conviction was quashed because the money was not relevant to any intent to supply in the future:

Commentary by Professor J. C. Smith on *Batt* [1994] Crim.L.R. 592–593.

The court does not seem to have questioned the admissibility of the possession of the scales and weights, presumably because these were evidence of an intention to sell cannabis in the future whereas the possession of the money was evidence only of past transactions. This distinction would be tenable if it was possible that B had acquired the weights and scales for dealing with the cannabis presently possessed but the fact that traces of cannabis were found on the scales seems to rule that out. The jury would inevitably conclude that the scales had been used for selling cannabis in the past, that they were kept for that purpose, and would have been so used in the future. If the evidence of possession of the money was unfair and prejudicial because it raised the suggestion that B was in the business of drug dealing generally, this was *a fortiori* true of the possession of the contaminated

[33] Federal Rules of Evidence, r.401.

[34] [1994] Crim.L.R. 592; *R. v. Wright* [1994] Crim.L.R. 55; *R. v. Simms* [1995] Crim.L.R. 304; *R. v. Lucas* [1995] Crim.L.R. 400; *R. v. Grant* [1995] Crim.L.R. 715; *R. v. Smith* [1995] Crim.L.R. 940; *R. v. Okunsaya* [1995] Crim.L.R. 941; *R. v. Nicholas* [1995] Crim.L.R. 942.

scales. But possession of the scales was very relevant evidence of an intent to supply and its exclusion would have been much too restrictive. Although it was undoubtedly evidence of an offence or offences by B on other occasions, it does not follow that it was inadmissible . . . the test of admissibility of evidence is that 'its probative force in support of the allegation that an accused person committed a crime is sufficiently great to make it just to admit the evidence, notwithstanding that it is prejudicial to the accused in tending to show that he was guilty of another crime.'[35] The evidence of the money in the kettle has less probative force — money may be kept in a kettle for all sorts of reasons — and it is correspondingly less 'prejudicial' (the two go together). By itself, it is probably insufficiently relevant . . . But it cannot be considered in isolation from the other evidence. If the evidence of the contaminated scales is admissible, it is because the evidence of past dealings is, in the circumstances, highly probative of present intention. Then supporting circumstantial evidence should also be admissible. An item of circumstantial evidence is nearly always susceptible of an innocent explanation.

This case is useful as it raises several issues, not least the relationship between relevance and fairness (discussed later) but also the difference between direct and circumstantial relevance. The finding of the drugs is directly relevant to the issue of the accused's possession whereas the finding of the money is at best only circumstantially relevant. It requires us to enter into a chain of inference, starting with an assumption that drug dealers habitually possess large sums of cash (and mobile phones![36]). From such an assumption, it is necessary to infer from the possession of £150 that B is a drug dealer and therefore is more likely to possess the cannabis with intent to supply. As the court decided, the relevance of the evidence of the money is tenuous. In this particular case, its admission is also prejudicial as it implies previous disreputable conduct on the part of the accused.

Relevance is not an inherent characteristic of any item of evidence but exists only as a relation between an item of evidence and some other matter which requires to be proved. It is sufficiently relevant when it renders the existence of the other matter "more or less probable". The appeal courts have tended not to lay down guidelines as to when evidence is admissible although, as here, they will interfere with the trial judge's discretion when the evidence is insufficiently relevant. But, as Professor Smith suggests, any item of evidence should not be considered in isolation but its relevance considered in the context of the evidence as a whole. If the scales are admissible, there is no longer a reason to exclude the evidence of the money on the grounds of prejudice nor should its limited relevance be a bar.

Diametrically opposed views on whether an item was relevant were expressed by members of the House of Lords in *R. v. Kearley*.[37] The Dorset police raided a flat occupied by the appellant, his wife and one other person. In the course of the raid they recovered a relatively small quantity

[35] *R. v. P.* [1991] 3 All E.R. 337.
[36] *Nicholas supra.*
[37] [1992] 2 All E.R. 345; see also *R. v. Harry* (1988) 86 Cr.App.R. 105.

of amphetamine. While on the premises, the police encountered visitors to the flat and answered the phone. Many of the callers requested drugs from "Chippie", the appellant's nickname. Since the actual amount of drugs and money discovered in the flat were not enough to raise an irresistible presumption that the accused was in possession of the drugs "with intent to supply", the prosecution sought to rely on the testimony of police officers who had heard these requests. The appeal raised issues of hearsay but also the question whether a telephone caller's belief that the accused was a drug supplier was at all relevant to proving the accused's intent to supply? The majority of the House regarded the evidence as irrelevant and excluded:

R. v. Kearley [1992] 2 All E.R. 345 *per* Lord Oliver, 370

The first inquiry must be: is it relevant evidence? For nothing that is not relevant is admissible. 'Relevant' cannot, I think, be better defined than in art. 1 of *Stephen's Digest of the Law of Evidence*,[38] that is to say that the word means that —

> Any two facts to which it is applied are so related to each other that according to the common course of events one either taken by itself or in connection with other facts proves or renders probable the past, present or future existence or non-existence of the other.

To put it, perhaps more succinctly, a fact to be relevant must be probative, and if one asks whether the fact that a large number of persons called at the premises seeking to purchase from 'Chippie' renders probable the existence of a person at the premises called 'Chippie' who is willing to supply drugs, the answer can, I think, only be in the affirmative. But the difficulty here is that it is only the combination of the facts (a) that persons called, (b) that they asked for 'Chippie' and (c) that they requested drugs which renders the evidence relevant. The mere fact that people telephoned or called, in itself, is irrelevant, for it neither proves nor renders probable any other fact. In order to render evidence of the calls relevant and therefore admissible there has to be added the additional element of what the callers said, and it is here that the difficulty arises. What was said — in each case a request for drugs — is, of course probative of the state of mind of the caller. But the state of mind of the caller is not the fact in issue and is, in itself, irrelevant, for it is not probative of anything other than its own existence. It becomes relevant only if and so far as the existence of other facts can be inferred from it . . .

Evidence of the callers' opinions was irrelevant to proving the accused's intent. Initially this argument is attractive especially when dealing with a single caller whose opinion would have so little probative weight as to make it inadmissible. But when the reasoning is extended to a significant number of callers, the argument that their opinions are irrelevant is more difficult to follow: if I testify to my belief, based on my own experience of you, that you possess a particular characteristic, it becomes more likely that you do. A single person's belief might have little probative weight but it

[38] 12th ed,. (1936) 4.

does have some. When many witnesses are willing to testify that you possess that characteristic, not only is such testimony sufficiently relevant but it has much more weight. Would the House have reached the same conclusion if the evidence related not to the accused possessing an intent to supply but a violent temper?

The minority agreed that the callers' beliefs were irrelevant as a means of directly proving the accused's intent but were relevant when it came to establishing the existence of a market for drugs:

R. v. Kearley, *op. cit.* at 383–384, *per* Lord Browne-Wilkinson

On that basis, [counsel for the appellant] submitted that such belief of third parties was irrelevant and inadmissible in deciding the intent of the accused. I accept that the opinions or beliefs of the callers were irrelevant and as such inadmissible. But in my judgment the calls prove more than the opinions or beliefs of the callers.

The evidence was, in my judgment, relevant because it showed that there were people resorting to the premises for the purposes of obtaining drugs from Chippie. Although evidence of the existence of such would-be buyers is not, by itself, conclusive, the existence of a substantial body of potential customers provides some evidence which a jury could take into account in deciding whether the accused had an intent to supply. The existence of a contemporaneous potential market to buy drugs from Chippie, by itself, shows that there was an opportunity for the accused to supply drugs.

In order to eliminate, for the purpose of considering relevance only, the complication that the purpose of the callers can only be demonstrated by the words that the callers use, I will seek to demonstrate the position by reference to a case where no such recourse is necessary. Suppose a shop which has a sole proprietor and sells only coffee. Say the issue is whether the proprietor had an intent to supply coffee. On a particular day there was a long queue of persons at the door of the shop waiting for it to open. Evidence of the existence of the queue would surely be admissible towards proving an intent to supply. The presence of potential purchasers is circumstantial evidence from which a jury can draw the inference that the shopkeeper was going to supply coffee. There can be no supply without persons to whom supply is made: if the existence of such persons is shown, that provides evidence of the opportunity for supply . . . .

. . . In my view therefore the fact that there were a number of people seeking to buy drugs was legally relevant and admissible as showing that there was a market to which the accused could sell, even though such evidence was also capable of giving rise to an impermissible secondary inference, viz that the callers believed Chippie supplied drugs. If the callers themselves had given evidence at the trial and said only that on the relevant day they had made a call for the purpose of obtaining drugs from Chippie, I can see no ground on which such evidence could have been excluded as being irrelevant.

The divergence in opinion in these two judgments may be reconciled by asking "Relevance as to what?" Lord Oliver wishes to establish direct relevance between the caller's opinion and a fact in issue, namely the intent of the accused. Lord Browne-Wilkinson, on the other hand, uses an indirect chain of inference: the caller's opinion is not evidence of intent but merely evidence of the existence of a market, not in itself a fact in issue but a fact relevant to a fact in issue, since the existence of a market for drugs at those premises compels the inference that there is a person supplying drugs at the flat. From that subsequent fact, a juror may infer that it was the accused who possessed the intent to supply drugs.

The threshold that an item of evidence must overcome to be sufficiently relevant is not a high one and allows considerable leeway to admit items that are essentially background in character and which are offered as an aid to understanding. But this can encompass marginal circumstantial evidence and the Royal Commission on Criminal Justice felt that the criterion of relevance was too widely interpreted by judges, allowing time-wasting by counsel and forcing juries to sit through evidence which adds little to what was already before them.[39] A more "robust" approach would be encouraged by the powers under the U.S. Federal Rules of Evidence:

403.—Although relevant, evidence may be excluded if its probative value is substantially outweighed by the danger of unfair prejudice, confusion of the issues or misleading the jury, or by considerations of undue delay, waste of time, or needless presentation of cumulative evidence.[40]

A final point is that *Batt* and *Kearley* show that relevance and probative value must be weighed against other key principles, in both cases, the prejudicial effect of introducing the evidence of the contamination of the scales and weights or the callers' requests. Although not told expressly, a sensible juror will inevitably conclude that the defendant has supplied drugs before and is doing it again. Express evidence of propensity and bad character is generally excluded for this reason, although the prejudice engendered must be balanced against the probative value.[41] For example, in *Batt*, even if there had been no trace of drugs on the scales, it is possible that the jury would have drawn the same conclusion that the scales were there for the purpose of dealing. The probative value of the very existence of the scales is considerable and, in the case itself, may be seen to outweigh any prejudice. In other words, the accused's past dealings revealed by the contamination are simply part of the background.

(h) weight: weight and relevance make up the probative value of evidence. The weight given to any item of evidence is a matter for the jury. It is for them to assess the credibility of a witness, the extent to which the information is consistent with other evidence in the case and the reliance that can be placed upon it. Although weight and relevance are logically distinct, the more direct and relevant an item of information, the greater weight attaches to it and the harder it is to rebut. For example, incriminating statements made in the police station are very difficult to retract at any later stage in the proceedings as judges and juries give such weight to the fact of a confession that they appear willing to overlook internal inconsistencies in the statement or evidence of oppressive circumstances in which it was made.

[39] Cm. 2263 (1993) para. 8.13.
[40] Federal Rules of Evidence, r. 403.
[41] See Chap. 14.

(j) prejudice: the term "prejudice" can be used in a general sense of "harm" but also in a more specific sense of pre-judging the issues. For example, where the defendant is charged with burglary, proof of previous convictions for burglary may well lead the jury to conclude that he or she is guilty of this offence as well.

Zuckerman A., *The Principles of Criminal Evidence* (1989) 222–223

At the simplest level such proof may lead to an exaggerated estimation of the probative value of previous crimes and other deviant conduct . . . Evidence of previous crimes might not only distort the inferential process; it could also threaten two central principles of our criminal justice. The first is that in any criminal trial the accused stands to be tried, acquitted or convicted only in respect of the offence with which he is charged. The second is that conviction must take place only if the jury are persuaded of the accused's guilty beyond all reasonable doubt . . .

On being informed that the accused has committed other crimes in the past a jury may decide that the accused deserves punishment whether or not he is guilty of the offence charged. As Wigmore put it, the 'deep tendency of human nature to punish, not because our victim is guilty this time, but because he is a bad man and may as well be condemned now that he is caught, is a tendency which cannot fail to operate with any jury, in or out of court.'[42] This could happen where there is a feeling that the accused got away on previous occasions without conviction or with unduly light punishment; or where the accused is charged with a particular act of prohibited homosexual conduct but a stigma attaches to the sexual inclination as such. In these situations — and there may be many others — there is a real possibility that the jury's verdict will reflect their judgment about the accused's character rather than their findings about the commission of the offence charged.

This is a particular problem in criminal proceedings. The rules of evidence seeks to combat prejudice by excluding those categories of evidence that are considered to be prejudicial. However, matters such as the accused's past disreputable conduct may firstly emerge indirectly as in *Batt* or *Kearley*, may secondly often have some direct relevance to the issues under the similar fact doctrine[43] or thirdly may be used in the cross-examination of the accused under section 1(f)(ii) of the Criminal Evidence Act 1898.[44] Juries are given no help in assessing their own prejudice:

When the accused's record is investigated under s.1(f)(ii) of the 1898 Act the jury are told that in law they must consider the criminal record only in relation to the accused's credibility and not his guilt. Since in common sense a criminal record would often be relevant to guilty, such a direction suggests that there is some special legal rule to be observed here. By creating a conflict between the normal standards familiar to the jury and legal standards, the judges have limited their own ability to guide the jury because juries are unlikely to defer to a legal standard which they do not understand or for which they have no sympathy.

A more effective way of combatting prejudice would be to bring into the open the scope of prejudice created by evidence of past criminal record and strive to

[42] Wigmore on Evidence (3rd ed., 1940) Vol. 1, s.57.

[43] See Chap. 14.

[44] See Chap. 15.

persuade juries that the principles of criminal justice, which require resisting prejudice, reflect their own perceptions of justice . . .[45]

(k) fairness: the principle that prejudicial evidence is excluded is part of the discretion which the trial judge exercises to ensure a fair trial.[46] At common law, this discretion was explored by the House of Lords in *R. v. Sang*[47] A majority in *Sang* restrict the boundaries of judicial discretion to ensuring that the probative weight of the evidence sufficiently outweighs any prejudicial effect and to excluding confessions (and analogous evidence) that have been obtained unfairly. The case concerned the role of an *agent provocateur* and the House considered that it was the function of judge to ensure the accused had a fair trial but not to exercise disciplinary powers over the police or prosecution. This limited notion of the principle of fairness has been significantly affected by the passage of section 78 of the Police and Criminal Evidence Act 1984:

> 78.—(1) In any proceedings the court may refuse to allow evidence on which the prosecution proposes to rely to be given if it appears to the court that, having regard to all the circumstances, including the circumstances in which the evidence was obtained, the admission of the evidence would have such an adverse effect on the fairness of the proceedings that the court ought not to admit it.

Section 78 was the result of an amendment tabled by Lord Scarman enabling courts to exclude evidence on the basis of police malpractice. It gives a wider discretion to the judge to exclude evidence on the basis of the judicial duty to ensure a fair trial. In this it reflects Lord Scarman's judgment in *Sang*:

> If the accused is misled or tricked into providing evidence (whether it be an admission or the provision of fingerprints or medical evidence or some other evidence), the rule against self-incrimination, *nemo tenetur se ipsum prodere*, is likely to be infringed. Each case must, of course, depend on its circumstances. All I would say is that the principle of fairness, though concerned exclusively with the use of evidence at trial, is not susceptible to categorisation or classification, and is wide enough in some circumstances to embrace the way in which, after the crime, evidence is obtained from the accused . . .[48]

Judicial concern with the fairness of the proceedings is no longer limited to the courtroom. The discretion to exclude evidence in the interests of fairness should encompass the treatment of the accused from the start of the investigation and any abuse of their position by the state agencies involved.

(l) exclusionary rules: even where the evidence proferred is relevant, with sufficient probative weight and non-prejudicial, it might still be the subject

[45] Zuckerman, *supra*, 245.
[46] The extent to which fairness is developing as a principle of evidence is discussed in Chap. 4.
[47] [1979] 2 All E.R. 1222.
[48] *supra* at 1247d.

of an exclusionary rule. The major rules of exclusion are ones dealing with opinion, character, public interest and hearsay. The first three are perhaps self-explanatory. Hearsay, though, is one of the most important concepts in evidence. The common law rule prevents adducing hearsay statements as evidence. The classic statement of the rule was formulated by Cross:

> an assertion other than one made by a person while giving oral evidence in the proceedings is inadmissible as evidence of any fact asserted.[49]

Despite considerable criticism, the rule remains stubbornly in force.[50] Witnesses are expected to testify from their own knowledge or belief. They are not expected to testify as to what they think others might know or believe. They give evidence of what they themselves perceived: what they saw, felt, tasted or heard. A witness cannot testify about another's perceptions. Were a witness permitted to retail another, absent, person's statement, the court could not investigate the probative value of that statement. It would, of course, be able to inquire whether the those actual words were spoken because that is within the witness's own perceptions. But the court could not explore other factors such as the absent witness's reliability or credibility. The court cannot assess whether the contents of the statement were likely to be true. The testimony is hearsay and is not admissible evidence.

The hearsay rule is mainly about excluding the evidence of an absent witness. But the rule does not only apply to repeating other people's statements. Witnesses cannot testify as to what they themselves said prior to the court proceedings. It does show the witness's consistency despite this but there are considerable limitations on introducing such prior consistent statements. The common law rule against hearsay is very broad, its rationale seemingly unclear to the judiciary and thus its boundaries indefinite.[51] It remains a *rule* of exclusion and the judge has no discretion to admit a hearsay statement simply on the grounds that, as evidence, it is relevant, reliable and probative.

(m) proof: evidence is not proof. The trier of fact, having heard the evidence, decided on the relevant facts, must come to a conclusion as to whether the facts in issue exist or not. Has the trier been persuaded of the correctness of a particular case? This question can be divided into two stages:

(1) which party has the task of persuading the trier? Must the accused satisfy the jury of his or her innocence or is it for the prosecution to

[49] Tapper C., *Cross and Tapper on Evidence* (8th ed., 1995) 46. This formula was approved by the House of Lords in *R. v. Sharp* [1988] 1 All E.R. 65 at 68b–c. The rule is discussed in Chap. 16.

[50] *Kearley supra*, although the scope of the rule is now limited to criminal trials as a result of the Civil Evidence Act 1995.

[51] *Woodhouse v. Hall* (1980) 72 Cr.App.R. 39.

convince them of her guilt? Does the plaintiff have to persuade the judge of the correctness of his or her suit or is it for the defence to rebut the allegations? This is the question of the *burden of proof.* In a criminal trial, it almost invariably rests upon the prosecution. In civil proceedings, the principle is that the party who asserts a particular fact must prove it.

(2) what level of proof is needed? Total certainty rarely happens and when lawyers talk about proof, they refer to the probability of a state of affairs existing. In a criminal trial with an individual's liberty at stake, a high standard is required and that occurs when the jury is satisfied "beyond reasonable doubt". In theory this seems a proper formula but in practice there are significant inadequacies. For example, juries are still allowed to convict even when the prosecution case rests wholly or mainly on an uncorroborated confession, on a single identification or on accomplice evidence. In *R. v. Silcott*[52] the appellant had been convicted of the murder of a police officer in the course of a riot in north London. The evidence against him consisted only of alleged verbal admissions, "You ain't got enough evidence", "I ain't saying no more and you've got a big surprise coming" and "No one will give evidence against me". The conviction was only quashed when forensic evidence showed these statements not to have been contemporaneously recorded as stated by the police witnesses. Yet it is difficult to see that such statements, even if accepted as true, could constitute proof beyond reasonable doubt.

A similar lack of evidence was present in the case of the Winchester Three when three young Irish people were sentenced to 25 years imprisonment for conspiring to murder the Secretary of State for Northern Ireland, Tom King. They were spotted lingering outside his farm:

> The police discovered driving licences in false names, a list of names and addresses of people prominent in British public life, and a list of car-numbers of vehicles arriving at King's estate. The three had some money, and had purchased a second-hand car. They had a radio and a woolly hat. That was more or less it. The jury were asked to believe that they were a major terrorist unit . . .[53]

The jury is not necessarily to blame and in many cases where justice has miscarried, the quality of evidence, accepted by the judge as evidence on which a reasonable jury might convict, has nowhere approached the requisite standard of proof. The ready acceptance of

[52] *The Guardian*, December 11, 1991.

[53] Woffinden B., "The Case of the Winchester Three" 140 New L.J. (1990) 164; see also Hilliard B. "Soldiers of Nothing" 140 New L.J. (1990) 160 for an analysis of the evidence in the case of the Birmingham Six.

circumstantial evidence has meant that sometimes not only the quality but the quantity of the evidence is wanting. The English legal system has always prided itself on its rules on proof of guilt but there remain real problems as to whether judicial supervision over the sufficiency of evidence is adequate.

In civil cases, the standard of proof is on the balance of probabilities: that is, whether a fact is more likely than not.

Some Logical Considerations

As discussion of these key concepts shows, evidence concerns legal rules. Simply because an item of evidence is relevant and fits into a logical pattern of proof does not automatically mean that it is admissible as evidence. But the study of evidence is a combination of law and logic. What can we rationally conclude from the evidence? There is a common sense world in which we constantly draw inferences, more or less logically, from observations that we make. Making this process transparent is central to the study of evidence.

The courtroom is seen as a forum where the production of evidence and logical argument will produce truth. Logic is the science of reasoning, proof, thinking, or inference, allowing us to analyse a piece of reasoning, and determine whether it is correct or not. A little basic knowledge of logic is often helpful when constructing or analysing an argument.[54] The initial building block of a logical argument is a proposition which is a statement which can be either true or false; for example:

The accused murdered the victim by shooting him at a particular time and place

Firstly, to decide on the truth or otherwise of this statement, we need to define "murder" which, at its most basic, requires proof that the accused caused the death of the victim with the intention of killing him or causing him serious harm. As we have seen, technically these are called *facta probanda* or the facts in issue. In a criminal case, the proposition is the charge and we now need an argument to establish this. There are three connected stages to an argument: premises, inference, and conclusion. The premises in a trial are the evidence that is produced.

The witness stated that she saw the accused stab the victim

In this case, this is direct evidence of the *actus reus*. The defendant can seek to deny the truth of the statement, possibly suggesting that the witness is deranged, has poor eyesight or malicious feelings towards him. Often, however, the testimony will be circumstantial:

[54] A detailed and valuable study of the principles of proof is to be found in Anderson T. and Twining W., *Analysis of Evidence* (1991) Chap. 2.

The witness saw the accused running from the scene of the stabbing

We might speculate that the accused was running because he did not want to be seen at the scene. Further speculation might lead us to suggest his reluctance to be seen there was because he was linked to the stabbing in some way, perhaps as the assailant. We are using the premises to obtain further propositions. This process is known as inference. In inference, we start with one or more propositions which have been accepted. We then derive a new proposition. The propositions arrived at by inference may then be used in further inference. As this shows, often the court may be dealing with chains of inferences.[55] Evidence leads the jury to an inferred fact from which a further inference can be drawn and so on through a series of intermediate stages until we reach the ultimate issue which has to be decided. In *Kearley*, the minority argued that the caller's requests for drugs established that there was a market at those premises; if that was accepted, it compels the inference that there was a person supplying that market, that the person could only be one of the occupants of the flat, namely the accused; if that is correct, we must conclude that the accused had the intent to supply drugs.

Clearly the process of inference can vary in strength and validity. Not least is the fact that there may be alternative valid explanations or inferences that can be drawn from the same information or that there may be other evidence which might contradict that inference. The chain of inference above (running suggests a reluctance to be seen at the scene, therefore some link to the stabbing, perhaps being the assailant) is scarcely one to be fully confident about. Alternative explanations on the basis of coincidence can easily be suggested: the accused was training for a marathon or rushing to catch a train. Wigmore has suggested that there may be four processes of proof:

Wigmore J., *The Science of Judicial Proof* (1937), para. 15

The first process, Assertion, consists in offering a fact tending to prove a specific conclusion of Probandum. This is subject to the test whether the claimed conclusion is a probable or a more probable one, having regard to conceivable other interpretations of the fact . . .

The second process, Explanation, consists in explaining away the original fact's force by showing the existence and probability of other hypotheses; for this purpose other facts affording such explanation are receivable from the opponent . . .

The third process, Denial, consists in negating the original proponent's evidentiary fact as such, either testimonially or circumstantially; and thus [the opponent] . . . offers a new witness or circumstance . . .

The fourth process, Rivalry, consists in adducing a new fact, circumstantial or testimonial, which by a rival inference tends to disprove the proponent's Probandum . . .

[55] Harry Kemelman's short story "The Nine Mile Walk" is a entertaining example of a chain of inference. It is reprinted in Anderson T. and Twining W., *op. cit.* 9.

Such are the forms of probative processes available for each single fact as offered. For each additional new fact the processes may be repeated, though they may not be actually used in each instance . . . amidst the multifarious varieties of evidence, our mental processes thereon are reducible to four fundamental types, constantly repeated.

The function of the trier of fact is to choose the right inference from all the possible rivals and as Wigmore suggests, any particular piece of information may gain significance when taken with the evidence as a whole:

The weapon used in the stabbing was found in a rubbish bin on the road that the accused ran along

Any inference that the accused was running away can gain strength from other circumstantial evidence. This was seen in *Batt*: where any inference that might be drawn from the possession of the money in the kettle by itself must be weak. However, when taken with the evidence of the scales and weights, the trier of fact might have more confidence in concluding that there was an intent to supply. Any such confidence must be balanced against other items of evidence which deny, explain or produce a rival to any particular inference: in *Batt*, the defendant testified that the drugs in the egg cup belonged to her husband.

Judges often describe the process of drawing inferences from evidence as one of common sense logic. But it might be argued that logic merely tells us whether an inference is valid or not. Whether it is the correct inference to draw is a more difficult exercise. A juror has to decide on the value of the evidence and the weight which he or she is willing to put on the inference. Did the witness really see the accused? Is it justified to conclude that he was running away? The process of inference necessarily involves recourse to generalisations:

Anderson T. and Twining W., *Analysis of Evidence* (1991), 68

Generalisations range over a broad spectrum. At one end are scientific laws (such as the law of gravity); well-founded scientific opinions (such as the conclusion of a qualified forensic expert based upon comparisons of handwriting alleged to have been written by the same individual); and widely shared conclusions based upon common experience (for instance, everyone knows that a driver must stop for a red light). In the middle are commonly held, but unproven or unprovable beliefs (for instance, fleeing the scene of a crime is evidence of a guilty conscience). At the other end are biases or prejudices that may be strongly held irrespective of available data (for instance, women do not make good trial lawyers; men are generally poor single parents; whites cannot fairly sit as jurors when a black is on trial, etc) and less strongly held but still operative beliefs (for instance, men's fixed designs are probably carried out). Some or all of these types of background generalisations are involved in factual adjudications.

It is probably better not to refer to "common sense" reasoning but to recognise that the trial court uses inductive argument, so-called to distinguish it from the other traditional type of argument, deductive argument. A deductive argument provides conclusive proof of its conclusions; if the premises are true, the conclusion must also be true. A deductive argument is either valid or invalid. A valid argument is defined as one where, if the premises are true, then the conclusion is true. On the other hand, an inductive argument is one where the premises provide some evidence for the truth of the conclusion. Inductive arguments are neither valid or invalid, but we can talk about whether they are better or worse than other arguments. We can also discuss how probable their premises are. In a court of law, verdicts are thus never "true" but are merely more or less probable. For lawyers to talk about the proof of a proposition is to discuss probabilities.

Some Common Fallacies

It may be useful to summarize the major pitfalls to be avoided when constructing an argument. These pitfalls are known as fallacies. In everyday English the term "fallacy" is used to refer to mistaken beliefs as well as to the faulty reasoning that leads to those beliefs. This is fair enough, but in logic the term is generally used to refer to a form of technically incorrect argument, especially if the argument appears valid or convincing.

(1) an argument *ad hominem* is literally "an argument directed at the man". The abusive variety occurs when, instead of trying to disprove the truth of an assertion, the arguer attacks the person or people making the assertion. This is invalid because the truth of an assertion does not depend upon the goodness of those asserting it. Sometimes in a court, doubt is cast upon the testimony of a witness by showing, for example, that he is a known perjurer. This is a valid way of reducing the credibility of the testimony given by the witness; however, it does not demonstrate that the witness's testimony is false, merely that it is more likely to be so.

(2) an *argument from ignorance* occurs whenever it is argued that something must be true simply because it has not been proved false. Equivalently, it may be argued that something must be false because it has not been proved true. This fallacy does not normally apply in a court of law, where one is generally assumed innocent until proven guilty. However, in section 35 of the Criminal Justice and Public Order Act 1994, where the prosecution have satisfied the court that there is a case to answer and a defendant declines to testify in his or her own defence, the judge, in the presence of the jury, is empowered to tell the defendant that the stage has been reached at which he or she can give evidence and to issue a warning that if he or she remain silent, that it will be permissible for the jury to draw whatever inferences appear to be proper. Although this can only come into play once the prosecution have supplied substantial evidence, logically this seems suspect. The main result of a refusal to testify, whatever the reason, would be the proposition that the defendant is guilty because he has not proved his innocence.

(3) *special pleading* is a classic defence ploy. This is committed when the arguer appeals to pity for the sake of getting a conclusion accepted. Pleas to reduce murder to manslaughter on the grounds of provocation might be examined for examples.

(4) lawyers often make a *populist appeal* to the gallery. To commit this fallacy is to attempt to win acceptance of an assertion by appealing to a large group of people. This form of fallacy is often characterized by emotive language. One example would be in the O.J. Simpson murder trial where the defence lawyer asserted that racism was the reason for the prosecution, that it was endemic in the Los Angeles police force and that the jurors' verdict was the means of combating this.

(5) *generalisation* is one of the commonest forms of reasoning, occurring when a general rule is applied to a particular situation in which the features of that particular situation render the rule inapplicable. Often, people will argue from assumptions which they do not bother to state. Juries often use inarticulated generalisations. These may be valid: people who hide goods in their clothing in shops rather than putting them in the basket provided tend to be dishonest. The principle is that all of the premises of an argument should be stated explicitly. It is not strictly a fallacy to fail to state all of one's assumptions; however, it is often viewed with suspicion.

It is moot how far courts go to uncover such generalisations and to assess their validity as opposed to their prejudicial quality. Sometimes there are formal rules — the shoplifter's previous convictions for theft, although relevant, are excluded. Any probative value such evidence might have is outweighed by the prejudice it would create in the minds of the jury. There is less protection from other stereotypes which exist in the minds of juries, sometimes based upon assumptions about race or nationality. There is some evidence for this proposition in the disproportionate numbers of young blacks prosecuted, convicted and given custodial sentences.

(6) the *fallacy of numbers* consists of asserting that the more people who support or believe a proposition, the more likely it is that that proposition is correct.

(7) an *appeal to greater authority* uses the admiration of the famous to try and win support for an assertion. However in courts, this line of argument is not always completely bogus, especially when there is reliance on expert testimony.

(8) the *false cause fallacy* occurs when one identifies something as the cause of an event but it has not actually been shown to be the cause. Likewise we talk of *post hoc, propter hoc* when something is assumed to be the cause of an event merely because it happened before the event. A similar situation occurs when it is asserted that because two events occur together, they must be causally related, and leaves no room for other factors that may be the cause(s) of the events.

(9) *begging the question* occurs when the premises are at least as questionable as the conclusion reached.

(10) *circular reasoning* occurs when one assumes as a premise the conclusion which one wishes to reach. Often, the proposition will be rephrased so that the fallacy appears to be a valid argument. For example:

(11) a lawyer's favourite is the *fallacy of presupposition* which is the interrogative form of begging the question. One example is the classic loaded question, "Have you stopped beating your wife?" The question presupposes a definite answer to another question which has not even been asked. This trick is often used by lawyers in cross-examination, when they ask questions like, "Where did you hide the money you stole?"

(12) a judicial favourite has been the *slippery slope* argument which states that should one event occur, so will other harmful events. There is no proof made that the harmful events are caused by the first event.

(13) the affirmation of the consequent is an argument of the form "*A implies B, B is true, therefore A is true.*" It is similar to the denial of the antecedent which takes the form "*A implies B, A is false, therefore B is false*".

(14) another judicial commonplace might be the *argument from antiquity* — the fallacy of asserting that something is right or good simply because it is old, or because "*That's the way it's always been*". The opposite is the fallacy of asserting that something is more correct simply because it is new or newer than something else.

(15) the *black and white* fallacy, occurs when one presents a situation as having only two alternatives, where in fact other options exist or can exist. The opposite, another favourite with the cross-examining advocate, is to demand the simple answer to a complex question.

(16) the *non-sequitur* is an argument where the conclusion is drawn from premises which are not logically connected with it.

(17) the *red herring* fallacy is committed when irrelevant material is introduced to the issue being discussed, so that everyone's attention is diverted away from the points being made, towards a different conclusion.

(18) a *burden of proof* is always on the person making an assertion or proposition. Shifting the burden of proof is the fallacy of putting the burden of proof on the person who denies or questions the assertion being made. The source of the fallacy is the assumption that something is true unless proven otherwise. The sections of the Criminal Justice and Public Order Act 1994 which modify the right to silence operate on this principle.

(19) the *straw man fallacy* is to misrepresent someone else's position so that it can be attacked more easily, then to knock down that misrepresented position, then to conclude that the original position has been demolished. It is a fallacy because it fails to deal with the actual arguments that have been made.

2

TRIAL PROCEDURE — THE JUDGE AND THE JURY

The Procedure of the Trial — Running Order

There are many issues of procedure that directly impinge upon the rules of evidence.[1] In this chapter we will be concerned with the organisation and running of the trial itself as this is the most significant context within which the rules of evidence operate.

In brief, in civil proceedings, there will be an opening speech by the plaintiff outlining the case. He or she will then produce evidence and call witnesses to be examined and cross-examined. If, at the close of the plaintiff's case, the defendant does not call any witnesses in reply, the plaintiff will sum up, to which the defendant has the right of reply. If the defence does call witnesses, there is no summing up at the conclusion of the plaintiff's case: the defence sums up at the conclusion of his or her case and the plaintiff is given the right to reply.

In criminal proceedings, there will be an opening speech by the prosecution which will be an overview of the issues and of the evidence supporting the allegations in the indictment. Whether such, often lengthy, openings are necessary was questioned by the Runciman Commission,[2] which supported the Law Commission's proposals for particularised indictments[3] which would remove the need for opening speeches in routine cases:

Royal Commission on Criminal Justice: *Report* (Cm. 2263) (1993) para. 8.7

We considered the practice in Scotland whereby the prosecution does not make an opening speech. There the judge, aided by narrative indictments,[4] may make a brief opening statement to the jury of the issues that they will be called upon to decide at the end of the trial. The prosecution then calls the first witness. If the Law

[1] Other pre-trial issues such as disclosure are discussed at 313, *et seq.*

[2] Royal Commission on Criminal Justice: *Report* (Cm. 2263) (1993) paras. 8.7ff.

[3] Law Commission: *Counts in an Indictment* (1992).

[4] A narrative indictment sets out each offence charged by giving an account of the facts alleged to constitute it. The facts are sometimes set out at some length.

Commission's proposals on particularised indictments are enacted, there will be no need for a prosecution opening speech in many trials in England and Wales. In the more complex cases an opening speech will almost certainly continue to be necessary. On the other hand, all that will be needed in routine and straightforward cases is the opening statement from the judge explaining the burden and standard of proof and such matters of law as he or she thinks necessary for the jury's understanding of the case. The judge should not, however, do more that identify, without discussing, the factual issues to be decided in the case. Those should be set out in the indictment.

Although Runciman accepted a need for an opening address in more complex cases, best practice should be to review the issues involved in the trial and not a comprehensive rehearsal of the evidence to be given by each witness.

The prosecution should present the case in an impartial manner, omitting reference to any evidence where the defence has given notice that it will be contested as inadmissible, especially confessions.[5] Where the prosecution cannot sensibly open the case without reference to such evidence, it is possible for there to be a preliminary hearing to settle the issue. In *R. v. Hammond*[6] in the opening speech for the prosecution, counsel referred to the defendant's confession. The defence immediately objected and the judge heard the objection to the admissibility of the confession in the absence of the jury. The Court of Criminal Appeal felt that the appropriate time to hear objections to evidence was just before the evidence was called:

> The ordinary practice in such a case, if there is any objection on the part of the counsel for the defence to the admissibility of a piece of evidence, is that he should inform the prosecution of that fact beforehand, and that that piece of evidence should not be opened to the jury . . . The court cannot lay down as a rule of practice that in no case should the judge decide to hear in advance arguments as to the admissibility of evidence. There may be cases in which it is convenient, and in which it cannot possibly result in any harm in its being done.[7]

Under the Criminal Procedure and Investigations Act 1996, there will be preparatory hearings in criminal cases at which time rulings may be made on the admissibility of evidence.[8]

It is much rarer for there to be an opening speech for the defence. This is an option (after the close of the prosecution case) where the defendant intends to call witnesses as to facts in addition to testifying himself or herself but not otherwise. At the close of defence evidence but before any closing speech, the prosecution will have a right to reply. The defence does have the right to the last word, (other, that is, than the judge's summing up). By the **Criminal Procedure (Right of Reply) Act 1964**:

[5] *R. v. Swatkins* (1831) 4 C. & P. 548; in civil proceedings the plaintiff must not mention facts with regard to which he cannot call evidence.
[6] [1941] 3 All E.R. 318.
[7] *ibid.* at 320, *per* Humphreys J.
[8] s.31.

1.—(1) Upon the trial of any person on indictment—

(a) the prosecution shall not be entitled to the right of reply on the ground only that the Attorney General or the Solicitor General appears for the Crown at the trial; and

(b) the time at which the prosecution is entitled to exercise that right shall, notwithstanding anything in section 2 of the Criminal Procedure Act 1865 be after the close of the evidence for the defence and before the closing speech,(if any) by or on behalf of the accused.

Under the adversarial system, in civil and criminal proceedings, it is the parties who decide what to litigate, what witnesses to call and what evidence to present. All parties have the opportunity to call and examine witnesses favourable to his or her case. This is known as examination-in-chief. The parties also have the opportunity to test the strength of the other side's evidence by examining their witnesses and this is known as cross-examination.

In civil cases, a party has to provide written proofs of evidence of the witnesses on which he or she intend to rely. But there is no obligation on a party in a civil case to call any witness or to be stopped from calling witnesses. If unnecessary and repetitious witnesses are called, there are sanctions, not least in the award of costs.[9] There is no particular order in which witnesses have to be called nor does the judge have the power to call witnesses on his or her own initiative.

In criminal proceedings, the prosecution must inform the defence (in trials on indictment) of the evidence on which they intend to rely. The accused also has certain obligations to reveal the line of the defence to the prosecution.[10] The prosecution's obligation to call witnesses is to ensure that all witnesses called at the committal proceedings were in court. But the prosecution has discretion whether to call such witnesses when counsel no longer believe them to be worthy of belief. This discretion is based on *R. v. Oliva*[11] where the witness was not called to testify, since he had testified at the committal hearing in a contradictory fashion:

> The prosecution do not, of course, put forward every witness as a witness of truth, but where the witness's evidence is capable of belief then it is their duty, well recognised, that he should be called, even though the evidence that he is going to give is inconsistent with the case sought to be proved. Their discretion must be exercised in a manner which is calculated to further the interest of justice, and at the same time be fair to the defence. If the prosecution appear to be exercising that discretion improperly, it is open to the judge of trial to

[9] *Connelly v. DPP* [1964] A.C. 1254 at 1301, *per* Lord Morris of Borth-y-Gest who suggests that the court has the power to "act effectively within its jurisdiction" to prevent abuse of its own proceedings.
[10] Under the provisions of the Criminal Procedure and Investigations Act 1996 — see Chap. 10.
[11] [1965] 3 All E.R. 116.

interfere and in his discretion in turn to invite the prosecution to call a particular witness . . .[12]

Defence witnesses should be called by the defence. In *R. v. Nugent*[13] it was argued that alibi witnesses for the defence (whose statements to the police had been included in the committal papers) should be called by the prosecution since the defendant's interests would otherwise be prejudiced. The trial judge held that there was no such obligation citing the judgment of Lord Roche in *Seneviratne v. R.*:

. . . [Their Lordships] cannot, speaking generally, approve of an idea that a prosecution must call witnesses irrespective of considerations of number and of reliability, or that a prosecution ought to discharge the functions of both prosecution and defence. If it does so confusion is very apt to result, and never is it more likely to result than if the prosecution calls witnesses and then proceeds almost automatically to discredit them by cross-examination. Witnesses essential to the unfolding of narratives on which the prosecution is based, must, of course, be called by the prosecution, whether in the result the effect of their testimony is for or against the case for the prosecution.[14]

The prosecution's discretion as to which witnesses to call is, to a limited extent, fettered and there is an obligation to call all witnesses whose testimony is essential to the narrative and who are capable of belief. Obviously the statements of witnesses on whom the Crown does not wish to rely should not find their way into the committal bundle. If they do the prosecution might well have to call the witness and tender him or her to the defence for cross-examination.[15]

Defence discretion is less restricted and they are able to call which witnesses they choose and in whatever order. The exception is that, if the defendant testifies, he or she must do so before other defence witnesses. Under the provisions of the Police and Criminal Evidence Act 1984:

79.—If at the trial of any person for an offence—

(a) the defence intends to call two or more witnesses to the facts of the case; and

(b) those witnesses include the accused, the accused shall be called before the other witness or witnesses unless the court in its discretion otherwise directs

Once any litigant has presented their evidence-in-chief, that is normally the end of the matter. In both civil and criminal proceedings, the parties should adduce all their evidence when presenting their case. Any opportunity to call further witnesses or present further evidence is very limited.

[12] *ibid.* at 122, *per* Lord Parker C.J.
[13] [1977] 3 All E.R. 662.
[14] [1936] 3 All E.R. 36 at 48.
[15] *R. v. Balmforth* [1992] Crim.L.R. 825; *R. v. Armstrong* [1995] Crim.L.R. 831; *R. v. Russell-Jones* [1995] Crim.L.R. 832.

In civil matters, there is a general discretion to allow evidence to be led at a later stage. In criminal proceedings, there is a limited discretion on the part of the judge to allow the prosecution call further evidence at the close of the defence case. This is known as the "*ex improviso*" rule and is restrictively interpreted in that it only permits such additional evidence in rebuttal of the defence case where no human ingenuity could have anticipated the line of the defence. However these constraints have recently been loosened. In *R. v. Milliken*,[16] the defence was based on allegations of fabrication of evidence by the police. The judge allowed the prosecution to call evidence in rebuttal and this course of action was upheld by the Court of Appeal. Rebuttal is permitted where a line of defence has emerged that could not have reasonably been foreseen. In *R. v. Hutchinson*[17] the defendant, accused of murder, dramatically pointed out a journalist sitting in the gallery as the "murderer". The prosecution had some inkling that such an allegation might be made but this did not prevent evidence being called in rebuttal. The court said:

> The *ex improviso* principle has to be applied by the court with a recognition that the prosecution are expected to react reasonably to what may be suggested as pre-trial warnings of evidence likely to be given which calls for denial beforehand, and for that matter to suggestions put in cross-examination of their witnesses. They are not expected to take notice of fanciful or unreal statements no matter from what source they emanate . . .[18]

There can be said to be two exceptions to the rule prohibiting the adducing of rebuttal evidence by the prosecution: firstly the modified *ex improviso* rule and secondly where the matter omitted is a mere formality. Apart from these the prosecution should not seek to remedy defects in its own case after the close of their case. But in *R. v. Francis*[19] a prosecution witness testified to picking out position 20 at an identity parade. However the prosecution failed to call evidence that the man standing at that position was in fact the accused. In making a submission of "no case to answer", defence counsel drew attention to this deficiency which could scarcely be said to have arisen *ex improviso*. The judge allowed the prosecution to recall the police inspector in charge of the parade in order to remedy the omission. The Court of Appeal upheld the conviction:

> The discretion of the judge to admit evidence after the close of the prosecution case is not confined to the two well established exceptions. There is a wider discretion. We refrain from defining precisely the limit of that discretion since we cannot foresee all the circumstances in which it might fall to be exercised. It is of the essence of any discretion that it should be kept flexible. But lest there be any misunderstanding and lest it be thought that we are opening the door too

[16] (1969) 53 Cr.App.R. 330.
[17] (1986) 82 Cr.App.R. 51.
[18] *ibid.* at 59.
[19] [1991] 1 All E.R. 225.

> wide . . . the discretion is one which should only be exercised outside the two established exceptions on the rarest of occasions.[20]

In a criminal trial, the judge has the power to call witnesses but these powers are very seldom used.[21] The Runciman Commission found that in 19 per cent of contested cases, the trial judge considered that there were one or more important witnesses that had not been called. The Commission recommended that judges should use their power more often to ensure that all relevant witnesses were heard by the jury.[22]

Although not strictly a matter of evidence, one glaring omission from the running order of a criminal trial is the victim: there is no right to speak, to be represented[23] nor even a place to sit. The crime is conceptualised as a wrong against society and once the complaint has been made, control is relinquished. The victim's wishes whether to prosecute or not may be taken into account by the police or the prosecution.[24] But the lack of protection may be seen across a range of cases, although illustrated at its worst by sexual assault cases where the defence is often a thinly-veiled attack on the character of the victim. The need for representation can become acute when the defendant asks for leave to cross-examine the rape victim on her past sexual history.[25] In such situations, the tactical interests of the prosecutor do not necessarily overlap with those of the victim.[26] Further examples can be seen in homicide cases: where the plea is one of provocation, this may involve an attack on the victim's character. The victim's relatives might wish to be independently represented in order to examine witnesses. Furthermore they may well object to the acceptance by the prosecution of a plea of "guilty" to manslaughter but of "not guilty" to murder but at present have no means of doing so.

The Role of the Judge

Within the court itself, the judge is, if not king, still a constitutional monarch. In criminal proceedings, once committal has taken place, discontinuance of the prosecution (*e.g.* by offering no evidence), amendment of the indictment or even the acceptance of a plea of guilty was always subject to the consent of the judge,[27] although there is an over-riding power of the

[20] *ibid.* at 229f, *per* Lloyd L.J.
[21] *R. v. Roberts* (1984) 80 Cr.App.R. 89.
[22] Royal Commission on Criminal Justice, *op. cit.* para. 8.18.
[23] This is not the case in certain European jurisdictions where the victim has a right to legal representation. In France the victim can be joined to an action as "*une partie civile*" and has *locus standi* in all preliminary matters and at the trial, able to argue that the charge is insufficient, to object to a certain line of questioning or to ask that certain questions be put to a witness.
[24] Code for Crown Prosecutors para. 6.7 ". . . Crown Prosecutors must always think very carefully about the interests of the victim".
[25] Under the Sexual Offences (Amendment) Act 1976, s.2 — this is discussed in Chap. 12.
[26] Temkin J.: *Rape and the Legal Process* (1987) 162 *et seq.*
[27] *R. v. Broad* (1979) 68 Cr.App.R. 281.

Attorney-General to stop a prosecution by entering a "*nolle prosequi*". However recently in *R. v. Grafton*[28] prosecution counsel sought to discontinue after part of the prosecution evidence had been heard. The Court of Appeal held that there was a common law power to discontinue proceedings even at this late stage and that the judge in such circumstances can only order an acquittal.

Within civil proceedings, actions can be halted at any time by the plaintiff by giving due notice to the defendant and to the court.

The judge acts as umpire, ensuring that the rules on procedure and evidence are followed. Thus, in a criminal case, he or she exercises control over the indictment, over the taking of the plea, over the admission of evidence; acts as the ultimate arbiter of any issue of law; summarises the evidence for the jury; explains the law and draws their attention to the issues that have to be decided. Judges do not normally call or question witnesses and, as discussed above, this can mean that the jury do not hear significant witnesses. The judge's functions are:

Admissibility of evidence

Parties to a case will put forward items of information (through witnesses, documents or objects) which they wish to have included in the case as evidence. Before any item is admitted as evidence, it must satisfy certain conditions. These may be conditions which generally pertain to all evidence, namely, that it is relevant, of sufficient weight and non-prejudicial or that a witness is competent. The conditions may be more specific to the particular class of evidence that is being offered: for example, a document must satisfy the conditions of section 27 of the Criminal Justice Act 1988 or section 8 of the Civil Evidence Act 1995. Another illustration may be taken from criminal cases where it is common for the prosecution to rely on incriminating statements, confessions, made by the defendant. There are conditions laid down by section 76 of the Police and Criminal Evidence Act 1984 before any confession can be admitted and the Crown must satisfy the court that these have been complied with. Those conditions are, namely, that the confession was obtained in circumstances which would not render it unreliable and that it was not obtained by oppression.[29]

Most of the time, such conditions for admissibility present no problems. However the judge will often have to consider whether the necessary conditions exist for evidence to be admitted. This is a preliminary question of fact for the judge and it can replicate the very question that the trier of fact later needs to decide. In *Doe d. Jenkins v. Davies*,[30] the issue in an

[28] [1992] 4 All E.R. 609 — the Crown Prosecution Service is able to discontinue prosecutions before committal under the Prosecution of Offences Act 1985, s.23. In magistrates' courts, they are also able to halt proceedings at any time — *R. v. Canterbury Justices ex parte Klisiak* [1981] 2 All E.R. 129.

[29] This is discussed at 43, *et seq.*

[30] (1847) 10 Q.B. 314.

action of ejectment was whether a dead person was legitimate. Before her death, she had made a declaration about this to her solicitor, at a time when she was handing him a document concerning her parents' marriage. The admissibility of that declaration, as an exception to hearsay, depended on whether it was made by a legitimate member of the family. Although her legitimacy was the substantive issue in the case, the judge can still decide on that very matter:

> There are conditions precedent which are required to be fulfilled before evidence is admissible for the jury. Thus, an oath, or its equivalent, and competence, are conditions precedent to admitting viva voce evidence; and the apprehension of immediate death to admitting evidence of dying declarations; a search to secondary evidence of lost writings; and stamps to certain written instruments; and so is consanguinity or affinity in the declarant to declarations of deceased relatives. The judge alone has to decide whether the condition has been fulfilled. If the proof is by witnesses, he must decide on their credibility. If counter-evidence is offered, he must receive it before he decides; and he has no right to ask the opinion of the jury on the fact of a condition precedent.[31]

Where the issue is the very one that has to be decided by the jury, the judge ought to come to a prima facie decision: whether sufficient evidence has been produced to admit the evidence or whether the objections are well founded. But this would not be a full hearing as the foundation of the defence could be heard in front of the jury who should decide the main question. In *Stowe v. Querner,*[32] the plaintiff sued on an insurance policy. The defence was that the policy had never been executed. The plaintiff sought to introduce, not the original policy which had been allegedly lost, but secondary evidence of its contents. To admit secondary evidence required the judge to decide whether the original had ever in fact existed. He admitted the evidence but still left to the jury the defence claim that the policy had never existed.

Where there is a dispute over the admissibility of evidence, the argument as to admissibility is often legal and can be disposed of on the basis of depositions and submissions of counsel. But the judge may have to conduct a factual inquiry to determine the question. These "trials within trials" are also known as hearings on the *voire dire*, taking their name from the special oath sworn by any witness testifying in such an inquiry. Such hearings should be in open court, not in the judge's chambers, and in the presence of the parties and their legal advisers.[33] The question arises whether they should be conducted in the jury's absence. The jury obviously should not be present where, for example, the subject of the *voire dire* is whether a confession should be admitted into evidence. Obviously to allow the jury to know that there was an incriminating statement of any kind, regardless of its details, would be prejudicial. It has been argued that different principles

[31] *ibid.* at 323, *per* Lord Denman C.J.

[32] (1870) L.R. 5 Exch. 155.

[33] *Lawrence v. R* [1933] A.C. 699 — the accused should be present throughout a trial.

should apply where the *voire dire* would disclose information that could usefully be taken into account by the jury in their overall assessment of the evidence. For example, with a young child, the judge might question the child to decide whether the child is competent. In *R. v. Hampshire*[34] the police videotaped an interview with the child victim of a sexual assault. The judge watched the recording and decided the child was a competent witness. The tape was admitted under section 32A of the Criminal Justice Act 1988. However the judge realised that he had not investigated the child's competence in front of the jury, recalled her and, in the presence of the jury, satisfied himself that she was a competent witness. On appeal:

R. v. *Hampshire* [1995] 2 All E.R. 1019 at 1026–1029, *per* Auld J.

The central question in this appeal is whether, when a judge considers it necessary to investigate a child's competence as a witness, he must do so in the presence of the jury. The rationale for the established practice of conducting such an exercise in their presence is said to be that, although the judge decides the issue of competence, they should see and hear the investigation, in addition to the evidence that follows it, to assist them in assessing the weight of that evidence. In our view, such authority as there is on the matter suggests that the practice is based more on the principle that an exercise of that sort is part of the trial and should, as a matter of openness and fairness, take place in open court and in the presence of the accused, rather than on its function in assisting the jury to determine the weight of the evidence given.

The present practice appears to have its origin in the view of the Court of Appeal in *R. v. Reynolds*[35] of an earlier decision of that court in *R. v. Dunne*.[36] In fact, nothing was said by the court in *Dunne* to justify that view of its reasoning. It was a case in which the court set aside a conviction which depended upon the uncorroborated sworn evidence of a child whom the judge had first examined privately in his room . . . *Reynolds* was a case in which a school attendance officer was examined in the absence of the jury on the question whether a child was fit to be sworn or was of sufficient intelligence to give evidence unsworn. She was permitted to give sworn evidence. The court quashed the conviction, citing *Dunne*, but attributed to the court in that case a reasoning not apparent from the short report of it. Lord Goddard C.J. . . . said:

> . . . it is most important that the jury should hear the answers which the child gives and see her demeanour when she is questioned by the court, for that enables them to come to a conclusion as to what weight they should attach to her evidence.

. . . with respect to the court in *Reynolds*, it was not necessary to its decision and it attributes a ratio to the court's judgment in *Dunne* which was not there and not necessary for its decision either.

. . . In *R. v. Deakin*[37] this court held that the evidence of third party experts on the issue of competence of a witness should be heard in the absence of the jury. It held that the calling of two educational psychologists to give evidence in the

[34] [1995] 2 All E.R. 1019.
[35] [1950] 1 All E.R. 335.
[36] (1929) 21 Cr.App.R. 176.
[37] [1994] 4 All E.R. 769.

presence of the jury as to the competence of a 34-year-old complainant who suffers from Downs Syndrome was an irregularity, though not a material one in the circumstances. In so ruling, the court distinguished between the calling of third party experts and evidence as to competence given by the complainant herself. In doing so, it acknowledged, though its reasoning on this was obiter, the well-established practice apparently resting on the decision in *Reynolds* that a child witness should be examined as to competence in the presence of the jury. Although the court in that case felt constrained by *Reynolds* and the need to distinguish it, the ratio of its decision is that the issue of competence of a witness is a matter for the judge, not the jury. This is how Farquharson L.J., giving the judgment of the court, put it.

> With diffidence we have come to the conclusion that in the circumstances of this case the evidence should have been heard in the absence of the jury for the following reasons. (1) Questions of admissibility of evidence are for the judge to decide. (2) If, after hearing the evidence and the submissions on the issue in the presence of the jury, the judge decides against admitting the evidence in question, the jury would have difficulty in excluding from their mind the evidence which the judge had ruled out. In the present case, this consideration was not significant as the prosecution would not have proceeded if the judge had decided not to admit the evidence of the complainant. (3) The rule, if it be a rule, that the jury should hear all the evidence given in a case does not here apply because at the time the evidence of the psychologists was given, the complainant was not a witness. It was of course only after hearing the evidence that the judge was able to rule on the complainant's competence to give evidence. (4) While acknowledging that it is right in law that questions relating to the competence of the witness in question should be answered by the witness himself in the presence of the jury, different considerations arise in relation to the evidence given by "third party" experts. In the former case, the jury may be assisted in deciding whether to accept the evidence of the complainant by observing the manner of his or her answers to the judge's questions. The evidence of the experts is in an altogether different category. (5) The jury would not be assisted in deciding the issue before them by hearing the expert evidence, which was concerned with the capacity of the complainant to tell the truth.

. . . where an issue arises as to the competence of a witness, he or she is not a witness until the judge has investigated and ruled on his or her competence, and that such an exercise is for the judge not the jury. Such reasoning appears to us to apply equally to the evidence as to competence given by a child complainant as to that given by a third party. In our view, *Reynolds* and the authorities following it do not, on analysis, necessitate or justify any distinction between them.

It follows, in our judgment, that a judge who considers it necessary to investigate a child's competence to give evidence in addition to or without the benefit of an earlier view of a videotaped interview . . . should do so in open court in the presence of the accused because it is part of the trial, but need not do so in the presence of the jury. The jury's function is to assess the child's evidence, including its weight, from the evidence he or she gives on the facts of the case after the child has been found competent to give it. The exercise of determining competence is not a necessary aid to that function . . .[38]

[38] *Hampshire supra* at 1026e–1029a, *per* Auld J.

Hearings on the *voire dire* can also take place in magistrates' courts. In *R. v. Liverpool Juvenile Court ex parte R.*,[39] the only evidence against a juvenile charged with burglary was the child's confession. The justices refused to consider its admissibility as a preliminary issue, presumably reasoning that, as triers of both law and fact who would hear all the evidence anyway, there was no reason to separate questions of admissibility from those of weight. The justices ruled that matters pertaining to the statement could be raised in the hearing proper and they could give appropriate weight to the statement. But the justices overlooked the fact that there were two advantages for a defendant in having a preliminary hearing. First, the accused could testify about the circumstances in which the confession was obtained but could not be questioned about the truth of the statement.[40] This would not be possible in the trial. Secondly the preliminary hearing allows the accused to assess the strength of the Crown case and decide whether or not to testify in the hearing proper. As a result, the Divisional Court held that the justices should hold a preliminary hearing if it is represented to them that the confession is in breach of section 76. The defendant may give evidence which is confined to the question of admissibility.

At the *voire dire,* the burden of proving that the conditions of admissibility have been met must lie on the party wishing to adduce the evidence. In criminal proceedings, where the prosecution bear the onus of proof, the evidence will not be admissible unless the conditions for admissibility are proved beyond reasonable doubt. However the standard of proof for the defence is on the preponderance of probabilities and this would be the same for parties in civil proceedings.[41]

Voire dire and the admissibility of confessions

One of the commonest issues for the judge in a criminal case is the admissibility of a confession. The most common situation is where such an incriminating statement has allegedly been made to a police officer. Under the conditions laid down by section 76 of the Police and Criminal Evidence Act 1984, the confession must not have been obtained in circumstances which would not render it unreliable nor by oppression:

> 76.—(2) If, in any proceedings where the prosecution proposes to give in evidence a confession made by an accused person, it is represented to the court that the confession was or may have been obtained —
>
> (a) by oppression of the person who made it; or
>
> (b) in consequence of anything said or done which was likely, in the circumstances existing at the time, to render unreliable any confession which might be made by him in consequence thereof,

[39] [1987] 2 All E.R. 668.
[40] *Wong Kam-ming v. R.* [1979] 1 All E.R. 939 — this is discussed at 45, *et seq.*
[41] This is discussed further at 89, *et seq.*

the court shall not allow the confession to be given in evidence against him except in so far as the prosecution proves to the court beyond reasonable doubt that the confession (notwithstanding that it may be true) was not obtained as aforesaid.

Section 78 is also relevant.[42] This is a provision which is not limited to confessions and requires that the admission of any evidence, including confessions, must not have an adverse effect on the fairness of the proceedings. Whether the preconditions laid down by either section 76 or section 78 are satisfied must be settled by *voire dire.* Where the prosecution proposes to offer a confession in evidence, normally defence counsel will notify the prosecution that the statement is to be challenged, in order to prevent any reference to the statement in the prosecution opening speech. However, even if there is no objection, the trial judge can act on his or her own initiative. Under the Police and Criminal Evidence Act 1984:

76.—(3) In any proceedings where the prosecution proposes to give in evidence a confession made by an accused person, the court may of its own motion require the prosecution as a condition of allowing it do so, to prove that the confession was not obtained as mentioned in subsection (2) above.

Where the judge initiates a hearing, a tactical problem confronts the defence. Should it actively seek to exclude the confession (which would alert the prosecution witnesses to the defence strategy) or should it keep its powder dry in order to attack the confession in the trial proper? If the confession is excluded, nothing more is heard of it. But, even if it is admitted, the defence may still wish to cross-examine the same witnesses, often police officers, on the same issues in front of the jury with the objective of undermining the weight that the jury might place on that confession.[43]

When the statement is admitted, the *voire dire* decision is not necessarily the end of the matter as the judge retains discretion at common law[44] to take steps to prevent injustice. In *R. v. Sat-Bhambra*[45] the defendant was charged with drug smuggling. There were several taped interviews, some of which were excluded because of the possible effect of medication given to the defendant who was diabetic. However, some of the tapes were admitted. During the course of the trial proper, the doctor, who had previously testified on *voire dire,* was more robust in his view that the defendant could have been suffering from hypoglycaemia at the time of the interviews. The judge declined to reconsider the question of the admissibility of the tapes on the grounds that the terms of section 76 precluded him from doing so. The Court of Appeal, although dismissing

[42] This is discussed further in Chap. 4.

[43] In magistrates' court, it should never be necessary to call prosecution evidence relating to the obtaining of a confession twice — *R. v. Liverpool Juvenile Court ex parte R.* [1987] 2 All E.R. 668 at 673b.

[44] Preserved by the Police and Criminal Evidence Act 1984, s.82(3).

[45] [1988] Crim.L.R. 453.

the appeal, did say that a judge has power to take such steps as are necessary to prevent injustice and this might involve directing the jury to disregard the statement or discharging the jury and ordering a new trial.

In order to challenge the admissibility of a confession, it is very likely that the defendant would give evidence as to the circumstances in which he or she made the statement. In *voire dire,* the relevant facts in issue are the conditions which attach to the admissibility of the evidence. Consequently the prosecution cannot examine the defendant on the truth or falsity of the alleged confession because, even if it is true, it may still have been obtained by oppression. In *Wong Kam-ming v. R.*,[46] six men were charged with murder and malicious wounding. The only evidence against the accused was a signed statement that he had been present at the scene and had "chopped" someone with a penknife. At *voire dire*, he admitted that he had been present at the attack but that he had been forced to copy out the statement and sign it. The confession was excluded but in the trial proper, the prosecution called two shorthand writers who had recorded the *voire dire* to testify that the defendant had admitted to being present. Also the accused was cross-examined on the discrepancies between what he had said at *voire dire* and what he was now saying in the course of his examination-in-chief. The Privy Council quashed the conviction:

Wong Kam-ming v. R. [1979] 1 All E.R. 939, at 942a–946d, _per_ Lord Edmund-Davies

Questions 1 and 2: relevance of truth of extra-judicial statements

In *R. v. Hammond*[47] prosecuting counsel was held entitled to ask the accused, when cross-examining him during the *voire dire*, whether a police statement which the accused alleged had been extorted by gross maltreatment was in fact true, and elicited the answer that it was . . .

Although much criticised, that decision has frequently been followed in England and Wales and in many other jurisdictions . . .

. . . But the basis of this assertion [that questions as to the truth of the confession go to the credibility of the defendant] is unclear. If the accused denies the truth of the confession or some self-incriminating admission contained in it, the question whether his denial is itself true or false cannot be ascertained until after the *voire dire* is over and the accused's guilt or innocence has been determined by the jury, an issue which the judge has no jurisdiction to decide. If, on the other hand, the accused made a self-incriminating admission that the statement is true, then, as one critic has expressed it, 'If the confession is true, this presumably shows that the accused tends to tell the truth, which suggests that he is telling the truth in saying the police were violent'.

The sole object of the *voire dire* was to determine the voluntariness of the alleged confession in accordance with principles long established . . . [T]he startling consequences of adopting the *Hammond* approach were well illustrated in the Canadian case of *R. v. Hnedish*[48] where Hall C.J. said:

[46] [1979] 1 All E.R. 939.
[47] [1941] 3 All E.R. 318.
[48] (1958) 26 W.W.R. 685.

> . . . I do not see how under the guise of 'credibility' the court can transmute what is initially an inquiry as to the 'admissibility' of the confession into an inquisition of an accused. That would be repugnant to our accepted standards and principles of justice; it would invite and encourage brutality in the handling of persons suspected of having committed offences.

It is right to point out that learned counsel for the Crown did not seek to submit that the prosecution could in every case properly cross-examine the accused during the *voire dire* regarding the truth of his challenged statement . . . But he was unable to formulate an acceptable test of its propriety, and their Lordships have been driven to the conclusion that none exists. In other words, in their Lordships' view, *R. v. Hammond* was wrongly decided . . .

Their Lordships turn to questions 3 and 4. As part of its case on the main issue, may the prosecution lead evidence regarding the testimony given by the accused on the *voire dire*? . . .

. . . in the instant appeal counsel for the Crown felt constrained to submit that, even were the trial judge to exclude a confession on the ground that torture had been used to extort it, any damaging statements made by the accused on the *voire dire* could nevertheless properly be adduced as part of the prosecution's case. Boldness could go no further.

Fortunately for justice, their Lordships have concluded that, where the confession has been excluded, the argument against ever admitting such evidence as part of the Crown case must prevail . . . But what if the confession is held admissible? . . . their Lordships have . . . concluded that the same exclusion of evidence regarding the *voire dire* proceedings from the main trial must be observed, regardless of whether the challenged confession be excluded or admitted . . .

Question 5 remains for consideration by their Lordships. Notwithstanding the answer to question 3, in the event of the accused giving evidence in the main trial, may he be cross-examined in respect of statements made by him during that *voire dire*? . . .

In *R. v. Treacy*,[49] where the accused's answers under police interrogation were held inadmissible, it was held that he could not be cross-examined to elicit that he had in fact given those answers . . . *R. v. Treacy* was undoubtedly correct in prohibiting cross-examination as to the contents of confessions which the court has ruled inadmissible. But what if during the *voire dire* the accused has made self-incriminating statements not strictly related to the confession itself but which nevertheless have relevance to the issue of guilt or innocence of the charge preferred? May the accused be cross-examined so as to elicit those matters? In the light of their Lordships' earlier conclusion that the Crown may not adduce as part of its case evidence of what the accused said during a *voire dire* culminating in the exclusion of an impugned confession, can a different approach here be permitted from that condemned in *R. v. Treacy*?

Subject to what was said to be the court's discretion to exclude it in proper circumstances, counsel for the Crown submitted that it can be, citing in support section 13 of the Hong Kong Evidence Ordinance, which was based on the familiar provision in section 4 of the Criminal Procedure Act 1865 of the United Kingdom, relating to the confrontation of a witness with his previous inconsistent statements. But these statutory provisions have no relevance if the earlier statements cannot be put in evidence. And, having already concluded that the *voire dire* statements of the accused are not admissible during the presentation of the prosecution's case, their Lordships find it impossible in principle to distinguish between such cross-examination of the accused on the basis of the *voire dire* as was permitted in the

[49] [1944] 2 All E.R. 229.

instant case by the trial judge and upheld by the majority of the Court of Appeal and that cross-examination based on the contents of an excluded confession which, it is common ground, was rightly condemned in *R. v. Treacy*.

But what if the *voire dire* resulted in the impugned confession being admitted, and the accused later elects to give evidence? If he then testifies to matters relating, for example, to the reliability of the confession (as opposed to its voluntariness, which ex hypothesi, is no longer in issue) and in so doing gives answers which are markedly different from his testimony given during the *voire dire*, may he be cross-examined so as to establish that at the earlier stage of the trial he had told a different story? Great injustice could well result from the exclusion of such cross-examination, and their Lordships can see no justification in legal principle or on any other ground which renders it impermissible. As has already been observed, an accused seeking to challenge the admissibility of a confession may for all practical purposes be obliged to testify in the *voire dire* if his challenge is to have any chance of succeeding, and his evidence is then (or certainly should be) restricted solely to the issue of the admissibility of the confession. But the situation is quite different where, the confession having been admitted despite his challenge, the accused later elects to give evidence during the main trial and, in doing so, departs materially from the testimony he gave in the *voire dire*. Having so chosen to testify, why should the discrepancies not be elicited and demonstrated by cross-examination? In their Lordships' view, his earlier statements made in the *voire dire* provide as acceptable as basis for this cross-examination to that end as any other earlier statements made by him, including, of course, his confession which, though challenged, had been ruled admissible. Indeed, for such purposes and in such circumstances, his *voire dire* statements stand on no different basis than, for example, the sworn testimony given by an accused in a previous trial where the jury had disagreed.

No doubt the trial judge has a discretion and, indeed, a duty to ensure that the right of the prosecution to cross-examine or rebut is not used in a manner unfair or oppressive to the accused, and no doubt the judge is under an obligation to see to it that any statutory provisions bearing on the situation . . . are strictly complied with. But, subject thereto, their Lordships hold that cross-examination in the circumstances predicated which is directed to testing the credibility of the accused by establishing the inconsistencies in his evidence is wholly permissible.

In the instant case, however, the challenged confession was excluded. It therefore follows that in the judgment of their Lordships no less than three substantial irregularities occurred in the trial: (1) in the *voire dire* the accused was cross-examined with a view to establishing that his extra-judicial statement was true; (2) in the trial proper, the Crown was permitted to call as part of its case evidence regarding answers given by the accused during the *voire dire*; and (3) the accused was permitted to be cross-examined so as to demonstrate that what he had said in chief was inconsistent with his statement in the *voire dire* . . .

Wong Kam-ming is persuasive authority that incriminating statements made by the accused at the *voire dire* are not admissible evidence in the trial proper, whether as evidence-in-chief or on cross-examination. This was supported by the House of Lords in *R. v. Brophy*[50] where the defendant was tried on charges of murder, of causing explosions and of being a member of the IRA. The only evidence against him was statements made to police officers. After a *voire dire*, all the statements were excluded. However, during examination-in-chief at the *voire dire*, the accused had

[50] [1981] 2 All E.R. 705.

admitted to being a member of the IRA. The trial judge allowed the prosecution to advance evidence of that statement. On appeal to the House of Lords:

R. v. Brophy [1981] 2 All E.R. 705 at 709a–f, _per_ Lord Fraser

I would rest my opinion of relevance also on a wider ground. Where, as in this case, evidence is given at the *voire dire* by an accused person in answer to questions by his counsel, and without objection by counsel for the Crown, his evidence ought in my opinion to be treated as relevant to the issue at the *voire dire*, unless it is clearly and obviously irrelevant. The accused should be given the benefit of any reasonable doubt. Of course, if the accused, whether in answer to questions from his own counsel or not, goes out of his way to boast of having committed the crimes with which he is charged, or if he uses the witness box as a platform for a political speech, his evidence so far as it relates to those matters will almost certainly be irrelevant to the issue at the *voire dire*, and different considerations will apply to its admissibility at the substantive trial. But on any reasonable view of the respondent's evidence in this case it cannot be said to be clearly and obviously irrelevant.

Once it has been held that the material part of the respondent's evidence was relevant to the issue at the *voire dire*, a necessary consequence is, in my opinion, that it is not admissible in the substantive trial. Indeed, counsel for the Crown did not argue to the contrary. If such evidence, being relevant, were admissible at the substantive trial, an accused person would not enjoy the complete freedom that he ought to have at the *voire dire* to contest the admissibility of his previous statements. It is of the first importance for the administration of justice that an accused person should feel completely free to give evidence at the *voire dire* of any improper methods by which a confession or an admission has been extracted from him, for he can almost never make an effective challenge of its admissibility without giving evidence himself. He is virtually compelled to give evidence at the *voire dire*, and if his evidence were admissible at the substantive trial, the result might be a significant impairment of his so-called 'right of silence' at the trial . . .

The result of these decisions is that, at common law, the prosecution is prevented from adducing incriminating statements made by the accused at the *voire dire* as part of the Crown case. But it has been argued[51] that decisions before 1984 could be reconsidered in light of the wording of section 76, since there is no question of a statement made in the course of a *voire dire*, such as that in *Brophy*, being obtained by oppression or in circumstances conducive to its unreliability. Such statements are consequently admissible under section 76. Even were this argument to be correct on strict construction of the statute, it is possible that the policy behind *Brophy* could be maintained by invoking section 78, an approach favoured in Australia,[52] but rejected by Lord Fraser:

> With all respect, I cannot regard that as satisfactory solution. The right of the accused to give evidence at the *voire dire* without affecting his right to remain silent at the substantive trial is in my opinion absolute and is not to be made conditional on an exercise of judicial discretion.[53]

[51] Tapper C., *Cross and Tapper on Evidence* (8th ed., 1995) 186.

[52] *R. v. Wright* [1969] S.A.S.R. 256.

[53] *Brophy* at 710d–e, *per* Lord Fraser. This principle is not affected by the derogation from the right of silence contained in the Criminal Justice and Public Order Act 1994, s.35 since the right must remain until, in the substantive trial itself, the prosecution has adduced sufficient admissible evidence.

Wong Kam-ming suggests, where the accused testifies at the trial proper, that the right of the prosecution to cross-examine the accused on testimony given at *voire dire* depends upon the outcome of that *voire dire*. Where the confession is excluded, the prosecution can use neither the confession itself[54] nor any statements made on *voire dire* in order to discredit the accused by using them as previous inconsistent statements. However, where the challenged confession is admitted into evidence, the whole evidence relating to the confession is rehearsed in front of the jury and the defendant's statements on oath on the *voire dire* are not to be differentiated by any other earlier statements made by him or her.

Judicial discretion to exclude evidence

As the last sections have shown, the judge has the capacity to exclude evidence as a matter of law. But the judge can also exercise a discretion to exclude evidence. This discretion arises as part of a general supervisory function over the trial and an obligation to ensure a fair trial. But, while judges can exclude admissible evidence by use of their discretionary powers, they do not have the power to admit inadmissible evidence. If evidence is inadmissible, that is the end of the matter, regardless of any considerations that may be put forward regarding the public interest or the administration of justice.

The discretion to exclude concerns evidence which is otherwise relevant, has sufficient probative value in relation to the time and trouble caused by its admission and is not subject to any other exclusionary rule. But even where these conditions exist, evidence may still be excluded. At common law, this can occur where the prejudicial effect of the evidence is so great as to outweigh any probative value. The scope of the judge's discretion at common law is discussed by the House of Lords in *R. v. Sang*.[55] This discretion has been retained by the Police and Criminal Evidence Act 1984:

> 82.—(3) Nothing in this part of the Act shall prejudice any power of a court to exclude evidence (whether by preventing questions from being put or otherwise) at its discretion.

But the judgment in *Sang* has undoubtedly been affected by the impact of section 78 of the Police and Criminal Evidence Act 1984 which requires a judge to take account of all the circumstances, including those in which the evidence was obtained, in deciding whether the admission of the evidence would have *"an adverse effect on the fairness of the proceedings"*. These questions are discussed later.[56]

[54] *Treacy supra.*
[55] [1979] 2 All E.R. 46.
[56] See 95, *et seq.*

Withdrawal of issues

As has been mentioned, the ultimate decision in any case rests with the trier of fact. But the judge exercises significant control by his or her ability to withdraw issues from the jury. This involves a judgment as to whether sufficient evidence on a particular point has been produced for that issue to be decided by the jury.[57] For example, in *Metropolitan Rly Co v. Jackson*,[58] the plaintiff sued for damages, having crushed a thumb in a carriage door. There was evidence that the train had been overcrowded but none that the overcrowding had caused the plaintiff's thumb to be in the wrong place at the wrong time. The judge correctly withdrew the issue from the jury:

***Metropolitan Rly Co. v. Jackson* (1877) 3 App. Cas. 193, at 196–197, *per* Lord Cairns L.C.**

The question is, was there at the trial any evidence of this negligence which ought to have been left to the jury? . . . the judge has a certain duty to discharge and the jurors have another and a different duty. The judge has to say whether any facts have been established by evidence from which negligence may be reasonably inferred; the jurors have to say whether, from those facts, when submitted to them, negligence ought to be inferred. It is, in my opinion, of the greatest importance to the administration of justice that these separate functions should be maintained, and should be maintained distinct. It would be a serious inroad on the province of the jury, if, in a case where there are facts from which negligence may reasonably be inferred, the judge were to withdraw the case from the jury upon the ground that, in his opinion, negligence ought not to be inferred; and it would, on the other hand, place in the hands of the jurors a power which might be exercised in the most arbitrary manner, if they were at liberty to hold that negligence might be inferred from any state of facts whatever . . .

This brings out the difference in function between the judge and jury. However in civil proceedings nowadays, the judge rarely sits with a jury. If, at the end of the plaintiff's case, the defendant makes a submission of "no case to answer". the judge would not rule on this unless the defendant elects not to call evidence.[59] The reasoning behind such a requirement to elect is that the judge in a civil matter is trier of fact as well as of law and a party should not expect the judge to express an opinion on the evidence until it is complete. However, where the judge sits with a jury, there is no such requirement.[60]

In criminal matters, at the end of the prosecution case, it is common for the defence to argue that there is no case to answer because the prosecution had failed to produce sufficient evidence on a constituent element of the offence. But what is "sufficient"? The leading authority is *R. v. Galbraith* [1981] 2 All E.R. 1060 at 1062e–g, *per* Lord Lane C.J.:

[57] This is discussed further in the next chapter in relation to the evidential burden of proof.
[58] (1877) 3 App. Cas. 193.
[59] *Alexander v. Rayson* [1935] 1 All E.R. Rep. 185.
[60] *Young v. Rank* [1950] 2 All E.R. 166.

How then should the judge approach a submission of 'no case'? (1) If there is no evidence that the crime alleged has been committed by the defendant, there is no difficulty. The judge will of course stop the case. (2) The difficulty arises where there is some evidence but it is of a tenuous character, for example, because of inherent weakness or vagueness or because it is inconsistent with other evidence. (a) Where the judge comes to the conclusion that the prosecution evidence, taken at its highest, is such that a jury properly directed could not properly convict upon it, it is his duty, upon a submission being made, to stop the case. (b) Where, however, the prosecution evidence is such that its strength or weakness depends on the view to be taken of a witness's reliability, or other matters which are generally speaking within the province of the jury and where on one possible view of the facts there is evidence upon which a jury could properly come to the conclusion that the defendant is guilty, then the judge should allow the matter to be tried by the jury . . .

The narrow limits allowed by *Galbraith* for judicial intervention have been criticised,[61] not least because there is a wider power to stop unmeritorious prosecutions in the magistrates' court. A Practice Direction from 1962[62] directs justices to uphold a submission where:

> . . . the evidence adduced by the prosecution has been so discredited as a result of cross-examination or is so manifestly unreliable that no reasonable tribunal could safely convict on it . . .

and there is little justification to distinguish between the two types of trial:

Pattenden R., "The Submission of No Case — Some Recent Developments" [1982] Crim.L.R. 564–565

The object of a submission of no case on a trial on indictment is two-fold. To avoid the risk of a perverse jury verdict and to protect the accused against a prosecutor who has failed to make out a prima facie case and hopes to make good the deficiency by cross-examining the witnesses for the defence. The accused needs this sort of protection as much in a case where the prosecution evidence is so unsound that no reasonable jury could believe the evidence against him as in a case where the prosecution has not mustered sufficient evidence, even if all the evidence is believed, for a lawful conviction. There is no good reason to trust the jury more in the first than in the second case and no inherent reason why a judge should be better equipped to deal with the second than the first matter. In some ways the judge is in a better position to decide the first point than an appellate court to whom the accused may eventually appeal. He sees the witnesses in person, though unlike the appellate court when it considers whether a conviction is unsatisfactory he has only the prosecution evidence to go on — the appellate court reviews all the evidence presented at the trial. An accused may feel genuinely aggrieved if an appellate court upholds a conviction where the trial judge has indicated that he considers a conviction unsupportable.

[61] Pattenden R., "The Submission of No Case — Some Recent Developments" [1982] Crim.L.R. 558.
[62] [1962] 1 All E.R. 448.

The Royal Commission on Criminal Justice accepted this position and recommended that the *Galbraith* rule be overturned.[63] However the Privy Council in *Daley v. R.*[64] rejected the opportunity to broaden the base for judicial intervention. In that case, the prosecution rested upon identification evidence considered by the judge to have serious weaknesses. Under the *Turnbull*[65] rule, a judge should warn the jury about the dangers of convicting on unsupported evidence of identification but, further, should withdraw the case from the jury altogether where that evidence is poor. This latter rule appears to clash with the *Galbraith* rule that the honesty and reliability of witnesses is a matter for the jury. Lord Mustill resolves this dilemma:

Daley v. R. [1993] 4 All E.R. 86 at 94g–j, _per_ Lord Mustill

A reading of the judgment in *R. v. Galbraith* as a whole shows that the practice which the court was primarily concerned to proscribe was one whereby a judge who considered the prosecution evidence as unworthy of credit would make sure that the jury did not have an opportunity to give effect to a different opinion. By following this practice the judge was doing something which . . . was not his job. By contrast, in the kind of identification case dealt with by *R. v. Turnbull* the case is withdrawn from the jury not because the judge considers that the witness is lying, but because the evidence even if taken to be honest has a base which is so slender that it is unreliable and therefore not sufficient to found a conviction: and indeed as *R. v. Turnbull* itself emphasised, the fact that an honest witness may be mistaken on identification is a particular source of risk. When assessing the 'quality' of the evidence, under the *Turnbull* doctrine, the jury is protected from acting upon the type of evidence which, even if believed, experience has shown to be a possible source of injustice. Reading the two cases in this way, their Lordships see no conflict between them . . .

Submissions of "no case" are not the only situations where a judge might withdraw an issue from the jury. For example, the defendant charged with murder might argue that he or she is not guilty of murder but guilty of manslaughter on the grounds of diminished responsibility under section 2 of the Homicide Act 1957. Subsection (2) places the persuasive burden on the defence and the judge might well refuse to allow that issue to go to the jury if the defendant had produced so little evidence that a reasonable jury, properly directed, could not on the balance of probabilities find in the accused's favour.

Summing up

One of the final stages of the trial is the judge summing up the case for the jury. This is also known as directing the jury. The summing up falls into two parts: a direction to the jury on the law to be applied and a summary

[63] Cm. 2263 (1993) para. 4.42.
[64] [1993] 4 All E.R. 86.
[65] *R. v. Turnbull* [1976] 3 All E.R. 549 — see 301, *et seq.*

of the evidence that has been put before them. A misdirection is frequently the basis of any appeal. As the final arbiter of the law, the judge must explain all the elements of the offence charged: in *R. v. McVey*[66] the accused was an employee suspected of stealing from his employer. A trap was set by marking all the bank notes at the accused's place of work and he was later found in possession of two marked £10 notes. His defence was that he had changed a £20 note. The judge told the jury that there was only one issue for them to consider, namely whether the accused was dishonest when he took the notes. The conviction was quashed as the jury had not been directed as to all the ingredients of the offence of theft. Obviously a judge must mention all such ingredients even if he or she places emphasis on those aspects that are related to the facts of the particular case.

The judge must also refer to any defences raised expressly by the accused or disclosed by the evidence, whether that evidence was led by the prosecution or the defence. He or she will also mention any necessary aspects of evidence: for example, the need for supportive evidence in certain situations; the dangers of convicting on identification evidence; the accused's right of silence and any inferences that may be drawn from a failure to testify. The summing up must also contain references to the burden and standard of proof. Failure to direct the jury that the prosecution bears the burden of proof beyond reasonable doubt can lead to any conviction being overturned by the Court of Appeal.[67]

The second aspect of the judge's direction will be an abbreviated version of the evidence that the jury have heard. However in *R. v. Wilson*[68] the judge told the jury, after a short case, that it was unnecessary for him to review the facts which must still be fresh in their minds. In that case, the Court of Appeal did not interfere but disapproved of this course in *R. v. Gregory*[69] saying that there must be a reminder of the facts in all cases. The difficulty is that any summary of the facts cannot be wholly neutral and must inevitably transmit the judge's opinions:

> It is not unknown for judges, while emphasising that matters of fact are for the jury and not for the judge, to comment on the facts in such a way as to attempt to influence the jury in one direction or another.[70]

The Royal Commission on Criminal Justice considered the possibility of introducing written jury charges, such as those used in New York State, which are in effect a string of explanatory notes by the judge. But the Royal Commission regarded any rule limiting the extent to which a judge should sum up on the facts as unnecessary, although they showed a

[66] [1988] Crim.L.R. 127.
[67] *R. v. Donoghue* (1987) 86 Cr.App.R. 267; *R. v. Edwards* (1983) 77 Cr.App.R. 5.
[68] [1991] Crim.L.R. 838.
[69] [1993] Crim.L.R. 623.
[70] Royal Commission on Criminal Justice *op. cit.* para. 8.21.

preference for the minimalist approach and the views of the Court of Appeal in *Wilson*.

A corollary to succinct directions is the need for a judge to be wholly neutral in any comment on the credibility of the evidence:

> It is appropriate for judges to identify for a jury questions, which are for them to decide, of a witness's credibility; it is inappropriate for judges to intrude their own views of whether or not a witness is to be believed. This is consistent with the need in some cases, for example where there is identification or confession evidence, for special guidance to be given as to its reliability. The precise balance between law and fact in a judge's summing up will be a matter for the judge to decide in the light of the facts of each case. We are well aware that summing up is an extremely difficult task, often calling for the exercise of great skill and judgment.[71]

The judge cannot direct the jury to accept his or her version of any disputed facts: in *R. v. Marr*[72] a conviction for indecent assault was quashed after the judge ridiculed the defence that the accused had stumbled and accidentally put his hand between the woman's legs:

> . . . however distasteful the offence, however repulsive the defendant, however laughable his defence, he is nevertheless entitled to have his case fairly presented to the jury both by counsel and by the judge.[73]

Nor can the judge direct the jury to bring in a verdict of guilty, although the opposite, as we have seen, is possible. There can be a directed acquittal after a defence submission of no case to answer at the close of the prosecution case. The "directed conviction" was discounted in *DPP v. Stonehouse*.[74] A prominent politician who was in financial difficulties arranged life insurance in favour of his wife and then faked his own death by drowning in Miami. No claims were made on the policies and, after the defendant was discovered in Australia and extradited, he was charged with attempting to obtain property by deception. At the trial the judge directed the jury to bring in a verdict of guilty if they were satisfied that he staged the death with a dishonest intention. By such a direction, the judge effectively withdrew from the jury another fundamental element of the offence, namely whether the act was sufficiently proximate to constitute an attempt.

DPP v. Stonehouse [1977] 2 All E.R. 909 at 927f–928c, *per* Lord Salmon

Whilst there is no doubt that, if a judge is satisfied that there is no evidence before the jury which could justify them in convicting the accused and that it would be perverse for them to do so, it is the judge's duty to direct them to acquit.

[71] *ibid.* para. 8.23.
[72] (1989) 90 Cr.App.R. 154.
[73] *ibid.* at 156, *per* Lord Lane C.J.
[74] [1977] 2 All E.R. 909.

> This rule, which has long been established, is to protect the accused against being wrongly convicted. But there is no converse rule, although there may be some who think that there should be. If the judge is satisfied that, on the evidence, the jury would not be justified in acquitting the accused and indeed that it would be perverse of them to do so, he has no power to pre-empt the jury's verdict by directing them to convict. The jury alone have the right to decide that the accused is guilty. In an appropriate case (and this was certainly such a case) the judge may sum up in such a way as to make it plain that he considers that the accused is guilty and should be convicted. I doubt however whether the most effective way of doing so would be for the judge to tell the jury that it would be perverse for them to acquit. Such a course might well be counter-productive.[75]

However in *R. v. Hill*[76] the defendant caused criminal damage to the fence of a U.S. naval base fence. The defence was that she had lawful cause in that by forcing the Americans to withdraw, she would be protecting her own property from the threat of nuclear attack. The trial court held that this was not lawful cause and thus directed the jury to convict. The Court of Appeal distinguished *Stonehouse* and did not interfere. Perhaps the consequences of the "uncontrolled" jury can be seen in a case in 1996 when women who broke into a British Aerospace factory and caused an estimated £1.5 million damage to a Hawk fighter jet were acquitted after claiming that their actions were justified on political grounds. A jury accepted the women's claim that they had a lawful excuse to damage the aircraft because they were using reasonable force to prevent a crime. The jet was to be sold to Indonesia and the accused feared that it would be used by the Government there against the people of East Timor.[77]

Functions of Juries

The jury is not a democratic part of the trial. Jurors are randomly selected, untrained and unpaid amateurs from all sections of the population and are, in theory, the least controlled aspect of criminal justice. There are very few jury trials in civil actions. They are unpaid.[78] Trial by jury has been regarded as a paradigm of English criminal law, described as a bulwark against oppression, a safeguard of our liberties since the common sense of the ordinary person prevails when all else fails.[79] The acquittal of Clive Ponting represents that. He was a senior civil servant who had sent documents to an opposition M.P. These related to the sinking of the Argentinean battleship, the Belgrano, in the course of the Falklands conflict. Prosecuted under the Official Secrets Act 1911, he admitted passing the documents. The judge virtually instructed the jury to convict yet they still acquitted.[80]

75 Lord Diplock and Viscount Dilhorne dissented.
76 [1989] Crim.L.R. 136.
77 *The Times*, July 31, 1996.
78 Although there is a financial loss allowance, wholly inadequate for the self-employed — Royal Commission on Criminal Justice, *op. cit.* para. 8.56.
79 Devlin P., *Trial By Jury* (1956).
80 *The Times*, February 12, 1985.

Whether the jury often live up to this ideal is moot.[81] Jackson wrote that the only cure for admiration of juries is to read *Howell's State Trials*, not least, the account of the conviction, by a jury, in 1792 of Thomas Paine for writing *The Rights of Man*. What is undoubted that it is *"the most ancient relic in any modern legal system"*,[82] dating from Anglo-Saxon and Anglo-Norman times. While the continental legal systems devised complex systems of logical proof, the English used the jury:[83]

Arnold T., *Symbols of Government* (1962) 144–45

In addition to the notion of fair hearing, the ceremonial trial must dramatize the impersonal application of logical rules to facts. Here we have the contradiction between the ideal of a permanent unyielding law which must be enforced without respect to persons, and the ideal of justice, which can never ignore persons. This conflict is resolved as most conflicts are resolved, by inventing a devil who can be blamed for the inconsistencies of the system. In the American trial the part of the devil is taken by the jury. We are constantly defending the jury as the best device for securing 'Justice' ever invented, and at the same time attacking it and seeking to limit its functions. The defense always refers to juries in general as an institution protecting our liberties, etc. The attack always centres about juries in particular types of cases, considered as an unpredictable body, moved by emotional considerations, and not careful of the fundamental principles of law because of ignorance, prejudice, etc. Yet the jury continues as the great symbol of justice, in spite of constant proof of its inadequacy in particular cases.

Actually, of course, the reason for the existence of the jury is to absorb the criticism of the numerous unsatisfactory results in the trial of cases, and thus to deflect it against the judicial system itself. When [a notorious criminal] is acquitted, we blame the jury if we do not like the result. We cannot blame the law, because according to the law there was a question of fact to be left to the jury which the law had no right to decide.

Apart from its role as a simple and understandable symbol, the jury has to listen to the testimony and other evidence provided by the prosecution or defence. It is their function to assess the credibility of a witness, to measure the weight that should be given to any piece of evidence and to determine the existence or non-existence of the facts in the case. Having determined the facts, the jury must apply those to the legal issues in the case, as explained to them by the judge, and, by applying the burden and standard of proof, come to a conclusion.

Often this process can require considerable clarity of thought on the part of the juror who may be told that he or she is entitled to use an accused's confession as evidence against that defendant but not as evidence against a co-accused; that the previous convictions which have been put to the defendant in cross-examination are not evidence of guilt but simply go to the defendant's credibility; that a previous statement consistent with present testimony is not evidence of the facts but can merely enhance the

[81] See discussion in Spencer J., *Jackson's Machinery of Justice* (8th ed., 1989) 390 *et seq.*
[82] Milsom H., *Historical Foundations of the Common Law* (1981) 413.
[83] *ibid.* 410.

weight the jury might give to that witness's evidence. The extent to which the jury understand and implement the judge's directions remains unclear.[84]

There is an apparently clear demarcation between the juror as the trier of fact and the judicial function as final arbiter of substantive and evidential law. But this distinction often becomes clouded as the definition of many offences include legal concepts which masquerade as "facts". Although there is a general rule that the construction of ordinary words in a statute is a question of fact for the trier of fact, these concepts are relatively imprecise in their definition. The key elements of theft, for example, are legal concepts of appropriation, property belonging to another and intent to deprive,[85] all of which may need explanation and definition by the judge because the law uses the terms in a manner which is outside any common usage of the terms themselves. But theft also requires "dishonesty" and this can be left, more or less straightforwardly,[86] as a matter of fact for the jury:

> Well, it is a matter for you to consider, members of the jury, but try to place yourselves in [the appellant's] position and answer the question whether in your view he thought he was acting honestly or dishonestly?[87]

While some terms have acquired a special meaning as a result of statute and of authority and the judge can direct the jury as to their meaning, others remain ordinary word which should be left to the jury to construe. How do we tell which terms fall into which category? In *Brutus v. Cozens*[88] the defendant, an anti-apartheid demonstrator, had interrupted Wimbledon by blowing whistles and distributing leaflets. He was charged under section 5 of the Public Order Act 1936 with using insulting behaviour in a public place. The justices (who, in summary trials, are the tribunal of fact and equivalent to the jury) held that the behaviour was not insulting and dismissed the information. The Divisional Court held that conduct which evinced disrespect for the rights of others so as to cause resentment was insulting within the meaning of the Act. The House of Lords reversed this approach, holding that the construction of the term was not a matter of law for the judge but for the trier of fact:

Brutus v. Cozens [1972] 2 All E.R. 1297, at 1299a–d, *per* Lord Reid

The meaning of an ordinary word of the English language is not a question of law. The proper construction of a statute is a question of law. If the context shows that a word is used in an unusual sense the court will determine in other words what that

[84] Not least because empirical research into the way juries function would be contempt of court under the Contempt of Court Act 1981, s.8.

[85] Smith J. and Hogan B.: *Criminal Law* (7th ed., 1992) Chap. 16.

[86] *R. v. Feely* [1973] 3 All E.R. 341 but matters have become more complex with *R. v. Ghosh* [1982] 2 All E.R. 689.

[87] Trial judge's direction to the jury in *R. v. Gilks* [1972] 3 All E.R. 280 at 283.

[88] [1972] 2 All E.R. 1297.

unusual sense is. But here there is in my opinion no question of the word 'insulting' being used in an unusual sense. It appears to me . . . to be intended to have its ordinary meaning. It is for the tribunal which decides the case to consider, not as law but as fact, whether in the whole circumstances the words of the statute do or do not as a matter of ordinary usage of the English language cover or apply to the facts which have been proved . . .

In *Stonehouse*, the issue was whether the defendant's acts (faking his own suicide) were "sufficiently proximate" to his wife's obtaining the insurance money to form the *actus reus* of the offence of an attempt to obtain that money by deception. This idea of "proximity"[89] was in itself is a fact which needed to be proved and decided by the jury:

DPP v. Stonehouse [1977] 2 All E.R. 909 at 918g–j, _per_ Lord Diplock

There are some crimes whose definition incorporates as a constituent element a concept which is imprecise in that it involves some matter of degree on which opinions of reasonable men may differ and as to which the legal training and experience of a judge does not make his opinion on the matter more likely to be right than that of a non-lawyer. Under our system of trial by jury the question whether the facts proved conform to such a concept is one for the jury despite its involving interpretation of the definition of a crime; because, it being a matter on which opinions may reasonably differ, an opinion shared by at least ten jurors is thought to be more reliable than that of a single judge.

Stonehouse and *Brutus v. Cozens* are both authority for the proposition that it is for the jury to decide upon and apply the meaning of ordinary English words. Thus the jury have an interpretative function but it only takes a cursory glance around the criminal law to see that these common sense concepts are frequently circumscribed by quite detailed definitions: in *R. v. Caldwell*,[90] the House of Lords define when a defendant may be "reckless"; in the decisions in *R. v. Hancock*[91] and *R. v. Nedrick*[92] it is when he or she is acting "intentionally". It is difficult to see why a court should interpret "intentional" for a jury but not the term "insulting". *Brutus v. Cozens* is honoured more in the breach than in its observance.

[89] The test for criminal attempts is now that of "more than merely preparatory" under the Criminal Attempts Act 1981.
[90] [1981] 1 All E.R. 961.
[91] [1986] 1 All E.R. 641.
[92] [1986] 3 All E.R. 1.

3

THE BURDEN AND STANDARD OF PROOF

What is Proof?

In both the everyday and the legal world, the term "proof" is used quite loosely. When we wish to test an assertion, we often say, "Have you any proof of that?". This question encompasses two senses of the term since we are asking "Do you have any evidence of what you say?" as well as "Can you prove the correctness of what you say?". This chapter uses the term in the latter sense: to prove an assertion is to demonstrate that the assertion is correct. But what do we regard as correct? Neither life nor law operates as a mathematical proof which, given certain assumptions and the operation of mathematical functions, produces the correct answer. In contrast, inferential logic requires that we test the strength of our assumptions and the inferences that are drawn from them. How strong must that inference be before we regard it as correct? How confident must we be in our conclusions?

In normal life, we do not lay down formal standards of "proof": if a person alleges that they "know" something or "believe" it, we test such statements by differing techniques. Firstly we may compare the assertion against other information available to us; secondly we may question the person on why he or she knows or believes; thirdly we may accept the person's word, presuming it to be true until there is other information which might confirm or refute the original statement; and finally we may disbelieve, presuming it to be untrue until other information becomes available. Often we invoke a moral language of "truth" or "honesty". For example, when we listen to an account of a child's misdeeds, they will be exhorted to give as accurate an account as possible. Sometimes we also recognise that it is difficult to "know" whether a state of affairs exists and we work on probabilities so that some courses of conduct, such as business decisions, involve conscious risk-taking.

In a court of law, these levels of confidence must be made explicit as one of the law job's is to resolve and define what is real.[1] The mere production of evidence is not proof and at the end of a trial, the trier of fact must

[1] Mansell W., Meteyard B., and Thomson A., *A Critical Introduction to Law* (1995), 20 *et seq.*

come to a conclusion — a verdict of guilty or not guilty or, in civil proceedings, a finding for one of the parties involved. In other words, the trier must decide whether the facts in issue have been *proved*. This is a two stage process:

(a) burden of proof: the first stage is to establish which party has the task of proving a fact? At its most basic level we need to ask, in civil proceedings, if no evidence at all were presented, which party would succeed? In a criminal trial, must the accused satisfy the jury of his or her innocence or must the prosecution convince them of his or her guilt? As soon as such questions are asked, there are, in general terms, straightforward answers. The person who mobilises the legal machinery has the obligation to demonstrate the correctness of any assertions. Thus it is normally accurate to say that the prosecution bear the burden of proof in criminal cases while the plaintiff bears that burden in civil actions.

But legal actions, civil and criminal, involve a plethora of issues. The burden of proof on any particular issue is not necessarily on the plaintiff or prosecution. For example, in a murder trial, the defendant might raise the defence of diminished responsibility under section 2 of the Homicide Act 1957 and proof of that condition lies with the accused. In a civil action for negligence, the defendant may well claim contributory negligence on the part of the plaintiff as a partial defence and again the proof of that would rest on the defendant.[2] But knowing who bears the burden of proving a fact does not tell us what *proof* is. That is a question of how a party can discharge any burden of proof cast upon them, *i.e.* the standard of proof.

(b) standard of proof: to prove something is to demonstrate that a fact or a state of affairs exists. But even historical or scientific facts get reassessed in the light of new information and theories, let alone decisions of courts of law. Although witnesses might say "I know . . ." or "I'm certain . . .", they should express themselves in terms of differing levels of probability.[3] Similarly any conclusion of the trier of fact can only be an assessment of likelihood. What is provable must be expressed in terms of what is probable. In trials, proof is merely the designation of a certain level of probability that a specific fact or state of affairs exists.

[2] Contributory negligence was a full defence until the Law Reform (Contributory Negligence) Act 1945, s.1 but the old common law which casts burden of proof on the defendant still applies — *Caswell v. Powell Duffryn Collieries* [1940] A.C. 152.

[3] Although in adversarial trial, such an approach would not lead to commendations for honesty but would invite the cross-examiner to ask "But you aren't sure . . . ?".

Eggleston R., *Evidence, Proof and Probability* (2nd ed., 1983) 8–9

The word 'probable', from which the term 'probability' is derived, originally meant 'provable' or 'capable of being tested'. In the course of time, however, it acquired the secondary meaning of 'likely to happen', so that when we speak of an event as being 'probable', we mean that we think the chances of its happening are at least better than even. We also mean that it is less than certain . . .

While we ordinarily use the term 'probability theory' as if it were a single thing, there are in fact several theories of probability . . . In 'classical' probability theory, probability is the ratio of favourable outcomes to all possible outcomes, where all outcomes have an equal likelihood of happening; the probability of throwing a six with a 'fair' die is one-sixth, since the die has six faces, and if the die is fair, each face has an equal chance of being uppermost.

For the statistician, probability refers to the frequency of occurrences of an event which happens a number of times. Thus, if a statistician is asked to estimate the probability of a person living to a certain age, he will refer to life tables that tell him what proportion of people of the same age as the subject have, in past experience, survived to the specified age.

There is a third concept of probability which is often referred to as a 'degree of belief' but which I would prefer to call a 'degree of likelihood' or 'degree of persuasion'. This is often called 'subjective probability' or 'psychological probability'. While probabilities of the first and second kind can be given mathematical equivalents, any attempt to put a figure on subjective probabilities is likely to meet with the criticism that it is incapable of quantification . . .

. . . the kind of probabilities that lawyers are mainly concerned with are of the subjective kind. They sometimes relate to the past and sometimes to the future, but except in rare cases they are not susceptible of verification. By contrast, if the assumptions of classical probability theory are accepted . . . the conclusions follow from the premisses; and for probabilities based on frequency, past experience offers a measure of frequency that can be applied to the case in hand . . .

In France, that "subjective probability" is expressed in the idea of "*intime conviction*". A judge should possess this before any finding of guilt. In England and Wales, in a criminal trial when an individual's liberty is at stake, proof of guilt requires a similar high standard and that occurs when the jury is "sure" or is satisfied "beyond reasonable doubt". In civil cases, the standard of proof is expressed in terms of the "balance of probabilities". Despite the language of probability, judges are reluctant to express such concepts of proof in mathematical language. However there is an increasing use (and abuse) of statistics in the courtroom as well as a complex literature on the extent to which probability theories have a part to play in the factual problems confronting courts.[4]

Redgrave M., "Science, Evidence and Logic", 69 M.L.R. (1996) 747

Modern debates about the role of mathematical models in adjudicative fact-finding are commonly traced back to *People v. Collins*.[5] The Collinses were accused of

[4] Eggleston, *op. cit.* Chap. 3; Cohen J., *The Probable and the Provable* (1977); Glanville Williams, "The Mathematics of Proof" [1979] Crim.L.R. 297 and 340; Cohen J., "The Logic of Proof" [1980] Crim.L.R. 91; Anderson T. and Twining W., *Analysis of Evidence* (1991) 385 *et seq.*; Robertson B. and Vignaux G., *Interpreting Evidence: Evaluating Forensic Science in the Courtroom* (1995).

[5] (1968) 68 Cal. 2d 319.

robbery, the case against them being largely that they fitted eyewitness descriptions of the robbers. The prosecutor identified several characteristics of the defendants, such as that the man had a moustache and that they drove a yellow car, which matched the eyewitness descriptions. The prosecutor assigned probabilities to the occurrence of each of the characteristics and, relying on the testimony of a mathematics instructor who had described the product rule, multiplied these probabilities together. He claimed that the resulting figure of 1/12,000,000 represented the probability of any couple possessing all of the characteristics of the defendants. The jury convicted.

While the newspapers triumphantly announced that 'Law of Probability Foils 2 Robbers in Tough Case,' the Collinses appealed and their convictions were overturned by the Supreme Court of California. There were two main problems with the prosecutor's strategy. First the figures he used seemed to have been plucked out of thin air: they lacked any objective grounding, while some of the characteristics chosen were not independent, making use of the product rule for independent events untenable. Secondly, even if the prosecutor could have proved the validity of the calculations underlying the 1/12,000,000 figure, it was not obvious what the figure meant: it does not necessarily follow that there was only a 1/12,000,000 probability that the Collinses were innocent.

The English Court of Appeal has also recently rejected the use of expert evidence from statisticians. In *R. v. Adams*[6] the prosecution in a rape case was based on DNA evidence which suggested that the probability of the defendant being innocent was 200 million to one. The defence were permitted to introduce expert evidence from a statistician to evaluate the relative probabilities of the non-DNA evidence and to incorporate that with the DNA evidence. This involved the use of Bayes Theorem which gives each separate piece of evidence a numerical percentage representing the ratio between the probability of circumstance A and the probability of circumstance B granted the existence of that evidence. The testimony looked at the probabilities of the culprit being a local man in the light of the alibi provided by the accused's girlfriend and the weakness of the identification evidence. The witness was even permitted to speculate as to the odds on the defendant being guilty. Quashing the conviction, Rose L.J. said:

R. v. Adams, The Times Law Reports, May 9, 1996

. . . the prosecution case rested entirely on expert evidence in relation to the DNA profile obtained from semen on a high vaginal swab taken from the complainant. At trial, the defence were permitted to lead evidence of the Bayes Theorem in connection with the statistical evaluation of the DNA profile.

Although their Lordships expressed no concluded view on the matter, they had very grave doubts as to whether that evidence was properly admissible, because it trespassed on an area peculiarly and exclusively within the jury's province, namely the way in which they evaluated the relationship between one piece of evidence and another.

[6] *The Times* Law Reports, May 9, 1996; a fuller account is on LEXIS, Court of Appeal, Criminal Division, April 24, 1996; [1996] Crim.L.R. 898.

The Bayes Theorem might be an appropriate and useful tool for statisticians, but it was not appropriate for use in jury trials or as a means to assist the jury in their task. In the first place, the theorem's methodology required that items of evidence be assessed separately according to their bearing on the guilt of the accused, before being combined in the overall formula. That in their Lordships' view was too rigid an approach to evidence of the nature which a jury characteristically had to assess. More fundamentally, the attempt to determine guilt or innocence on the basis of a mathematical formula, applied to each separate piece of evidence, was simply inappropriate to the jury's task. Jurors evaluated evidence and reached conclusions not by means of a formula, mathematical or otherwise, but by the joint application of their individual common sense and knowledge of the world to the evidence before them.

It was common for juries to evaluate scientific evidence but their Lordships had never heard it suggested that a jury should consider the relationship between such scientific evidence and other evidence by reference to probability formulae.

The Burden of Proof

The burden of proof has been described as "Whose task is it to establish a fact?" but there are preceding questions, namely, "What fact?" and "Why does that fact have to be established?" For example, in criminal law, the summons or indictment will specify an offence which has particular elements as part of its definition: murder involves causing death with an intent to kill or cause serious harm. It is the prosecution's task to prove those elements which are, so to speak, already on the court's agenda. But in response to the charge, the accused may wish to raise any number of legally recognised defences: self-defence, duress, provocation. It is not part of the prosecution's task in presenting its evidence-in-chief to disprove all possible defences. These issues are not on the agenda until the defendant has produced some evidence that a particular defence applies in this case.

An example of this can be seen in *Hill v. Baxter*[7] the defendant was charged with a road traffic offence and claimed that he had blacked out just before the incident. This raised a possible defence of non-insane automatism:

Hill v. Baxter [1958] 1 Q.B. 277 at 284–5, *per* Devlin J.

I am satisfied that even in a case in which liability depended upon full proof of mens rea, it would not be open to the defence to rely upon automatism without providing some evidence of it. If it amounted to insanity in the legal sense, it is well established that the burden of proof would start with and remain throughout upon the defence. But there is also recognised in the criminal law a lighter burden which the accused discharges by producing some evidence, but which does not relieve the prosecution from having to prove in the end all the facts necessary to establish guilt . . . It would be quite unreasonable to allow the defence to submit at the end of the prosecution's case that the Crown had not proved affirmatively and beyond a reasonable doubt that the accused was at the time of the crime sober, or not sleepwalking or not in a trance or black-out. I am satisfied that such matters ought

[7] [1958] 1 Q.B. 277: see also *R. v. Acott* [1997] 1 All E.R. 706.

not to be considered at all until the defence has produced at least prima facie evidence . . .

This demonstrates that the term "burden of proof" can be broken down into two processes:

(a) evidential burden: the first of these processes (which may be described as agenda-setting) is the burden a party bears to adduce enough evidence for the judge to be satisfied that the issue should be left to the trier of fact. All issues in an action must be established in this way. This is known as imposing an evidential burden and might be referred to as the problem of "passing the judge" as any failure to satisfy the evidential burden means that the issue will never reach the jury. The issue is bound up with that of the judge's role in withdrawing issues from the jury, discussed earlier.[8]

(b) legal burden: simply adducing enough evidence to raise an issue must be distinguished from the burden placed on a party to persuade the trier of fact to find for him or her on any particular issue. This latter stage is the burden of *proof* in a strict sense and is also known as the persuasive or probative burden.

> . . . the peculiar duty of him who has the risk of any given proposition on which the parties are at issue — who will lose the case if he does not make this proposition out, when all has been said and done.[9]

Certain further preliminary points should be emphasised: firstly, burdens relate not to the action as a whole but to particular issues within a case; secondly, in general, the evidential burden and the legal burden on any issue will both be borne by the same party but, as *Hill v. Baxter* shows, even in the criminal law, the burdens can rest on different parties. In that case, the accused had the evidential burden to adduce enough evidence to raise the issue of automatism but the prosecution bore the legal burden of disproving this defence. Thirdly, the discharge of any burden obviously involves adducing sufficient evidence but what is "sufficient" will vary. The test of evidential sufficiency when raising the defence of automatism is clearly very different to that required to prove the guilt of an accused.

Does the burden of proof shift in the course of a trial? The evidential burden and the legal burden attach themselves to parties at the beginning of a trial as a matter of law, allocated either at common law or by statute. These burdens do not shift. What does change in the course of a trial is the tactical balance between the parties. In a rape case, the prosecution may produce sufficient evidence that the accused had intercourse with the

[8] see 50.

[9] Thayer J., *Preliminary Treatise on Evidence at Common Law* 355 (although the substitution of "issue" for "case" would be wise).

victim without her consent. If this remained unchallenged, the defendant is at serious risk of being convicted. He is at a tactical disadvantage and thus should meet the Crown case either by cross-examining the prosecution witnesses to destroy their credibility or by adducing evidence of his own. But there has been no shifting of the burden of proof:

> If [the prosecution] adduces evidence to show that intercourse took place and that the woman did not consent to it, then in the absence of any evidence from the defendant the jury will certainly draw the inference that he was aware that she was not consenting. So as a practical matter he is bound — if he wishes to raise the point — to give evidence to the effect that he believed that she was consenting and as to his reason for that belief; and the weaker those reasons are, the more likely the jury are to conclude that he had no such belief. But the issue as to the accused's belief in the woman's consent is before the jury from the beginning, and is an issue in respect of which the evidential burden is on the Crown from the first to the last. There is never any question of any evidential burden with regard to it being on the accused or of the judge withdrawing it from the jury.[10]

The only situation when the legal burden may be said to shift is where there is the operation of another rule of law, such as the impact of a rebuttable presumption. For example, where a litigant bears the burden of showing that a third party is dead, they may adduce proof that the third party has been seven years absent without being heard from. This raises a rebuttable presumption of death and the burden of proving that the third party is still alive now rests on the other party to the action.[11]

Allocation of the legal burden

The allocation of the legal burden is determined by the rules of substantive law.[12] It is straightforwardly the allocation of risk which means that the party shouldering the burden loses if there is no evidence at all or if the evidence does not satisfy the finder of fact. It is often called the probative or persuasive burden and it has various effects:

- in specifying the right to start calling evidence[13]
- in dictating who can make submissions of "no case to answer"
- in settling doubts for the trier of fact

The common law principle is that "he who asserts must prove". In *Wakelin v. London and South Western Rly*,[14] a man was killed on a railway level

[10] Submission of appellant in *DPP v. Morgan* [1975] 2 All E.R. 347 at 349j–350b, *per* Lord Cross.
[11] See section on presumptions at 68, *et seq.*
[12] For a discussion of such rules, see Kiralfy A., *The Burden of Proof* (1987).
[13] R.S.C., Ord. 35, r.7 spells out the order of speeches in civil actions.
[14] (1887) 12 App.Cas. 41.

crossing. The widow sued. The defendant railway admitted that he had been run over by a train and also that they had neglected certain warnings. But they called no evidence and submitted that there was no case to answer, since there was no proof as to whether the man had been killed because of their fault or because he had run against the train.

Wakelin v. London and South Western Rly (1887) 12 App. Cas. 41

. . . the plaintiff must allege and prove, not merely that they were negligent but that their negligence caused or materially contributed to the injury . . . The evidence . . . affords ample material for conjecturing that the death may possibly have been occasioned by that negligence, but it furnishes no data from which an inference can reasonably be drawn that as a matter of fact it was so occasioned.[15]

My Lords, it is incumbent upon the plaintiff in this case to establish by proof that the husband's death had been caused by some negligence of the defendants . . . That is the fact to be proved. If the fact is not proved, the plaintiff fails, and if in the absence of direct proof the circumstances which are established are equally consistent with the allegation of the plaintiff as with the denial of the defendant, the plaintiff fails for the very simple reason that the plaintiff is bound to establish the affirmative of the proposition . . .[16]

(a) Legal burden in criminal cases

Although the prosecution will bear the burden of proof in relation to most issues in any criminal trial, in a few situations the defence will bear it. For example, in a murder trial, the prosecution has to prove the issues of causing death and the intent to kill or cause serious harm. But at common law, if the accused is seeking a verdict of "not guilty through reason of insanity",[17] the burden of proof is on the defence. Similarly under statute, if the accused has pleaded "not guilty" to murder but is arguing for a conviction for manslaughter on the grounds of diminished responsibility, section 2(2) of the Homicide Act 1957 places the legal burden of proof on that issue on the accused, again on the preponderance of probabilities.

But the basic common law rule in criminal cases was laid down by Lord Sankey in *Woolmington v. DPP*.[18] The accused was charged with murdering his wife from whom he was separated. He called at her mother's house and shot her dead. His story was that he decided to take a gun, show it to his wife and threaten to shoot himself if she did not return. He attached the gun with wire flex under his coat and, as he brought it out, it somehow went off. The trial judge directed the jury:

[15] *ibid.* at 49, *per* Lord Watson.
[16] *ibid.* at 44–45, *per* Lord Halsbury L.C.
[17] There is a presumption of sanity — the defendant must prove on the balance of probabilities that he or she is insane within the meaning of the *M'Naghten Rules* (1843) 10 Cl. & F. 200.
[18] *Woolmington v. DPP* [1935] A.C. 462.

> The Crown has got to satisfy you that this woman . . . died at the prisoner's hands. They must satisfy you of that beyond any reasonable doubt. If they satisfy you of that, then he has to show that there are circumstances to be found in the evidence which has been given from the witness box in this case which alleviate the crime so that it is only manslaughter, or which excuse the homicide altogether by showing that it was a pure accident.

This placed the burden of proving that the incident was an accident on the accused. In the House of Lords, the conviction was quashed:

Woolmington v. DPP [1935] A.C. 462 at 473–481, *per* Lord Sankey

It is true, as stated by the Court of Criminal Appeal, that there is apparent authority for the law as laid down by the learned judge . . . Rather would I invite your Lordships to begin by considering the proposition of law which is contained in *Foster's Crown Law*, written in 1762 . . .

> In every charge of murder, the fact of killing being first proved, all the circumstances of accident, necessity, or infirmity, are to be satisfactorily proved by the prisoner, unless they arise out of the evidence produced against him; for the law presumeth the fact to have been founded in malice until the contrary appeareth. And very right it is, that the law should so presume. The defendant in this instance standeth upon just the same foot that every other defendant doth; the matters tending to justify, excuse, or alleviate must appear in evidence before he can avail himself of them.

. . . The question arises: Is that statement correct law? . . . If at any period of a trial it was permissible for the judge to rule that the prosecution had established its case and that the onus was shifted on the prisoner to prove that he was not guilty, and that, unless he discharged that onus, the prosecution was entitled to succeed, it would be enabling the judge in such a case to say that the jury must in law find the prisoner guilty and so make the judge decide the case and not the jury, which is not the common law . . .

. . . Throughout the web of English criminal law one golden thread is always to be seen — that it is the duty of the prosecution to prove the prisoner's guilt subject to what I have already said as to the defence on insanity and subject also to any statutory exception. If, at the end of and on the whole of the case, there is a reasonable doubt, created by the evidence given by either the prosecution or the prisoner, as to whether the prisoner killed the deceased with a malicious intention, the prosecution has not made out the case and the prisoner is entitled to an acquittal. No matter what the charge or where the trial, the principle that the prosecution must prove the guilt of the prisoner is part of the common law of England and no attempt to whittle it down can be entertained.

It is not for the accused to prove that it was an accident. There is neither a legal burden nor an evidential burden on the accused here. Unlike, say, self-defence, accident is not an additional issue but is merely a denial of intention, proof of which is the function of the prosecution. It was for the prosecution to prove beyond reasonable doubt that Woolmington had intended to fire the gun and to kill his wife. Of course, having proved the shooting, the prosecution is entitled to rely on an inference that the defendant intended to kill and if he chose not to testify, he would take a considerable risk of conviction. But he would not inevitably lose because the jury must still be directed by the judge that the prosecution must prove malice aforethought and the jury might not have been convinced by the prosecution witnesses. There is a tactical reason why the accused would wish to testify in order to implant a doubt in the jury's mind about whether the shooting was intentional or accidental. But such tactical decisions must be distinguished from legal or evidential burdens.

In *Woolmington*, Lord Sankey mentions specifically two exceptions to this "golden thread", namely the defence of insanity and any statutory exceptions which place a burden on the accused:

(1) as a result of *M'Naghten's Case*[19] the accused raising the defence of insane automatism bears the burden of proof. That burden is discharged by proof on the balance of probabilities.[20]

(2) there are many express statutory exceptions which place the burden of proof on the defendant. An example is section 2 of the Prevention of Corruption Act 1916 which requires that a public servant, charged with corruption, would have to prove that any money or gift was not received corruptly:

> 2.—Where in any proceedings against a person for an offence under the Prevention of Corruption Act 1906, or the Public Bodies Corrupt Practices Act 1889, it is proved that any money, gift, or other consideration has been paid or given to or received by a person in the employment of His Majesty or any Government Department or a public body by or from a person, or an agent of a person, holding or seeking to obtain a contract from His Majesty or any Government Department or public body, the money, gift, or consideration shall be deemed to have been paid or given and received corruptly as such inducement or reward as is mentioned in such Act unless the contrary is proved.

Similarly under section 1 of the Prevention of Crimes Act 1953 it is for the accused to show that he or she has a lawful excuse for carrying an offensive weapon;[21] under section 30 of the Sexual Offences Act 1956 where the accused is living with a prostitute, he or she is presumed to be living off immoral earnings unless he or she proves the contrary; and under section 2 of the Homicide Act 1957 it is for the accused to prove that he or she is suffering from diminished responsibility.

More controversially, the courts have developed a third category, the "implied" exception. The principle that the prosecution must prove the guilt of the accused has been "whittled away" by an acceptance that Lord

[19] (1843) 10 Cl. & F. 200.

[20] *R. v. Podola* [1959] 3 All E.R. 418.

[21] This is also the case with analogous offences created by sections 4 and 6 of the Offensive Weapons Act 1996.

Sankey's statutory exceptions were not limited to those statutes which expressly cast the burden of proof on the accused but extended to those which did it by implication. An early example of this is *R. v. Turner*[22] where the defendant was charged with having pheasants in his possession without the necessary authorisation. The statute creating the offence also provided a list of situations where an accused might be authorised to possess the pheasants and Bayley J. said:

> If a negative averment be made by one party, which is peculiarly within the knowledge of the other, the party within whose knowledge it lies and who asserts the affirmative, is to prove it and not he who asserts the negative.[23]

The modern statement of an "implied statutory exception" to the normal allocation of the burden of proof can be found in the Magistrates' Courts Act 1980:

> 101.—Where the defendant to an information or complaint relies for his defence on any exception, exemption, proviso, excuse or qualification, whether or not it accompanies the description of the offence or matter of complaint in the enactment creating the offence or on which the complaint is founded, the burden of proving the exception, exemption, proviso, excuse or qualification shall be on him; and this notwithstanding that the information or complaint contains an allegation negativing the exception, exemption, proviso, excuse or qualification.

Section 101 lays down a rule which changes the burden of proof in certain circumstances for summary trial. However the section has been interpreted by *R. v. Edwards*[24] to be an expression of a common law rule. The argument runs: the origins of section 101 are to be found in the establishment of a new system of summary jurisdiction in the Summary Jurisdiction Act 1848, section 14 of which was in similar terms to section 101, stating:

> . . . it shall not be necessary for the Prosecutor or Complainant in that behalf to prove such Negative, but the Defendant may prove the Affirmative thereof in his Defence, if he would have Advantage of the Same.

It must be assumed that, in passing the 1848 legislation, Parliament was applying the common law rules as to proof as then applied by the judges hearing trials on indictment. If that was the case, those common law rules must be applicable to modern trials on indictment.

Although section 101 (and thus the common law) is limited to offences created by enactments, this is scarcely restrictive since the majority of criminal offences are contained in statute. In *Edwards*, the defendant was convicted under section 160 of the Licensing Act 1964 of selling alcohol

[22] (1816) 5 M.&S. 206.
[23] *ibid.* at 211.
[24] [1974] 2 All E.R. 1085.

without a justices' licence. The prosecution did not call evidence that the appellant did not hold a justices' licence, leaving the appellant to show, if he could, that he did possess one. The conviction was upheld by the Divisional Court:

R. v. Edwards [1974] 2 All E.R. 1085, at 1095a–d, _per_ Lawton L.J.

In our judgment this line of authority establishes that over the centuries the common law, as a result of experience and the need to ensure that justice is done both to the community and the defendants, has evolved an exception to the fundamental rule of our criminal law. This exception, like so much else in the common law, was hammered out on the anvil of pleading. It is limited to offences arising under enactments which prohibit the doing of an act save in specified circumstances or by persons of specified classes or with specified qualifications or with the licence or permission of specified authorities. Whenever the prosecution seeks to rely on this exception, the court must construe the enactment under which the charge is laid. If the true construction is that the enactment prohibits the doing of acts, subject to provisos, exemptions and the like, then the prosecution can rely on the exception.

In our judgment its application does not depend upon either the fact or the presumption that the defendant has peculiar knowledge . . .

At first glance, the result accords with common sense, since in the circumstances of the case, it would have been no hardship for the defendant to produce his justices' licence, if such existed. On the other hand, it would have been equally easy for the prosecution to conduct a search of the relevant register and adduced evidence that no record could be found.[25] But the ratio is much broader than "common sense" requires since, unlike *Turner*, this transfer of the burden of proof is not limited to those cases where the defendant has "peculiar knowledge" and where it would be difficult for the prosecution to prove a negative. Basing the decision on such elements would have been both practical and also corresponded with principles of fairness: the statute would have been narrowly interpreted[26] and the ratio would have accorded with the principle of ease of proof.[27] Instead the decision was based on the linguistic structure of the statute.

In *R. v. Hunt*[28] the accused was charged with possession of morphine. Possession is only illegal where the preparation contained more than 0.2 per cent morphine. The defendant argued that the prosecution had not adduced any evidence as to the strength of the preparation but was still convicted on the basis that the burden of proving that the concentration of the preparation was less than this lay on the defence. The House of Lords

[25] Although such testimony would be hearsay (*R. v. Patel* [1981] 3 All ER 94), such a register would be admissible under Criminal Justice Act 1988, s.24. Oral testimony to the effect that "No such record exists" might still be hearsay.

[26] This should be the fundamental approach with any penal statute — Ashworth A., *Principles of Criminal Law* (2nd ed, 1995) 76.

[27] Ashworth A., *ibid.* 82.

[28] [1987] 1 All E.R. 1.

(while allowing the appeal) accepted that statutes could by implication cast the burden of proof on the accused even in indictable offences:

R. v. Hunt [1987] 1 All E.R. 1 at 10e–12a, *per* Lord Griffiths

I would summarise the position . . . by saying that *Woolmington v. DPP* did not lay down a rule that the burden of proving a statutory defence lay only on the defendant if the statute specifically so provided, that a statute can, on its true construction, place a burden of proof on the defendant although it does not do so expressly and that if a burden of proof is placed on the defendant it is the same burden whether the case be tried summarily or on indictment, namely a burden that has to be discharged on the balance of probabilities.

The real difficulty in these cases lies in determining on whom Parliament intended to place the burden of proof when the statute has not expressly so provided. It presents particularly difficult problems of construction when what might be regarded as a matter of defence appears in a clause creating the offence rather than in some subsequent proviso from which it may more readily be inferred that it was intended to provide for a separate defence which a defendant must set up and prove if he wishes to avail himself of it. This difficulty was acutely demonstrated in *Nimmo v. Alexander Cowan & Sons Ltd.*[29] s.29(1) of the Factories Act 1961 provides:

> There shall, so far as is reasonably practicable, be provided and maintained safe means of access to every place at which any person has at any time to work and every such place shall, so far as is reasonably practicable, be made and kept safe for any person working there.

The question before the House was whether the burden of proving that it was not reasonably practicable to make the working place safe lay on the defendant or the plaintiff in a civil action. However, as the section also created a summary offence, the same question would have arisen in a prosecution. . . . their Lordships were in agreement that if the linguistic construction of the statute did not clearly indicate on whom the burden should lie the court should look to other considerations to determine the intention of Parliament, such as the mischief at which the Act was aimed and practical considerations affecting the burden of proof and, in particular, the ease or difficulty that the respective parties would encounter in discharging the burden. I regard this last consideration as one of great importance, for surely Parliament can never lightly be taken to have intended to impose an onerous duty on a defendant to prove his innocence in a criminal case, and a court should be very slow to draw any such inference from the language of a statute . . .

In *R. v. Edwards* the Court of Appeal expressed its conclusion in the form of an exception to what it said was the fundamental rule of our criminal law that the prosecution must prove every element of the charge. It said that the exception:

> . . . is limited to offences arising under enactments which prohibit the doing of an act save in specified circumstances or by persons of specified classes or with specified qualifications or with the licence or permission of specified authorities.

I have little doubt that the occasions on which a statute will be construed as imposing a burden of proof on a defendant which do not fit within this formulation are likely to be exceedingly rare. But I find it difficult to fit *Nimmo v. Alexander*

[29] [1967] 3 All E.R. 187.

Cowan & Sons Ltd into this formula, and I would prefer to adopt the formula as an excellent guide to construction rather than as an exception to a rule. In the final analysis each case must turn on the construction of the particular legislation to determine whether the defence is an exception within the meaning of section 101 of the 1980 Act, which the Court of Appeal rightly decided reflects the rule for trials on indictment. With this one qualification I regard *R. v. Edwards* as rightly decided.

My Lords, I am, of course, well aware of the body of distinguished academic opinion that urges wherever a burden of proof is placed on a defendant by statute the burden should be an evidential burden and not a persuasive burden, and that has the support of the distinguished signatories to the 11th Report of the Criminal Law Revision Committee . . . [30] My Lords, such a fundamental change is, in my view, a matter for Parliament and not a decision of your Lordships' House . . .

The problem is treated here, not as one involving the erosion of the presumption of innocence, but as one of statutory construction. The worst effects of *Edwards* are avoided as Lord Griffiths states that the language of exceptions or provisos does not automatically place the burden of proof on the accused. Indeed he placed stress on practical considerations such as the ease or difficulty that a defendant might have in discharging this burden. In a drugs case, it would be rare for the prosecution not to have the substance analysed nor does the defendant have any right to a sample for his or her own analysis. The House also made it clear that in any serious criminal offence, it was right to resolve any ambiguity in favour of the defendant.

Despite this, the potential scope of *Hunt* and *Edwards* is enormous as a multitude of statutes use the language of "excuse, proviso, exemption or qualification". To allow an implied reversal of the burden of proof undermines the presumption of innocence expressed in *Woolmington*.[31]

Mirfield P. "The Legacy of *Hunt*" [1988] Crim.L.R. 19 at 29

. . . *Hunt* takes insufficient account of the *Woolmington* policy or principle. Even in the straightforward context of questions about the incidence of the burden of proof, *Woolmington* has dual significance. It states a legal rule that the prosecution must always disprove accident, certainly in murder cases and probably in all cases. But, it also states a broader policy or principle in relation to the burden of proof. In my view [their Lordships] fail to accord appropriate and sufficient weight to that policy or principle. One may well regret that failure simply because it is a policy or principle one regards as rightly held dear by the common law as an important buffer between the practical power of the state and the comparative weakness of the individual. It is another argument for *Woolmington* which has been stressed here; a strong *Woolmington* 'presumption' has enormous practical advantages so far as the judges and magistrates considering novel statutory provisions are concerned. There should surely not be a wilderness of single instances here. In effect, [the House of Lords] leave, at least in theory, too much in doubt in relation to statutory offences.[32]

[30] (1972) Cmnd. 4991.

[31] A summary of criticisms is given in Tapper C., *Cross and Tapper on Evidence* (8th ed., 1995) 150 *et seq.* and n.14; Zuckerman A.: *Principles of Criminal Evidence* (1989) Chap. 9.

[32] See the reply by Birch D., "Hunting the Snark: the Elusive Statutory Exception" [1988] Crim.L.R. 221.

This derogation from the strict criteria of *Woolmington* leads to policy decisions by judges on the construction of statutes. Such policies are only based on vague criteria. Furthermore a failure to construe penal statutes in a strict fashion can only encourage legislative draftsmen routinely to place probative burdens on the defence. But *Hunt* has its supporters:

Zuckerman A., *The Principles of Criminal Evidence* (1989) 148–149

. . . *Hunt* is a progressive decision. Broadly speaking, it establishes that a statutory interpretation imposing a burden on the accused is justified only where, first, the statute prohibits an act generally but goes on to allow it to be performed by specified classes of persons or by persons with special permits, and, secondly, it is easy for the accused to prove that he belongs to the designated class or that he possesses the requisite permit. From a practical point of view the imposition of such a burden on an accused is of limited consequence. Suppose that an activity is prohibited in the absence of a licence to engage in it. Suppose also that, contrary to *Hunt*, the law imposed the burden of proving the absence of a licence entirely on the prosecution rather than on the accused. To discharge its burden, it would usually be sufficient for the prosecution to call evidence that the accused had been asked to produce his licence and had declined to do so. If at his trial the accused still fails to come forward with a licence or any credible explanation for its absence, the prosecution will have gone a long way towards discharging its burden of persuasion on this point. Consequently to say, as *Hunt* does, that it is upon the accused, rather than the prosecution, to prove the licence does not make much practical difference. The accused has to do much the same as he would have had to do had the burden rested on the prosecution: to produce his licence or a credible explanation for its absence . . .

(b) Legal burden in civil cases:

In civil cases the general rule is that he or she who asserts must prove. On its face, this suggests that the burden is borne by the party who makes the positive assertion. This does not mean that a party cannot bear the onus of proving a negative. Thus it is probably better expressed that a party who wishes the court to take action on a particular issue should bear the responsibility of showing why action should be taken. In *Soward v. Leggatt*[33] the plaintiff was the landlord of the defendant and his claim was that the latter had not properly repaired and maintained the premises in question. The defendant in the pleadings positively stated that he had done so. Even though linguistically the defence case was a positive assertion, the burden of proof still rested on the plaintiff:

> Looking at these things according to common sense, we should consider what is the substantive fact to be made out, and on whom it lies to make it out. It is not so much the form of the issue which ought to be considered, as the substance and effect of it. In many cases, a party, by a little difference in the drawing of his pleadings might make it either affirmative or negative, as he pleased. The plaintiff here says, 'You did not repair'; he might have said, 'You let the house

[33] (1836) 7 C.&P. 613.

> become dilapidated.' I shall endeavour by my own view to arrive at the substance of the issue, and I think in the present case that the plaintiff's counsel should begin.[34]

A similar point arose in *Abrath v. North Eastern Rly*[35] which involved an action for malicious prosecution. In such a case, it is necessary for the plaintiff to prove not only the fact of prosecution but also the lack of reasonable and probable cause for the prosecution:

Abrath v. North Eastern Rly (1883) 11 Q.B.D. 440 at 457–458, *per* Bowen L.J.

Now in an action for malicious prosecution the plaintiff has the burden throughout of establishing that the circumstances of the prosecution were such that a judge can see no reasonable or probable cause for instituting it. In one sense this is the assertion of a negative, and we have been pressed with the proposition that when a negative is to be made out the onus of proof shifts. That is not so. If the assertion of a negative is an essential part of the plaintiff's case, the proof of the assertion still rests upon the plaintiff. The terms 'negative' and 'affirmative' are after all relative and not absolute. In dealing with a question of negligence that term may be considered either as negative or affirmative according to the definition adopted in measuring the duty which is neglected. Wherever a person asserts affirmatively as part of his case that a certain state of facts is present or is absent, or that a particular thing is insufficient for a particular purpose, that is an averment that he is bound to prove positively. It has been said that an exception exists in those cases where the facts lie peculiarly within the knowledge of the opposite party. The counsel for the plaintiff have not gone the length of contending that in all those cases the onus shifts, and that the person within whose knowledge the truth peculiarly lies is bound to prove or disprove the matter in dispute. I think a proposition of that kind cannot be maintained, and that the exceptions supposed to be found amongst cases relating to the game laws may be explained on special grounds . . .

In civil actions generally, the legal burden rests on the plaintiff: in a negligence action, the plaintiff would bear the burden of proving the existence and the breach of the duty of care as well as the extent of the injuries and damage. In *Bonnington Castings Ltd v. Wardlaw*,[36] an employee contracted an industrial disease in the course of work in a factory owned by the defendants. The employers were in breach of certain safety regulations although it was unclear that these breaches caused the harm:

> It would seem obvious in principle that a plaintiff must prove not only the negligence or breach of duty but also that such fault caused or materially contributed to his injury, and there is ample authority for that proposition. I can find neither reason nor authority for the rule being different when there is a breach of a statutory duty . . . In my judgment the employee must in all cases

[34] *ibid.* at 615, *per* Lord Abinger C.B.
[35] (1883) 11 Q.B.D. 440.
[36] [1956] A.C. 613.

prove his case by the ordinary standard of proof in civil actions: he must make it appear that at least on a balance of probabilities the breach of duty caused or materially contributed to his injury.[37]

The defendant in a civil action may bear the burden of proof where the defence goes beyond mere denial. In a negligence action, for example, where questions of *volenti* or contributory negligence arise, the burden of proving those issues rests upon the defendant. Thus the defence of contributory negligence has been raised in a number of cases where a motorist was not wearing a seat belt and suffered more serious injuries than would otherwise have been the case. In such cases the onus of proving negligence on the part of the plaintiff rests on the defendant.[38]

In contract litigation, likewise, the plaintiff must bear the burden of proving the existence of the contract, its breach and the extent of any damages. But the incidence of the burden of proof is rarely decisive, although it proved to be in *Rhesa Shipping Co. SA v. Edmunds*.[39] The plaintiff shipowners sought to recover from the underwriters under a policy of insurance for the total loss of their ship. The plaintiffs argued that the cause was a collision with a submarine and thus came under the "perils of the sea" clause while the underwriters argued that it was prolonged wear and tear over many years. There was no direct evidence of either contention:

Rhesa Shipping Co. SA v. Edmunds [1985] 2 All E.R. 712, at 718a, _per_ Lord Brandon

My Lords, the late Sir Arthur Conan Doyle in his book, *The Sign of Four*, describes his hero, Mr Sherlock Holmes, as saying to the latter's friend, Dr Watson: 'How often have I said to you that, when you have eliminated the impossible, whatever remains, however improbable, must be the truth?' It is, no doubt, on the basis of this well-known but unjudicial dictum that [the trial judge] decided to accept the shipowners' submarine theory, even though he regarded it . . . as extremely improbable.

In my view there are three reasons why it is inappropriate to apply the dictum of Mr Sherlock Holmes . . . to the process of fact-finding which a judge of first instance has to perform at the conclusion of a case of the kind here concerned.

The first reason is one which I have already sought to emphasise as being of great importance, namely that the judge is not always bound to make a finding one way or the other with regard to the facts averred by the parties. He has open to him the third alternative of saying that the party on whom the burden of proof lies in relation to any averment made by him has failed to discharge that burden. No judge likes to decide cases on burden of proof if he can legitimately avoid having to do so. There are cases, however, in which, owing to the unsatisfactory state of the evidence or otherwise, deciding on the burden of proof is the only just course for him to take.

The second reason is that the dictum can only apply when all the relevant facts are known, so that all possible explanations, except a single extremely improbable

[37] *ibid.* at 620, *per* Lord Reid.
[38] e.g. *Froom v. Butcher* [1976] Q.B. 286.
[39] [1985] 2 All E.R. 712.

one, can properly be eliminated. That state of affairs does not exist in the present case: to take but one example, the ship sank in such deep water that a diver's examination of the nature of the aperture, which might well have thrown light on its cause, could not be carried out.

The third reason is that the legal concept of proof of a case on a balance of probabilities must be applied with common sense. It requires a judge of first instance, before he finds that a particular event occurred, to be satisfied on the evidence that it is more likely to have occurred than not. If such a judge concludes . . . that the occurrence of an event is extremely improbable, a finding by him that it is nevertheless more likely to have occurred than not, does not accord with common sense. This is especially so when it is open to the judge to say simply that the evidence leaves him in doubt whether the event occurred or not, and that the party on whom the burden of proving that the event occurred lies has therefore failed to discharge such burden.

The defendant might carry a burden on a particular issue in a breach of contract action. This might be the case with affirmative defences, for example, an assertion that there was a material non-disclosure on the part of the plaintiff.[40] In *Joseph Constantine Steamship Line Ltd v. Imperial Smelting Corp Ltd*[41] a ship on charter was destroyed in an explosion, the cause of which was unknown. The plaintiff charterers claimed damages from the owner for failure to load. The owners' defence was that the charterparty had been frustrated by the explosion. The House of Lords decided that, where the defendant establishes a frustrating event, the burden rested on the plaintiff charterers to show that event had occurred and the contract had been broken as a result of the owners' fault:

Joseph Constantine Steamship Line Ltd v. Imperial Smelting Corp. Ltd [1941] 2 All E.R. 165 at 179a–180a, *per* Viscount Maugham

I think the burden of proof in any particular case depends on the circumstances under which the claim arises. In general, the rule which applies is '*Ei qui affirmat non ei qui negat incumbit probatio*'. It is an ancient rule founded on considerations of good sense and it should not be departed from without strong reasons. The position as to proof of non-responsibility for the event in such a case as the present is not very different from the position of a plaintiff in an action for negligence where contributory negligence on his part is alleged. In such a case the plaintiff must prove that there was some negligent act or omission on the part of the defendant which caused or materially contributed to the injury, but it is for the defendant to prove affirmatively, if he so contends, that there was contributory negligence on the part of the person injured, though here again the onus may easily be shifted . . .

If, however, I am right in the opinion above expressed that the onus of establishing absence of default did not rest on the appellants, the mere possibility of default on their part is not sufficient to disentitle them to rely on the principle of frustration . . .

[40] *Everett v. Hogg, Robinson and Gardner Mountain (Insurance) Ltd* [1973] 2 Lloyd's Rep. 217.

[41] [1941] 2 All E.R. 165.

Is this as straightforward as it seems? The charterers had shown breach of contract. It may be as legitimately argued that it should have been for the owners pleading frustration to show that that breach was beyond their control? The House placed some stress on the difficulty of proving a negative but it has been suggested that the decision was one of policy since most frustrating events occur without fault on the part of the defendant. Less injustice is likely to be caused by placing the burden of proving fault on the plaintiff.[42] But this situation might be contrasted with that in bailment: where there is a contract of bailment and the goods are lost, the bailor merely has to show the bailment and the failure to restore the goods. The legal burden is on the bailee to show lack of fault on his part.[43]

Contracts can expressly or impliedly vary the incidence of the burden of proof. With insurance contracts, insurers sometimes seek to show that a loss falls within an exception to the contract: the policy may expressly put the burden on the insured to prove that the loss falls outside the exception. Even where this is not done expressly, the courts have sometimes held that the insured bears the burden of proof in showing that it falls outside any proviso. [44] But in *Munro, Brice & Co v. War Risks Association*[45] a policy of marine insurance covered loss of a ship through perils of the sea but with an exception in the case of loss by enemy action. The ship had simply disappeared and the court held that the insurers bore the burden of proof of showing that the ship had been lost in that way.

In *The Glendarroch*[46] a ship was lost when it struck a rock and the plaintiff sued for non-delivery of the sacks of cement it was carrying. The contract expressly provided that the shipowners were not liable in respect of loss caused by perils of the sea, provided that the owners were not negligent. If the plaintiff proved the contract and breach, the burden was on the owners to show that it was "peril of the sea". However once it had been shown that the ship had sank because of a "peril of the sea" it was for the plaintiffs to show negligence, if they were to rely upon the proviso.

> The plaintiffs would have to prove the contract and the non-delivery. If they leave that in doubt, of course they fail. The defendants' answer is 'Yes; but the case was brought within the exception — within its ordinary meaning'. That lies upon them. Then the plaintiffs have a right to say there are exceptional circumstances, viz, that the damage was brought about by the negligence of the defendants' servants, and it seems to me that it is for the plaintiffs to make out the second exception.[47]

In civil cases, as in criminal, statutes can affect the burden of proof.[48] For example, in unfair dismissal cases, after proof of dismissal, the burden of

[42] Stone J., "Burden of proof and the judicial process . . ." (1944) 60 L.Q.R. 262.
[43] *Coldman v. Hill* [1919] 1 K.B. 443; *Levison v. Patent Steam Carpet Cleaning Co Ltd* [1977] 3 All E.R. 498.
[44] *Hurst v. Evans* [1917] 1 K.B. 352.
[45] [1918] 2 K.B. 78.
[46] [1894] P.226.
[47] *ibid.* at 231, *per* Lord Esher.
[48] Examples include the Consumer Credit Act 1974, s.171(7) and the Bills of Exchange Act 1882, s.30(2).

proving that it was objectively fair lay on the employer. In 1974[49] the employer also had to prove that he or she had acted reasonably in all the circumstances but this requirement was removed in 1980.[50] It is now governed by section 57 of the Employment Protection (Consolidation) Act 1978 (as amended):

> 57.—(1) In determining for the purposes of this part whether the dismissal of an employee was fair or unfair, it shall be for the employer to show —
>
> (a) what was the reason (or, if there was more than one, the principal reason) for the dismissal, and
> (b) that it was a reason falling within subsection (2) or some other substantial reason of a kind such as to justify the dismissal of an employee holding the position which that employee held . . .
>
> (3) Where the employer has fulfilled the requirements of subsection (1), then . . . the determination of the question whether the dismissal was fair or unfair, having regard to the reason shown by the employer, shall depend on whether in the circumstances (including the size and administrative resources of the employer's undertaking) the employer acted reasonably in treating it as a sufficient reason for dismissing the employee; and that question shall be determined in accordance with equity and the substantial merits of the case.

The employer has to adduce a reason for dismissal under subsection (1) but, although this appears to be simply an evidential burden, the real onus still lies on the employer.[51]

Allocation of the evidential burden

The allocation of the legal burden normally determines the incidence of the evidential burden. The party shouldering the evidential burden on a particular issue carries the risk that, if there is no evidence on that issue or if the evidence does not satisfy the judge, the issue will be withdrawn from the trier of fact.

(a) Evidential burden in criminal cases:

As will be seen later, it is a significantly lesser hurdle to adduce enough evidence to satisfy the judge to leave an issue to the jury than it is to convince the jury. Simply clearing the hurdle of the evidential burden does not mean that the party will therefore succeed in that issue.

The general rule is that whosoever carries the legal burden also bears the evidential burden. The prosecution in a criminal case will bear both burdens in relation to most issues: in other words, the Crown must adduce enough evidence in relation to each and every element of the offence that a

[49] Trade Union and Labour Relations Act, Sched. 1, para. 6(8).
[50] Employment Act, s.6.
[51] But see Tapper C., *Cross and Tapper on Evidence* (8th ed., 1995) 142–143.

defence submission of no case to answer at the end of the prosecution case would be unsuccessful and since the judge would consider that there was evidence on which a reasonable jury, properly directed, could convict.[52] But where the defence bear the legal burden, on such issues as insanity or diminished responsibility, they would also bear the evidential burden.

There are issues on which the accused will bear an evidential burden, although the legal burden of disproof will rest on the prosecution. This occurs when the defendant raises certain positive defences, over and above a denial of a definitional element of the offence, such as self-defence, provocation, or duress. He or she may have to bear an evidential burden if that defence is to be left to the jury. In *Bratty v. Attorney-General for Northern Ireland*[53] the accused was charged with murder, having strangled a young girl. His defences, based on some evidence of psychomotor epilepsy, were either insanity (an issue left to and rejected by the jury) or non-insane automatism. The latter was not left to the jury and the appeal was rejected by the House of Lords:

Bratty v. Attorney-General for Northern Ireland [1961] 3 All E.R. 523 at 527f–530f, _per_ Viscount Kilmuir L.C.

. . . 'Automatism' was defined by the Court of Criminal Appeal in this case 'as connoting the state of a person who, though capable of action, is not conscious of what he is doing . . . It means unconscious involuntary action, and it is a defence because the mind does not go with what is being done'

. . . The first portion of the argument before them that 'automatism' should have been left to the jury was summarised by the Court of Criminal Appeal as being that the whole of the evidence on the issue of insanity was relevant on the issue whether automatism itself existed, however it was caused; in view of the onus being on the defence to show on a preponderance of probabilities that the necessary constituents of the M'Naghten formula were present, it was therefore submitted that, although the evidence might have failed to prove some constituent of insanity, the lack of consciousness itself might have seemed a genuine possibility to the jury, and the jury might at least have had a reasonable doubt as to whether the appellant was conscious of his acts so as to be guilty of murder . . .

The Court of Criminal Appeal rejected that 'first portion of the argument' on the ground that the learned judge was right in not leaving to the jury the defence of automatism, in so far as it purported to be founded on a defect of reason from disease of the mind within the M'Naghten Rules. In this I think they were right . . .

What I have said does not mean that, if a defence of insanity is raised unsuccessfully, there can never, in any conceivable circumstances, be room for an alternative defence based on automatism. For example, it may be alleged that the accused had a blow on the head, after which he acted without being conscious of what he was doing or was a sleepwalker. There might be a divergence of view as to whether there was a defect of reason from disease of the mind . . . The jury might not accept the evidence of a defect of reason from disease of the mind, but at the same time accept the evidence that the prisoner did not know what he was doing. If the jury should take that view of the facts they would find him not guilty. But it

[52] *R v. Galbraith* [1981] 2 All E.R. 1060; see Chap. 2 for further discussion.
[53] [1961] 3 All E.R. 523.

should be noted that the defence would only have succeeded because the necessary foundation has been laid by positive evidence which, properly considered, was evidence of something other than a defect of reason from disease of the mind. In my opinion, this analysis of the two defences (insanity and automatism) shows that where the only cause alleged for the unconsciousness is a defect of reason from disease of the mind, and that cause is rejected by the jury, there can be no room for an alternative defence of automatism. Like the Court of Criminal Appeal, I cannot therefore accept the submission that the whole of the evidence directed to the issue of insanity should have been left to the jury to consider whether there was automatism due to another cause. It was conceded . . . that there was nothing to show or suggest that there was any other pathological cause for automatism . . .

It is necessary that a proper foundation be laid before a judge can leave 'automatism' to the jury. That foundation, in my view, is not forthcoming merely from an unaccepted evidence of a defect of reason from disease of the mind. There would need to be other evidence on which a jury could find non-insane automatism . . .

Certain very relevant problems were discussed in *Hill v. Baxter* where the court . . . held that, in spite of the justices accepting the defendant's evidence that he became unconscious while driving, there was no evidence which justified the justices in finding that the defendant was not fully responsible for his actions . . . Devlin J. used these words with which I respectfully agree and which are relevant to the present case,

> It would be quite unreasonable to allow the defence to submit at the end of the prosecution's case that the Crown had not proved affirmatively and beyond a reasonable doubt that the accused was at the time of the crime sober, or not sleep-walking or not in a trance or a blackout . . . In my judgment there is not to be found in the case stated evidence of automatism of a character which would be fit to leave to a jury . . . he was not saying that he was a victim of a disease of the mind. Unless there was evidence that this irrationality was due to some cause other than disease of the mind, the justices were not entitled simply to acquit . . .

. . . I am of the opinion that there was not any evidence on which a jury could properly have considered the existence of automatism. Counsel for the petitioner directed our attention to the petitioner's statement, to his evidence and to his previous conduct. In my view they do not provide evidence fit to be left to a jury on this question. They could not form the basis of reasonable doubt . . .

In *Bratty* the accused bore firstly the legal burden of proving insanity. He adduced evidence of psychomotor epilepsy that satisfied the evidential burden cast on him so that the issue was left to the jury who, on the preponderance of probabilities, decided that he was, in fact, sane. Secondly the defendant bore the evidential burden of raising the issue of non-insane automatism: the only evidence of a possible cause of his (allegedly) involuntary conduct was psychomotor epilepsy. As a matter of law, the trial judge had already ruled that this was a disease of the mind and therefore evidentially could only form the foundation for a defence of insane automatism. As no other possible cause had been put forward, the judge was correct in withdrawing the issue from the jury.

This requirement to lay an evidential foundation applies to other defences, whether common law such as self-defence or duress or statutory defences such as provocation. The accused has to produce enough cogent evidence to satisfy the judge that the issue should be left to the jury. Once the defence has raised such an issue, it is for the prosecution to disprove it beyond reasonable doubt.

There is a difficult distinction to be drawn here. Where the defence is based on a denial of one of the constituent elements of the offence, the prosecution bear both burdens and the jury must be directed on the requirement for proof beyond reasonable doubt on each and every element. The accused in *Woolmington* was entitled to a direction on the lack of intention, regardless of the quality of his own evidence or indeed of whether he had testified at all. But where the defence raises issues other than those expressly or impliedly contained in the offence itself, it is for the accused to raise the issue and to surmount an evidential burden. Such was the case in *Hill v. Baxter* and yet the defendant in that case was simply pleading lack of volition as opposed to Woolmington's lack of intention?

The difficulty is that the criminal law provides no satisfactory analytical distinction between *offence* and *defence*. The fine line that needs to be drawn can be seen in relation to the question of consent in rape. What constitutes the elements of an offence is a question of substantive law and the Crown obviously bear the onus of showing intercourse and the lack of the victim's consent. But *DPP v. Morgan*[54] decided that the mental ingredient of the offence was an intention to have non-consensual intercourse with the victim. The accused's belief in consent was not a separate defence in itself but was simply a denial of the requisite mens rea. As a result, there is no evidential burden on the defendant in a rape case to raise the issue of consent. Whether a similar argument would apply to consent in a non-sexual assault is moot.[55]

(b) Evidential burden in civil cases:

In civil proceedings, the allocation of the evidential burden runs with that of the legal burden. Normally defences aimed at defeating a claim need to be proved by the party asserting them. For example, where a party to a contract alleges it is voidable for duress or undue influence, the burden of proving the necessary facts falls on the party alleging them. However there are some cases where equity will presume undue influence from the fact of the relationship and, although there is an evidential burden on the party alleging the undue influence, the legal burden falls on the party seeking to show that no such influence was exerted.[56]

[54] [1975] 2 All E.R. 347.
[55] The decision of the House of Lords in *R. v. Brown* [1993] 2 All E.R. 75 restricts the scope for such a defence to common law assault or battery — perhaps an unwanted kiss?
[56] *Allcard v. Skinner* (1887) 36 Ch.D. 145; explained by Lord Scarman in *National Westminster Bank PLC v. Morgan* [1985] 1 All E.R. 821.

The Standard of Proof

A court is concerned with the problem of reconstructing the past and attempting to discover the truth. Such an exercise is at best an approximation and any conclusions are not certainties but exist only at varying levels of likelihood. For the benefit of the trier of fact, courts need to specify the level of probability that constitutes proof and this is referred to as the standard of proof. There are two levels: proof beyond reasonable doubt or proof on the balance of probabilities. Although formally there are only two standards of proof, Tapper[57] points out that some acts are inherently less likely than others and the consequences of some decisions are more serious than others. Thus the prosecutor in a murder case should have a higher hurdle to surmount since people are less likely to kill and the consequences are life imprisonment, than one prosecuting a less serious charge. But such reasoning has not led the appellate courts to develop flexible standards and we are left with standard formulae.

(a) Discharge of evidential burden in criminal cases

As has been explained, the first stage of "proof" is to overcome the evidential burden, to "pass the judge". If the judge does not believe that sufficient evidence has been adduced by the prosecution on each element of the offence so that a reasonable jury, properly directed, might convict, he or she might direct the jury to acquit. This often happens at the end of the prosecution case on a submission by the defence of "no case to answer". This is a common occurrence — in Crown Court approximately 40 per cent of all acquittals are the result of the prosecution offering no evidence or the judge directing the jury to return a verdict of "not guilty" at the conclusion of the Crown case. This can be the result of such matters as prosecution witnesses not turning up to testify or failing to testify as effectively as had been expected or simply bad preparation of the case.[58]

The evidential burden is discharged if the judge feels that there is:

> such evidence as, if believed, and if left uncontradicted and unexplained, could be accepted by the jury as proof.[59]

The judge should assume that the jury will accept the evidence and should draw any inferences which favour the prosecution. At the end of the day, of course, the jury do not have to accept it and might still acquit. The test for the discharge of the evidential burden is whether the judge considers that there is evidence which he or she regards as capable of sustaining a verdict beyond reasonable doubt.

Discharging the evidential burden, when it rests on the defendant, is not onerous, merely needing to produce enough evidence to leave a jury with a

[57] Tapper C., *Cross on Evidence* (8th ed., 1995) 171–172.
[58] Uglow S., *Criminal Justice* (1995) 176.
[59] *Jayasena v. R.* [1970] 1 All E.R. 219 at 221g–h, *per* Lord Devlin.

reasonable doubt on the issue. If the judge does not believe that sufficient evidence has been adduced by the defendant and that a reasonable jury, properly directed, could not find a reasonable doubt, the judge can withdraw that issue from the jury. This was discussed in *Hill v. Baxter*[60] where the Court of Appeal held that, in spite of the justices accepting the defendant's evidence that he became unconscious while driving, this did not constitute evidence which was a proper foundation for a defence of non-insane automatism. Devlin J. said:

> It would be quite unreasonable to allow the defence to submit at the end of the prosecution's case that the Crown had not proved affirmatively and beyond a reasonable doubt that the accused was at the time of the crime sober, or not sleep-walking or not in a trance or a blackout . . . In my judgment there is not to be found in the case stated evidence of automatism of a character which would be fit to leave to a jury . . . he was not saying that he was a victim of a disease of the mind. Unless there was evidence that this irrationality was due to some cause other than disease of the mind, the justices were not entitled simply to acquit . . .[61]

But why was it necessary for the defendant to show the cause of the blackout? The defendant's sworn evidence, believed by the justices, that he suffered a blackout, surely raises at least a reasonable doubt that it occurred?

(b) Discharge of evidential burden in civil cases

Similarly in civil cases, a party, normally the defence, might make a "no case" submission at the close of the opposing case. The judge would regard the evidential burden as discharged if sufficient evidence has been adduced that would justify the trier of fact in concluding that the legal burden (on the preponderance of probabilities) on that issue has been discharged.

(c) Discharge of legal burden in criminal cases

At the close of a criminal trial, the party with the legal burden must persuade the trier of fact of the "truth" of the assertions. There are two levels: for the prosecution, that level of persuasion is that proof must be beyond reasonable doubt; for the defence, that standard is proof on the balance of probabilities.[62] The standard of proof of "beyond reasonable doubt" is seen as one of the cornerstones of the presumption of innocence.

Stephen F., *History of the Criminal Law* Vol. 1, 354

If it be asked why an accused person is presumed to be innocent, I think the true answer is, not that the presumption is probably true, but that society in the present

[60] [1958] 1 All E.R. 193.
[61] *ibid.* at 196h–197b: *R. v. Acott* [1997] 1 All E.R. 706.
[62] *R v. Carr-Briant* [1943] 2 All E.R. 156.

day is so much stronger that the individual, and is capable of inflicting so very much more harm on the individual than the individual as a rule can inflict upon society, that it can afford to be generous. It is, however, a question of degree, varying according to time and place, how far this generosity can or ought to be carried . . .

The presumption of innocence in criminal law is linked closely to the strict requirements of the standard of proof. Heretics occasionally question it, pointing out that the acquittal of the guilty is as great a miscarriage of justice as the conviction of the innocent. Is it true that the acquittal of ten heroin dealers is better than the unjust conviction of one innocent person?

The nature of the two standards of proof was discussed in *Miller v. Ministry of Pensions*.[63] The widow of an army officer was appealing from the decision of a pensions tribunal that she was not entitled to the higher pension awarded to widows of soldiers who had died in war service.

Miller v. Ministry of Pensions [1947] 2 All E.R. 372 at 373f–374b, *per* Denning J.

The first point of law in the present appeal is whether the tribunal properly directed itself as to the burden of proof. The proper direction is covered by decisions of this court. It is as follows,

1. In cases falling under art 4(2) and art 4(3) of the Royal Warrant Concerning Pay, Pensions etc, 1943 (which are generally cases where the man was passed fit at the commencement of his service, but is later afflicted by a disease which leads to his death or discharge) there is a compelling presumption in the man's favour which must prevail unless the evidence proves beyond reasonable doubt that the disease was not attributable to or aggravated by war service, and for that purpose the evidence must reach the same degree of cogency as is required in a criminal case before an accused person is found guilty. That degree is well settled. It need not reach certainty, but it must carry a high degree of probability. Proof beyond reasonable doubt does not mean proof beyond the shadow of a doubt. The law would fail to protect the community if it admitted fanciful possibilities to deflect the course of justice. If the evidence is so strong against a man as to leave only a remote possibility in his favour which can be dismissed with the sentence 'of course it is possible, but not in the least probable,' the case is proved beyond reasonable doubt, but nothing short of that will suffice.

2. In cases falling under art 4(2) and art 4(4) (which are generally cases where the man was fit on his discharge, but incapacitated later by a disease) there is no compelling presumption in his favour, and the case must be decided according to the preponderance of probability. If at the end of the case the evidence turns the scale definitely one way or the other, the tribunal must decide accordingly, but if the evidence is so evenly balanced that the tribunal is unable to come to a determinate conclusion one way or the other, then the man must be given the benefit of the doubt. This means that the case must be decided in favour of the man unless the evidence against him reaches the same degree of cogency as is required to discharge a burden in a civil case. That degree is well settled. it must carry a reasonable degree of probability, but not so high as is required in a criminal case. If the evidence is such that the tribunal can say: 'We think it more probable than not,' the burden is discharged, but, if the probabilities are equal, it is not . . .

[63] [1947] 2 All E.R. 372.

In *R. v. Hepworth*,[64] Lord Goddard C.J. expressed his misgivings about "reasonable doubt":

R. v. *Hepworth* [1955] 2 All E.R. 918 at 919–920, *per* Lord Goddard C.J.

. . . it is very difficult to tell a jury what is a reasonable doubt. To tell a jury that it must not be a fanciful doubt is something that is without real guidance. To tell them that a reasonable doubt is such a doubt as to cause them to hesitate in their own affairs never seems to me to convey any particular standard . . . It may be that in some cases the word 'satisfied' is enough. Then, it is said that the jury in a civil case has to be satisfied and, therefore, one is only laying down the same standard of proof as in a civil case. I confess that I have had some difficulty in understanding how there is or there can be two standards; therefore one would be on safe ground if one said in a criminal case to a jury: 'You must be satisfied beyond reasonable doubt' and one could also say: 'You, the jury, must be completely satisfied,' or better still: 'You must feel sure of the prisoner's guilt.' But I desire to repeat what I said in *R. v. Kritz*[65]: 'It is not the formula that matters: it is the effect of the summing up. If the jury are made to understand that they have to be satisfied and must not return a verdict against a defendant unless they feel sure, and that the onus is all the time on the prosecution and not on the defence, that is enough.

This difficulty was shown in *R. v. Yap Chuan Ching*[66] where the jury had difficulty in reaching a verdict and asked for help. They were told by the judge:

> . . . a reasonable doubt, it has been said, is a doubt to which you can give a reason as opposed to a mere fanciful sort of speculation such as 'Well, nothing in this world is certain, nothing in this world can be proved.' As I say, that is the definition of a reasonable doubt — something to which you can assign a reason. It is sometimes said the sort of matter which might influence you if you were to consider some business matter. A matter, for example, of a mortgage concerning your house, or something of that nature . . .

The Court of Appeal accepted this but felt that judges should not seek to define further "sure" or "beyond reasonable doubt":

R. v. *Yap Chuan Ching* [1976] 63 Cr.App.R. 7 at 9–10, *per* Lawton J.

> [The appellant] attacked the final direction on three grounds. He said that it was unsatisfactory for a judge to define a 'reasonable doubt' as one for which a reason could be given: he pointed to a criticism of that phrase which was made by Edmund Davies L.J. . . . in *Stafford and Luvaglio*[67] [who] said: 'We do not, however, ourselves agree with the trial judge when directing the jury upon the standard of proof, he told them to 'Remember that a reasonable doubt is one for which you could give reasons if you were asked,' and we dislike such a description or definition.' So do we. It does not help juries. But that is not the

[64] [1955] 2 All E.R. 918.
[65] [1949] 2 All E.R. 406.
[66] (1976) 63 Cr.App.R. 7.
[67] [1968] 3 All E.R. 752.

problem in this case. the problem is whether its use made this conviction unsafe. The next ground of complaint was that by using the mortgage of a house analogy, the learned judge was doing something which had been condemned a number of times in this Court . . . In the past this Court has criticised trial judges for using that kind of analogy. The use of any analogy is to be avoided whenever possible. The final criticism was that when giving the direction of which complaint is made, the judge did not emphasise once again that the jury had to be sure. But we have no doubt that by the time the jury had retired for the last time, they must have appreciated that they had to be sure before they could return a verdict of guilty. Nevertheless, in most cases . . . judges would be well advised not to attempt any gloss upon what is meant by 'sure' or what is meant by 'reasonable doubt'.[68]

The appellate courts tend to dislike specifying a formula but the "reasonable doubt" and "sure" have attained a traditional status. The Judicial Studies Board preferred direction emphasises that the jury has to be sure before bringing in a verdict of guilty and that the phrase "reasonable doubt" may have a much smaller part to play in criminal trials.

Where the legal burden is on the accused, that burden is discharged by proof on the balance of probabilities. *R. v. Carr-Briant*[69] involved a charge under the Prevention of Corruption Acts 1906 and 1916 which placed the legal burden on the accused to show that a gift to him or her as a public servant was in fact not made corruptly. The trial judge directed the jury that the defendant had to discharge this burden on the same standard as that resting on the prosecution:

R. v. *Carr-Briant* [1943] 2 All E.R. 156 at 158a–h, *per* Humphreys J.

We see no reason why the rebuttable presumption created by the section should not be construed in the same manner as similar words in other statutes or similar presumptions at common law, for instance, the presumption of sanity in the case of an accused person who is setting up the defence of insanity . . . In our judgment, in any case where, either by statute or at common law, some matter is presumed against an accused person 'unless the contrary is proved', the jury should be directed that it is for them to decide whether the contrary is proved, that the burden of proof required is less than that required at the hands of the prosecution in proving the case beyond a reasonable doubt, and that the burden may be discharged by evidence satisfying the jury of the probability of that which the accused is called upon to establish.

(d) Discharge of legal burden in civil cases

In *Miller*, Denning J. said:

. . . the case must be decided according to the preponderance of probability. If at the end of the case the evidence turns the scale definitely one way or the other, the tribunal must decide accordingly, but if the evidence is so evenly

[68] *Yap Chuan Ching supra* at 9–10, *per* Lawton L.J.
[69] [1943] 2 All E.R. 156.

> balanced that the tribunal is unable to come to a determinate conclusion one way or the other, then the man must be given the benefit of the doubt.[70]

It is settled that in civil cases the burden of proof is discharged on proof on the preponderance of probabilities. This is not a matter of the relative quantity of evidence adduced by the parties but whether the party bearing the burden has shown in absolute terms that his or her proposition is more likely than not. The burden is not successfully discharged by merely showing that your account of the events is more likely than that of your opponent.

> . . . the legal concept of proof of a case on a balance of probabilities must be applied with common sense. It requires a judge of first instance, before he finds that a particular event occurred, to be satisfied on the evidence that it is more likely to have occurred than not. If such a judge concludes . . . that the occurrence of an event is extremely improbable, a finding by him that it is nevertheless more likely to have occurred than not, does not accord with common sense. This is especially so when it is open to the judge to say simply that the evidence leaves him in doubt whether the event occurred or not, and that the party on whom the burden of proving that the event occurred lies has therefore failed to discharge such burden.[71]

There are some exceptions to the principle that the standard of proof in civil proceedings is on the preponderance of probabilities:

(1) the standard of proof in *contempt of court cases*, whether occurring in a criminal or civil court, is the criminal standard beyond reasonable doubt. In a passing off case, *Comet Products U.K. Ltd v. Hawkex Plastic Ltd*,[72] the plaintiffs applied to the court for the committal of the defendants for contempt of court. The question arose whether the defendant could be cross-examined.

> . . . A criminal contempt is one which takes place in the face of the court, or which prejudices a fair trial and so forth. A civil contempt is different. A typical case is disobedience to an order made by the court in a civil action . . . . Although this is a civil contempt, it partakes of the nature of a criminal charge. The defendant is liable to be punished for it. He may be sent to prison. The rules as to criminal charges have always been applied to such a proceeding. . . . .we ourselves in this court, in *Re Bramblevale Ltd*,[73] said that it must be proved with the same degree of satisfaction as in a criminal charge. It follows that the accused is not bound to give evidence unless he chooses to do so.[74]

(2) *certain statutes* may require a higher standard of proof.

[70] *Miller supra* at 374a.
[71] *Rhesa Shipping Co SA v. Edmunds* [1985] 2 All E.R. 712 at 718f, *per* Lord Brandon.
[72] [1971] 1 All E.R. 1141.
[73] [1969] 3 All E.R. 1062.
[74] *Comet Products supra* at 1143j–1144a, *per* Lord Denning M.R.

(3) where *allegations of crime* are made in civil proceedings, the standard of proof is the preponderance of probabilities. In *Hornal v. Neuberger Products Ltd*,[75] the plaintiff claimed damages for breach of warranty or, alternatively, for fraudulent misrepresentation after the defendant had sold the plaintiff a lathe on the representation that it had been reconditioned by certain toolmakers. The judge awarded damages on the basis of a fraudulent misrepresentation, stating that he had been satisfied on the balance of probabilities that fraud had occurred but had not been satisfied beyond reasonable doubt. Should he have been satisfied beyond reasonable doubt? The Court of Appeal held that in civil proceedings, proof of an allegation of crime need only be on the basis of the balance of probabilities:

> I must say that, if I was sitting as a judge alone, and I was satisfied that the statement was made, that would be enough for me, whether the claim was put in warranty or on fraud. I think it would bring the law into contempt if a judge were to say that on the issue of warranty he finds the statement was made, and that on the issue of fraud he finds it was not made.
>
> Nevertheless, the judge having set the problem to himself, he answered it, I think, correctly; he reviewed all the cases and held rightly that the standard of proof depends on the nature of the issue. The more serious the allegation the higher the degree of probability that is required: but it need not, in a civil case, reach the very high standard required by the criminal law.[76]

Although the decision establishes that allegations of crime in civil proceedings need only be established on the balance of probabilities, where that allegation is very serious, different considerations come into play. In *Re Dellow's Will Trusts*[77] the issue was whether a wife had murdered her husband before killing herself:

> It seems to me that in civil cases it is not so much that a different standard of proof is required in different circumstances varying according to the gravity of the issue, but . . . the gravity of the issue becomes part of the circumstances which the court has to take into consideration in deciding whether or not the burden of proof has been discharged. The more serious the allegation the more cogent is the evidence required to overcome the unlikelihood of what is alleged and thus to prove it . . .[78]

In wardship cases, the welfare of the child is the paramount issue. In *Re G*[79] there were suspicions of sexual abuse by a father and the local authority, who had taken the child into care, issued wardship proceedings:

[75] [1956] 3 All E.R. 970.
[76] *ibid.* at 973a–f, *per* Denning L.J.
[77] [1964] 1 All E.R. 771.
[78] *ibid.* at 773c, *per* Ungoed-Thomas J.
[79] [1987] 1 W.L.R. 1461.

Re G. [1987] 1 W.L.R. 1461 at 1466f–1467b, per Sheldon J.

In wardship proceedings . . . although alleged wrongdoing by an individual may be an issue, the predominant consideration is the welfare of the child and not the behaviour of any particular adult. They are also civil proceedings.

. . . in general terms the standard of proof to be applied in such proceedings as these is based on the balance of probabilities. On the other hand, having regard to the diversity of issues that might be raised in such proceedings, I also take the view . . . that the 'degree of probability' required in any particular context may vary and must be 'commensurate with the occasion' or 'proportionate to the subject matter'. Thus in my opinion, such proceedings as the present, a higher degree of probability is required to satisfy the court that the father has been guilty of some sexual misconduct with his daughter than would be needed to justify the conclusion that the child has been the victim of some such behaviour of whatever nature and whoever may have been its perpetrator.

In the latter context, indeed, I am of the opinion that the gravity of the matter is such from the child's point of view that any tilt in the balance suggesting that she has been the victim of sexual abuse would justify a finding to that effect. In my view, indeed, there may also be circumstances in which the application of a 'standard of proof' as that phrase is commonly understood, is inapt to describe the method by which the court should approach the particular problem; as, for example, where the suspicion of sexual abuse or other wrong-doing, although incapable of formal proof, is such as to lead to the conclusion that it would be an unacceptable risk to the child's welfare to leave him in his previous environment or . . . where, although the court may be satisfied that no sexual abuse has taken place, the very fact that it has been alleged by a child against a parent suggests that in the child's interests, some change in, or control over the existing regime is required . . .

(4) *matrimonial cases*, for many years, were decided on the basis of a "matrimonial offence" and early decisions certainly favoured a criminal standard for proof. Adultery, for example, had to be proved beyond reasonable doubt.[80] But the old cases have to be read in the light of reform legislation: section 26 Family Law Reform Act 1969 provides that any presumption of law as to legitimacy or illegitimacy may be rebutted on the civil standard of proof; the Divorce Reform Act 1969 (now the Matrimonial Causes Act 1973) allows for the parties to prove "irretrievable breakdown" of the marriage and this is established if the court is "satisfied" as to one of five basic facts. The modern divorce court is best regarded as a civil court which should not adopt the rules and standards of the criminal court.

[80] *Ginesi v. Ginesi* [1948] 1 All E.R. 373; *Preston-Jones v. Preston-Jones* [1951] 1 All E.R. 124 but see *Blyth v. Blyth* [1966] 1 All E.R. 524; *Bastable v. Bastable* [1968] 3 All E.R. 701.

Discharge of burden in voire dire

At the *voire dire*, the burden of proving that the conditions of admissibility have been met must lie on the party wishing to adduce the evidence. Sometimes that burden will be allocated by statute.[81] Proof must be by admissible evidence.[82] In criminal proceedings, where the prosecution bear the onus of proof, the evidence will not be admissible unless the conditions for admissibility are proved beyond reasonable doubt. In *R. v. Yacoob*[83] the competence and compellability of a prosecution witness depended on whether or not she was married to the defendant. She had been through a ceremony of marriage with him in 1971 but there was also a certificate of another marriage in 1968. The judge held that the presumption of validity of the 1971 marriage was rebutted by the evidence relating to the 1968 ceremony and the burden was on the defence to prove that the witness was incompetent.

> As to the burden of proof in this context, it is for the prosecution, once the issue of competence of one of its witnesses is raised, to prove that that person is competent to testify . . . The burden will be discharged if the trial judge is satisfied beyond a reasonable doubt upon admissible and sufficient evidence of competence.[84]

R. v. Ewing[85] involved expert comparison of handwriting under section 8 of the Criminal Procedure Act 1865:

> 8.—Comparison of a disputed writing with any writing proved to the satisfaction of the judge to be genuine shall be permitted to be made by witnesses; and such writings, and the evidence of witnesses respecting the same, may be submitted to the court and jury as evidence of the genuineness or otherwise of the writing in dispute.

Under the section, the judge has to be satisfied that the writing alleged to be by the accused was in fact by the accused before expert comparison can take place. Was the standard one of balance of probabilities or did the judge have to be satisfied beyond reasonable doubt?

R. v. Ewing [1983] 2 All E.R. 645 at 652j–653c, *per* O'Connor L.J.

In our judgment, the words in section 8 of the 1865 Act, 'any writing proved to the satisfaction of the judge to be genuine', do not say anything about the standard of

[81] Police and Criminal Evidence Act 1984, s.76.
[82] *R. v. O'Loughlin* [1988] 3 All E.R. 431 — in construing the Criminal Justice Act 1925, s.13(3) police officers' evidence that the witnesses were frightened was direct evidence and admissible but their statements as to what the witnesses had said about the specific threats was hearsay.
[83] (1981) 72 Cr.App.R. 313.
[84] *ibid.* at 317, *per* Watkins L.J.
[85] [1983] 2 All E.R. 645.

proof to be used, but direct that it is the judge, and not the jury, who is to decide, and the standard of proof is to be governed by common law . . . It follows that when the section is applied in civil cases, the civil standard of proof is used, and when it is applied in criminal cases, the criminal standard should be used. Were it otherwise, the situation created would be unacceptable, where conviction depends on proof that disputed handwriting is that of the accused person and where that proof depends on comparison of the disputed writing with samples alleged to be genuine writings of the accused; we cannot see how this case can be said to be proved beyond reasonable doubt, if the Crown only has to satisfy the judge on a balance of probabilities, that the allegedly genuine samples were in fact genuine. The jury may be satisfied beyond reasonable doubt that the crucial handwriting is by the same hand as the allegedly genuine writings, but if there is a reasonable doubt about the genuineness of such writings, then that must remain a reasonable doubt about the fact the disputed writing was that of the accused and the case is not proved . . .[86]

When the issue is one of the preconditions for admissibility of evidence tendered by the defendant or of evidence tendered in civil proceedings, the test is one of the balance of probabilities. In *R. v. Mattey and Queeley*[87] the defence sought to rely on the written statements of witnesses now in France and unable to be present for the trial. Under the Criminal Justice Act 1988:

23.—(1) . . . a statement made by a person in a document shall be admissible in criminal proceedings as evidence of any fact of which direct oral evidence by him would be admissible if . . .

(2) . . .

b) that —

i) the person who made the statement is outside the United Kingdom; and

ii) it is not reasonably practicable to secure his attendance;

It is for the defence to show that the witnesses were abroad and that it was not reasonably practicable for them to attend court. There should be independent and admissible evidence on this issue. This probably requires more evidence than statements by the absent witnesses contained in the document in question. But the evidence, of whatever nature, when proffered by the defence, merely has to satisfy the judge on the balance of probabilities.

[86] Not following *R. v. Angeli* [1978] 3 All E.R. 950 and following the reasoning of the House of Lords in *Blyth v. Blyth* [1966] 1 All E.R. 524.

[87] [1995] Crim.L.R. 308.

4

POLICE INVESTIGATION, INTERROGATION AND CONFESSION

JUDICIAL DISCRETION AND EXCLUSION OF EVIDENCE

One of the key judicial functions in the course of a trial will be the exercise of discretion in relation to the admissibility of evidence. Evidence which is otherwise admissible may still be excluded, normally on grounds that it is unduly prejudicial or unfair. This chapter deals with the principles under which the judge may exercise that exclusionary discretion. The use of the discretion is most often to be found in a contested criminal trial in which many of the evidential issues will concern the police conduct of the investigation.[1] Police powers form the backdrop of this discussion and although the details are not relevant here,[2] it is necessary to sketch an outline.

Police powers at common law: there were few, if any, special powers for police or any state officials which were distinguishable from those exercisable by the ordinary citizen. The core powers were:

- arrest: this is the detention of a person and common law required that there had to be reasonable suspicion that a serious offence had been committed. There was no power to stop, search or detain people outside of arrest
- questioning: there was no obligation to answer questions put to you by police officers
- search of the person: this could only take place on arrest
- search of premises: this required a magistrate's warrant

[1] Issues concerning judicial discretion can also emerge in the context of the admission of similar fact evidence — see Chap. 14.
[2] Lidstone K. and Palmer C., *Bevan and Lidstone's The Investigation of Crime* (2nd ed., 1996); Uglow S., *Criminal Justice* (1995) Chap. 3.

- detention of the person: this was only possible after a lawful arrest and the detainee had to be taken before magistrates as soon as possible, normally within 24 hours
- questioning suspects; this was initially not seen as police job but as a matter for magistrates. It became normal for the police to interview suspects and the questioning and treatment of suspects was regulated by the Judges' Rules 1912, amended in 1964

Police powers under statute: the legal powers of the police at common law were restricted. Throughout the last century they were added to in a piecemeal fashion but are now codified under Police and Criminal Evidence Act 1984, which covers most of the pre-trial criminal process. The statutory powers under the Act are supplemented by Codes of Practice promulgated under section 66 covering areas such as stop and search, road blocks, detention and questioning of suspects, identification and tape recording of interviews. As a result of the Act, police powers can now be clearly distinguished, both in quantity and kind, from those of the citizen. Some of the most significant powers are:

- stop and search: section 1 allows a police officer in uniform to stop and search (without arresting them) persons and vehicles for a range of contraband material
- road blocks: section 4 provides much greater powers than previously existed for the police to mount roadblocks
- arrest: sections 24 and 25 define and extend the powers of arrest. The police officer's powers now are much broader than the ordinary person, in particular under the general arrest conditions for minor offences under section 25
- detention: section 42 allows police officers extended powers to detain an arrested person for up to 96 hours
- questioning: although there is still no obligation to answer police questions, a failure to mention salient facts may now prejudice one's defence in court as a result of section 34 of the Criminal Justice and Public Order Act 1994
- searching premises: there are additional powers to search premises, especially under section 18 which allows a search where it is suspected that there is evidence which relates to the offence
- intimate searches: section 55 gives the power to make intimate body searches without consent
- non-intimate samples: although section 62 only allows the police to take intimate samples with consent, the taking of non-intimate samples does not. These include samples of saliva and mouth swabs[3]

[3] Police and Criminal Evidence Act 1984, s.65 as amended by the Criminal Justice and Public Order Act 1994.

Abuse of police powers can result in evidence being acquired which would otherwise not have been obtained. This in turn raises issues as to whether such evidence should be excluded by the exercise of the judge's discretion. But police techniques of investigation are not limited to the powers described above. Officers can act in any manner not prohibited by the civil or criminal law and use systems of aural and visual surveillance, perhaps misinformation and deception and to some extent can participate in the commission of the crime. When considering the admissibility of evidence, a court might be concerned about any abuse of police powers or the employment of underhand tactics. The court might question, for example, the nature of the surveillance, the techniques of identification or arrest, let alone the conditions for the questioning of the suspect.

Discretion at common law

There is a range of approaches which the law might adopt when asked to accept evidence which has gathered by questionable methods: firstly there can be rules to exclude any evidence which has been inappropriately obtained; secondly it may be left as a matter for the discretion of the judge as to whether to ensure fairness to the accused; or finally, the courts might concern themselves only with the quality of the evidence (is it relevant and reliable?) and not consider its provenance at all.

The common law tradition embraced this latter approach. Although judges often condemned such police tactics, this concern rarely led to the exclusion of evidence. In *Jeffery v. Black*,[4] two drugs squad officers arrested the accused for the theft of a sandwich in a pub. Having charged him with that offence, they took him to his rooms which they searched illegally, without his consent and without a warrant, discovering cannabis. The Divisional Court were willing to admit the evidence of finding the drugs despite the officers lacking the appropriate authority:

Jeffery v. Black [1978] 1 All E.R. 555 at 558j–559g, _per_ Lord Widgery C.J.

It is firmly established according to English law that the mere fact that evidence is obtained in an irregular fashion does not of itself prevent that evidence from being relevant and acceptable to a court. The authority for that is *Kuruma Son of Kaniu v. R.*[5] and I need only refer to one passage to make good the proposition which I have already put forward:

> In their Lordships' opinion, the test to be applied in considering whether evidence is admissible is whether it is relevant to the matters in issue. If it is, it is admissible and the court is not concerned with how the evidence was obtained. While this proposition may not have been stated in so many words in any English case, there are decisions which support it and, in their Lordships' opinion, it is plainly right in principle.[6]

[4] [1978] 1 All E.R. 555.
[5] [1955] 1 All E.R. 236.
[6] *ibid.* at 239b.

> There one has that pronouncement from the Privy Council, and I have not the least doubt that we must firmly accept the proposition that an irregularity in obtaining evidence does not render the evidence inadmissible. Whether or not evidence is admissible depends on whether or not it is relevant to the issues in respect of which it is called.
>
> But . . . the magistrates sitting in this case, like any other criminal tribunal in England sitting under English law, have a general discretion to decline to allow any evidence to be called by the prosecution if they think it would be unfair or oppressive to allow that to be done . . . It is a discretion which every criminal judge has all the time in respect of all the evidence which is tendered by the prosecution. It would probably give magistrates some idea of the extent to which this discretion is used if one asks them whether they are appreciative of the fact that they have the discretion anyway, and it may well be that a number of experienced magistrates would be quite ignorant of the possession of this discretion. That gives them, I hope, some idea of how relatively rarely it is exercised in our courts. But if the case is exceptional, if the case is such that not only have the police officers entered without authority, but they have been guilty of trickery or they have misled someone, or they have been oppressive or they have been unfair, or in other respects they have behaved in a manner which is morally reprehensible, then it is open to the justices to apply their discretion and decline to allow the particular evidence to be let in as part of the trial.

Lord Widgery's proposition was that if evidence was relevant, it was admissible notwithstanding its provenance. This ready acceptance was qualified by Lord Widgery's statement that there was judicial discretion to exclude evidence, albeit a discretion to be used rarely where there had been trickery, oppression or unfairness. It was unclear why his Lordship felt that the facts in front of him did not amount to oppressive conduct by the police.

Shortly afterwards, in *R. v. Sang*,[7] the House of Lords reduced the scope of this discretion still further. This time their Lordships were considering the police technique of using an *agent provocateur*, a situation whereby a police agent participates in or incites the commission of an offence. For example, in *Brannan v. Peek*[8] a policeman entered a public house where illegal gambling was in progress and persuaded the appellant to accept a bet from him. As that decision showed, in substantive criminal law, there is no defence of entrapment although the courts have consistently expressed strong disapproval of such police methods. But for the defendant, the desired result may also be reached by evidential means, if the court can be persuaded to exclude any evidence obtained by the use of an agent provocateur.

In *Sang* the issue was whether the judge had a common law discretion to exclude evidence which was both relevant and of more than minimal probative value but which had been unfairly obtained. In the case, the accused had been in Brixton prison where he met a fellow inmate, S, alleged to be a police informer. Shortly before the accused was about to be

[7] [1979] 2 All E.R. 1222.
[8] [1947] 2 All E.R. 572.

released, S, who was aware that the accused's business was dealing in forged banknotes, told the accused that he knew of a safe buyer who would get in touch with the accused by telephone. After the accused left prison, he was telephoned by a man who inquired whether the accused would sell him any forged banknotes. A rendezvous was arranged but the accused had no idea that the man was a sergeant in the police force. The accused and some of his associates went to the rendezvous carrying with them a large number of forged American dollars and walked straight into a police trap. The appellant argued that, where the judge was satisfied at *voire dire* that the offence was instigated by an *agent provocateur* acting on the instructions of the police, the judge had a discretion to refuse to allow the prosecution to prove its case by evidence.

R. v. Sang [1979] 2 All E.R. 1222 at 1227d–1231b, *per* Lord Diplock

What [this submission] really involves is a claim to a judicial discretion to acquit an accused of any offences in connection with which the conduct of the police incurs the disapproval of the judge. The conduct of the police where it has involved the use of an *agent provocateur* may well be a matter to be taken into consideration in mitigation of sentence; but under the English system of criminal justice it does not give rise to any discretion on the part of the judge himself to acquit the accused or to direct the jury to do so, notwithstanding that he is guilty of the offence.

Recognition that there may be circumstances in which in a jury trial the judge has a discretion to prevent particular kinds of evidence that is admissible from being adduced before the jury has grown up piecemeal. It appears first in cases arising under section 1 proviso (f) of the Criminal Evidence Act 1898, which sets out the circumstances in which an accused may be cross-examined as to his previous convictions or bad character. The relevant cases starting in 1913 with *R. v. Watson*[9] are conveniently cited in the speech of Lord Hodson in *Selvey v. DPP*,[10] a case in which this House accepted that in such cases the trial judge had a discretion to prevent such cross-examination, notwithstanding that it was strictly admissible under the statute, if he was of opinion that its prejudicial effect on the jury was likely to outweigh its probative value.

Next the existence of a judicial discretion to exclude evidence of 'similar facts', even where it was technically admissible, was recognised . . . in *Harris v. DPP*.[11] Viscount Simon, with whose speech the other members of this House agreed, said that the discretion to exclude 'similar facts' evidence should be exercised where 'the probable effect [sc prejudicial to the accused] would be out of proportion to the true evidential value'.

That phrase was borrowed from the speech of Lord Moulton in *R. v. Christie*.[12] That was neither a 'previous conviction' nor a 'similar facts' case, but was one involving evidence of an accusation made in the presence of the accused by the child victim of an alleged indencent assault and the accused's failure to answer it, from which the prosecution sought to infer an admission by the accused that it was true. Lord Moulton's statement was not confined to evidence of inferential confessions but was general in its scope . . . So I would hold that there has now developed a general rule of practice whereby in a trial by jury the judge has a

[9] (1913) 8 Cr.App.R. 249.
[10] [1968] 2 All E.R. 497.
[11] [1952] 1 All E.R. 1044.
[12] [1914–15] All E.R. Rep 63.

discretion to exclude evidence which, though technically admissible, would probably have a prejudicial influence on the minds of the jury, which would be out of proportion to its true evidential value.

Ought your Lordships to go further and to hold that the discretion extends more widely than this, as the comparatively recent dicta . . . suggest? [*Kuruma Son of Kaniu v. R.*[13]] was a case in which the evidence of unlawful possession of ammunition by the accused was obtained as a result of an illegal search of his person. The Board held that this evidence was admissible and had rightly been admitted; but Lord Goddard C.J., although he had earlier said that if evidence was admissible 'the court is not concerned with how the evidence was obtained', nevertheless went on to say:

> No doubt in a criminal case the judge always has a discretion to disallow evidence if the strict rules of admissibility would operate unfairly against the accused . . . If, for instance, some admission of some piece of evidence, eg, a document, had been obtained from the defendant by a trick, no doubt the judge might properly rule it out.[14]

Up to the (final) sentence . . . there is nothing in this passage to suggest that when Lord Goddard spoke of admissible evidence operating 'unfairly' against the accused he intended to refer to any wider aspect of unfairness that the probable prejudicial effect of the evidence on the minds of the jury outweighing its true evidential value; though he no doubt also had in mind the discretion that had long been exercised in England under the Judges' Rules to refuse to admit confessions by the accused made after the crime even though strictly they may be admissible. The instance given in the (final sentence) appears to me to deal with a case which falls within the latter category since the document 'obtained from a defendant by a trick' is clearly analogous to a confession which the defendant has been unfairly induced to make, and had, indeed, been so treated in *R. v. Barker*[15] where an incriminating document obtained from the defendant by a promise of favours was held to be inadmissible.

(Lord Diplock made a similar point with regard to *R. v. Payne*[16] and continued . . .) Nevertheless it has to be recognised that there is an unbroken series of dicta in judgments of appellate courts to the effect that there is a judicial discretion to exclude admissible evidence which has been 'obtained' unfairly or by trickery or oppressively, although except in *R. v. Payne* there never has been a case in which those courts have come across conduct so unfair, so tricky or so oppressive as to justify them in holding that the discretion ought to have been exercised in favour of exclusion . . . the dicta can be traced to a common ancestor in Lord Goddard's statement in *Kuruma Son of Kaniu v. R.* . . . That statement was not, in my view, ever intended to acknowledge the existence of any wider discretion than to exclude (1) admissible evidence which would probably have a prejudicial influence on the minds of the jury that would be out of proportion to its true evidential value and (2) evidence tantamount to a self-incriminatory admission which was obtained from the defendant, after the offence had been committed, by means which would justify a judge in excluding an actual confession which had the like self-incriminating effect. As a matter of language, although not as a matter of application, the subsequent dicta go much further than this; but in so far as they do so they have never yet been considered by this House.

My Lords, I propose to exclude, as the certified question does, detailed consideration of the role of the trial judge in relation to confessions and evidence

[13] [1955] 1 All E.R. 236.
[14] *ibid.* at 239.
[15] [1941] 3 All E.R. 33.
[16] [1963] 1 All E.R. 848.

obtained from the defendant after commission of the offence that is tantamount to a confession. It has a long history dating back to the days before the existence of a disciplined police force, when a prison on a charge of felony could not be represented by counsel and was not entitled to give evidence in his own defence either to deny that he had made the confession, which was generally oral, or to deny that its contents were true. The underlying rational of this branch of the criminal law, though it may originally have been based on ensuring the reliability of confessions is, in my view, now to be found in the maxim, *nemo debet prodere se ipsum*, no one can be required to be his own betrayer, or in its popular English mistranslation 'the right to silence'. That is why there is no discretion to exclude evidence discovered as the result of an illegal search but there is discretion to exclude evidence which the accused has been induced to produce voluntarily if the method of inducement was unfair.

Outside this limited field in which for historical reasons the function of the trial judge extending to imposing sanctions for improper conduct on the part of the prosecution before the commencement of the proceedings in inducing the accused by threats, favour or trickery to provide evidence against himself, your Lordships should, I think, make it clear that the function of a judge at a criminal trial as respects the admission of evidence is to ensure that the accused has a fair trial according to law. It is no part of a judge's function to exercise disciplinary powers over the police or prosecution as respects the way in which evidence to be used at the trial is obtained by them . . .

I would accordingly answer the question certified in terms which have been suggested by my noble and learned friend, Lord Dilhorne, in the course of our deliberations on this case. (1) A trial judge in a criminal trial has always a discretion to refuse to admit evidence if in his opinion its prejudicial effect outweighs its probative value. (2) Save with regard to admissions and confessions and generally with regard to evidence obtained from the accused after commission of the offence, he has no discretion to refuse to admit relevant admissible evidence on the ground that it was obtained by improper or unfair means. The court is not concerned with how it was obtained. It is no ground for the exercise of discretion to exclude that the evidence was obtained as the result of the activities of an agent provocateur.

A majority in *Sang* expressly agree with Lord Diplock, although some are less strict in this delineation of the boundaries of the discretion of the judge to exclude evidence at common law. The effect of the judgment is that discretion at common law is limited to ensuring that the probative weight of the evidence sufficiently outweighs any prejudicial effect[17] and to excluding confessions (and analogous evidence) that have been obtained unfairly. The function of the judge is to ensure the accused has a fair trial and it is no part of that function to exercise disciplinary powers over police or prosecution as the defendant has available civil and disciplinary remedies.

But the House of Lords are willing to exercise discipline over unfair methods employed in the interview room and to exclude unfairly obtained confessions. *Sang* draws a distinction which is perhaps difficult to justify in principle since the House is willing to exclude the product of illegal

[17] It is this element in the ratio in *Sang* that is retained by the Police and Criminal Evidence Act 1984, s.82(3), "Nothing in this Part of this Act shall prejudice any power of a court to exclude evidence (whether by preventing questions from being put or otherwise) at its discretion."

interviews and thus protect the accused's right of silence but is not willing to exclude the product of illegal searches in order to protect his or her right to privacy.

American decisions show no such reluctance. The Supreme Court has on several occasions excluded evidence which has been illegally obtained acting under the Fourth Amendment to the Constitution which forbids unreasonable searches and seizures. The key case is *Mapp v. Ohio*.[18]

Stuntz W., "The American Exclusionary Rule and Defendants' Changing Rights" [1989] Crim.L.R. 117 at 118–119

Police officers broke into Dollree Mapp's boarding house, in search of both gambling paraphernalia and a fugitive. When Ms. Mapp asked to see a warrant (it was clear that a warrantless search was not authorised under the circumstances), one of the officers produced a piece of paper but would not let Ms Mapp read it; in subsequent proceedings the state all but conceded that the 'warrant' was fraudulent. The police proceeded to ransack the whole house, examining, among other things, all of Ms Mapp's books and papers. During this process, they found four books that under then-governing state law were deemed obscene, though today they would probably be protected by the First Amendment. Ms Mapp was prosecuted for possession of obscene materials, an offence that the Supreme Court has since invalidated as infringing constitutionally protected freedom of thought (no matter how obscene the materials).[19]

The Court chose this combination of a questionable offence and egregious police misconduct to hold that the states are bound not only by the Fourth Amendment but by its exclusionary remedy as well. The majority opinion gave a host of reasons for this conclusion, but three stand out as particularly important. The first, and most obvious is deterrence: exclusion removes the incentive for police to conduct illegal searches. The second is 'the imperative of judicial integrity', the notion being that it is dishonest and hypocritical for courts to admit illegally obtained evidence. The third ground is one that permeates the entire *Mapp* opinion: that exclusion of illegally obtained evidence is in some normative sense the defendant's entitlement, that it does no more than right the wrong the police have done. Though not framed in these terms, the argument is that the exclusionary rule serves a necessary compensatory purpose . . .

The legal structure *Mapp* created endures, at least in its basic outline, today. As a precaution against police overreaching, the Fourth Amendment requires a police officer to obtain a warrant from a neutral and detached magistrate before undertaking any major search, unless doing so is plainly infeasible. Violation of this requirement leads automatically to the suppression of evidence obtained as a result of the search . . .

Recent U.S. decisions have restricted this exclusionary rule to criminal proceedings[20] and treated the primary rationale as that of deterring illegal police conduct. In *U.S. v. Leon*[21] the warrant was technically improperly issued by the magistrate but on its face valid. Evidence resulting from a

[18] 367 U.S. 643 (1961).
[19] *Stanley v. Georgia* 394 U.S. 557 (1969).
[20] *U.S. v. Janis* 428 U.S. 433 (1976) where the rule was inapplicable in civil tax proceedings.
[21] 468 U.S. 897 (1984).

search by police officers relying in good faith on the warrant was not excluded. The rationale of such a limitation is that magistrates do not need to be forced to apply the proper standards of "probable cause" in issuing warrants. While police officers do need policing by the courts, the deterrent force of the exclusionary rule only operates where the police officer can do something to prevent the illegality. In *Leon* the only error was by the issuing magistrate which could not be detected by the officers involved.

The divergence between the English and American courts shows the differing public interests involved: on the one hand, the proper determination of cases requires that all relevant and reliable evidence is before the courts whereas, on the other, the due process of law states that the proper administration of justice requires respect for the rights of the accused (with the corollary that state officials must be deterred from committing illegal acts).

Discretion under section 78

The common law rejection of judicial discretion has been significantly affected by the passage of Police and Criminal Evidence Act 1984, section 78:

78.—(1) In any proceedings the court may refuse to allow evidence on which the prosecution proposes to rely to be given if it appears to the court that, having regard to all the circumstances, including the circumstances in which the evidence was obtained, the admission of the evidence would have such an adverse effect on the fairness of the proceedings that the court ought not to admit it.

(2) Nothing in this section shall prejudice any rule of law requiring a court to exclude evidence.

Section 78 did not appear in the original bill but was the result of an amendment tabled by Lord Scarman enabling courts to exclude evidence on the basis of police malpractice. The government accepted the need for such an exclusionary clause but watered down the original with the eventual, rather obscure, text. Lord Scarman's judgment in *Sang* differed from that of Lord Diplock as he was more willing to cede a wider discretion to the judge to exclude evidence on the basis of the judicial duty to ensure a fair trial:

R. v. Sang [1979] 2 All E.R. 1222 at 1247d–1248c, _per_ Lord Scarman

If an accused is misled or tricked into providing evidence (whether it be an admission or the provision of fingerprints or medical evidence or some other evidence), the rule against self-incrimination, *nemo tenetur se ipsum prodere*, is likely to be infringed. Each case must, of course, depend on its circumstances. All I would say is that the principle of fairness, though concerned exclusively with the use of evidence at trial, is not susceptible to categorisation or classification, and is wide enough in some circumstances to embrace the way in which, after the crime, evidence is obtained from the accused . . .

> In reaching my conclusion that the discretion is a general one designed to ensure the accused a fair trial, I am encouraged by what I understand to be the Scots law. Such research as I have been able to make makes clear that the Scots judges recognise such a discretion. Indeed, I think they go further than the English law, the Scots principle being that evidence illegally or unfairly obtained is inadmissible unless in the exercise of its discretion the court allows it to be given. Sheriff MacPhail . . . describes the existing law in these terms:
>
> > In criminal cases, on the other hand, evidence illegally or irregularly obtained is inadmissible unless the illegality or irregularity associated with its procurement can be excused by the court.
>
> It would appear that the principal authority is the Full Bench case of *Lawrie v. Muir*[22] in which Lord Justice-General Cooper, after saying that the irregularities require to be excused, continued:
>
> > In particular, the case may bring into play the discretionary principle of fairness to the accused which has been developed so fully in our law in relation to the admission in evidence of confessions or admissions by a person suspected or charged with crime. That principle would obviously require consideration in any case in which the departure from the strict procedure had been adopted deliberately with a view to securing the admission of evidence obtained by an unfair trick.
>
> How far the Scots judges have extended 'the discretionary principle of fairness to the accused' I am not qualified to say. It is, however, plain that by the law of Scotland it may be invoked in a case where, after the commission of a crime, illegal or irregular methods have been used to obtain evidence from the accused . . . Though differences of emphasis and scope are acceptable, it would be, I think, unfortunate if 'the discretionary principle of fairness to the accused' was not recognised in all the criminal jurisdictions of the United Kingdom. Indeed, it must be a fundamental principle in all British criminal jurisdictions that the court is under the duty to ensure the accused a fair trial, and I do not believe that a judge can effectually discharge his duty without, at the very least, the availability of the discretion I have endeavoured to describe.

It is this "the discretionary principle of fairness to the accused" that Lord Scarman sought to incorporate into law by tabling his amendment. However, in his judgment, his Lordship was clearly concerned with illegalities and irregularities *after* the commission of a crime. The final wording of section 78 allows the court to consider whether police conduct prior to the offence, whether perhaps by illegal bugging or by entrapment, affects the overall fairness of the proceedings.

Entrapment still does not exist as a defence in criminal law and the appellate courts have remained reluctant to allow such a defence through the back door of the rules of evidence. To a large extent the courts adhere to the position laid down by Lord Salmon in *Sang*:

[22] 1950 J.C. 19 at 27.

> I would now refer to what is, I believe, and hope, the unusual case, in which a dishonest policeman, anxious to improve his detection record, tries very hard with the help of an agent provocateur to induce a young man with no criminal tendencies to commit a serious crime; and ultimately the young man reluctantly succumbs to the inducement. In such a case, the judge has no discretion to exclude the evidence which proves that the young man has committed the offence.[23]

In *DPP v. Marshall*[24] police officers in plain clothes purchased four cans of lager and a bottle of wine from the respondent's shop. The respondents were licensed to sell the liquor by the case but not to sell individual cans and bottles and were charged with having sold the beer and the wine without having the requisite licence. At the hearing, the respondents contended that the police officers' evidence should be excluded under section 78(1) as having "an adverse effect on the fairness of the proceedings" because the officers had not at the time of the purchase made it known that they were police officers. The magistrates accepted that contention but the Divisional Court held that the evidence of the police officers had been wrongly excluded. It had not been shown that the evidence of police officers who had made test purchases in plain clothes would have an adverse effect on the fairness of the proceedings. The appeal was therefore allowed and the case remitted to the magistrates with a direction to proceed with the hearing of the information. Woolf L.J. distinguished *R. v. Mason*,[25] saying:

> In that case a deceit was practised by the police on the appellant and on his solicitor with regard to the police having evidence of a fingerprint which had not in fact been found and in those circumstances the Court of Appeal, Criminal Division, indicated that the evidence could be admissible under section 78 of the 1984 Act. There, however, was an express misrepresentation and a clear deception practised and you can understand how, if a deception of this type occurs, it could have an effect on the fairness of the trial, but here it is difficult to see how the fact that the police officers did not reveal their identity could have any effect on the trial.[26]

In *R. v. Christou*[27] an undercover police operation in London set up a shop to buy and sell jewellery commercially. It was staffed solely by undercover officers purporting to be shady jewellers willing to buy stolen property. Discreetly sited cameras and sound equipment recorded all that occurred over the counter. The object was to recover stolen property for the owners and obtain evidence against persons who had either stolen or dishonestly handled it. The cameras clearly identified the property on the counter and the vendors who produced it. The conversations between the

[23] *ibid.* at 1236c–e.
[24] [1988] 3 All E.R. 683.
[25] [1987] 3 All E.R. 481.
[26] *Marshall supra* at 685d–e.
[27] [1992] 4 All E.R. 559.

officers and the vendors essentially concerned bartering about price. To maintain their cover, the officers asked questions such as the area of London in which it would be unwise to resell the goods. They also required the signing of receipts recording the money paid for specified goods. The appellants, who each made repeated sales at the shop, pleaded not guilty to indictments charging burglary and handling stolen goods and challenged the admissibility of the evidence resulting from the undercover operation on the grounds that it should be excluded under section 78.[28] The evidence was admitted and the appeal was dismissed.

R. v. Christou [1992] 4 All E.R. 559 at 564e–j, *per* Lord Taylor C.J.

The learned judge held that discretion under section 78 may be wider than the common law discretion identified in *R. v. Sang*, the latter relating solely to evidence obtained from the defendant after the offence is complete, the statutory discretion not being so restricted. However he held that the criteria of unfairness are the same whether the trial judge is exercising his discretion at common law or under the statute. We agree. What is unfair cannot sensibly be subject to different standards depending on the source of the discretion to exclude it.

In the result the learned judge concluded that to admit the challenged evidence would not have an adverse effect on the fairness of the trial. He said:

> Nobody was forcing the defendants to do what they did. They were not persuaded or encouraged to do what they did. They were doing in that shop exactly what they intended to do and, in all probability, what they intended to do from the moment they got up that morning. They were dishonestly disposing of dishonest goods. If the police had never set up the jewellers shop, they would, in my judgment, have been doing the same thing, though of course they would not have been doing it in that shop, at that time. They were not tricked into doing what they would not otherwise have done, they were tricked into doing what they wanted to do in that place and before witnesses and devices who can now speak of what happened. I do not think that is unfair or leads to an unfairness in the trial.

Putting it in different words, the trick was not applied to the appellants; they voluntarily applied themselves to the trick. It is not every trick producing evidence against an accused which results in unfairness. There are, in criminal investigations, a number of situations in which the police adopt ruses or tricks in the public interest to obtain evidence. For example, to trap a blackmailer the victim may be used as an agent of the police to arrange an appoitment and false or marked money may be laid as a bait to catch the offender. A trick, certainly; in a sense too, a trick which results in a form of self-incrimination; but not one which could reasonably be thought to involve unfairness.

Lord Taylor felt that such operations were not contrary to public policy. The operation allowed the offenders to commit further offences which may

[28] An alternative ground of appeal was that the police had infringed the Code of Practice on the conduct of interviews. The court held that what occurred was not an interview within the meaning of the Code. Were police officers to adopt or use an undercover pose or disguise to enable themselves to ask questions about an offence uninhibited by the requirements of the Code and with the effect of circumventing it, the product of such an interview would be inadmissible under s.78 — *R. v. Bryce* [1992] 4 All E.R. 567.

have been obviated had they been arrested earlier. In other words, the existence of the shop facilitated, if it did not directly encourage, the commission of the crime.

> Clearly, it must be a matter for policy and operational decision by the police as to how they reconcile and balance the need on the one hand to bring an individual offender swiftly to book and deter crime, and on the other, the desirability of apprehending a larger number of offenders and recovering property.[29]

R. v. Smurthwaite[30] involved allegations that the defendant had solicited another to murder his wife. An undercover police officer was introduced to the defendant by a third party and pretended to be a contract killer. Conversations incriminating the defendant were then recorded by a tape recorder concealed by the police officer. Evidence of the conversations was admitted. The Court of Appeal held that section 78 had not altered the substantive rule that entrapment or use of an *agent provocateur* did not *per se* afford a defence in law to a criminal charge. However, that was not to say that the use of such methods was irrelevant to the application of section 78. If obtaining evidence in that way would have an adverse effect on the fairness of the proceedings, the court may exclude it.

R. v. *Smurthwaite* [1994] 1 All E.R. 898 at 903a–d, *per* Lord Taylor C.J.

In exercising his discretion whether to admit evidence of an undercover officer, some, but not an exhaustive list, of the factors that the judge may take into account are as follows. Was the officer acting as an *agent provocateur* in the sense that he was enticing the defendant to commit an offence he would not have otherwise committed? What was the nature of any entrapment? Does the evidence consist of admissions to a completed offence, or does it consist of the actual commission of an offence? How active or passive was the officer's role in obtaining the evidence? Is there an unassailable record of what occurred, or is it strongly corroborated? In *R. v. Christou* this court held that discussions between suspects and undercover officers, not overtly acting as police officers, were not in the ambit of the codes under the 1984 Act. However, officers should not use their undercover pose to question suspects so as to circumvent the code. In *R. v. Bryce* the court held that the undercover officer had done just that. Accordingly a further consideration for the judge in deciding to admit an undercover officer's evidence is whether he has abused his role to ask questions which ought properly to have been asked as a police officer and in accordance with the codes.

These authorities demonstrate that the Court of Appeal is using its exclusionary power to lay down guidelines for the police so that traps will only yield admissible evidence when phone calls are recorded and crucial

[29] *ibid.* at 567c; the House of Lords also has held that a trick to lure a defendant into the jurisdiction is not an abuse of process in *R. v. Latif* [1996] 1 All E.R. 353 although a stay to proceedings is appropriate where the defendant is forcibly abducted and brought to this country — *R. v. Horseferry Road Magistrates' Court ex parte Bennett* [1993] 3 All E.R. 138.
[30] [1994] 1 All E.R. 898.

meetings taped. It is a pragmatic approach, preferable to the chains of *Sang* but which lacks guiding principle. It has been argued that society has a real interest in limiting the use of entrapment techniques:

> One reason is that the State does not have unlimited power to intrude into our personal lives or to randomly test the virtue of individuals. Another is the concern that entrapment techniques may result in the commission of crimes by people who would not otherwise become involved in criminal conduct . . . Ultimately we may be saying that there are inherent limits on the power of the State to manipulate people and events for the purpose of attaining the specific objective of obtaining convictions.[31]

The consequence of this approach has been that in Canada and Australia, courts have the power to exclude evidence or to stay proceedings for abuse of process. English courts have not gone so far. The authorities show:

- that the statutory discretion to exclude evidence bestowed on the courts by section 78 applies to a broader range of circumstances than the common law discretion of *Sang*
- that the criteria of unfairness are the same whether the judge is exercising his discretion at common law or under statute

In practice the courts are unwilling to use their statutory discretion in any radically different way than the common law discretion which existed under *Sang*:

(a) tricks leading to incriminating statements: police deception which leads to the accused making an incriminating statement is certainly envisaged in the judgments in *Sang* and the enactment of section 78 has made little difference. The example given in *Sang* is *R. v. Payne*[32] where the defendant, charged with drunk driving, was induced to see a doctor on the understanding that the doctor would not examine him for the purpose of seeing whether he was fit to drive. The doctor later testified that he was in fact unfit to drive. Lord Diplock treated this as analogous to unfairly inducing the defendant to confess.[33] Section 78 does not change this position. In *R. v. Mason*[34] the police falsely told the defendant, accused of arson of a car, in the presence of his solicitor that they had the defendant's fingerprints on a fragment of glass. As a result he made a confession. The conviction was quashed and the Court of Appeal stressed the need to balance the gravity of the charge, the public interest, the position of the defendant and the nature of the police illegality. This was a significant deception on a minor charge, not only of the defendant but also of his lawyer.

[31] *Mack v. The Queen* (1988) 44 C.C.C. 3d 513 at 541; cited in Robertson G., "Entrapment Evidence: Manna from Heaven or Fruit of the Poisoned Tree?" [1994] Crim.L.R. 805.
[32] [1963] 1 All E.R. 848.
[33] *Sang* supra at 1229 c–d.
[34] [1987] 3 All E.R. 481.

Another trick leading to self-incriminating statements was perpetrated in *R. v. Bailey and Smith*[35] when the police put the two suspects into the same cell and then staged a pantomime to convince the men that this was being forced on them by an uncooperative custody officer. The men made damaging admissions which were recorded, despite having been warned by their solicitor that the police were likely to act in exactly this fashion.The balance of fairness is harder to assess: it was a serious charge and suspects in police stations can have no justified expectation of privacy and this was reinforced by their solicitor's warning. There was also no illegality on the part of the police.[36] However there is an expectation that within the police station, officers will behave, not only in strict accordance with the Codes but perhaps in a "proper" fashion. An express deception (for example, telling the suspects that they could consult together without fear of eavesdropping) would surely rule out the admissibility of any damaging statements. On the facts there is an intentional, implied, deception to lure the suspects into a false sense of security. Should the fact that the deception is implied rather than express make a difference?

(b) tricks outside the station: police deception, resulting in acquisition of incriminating evidence, will not normally trigger the exclusionary discretion. In *R. v. Maclean and Kosten*[37] the customs had arrested a drugs courier with a carload of cannabis but wished to implicate the real importer. By an elaborate hoax, the accused was inveigled into arranging the safe garaging of the car, thus demonstrating guilty knowledge. Outside the police station, there can be no expectation of privacy nor that the people with whom you are dealing are honest, especially if you are engaged in illegal activity. Where the police officer becomes involved in an ongoing offence (as was the case in *Christou* and *Smurthwaite*), is relatively passive and an accurate record is provided, it is difficult to argue that the fairness of the proceedings has been affected.

The problem case is where the offence is instigated by the police. Common law discretion is irrelevant and the accused must rely on section 78. In *Williams v. DPP*[38] the police left a Transit van apparently loaded with cigarettes in public view, arresting the appellants when they attempted to take some of the cartons. The court held that they had not acted as agents provocateurs and admitted the evidence but it is clear that the police procured the commission of an offence which would not otherwise have been committed. To set up offences and then bring criminal proceedings would appear to satisfy the criteria laid down in *Smurthwaite* and in any case must be close to abuse of process.[39]

[35] [1993] 3 All E.R. 513.
[36] But see *R v. Khan* [1994] 4 All E.R. 426 where the police trespassed (although within Home Office guidelines) to install a listening device on a private house and were still permitted to use the incriminating recordings in evidence.
[37] [1993] Crim.L.R. 687.
[38] [1993] 3 All E.R. 365.
[39] *ex parte Bennett supra.*

Another case which falls close to the *Smurthwaite* guidelines is *R. v. Wilson*[40] where a police informer enticed the accused into forging large quantities of Amercian Express traveller cheques. Although the judge refused to exclude the evidence, he merely imposed suspended sentences, a clear comment on the propriety of the proceedings.

(c) straightforward illegality: such conduct by the police is rarely seen in reported cases and there are few, if any, recent authorities where evidence is gathered as a result of a tort, breach of contract or crime. In *Jeffery v. Black*[41] Lord Widgery preferred to use the expression "irregular" rather than "illegal" for the obviously tortious search without a warrant. It is a moot point whether that common law decision would be the same under section 78. In some ways the lack of authority is encouraging as it suggests that the police observe the formalities for stopping and searching, for arrests or for searching premises. But again, and not surprisingly, the point is rarely taken that there was no "reasonable cause" for the police action, as the finding of the contraband material, be it drugs, stolen property or an offensive weapon, *de facto* legitimises the search.

(d) covert surveillance: this is not in itself illegal. There exist, in strict law, no police "powers" of surveillance and information gathering.[42] These activities are rarely carried out under any direct statutory or common law authority and are, in effect, based upon the common law principle that whatever is not expressly forbidden by law is permissible. Such activities are not forbidden because they do not, in general, infringe interests of the citizen which are recognised by the common law and Parliament has shown itself reluctant to extend those interests. There is a limited protection provided by recent legislation such as the Interception of Communications Act 1985[43] and the Data Protection Act 1984.

There are thus few legal constraints on the police and correspondingly considerable legal and practical difficulties in obtaining remedies against them. Common law has never recognised a right to privacy as such. The practice of intercepting letters under the Home Secretary's warrant is of very long standing although the authority for doing so is obscure. The Home Secretary's power to authorise telephone tapping was challenged in *Malone v. Metropolitan Police Commissioner*[44] when the plaintiff failed in his domestic action when he sued after the prosecution had admitted tapping his telephone in a criminal trial. The Interception of Communications Act 1985 now regulates interception of the post, telephone tapping

[40] *The Guardian*, December 15, 1994.
[41] [1978] 1 All E.R. 555.
[42] Such acts will be authorised under Part III of the Police Bill before Parliament at the time of writing.
[43] See the decisions in *R. v. Effik* [1994] 3 All E.R. 458 and *R. v. Preston* [1993] 4 All E.R. 638.
[44] [1979] Ch. 344 at 366; *Malone v. U.K.* (1984) 7 E.H.R.R. 14.

and any communications sent by a public[45] telecommunications system.[46] It is now a criminal offence for a person intentionally to intercept a communication unless he was doing so under a warrant issued by the Secretary of State or he had reasonable grounds to believe that the sender or recipient of the communication consented.[47]

At the moment the police can also rely on the product of listening devices not coming under the Interceptions of Communications Act. In *R. v. Khan*[48] the Court of Appeal gave firm approval for bugging as a technique used in targeting known offenders, even where, as in this case, this involved trespass. The test for admissibility is relevance and the product is admissible if relevant. In other cases, there may well be more compelling considerations of invasion of privacy or even of tort through trespass and of criminal damage. But such considerations must be weighed against the probative value of the evidence. Lord Taylor discussed the nature of the judicial discretion exercised under section 78 when confronted with illegally obtained evidence:

R. v. Khan [1994] 4 All E.R. 426 at 435h–438a, _per_ Lord Taylor

The nature of the arguments advanced by counsel for the appellant under this head (that the evidence should be excluded as a matter of judicial discretion) are . . . (1) The conduct of the police in fitting the device which enabled them to obtain the evidence was unlawful . . . (2) There are no statutory provisions and no readily accessible published criteria to inform the public as to the circumstances in which such intrusions on privacy may occur. Unless the terms on which such conduct is to be permitted are, by some such means, known to all, it is unfair to permit the product of it to be used in evidence. (3) Previous practice has been against such material being used in evidence to secure a conviction; its legitimate use has been confined to detection and prevention of crime. (4) Parliament has decided that the product of telephone tapping should not be used in evidence and, since this material was obtained in closely analogous circumstances, the use of it would be unfair. (5) There are grounds for thinking, on the strength of the decision in *Malone v. U.K.*, that the European Court of Human Rights would conclude that there had in the present case been a breach of art. 8 of the 1950 convention . . .

Counsel for the Crown point out that in the present case no crime was incited; no deliberate deceit was practised on the appellant; no misleading information was advanced or pressure placed upon him to induce him to speak; the police did not act oppressively towards him; at the time the conversation was taped the appellant had neither been arrested, interviewed, nor charged; the tape provided a clear record of what was admittedly said by the appellant; and no question arose of the breach of any Codes of Practice under the 1984 Act . . .

Counsel argued that, in the circumstances, the factors of trespass, damage and the matters relating to art 8 and the intrusion on privacy were of insufficient gravity to outweigh the other factors to which they had been referred, all of which militated in favour of concluding that fairness to both sides required the admission of the evidence. We agree with this submission. We would emphasise, in particular, the

[45] As defined in s.9 of the Telecommunications Act 1984.
[46] As defined in s.4(1) of the Telecommunications Act 1984.
[47] Interception of Communications Act 1985, s.1(1) & (2).
[48] [1994] 4 All E.R. 426.

fact that in proceeding as they did the police were, so far from acting in an arbitrary or uncontrolled manner, proceeding in accordance with the relevant Home Office guidelines . . . Moreover, what was under investigation was a type of criminal conduct of great gravity. The issues of trespass and damage . . . are in the circumstances of this case of limited importance, save for their impact upon the issues of privacy and the inviolability of the home which have rightly been emphasised. We would expect there to be devices available now or in the future, which can pick up even the most private conversations without the need for a trespass. There are, as art. 8 recognises, circumstances in which such intrusion is necessary and therefore justifiable in a democratic society. In the circumstances we cannot but think that the judge was right in concluding, as he plainly did, that the invasion of privacy with the attendant trespass and damage was outweighed by other considerations and should plainly not be regarded as having such an adverse effect on the fairness of the proceedings that the court ought to exclude the evidence.

Discretion and European law

The significant restraints on police surveillance are likely to be the result of applications under the European Convention on Human Rights which protects a range of human rights, especially Article 8:

8.—1. Everyone has the right to respect for his private and family life, his home and his correspondence.
2. There shall be no interference by a public authority with the exercise of this right except such as is in accordance with the law and is necessary in a democratic society in the interests of national security, public safety or the economic well-being of the country, for the prevention of disorder or crime, for the protection of health or morals, or for the protection of the rights and freedoms of others.[49]

United Kingdom police practices of visual and aural surveillance are very likely in breach of the right to privacy under Article 8, as these practices are regulated only by administrative guidelines formulated by the Home Office and therefore contravene the Convention as they are not clearly formulated and accessible for citizens to be aware of the conditions under which the authorities are empowered to resort to secret interference with the right to privacy.[50] In *Malone v. U.K.*,[51] the applicant brought proceedings under the Convention, claiming that telephone tapping had violated the European Convention on Human Rights. The European Court of Human Rights unanimously decided that the British Government had breached Article 8 of the Convention since telephone tapping was not in accordance with the law. It ruled that the law had to be sufficiently clear in terms to give citizens an adequate indication of the circumstances in which and the conditions under which telephone tapping could be carried out. The law had to indicate the scope of any executive discretion and the

[49] See Joubert C., "Undercover Policing — A Comparative Study" [1994] European Journal of Crime, Criminal Law and Criminal Justice 18.
[50] *Malone v. U.K.* (1984) 7 E.H.R.R. 14 at 39–41.
[51] *ibid.*

manner of its existence in order to give the citizen protection against arbitrary interference.

By analogy, similar arguments apply to police practices of "aural" and "visual" surveillance covering matters such as the planting of "electronic bugs" and the use of video cameras to observe the activities of people in private places. Such practices are clearly violations of the rights to "respect for private life" in Article 8 and are not "in accordance with the law", being governed only by administrative guidelines.[52] Police surveillance may indeed breach the guarantee of privacy contained in Article 8. In *Klass v. Germany*[53] the European Court acknowledged the significance of the technical advances made in surveillance as well as the development of terrorism; that the state must be entitled to counter terrorism with secret surveillance of mail, post and telecommunications under exceptional circumstances does not however give it the right to adopt whatever measures it thinks it appropriate in the name of counteracting espionage and terrorism.

In *Klass* the Court provided the following general guidance as to the application of Article 8 to legislation authorising surveillance:

- the legislation must be designed to ensure that surveillance is not ordered haphazardly, irregularly or without due and proper care
- surveillance must be reviewed and must be accompanied by procedures which guarantee individual rights
- it is in principle desirable to entrust the supervisory control to a judge in accordance with the rule of law, but other safeguards might suffice if they are independent and vested with sufficient powers to exercise an effective and continuous control
- if the surveillance is justified under Article 8(2) the failure to inform the individual under surveillance of this fact afterwards is, in principle, justified.[54]

[52] This position may change as a result of the Police Bill currently before Parliament.

[53] (1978) 2 E.H.R.R. 214; legislation in Germany permitted the State authorities to open and inspect mail and listen to telephone conversations in order to protect against, inter alia, "imminent dangers" threatening the "free democratic constitutional order" and "the existence or the security" of the State . . . The applicants, five German lawyers, claimed that the legislation infringed Articles 6 (right to a fair hearing), 8 (right to respect for correspondence) and 13 (effective remedy before a national authority in respect of breaches of the Convention) of the European Convention on Human Rights. They accepted the State's right to have recourse to such measures, but challenged the legislation on the grounds that it contained no absolute requirement to notify the persons after surveillance of their mail, etc. had ceased and that it excluded any remedy before the courts against the ordering and implementation of the measures. The Government denied that the legislation infringed the Convention and questioned whether the applicants were "victims of a violation" within the terms of Article 25(1), since they had not themselves been subject to surveillance. The Commission declared that the secret nature of the exercise made it necessary to regard the applicants as possible victims for the purpose of Article 25, but decided that no breaches of the Convention were disclosed.

[54] *ibid.* at 232–6.

The European Court has recently ruled that telephone tapping carried out on the instructions and under the supervision of investigating judges in France violated Article 8, because there were inadequate safeguards against various possible abuses. In *Huvig v. France*[55] and *Kruslin v. France*,[56] the following deficiencies were identified:

- there had been no definition for the categories of people liable to have their telephones tapped nor the nature of the offence which might give rise to such order
- the investigating judge had not been under an obligation to set a limit on the duration of the tapping
- the procedure for drawing up the summary reports of the intercepted conversations was unspecified
- the precautions to be taken with regard to the communication of the recordings intact and in their entirety for possible inspection by the judge and by the defence were unspecified
- the destruction of the recordings, particularly where the accused had been discharged or acquitted were unspecified.

By contrast, in *Leander v. Sweden*,[57] the European Court held that in the gathering of information in a secret police register and its release to the public service, the applicant's prospective employer had not violated Article 8 even though it was held that there had been an interference with the applicant's rights under Article 8(1). The Court was, however, satisfied that the Swedish personnel control system had the legitimate aim of protecting national security and that it was "in accordance with the law." The Court's decision, was in this case, influenced by the involvement of parliamentarians, the Parliamentary Ombudsman and the Parliamentary Committee on Justice in the supervision of the system.

[55] (1990) 12 E.H.R.R. 528 — the applicants were suspected of, and subsequently convicted of, various offences of tax evasion by the use of forged invoices. In the course of the judicial investigating the investigating judge authorised a senior police officer to have the applicants' business and private telephone lines tapped. The applicants complained of a violation of Article 8 of the Convention. It was held unanimously, that indeed, there had been a breach of Article 8.

[56] (1990) 12 E.H.R.R. 547 — the applicant was convicted of, inter alia, armed robbery. One decisive piece of evidence against him was a taped record of his telephone conversation with another person whose telephone line was tapped in relation to other proceedings. The applicant argued that the interception and recording of his telephone conversation violated Article 8 of the Convention.' Again, it was held unanimously that there had been a breach of Article 8.

[57] (1987) 9 E.H.R.R. 433 — the applicant had been refused permanent employment as museum technician with the Naval museum on account of certain secret information which allegedly made him a security risk. He contended that the vetting had involved an attack on his reputation and that he should have had the opportunity of defending himself before a tribunal. It was held that there had been no breach of Article 8.

THE ADMISSIBILITY OF CONFESSIONS

Police interrogation and reliability

One of the key items of evidence in a criminal trial will be the answers by the accused to police questions. Often these will be incriminating statements and interrogation designed to obtain such admissions has always been a major investigative technique for the police. Despite developments in police crime strategies, emphasising the targeting of offences and offenders, which should lead to the gathering of more tangible forms of evidence, interviewing remains an essential police task. Compared to other forms of acquiring evidence, it is cheap and the end result, a confession, is evidence that is seen as reliable and convincing. Most suspects (especially those detained in the police station) talk to the police and many make either complete or partial, verbal or written admissions of guilt.[58] The amendments to the right of silence made by the Criminal Justice and Public Order Act 1994 will presumably increase this proportion.

The use of confessions as evidence at first sight infringes the rule against hearsay. That rule prohibits a witness repeating an out-of-court oral or written statement in order that the court should rely on the truth of that statement. This is exactly what a police officer does when he or she repeats a defendant's confession. This is so whether that confession has been taped, written down or merely remembered by the officer. But confessions are admissible because they form the most important exception to the hearsay rule: an incriminating statement is admissible evidence whether it is a full confession or simply a partial admission or a statement by the accused which is against his or her interest.

Indeed all statements made by a suspect to the police, whether exculpatory or inculpatory, are accepted into evidence.[59] Once admitted, such statements are very harmful to the defendant's case since the psychology of the juror will often, not unreasonably, lead to greater weight being given to the confession and less attention being paid to the extent to which any other independent evidence supports or undermines that confession.

The rationale for the rule against hearsay is explored later but in essence it has two aspects: firstly, hearsay is regarded as unreliable and consequently less probative value can be placed upon it; secondly, to admit the evidence of an absent witness denies the defendant the opportunity to confront his or her accusers, or in other words to cross-examine those giving evidence which is adverse to him or her. Both carry less weight when considering confessions: firstly, confessions are more reliable and therefore probative since people are unlikely to admit a state of affairs which is contrary to their own interests unless that admission is true; secondly, all the relevant people are in court so defendants are able both to

[58] Mitchell B.: "Confessions and Police Interrogation of Suspects" [1983] Crim.L.R. 596.
[59] *R. v. Sharp* [1988] 1 All E.R. 65.

confront the officer who took the statement and, should they choose to do so, can testify on their own behalf.

Although confessions may be more reliable, in practice over-reliance on them can be dangerous. The trail of false confessions by vulnerable suspects is well documented: the young as in the Confait Case,[60] the disturbed,[61] the mentally subnormal[62] let alone those subject to brutality and intimidation.[63] But under hostile interrogation in the psychologically intimidating environment of a police station, even non-vulnerable people are also likely to make admissions which are not true,[64] not realising that once a statement had been made, there is great difficulty in retracting it:

Sanders A. and Young R., *Criminal Justice* (1994) 183–187

From the due process perspective . . . protections for suspects are justified in themselves and should not be dependent on whether or not oppressive behaviour or inducements really do lead to false confessions. On the other hand, since all systems have some false confessions and some wrongful convictions . . . the fact that there are some false confessions does not automatically mean that the system must be changed. For while the due process adherent will want to minimise the incidence of false confessions (and minimise the reliance of the system on them) knowing that the result will be the conviction of fewer guilty people, the crime control adherent will wish to maintain the processes which produce false confessions as long as they produce even greater numbers of reliable confessions and expeditious convictions.

In discussing false confessions we need to distinguish between innocent people who confess 'voluntarily'; people whose innocence or otherwise is unknown who 'confess' through coercion; and people again whose innocence is unknown, who allegedly confess but who in fact do not. The last category concerns fabricated confessions . . . There are a number of reasons why people who are, or may be, innocent confess.[65]

"Coerced-compliant" confessions

Here the suspect knows that the confession is false, but is prepared to confess to escape pressure. This pressure will sometimes be oppressive interrogation tactics, or sometimes just the experience of custody and interrogation. This was what apparently happened in the 'Confait Affair' and probably in the 'Cardiff Three' case[66] and several of the other infamous miscarriage cases. Many of these cases

[60] *R. v. Lattimore* (1976) 62 Cr.App.R. 53.
[61] *R. v. Ward* [1993] 2 All E.R. 577.
[62] Timothy Evans confessed to killings of his wife and child committed by John Christie — Kennedy L., *Ten Rillington Place* (1961).
[63] The Birmingham Six were seriously assaulted before they made any statements — Mullin C., *Error of Judgment* (1986).
[64] Irving B. and Hilgendorf L., *Police Interrogation: The Psychological Approach* (Royal Commission on Criminal Procedure Research Study No. 1 1980); Irving B.: *Police Interrogation* (Royal Commission on Criminal Procedure Research Study No. 2 1980); Irving B. and McKenzie I., *Police Interrogation: The Effects of PACE* (1989); Gudjonsson G., *Persons at Risk During Interviews in Police Custody* (Royal Commission on Criminal Justice Research Study No. 12, 1992); McConville M. et al, *The Case for the Prosecution* (1991) 56 *et seq.*
[65] The first two categories which follow were developed by G Gudjonsson, *The Psychology of Interrogation, Confessions and Testimony* (1992).
[66] *R. v. Paris* (1992) 97 Cr.App.R. 99.

involve vulnerable suspects, but people with average IQ and normal personality characteristics are also vulnerable to tactics of this type . . . [67]

"Coerced-internalised" confessions

Here, suspects begin to doubt their own memory. They temporarily believe in their own guilt because of disorientation. Carol Richardson, one of the 'Guildford Four' (imprisoned for terrorist offences for 14 years before having their convictions quashed), reported this experience after being told of the alleged confession of a fellow suspect. In establishing control, interrogators frequently try to throw suspects off balance, creating the continual danger that the suspect will be completely unbalanced.

"Coerced-passive" confessions

Here interrogation leads suspects to 'admit' to committing an offence without necessarily adopting or even understanding the substance of this admission. Given the extent to which interrogations centre on repetitious accusations, the pressure simply to agree is enormous. In one case . . . it was accepted that the suspect broke a car windscreen in the course of an argument. The question was, why?

> 'Did you intend to smash the windscreen?'
> 'No.'
> 'So you just swung your hand out in a reckless manner?'
> 'Yes, that's it, just arguing . . . Just arguing, reckless, it wasn't intentional to break it.'[68]

In other examples, suspects agreed that they 'stole' goods simply because they took them (not necessarily with intent permanently to deprive the owner), without understanding the legal implications of the term.

Interrogative suggestibility

This involves suspects receiving messages in ways which affect 'their subsequent behavioural response'.[69] This can occur in all three of the confession types discussed above. 'Vulnerable' suspects are particularly susceptible. Stefan Kiszko had a mental age of 12, and was jailed for life in 1976 for murdering a schoolgirl. He had been interrogated repeatedly, and eventually 'confessed' after his sixth interrogation. In 1992, his conviction was quashed after it was found that the semen on the victim's body could not have been his. This evidence was available at the time of the trial, but was not revealed. Kiszko died, aged 41, less than two years after his release . . .

Vulnerable people now have the additional protection during interrogation of an 'appropriate adult'. But . . . the police often fail to identify vulnerable suspects. This was so in the 'Tottenham Three' case,[70] and lower profile examples include *Brine*[71] and *Miller*.[72] In the first two of these cases, confessions were rejected by the

[67] See Gudjonsson G. and Mackeith J., "A Proven Case of False Confession: Psychological Aspects of the Coerced-Compliant Type" (1990) 30 Med. Sci. Law 329.
[68] McConville M., (1991) *op. cit.* 70.
[69] Gudjonsson G. and Clark N. "Suggestibility in Police Interrogation: a Social Psychological Model" (1986) 1 Soc. Behav. 83.
[70] *R. v. Raghip*, *The Times*, December 9, 1991.
[71] [1992] Crim.L.R. 122.
[72] [1986] 3 All E.R. 119.

Court of Appeal because of the vulnerability of the defendants, but this was not the result in *Miller*. Further, neither appropriate adults nor legal advice prevents the police from placing on suspects the kinds of pressures faced by Kiszko. Indeed, the point of many police tactics is to identity and exploit vulnerabilities in 'ordinary' people . . .

The dangers of interrogative suggestibility are enhanced by the types of question commonly asked. If interrogations were primarily fact finding, questions would generally be of the open kind ('what did you see?', 'what did you do?') where there would be few dangers of false confessions, if only because the criminal alone would be able to provide the correct details . . . The important question is what happens in interrogations where suspects do not readily confess? McConville and Hodgson[73] argue that the questions then turn to admission seeking. The most important question forms of this type which they identify are, firstly, leading questions. These seek particular answers by foreclosing others (for example, 'You went down there to get the stuff and assaulted her, didn't you?'). Secondly, there are statement questions (such as, 'You did it. You went there. There is no sign of entry, no force; whoever did it, did it by key.'); thirdly, there are legal closure questions ('So you stole the goods?'); fourthly, there are questions seeking the adoption of police opinions ('You are not innocent, you know what goes on.') Finally, there are accusatory questions.

In the process of 'asking' these questions, the police sometimes let information slip which suspects may incorporate into their answers. And sometimes as the police ask for detail, and the innocent suspect gets it wrong, the suspect is contradicted until, by chance, the current answer is produced . . . What many researchers . . . have described as inadequate interview technique is, in reality, entirely adequate for the purposes of the police. It is the establishment of proof, regardless of truth. The same is true of hectoring, accusatorial questioning. Much of the time it is . . . .within the law, and it is consistent with the adversarial role of the police. Yet the Runciman Commission stated that: 'In our view the safeguards under PACE against false confessions are comprehensive and, while not foolproof, are substantially sound.'[74]

A central question for the Runciman Commission was whether independent corroborative evidence should be required for all confession cases. An independent study suggested that 95 per cent of such cases had such supporting evidence[75] which indicated that a rule requiring corroboration would lead to few additional acquittals. Although three members of the Commission felt that there should never be a conviction based solely on a confession, the majority were satisfied with a recommendation that the judge in all cases should give a strong warning that care was needed before convicting on the basis of the confession alone,[76] explicitly referring to

[73] McConville M. and Hodgson J.: *Custodial Legal Advice and the Right to Silence* (Royal Commission on Criminal Justice Research Study 16, 1993) 137.

[74] Sanders A. and Young R. *Criminal Justice* (1994) 183–187.

[75] McConville M., *Corroboration and Confessions: The Impact of a Rule Requiring that no Conviction be sustained on the Basis of Confession Evidence Alone* (Royal Commission on Criminal Justice Research Study No. 13, 1993). Corroboration is not a panacea against wrongful conviction — in the Birmingham Six case, there were confessions to the pub bombings and there was independent forensic evidence, later proved fatally flawed, that the defendants had handled explosives.

[76] Such a development does not need legislation and a similar warning was implemented in the case of identification evidence by the Court of Appeal in *R. v. Turnbull* [1977] Q.B. 224.

reasons why people might confess to crimes that they did not commit.[77] Such a provision already exists under the Police and Criminal Evidence Act 1984, but only in regard to a confession made by a mentally handicapped person:

> 77.—(1) Without prejudice to the general duty of the court at a trial on indictment to direct the jury on any matter on which it appears to the court appropriate to do so, where at such a trial—
>
> (a) the case against the accused depends wholly or substantially on a confession by him; and
>
> (b) the court is satisfied—
>
> (i) that he is mentally handicapped; and
>
> (ii) that the confession was not made in the presence of an independent person,
>
> the court shall warn the jury that there is a special need for caution before convicting the accused in reliance on the confession, and shall explain that the need arises because of the circumstances mentioned in paragraphs (a) and (b) above.

The development of safeguards

At common law, the judge had the discretion to exclude a confession if it was involuntary:[78]

> It has long been established as a positive rule of English law that no statement by an accused is admissible in evidence against him unless it is shown by the prosecution to have been a voluntary statement, in the sense that it has not been obtained from him by fear of prejudice or hope of advantage exercised or held out by a person in authority.[79]

The considerable uncertainty, not to say hostility, with which nineteenth century judges regarded police powers to detain and to question suspects led to divergent attitudes towards statements made to the police while in police custody, some happy to admit such statements as evidence while others excluded them.[80] Generally arrest signalled the end of police interrogation. The courts sought to limit the police powers of interrogation and insisted that a suspect should be taken before a magistrate with all speed, normally within 24 hours. Eventually it was the judges themselves who took the initiative to resolve this uncertainty by issuing the Judges' Rules in 1912 to regulate police procedure over the treatment of detained persons. Although these Rules had neither the authority of common law nor of statute and thus in legal theory possessed no legal force, they

[77] Royal Commission on Criminal Justice: *Report* Cm. 2263 (1993) paras. 4.56–4.87.
[78] *Ibrahim v. R.* [1914] A.C. 599.
[79] *ibid.* at 610, *per* Lord Sumner.
[80] *R. v. Knight and Thayre* (1905) 20 Cox C.C. 711.

remained as influential guidelines until 1984 and a basis for the courts to decide on whether to admit incriminating statements into evidence. Originally they prohibited police questioning after arrest, still reflecting the nineteenth century distrust of the "new" policing arrangements. It was not until the revision of the Rules in 1964 that the police power to question while the suspect was in custody was recognised. But by the 1960s, the judicial attitude towards breaches of the Rules had become very permissive and rarely did police misconduct lead to the exclusion of the evidence. By the 1970s, although police powers appeared quite restricted as a matter of law, in practice they were relatively wide: the power to stop, search and question on the streets was exercised *de facto*; premises were often searched without the "technicality" of a warrant; people "assisted the police with their enquiries" at police stations (although the courts did not recognise the legal concept of "detention for questioning"); suspects were held for extended periods without access to legal advice. The Judges' Rules provided no barrier to miscarriages of justice and many of the most notorious cases date from this period.[81]

The modern law is contained in the Police and Criminal Evidence Act 1984 which codifies pre-trial procedures including the powers of the police to stop people, search them, arrest them, hold them in police custody and interrogate them. It also lays down the suspect's privileges. The statute's history was tortuous.[82] The need for reform had been recognised for many years but the spark came in Catford, South London in April 1977 where Confait, a homosexual, was found strangled with electric flex in a burning house. Three boys (14, 15 and 18 and in the latter case, educationally subnormal) were arrested, interrogated without legal advice and, as a result of their confessions, charged with murder. Three years later, they were all released after the Fisher Report concluded that they had nothing to do with the killing.[83]

The Labour government set up the Royal Commission on Criminal Procedure[84] to examine police procedures. The establishment of the Commission was claimed as a victory for civil liberty groups but it rapidly became apparent that the most coherent evidence and proposals were coming from the police and Home Office. The Police Federation and ACPO were able to alter the Commission's focus, away from the abuses of police powers and onto the artificial restrictions on those powers that were alleged to hamper the police's fight against the rising crime rates.[85]

The recommendations in the Commission's Report were presented as balancing the "interests of the community" (sufficient police powers to

[81] Stefan Kiszko, Judith Ward, the Maguires, the Guildford Four and the Birmingham Six were all 1970s investigations.

[82] de Gama K., "Police Process and Public Prosecutions: Winning by Appearing to Lose?" 16 Int. J. Soc. L. (1988) 339.

[83] Fisher Sir H., *The Confait Case: Report* (HMSO 1977) HCP 1977/78 90.

[84] Royal Commission on Criminal Procedure: *Report* (HMSO 1981) Cmnd. 8092.

[85] There is no evidence that changes in police powers affect crime rates in any way.

tackle the crime problem) with the "liberties of the individual" (providing safeguards for suspects in the police station). This balance is shown in the statute itself which extended police powers, especially in the areas of stop and search, arrest and detention at the police station but provided a more rigorous regime once the suspect was in custody. There were new controls especially the role of the custody officer, the documentation procedures, tape-recording of interviews, access to legal advice, a duty solicitor scheme and, in 1985, an independent prosecution service.[86]

Where the accused has made a confession which the prosecution seek to adduce as evidence, the position is regulated by sections 76 and 78. Where a confession is challenged, the court should firstly consider section 76(2), namely, whether the prosecution has proved beyond reasonable doubt that a confession was not obtained by oppression or in circumstances which might render it unreliable:

> 76.—(1) In any proceedings a confession made by an accused person may be given in evidence against him in so far as it is relevant to any matter in issue in the proceedings and is not excluded by the court in pursuance of this section
>
> (2) If, in any proceedings where the prosecution proposes to give in evidence a confession made by an accused person, it is represented to the court that the confession was or may have been obtained—
>
> (a) by oppression of the person who made it; or
> (b) in consequence of anything said or done which was likely, in the circumstances existing at the time, to render unreliable any confession which might be made by him in consequence thereof,
>
> the court shall not allow the confession to be given in evidence against him except in so far as the prosecution proves to the court beyond reasonable doubt that the confession (notwithstanding that it may be true) was not obtained as aforesaid

A confession is defined in section 82(1) as including:

> 82.—(1) . . . any statement wholly or partly adverse to the person who made it it, whether made to a person in authority or not and whether made in words or otherwise.

Unlike the rule in *Ibrahim*, section 76 covers all incriminating statements, however and to whomever made. Oppression is defined by section 76(8) as including torture, inhuman or degrading treatment or the use or threat of violence.

Section 76 demonstrates the law's ambivalence towards confession evidence. It is highly regarded and admissible as relevant and reliable evidence on one hand and yet is treated with suspicion and still to be excluded unless the prosecution meets the strict conditions for admissibility. Judges use different strands of reasoning to explain this:

[86] Prosecution of Offences Act 1985.

(1) state power must not be abused and the guardians of the law must themselves respect it. The Crown must not be allowed to take advantage of evidence obtained by improper conduct. Regardless of the relevance and reliability of the confession,wherever there is improper conduct, the confession should be excluded:

> . . . Any civilised system of criminal jurisprudence must accord to the judiciary some means of excluding confessions or admissions obtained by improper methods. This is not only because of the potential unreliability of such statements, but also, and perhaps mainly, because in a civilised society it is vital that persons in custody or charged with offences should not be subjected to ill treatment or improper pressure in order to extract confessions.[87]

(2) morally a society should never compel a person to incriminate themselves since within a liberal society the autonomy of the individual must always be given precedence over the power of the collective. But if there is no compulsion and the statement is genuinely voluntary, there is no reason to exclude it

(3) proper adjudication of disputes requires that standards of fairness be met. Although this incorporates elements of the two preceding points (abuse of a dominant position and the right of silence), it also stands by itself:

> Though differences of emphasis and scope are acceptable, it would be, I think, unfortunate if the 'the discretionary principle of fairness to the accused' was not recognised in all the criminal jurisdictions of the United Kingdom. Indeed, it must be a fundamental principle in all British criminal jurisdictions that the court is under the duty to ensure the accused a fair trial, and I do not believe that a judge can effectually discharge his duty without, at the very least, the availability of the discretion I have endeavoured to describe.[88]

After consideration of section 76, there can be a second stage as these provisions are not the only criteria by which the court can rule a confession inadmissible. The court's power to exclude evidence at its discretion is expressly preserved by section 82(3):

> 82.—(3) Nothing in this Part of this Act shall prejudice any power of a court to exclude evidence (whether by preventing questions from being put or otherwise) at its discretion.

That discretion, as we have seen, has been extended by section 78 so that, even where there is neither oppression nor circumstances likely to render the confession unreliable under section 76, it may still be that the admission of the evidence would have an adverse effect on the fairness of the proceedings.

[87] *Wong Kam-ming v. R.* [1979] 1 All E.R. 939 at 946g, *per* Lord Hailsham.
[88] *R. v. Sang* [1979] 2 All E.R. 1222 at 1248b–c, *per* Lord Scarman.

All these statutory provisions must be read with the Codes of Practice which are promulgated under section 66 of the Police and Criminal Evidence Act 1984, in particular Code C which governs the detention, treatment and questioning of suspects. A breach of the Code's procedures may lead to the exclusion of an incriminating statement allegedly made by the accused. Adherence to the procedure laid down in the Code is necessary before any transcript of a police interview becomes admissible evidence. This had been the concern of the Royal Commission in 1981 to ensure that the transcript was valid evidence both in terms of reliability and in terms of fairness.[89] While many other countries use an intermediary judicial official[90] to compile this record, the Royal Commission were unwilling to take this step towards a more inquisitorial role for the courts. Instead it is the police who have been placed in a quasi-judicial role in interrogating suspects inside the police station.

This combination of the Codes of Practice and sections 76 and 78 has brought a sea-change in appellate courts' attitudes. The previous strategy, demonstrated by *Jeffery v. Black*, was a "crime-control" model since, for the courts, the end (of convicting the guilty by accepting any relevant evidence regardless of its provenance) was more important than the means (since the protection of a defendant's rights was subordinated to that end). There is now a limited "due-process" model in the English courts whereby violation of the defendant's rights will frequently lead to the exclusion of the evidence, even where that evidence is highly relevant. The courts have been driven in particular by the fairness criterion contained in section 78. But there is still considerable pragmatism about the Court of Appeal's approach: any breach of the Act or of the Code must be serious and substantial[91] so that the suspect's right to a fair trial would be put in jeopardy.

Tape-recording of interviews under section 60 is now mandatory for all indictable and either way cases.[92] The recording of interviews is governed by Code of Practice E and this should reinforce the objective of the reliability and fairness of the record. Designated police stations[93] will have specially equipped interview rooms in which everything said will be recorded. A master tape is made which is signed and sealed by all parties and will normally remain unopened.[94] There will be copies for the CPS and defendants, if they are informed that they will be prosecuted. It must be

[89] Royal Commission on Criminal Procedure, *op. cit.* paras. 4.2ff.

[90] Such as the *juge d'instruction* in France — see the Royal Commission on Criminal Procedure, *op. cit.* para. 6.25ff; any move to an inquisitorial system was also rejected by the Royal Commission on Criminal Justice, *op. cit.* paras. 1.11–1.15.

[91] *R. v. Walsh* (1989) 91 Cr.App.R. 161 — denying access to a solicitor would usually mean denial of a fair trial (cf. *R. v. Oliphant* [1992] Crim.L.R. 40) but a technical breach of detention rules would not.

[92] Code E 3.

[93] Under s.35 of the Police and Criminal Evidence Act 1984, certain police stations are designated for the purpose of detention and questioning of arrested suspects.

[94] Code E 6.

remembered that the recording is only part of the interaction between suspect and police officer and conversations take place outside the interview room. The recording is never wholly satisfactory.[95]

Despite all these changes, as we shall see, the courts still do not automatically exclude anything said by the suspect outside the interview room, thus allowing "spontaneous" admissions to occur in the patrol car as it takes the scenic route to the station.[96] Informal interviews[97] prior to the recorder being switched on is another ploy. Even in the interview room, the police still use oppressive questioning with the recorder switched on and with a solicitor present.[98]

The right to silence

Fundamental to any discussion of interviewing is the concept of the right to silence. This right consists of a conglomerate of different ideas, several of which have been affected by the Criminal Justice and Public Order Act 1994 and the Criminal Procedure and Investigations Act 1996:

(1) there is the requirement of a caution: that is, the police must warn a suspect that he or she need not say anything and that whatever is said might be used in evidence. This has to be given initially when the investigating officer has grounds for suspecting that that person has committed an offence and the purpose of the questions is to obtain evidence to use in court.[99] Furthermore a caution has to be given on arrest.[1] If the person is interviewed at a police station, the interviewer has to remind the interviewee at the start and after every break that he or she is still under caution. The caution is repeated at formal charge. The wording of the caution has been affected by sections 34-37 of the Criminal Justice and Public Order Act 1994 which are discussed below.

(2) there is also the evidential rule that places a burden of proof on the prosecution that they should prove the defendant's guilt beyond reasonable doubt.[2] Such a presumption of innocence means that there is no obligation on the accused to produce evidence or to testify. This has been affected by section 35 Criminal Justice and

[95] Moston S. and Stephenson G., *The Questioning and Interviewing of Suspects Outside the Police Station* (Royal Commission on Criminal Justice Research Study No. 22, 1993).

[96] Maguire M. and Norris C., *The Conduct and Supervision of Criminal Investigations* (Royal Commission on Criminal Justice Research Study No. 5, 1992).

[97] McConville et al. (1991): *op. cit.* 60.

[98] *Paris supra* — Royal Commission on Criminal Justice: *op. cit.* para. 1.22 were concerned at the endless repetitive questioning that the tapes revealed.

[99] Code C 10.1 — there is no need to caution a person if questions are being put prior to a search and in exercise of stop and search powers under PACE, s.1.

[1] Code C 10.3 — unless it is impracticable or if the person has been cautioned immediately before in accordance with Code C 10.1.

[2] *Woolmington v. DPP* [1935] A.C. 462.

Public Order Act 1994, discussed below, and by Part I Criminal Procedure and Investigations Act 1996.[3]

(3) the defendant is not a compellable witness for the prosecution and again is under no duty to reveal information.

(4) the police and prosecution were not permitted to comment on the defendant's decision to remain silent in the police station[4] or not to testify.[5] There were some limited exceptions: the prosecution could adduce evidence of silence when accusation was made by victim[6] or parent[7] or where the accused was on 'level terms' with the police.[8] This position has been significantly changed by sections 34-37 of the Criminal Justice and Public Order Act 1994 which are discussed below.

(5) the judge is entitled to comment on the accused's silence[9] but he or she has to do so in measured terms and had to warn the jury that they must not assume guilt from the defendant's silence. The Judicial Studies Board's specimen direction was quoted in *R. v. Martinez-Tobon:*[10]

> The defendant does not have to give evidence. He is entitled to sit in the dock and require the prosecution to prove its case. You must not assume that he is guilty because he has not given evidence. The fact that he has not given evidence proves nothing one way or the other. It does nothing to establish his guilt. On the other hand, it means that there is no evidence from the defendant to undermine, contradict or explain the evidence put before you by the prosecution.[11]

This direction has been affected by the Criminal Justice and Public Order Act 1994 and can be contrasted with the new guidelines in *R. v. Cowan*,[12] discussed below.

(6) there also exists a general maxim and a more technical privilege against self-incrimination[13]

Over the past 25 years, there has been a constant debate about the right to silence. Attempts at reform started with the Criminal Law Revision Committee in 1972[14] whose arguments were rejected by the Royal

[3] See 321, *et seq.*
[4] *Hall v. R.* [1971] 1 All E.R. 322.
[5] Criminal Evidence Act 1898, s.1(b) — the failure of any person charged with an offence to give evidence shall not be made the subject of any comment by the prosecution.
[6] *R. v. Horne* [1990] Crim.L.R. 188.
[7] *Parkes v. R.* [1976] 3 All E.R. 380 .
[8] *R. v. Chandler* [1976] 3 All E.R. 105.
[9] *R. v. Bathurst* [1968] 1 All E.R. 1175; *R. v. Sparrow* [1973] 2 All E.R. 129 although see Rupert Cross's forthright comments on "gibberish" — "The Evidence Report: Sense or Nonsense . . ." [1973] Crim.L.R. 329 at 333.
[10] [1994] 2 All E.R. 90.
[11] *ibid.* at 96c–d, *per* Lord Taylor C.J.
[12] [1995] 4 All E.R. 939.
[13] See 239.
[14] *11th Report* (HMSO 1972) Cmnd. 4991 paras. 28–52.

Commission on Criminal Procedure in 1981.[15] Since the Police and Criminal Evidence Act 1984, the police have argued that the safeguards introduced, especially the suspect's access to legal advice, have tipped the balance in favour of suspects. The suggestion was that there was an increase in the number of prosecution for serious offences which were either being discontinued or were ending in acquittals, especially because of 'ambush' defences. This latter term meant that at trial the defence relied on significant facts which had not been mentioned to the police at the time of the investigation and which the prosecution were subsequently in no position to rebut. A Home Office Working Group[16] again favoured the idea of abolition, only for its arguments to be rejected in their turn by the Royal Commission on Criminal Justice in 1993 which commissioned two separate reports.[17] The empirical evidence[18] put forward did not suggest that there was either an unacceptable acquittal rate or "no further action" rate for those few defendants, charged with serious crimes, who choose to remain silent.[19] Nor did the research studies consider that there was any serious problem of "ambush" defences. The Royal Commission Report did suggest that the defence should be under an obligation to disclose aspects of its case but stood firm against the wholesale abolition of the right to silence. Despite this, the Criminal Justice and Public Order Act 1994 introduced sweeping changes to allow juries to use silence as evidence against the accused. This is very similar to position in Northern Ireland.[20]

The argument to retain the right of silence has many different facets:

Ashworth A., *The Criminal Process* (1994) 112–114

The link between the presumption [of innocence] and the right to remain silent during police questioning has been recognised many times, notably by the Royal Commission on Criminal Procedure in 1981 and by the European Court of Human Rights in 1993.[21] If there is to be a presumption that a person is innocent until proved guilty by the prosecution, there appears to be some inconsistency in holding that the defendant can through his or her silence supply an element in that case. Whether this is a true or absolute inconsistency is for analysis elsewhere; because Parliament has introduced a few particular obligations on defendants to deliver records or submit to searches, it has been argued that to take the further step of requiring defendants to answer questions or to risk adverse inferences is 'incremental rather than fundamental'.[22] This seems less than persuasive. The Royal Commissions of both 1981 and 1992 took the 'middle line' that adverse inferences from

[15] Royal Commission on Criminal Procedure, *op. cit.* paras. 4.33 ff.
[16] Zuckerman A., "Trial By Unfair Means" [1989] Crim.L.R. 855 .
[17] Leng R., *The Right to Silence in Police Interrogation* (Royal Commission on Criminal Justice Research Study 10, 1993); McConville M. and Hodgson J., *Custodial Legal Advice and the Right to Silence* (Royal Commission on Criminal Justice Research Study 16, 1993).
[18] This is summarised in Leng, *op. cit.* Chap. 2.
[19] Zander M., "The Investigation of Crime: a study of cases tried at the Old Bailey" [1979] Crim.L.R. 203.
[20] Criminal Evidence Order (No. 1987 of 1988); for its impact, see Jackson J., "Curtailing the Right of Silence: Lessons from N. Ireland" [1991] Crim.L.R. 404.
[21] *Funke, Cremieux and Miailhe v. France* (1993) E.H.R.R. A.256.
[22] Galligan D., "The Right to Silence Reconsidered" [1988] CLP 69 at 88.

silence would be permissible once the defendant has received full notice of the prosecution case and has declined to comment on it. But both Royal Commissions argued that it would be inappropriate to permit adverse inferences to be drawn from silence in the face of police questioning, since the defendant is unlikely to know what evidence the police have and police stations are known to be percevied by many suspects as intimidating. The availability of legal advisers — who . . . are often not qualified lawyers — may not be sufficient to offset this disadvantage.

The right of silence at the police station does not derive strength merely from the presumption of innocence, but also from the privilege against self-incrimination and the right of privacy. There is no constitutional or statutory declaration of the privilege against self-incrimination in English law, but it has been recognised judicially in the House of Lords: 'The underlying rationale . . . is, in my view, now to be found in the maxim *nemo debet prodere se ipsum,* no one can be required to be his own betrayer or in its popular English mistranslation "the right to silence" '.[23] Although spoken in a different context, these words recognise the place of the privilege against self-incrimination in the English criminal process. It can be justified by arguing that the State should not indulge in the unfairness of forcing on defendants a choice between speaking and convicting themselves out of their own mouths, or not speaking and being convicted by default. Whilst it should be said that most modern formulations make it clear that guilt is not the only thing that may be inferred from a person's failure to speak — other reasons, such as shame or shielding others from harm are often mentioned — it is believed that courts will often draw adverse inferences if invited to do so.

A third argument, based on privacy, has been developed by Dennis Galligan and receives support from Article 8 of the European Convention: 'everyone has the right to respect for his private and family life, his home and his correspondence.' Galligan argues that the right not to be compelled to vouchsafe one's secrets is particularly important when the aim of questioning is to obtain evidence for use against the person. If the right of privacy is to have any meaning, then these are surely the cases in which it should be asserted. We should no more approve of the imposition of a requirement to answer questions, on pain of adverse inferences, than of the compulsory use of machines that can extract information directly from the human memory. This rationale can claim to be more fundamental than the privilege against self-incrimination and the presumption of innocence, since it is directly connected with concepts of personhood and respect for individual autonomy. However, Galligan recognises that privacy cannot be regarded as an absolute right, although he argues strongly that the propriety of derogating from it cannot be left to the judgement of police officers and ought to be settled at the level of general policy.

A fourth argument starts from a factual rather than a theoretical proposition. It is that the balance of power in the pre-trial stages of the criminal process is so much in favour of the investigators that the right of silence is needed to protect suspects from being overborne. Among the evidence led in support of this are the findings on the psychological effects of police interrogation; the finding that the police still sometimes fail to inform suspects of their full rights or, when they do give the information, convey it in a manner calculated to persuade them to waive some rights; and the superior access of police to forensic science laboratories and other expert services. This is challenged by those who want to see the right of silence removed or curtailed. They argue that the spread of legal aid and duty solicitor schemes now puts suspects on a par with the police, and that the provisions for an 'appropriate adult' afford sufficient protection for vulnerable suspects. In favour of this reply are those cases in which a defendant arrives at a police station with his or

[23] *Sang supra* at 1230c, *per* Lord Diplock.

her own solicitor, with the result that the constable questioning the suspect may feel under greater pressure than the suspect. This was the position described by Lawton L.J. in the judgment in *Chandler*.[24] However, it is an unusual situation, and the implication that it is becoming the norm can be dispelled by the findings of research for the 1993 Royal Commission that many defendants waive their right to a lawyer, that many 'legal advisers' are not legally qualified, and also that defence access to expert evidence is limited.

Such arguments have failed to convince and as a result of sections 34-37 Criminal Justice and Public Order Act 1994, the right of silence has been considerably modified.[25]

(a) ambush defences: section 34 is aimed at forcing the suspect to reveal the nature of the defence, by allowing a court to 'draw such inferences as appear proper' from a failure to mention a relevant fact relied on in the defence when it might reasonably have been mentioned during police questioning. The suspect must have been cautioned:[26]

34.—(1) Where, in any proceedings against a person for an offence, evidence is given that the accused—

(a) at any time before he was charged with the offence, on being questioned under caution by a constable trying to discover whether or by whom the offence had been committed, failed to mention any fact relied on in his defence in those proceedings; or

(b) on being charged with the offence or officially informed that he might be prosecuted for it, failed to mention any such fact,

being a fact which in the circumstances existing at the time the accused could reasonably have been expected to mention when so questioned, charged or informed, as the case may be, subsection (2) below applies.

(2) Where this subsection applies—

(a) a magistrates' court, in deciding whether to grant an application for dismissal made by the accused under section 6 of the Magistrates' Court Act 1980 (application for dismissal of charge in course of proceedings with a view to transfer for trial);

(b) a judge, in deciding whether to grant an application made by the accused under—

(i) section 6 of the Criminal Justice Act 1987 (application for dismissal of charge of serious fraud in respect of which notice of transfer has been given under section 4 of that Act); or

[24] *supra.*
[25] Dennis I., "The Criminal Justice and Public Order Act 1994 . . ." [1995] Crim.L.R. 4.
[26] Code C 10.4 "You do not have to say anything. But it may harm your defence if you do not mention when questioned something which you later rely on in court. Anything you do say may be given in evidence."

(ii) paragraph 5 of Schedule 6 to the Criminal Justice Act 1991 (application for dismissal of charge of violent or sexual offence involving a child in respect of which notice of transfer has been given under section 53 of that Act);

(c) the court, in determining whether there is a case to answer; and

(d) the court or jury, in determining whether the accused is guilty of the offence charged,

may draw such inferences from the failure as appear proper.

The impact of section 38(3) means that a person should not be convicted solely on the basis of an inference drawn from this failure. In principle such inferences should only be drawn where the prosecution have supplied substantial evidence linking the accused with the offence and on which a reasonable jury could convict. A jury would thus be told to attach less weight to issues raised by the defence which have only been revealed at the trial, where such issues presumably have little, if any, supporting evidence, and which, logically, can be treated as less credible. Even legal advice not to answer police questions will not exclude the operation of section 34.[27] The prosecution is entitled to comment on this failure since the prohibition on such comment in section 1(b) of the Criminal Evidence Act 1898 has been repealed by section 168(3) and Schedule 11 of the Act.

There are logical arguments for such a provision but the practical effect will be to place unfair pressure on the accused to disclose his or her defence at a very early stage before the suspect would have any knowledge of the prosecution case. But section 34 has already been rendered effectively redundant by the new provisions for disclosure. Advance disclosure of the defence case was a key recommendation of the Royal Commission Report.[28] The majority defended this on the grounds that it might lead to discontinuances by the prosecution, early guilty pleas by the defence and thus allow earlier fixing of trial dates and permit accurate estimates of trial lengths. Dissentients have pointed out that likely defences are usually apparent on the face of the witness statements,[29] that trials might degenerate into issues as to why the accused failed to mention a particular fact and that genuine "ambush" defences are so infrequent that they provide no justification for making such a fundamental change. But the Royal Commission recommendations were adopted by the Criminal Procedure and Investigations Act 1996 which creates a statutory scheme for disclosure by both prosecution and defence.[30] Now a failure by the

[27] *R. v. Condran* [1997] Crim.L.R. 215.

[28] Royal Commission on Criminal Justice: *op. cit.* paras. 57–73, but see note of dissent by Zander, 221 paras. 1–12.

[29] These are often ignored by the police — "It is routine police work not to follow up evidence raised by an accused which may support a defence." McConville et al. (1991): *op. cit.* 77.

[30] see Chap. 10. These should be brought into effect in 1997.

defence to disclose relevant matters or to comply with the statutory obligations can lead to prosecution comment and adverse inferences being drawn by the trier of fact. Despite this new legislation, section 34 was not repealed.

(b) failure to testify: section 35 applies where the prosecution have satisfied the court that there is a case to answer and a defendant declines to testify in his or her own defence. The judge, in the presence of the jury, is empowered to tell the defendant that the stage has been reached at which he or she can give evidence and to issue a warning that if he or she remains silent, that it will be permissible for the jury to draw whatever inferences appear to be proper:

35.—(1) At the trial of any person who has attained the age of fourteen years for an offence, subsections (2) and (3) below apply unless—

(a) the accused's guilt is not in issue; or

(b) it appears to the court that the physical or mental condition of the accused makes it undesirable for him to give evidence;

but subsection (2) below does not apply if, at the conclusion of the evidence for the prosecution, his legal representative informs the court that the accused will give evidence or, where he is unrepresented, the court ascertains from him that he will give evidence.

(2) Where this subsection applies, the court shall, at the conclusion of the evidence for the prosecution, satisfy itself (in the case of proceedings on indictment, in the presence of the jury) that the accused is aware that the stage has been reached at which evidence can be given for the defence and that he can, if he wishes, give evidence and that, if he chooses not to give evidence, or having been sworn, without good cause refuses to answer any question, it will be permissible for the court or jury to draw such inferences as appear proper from his failure to give evidence or his refusal, without good cause, to answer any question.

(3) Where this subsection applies, the court or jury, in determining whether the accused is guilty of the offence charged, may draw such inferences as appear proper from the failure of the accused to give evidence or his refusal, without good cause, to answer any question.

As a result of section 38(3), a person should not be convicted solely on the basis of an inference drawn from this failure.

To use a failure to testify as an element in the prosecution case is, in an evidential and logical sense, suspect, even though this section can only come into play once the prosecution have supplied substantial evidence. There is some basis in logic for the changes introduced in sections 34, 36 and 37: a defence raised late in the proceedings may be less credible; a refusal to account for one's presence in a particular place or one's possession of articles may justifiably lead to an inference of guilty knowledge. These sections also focus on specific facts in issue. Under section 35, while the prosecution have satisfied the evidential burden placed on them, there is no requirement that the accused's failure to testify strengthens any particular element of the prosecution case and thereby creates any specific inference, the strength and validity of which can be identified. The main result of a refusal to testify, in most cases, would be a general presumption of guilt by the jury.

There are other concerns about any legislation where the state pressures individuals into answering questions, let alone testifying. Briefly these can be framed first, as constitutional arguments since the right to silence is the final guarantee of the autonomy of the individual, in itself a central concept of a liberal society. Such arguments underlie the principle of the rule of law that the prosecution should prove guilt and thereby the presumption of innocence. Secondly, there are ethical considerations whether the state should ever use evidence obtained in such a manner as the basis of a conviction. Section 35 is a major breach of the privilege against self-incrimination: accused persons are damned if they answer and damned if they don't. Thirdly, section 35 sits uneasily alongside the old common law rule in *Sang* that if the prejudicial effect of a piece of evidence outweighs its probative value, it should be excluded. Here the prejudicial effect on the jury of the failure to testify must far outweigh any probative weight and section 35 necessarily infringes this principle. To an extent this has been recognised by the caution shown in Northern Ireland where failure to testify has been taken into account only where the prosecution case just rests on the brink of the necessary standard of proof.[31]

The impact of section 35 was considered by the Court of Appeal in *R. v. Cowan*[32]:

R. v. Cowan [1995] 4 All E.R. 939 at 942f–945d, *per* Lord Taylor C.J.

The issues raised are: (1) whether the discretion to draw inferences from silence under section 35(3) should be open in the generality of cases or only exceptionally, and (2) if it is to apply in a jury trial, what directions should the judge give?

. . . the judge has a discretion as to whether and in what terms he should advise a jury for or against drawing inferences. In what circumstances, then, should the court or jury be prepared to draw an adverse inference? [Counsel for the appellant's] answer is: 'only exceptionally where there is no reasonable possibility of an innocent explanation for the defendant's silence'. He suggested a number of possible reasons for silence at trial which may be consistent with innocence. They were: (1) a weak case barely surviving a submission of no case; (2) other defence evidence contradicting prosecution evidence; (3) if the defendant is nervous, inarticulate or unlikely to perform well; (4) if the defendant's medical condition is abnormal although not within section 35(1); (5) fear, duress or the protection of others; (6) previous convictions of the defendant where he is liable to be cross-examined on them; . . .

If any of these reasons or excuses exist or may do so, it is submitted the court should not draw, or the jury should be directed not to draw, an adverse inference. Moreover [counsel for the appellant] suggests such reasons or excuses could properly be advanced by defending counsel without the need for evidence.

[31] Jackson, *op. cit.* 410–412.
[32] [1995] 4 All E.R. 939.

The breadth of these propositions is patently inconsistent with the scheme and plain words of section 35. To use the inevitable cliche, they would drive a coach and horses through the statutory provisions . . . We cannot agree.

. . . the general proposition that a previous criminal record upon which a defendant could be cross-examined (if he has attacked prosecution witnesses) is a good reason for directing a jury that they should not hold his silence against him, would lead to a bizarre result. A defendant with convictions would be in a more privileged position than one with a clean record. The former could avoid submitting himself to cross-examination with impunity; the latter could not. We reject that proposition.

We accept that, apart from the mandatory exceptions in section 35(1), it will be open to a court to decline to draw an adverse inference from silence at trial and for a judge to direct or advise a jury against drawing such inference if the circumstances of the case justify such a course. But in our view there would need either to be some evidential basis for doing so or some exceptional factors in the case making that a fair course to take. It must be stressed that the inferences permitted by the section are only such 'as appear proper'. The use of that phrase was no doubt intended to leave a broad discretion to a trial judge to decide in all the circumstances whether any proper inference is capable of being drawn by the jury. If not, he should tell them so; otherwise it is for the jury to decide whether in fact an inference should properly be drawn.

By way of guidance, a specimen direction has been suggested by the Judicial Studies Board in the following terms:

> The defendant has not given evidence. That is his right. but, as he has been told, the law is that you may draw such inferences as appear proper from his failure to do so. Failure to give evidence on its own cannot prove guilt but depending on the circumstances, you may hold his failure against him when deciding whether he is guilty. [There is evidence before you on the basis of which the defendant's advocate invites you not to hold it against the defendant that he has not given evidence before you namely . . . . If you think that because of this evidence you should not hold it against the defendant that he has not given evidence, do not do so. But if the evidence he relies on presents no adequate explanation for his absence from the witness box then you may hold his failure to give evidence against him. You do not have to do so.] What proper inferences can you draw from the defendant's decision not to give evidence before you? If you conclude that there is a case for him to answer, you may think that the defendant would have gone into the witness box to give you an explanation for or an answer to the case against him. If the only sensible explanation for his decision not to give evidence is that he has no answer to the case against him, or none that could have stood up to cross-examination, then it would be open to you to hold against him his failure to give evidence. It is for you to decide whether it is fair to do so.

. . . there are certain essentials which we would highlight.

(1) The judge will have told the jury that the burden of proof remains upon the prosecution throughout and what the required standard is.

(2) It is necessary for the judge to make clear to the jury that the defendant is entitled to remain silent. That is his right and choice. The right of silence remains.

(3) An inference from failure to give evidence cannot on its own prove guilt . . .

(4) Therefore, the jury must be satisfied that the prosecution have established a case to answer before drawing any inferences from silence. Of course, the judge must have thought so or the question whether the defendant was to give evidence would not have arisen. But the jury may not believe the witnesses whose evidence the judge considered sufficient to raise a prima facie case. It must therefore be made

clear to them that they must find there to be a case to answer on the prosecution evidence before drawing an adverse inference from the defendant's silence.

(5) If, despite the evidence relied upon to explain his silence or on the absence of any such evidence, the jury conclude the silence can only sensibly be attributed to the defendant's having no answer or none that would stand up to cross-examination, they may draw an adverse inference.

The Court of Appeal rejected any attempt to restrict the operation of section 35 but stressed that the nature, extent and degree of inferences to be drawn from silence lay within the discretion of the trial judge. In *Murray v. U.K.*[33] the Commission on Human Rights considered that, where a prima facie case was established and the burden of proof remained on the prosecution, adverse inferences may be drawn from a failure to testify.

(c) failure to account for objects, substances or marks: section 36 applies where the suspect gives no explanation to police about certain specific facts such as objects, substances or marks on clothing which tend to suggest the accused's participation in the offence. This section only comes into play after arrest and thus the suspect will have been cautioned and told in ordinary language what the consequences were of any failure to give an explanation.[34]

36.—(1) Where—

(a) a person is arrested by a constable, and there is—

(i) on his person; or
(ii) in or on his clothing or footwear; or
(iii) otherwise in his possession; or
(iv) in any place in which he is at the time of his arrest,

any object, substance or mark, or there is any mark on any such object; and

(b) that or another constable investigating the case reasonably believes that the presence of the object, substance or mark may be attributable to the participation of the person arrested in the commission of an offence specified by the constable; and

(c) the constable informs the person arrested that he so believes, and requests him to account for the presence of the object, substance or mark; and

(d) the person fails or refuses to do so,

then if, in any proceedings against the person for the offence so specified, evidence of those matters is given, subsection (2) below applies.

(2) [This is in identical terms to section 34(2) *supra*]

One of the possible inferences that the prosecution will be seeking to draw in these circumstances (and in those envisaged in section 37) will be

[33] (1994) 18 E.H.R.R. C.D. 1.
[34] s.36(4).

that of guilty knowledge: that the accused knew what the substance was or that the article was stolen. In many offences this is a central fact in issue and the failure to give an explanation will be relied on by the prosecution as evidence of that fact. In this way, it is similar to the common law rule that allows inferences to be drawn from silence on an accusation.[35] But this section (and section 37) differs from the preceding sections in the sense that a fact in issue can be proved solely on the basis of the failure to explain: where the charge is handling stolen goods, a jury might reasonably convict on proof of possession of the stolen goods and a refusal to account for that possession. Although section 38(3) states that a person should not be convicted solely on the basis of an inference drawn from such a failure, there would be other evidence, namely of the possession, and the inference could be used to supply the lack of evidence on the question of knowledge.

In any case the prosecution is entitled to comment on this failure since the prohibition on such comment in section 1(b) of the Criminal Evidence Act 1898 has been repealed by section 168(3) and Schedule 11 of the Act.

(d) failure to account for presence: section 37 applies where the suspect gives no explanation to police about his or her presence at a particular place and this refusal tends to suggest participation in an offence. This section only comes into play after arrest and thus the suspect will have been cautioned and told in ordinary language what the consequences were of any failure to give an explanation.[36]

> 37.—(1) Where—
>
> (a) a person arrested by a constable was found by him at a place ar or about the time the offence for which he was arrested is alleged to have been committed; and
>
> (b) that or another constable investigating the case reasonably believes that the presence of the person at that place and at that time may be attributable to the participation of the person arrested in the commission of the offence; and
>
> (c) the constable informs the person that he so believes, and requests him to account for that presence; and
>
> (d) the person fails or refuses to do so,
>
> then if, in any proceedings against the person for the offence, evidence of those matters is given, subsection (2) below applies
>
> (2) [This is in identifical terms to section 34(2) *supra*]

Obviously this is very similar in structure to section 36. There may be different inferences which the prosecution will be seeking to draw: perhaps the silence might be used, on a charge of burglary, to suggest that the

[35] *R. v. Cramp* (1880) 14 Cox C.C. 390.
[36] s.37(3).

accused, without any lawful reason to be on the premises, had an intent to steal; perhaps where drugs have been abandoned nearby, the proper inference is that the accused had just abandoned them. The silence will be used to prove a central fact in issue and the failure to give an explanation will be relied on by the prosecution as evidence of that fact. If this is correct, a fact in issue can be proved solely on the basis of the failure to explain. Again section 38(3) does not apply because there is other evidence, although not necessarily relating to that particular element of the offence. In any case the prosecution is entitled to comment on this failure to account for presence in a particular place.

Sections 34, 36 and 37 require the accused to have been arrested and to have been warned about the consequences of a failure to answer. Although this indicates that the objective threshold of "reasonable grounds" for arrest should have been satisfied, the police often have a lot of suspicion and very little hard evidence. They already use arrest as a technique to gain that evidence by putting pressure on a suspect, through interrogation.[37] These sections will encourage this practice, putting even greater pressure on the suspect since a refusal can be part of the prosecution's case, contributing to proof beyond reasonable doubt. While silence to questions has some weight, it is very far from conclusive. There are defendants who are confused and vulnerable, defendants who wish to protect others, let alone those who are just unwilling to co-operate. Can a jury ever regard silence as sufficient to quash a reasonable doubt they might harbour about the prosecution case?

These changes will increase the pressure brought on people detained in police stations to answer questions. Alhough Bentham bears the burden of suggesting that the right to silence only protects the guilty and the criminally sophisticated when he wrote:

> Innocence claims the right of speaking as guilt invokes the privilege of silence.

He did so at a time when the right to silence as we know it did not exist, when the defendant was not permitted to testify in his own defence and when police interrogation did not exist. The pressure to answer police questions will necessarily bear on the innocent as well as the guilty. The controversy surrounding the right to silence encompasses empirical questions and evidential problems but ultimately it should be a decision based on concepts of due process of law and proper constitutional principles. It is another of those important markers which define the relationship of State and citizen, delineating constraints on the State and our moral choice that prosecution and punishment should not be based on evidence from the accused.

[37] This practice has been approved by the House of Lords in *Mohammed-Holgate v. Duke* [1984] A.C. 437 — it was not unreasonable to arrest someone against whom there were reasonable grounds for suspicion but with the predominant motive that they were more likely to confess in the police station than if interviewed elsewhere.

Interviews outside the station

The Codes of Practice were intended to eliminate the damning unrecorded verbal admission[38] by focusing on the interview in a designated police station where there were the central safeguards of the caution, notification of the right to legal advice and the recording of interviews. An arrested person shall be taken to a police station as soon as practicable after the arrest.[39] Where practicable, the interview of an arrested person should always take place at a police station. Under Code C:

11.1—Following a decision to arrest a suspect he must not be interviewed about the relevant offence except at a police station (or other authorised place of detention) unless the consequent delay would be likely:

(a) to lead to interference with or harm to evidence connected with an offence or interference with or physical harm to other persons; or

(b) to lead to the alerting of other persons suspected of having committed an offence but not yet arrested for it; or

(c) to hinder the recovery of property obtained in consequence of the commission of an offence.

Interviewing in any of these circumstances shall cease once the relevant risk has been averted or the necessary questions have been put in order to attempt to avert that risk.[40]

Under section 30(10) of the Police and Criminal Evidence Act the police officer is entitled to delay taking the suspect to the police station in order to carry out investigations which reasonably can be carried out. Going to a shop to check whether the suspect had bought the goods or to his or her home to inspect papers or assess an alibi would all be reasonable courses of action for the constable.

If a suspect is questioned outside the station or makes a spontaneous statement, these may well be admissible. In *R. v. Parchment*[41] the suspect was discovered naked in the cupboard in his flat. Arrested and cautioned over some burglaries, he made spontaneous admissions, allegedly repeated in the police car, which were only written up by the officers later in a joint note which was neither shown to nor signed by the defendant. By the time of the formal interview, he was denying the offences. The Crown Court admitted the statements arguing that, while the police were operating within the Police and Criminal Evidence Act 1984 and its Codes, they could not be said to be acting unfairly under section 78. But at that time, there was no obligation under Code C to show the accused the joint note.

[38] *R. v. Pattinson* (1973) 58 Cr.App.R. 417 at 425 where Lawton L.J. stigmatised this practice.

[39] Police and Criminal Evidence Act 1984, s.30(1).

[40] Code C 11.1.

[41] [1989] Crim.L.R. 290.

The Code has been amended so that interviews outside the police station are subject to safeguards similar to those applying to interviews inside the station.[42] Under C 11.2A, significant statements, whether in an interview or not, that occur before arrival at the police station must be put to the suspect at the beginning of the formal interview. Failure to do this may well lead to such previous statements, however spontaneous, being excluded by section 78. The rationale would be that the accused, even where cautioned, will have had no notification of any right to see a solicitor nor will the record have been taped or been noted contemporaneously. It will simply be an unverified police account.

Spontaneous statements will not be automatically excluded by section 78. But the police cannot evade the Code's requirements by questions at the scene on the ground that such questions do not constitute an interview and are thus not bound by the Code. An interview is defined in Code C as:

> 11.1A—. . . the questioning of a person regarding his involvement or suspected involvement in a criminal offence or offences.[43]

An interview can take place inside or outside a police station. Initially the courts took a restrictive view of when an interview occurred: in *R. v. Maguire*[44] the police officer arrested the suspect for attempted burglary. In the police car, the officer advised him to "tell the truth" and the accused said that ". . . we were only going in to have a look around . . . for anything, for money, whatever." The Court of Appeal held that although the Code did not apply only to interviews in police stations, in this case, this questioning did not constitute an "interview" since there were no questions asked. But this was post-arrest questioning and the suspect was prompted for an explanation about his involvement. Were courts to permit such statements to be admitted into evidence, the Police and Criminal Evidence Act safeguards would be largely by-passed as "verbals" would move from the police station to the scene of crime and police car, before the Code of Practice started to run.[45]

A preferable and broader approach was taken in *R. v. Hunt*[46] where police officers saw the defendant in a garden with a flick knife. He was searched and asked, without caution, what it was for, replying that it was his. He ran off but was arrested. In the police car, he was again asked why he had the knife and made certain admissions. The Court of Appeal held that even at the time of the original search, the officer had evidence of an offence and should have cautioned at that point. Certainly in the car, the single question and answer constituted an interview and the statements

[42] Code C 11.5 *et seq.*
[43] Code C 11.1A.
[44] [1989] Crim.L.R. 815.
[45] Royal Commission on Criminal Justice, *op. cit.* paras. 3.7ff.; Moston S. and Stephenson G.: *The Questioning and Interviewing of Suspects Outside the Police Station* (Royal Commission on Criminal Justice Research Study No. 22, 1993); McConville et al., (1991) 83 *et seq.*
[46] [1992] Crim.L.R. 582.

should have been excluded under section 78. A similar approach is taken in *R. v. Goddard*[47] where the appellant was arrested and cautioned and then questioned about three polythene wraps that he had thrown away. He admitted that these contained heroin. The Court of Appeal quashed the convictions, holding that the questions were an interview designed to obtain admissions and that the appellant had been denied the protection of the Code.

An officer must be able to ask questions which do not comprise an "interview". At an early stage of any investigation, the police are endeavouring to discover whether an offence has been committed and whether the suspect is involved. Once they are satisfied about these, a caution must be administered and any further questions must be an interview within the meaning of Code C. But questioning only to obtain information or an explanation or in the ordinary course of an officer's duties does not constitute an interview.[48] Nor do questions which are confined to the proper conduct of a search.[49] In *R. v. Park*[50] the appellant was convicted of burglary. The car he was driving (with the stolen goods in it) had been stopped because of a defective rear light. The appellant told the police officer that the car belonged to his father, that the electrical goods on the rear seat were his and that he was moving home. The police officer cautioned and arrested him. The answers given at the roadside were not to be excluded by section 78 and could be put to the appellant in cross-examination as statements inconsistent with his testimony. The officer had asked some exploratory questions which were merely an inquiry. That stopped when the officer felt that there was evidence on which the appellant could be arrested and cautioned. However a record must still be made, even if not contemporaneously, and the suspect given the opportunity to check the record.

The Royal Commission found that about 30 per cent of suspects report being questioned prior to arrest and there was evidence that negotiations took place off-record inside the police station as to what was to be said on the record.[51] Despite the dangers involved in the use of such informal interviewing, the Royal Commission did not consider recommending the exclusion of all except formal, recorded interviews, but instead contented themselves merely with discussing the possibilities of extending tape-recording to all transactions between officer and suspect.

[47] [1994] Crim.L.R. 46.

[48] But seeking information in the course of duties might well be questioning about a person's involvement in an offence — *R. v. Cox* [1993] Crim.L.R. 382; *R. v. Marsh* [1991] Crim.L.R. 455.

[49] *R. v. Langiert* [1991] Crim.L.R. 777; *R. v. White* [1991] Crim.L.R. 779; *R. v. Chung* [1991] Crim.L.R. 622.

[50] [1994] Crim.L.R. 285.

[51] Moston S. and Stephenson G., *op. cit.* ; Irving B. and Dunnighan C., *Human Factors in the Quality Control of CID Investigations* (Royal Commission on Criminal Justice Research Study No.21 HMSO 1993); Sanders A. and Young R., *Criminal Justice* (1994) 176 *et seq.*

Interviews in the police station — access to legal advice[52]

Within the police station, there are various statutory safeguards under the Police and Criminal Evidence Act:

- **section 56** provides for a right for a person to be informed of the fact of your arrest.[53] This can be delayed under similar conditions to section 58.

- **section 58** gives a right to legal advice:

  58.—(1) A person arrested and held in custody in a police station or other premises shall be entitled, if he so requests, to consult a solicitor privately at any time.

  Access can be delayed (but never refused altogether) under section 58(6) and (8) if the person is suspected of a serious arrestable offence and access might lead to interference with evidence, alerting of accomplices or hindering recovery of property.

- **section 59** originally established a duty solicitor scheme and the Legal Aid Board now is responsible for arrangements which cover the whole country

Under Code C 3.1 a detained person must be clearly informed of these rights as well as the opportunity to consult the Codes of Practice and a copy of the Custody Record. Detainees will also be given a written notice stating these rights. They will be asked if they wish to consult a solicitor and if they do not, they will sign the custody record to that effect.

The right to legal advice was previously enshrined in the Judges Rules and has recently been acknowledged as a right in common law.[54] The irony here was that previously the right was more honoured in the breach[55] with few convictions being overturned as a result. The defendant isolated in the police station is vulnerable and capable of being manipulated by interrogators even without malpractice on their part.[56] This remains the case

[52] Royal Commission on Criminal Justice, *op. cit.* paras. 3.46–3.64; Baldwin J.: *The Role of Legal Representatives at the Police Station* (Royal Commission on Criminal Justice Research Study No. 3, 1992); McConville M. and Hodgson J., *Custodial Legal Advice and the Right to Silence* (Royal Commission on Criminal Justice Research Study No. 16, 1993).

[53] Previously Criminal Law Act 1977, s.62.

[54] *R. v. Chief Constable of South Wales ex parte Merrick* [1994] 2 All E.R. 560 — s.58 does not apply to a prisoner held on remand in police cells but there is a common law right to legal advice which must be allowed by the police if reasonably practicable.

[55] Zander M., "Access to a Solicitor in the Police Station" [1972] Crim.L.R. 342; Baldwin J. and McConville M., "Police Interrogation and the Right to See a Solicitor" [1979] Crim.L.R. 145.

[56] Softley P., *Police Interrogation* (Royal Commission on Criminal Procedure Research Study No. 4, 1980); Gudjonsson G., *The Psychology of Interrogation, Confessions and Testimony* (1992).

especially so given the police have no obligation to reveal the nature of the case against the suspect. The police remain very hostile to a solicitor's intervention which is seen as increasing a suspect's resistance to questioning and reducing their control.[57]

Despite these provisions and the fact that custody officers do advise suspects of their rights,[58] there is a low take-up rate of legal advice of between 25-30 per cent. The extent of protection is still limited and it has been suggested[59] that defendants are not always given the leaflet advising them of their rights, that they are told to "sign here" on the custody record without realising that they are waiving their right to see a solicitor or that they are told that a solicitor will not be available for some hours and it may be necessary to be detained in a cell. The Royal Commission's recommendations included the video-recording of events in a custody suite and interviewers both reminding suspects of their rights to advice at the beginning of an interview and asking for their reasons for waiving those rights, reasons which would be recorded on tape.[60]

Where advice is given, it can be over the telephone. The police can interview before or after a lawyer's visit, thus negating the value of the advice. Further doubts have been raised[61] about the quality of the legal work and advice given, with solicitors or their representatives failing to obtain information from the investigating officers, often failing to acquire important facts from their own client and intervening in the interview on the client's behalf in less than one third of cases.

But the right to legal advice has become a substantial safeguard. Failure to observe the correct procedure in the Code of Practice, especially in relation to the provision of legal advice, can lead to the evidence obtained from the subsequent interview being excluded. In *R. v. Absolam*[62] the accused was arrested for threatening behaviour and taken to a police station. He emptied his pockets but the custody officer, knowing that the defendant had previously been arrested for possession of cannabis, said "Put the drugs on the table". The accused took a packet from inside his trousers and also admitted selling the drugs. Only then was he reminded of the caution and of his rights to legal advice under section 58. The conviction was quashed on appeal since not only was the defendant denied legal advice but the custody officer's questions constituted an interview and the Code specifies the sequence of events which should not be overridden. The Court of Appeal considered this to be a "serious and substantial breach" and excluded the evidence under section 78.[63]

[57] McConville M. et al. (1991), *op. cit.* 47–54.

[58] Irving B. and McKenzie I., *Police Interrogation* (1989): Sanders A. et al., *Advice and Assistance at Police Stations* (1989).

[59] Sanders et al. (1989), *op. cit.*

[60] Royal Commission on Criminal Justice, *op. cit.* para. 3.47.

[61] Royal Commission on Criminal Justice: *op. cit.* paras. 3.56ff. Baldwin J., *Preparing the Record of Taped Interview* (Royal Commission on Criminal Justice Research Study No. 2, 1992); McConville M. and Hodgson J. (1993): *op. cit.*

[62] [1988] Crim.L.R. 748.

[63] See also *R. v. Williams* [1989] Crim.L.R. 66 and *R. v. Sanusi* [1992] Crim.L.R. 43.

The early cases[64] suggested that any serious breach should lead to exclusion of evidence under section 78. That has been affected by the benchmark decision in *R. v. Walsh*.[65] This involved an allegation of robbery. There was an interview in the cell which was not contemporaneously recorded and there had been no legal advice. The judge admitted the evidence as there was no material that suggested that the police were not acting in good faith. Again the conviction was quashed. The Court of Appeal held that the main objective of section 58 was to achieve fairness to the suspect and to the Crown. Where there were significant and substantial breaches, prima facie those standards of fairness have not been met and to admit evidence obtained in such circumstances meant that there would be an adverse effect on the fairness of the proceedings. But a breach of section 58 does not lead to the automatic exclusion of the statements and the breach must be shown to affect fairness to an extent that justice required that the evidence should not be admitted. In this case the breach had made a difference and the good faith or otherwise of the officers did not affect this.

This different approach is seen in *R. v. Dunford*[66] where a senior officer refused access to a solicitor in breach of section 58 and the prosecution claimed that the suspect admitted acting as a lookout on a robbery. At the *voire dire* stage the judge was entitled to take account of the accused's criminal record and his awareness of the arrest and detention procedures, so that the absence of the solicitor did not affect the fairness of the proceedings so adversely so as to require the exclusion of the evidence. It is useful to compare *R. v. Chahal*[67] and *R. v. Franklin*.[68] In both cases the accused initially chose not to see a solicitor and in both cases, the family arranged for one to be present. However the police did not inform the accused until the interviews were concluded. The conviction was upheld in *Chahal* where the defendant was a mature businessman who knew the position and suffered no prejudice. However in *Franklin* the defendant was a young unemployed man who had never been in a police station before and the Court of Appeal held that the judge had exercised his discretion wrongly and should have excluded the admissions.

Access to a duty solicitor was the issue in *R. v. Vernon*[69] where the accused nominated a solicitor who was unavailable since it was late at night. She agreed to be interviewed without legal advice but was not told of the availability of the duty solicitor. The record of the interview was deemed inadmissible under section 78 as she would not have consented to be interviewed but for this breach.

The police are empowered to delay access to a solicitor under the provisions of section 58(8) mentioned above. Delaying access to a solicitor

[64] *R. v. Keenan* [1989] 3 All E.R. 598.
[65] [1989] Crim.L.R. 822.
[66] [1991] Crim.L.R. 370; also *R. v. Oliphant* [1992] Crim.L.R. 40.
[67] [1992] Crim.L.R. 124.
[68] *The Times*, June 16, 1994.
[69] [1988] Crim.L.R. 445.

requires that the police believe that this individual solicitor would alert other suspects or hinder the recovery of evidence, albeit inadvertently. Such a belief could only be rarely held and the courts regard access to legal advice as a fundamental right. The police cannot refuse to allow a suspect access to legal advice on the grounds that legal advice will be to remain silent. In *R. v. Samuel*,[70] there were allegations of robbery and of burglary. The suspect had asked for a solicitor but this was denied under section 58(8). After 24 hours, he admitted involvement in two burglaries and was charged with those. Relatives and lawyers were informed at this point but police continued questioning until the accused confessed to the robbery as well. The Court of Appeal quashed the robbery conviction under section 78 because although the initial refusal of access to a solicitor was justified, that refusal could not be justified after charging the defendant with the burglaries.[71] Legal advice was seen as *"one of the most important and fundamental rights of the citizen"*.[72]

The *Walsh* approach was seen in *R. v. Alladice*,[73] again an armed robbery case. While *Samuel* adopts a "rights" approach, (so that the accused's rights should be protected by putting him into a position that he would have been in if his rights had been observed), *Alladice* displays a slightly harder Court of Appeal line. The nature of the right interfered with and the causal link between that interference and the evidence obtained are factors to be taken into account under section 78 in reaching a solution which reflects "justice". In *Alladice* the suspect was accustomed to police interviews and thus the court felt that a solicitor's presence would not have made a difference.

Such cases suggest that the Court of Appeal is weaving a rather uneasy road between the two rationales for excluding evidence. Although they have turned their backs on the strict "reliability" approach (which would test the quality of the statement regardless of the infringement of the defendant's rights), they find it hard to embrace the full American "fairness" model which would lead to exclusion whenever the suspects' rights are infringed. The pragmatic approach in *Walsh* appears preferable as it allows the judge discretion to measure the significance of the breach with the adverse affect on the fairness of the proceedings created.

Interviews in the police station — other matters

General breaches of Code C other than those relating to legal advice might lead to the exclusion of evidence. When taken to a police station, the arrested person is taken before the custody officer.[74] In brief the custody

[70] [1988] 2 All E.R. 135; see also *R. v. Parris* [1989] Crim.L.R. 214.

[71] The Court of Appeal is quite strict on further questioning once charged although if the suspect makes voluntary statement, that can be admitted — *R. v. Pall* [1992] Crim.L.R. 126.

[72] *Samuel supra* at 147c, *per* Hodgson J.

[73] [1988] Crim.L.R. 608.

[74] s.36 outlines the role of the custody officer; s.37 defines the custody officer's duties before charge; s.38 defines the custody officer's duties after charge and s.39 outlines the custody officer's responsibilities to the arrested person. The custody officer will not be involved in the investigation.

officer must decide whether sufficient evidence exists either to charge the person or to warrant further detention for the purpose of obtaining evidence through interview.[75] The custody officer must ensure that the person is aware of their rights to legal advice, to notify someone of the fact of their arrest and to see that the Codes of Practice are observed by monitoring the conditions of the custody: how long and how often a person is interviewed; whether medical advice is required; and whether proper sleep and refreshment has been provided. Custody officers must be aware of the special provisions regarding the mentally handicapped, those with sight or speech impediments, the ill, foreigners and juveniles. All of this should be recorded on the custody record,[76] an essential source of information for the defendant and the court in the event of, say, a disputed confession. Proper documentation was seen by the Royal Commission to be a critical safeguard for both police and suspect, not just the custody record but also a proper interview record.[77]

The custody officer is initially responsible for the length of time that a person is detained in a police station. That detention must be periodically reviewed.[78] Prior to the Act, the police probably had to bring a suspect before a court within 24 hours. Now, with certain safeguards, it is possible to hold people without charge for up to four days. Although section 41 lays down the principle that a person should not be held without charge for more than 24 hours, this can be derogated from in certain circumstances. Continued detention for a further 12 hours can be authorised by a senior officer (a superintendent or above) if the detention is necessary to secure or preserve evidence, if the offence is a serious arrestable offence[79] and if the investigation is being conducted "diligently and expeditiously".[80] Further periods of continued detention up to 96 hours are possible with approval from the magistrates' court.[81]

The basic rights[82] of a suspect being interviewed allow for a minimum eight hour continuous period of rest without interrogation in any 24 hour period with properly heated, ventilated and lit interview rooms, with no requirement to stand and with proper breaks for refreshment at recognised mealtimes. The interview will be tape-recorded. Breaches of the Code might lead to the exclusion of any admissions by the defendant but these

[75] In practice, detention is almost never refused — McKenzie I. et al: "Helping the Police with their Inquiries" [1990] Crim.L.R. 22.

[76] s.37(4) — in Kent there are five copies: for the station record, for the suspect, for case papers, a transit copy and finally for the local intelligence liaison officer.

[77] A major complaint by the police has been the bureaucracy engendered by the Police and Criminal Evidence Act 1980 — see Audit Commission: *Tackling Crime Effectively* (Police Paper No. 12). Exhibit 17 "The Paper Chase" on 29 indicates that some 40 forms need to be completed after arrest for even a minor offence.

[78] s.40 — the extent to which such reviews are carried out is doubtful — Dixon D. et al.: "Safeguarding the rights of the accused . . ." 1 *Policing and Society* 115 (1990).

[79] These are listed in Schedule 3 of the Police and Criminal Evidence Act 1984.

[80] s.42.

[81] s.43.

[82] Code C 12.2.

must be significant and substantial and not merely technical. In *R. v. Taylor*[83] there was a breach of length of detention regulations as a result of delay in organising an identification parade. It was a minor delay and a technical infraction would not lead to the exclusion of evidence.

But presence in the police station does not mean that all the safeguards are observed. Informal interviewing is a substantial breach of the Code and yet statements are still sometimes admitted. In *R. v. Matthews*,[84] the accused was remanded in police cells (the remand centre was full) and she was alleged to have made incriminating statements, neither contemporaneously recorded, shown on the custody sheet nor was any note shown to the defendant. It is a matter for the trial judge's discretion whether such unverified accounts should be admitted, and as long as the judge addresses his or her mind to the correct issues under section 78, the appellate court will not interfere with the decision although other trial judges might well have considered the breaches in this case substantial and significant. However the accused's statement led directly to the discovery of the victim's clothes and it is hard to resist the conclusion that the judge must have considered that this confirmed the reliability of the statement, although its reliability should not be a relevant issue for the purposes of section 78.

As a result of their unwillingness to interfere in the exercise of judicial discretion, the Court of Appeal decisions on sections 76 and 78 are difficult to fit into a clear pattern. In *R. v. Trussler*[85] the suspect was a drug addict who was arrested at 9 a.m. and eventually made a statement at 2 a.m. the following morning. A doctor had been provided and the suspect had talked to his lawyer on the phone but there were long periods of questioning without adequate rest periods and the statements were eventually excluded as potentially unreliable under section 76(2)(b). But in *R. v. Crampton*[86] the defendant made admissions some 19 hours after arrest and was possibly suffering from withdrawal symptoms, the Court of Appeal emphasised that the trial court must look for potential unreliability. Had the police officers said or done anything which might render the confession unreliable?

The discretion to exclude evidence is exercised freely with regard to vulnerable defendants. In *R. v. Lamont*[87] the interrogation was of a mentally retarded suspect with an IQ of 73 and acting under section 77, the Court of Appeal excluded evidence of a confession which provided the only evidence of intention in an attempted murder case. But in *R. v. Clarke*,[88] the accused admitted attempted theft while being taken to the police station. A record of the conversation was made and signed but at

[83] [1991] Crim.L.R. 541.
[84] [1990] Crim.L.R. 190.
[85] [1988] Crim.L.R. 446.
[86] [1991] Crim.L.R. 277.
[87] [1989] Crim.L.R. 813.
[88] [1989] Crim.L.R. 892.

trial the defendant alleged that he was deaf and thus there had been a breach of the Codes.[89] On appeal, this argument was rejected. There was no breach of the Codes if the officer had been unaware that the suspect was deaf but if shown as fact that the defendant was deaf, it could still be excluded under section 78. Exclusion of evidence is not predicated on proof of police misconduct as could be seen in *R. v. Brine*[90] where the suspect was properly interviewed but the interview was excluded after medical evidence that the accused was suffering from a mild form of paranoid psychosis.

When the police do act unethically, the Court of Appeal again fails to give a clear guide. In *R. v. Fulling*,[91] the police told the defendant that her lover had been unfaithful to her with another woman (being held in the next cell). The accused made a statement which was not excluded since this was not "oppressive" behaviour under section 76. The conviction was upheld but some questions remain. Could the statement be said to be "reliable" in such circumstances for the purpose of section 76? Or could it be said that deliberately (but not illegally) undermining the willpower of a suspect in this manner has an "adverse effect on the fairness of the proceedings"? This can be contrasted with *R. v. Mason*[92] which involved arson of a car. The police told the defendant in the presence of his lawyer that they had his fingerprints on a fragment of glass from the scene and as a result, he made incriminating statements. The conviction was quashed with the Court of Appeal stressing the need to balance the gravity of the charge, the public interest, the position of the defendant and the nature of the police illegality. This was regarded as a significant deception on a minor charge, not merely to deceive the defendant but also his lawyer. General oppressive conduct can lead to exclusion as in *R. v. Beales*[93] where the officer "hectored and bullied" and fabricated evidence.

Inadmissible statement followed by proper interview

If a statement is excluded because of a breach of the Codes, this does not automatically lead to exclusion of a second statement occurring in course of a properly conducted interview.[94] But if the grounds for impugning the first statement still exist, then the second statement suffers the same fate. In *R. v. Canale*,[95] the officers deliberately broke the rules and the court refused to permit the prosecution from gaining advantage. In *R. v.*

[89] Code C 13.5 which specifies that if a person appears to be deaf, he must not be interviewed in the absence of an interpreter.

[90] [1992] Crim.L.R. 122 .

[91] [1987] Crim.L.R. 492.

[92] [1987] Crim.L.R. 757 but cf. *R. v. Bailey* [1993] Crim.L.R. 681 where play-acting by the police convinced the suspects that their cell had not been bugged and they made incriminating statements.

[93] [1991] Crim.L.R. 118.

[94] *Y. v. DPP* [1991] Crim.L.R. 917.

[95] [1990] Crim.L.R. 329.

McGovern[96] (that the impact of the first statement could not be excluded from affecting reliability of the second statement even though this latter was in the presence of his solicitor.

Evidence found in consequence of inadmissible confession

At common law, the inadmissibility of the confession made no difference to the admissibility of any evidence which was discovered as a consequence of that confession. In *R. v. Warwickshall*[97] the accused was charged as an accessory after the fact, with having received stolen property knowing it to have been stolen. As a result of her confession, the stolen property was recovered having been hidden in her bedroom. But the confession had been obtained as a result of inducements and was held to be inadmissible. Was evidence of the finding of the property also inadmissible?

R. v. Warwickshall (1783) 1 Leach 263 at 264, _per_ Nares J.

A free and voluntary confession is deserving of the highest credit, because it is presumed to flow from the strongest sense of guilt, and therefore it is admitted as proof of the crime to which it refers; but a confession forced from the mind by the flattery of hope, or by the torture of fear, comes in so questionable a shape when it is to be considered as evidence of guilt, that no credit ought to be given to it; and therefore it is rejected. This principle respecting confessions has no application whatever as to the admission or rejection of facts, whether the knowledge of them be obtained in consequence of an extorted confession, or whether it arises from some other source; for a fact, if it exists at all, must exist invariably in the same manner, whether the confession from which it is derived be in other respects true or false. Facts thus obtained, however, must be fully and satisfactorily proved, without calling in aid of any part of the confession from which they have been derived . . .

This rule is preserved in the Police and Criminal Evidence Act 1984:

76.—(4) The fact that a confession is wholly or partly excluded in pursuance of this section shall not affect the admissibility in evidence—

(a) of any facts discovered as a result of the confession;

(b) where the confession is relevant as showing that the accused speaks, writes or expresses himself in a particular way, of so much of the confession as is necessary to show that he does so.[98]

In *Warwickshall*, the discovery of the property in the accused's bedroom necessarily linked her with the crime without reference to the confession. In *Chalmers v. H.M. Advocate*,[99] the accused made an inadmissible

[96] [1991] Crim.L.R. 124.
[97] (1783) 1 Leach 263.
[98] subsection (b) preserves the common law as demonstrated by the facts in *R. v. Voisin* [1918] 1 K.B. 531.
[99] 1954 S.L.T. 177.

confession to murder and then accompanied police officers to a cornfield where he pointed out the victim's purse. The High Court of Justiciary held that evidence of the defendant pointing to the purse was inadmissible since it was part of the same transaction as the interrogation itself and that if that confession was unfairly obtained, so was the visit to the cornfield. But the purse itself was admissible, although of little probative value. It would be necessary to find another link to the accused, such as his fingerprints having been found on the object.

If the facts are equivalent to a confession, then they are not admissible. In *R. v. Payne*[1] the defendant, charged with drunk driving, was induced to see a doctor on the understanding that the doctor would not examine him for the purpose of seeing whether he was fit to drive. The doctor later testified that he was in fact unfit to drive. This can also be seen in *R. v. Barker*[2] where the defendant was charged with tax fraud. He had been implicitly promised immunity from prosecution and as a result, produced papers and documents which disclosed tax irregularities. The Court of Appeal quashed the conviction as the documents stood on exactly the same footing as an oral or written confession which was brought about as a result of a promise or a threat.[3]

[1] [1963] 1 All E.R. 848.
[2] [1941] 2 K.B. 381.
[3] The decision itself was negatived by the Taxes Management Act 1970, s.105.

5

DOCUMENTARY AND REAL EVIDENCE

Documentary Evidence

Evidence which is placed in front of a court can take three basic forms, namely documentary evidence, real evidence or the testimony of witnesses. Real evidence is considered at the end of this chapter and oral testimony is examined in the following chapters. The admissibility of evidence, in whatever form, is subject to the general principles of relevance, probative weight and avoidance of prejudice as well as to the exclusionary rules such as hearsay, public interest or opinion. But when the information which a party wishes to rely on is contained in a document, there are two additional preconditions which must be met before the document will be admitted as evidence:

(1) the first of these is known as "*proof of contents*". At common law, a document was only evidence of its contents if it was the original document, although in certain circumstances, copies or oral testimony of the contents was permitted. This rule, itself an aspect of the old "*best evidence*" rule, has been significantly changed by statute.[1]

(2) the second requirement is "*proof of due execution*" by which is meant proof that the document was signed or written by the person by whom it purports to have been signed or written.

These conditions need to be met with regard to any document.

What is a document?

Everyday language would confine the term "documentary evidence" to statements recorded on paper in some form but in *R. v. Daye*[2] Darling J. talked of a document as any *'written thing capable of being evidence'* and pointed out that paper has been preceded by parchment, stone, marble,

[1] In particular the Criminal Justice Act 1988, s.27 and the Civil Evidence Act 1995, s.8.
[2] [1908] 2 K.B. 333.

clay and metal. Nowadays even the adjective "written" is too restrictive and there is an even wider meaning. Under the Civil Evidence Act 1995:

> 13.—. . . 'document' means anything in which information of any description is recorded, and 'copy', in relation to a document, means anything onto which information recorded in the document has been copied, by whatever means and whether directly or indirectly[3]

The legal definition of the term no longer bears much resemblance to its everyday meaning. Film, photographs, video tape, audio tape, computer disks, a fax, all are capable of being documents within the meaning of the Civil Evidence Act. In *Senior v. Holdsworth ex parte Independent Television News*[4] the plaintiffs sought damages against the police for assault and sought to make ITN produce film of a pop festival which had been held in Windsor Great Park. The Court of Appeal held that the film was a document within the county court rules[5] and that a witness could be compelled by the issue of a summons *duces tecum* to produce the film in court.

In *Derby & Co Ltd v. Weldon (No. 9)*[6] the court was asked to decide whether a computer database was a document for the purposes of discovery under R.S.C. Ord. 24, which provides for the discovery of documents:

Derby & Co. Ltd v. Weldon (No. 9) [1991] 2 All E.R. 901 at 905h–906d, per Vinelott J.

> The first question raised by this application is whether the database of a computer's on-line system which is recorded in back-up files is a document within the meaning of R.S.C. Ord. 24. An analogous question came before Walton J. in *Grant v. Southwestern and County Properties Ltd.*[7] The question there was whether a tape recording of a telephone conversation was a document. In *Beneficial Finance Corp Co v. Conway*[8] McInerney J. had held that it was not, on the ground that, although a tape recording records information and serves a function corresponding to that of a document, it is not a document because the information is not capable of being visually inspected. Walton J. took the opposite view and pointed to the absurdity of the conclusion that if two parties to litigation recorded a conversation, one on a tape recorder and one in shorthand, the one record would and the other record would not be discoverable, though both were ways of recording the same conversation and although, if the second was written in a private shorthand system, both would need a key before the message could be read. He said:

[3] Civil Evidence Act 1995, s.13 implementing the recommendations of the Law Commission Report *The Hearsay Rule in Civil Proceedings* (1993 No. 216). Compare this section with the cumbersome approach in s.5 and s.10(1) of the Civil Evidence Act 1968.
[4] [1975] 2 All E.R. 1009.
[5] C.C.R. (1981) Ord. 20, r.12 which allows a witness to be summoned to attend and produce a document in his or her possession.
[6] [1991] 2 All E.R. 901.
[7] [1974] 2 All E.R. 465.
[8] [1970] V.R. 321.

> . . . the mere interposition of necessity of an instrument for decyphering the information cannot make any difference in principle. A litigant who keeps all his documents in microdot form could not avoid discovery because in order to read the information extremely powerful microscopes or other sophisticated instruments would be required. Nor again, if he kept them by means of microfilm which could not be read without the aid of a projector.
>
> I respectfully adopt that statement of principle. It must, I think, apply *a fortiori* to the tape or discretionary on which material fed into a simple word processor is stored. In most businesses, that takes the place of the carbon copy of outgoing letters which used to be retained in files.

In criminal proceedings, the definition of document provided by section 8 of the Civil Evidence Act 1995 is now incorporated into the Police and Criminal Evidence Act 1984[9] and into the Criminal Justice Act 1988.[10] A more limited definition had apparently been applied in *Kajala v. Noble*[11] in which the defendant was charged with using threatening behaviour likely to cause a breach of the peace. A prosecution witness who was familiar with the accused testified that he had recognised him on a BBC television news programme. The BBC supplied a video cassette recording of the incident but not the original footage. This copy was admitted into evidence. The normal rule is that a party seeking to rely upon the contents of a document must adduce primary evidence of that document, generally the original document itself. Ackner L.J. held that this rule, known as the "best evidence" rule, was confined to written documents in the strict sense and did not apply to tapes or films. This is not a narrower definition of "document" for the general purposes of the common law but simply for the purpose of the "best evidence" rule in criminal proceedings.

As the definition of "document" broadens, so do the difficulties of demonstrating authenticity. While computer-generated information should be treated similarly to other records, its weight depends on its reliability and parties might need to provide information as to the security of their computer system. In criminal proceedings, the proper functioning of the machine needs to be proved to the court under the provisions of section 69 of the Police and Criminal Evidence Act 1984. Similar safeguards were provided by section 5 of the Civil Evidence Act 1968 but this section was repealed by Civil Evidence Act 1995 and not replaced. Computerised records are admissible in the same manner as other records. These issues are discussed later in this chapter.

Original documents and hearsay documents

A party will normally introduce a document into evidence in order to rely upon the contents of that document. The document may record a state of affairs in words, whether spoken or written, or in numbers; it may do so by

[9] s.118(1) as amended by the Civil Evidence Act 1995, Sched. 1.
[10] Sched. 2, para. 5 as amended by the Civil Evidence Act 1995, Sched. 1.
[11] (1982) 75 Cr.App.R. 149.

means of a chart or a graph; it may do so pictorially by film or photo; it may be a map or even an artist's representation. A litigant may seek to demonstrate the truth or falsity of those contents or simply their existence. In considering the conditions under which such documents become admissible, we must distinguish:

- documents admissible in their own right
- documents containing admissible hearsay.

The requirements relating to the proof of the contents of the document and to the proof of the proper execution of the document apply to both categories. But if the document contains hearsay, before it is admissible, it must also satisfy the conditions laid down by the Civil Evidence Act 1995, by the Criminal Justice Act 1988 or by some other common law or statutory exception to hearsay.

The classic statement of the hearsay rule was formulated by Cross:

> an assertion other than one made by a person while giving oral evidence in the proceedings is inadmissible as evidence of any fact asserted[12]

The rule against hearsay is discussed later[13] but as a general rule, documents containing a person's writing (letters, memos, etc) or speech (such as a tape recording) are likely to be hearsay. Increasingly courts are faced with documents produced by mechanical devices, such as cameras, speed guns, devices that test alcohol levels in the blood, etc. Again as a rule of thumb, because these do not purport to be a person's statements, they are original rather than hearsay evidence. For example, the videotape on which there is a visual record of an event is original evidence of that incident, or a printout which details a computer's analysis of a substance is evidence of the constituent elements of that compound.[14] If the evidence is original, the jury can draw inferences from the thing itself, although they will normally be assisted by expert testimony.

In *The Statue of Liberty*[15] a film record of a radar screen showed two ships' courses before a collision in the Thames. This was admitted as real evidence:

> If tape-recordings are admissible, it seems that a photograph of radar reception is equally admissible — or indeed any other type of photograph. It would be an absurd distinction that a photograph should be admissible if the camera were operated manually by a photographer, but not if it were operated by a trip or clock

[12] Tapper C. (ed), *Cross and Tapper on Evidence* (8th ed., 1995) 46. This formula was approved by the House of Lords in *R. v. Sharp* [1988] 1 All E.R. 65 at 68b–c.
[13] See Chap. 16.
[14] *R. v. Wood* (1982) 76 Cr.App.R. 23.
[15] [1968] 2 All E.R. 195 — the case was decided before the Civil Evidence Act 1968 allowed the admission of much hearsay evidence in civil proceedings.

mechanism. Similarly, if evidence of weather conditions were relevant, the law would affront common sense if it were to say that those could be proved by a person who looked at a barometer from time to time, but not by producing a barograph record. So, too, with other types of mechanical recordings. Again, cards from clocking-in-and-out machines are frequently admitted in accident cases. The law is now bound to take cognizance of the fact that mechanical means replace human effort.[16]

If the radar map can be termed an "assertion" or a "statement", it is a statement by a machine automatically tracking the ships and is not a hearsay statement which must be by a person. Where a machine is being used to collect, process and output information without any human input (apart from the original building and programming of the machine), the output is original evidence.[17]

Proof of Contents

Criminal proceedings

Where a party seeks to introduce a document into evidence in a criminal case, this is governed by the Criminal Justice Act 1988:

27.—Where a statement contained in a document is admissible as evidence in criminal proceedings, it may be proved —

a) by the production of that document; or

b) (whether or not that document is still in existence) by the production of a copy of that document, or of the material part of it,

authenticated in such manner as the court may approve; and it is immaterial for the purposes of this subsection how many removes there are between a copy and the original[18]

The common law rule was that where a party wishes to rely on the contents of a document as direct evidence, he or she must adduce primary evidence of the contents of that document. This is the "*primary evidence*" rule. In criminal proceedings, section 27 abolishes that rule. A party is now entitled to introduce a copy of the document, regardless of whether the original exists, as long as that copy is properly authenticated by the court. Furthermore the section does not allow the argument that it is not a direct

[16] *ibid.* at 196g–h, *per* Sir Jocelyn Simon P.

[17] This formulation might well cast doubt on the example of the "clocking-in-and-out machine" given by Sir Jocelyn Simon P. — this is surely no different to the worker writing down the times of arrival and departure on a card. This in turn must be distinguished from machines that can recognise a palmprint or thumbprint!

[18] "Document" and "copy" bear the same meaning as in the Civil Evidence Act 1995, s.13 — the Criminal Justice Act 1988, Sched. 2, para. 5, has been amended by the Civil Evidence Act 1995, Sched. 1.

copy as it is immaterial how many removes there are between the copy and the original. On its wording, the section applies to all documents, whether constituting original evidence or hearsay evidence. In *Kajala*, the "document" (*i.e.* the film) was original evidence and, had section 27 been in force, a videotape copy would have been admissible. If section 27 applies in cases of original evidence, this would leave no scope in criminal proceedings for the operation of a "primary evidence" rule.

But the section might be interpreted in a narrower manner. Part II of the 1988 legislation deals with documentary hearsay and thus section 27 might be read legitimately as applying only to the proof of documents containing hearsay and not to the proof of documents containing original evidence. Such authority as exists suggests a broader approach. In *R. v. Foxley*[19] copies of credit notes were advanced as evidence of certain corrupt payments. These notes were not hearsay statements but original evidence of the payments themselves and yet copies were permitted to be adduced in evidence. Commenting, Professor Smith argues that section 27 is in point because the section is concerned, not with hearsay, but with the best evidence rule, allowing admission of copies authenticated in such manner as the court may approve. He suggests persuasively that the question of authenticity is substantially the same whether the document is tendered as hearsay or as direct evidence.[20]

Even where section 27 applies, it does not override certain common law or statutory provisions:

(1) at common law, the contents of a document may be proved not merely by copies of the document but by other forms of secondary evidence, including oral evidence. Where the document and any copies are lost, other secondary evidence might be admissible. The conditions for the admission of such evidence are the same in criminal and in civil proceedings and are discussed below.
(2) there are a range of statutory exceptions to the general rule, mainly relating to public and judicial documents, including bankers books. These permit proof of contents by copies but such copies normally have to be in a specific form. Such specificity is unnecessary under section 27 but is not overridden by that section.

An additional statutory provision is to be found in the Police and Criminal Evidence Act 1984:

> 71.—In any proceedings the contents of a document may (whether or not the document is still in existence) be proved by the production of an enlargement of a microfilm copy of that document or of the material part of it, authenticated in such manner as the court may approve.

[19] [1995] Crim.L.R. 636.
[20] The editor of Cross also prefers the broader interpretation — Tapper C., *Cross and Tapper on Evidence* (8th ed., 1995) 705.

The extended interpretation of "copy" in the Civil Evidence Act 1995:

> ... 'copy', in relation to a document, means anything onto which information recorded in the document has been copied, by whatever means and whether directly or indirectly.[21]

appears to make this provision redundant.

Civil proceedings — primary evidence

The common law rule is that where a party wishes to rely on the contents of a document as direct evidence, he or she must adduce primary evidence of the contents of that document. It was a rule that arose when documents were mainly handwritten and there was a greater risk of fraud and forgery, let alone of the potential inaccuracy of the copy.

In *Augustien v. Challis*[22] the debtor owed a sum of money to the plaintiff. The plaintiff obtained a judgment against him and sought to recover the money through a writ of *fieri facias*. The sheriff withdrew this writ and the plaintiff sued the sheriff who, he alleged, had withdrawn the writ negligently. The sheriff argued that the debtor also owed rent to his landlord who had priority over the plaintiff's judgment debt. The landlord testified that rent was due to him under a lease and the court held that the original lease had to be produced as primary evidence of the rent payable,[23] without which the landlord's testimony was inadmissible.

In *MacDonnell v. Evans*[24] the defence produced a letter purporting to have been written by a witness called by the plaintiff. That witness was asked in cross-examination whether he had written that letter in response to another letter accusing the witness of forgery. The prior letter was not produced and defence counsel was thus seeking to prove its contents by secondary evidence, namely the oral testimony of the witness. The question was disallowed since letter had to be proved by production of the original:

MacDonnell v. Evans (1852) 11 C.B. 930 at 943, *per* Maule J.

> It is a general rule ... that, if you want to get at the contents of a written document, the proper way is, to produce it, if you can. That is a rule in which the common sense of mankind concurs. If the paper is in the possession of the party who seeks to have the jury infer something from its contents, he should let them see it. That is the general and ordinary rule; the contents can only be proved by the writing itself. If the document does not exist, or the party seeking to show its contents cannot get at it, he is at liberty to give secondary evidence, because in that case no better is to be had ... Here the very form of the question, 'Did you not

[21] These definitions also apply to proof of contents in criminal cases under Criminal Justice Act 1988, s.27, by virtue of Sched. 1 of the 1995 Act.
[22] (1847) 1 Exch. 279.
[23] Similarly to prove the length of a tenancy — *Twyman v. Knowles* (1853) 13 C.B. 222.
[24] (1852) 11 C.B. 930.

write that letter in answer to a letter containing so and so?' assumes that there is another letter in existence, the production of which would be the best proof of its contents. There was nothing to show why that letter was not forthcoming . . .

The contents of the document, namely the amount of rent payable, needed to be proved. But if the intent is not to prove the contents but some other purpose, the rule does not apply. In *R. v. Holy Trinity, Hull*[25] it was necessary to prove the existence of a tenancy. Although that relationship had been created by a document, the fact that a tenancy existed could be proved by parol evidence on payment of rent or possession of land. It did not need proof of the written tenancy agreement. Similarly in *R. v. Elworthy*[26] a solicitor was prosecuted for perjury, having denied on oath that he had prepared a draft of a statutory declaration. The prosecution produced oral evidence to show, firstly, that the draft existed and secondly, that the defendant had altered it. The conviction was quashed: secondary evidence was admissible to show the existence of the document itself but not to show the alterations because the prosecution would then be relying on the testimony to prove the contents of the document rather than its mere existence.

Civil proceedings — original documents

In common law, the original of a document can be in different forms:

(1) signed duplicates and signed copies: these are equivalent to originals.[27] Unsigned versions or photocopies would not be treated as originals where the issue is the contents of the signed copy. Thus in *R. v. Regan*,[28] the original of a telegram was the written message handed in at the Post Office and not the message as delivered. However, if the issue is, for example, the contents of a pamphlet handed out in the street, any of the copies could be treated as the original. It should be noted that in *Derby & Co Ltd v. Weldon (No. 9)*[29] it was the computer database itself that was treated as the original document
(2) enrolled documents: if the original document has to be enrolled by being filed in a court or other public office. An example would be a will where an official copy is sufficient as primary evidence of its contents.
(3) admission of contents: where there is an admission (whether (formal or informal, oral or written) made by a party about the contents of a private document, this admission is primary evidence of the

[25] (1827) 7 B&C 611.
[26] (1867) L.R. 1 C.C.R. 103.
[27] *Forbes v. Samuel* [1913] 3 K.B. 706.
[28] (1887) 16 Cox C.C. 203.
[29] [1991] 2 All E.R. 901.

contents of that document. In *Slatterie v. Pooley*[30] the plaintiff sued on a covenant which created an indemnity in respect of certain debts, covered in a schedule to the deed. The schedule was inadmissible but there was an oral admission by the defendant that a particular debt was included in that schedule and that admission was binding on the defendant.

The common law rule can be very restrictive and where, as in the U.S.A., there is a broad definition of originals and duplicates, the primary evidence rule is less constraining. Under the Federal Rules of Evidence:

1001.—For the purpose of this article the following definitions are applicable:

(1) Writings and recordings. 'Writings' and 'recordings' consist of letters, words, or numbers, or the equivalent, set down by handwriting, typewriting, printing, photostating, photographing, magnetic impulse, mechanical or electronic recording, or other form of data compilation

(2) Photographs. 'Photographs' include still photographs, X-ray films, video tapes, and motion pictures.

(3) Original. An 'original' of a writing or recording is the writing or recording itself or any counterpart intended to have the same effect by a person executing or issuing it. An 'original' of a photograph includes the negative or any print therefrom. If data are stored in a computer or similar device, any printout or other output readable by sight, shown to reflect the data accurately is an 'original'.

(4) Duplicate. A 'duplicate' is a counterpart produced by the same impression as the original, or from the same matrix, or by means of photography, including enlargements and miniatures, or by mechanical or electronic re-recording, or by chemical reproduction, or by other equivalent techniques which accurately reproduces the original.[31]

Civil proceedings — admissibility of secondary evidence

There are exceptions to the primary evidence rule where secondary evidence is admitted, whether it be oral evidence, copies or copies of copies, all of which are acceptable. There must be evidence that the copy is a true copy of the original. Before discussing those exceptions, it is necessary to consider section 8 of the Civil Evidence Act 1995:

8.—(1) Where a statement contained in a document is admissible as evidence in civil proceedings, it may be proved —

a) by the production of that document; or
b) (whether or not that document is still in existence) by the production of a copy of that document, or of the material part of it,

authenticated in such manner as the court may approve.

[30] (1840) 6 M&W 664.
[31] Federal Rules of Evidence, r.1001.

(2) It is immaterial for this purpose how many removes there are between a copy and the original.[32]

In proposing this section the Law Commission were not intending to depart from the policy of section 6(1) of the Civil Evidence Act 1968, apart from the provisions in subsection (2).[33] Commentators have treated section 6 as restricted to the proof of hearsay statements in documents.[34] But to restrict section 8 in this fashion would be absurd: the 1995 Act abolishes the hearsay rule in civil proceedings and there will be virtually no difference between the admissibility of hearsay and non-hearsay statements. It would be counter-productive to have different conditions for the proof of the contents of documents admissible in their own right as opposed to the conditions for the proof of contents of documents which contain hearsay statements. Moreover the argument that section 8 is applicable to all documents gains weight from the fact that it is obviously modelled on section 27 Criminal Justice Act 1988 which, as has been argued above, is of general application.

The conclusion from this is that the primary evidence rule in civil proceedings has been undermined as has the same rule in criminal proceedings and the following discussion should be read with this in mind. A document, whether containing original or hearsay evidence, can be proved by producing a copy, no matter at how many removes from the original that copy is. This resolves some doubts as to whether a copy of a copy was admissible.[35] Nor is the definition of "copy" limited as the extended interpretation of "copy" is to be found in the Civil Evidence Act 1995:

13.—. . . 'copy', in relation to a document, means anything onto which information recorded in the document has been copied, by whatever means and whether directly or indirectly.

Even if section 8 is given this broad interpretation, it does not override certain common law or statutory provisions:

(1) at common law, the contents of a document may be proved not merely by copies of the document but by other forms of secondary evidence, including oral evidence. As was seen with regard to criminal proceedings, where the document and any copies are lost, other secondary evidence might be admissible.
(2) there are a range of statutory exceptions to the general rule, mainly relating to public and judicial documents, including bankers books, which lay down criteria for admissibility of such documents.

[32] "Document" and "copy" are defined in Civil Evidence Act 1995, s.13.
[33] Law Commission, *The Hearsay Rule in Civil Proceedings* (1993 Law Comm. No. 216) para. 4.37.
[34] Tapper C., *Cross and Tapper on Evidence* (8th ed., 1995) 611 — certainly section 6 was headed "Provisions supplementary to sections 2–5 in the Act".
[35] *Everingham v. Roundell* (1838) 2 M. & R. 138.

The exceptions to the primary evidence rule which allow secondary evidence of the contents of a document are as follows:

(a) failure to produce: where the opponent is given notice and fails to produce the original document, a party is entitled to rely on secondary evidence. A party cannot prevent an opponent from using a document by withholding the original. Thus where a party wishes to rely on correspondence with his or her opponent, the letters would normally be disclosed in the opponent's list of documents and he or she would be obliged to produce the original at trial. Failure to do so means that the other party can give secondary evidence, either orally or by producing a copy of the original:

> A party to a cause or matter by whom a list of documents is served on any other party in pursuance of any provision of Order 24 shall be deemed to have been served by that other party with a notice requiring him to produce at the trial of the cause or matter such of the documents specified in the list as are in his possession, custody or power.[36]

In civil proceedings, this procedure normally negates any need for a formal notice to produce. If such a notice is served,[37] it is for the purpose of laying a foundation for adducing secondary evidence as much as to compel the production of the original. The opposing party cannot later rely on the original if secondary evidence proves to be at variance with original document. There is a risk however, since formal notice to produce does compel the party to put the document in evidence even if it proves unfavourable. The procedure cannot be used simply as a means of inspecting a document. The purpose of notice was explained in *Dwyer v. Collins*[38] which was an action on a bill of exchange. The plaintiff's lawyer was called by the defendant to testify. He admitted that he had the bill in court but declined to produce it.

Dwyer v. Collins (1852) 7 Ex. 639 at 648–649, _per_ Parke B.

The next question is, whether the bill being admitted to be in court, parol evidence was admissible on its non-production by the attorney on demand, or whether previous notice to produce was necessary. On principle the answer must depend on this: why the notice to produce is required. If it be to give the opponent notice that such a document would be used by the party to the cause, so that the opponent may be enabled to prepare evidence to explain or confirm it, then, no doubt, a notice at the trial, although the document be in court, is too late; but if it be merely to enable the party to have the document in court, to produce it if he likes, and if he does not, to enable his opponent to give parol evidence — if it be merely to exclude the argument that the opponent has not taken all reasonable means to procure the original, which he must do before he can be permitted to make use of secondary evidence, then the demand of production at the trial is sufficient . . .

[36] R.S.C. Ord. 27, r.4(3).
[37] R.S.C. Ord. 24, r.10.
[38] (1852) 7 Ex. 639.

> We think the plaintiff's alleged principle is not the true one on which the notice to produce is required, but that it is merely to give sufficient opportunity to the opposite party to produce it if he pleases, and thereby to secure the best evidence of its contents, and the request to produce it immediately is quite sufficient for that purpose if the document be in court . . .

In criminal proceedings, an accused cannot be compelled (by serving a *subpoena duces tecum*) to produce a document, as any failure would be excused because of the privilege against self-incrimination. But a refusal to produce after notice can lead to secondary evidence being given. In *R. v. Collins*[39] the accused was charged with deception offences, having cashed a cheque on an account that he knew to be closed. He was called on to produce the letter closing the account but refused. As a result a carbon copy would have been admissible on behalf of the Crown. In this case, the Court of Criminal Appeal quashed the conviction since the witness did not prove that it was a true copy. This aspect of the decision has to be read in the light of section 27 Criminal Justice Act 1988 which provides that any copy may be authenticated in a manner approved by the court.

(b) lawful refusal to produce by a stranger: a stranger to the proceedings may be served with a *subpoena duces tecum*, ordering him or her to attend court and to produce a document. That person may lawfully refuse to produce such documents: for example, where the documents are privileged through legal professional privilege or public interest immunity; where diplomatic immunity exists or where the person is outside the jurisdiction.[40] If the refusal is lawful, secondary evidence of the contents of the document is admissible. In *R. v. Nowaz*[41] the accused was charged with making a false declaration contrary to the Perjury Act 1911. The Crown sought to adduce evidence of a photograph and an application for a passport submitted to the Pakistani consulate. The consul refused to produce the documents and the prosecution relied on the oral evidence of a police officer to whom the consul had shown the documents in question. The conviction was upheld since secondary evidence of the contents was permissible where production of the original was impossible.

But where the refusal is unlawful, secondary evidence is not permitted because production can be compelled. In *R. v. Llanfaethly (Inhabitants)*[42] a *subpoena* had been served on a witness to produce a rate-book supposed to be in his possession. The witness did not attend and it was held that oral evidence of rating was not permitted:

> It has been held that if, under a *subpoena duces tecum*, the witness appears and stands on his privilege and refuses to produce the document, and the judge admits the objection, secondary evidence is then admissible. But here no

[39] (1960) 44 Cr.App.R. 170.
[40] *Kilgour v. Owen* (1889) 88 L.T. Jo. 7.
[41] [1976] 3 All E.R. 5.
[42] (1853) 2 E&B 940.

privilege existed, and the witness would have been bound to produce the rate-book, and would have been punishable for contempt if he had refused to do so . . .[43]

(c) lost documents: where a party is seeking to introduce secondary evidence of the contents of a document because that document has been lost, it is necessary to show that all reasonable steps to search for that document have been taken. In *Brewster v. Sewell*[44] there had been a fire at the plaintiff's premises in 1813 and the insurance company had paid out on the policy. Afterwards a new policy was taken out. The plaintiff had reason to testify about the original policy but could not produce the original. He gave evidence that he had searched but had been unable to find it. Secondary evidence of the contents was permitted:

***Brewster v. Sewell* (1820) 3 B. & Ald. 297 at 299, *per* Abbott C.J.**

All evidence is to be considered with regard to the matter with respect to which it is produced. Now it appears to be a very different thing, whether the subject of inquiry be a useless paper, which may reasonably be supposed to be lost, or whether it be an important document which the party might have an interest in keeping, and for the non-production of which no satisfactory reason is assigned. This is the case of a policy of insurance by which a company undertook to indemnify the plaintiff against losses by fire. A fire took place, and a loss was paid. That having taken place, the original policy became mere waste paper. There was no reason to suppose that the policy could, at any future time, be called for, to answer any reasonable purpose whatever . . . This being a case, therefore, where the loss or destruction of the paper may almost be presumed, very slight evidence of its loss or destruction is sufficient . . .

In *R. v. Wayte*[45] two letters were lost and a photocopy of one and a photocopy of a carbon of the other were held to be admissible.

(d) production of the original is impractical: in *Owner v. Bee Hive Spinning*[46] there was a notice giving the times of meal breaks which was affixed to the wall of a factory. Statute required that it remained fixed there at all times and secondary evidence of its contents was admissible. Another example might be photographic evidence of the 'tags' of graffiti artists facing criminal damage charges. Such tags might well be on walls, bridges or even tube trains.

(e) proof of public and judicial documents[47]: in *Mortimer v. M'Callan*[48] the issue was whether the defendant had accepted certain stock. There was

[43] *ibid.* at 944, *per* Lord Campbell C.J.
[44] (1820) 3 B&Ald 297.
[45] (1983) 76 Cr.App.R. 110.
[46] [1914] 1 K.B. 105.
[47] Often such documents are also hearsay but they come under a common law exception to the rule against hearsay as well as forming an exception to the primary evidence rule — see 528, *et seq.*
[48] (1840) 6 M&W 58.

evidence that a person, unknown to the clerk in the Bank of England, had come to the bank with one Taylor and had made an entry accepting the stock. Another witness testified that he had inspected the bank's books and that the signature to the acceptance of the stock was in the defendant's handwriting. It was held that the books themselves did not have to be produced:

Mortimer v. M'Callan **(1840) 6 M. & W. 58 at 72, *per* Lord Abinger C.B.**

The Bank books are not capable of being produced without so much inconvenience, that the courts have directed them to remain in the Bank, and copies of them to be received in evidence for the purpose for which the books are receivable. Then, if they are not removable on the ground of public inconvenience, that is upon the same footing in point of principle as in the case of that which is not removable by the physical nature of the thing itself. Inscriptions upon tombstones or on a wall are proved every day in this way for that reason. The necessity of the case in the one instance and in the other case the general inconvenience which would follow from the books being removed, supplies the reason of the rule . . .

Thus at common law, a range of public documents can be proved by copies under this principle. However there are also many statutes which regulate the proof of public documents:

(1) **legislation:** private and local and personal Acts of Parliament are proved by the Queen's Printer's or Stationery Office copies.[49] Judicial notice is taken of all public Acts under section 3 Interpretation Act 1978. As a general rule, the content of foreign law cannot be proved by the production of the record but has to be proved by oral testimony of an expert witness.[50]
(2) **proclamations**: royal proclamations and orders or regulations issued by the government are proved by Queen's Printer's or Stationery Office copies.[51]
(3) **statutory instruments**: these are proved by Queen's Printer's or Stationery Office copies.[52]
(4) **foreign proclamations**: proclamations, treaties and other acts of state of foreign states or British colonies are proved by an examined copy (that is, a copy proved by oral evidence to have been examined with and to correspond to the original) or by a copy authenticated with the seal of the state or colony.[53]
(5) **by-laws:** these are proved by certified printed copies. That is, a copy signed and certified as correct by officials having custody of the

[49] Evidence Act 1845, s.3; Documentary Evidence Act 1882, s.2.
[50] *Sussex Peerage Case* (1844) 11 Cl and Finn 85.
[51] Documentary Evidence Act 1868, ss.2–6; Documentary Evidence Act 1882, s.2.
[52] Documentary Evidence Act 1868, s.2; Documentary Evidence Act 1882, s.2; Statutory Instruments Act 1946, s.3.
[53] Evidence Act 1851, s.7.

originals.[54] This method is also used in the case of entries in registers[55] or company proceedings.

(6) **judicial proceedings**: in the superior court under R.S.C. Ord. 38, r.10, these may be proved by office copies, that is, copies made by officials having custody of the documents and sealed with the seal of the court;[56] in the county court, records can be proved by certified copies;[57] in the magistrates' court, the Magistrates' Courts Rules 1981, r. 68 provides that the register of a magistrates' court or any document purporting to be an extract from the register and to be certified by the clerk as a true extract, shall be admissible as evidence of the proceedings of the court.

(7) **convictions and acquittals**: these are proved under the Police and Criminal Evidence Act 1984:

> 73.—(1) Where in any proceedings the fact that a person has in the United Kingdom been convicted or acquitted of any offence otherwise than by a Service court is admissible in evidence, it may be proved by producing a certificate of conviction or, as the case may be, of acquittal relating to that offence, and proving that the person named in the certificate as having been convicted or acquitted of the offence is the person whose conviction or acquittal is to be proved.

(8) **public records**: records in the Public Record Office are proved by copies certified by the Keeper of the Public Records.[58]

Two further provisions are of importance: section 1 of the Evidence Act 1845 provides that, where a document may be proved by a certified, signed or sealed copy, any copy bearing the signature, seal or stamp should be admissible without any further proof. In other words the copy is presumed to be authentic. Furthermore under section 14 of the Evidence Act 1851, where there is a public document not covered by a statutory provision, a certified or examined copy will be admissible evidence:

> 14.—Whenever any book or other document is of such a public nature as to be admissible in evidence on its mere production from proper custody, and no statute exists which renders its contents provable by means of a copy, any copy thereof or extract therefrom shall be admissible in evidence in any court of justice, or before any person now or hereafter having by law or by consent of parties authority to hear, receive, and examine evidence, provided it be proved to be an examined copy or extract, or provided it purport to be signed and certified as a true copy or extract by the officer to whose custody the original is entrusted, and which officer is hereby required to furnish such certified copy or extract to any person applying at a reasonable time for the same, upon payment of a reasonable sum for the same.

[54] Local Government Act 1972, s.238.
[55] For example, births, deaths and marriages under Births and Deaths Registration Act 1953, s.34.
[56] See also Supreme Court Act 1981, s.132.
[57] County Courts Act 1984, s.12.
[58] Public Records Act 1958, s.9.

Bankers' books

With the exception of the records of the Bank of England, the records of banks are private documents. By the Bankers Books Evidence Act 1879:

3.—Subject to the provisions of this Act, a copy of any entry in a banker's book shall in all legal proceedings be received as prima facie evidence of such entry, and of the matters, transactions, and accounts therein recorded.[59]

Under section 5, copies of entries are admissible as long as they are an examined copies. An officer of the bank would need to prove the copy but would not have to prove the particular entry.

Under section 4, the 'book' must be one of the ordinary books in the control and custody of the bank and the entry was made in the usual course of business. *Barker v. Wilson*[60] held that microfilmed records (and presumably printouts from computerised databases) were sufficient and this is now incorporated in section 9 of the 1879 Act by the Banking Act 1979. But this relaxation of the primary evidence rule only applies to "bankers' books" and does not apply to other banking business. In *R. v. Dadson*[61] the defendant was charged with offences relating to the misuse of a cheque card and copies of the bank's letters to the defendant about the state of his account were admitted in reliance on the 1879 Act. The Court of Appeal quashed the conviction as these were not "books" even under the broad interpretation employed in *Barker v. Wilson*. As *R. v. Collins*[62] showed, the fact that such letters were sent is admissible evidence of the defendant's mens rea but are not admissible under section 3. Notice to the defendant to produce the originals would be necessary and, if he or she failed to do so, production of copies would be possible.

In *Williams v. Williams*[63] the Court of Appeal considered whether the 1879 Act extended to paid cheques and paying-in slips. A wife sought inspection of her husband's bank account under section 7 of the Act, including bundles of paid cheques and paying-in slips as these would reveal more information than a bank statement:

Williams v. Williams [1987] 3 All E.R. 257 at 261a–d, *per* Donaldson M.R.

In this situation counsel for Mrs Williams has to submit, and does submit, that the bundles of cheques and paying-in slips constitute bankers' books within the modern definition and that adding each cheque or paying-in slip to the bundle constitutes making an entry in those books. Whilst I would be prepared to accept that the

[59] This section also creates an exception to hearsay as the entry is prima facie admissible evidence of the matters it records.
[60] [1980] 2 All E.R. 81.
[61] (1983) 77 Cr.App.R. 91.
[62] (1960) 44 Cr.App.R. 170.
[63] [1987] 3 All E.R. 257.

cheques constitute part of the bank's records used in the ordinary business of the bank, . . . I am quite unable to accept that adding an individual cheque or paying-in slip can be regarded as making an 'entry' in those records. Putting the matter in another way, 'other records' in the new definition has, I think, to be construed *eiusdem generis* with 'ledgers, day books, cash books [and] account books' and unsorted bundles of cheques and paying-in slips are not 'other records' within the meaning of the Act.

This case also involves the power of inspection of bankers' books under section 7 of the 1879 Act. This power is extremely wide:

7.—On the application of any party to a legal proceedings a court or judge may order that such party be at liberty to inspect and take copies of any entries in a banker's book for any of the purposes of such proceedings. An order under this section may be made either with or without summoning the bank or any other party, and shall be served on the bank three clear days before the same is to be obeyed, unless the court or judge otherwise directs.

Any party to legal proceedings can inspect and take copies of any entry in a banker's book. This power can be exercised *ex parte* and does not even require notice to the bank or any other party affected. The account to be inspected may be that of a person not party to the case. In *R. v. Andover Justices ex parte Rhodes*[64] the accused was charged with theft and told the police that the money was in her husband's bank account. The Divisional Court upheld a section 7 order in respect of that account, noting in addition that the husband was not a competent witness against his wife.

However section 7 orders should only be made in exceptional circumstances where the public interest outweighs the interest in the confidentiality of banking transactions: *R. v. Grossman*[65] limits it to inspecting bankers' books within the jurisdiction. In *Williams v. Summerfield*[66] Lord Widgery C.J. said:

Williams v. Summerfield [1972] 2 All E.R. 1334 at 1337g–1338g, *per* Lord Widgery C.J.

So far as civil proceedings are concerned a working rule has long since been established, and it is conveniently expressed in *Re Bankers' Books Evidence Act 1879, R. v. Bono*[67] . . . The effect of the judgment in Bono's case and other authorities is that the courts have set their face against section 7 being used as a kind of searching enquiry or fishing expedition beyond the ordinary rules of discovery.

In civil proceedings the normal approach to the use of section 7 is that documents which would not be discoverable under the ordinary rules are not to be disclosed by a side wind, as it were, by the application of s.7. It is quite clear that the section applies to ordinary criminal proceedings, and counsel for the appellants

[64] [1980] Crim.L.R. 644.
[65] (1981) 73 Cr.App.R. 302.
[66] [1972] 2 All E.R. 1334.
[67] (1913) 29 T.L.R. 635.

has really put his argument as high as this. He refers us to the well-known principle that an accused is not bound to incriminate himself, and he says that an order under section 7 against an accused in criminal proceedings for the disclosure of his bank account is a means of requiring him to incriminate himself.

When pressed on this argument, counsel for the appellants, it seems to me, had to retreat to the position in which he was really contending that section 7 could have no effective application to criminal proceedings. For my part I was unable to discover in the way in which he was putting his argument before us, any practical example in which such an application would not be met by the objection that it was a means of requiring the accused to incriminate himself. For my part I do not think that the application of the section can be restricted to that extent or in that way.

On the other hand, one must I think recognise that an order under section 7 can be a very serious interference with the liberty of the subject. It can be a gross invasion of privacy; it is an order which clearly must only be made after the most careful thought and on the clearest grounds . . .

I think that in criminal proceedings, justices should warn themselves of the importance of the step which they are taking in making an order under s.7; should always recognise the care with which the jurisdiction should be exercised; should take into account amongst other things whether there is other evidence in the possession of the prosecution to support the charge; or whether the application under section 7 is a fishing expedition in the hope of finding some material on which the charge can be hung.

. . . if [justices] are always alive to the requirement of not making the order extend beyond the true purposes of the charge before them, and if in consequence they limit the period of the disclosure of the bank account to a period which is strictly relevant to the charge before them; and if finally they recognise the importance of considering whether there is other evidence in the possession of the prosecution before they provide the bank account as perhaps the only evidence, I feel . . . they will in fact produce a situation in which the section is used properly, wisely and in support of the interests of justice, and will not allow it to be used as an instrument of oppression . . .

Courts should only make an order under section 7 under 'careful consideration' and only when it is to strengthen an existing case. In *R. v. Nottingham Justices ex p. Lynn*,[68] it was stated that applications under section 7 should not be used as fishing expeditions to create a case.

Proof of Due Execution

Producing the document itself (or secondary evidence of it) is one matter. It is also necessary to prove that it was made at the time and in the manner alleged by the person adducing the document as evidence. In other words, a proper foundation must be laid. For example, there are statutory guidelines where the document is produced by a computer. Under the Police and Criminal Evidence Act 1984:

69.—(1) In any proceedings, a statement in a document produced by a computer shall not be admissible as evidence of any fact stated therein unless it is shown —

[68] (1984) 79 Cr.App.R. 238.

a) that there are no reasonable grounds for believing that the statement is inaccurate because of improper use of the computer;

b) that at all material times the computer was operating properly, or if not, that any respect in which it was not operating properly or was out of operation was not such as to affect the production of the document or the accuracy of its contents; . . .

The conditions in section 69 can be satisfied by a certificate from "a person in a responsible position in relation to the operation of the computer" that the computer was properly used and in proper working order and the original supplier of the information must not be available to give evidence.[69] However evidence of the proper working of the computer can also be given orally by a wider range of witnesses.[70]

In *R. v. Shepherd*[71] the charge was shoplifting. The store used computerised checkouts which read the bar code on the item being purchased to recognise the item being bought, to know the price and to generate a till roll. The evidence against the alleged shoplifter was that the till roll showed no trace of the items found in her possession. The provenance of the till rolls was explained to the court by the store detective who described the computer operations, having collected all the till rolls and examined them without finding any trace of the relevant items. The court accepted this as satisfying the requirements of section 69. But it is not evident whether the till rolls were produced in court. If they were, the oral testimony was adequate for the "proof of due execution" and the till rolls themselves were the original documents satisfying the primary evidence rule for "proof of contents". But if the till rolls (nor copies of them) were not produced in court, it is difficult to see that the oral evidence of the detective was admissible as secondary evidence of the contents.

In civil proceedings, there are no such preconditions laid down for computer generated documents. These previously existed under section 5 of the Civil Evidence Act 1968 but this section was repealed and not replaced in 1995. The Law Commission questioned whether the requirements provided any real safeguards in relation to the reliability of the hardware or software concerned and provided no protection against the inaccurate inputing of data:

Law Commission Report: *The Hearsay Rule in Civil Proceedings* (1993 Law Comm. No. 216) paras. 3.14–3.21, at para. 3.17

A particular example is automatic stock control systems, which are now in common use and which allow for purchase orders to be automatically produced. Under such systems evidence of contract formation will lie solely in the electronic messages automatically generated by the seller's and buyer's computers. It is easy to see how

[69] Police and Criminal Evidence Act 1984, Sched. 3, para. 8.
[70] *R. v. Shepherd* [1993] 1 All E.R. 225 at 231b.
[71] [1993] 1 All E.R. 225.

uncertainty as to how the courts may deal with the proof and enforceability of such contracts is likely to stifle development and effective use of such technology. Furthermore, uncertainty may deter parties from agreeing that contracts made in this way are to be governed by English law and litigated in the English courts.

The uncertainty generated by section 5 was not to be resolved by creating new and inevitably complex conditions of admissibility. The common law had survived without guidelines for verifying these, non-written, forms of document, although a witness should testify to the circumstances in which a security video was recorded, a photo was taken or news film produced.

Law Commission, *op. cit.*

It is interesting to compare the technical manner in which the admissibility of computer-generated records has developed, compared with cases concerning other forms of sophisticated technologically produced evidence, for example, radar records.[72] In the *Statue of Liberty* case radar records, produced without human involvement and reproduced in photographic form, were held to be admissible to establish how a collision of two ships occurred. It was held that this was 'real' evidence, no different in kind from a monitored tape recording of a conversation. Furthermore, in these cases, no extra tests of reliability need to be met and the common law rebuttable presumption is applied, that the machine was in order at the material time. The same presumption[73] has been applied to intoximeter printouts.

In civil proceedings, where the document is generated by technology, the Commission suggests that there is a rebuttable presumption[74] that the machinery is in proper working order. Where the document is a more traditional, written document, the common law has more specific, positive, demands in relation to proof of handwriting or proof of attestation.

(a) evidence of handwriting: it is necessary to prove that a letter, a contract or a lease was written or signed by the person that purported to write or sign it. This can be done:

(1) by direct evidence by the signatory, witnesses or someone who saw the execution of the document;
(2) by the opinion of a non-expert who is familiar with the handwriting in question. In:

***Doe d. Mudd v. Suckermore* (1837) 5 Ad. & El. 703 at 739, *per* Lord Denman C.J.**

He did not see him sign it; nor has he ever seen him write; but this is professedly immaterial, if he has had other adequate means of obtaining a

[72] *Statue of Liberty supra.*
[73] *Castle v. Cross* [1985] 1 All E.R. 87.
[74] This could only place an evidential burden on the opposing party.

knowledge of his hand . . . The clerk who constantly read the letters, the broker who has ever consulted upon them, is as competent to judge whether another signature is that of the writer of the letters, as the merchant to whom they were addressed. The servant who has habitually carried letters addressed by me to others has an opportunity of obtaining a knowledge of my writing though he never saw me write, or received a letter from me . . .

(3) by means of the Criminal Procedure Act 1865:

8.—Comparison of a disputed writing with any writing proved to the satisfaction of the judge to be genuine shall be permitted to be made by witnesses; and such writings, and the evidence of witnesses respecting the same, may be submitted to the court and jury as evidence of the genuineness or otherwise of the writing in dispute.

This is applicable in civil or criminal proceedings. In *R. v. Ewing*[75] the Court of Appeal had to decide on the meaning of the phrase "satisfaction of the judge":

R. v. Ewing [1983] 2 All E.R. 645 at 652j–653d, _per_ O'Connor L.J.

In our judgment, the words in section 8 of the 1865 Act, 'any writing proved to the satisfaction of the judge to be genuine', do not say anything about the standard of proof to be used, but direct that it is the judge, and not the jury, who is to decide, and the standard of proof is governed by common law . . . It follows that when the section is applied in civil cases, the civil standard of proof is used, and when it is applied in criminal cases, the criminal standard should be used . . .

. . . We hold that in a criminal trial, where handwriting is to be used for comparison under s.8, it should be proved to the satisfaction of the judge to be genuine, and the standard of proof should be the ordinary criminal standard, namely proof beyond reasonable doubt.

Expert witnesses are permitted to state opinion on authorship and juries should not be invited to make comparison without expert assistance — as in *R. v. Tilley*[76] where jurors were supplied with photographs and a magnifying glass! But jurors should also not be directed to accept inevitably the evidence of an expert witness, even where that is uncontradicted, although there is a fine line for the judge to draw and he or she must not invite juries to disregard such testimony in favour of their own unaided lay opinion.

(b) proof of attestation: due execution sometimes requires witnesses to the signatures on the document. To prove a will at common law, for example, one of the attesting witnesses should be called to prove attestation. An attesting witness is a witness of the court and can be cross-examined or

[75] [1983] 2 All E.R. 645 overruling *R. v. Angeli* [1978] 3 All E.R. 950.
[76] [1961] 3 All E.R. 406.

contradicted even by the party seeking to rely on the document. Such a witness cannot claim legal privilege. Only if the witnesses are dead, mad, beyond jurisdiction or untraceable can the document be proved by other means such as proof of handwriting of one of the witnesses.

Section 3 of the Evidence Act 1938 now allows such documents to be proved by other means:

> 3.—Subject as hereinafter provided, in any proceedings, whether civil or criminal, an instrument to the validity of which attestation is requisite may, instead of being proved by an attesting witness, be proved in the manner in which it may be proved if no attesting witness were alive;
>
> Provided that nothing in this section shall apply to proof of wills or other testamentary documents.

In contrast to these positive requirements for authentification, there are some exceptions:

(a) public documents: it is necessary to distinguish public from private documents. For public documents, mere production of an admissible copy is normally sufficient as the statutes, such as those mentioned above, which provide for the admissibility of the copy, often dispense with the need to prove due execution. This reflects a common law rebuttable presumption that official documents which prima facie are properly executed are assumed to be in fact properly executed in the absence of the party adversely affected by such a document producing evidence to the contrary

(b) ancient private documents: for private documents, a presumption that they have been properly executed only arises when the document is shown to be over 20 years old[77] and has been in proper custody for that period. Proper custody does not require proof that the document was in the best and most proper place, as long as the custody was reasonable and natural in the circumstances. In *Meath (Bishop) v. Winchester (Marquis)*[78] documents which had belonged to a dead bishop and which should have gone to his successor were found amongst his private papers held by his family. Was this "proper custody"?

Meath (Bishop) v. Winchester (Marquis) (1836) 3 Bing N.C. 183 at 201, _per_ Tindal C.J.

These documents were found in a place in which, and under the care of persons with whom, papers of Bishop Dopping might naturally and reasonably be expected to be found; and that is precisely the custody which gives authenticity to documents found within it; for it is not necessary that they should be found in the best and

[77] At common law, the period was 30 years but 20 years was substituted by the Evidence Act 1938.

[78] (1836) 3 Bing N.C. 183.

most proper place of deposit. If documents continue in such custody there never would be any question as to their authenticity; but it is when documents are found other than in their proper place of deposit that investigation commences, whether it was reasonable and natural under the circumstances in the particular case, to expect that they should have been in the place where they are actually found; for it is obvious that whilst there can only be one place of deposit strictly and absolutely proper, there may be various and many that are reasonable and probable . . .

There are other presumptions relating to all (not necessarily ancient) documents: a document is presumed to have been executed on the date it bears[79] and that any alterations to the document were made before the execution of that document. However this latter presumption does not apply to wills where it is presumed that any alterations are made after execution.[80] Where such presumptions apply, it normally changes the legal burden of proof on that issue so that burden falls on the party adversely affected to adduce evidence and prove that the document was executed on a different date or was altered after execution.

(c) admitted by opponent: in civil proceedings due execution can be admitted under R.S.C., Ord. 27, rr.1 and 2 and in criminal proceedings under section 10 of the Criminal Justice Act 1967.

(d) failure to deny authenticity: in civil proceedings, a party is deemed to admit authenticity where a list of documents is served by way of discovery and the party fails to deny that authenticity by way of pleadings or notice. This comes under R.S.C., Ord. 27, r.4.

Real Evidence

As has been explained, information can be presented to the court in different forms: through the oral evidence of a physically present witness, through documents or through real evidence such as material objects produced in court from the nature and condition of which the jury is invited to draw conclusions. But real evidence is not restricted to physical objects but also encompasses facts such as the demeanour of witnesses or visits to the site of an occurrence.

Material objects

The trier of fact can draw conclusions from the object itself. For example, under section 1(4) of the Prevention of Crime Act 1953, an offensive weapon includes items that have been adapted to cause injury. The jury can draw their own conclusions as to whether the item has been adapted from

[79] *Anderson v. Weston* (1840) 6 Bing N.C. 296.
[80] *Doe d. Tatum v. Catomore* (1851) 16 Q.B. 745.

the production in court, say, of the nail-studded baseball bat. In *Line v. Taylor*[81] there was an action for keeping a fierce and mischievous dog. The judge allowed the dog to be brought into court and told the jury that they might assess whether it was vicious from their own experience of dogs and from their observations of this particular animal. However a jury will often need expert assistance on the inferences that can be properly drawn from the object.

An object is admissible under general conditions of admissibility, that is, if it is relevant, possesses sufficient probative weight and its admission would not be unduly prejudicial. A proper foundation would need to be laid to establish that relevance. No further criteria need to be satisfied. Thus the boundary between real evidence and documents must be properly demarcated. In *R. v. Hunt*[82] the charge was one of seditious meeting and riot. Part of the prosecution case was that there were various banners with inflammatory slogans. Oral evidence was admitted of the wording on the banners:

R. v. Hunt (1820) 3 B. & Ald. 566 at 574, _per_ Abbott C.J.

. . . I think it was not necessary either to produce the flags or to give notice to the defendants to produce them. The cases requiring the production of a writing itself will be found to apply to writings of a very different character. There is no authority to show that in a criminal case ensigns, banners, or other things exhibited to public view, and of which the effect depends upon such public exhibition, must be produced or accounted for on the part either of the prosecutor or of the defendants. And in many instances the proof of such matters from eyewitnesses, speaking to what they saw on the occasion, has been received, and its competency was never, to my knowledge, called in question until the present time. Inscriptions used on such occasions are the public expression of the sentiments of those who bear and adopt them, and have rather the character of speeches than of writings. If we were to hold that words inscribed on a banner so exhibited could not be proved without the production of the banner, I know not upon what reason a witness should be allowed to mention the colour of the banner or even to say that he saw a banner displayed, for the banner itself may be said to be the best possible evidence of its existence and its colour. And if such parol proof may be received generally, the proof at this trial was properly received . . .

It is difficult not to see the banner as a document which should nowadays require the prosecution to produce primary evidence, *i.e.* the banner itself.[83] However although that part of the decision can be criticised, *Hunt* is some authority for the proposition that the best evidence rule does not apply to material objects and there is no requirement to produce the thing itself. Secondary and oral evidence is admissible.[84]

[81] (1862) 3 F&F 731.
[82] (1820) 3 B&Ald 566.
[83] Under section 27 of the Criminal Justice Act 1988, a copy would suffice — would a photograph of the banner be a copy?
[84] *R. v. Francis* (1874) 12 Cox C.C. 612.

Appearance of persons or animals

The height, weight, colour of eyes or hair or other personal characteristics of a person, such as poor hearing or sight can be important items of information as can a particular local accent. Frequently juries might view security videos and draw their own conclusions by comparing them with their observation of the defendant in court.

Demeanour of witness

Courts have always accepted that the demeanour of witnesses (their frankness, anxiety, evasiveness or attitude to the court) is an element of information that can be used to give greater or lesser weight to the credibility of the testimony. Appeal courts have often refused to interfere with jury verdicts on the ground that the jurors had had the opportunity to see and assess the witnesses. Yet this common sense that jurors are able to differentiate between the truthful and untruthful witness is increasingly being doubted.[85]

Stone M., "Instant Lie Detection? Demeanour and Credibility in Criminal Trials" [1991] Crim.L.R. 821 at 829

There is no sound basis for assessing credibility from demeanour. There is no known physiological connection between the brain processes of a lying person and any bodily or vocal signs. Also, psychological research confirms that there are no specific physical signs of lying, although there are physical expressions of emotions, including anxiety. Bodily or vocal emotional clues to sincerity in normal relationships tend to be neutralised in court. Witnesses are strangers. They are controlled, can only answer questions and give edited testimony. Witnesses tend to be inhibited and to lose their spontaneity. The demeanour of witnesses tends to be flattened and sterilised so that it has minimal, if any, value for assessing credibility.

Anxiety or relaxation, even if detected correctly, cannot be relied on to indicate veracity. Truthful witnesses may be anxious, and liars may be, or seem to be, relaxed.

Evidence is evaluated holistically by integrating all of it from every angle. This includes assessing witnesses' personalities, characters and motives as well as objective analysis of evidence, *i.e.* its consistency and probability.

Any significance of demeanour for veracity, would, at best, be relatively minor in this context. Courts should refrain from practising 'instant lie detection; from the demeanour of a single witness. This should never be the basis of crucial decisions, particularly convictions.

Views

This is an inspection by the court of a relevant physical location or of an object that it is too inconvenient to bring to court.[86] All interested parties,

[85] Ekman P., *Telling Lies* (1986).
[86] In *London General Omnibus Co Ltd v. Lavell* [1901] 1 Ch. 135, the item was a bus.

legal representatives and jurors (if involved) should attend. In *R. v. Gurney*[87] the conviction was quashed when one juror was deputed to view and to report back to the other jurors. It was said in *R. v. Hunter*[88] that the judge should always be present at a view. In that case the accused was charged with importing cannabis through Newport docks and the judge sent the jury to see the docks but did not accompany them.

In *Buckingham v. Daily News Ltd*[89] the plaintiff was injured while cleaning a machine at his place of work. He sued his employers. The court inspected the machine and watched a demonstration of the operation. Judgment was given for the defendants:

Buckingham v. Daily News Ltd [1956] 2 Q.B. 534 at 539–543, *per* Birkett L.J.

[The] substantial submission that [counsel] makes is that what the judge did in this case was something forbidden by law, according to the authorities; namely, that he cast to the winds the evidence that was given for the plaintiff in this case and substituted for that evidence the impression which he had gained when he made the view . . .

In a case which I tried it was alleged that an accident had been caused by a defective stairway. The parties said: We would like you to see it; you can form your own view by seeing the stairway. I went to see the stairway. I had in mind what was said upon the one side and the other, and could make up my own mind whether, in my view, every relevant fact being before me, it was a reasonable thing to say it was a dangerous stairway or a dangerous floor, a too-highly polished floor, and matters of that kind. As a judge of first instance, I visited factories, workshops, shops, cinemas — all for the purpose of seeing for myself the nature of the place where the accident occurred — the very material upon which the accident was itself founded.

Then, in addition to that, there are the exhibits that are brought into court. I have seen the model of the side of a house, with all the elaborate modern scaffolding, in order to save me and the parties making a journey to where the house was, the parties having agreed that that model was a faithful representation of the scaffolding and the house. I have seen models of aeroplanes in which it was alleged that accidents had occurred, such models being brought into court by the wish of the parties, so that I could see for myself and form my own opinion.

My own view in that respect is supported by what was said by Denning L.J. in *Goold v. Evans & Co.*[90] . . . Denning L.J. said:

> It is a fundamental principle of our law that a judge must act on the evidence before him and not on outside information; and further, the evidence on which he acts must be given in the presence of both parties, or, at any rate, each party must be given an opportunity of being present. Speaking for myself, I think that a view is part of the evidence, just as much as an exhibit. It is real evidence. The tribunal sees the real thing instead of having a drawing or a photograph of it. But, even if a view is not evidence, the same principles apply.

[87] [1976] Crim.L.R. 567.
[88] [1985] 2 All E.R. 173.
[89] [1956] 2 Q.B. 534.
[90] [1951] 2 T.L.R. 1189.

> I would very respectfully adopt that language and say that when a judge goes to see machinery, and sees it in operation when the parties are present and everything is done regularly and in order, it is just the same as though the machinery were brought into court and the demonstration made in the well of the court . . .

Demonstrations can also include reconstructions of a crime. In *Li Shu-ling v. R.*[91] the appellant reconstructed the crime on video. The Privy Council accepted the video as admissible evidence of the accused's confession. In *R. v. Thomas*[92] the police made a video of the route of a car chase as evidence of the defendant's reckless driving. As such it was no different in principle from the use of maps and photographs to illustrate the events to the jury. However this has to be distinguished from *R. v. Quinn*[93] where the prosecution sought to introduce a film purporting to be a reconstruction of the actual events of the night in question. This was held to be inadmissible as such a film could never be sufficiently accurate.

[91] [1988] 3 All E.R. 138.
[92] [1986] Crim.L.R. 682.
[93] [1961] 3 All E.R. 88.

6

IMMUNITIES FROM TESTIFYING: PUBLIC INTEREST IMMUNITY

Access to Evidence

Zuckerman A., "Privilege and public interest" in Tapper C. (ed), *Crime, Proof and Punishment* (1981) 248 at 248–249

It is a fundamental principle in the administration of justice that parties to litigation have a right to bring before the court all evidence relevant to their case and to call on others to produce such evidence as they may have. This right is derivative from the right to equal and just trial. Without it the efficacy of substantive rights would be much reduced and rendered uncertain. This principle — which may for convenience be termed the principle of unimpeded access to evidence — is therefore of cardinal constitutional significance and bears close relation to the constitutional right of unimpeded access to the courts of law generally. Although these two principles have much in common, both on account of their goals and their supremacy over other, lesser, principles, the courts have not been nearly as zealous in upholding the former as they have been in relation to the latter. The principle of access is particularly important in an adversary system of adjudication where litigants have to rely on their own efforts to find and present evidence. More specifically, this principle serves two basic goals: securing the correctness of legal decisions on question of fact and promoting procedural fairness. Although partially overlapping, these two goals are somewhat distinct. The first goal has to do with ensuring that the correctness of the actual result of litigation is not distorted by the absence of a relevant piece of evidence, as would be the case if access to the only evidence in support of an allegation was barred. The cogency of an inference of fact is a function of two factors: first, the logical correctness of the conclusion on the evidence presented to the court and, secondly, the extent to which such evidence as was presented was complete. The conclusion may well be logically flawless on the evidence presented, but if there is further relevant evidence which was not presented, this logically correct conclusion may be in fact unreliable, and at least the weight of the conclusion is reduced; it is therefore less certain that justice will be done. The second goal is that of promoting confidence in the machinery of justice as a just and efficient means of resolving disputes. When a litigant is denied access to relevant evidence he may understandably feel aggrieved, whether or not such evidence would have affected the actual result of the litigation; whether or not justice has been done, it would not appear to have been done.

The principle of access to evidence is embodied in the statement that all witnesses who are competent to testify can be compelled to testify through subpoena or witness summons. This must be qualified:

(1) there are certain competent witnesses who cannot be compelled to give evidence, especially the accused and the accused's spouse.[1]
(2) there are other witnesses who cannot be compelled to give information about certain subjects and are able to claim immunity from testifying. If, as is often the case, that information is contained in a document, that document also cannot be received into evidence.

In this latter group, there are three central immunities: there is the privilege against self-incrimination; there is the privilege that attaches to legal advice and to litigation; and there is public interest immunity. There is also a limited concept of confidentiality.

Immunity is an issue which emerges in relation to the provision of information in advance of trial, particularly in relation to discovery of documents.[2] It is a question which can arise in the context of both criminal and civil proceedings although legal professional privilege tends to be of more significance in civil work. Public interest immunity has become of greater importance in criminal proceedings as a result of the increase in the proactive and intelligence-based side of police work which means that the police are less willing to release information about informants or police procedures. The enhanced duty of the prosecution to disclose unused material[3] has meant more claims by the police for immunity and non-disclosure.

Public Immunity versus Private Privilege

We have seen that it is a major principle of litigation that parties should disclose all relevant evidence for inspection. This rule is based on the public interest involved in the proper administration of justice. But it can be overridden by broader public interests or by certain private interests, principally legal professional privilege, the privilege against self-incrimination and a limited press privilege. There are differences between the public and the private:

(a) waiver of privilege: when privilege is based upon a private interest, the party to whom the privilege attaches has to assert it but he or she can also waive it.[4] Waiver can be express or it can be implied through disclosure.

[1] See 263, *et seq.*
[2] See 313, *et seq.*
[3] See 321, *et seq.*
[4] See 215, *et seq.*

This is not the case with public interest immunity. Anyone, including the court and those not party to the proceedings, can object to disclosure on the ground of public policy. It is doubtful that the public policy objection can be waived. In *Rogers v. Secretary of State for the Home Department*[5] Lord Simon stated categorically[6] that it is not a privilege that can be waived by the Crown or by anyone else. But in *Hehir v. Metropolitan Police Commissioner*,[7] the plaintiff was suing the police for false imprisonment. He had previously and unsuccessfully complained about his treatment and there had been an inquiry under section 49 of the Police Act 1964. At the hearing, the police sought to cross-examine him on his statement to the inquiry. The Court of Appeal considered that, although in this case such material was immune from disclosure, it was arguable that public interest immunity might cease to apply if the maker of the statement wished disclosure to be made.[8]

There are other dicta suggesting that public interest immunity could be waived where the maker of the statement is willing for the information to be disclosed.

Campbell v. Tameside Metropolitan Borough Council [1982] 2 All E.R. 791 at 795e–g, _per_ Lord Denning M.R.

I know that in the days of the old Crown privilege it was often said that it could not be waived. That is still correct when the documents are in the vital category spoken of by Lord Reid in *Conway v. Rimmer*.[9] This category includes all those documents which must be kept top secret because the disclosure of them would be injurious to national defence or to diplomatic relations or the detection of crime (as the names of informers). But not where the documents come within Lord Reid's lower category. This category includes those documents which are kept confidential in order that subordinates should be frank and candid in their reports, or for any other good reason. In those cases the privilege can be waived by the maker and recipients of the confidential document.[10]

Lord Denning's suggestion that there were two categories of documents (secret documents which were wholly immune and confidential documents where public interest immunity might be waived) fell on stony ground. In essence, his Lordship was putting the cart before the horse. The first decision for the court is whether this is a case where public interest immunity applies. This decision, as we shall see, involves the court performing a balancing act between, on the one hand, the public interest in

[5] [1972] 2 All E.R. 1057.
[6] *ibid.* at 1066d–e.
[7] [1982] 2 All E.R. 335.
[8] This argument also found favour with Lord Cross in *Alfred Crompton Amusement Machines Ltd v. Customs and Excise Commissioners (No. 2)* [1973] 2 All E.R. 1169 at 1185e.
[9] [1968] 1 All E.R. 874.
[10] The old term of "Crown Privilege" has long since been superseded by the phrase "public interest immunity".

the proper administration of justice (that is, putting all relevant information before the court) and, on the other, the specific public interest in not disclosing this specific item of information. Many factors are involved in this balancing process, not least the nature of the document, its significance to the case and whether the information is in the public domain or whether the makers or recipients of the statements object to disclosure. There is little point in keeping information secret where "owners" of that information are willing for it to be revealed. In other words, the fact of the maker's willingness to give evidence or to reveal the information goes to the question of the weight of the public interest involved and not to the issue of whether that public interest should be waived.

The better view is that, once such an interest does exist, it cannot be waived.

Makanjuola v. Commissioner of Police of the Metropolis [1992] 3 All E.R. 617 at 623e–j, *per* Bingham L.J.

> . . . Where a litigant asserts that documents are immune from production or disclosure on public interest grounds he is not (if the claim is well founded) claiming a right but observing a duty. Public interest immunity is not a trump card vouchsafed to certain privileged players to play when and as they wish. It is an exclusionary rule, imposed on parties in certain circumstances, even where it is to their disadvantage in the litigation. This does not mean that in any case where a party holds a document in a class prima facie immune he is bound to persist in an assertion of immunity even where it is held that, on any weighing of the public interest, in withholding the document against the public interest in disclosure for the purpose of furthering the administration of justice, there is a clear balance in favour of the latter. But it does, I think, mean: (1) that public interest immunity cannot in any ordinary sense be waived, since, although one can waive rights, one cannot waive duties; (2) that, where a litigant holds documents in a class prima facie immune, he should (save perhaps in a very exceptional case) assert that the documents are immune and decline to disclose them, since the ultimate judge of where the balance of public interest lies is not him but the court; and (3) that, where a document is, or held to be, in an immune class, it may not be used for any purpose whatever in the proceedings to which the immunity applies, and certainly cannot (for instance) be used for the purposes of cross-examination.

The argument is that public interest immunity involves the observance of a duty which cannot be waived. This raises the question as to the extent to which a person asserting the immunity, be he or she a senior police officer or a minister, of the Crown, should inquire into the weight of the public interest factors involved. This is discussed below.

(b) the use of secondary evidence: when a document (or testimony) is excluded, is it just that document itself that is the subject of that exclusion or can the contents be proved by some other means? With regard to private privilege, documents must be guarded carefully since if their contents become known, secondary evidence may be admissible.[11]

[11] See 217, *et seq.*

Where public interest immunity applies, a party cannot use secondary evidence. Looking at the facts of *Rogers*[12] the applicant had requested a gaming licence from the responsible public body, the Gaming Board. The Board had taken advice from the police and refused to grant the licence. The applicant obtained, by improper means, a copy of the letter from the police to the Board which he considered libellous and brought a private prosecution for criminal libel. He sought to call the secretary of the Gaming Board as a witness in order that he might produce the letter. The House of Lords held that the letter was covered by public interest immunity and its contents could be proved neither by the oral testimony of the secretary nor by production of the purloined copy. Where facts are excluded on grounds of public policy, they cannot be proved by secondary evidence.

Sometimes it would be against the public interest to disclose the facts that are contained in the document. No wartime court would have permitted proof of the method of construction of the submarine *Thetis*, the subject of the action in *Duncan v. Cammell Laird & Co Ltd*,[13] whether by production of the plans or by the testimony of workmen who built it. But such a blanket ban is inappropriate in many other cases. In *Makanjuola*[14] the plaintiff alleged that she had been assaulted by a police officer. She complained and there was an investigation, leading to a disciplinary tribunal and further to a disciplinary appeals tribunal. The plaintiff sought, *inter alia*, the witness statements taken in the course of the investigation and the evidence given before the tribunals. The Court of Appeal held that these documents were covered by public interest immunity.[15] Yet in any actual trial of the action for assault, the plaintiff (and any other witness) would be able to testify as to her recollection of the assault even though these facts would have been covered in her witness statement and in any evidence to the disciplinary tribunal. Presumably no witness could be cross-examined on any previous inconsistent statement made in a witness statement or given in evidence before the tribunal.

There is obviously a distinction here between the *Thetis* situation where public interest immunity applies not only to the discovery of the documents but also to their contents — had a victim of the tragedy survived, testimony which revealed aspects of the construction of the submarine, however relevant, would be excluded as a result of the public interest rule. Can this be contrasted with a police complaints scenario where public interest immunity applies only to the discovery of the document? Information already in the hands of the parties, although replicated in the document, can be reproduced. In *Air Canada v. Secretary of State for Trade (No. 2)*,[16] airlines using Heathrow challenged increased landing charges

[12] See *supra*.
[13] [1942] 1 All E.R. 587.
[14] See *supra*.
[15] Although now see the House of Lords' decision in *R. v. Chief Constable of the West Midlands ex parte Wiley* [1994] 3 All E.R. 420.
[16] [1983] 1 All E.R. 910.

and brought an action against the Trade Secretary and the British Airports Authority arguing that he had forced the BAA into this action and had taken irrelevant considerations into account. They sought discovery of ministerial documents which related to the formulation of the policy. The House of Lords rejected an argument that Cabinet minutes were automatically immune from disclosure but considered that the information contained in the minutes added little to the plaintiffs' case:

Air Canada v. Secretary of State for Trade (No. 2) [1983] 1 All E.R. 910 at 920f–j, _per_ Lord Wilberforce

There is . . . the allegation that the Secretary of State took 'irrelevant' considerations into account in that his dominant purpose was to contain the public sector borrowing requirement and to implement government policy in accordance with a White Paper. As to this allegation, there is available the White Paper on *The Nationalised Industries* (Cmnd 7131), there is also available the text of the statement made by the Secretary of State in the House Of Commons on 26 February 1980, and a letter dated 13 December 1979 from the Department of Trade to the managing director of BAA. These documents are direct and primary evidence as to the policy in fact followed by the Secretary of State in relation to the matters complained of and the appellants' case . . . for good or ill, must primarily depend on them. By contrast, the documents of which inspection is sought relate to the formulation of this policy . . . As compared with the pronouncements I have referred to, they are of a wholly secondary character. I am unable to see that any case, still less any convincing case, can be made for saying that, even assuming that they are admissible at all, they would add, in any material way to the first hand evidence which has been provided.

PUBLIC INTEREST IMMUNITY

In conflict with the principle that all relevant information should be disclosed to the court is the equally important idea that information should not be publicly revealed in court that is injurious to the public interest. As already discussed, this principle cannot be waived and, if neither party to the proceedings claims the immunity, the court or another person such as a government minister should assert it.

A brief history — ministerial certificates

There are two themes in the development of public interest immunity. The first issue is the substantive one as to how wide the net of immunity is cast: what categories of information attract it? Secondly comes a procedural point as to who should decide whether a particular document is covered by public interest immunity: is this the province of the court of trial or of the relevant minister of the Crown? These two questions were linked in the sense that until the 1960s, there was a clear rule that where such public interest was claimed by the requisite certificate from a minister, that would be accepted by the courts. This was normally claimed, not on the basis of the contents of the particular document, but on the class to which the document belonged. Consequently this meant that public interest immunity (or Crown privilege, as it was known) covered a broad range of public service records that had little to do with national defence or vital state interests.

Documents with a genuine sensitivity can be seen in early cases such as *Asiatic Petroleum Co Ltd v. Anglo-Persian Oil Co Ltd*[17] where the court refused to permit disclosure of documents which would reveal military plans. Similarly, *Duncan v. Cammell Laird* involved the sinking of the submarine, *Thetis*. There was an action for damages for personal injury and the plaintiffs sought discovery of documents including contracts with the Admiralty which would reveal the design of a new submarine. Lord Simon spelt out the rule:

> The rule that the interest of the State must not be put in jeopardy by producing documents which would injure it is a principle to be observed in administering justice, quite unconnected with the interests or claims of the particular parties in litigation . . . [18]

It is suggested that this case is early authority that judges may inspect and decide upon a claim of privilege but Lord Simon did say that a minister:

> . . . ought not to take the responsibility of withholding production except in cases where the public interest would otherwise be damnified, for example, where disclosure would be injurious to national defence, or to good diplomatic relations, or where the practice of keeping a class of documents secret is necessary for the proper functioning of the public service.[19]

The practice developed that the minister's decision was dispositive and that public interest immunity covered defence, diplomatic relations and the proper functioning of public service. If Lord Simon intended all three to be of a similar level of importance, it is doubtful whether he ever meant for routine, low-level, administrative communications to be included in this latter category. However, he talked of:

> . . . the view that the public interest requires a particular class of communications with, or within, a public department to be protected from production on the ground that the candour and completeness of such communications might be prejudiced if they were ever liable to be disclosed in subsequent litigation rather than upon the contents of the particular document itself.[20]

[17] [1916–1917] All E.R. Rep 637.
[18] [1942] 1 All E.R. 587 at 592.
[19] *ibid.* at 595g.
[20] *ibid.* at 592b.

The result was that the contents of the document itself were not considered and instead whole classes of innocuous records were protected by ministerial fiat. The rationale was that civil servants would not communicate fully and candidly with each other unless they had the shield of immunity from disclosure. In *Ellis v. Home Office*[21] the plaintiff sued the Home Office when he was assaulted by another prisoner. He sought but was refused medical reports on the attacker's mental state. Similarly in a divorce action, *Broome v. Broome*,[22] reconciliation reports, written by the social welfare service for the armed services, were treated as subject to Crown privilege. Forty years later, class claims still caused problems:

> . . . experience suggests that if public interest immunity class claims are sanctioned, Whitehall departments will inevitably seek to bring within the recognised classes an increasing range of documents. I do not believe that the instinctive Whitehall reaction to seek to withhold Government documents from public inspection is likely to change.[23]

The civil service's desire for secrecy and such decisions as *Ellis* raised the questions of whether the judge should have the discretionary power to go behind the ministerial certificate, to inspect the document for himself or herself and to decide whether the public interest in the administration of justice outweighs any injurious effects of disclosure on the State. Were judges to inspect and review the contents of documents, they would necessarily need to review those areas which might attract public interest immunity.

Modern times — the right to inspect

The starting point in modern law is *Conway v. Rimmer*[24] where a probationer police officer was charged and acquitted of theft. Shortly afterwards he was sacked. He brought an action for malicious prosecution against his former superintendent. Both parties wished for various documents to be produced, including the internal reports on the plaintiff's performance as a probationary constable. The Home Secretary certified that he had personally inspected the documents and regarded them as belonging to a class of documents, the production of which would be injurious to the public interest:

Conway v. Rimmer [1988] 1 All E.R. 874 at 880f–889a, *per* Lord Reid

It is universally recognised that here there are two kinds of public interest which may clash. There is the public interest that harm shall not be done to the nation or

[21] [1953] 2 Q.B. 135.
[22] [1955] P. 190.
[23] Sir Richard Scott, *Report of the Inquiry into the Export of Defence Equipment and Dual Use Goods to Iraq and Related Prosecutions* (H.C.P. 1995–96 115), para. K6.16 at 1789.
[24] [1968] 1 All E.R. 874.

the public service by disclosure of certain documents, and there is the public interest that the administration of justice shall not be frustrated by the withholding of documents which must be produced if justice is to be done. There are many cases where the nature of the injury which would or might be done to the nation, or the public service is of so grave a character that no other interest, public or private, can be allowed to prevail over it. With regard to such cases it would be proper to say, as Lord Simon did, that to order production of the document in question would put the interest of the state in jeopardy; but there are many other cases where the possible injury to the public service is much less and there one would think that it would be proper to balance the public interests involved. I do not believe that Lord Simon really meant that the smallest probability of injury to the public service must always outweigh the gravest frustration of the administration of justice.

It is to be observed that . . . Lord Simon referred to the practice of keeping a class of documents secret being 'necessary for the proper functioning of the public service'. But the certificate of the Home Secretary in the present case does not go nearly so far as that. It merely says that the production of a document of the classes to which it refers would be 'injurious to the public service': it does not say what degree of injury is to be apprehended. It may be advantageous to the functioning of the public service that reports of this kind should be kept secret — that is the view of the Home Secretary — but I would be very surprised if anyone said that was necessary . . .

Two questions will arise: first, whether the court is to have any right to question the finality of a Minister's certificate and secondly, if it has such a right, how and in what circumstances that right is to be exercised and made effective.

A Minister's certificate may be given on one or other of two grounds: either because it would be against the public interest to disclose the contents of the particular document or documents in question, or because the document belongs to a class of documents which ought to be withheld whether or not there is anything in the particular document in question disclosure of which would be against the public interest. It does not appear that any serious difficulties have arisen or are likely to arise with regard to the first class. However wide the power of the court may be held to be, cases would be very rare in which it could be proper to question the view of the responsible Minister that it would be contrary to the public interest to make public the contents of a particular document . . . In the present case your lordships are directly concerned with the second class of documents . . .

. . . In this field, however, it is more than ever necessary that in a doubtful case the alleged public interest in concealment should be balanced against the public interest that the administration of justice should not be frustrated. If the Minister, who has no duty to balance these conflicting public interests, says no more than that in his opinion the public interest requires concealment, and if that is to be accepted as conclusive in this field as well as with regards to documents in his possession, it seems to me that not only very serious injustice may be done to the parties, but also that the due administration of justice may be gravely impaired for quite inadequate reasons.

. . . I would therefore propose that the House ought now to decide that the courts have and are entitled to exercise a power and duty to hold a balance between the public interest, as expressed by a Minister, to withhold certain documents or other evidence, and the public interest in ensuring the proper administration of justice. That does not mean that a court would reject a Minister's view: full weight must be given to it in every case, and if the Minister's reasons are of a character which judicial experience is not competent to weigh then the Minister's view must prevail; but experience has shown that reasons given for withholding whole classes of documents are often not of that character . . .

I do not doubt that there are certain classes of documents which ought not to be disclosed whatever their content may be. Virtually everyone agrees that cabinet minutes and the like ought not to be disclosed until such time as they are only of

> historical interest; but I do not think that many people would give as the reason that premature disclosure would prevent candour in the cabinet . . .
>
> It appears to me that, if the Minister's reasons are such that a judge can properly weigh them, he must on the other hand consider what is the probable importance in the case before him of the documents or other evidence to be withheld. If he decides that on the balance the documents probably ought to be produced, I think it would generally be best that he should see them before ordering production and, if he thinks that the Minister's reasons are not clearly expressed, he will have to see the documents before ordering production. I can see nothing wrong in the judge seeing documents without their being shown to the parties . . .

The House of Lords unanimously agreed that the judges had to regain their control over such issues. They held that the minister's certificate was no longer dispositive and that the trial judge has a residual power to inspect and to balance the state interest against the public interest in the proper administration of justice. The House considered the consequences of the *Conway* decision in *Rogers*,[25] concluding that the Gaming Board needed full information in order to identify persons of dubious character and to prevent them from obtaining a gaming licence. Consequently there was a public interest that required that documents of this kind should not be disclosed. But again, as in *Conway v. Rimmer*, there were dicta which suggested that there were certain classes of document that ought never to be disclosed:

> There are also classes of documents and information which for years have been recognised by the law as entitled in the public interest to be immune from disclosure. In such cases the affidavit or certificate of a Minister is hardly necessary. I refer to such documents as Cabinet minutes, minutes of discussions between heads of government departments and despatches from ambassadors abroad. Although different in nature, any evidence as to the sources from which the police obtain their information has always been recognised by the courts as entitled to the same immunity.[26]

Despite such dicta, modern courts have been reluctant to countenance the view that there are any classes of documents that are automatically immune from disclosure, reflecting a public wish to see more open government. In *Burmah Oil Co Ltd v. Bank of England*,[27] an agreement was made between Burmah Oil and the Bank of England. The Bank was acting under the direction of the government with a view to rescuing the company from financial difficulties. One part of the agreement was the sale in 1975 of shares in British Petroleum to the Bank at a price below the current market valuation. As BP shares continued to rise, the company sought to set aside the sale. The Bank's list of documents disclosed the part played by the government in the transaction. These included Bank memos of high level meetings attended by government ministers as well as others

[25] See *supra*.
[26] *Rogers supra* at 1070j–1071b, *per* Lord Salmon.
[27] [1979] 3 All E.R. 700.

of meetings at which government officials but not ministers were present. Ought these to be disclosed? The trial judge refused the company's application for discovery and this was upheld by the House of Lords, but only after they had inspected the documents in question:

Burmah Oil Co. Ltd v. Bank of England [1979] 3 All E.R. 700 at 727f–735g, _per_ Lord Scarman

The truth is that the appeal raises a question of law of great importance. Your Lordships are asked to determine the respective spheres of the executive and the judiciary where the issue is whether documents for which 'public interest immunity' is claimed are to be withheld from disclosure in litigation to which they are relevant. More specifically, the House has to decide whether *Conway v. Rimmer* is definitive of the law, *i.e.* sets limits statute-wise to the power of the court, or is an illustration on its particular facts of a broader principle of judicial review.

. . . Although in the High Court discovery of documents is automatic in most civil litigation, this is no more than a convenient practice ordered and regulated by rules of the court: see R.S.C., Ord. 24, and the recent decision of this House in *Science Research Council v. Nassé*.[28] Discovery of documents remains, ultimately, a matter for the discretion of the court. It is a discretion governed by two general rules of law. The first is that discovery is not to be ordered unless necessary for fairly disposing of the case or for saving costs: R.S.C., Ord. 24.

The second is that only documents in a party's possession and control which relate to the matters in issue are required to be disclosed, but all such documents, subject to certain exceptions, are to be disclosed, whether or not admissible in evidence. Public interest immunity is, of course, an exception. The case law has given an extended meaning to the qualifying clause 'which relate to the matters in issue'. It embraces not only documents directly relevant but also documents which may well lead to a relevant train of enquiry: see *Compagnie Financière Commerciale du Pacifique v. Peruvian Guano Co.*[29] This extended meaning is a vital part of the law of discovery, enabling justice to be done where one party knows the facts and possesses the documents and the other does not.

. . . It is said, and this view commended itself to the majority of the Court of Appeal, that the Bank has given very full discovery of the documents directly relevant to the critical issue in the action, namely the conduct by the Bank of the negotiations with Burmah, that Burmah knows as much about this issue as does the Bank, and that it can be fully investigated and decided on the documents disclosed and the evidence available to Burmah without recourse to documents noting or recording the private discussions between the Bank and the government. On this view, Burmah's attempt to see these documents is no more than a fishing expedition.

I totally reject this view of the case. First, as a matter of law, the documents for which immunity is claimed, relate to the issues in the action and, according to the *Peruvian Guano* formulation, may well assist towards a fair disposal of the case. It is unthinkable that in the absence of a public immunity objection and without a judicial inspection of the documents disclosure would have been refused. Secondly, common sense must be allowed to creep into the picture. Burmah's case is not merely that the Bank exerted pressure: it is that the Bank acted unreasonably, abusing its power and taking an unconscionable advantage of the weakness of Burmah. On these questions the withheld documents may be very revealing. This is not 'pure speculation'.

[28] [1979] 3 All E.R. 673.
[29] (1882) 11 Q.B.D. 55.

. . . the advance made in the law by *Conway v. Rimmer* was that the certificate was not final. I think, therefore, that it would now be inconsistent with principle to hold that the court may not, even in a case like the present, review the certificate and balance the public interest of government to which it alone refers, against the public interest of justice, which is the concern of the court.

I do not therefore accept that there are any classes of documents which, however harmless their contents and however strong the requirement of justice, may never be disclosed until they are only of historical interest. In this respect I think there may well be a difference between a 'class' objection and a 'contents' objection, though the residual power to inspect and to order disclosure must remain in both instances. A Cabinet minute, it is said, must be withheld from production. Documents relating to the formulation of policy at a high level are also to be withheld. But is the secrecy of the 'inner workings of the government machine' so vital a public interest that it must prevail over even the most imperative demands of justice? If the contents of a document concern the national safety, affect diplomatic relations or relate to some sort of state secret of high importance, I can understand an affirmative answer. But if they do not (and it is not claimed in this case that they do), what is so important about secret government that it must be protected even at the price of injustice in our courts?

The reasons given for protecting the secrecy of government at the level of policy-making are two. The first is the need for candour in the advice offered to Ministers; the second is that disclosure 'would create or fan ill-informed or captious public or political criticism'. Lord Reid in *Conway v. Rimmer* thought the second 'the most important reason'. Indeed he was inclined to discount the candour argument.

I think both reasons are factors legitimately to be put into the balance which has to be struck between the public interest in the proper functioning of the public service (*i.e.* the executive arm of government) and the public interest in the administration of justice. Sometimes the public service reasons will be decisive of the issue; but they should never prevent the court from weighing them against the injury which would be suffered in the administration of justice if the document was not to be disclosed. And the likely injury to the cause of justice must also be assessed and weighed. Its weight will vary according to the nature of the proceedings in which disclosure is sought, the relevance of the documents and the degree of likelihood that the document will be of importance in the litigation. In striking the balance, the court may always, if it thinks necessary, itself inspect the documents.

Inspection by the court is, I accept, a power to be exercised only if the court is in doubt, after considering the certificate, the issues in the case and the relevance of the documents whose disclosure is sought. Where documents are relevant (as in this case they are), I would think a pure 'class' objection would by itself seldom quieten judicial doubts, particularly if, as here, a substantial case can be made for saying that disclosure is needed in the interest of justice.

I am fortified in the opinion which I have expressed by the trend towards inspection and disclosure to be found both in the United States and in Commonwealth countries. [His Lordship considered *Nixon v. USA*[30] and *Sankey v. Whitlam*[31]]

For these reasons I was one of a majority of your Lordships who thought it necessary to inspect the ten documents. Having done so, I have no doubt that they are relevant and, but for the immunity claim, would have to be disclosed, but their significance is not such as to override the public service objections to their production. Burmah will not suffer injustice by their non-disclosure, while their

[30] (1975) 418 U.S. 683.
[31] (1978) 21 A.L.R. 505.

disclosure would be, in the opinion of the responsible Minister, injurious to the public service. I would, therefore, dismiss the appeal.

Lord Scarman suggests that there is no class which is automatically excluded from inspection, "I do not accept that there are any classes of document which . . . may never be disclosed". This argument applies even with regard to cabinet minutes, ". . . what is so important about secret government that it must be protected even at the price of injustice in our courts?" The majority the House agreed that the documents could be inspected but having done so, refused to order disclosure. Lord Wilberforce dissented on the issue of inspection, feeling that the need for "candour" was still relevant and underestimated.

The modern authorities are clear that a court can question a claim to withhold disclosure of a document and that a court will inspect the document and decide on the balance between the public interest in full disclosure and the administration of justice as opposed to the public interest which may be damaged by revealing the document. In *Air Canada v. Secretary of State for Trade (No. 2)*,[32] the House of Lords was quite prepared to inspect ministerial papers on the formulation of government policy. Lord Fraser said that ". . . even Cabinet minutes are [not] completely immune from disclosure in a case where, for example, the issue in litigation involves serious misconduct by a Cabinet Minister".[33]
The "class claim" appears to have received its quietus and there is no category of document which in all circumstances is automatically exempt. Until recently there was a presumption of exclusion with regard to one class of documents, namely those related to inquiries into police misconduct under Pt. 9 of the Police and Criminal Evidence Act 1984.[34] This exemption was originally based on the long-recognised refusal to disclose the names of informants to crime.[35] But immunity from disclosure had become automatic, without consideration of the original purpose, covering those who co-operated with such investigations and who were unconcerned by the release of their identity as well as other informants who did wish to remain anonymous. There have been many actions when the court has needed to decide whether to make the documentation from the complaint procedure available to civil litigants suing the police.[36] The general view of the authorities was that adopted by the Court of Appeal in *Makanjuola*:[37]

[32] [1983] 1 All E.R. 910.
[33] *ibid.* at 915c.
[34] Now replaced by the Police Act 1996, ss.65–88.
[35] *Marks v. Beyfus* (1890) 25 Q.B.D. 494; *D v. National Society for the Prevention of Cruelty to Children* [1977] 1 All E.R. 589.
[36] For example, *Neilson v. Laugharne* [1981] 1 All E.R. 829; *Hehir v. Metropolitan Police Commissioner* [1982] 2 All E.R. 335; *Peach v. Metropolitan Police Commissioner* [1986] 2 All E.R. 129; *ex parte Coventry Newspapers Ltd* [1993] 1 All E.R. 86.
[37] See *supra*.

***Makanjuola v. Commissioner of Police of the Metropolis* [1992] 3 All E.R. 617 at 622a–e, *per* Bingham L.J.**

The claim [to public interest immunity] raised an issue on which this court might have taken either one or other of two views. One view, urged by the plaintiff in that action, was that any statement made for the purposes of a section 49 investigation[38] might be used either in disciplinary proceedings or in a criminal prosecution against a police officer and so its contents might become known to the police officer, other witnesses and members of the public at large in the ordinary course of events. Since these consequences would be foreseeable from the outset such statements could not be regarded as confidential and would not be appropriate subjects for public interest immunity.

The competing view was that, in the public interest, statements made for the purposes of a section 49 investigation should be available for use to further those purposes (whether disciplinary and private, or criminal and public) but no other. The underlying public interest asserted was (one infers) in the maintenance of an honourable, disciplined, law-abiding and uncorrupt police force. The protection of that public interest required that allegations of improper or criminal conduct by police officers should be investigated and appropriate action taken. To that end it was necessary that members of the public or other police officers should be encouraged to give any relevant information they had to the appropriate authority without fear of harassment, intimidation or use of any statement in any other proceedings. It was therefore desirable in the public interest that statements made to the appropriate authority investigating a complaint against a police officer should not be liable to be produced or disclosed or referred to in any proceedings save disciplinary or criminal proceedings officially brought against the police officer in question. To hold otherwise would frustrate the statutory purpose of any investigation under this Act.

This view was that immunity was required to uphold the public interest in ". . . an honourable, disciplined, law-abiding and uncorrupt police force". It was reconsidered by the House of Lords in *R. v. Chief Constable of the West Midlands Police ex parte Wiley*[39] in rather different circumstances. The applicant had made complaints against the police which were being investigated by the Police Complaints Authority. The applicant requested that the chief constable give an undertaking not to use the documents arising out of the investigations or to rely on any information in those documents in civil proceedings by the applicant. The applicant sought judicial review of this refusal to give an undertaking. The House of Lords held that a class claim to public interest immunity did not attach generally to all documents coming into existence in consequence of an investigation into a complaint against a police officer:

[38] This refers to the Police Act 1964, s.49, which governed investigations of complaints into the police until replaced by the Police and Criminal Evidence Act 1984, Pt. 9 and subsequently by the Police Act 1996.
[39] [1994] 3 All E.R. 420.

R. v. Chief Constable of the West Midlands Police ex parte Wiley [1994] 3 All E.R. 420 at 445j–446j, per Lord Woolf

. . . the [Police Complaints] authority has accepted that in general the class immunity created by the *Neilson* decision can no longer be justified. However, in my opinion, this is the case, not because of any change in the balance of public interest or change in attitudes since the *Neilson* decision, but because establishing a class of public interest immunity of this nature was never justified. This lack of justification is part of the explanation for the problems which the courts have since had in finding a logical limit to the application of the class and creating a sensible balance between the interest of those involved in subsequent legal proceedings and the interest of those responsible for conducting the investigations into police complaints.

The recognition of a new class-based public interest immunity requires clear and compelling evidence that it is necessary. Yet as the present case has demonstrated, the existence of this class tends to defeat the very object it was designed to achieve. The respondents to the present appeal only launched their proceedings for judicial review to avoid the existence of a situation where their position would be prejudiced as a result of their not being given access to material to which the police had access. Their non-co-operation was brought about because of the existence of the immunity . . . While I agree with Lord Hailsham . . . in *D. v. National Society for the Prevention of Cruelty to Children*[40] that:

> The categories of public interest are not closed, and must alter from time to time whether by restriction or extension as social conditions and social legislation develop.

In my opinion no sufficient case has ever been made out to justify the class of public interest immunity recognised in *Neilson*

The *Neilson* case and the cases in which it was subsequently applied should therefore be regarded as being wrongly decided. This does not, however, mean that public interest immunity can never apply to documents that come into existence in consequence of a police investigation into a complaint. There may be other reasons why because of the contents of a particular document it would be appropriate to extend immunity to that document . . .

This finally clears away the absurdity of this particular blanket immunity, allowing the trial court to determine whether a claim to public interest immunity should be upheld. One of the recommendations of the Scott Report on the Matrix Churchill case[41] was that public interest immunity claims should never be made on a class basis.

Judicial determination of claim

There must, of course, be an objection to disclosure, identifying the documents and the grounds for withholding them. Did the holder of potentially immune material have a duty to lodge an objection? This issue recently arose in the context of the Matrix Churchill case, in which

[40] [1977] 1 All E.R. 589 at 605.
[41] Sir Richard Scott, *op. cit.* para. K6.18 at 1790.

company directors were prosecuted for exporting defence equipment to Iraq and concealing the fact that it would be used for military purposes. Ministers signed public interest immunity certificates for various documents. These documents showed that the Government, in granting licences to the company, were aware of the use to which the equipment would be put. However the Attorney-General's advice to ministers[42] was that they were obliged to resist disclosure even where the documents might prove the innocence of the defendants.[43] In the case itself, the trial judge rejected the claim and the prosecution collapsed. Should the ministers have automatically claimed immunity, as suggested by Bingham L.J. in *Makanjuola*?

***Makanjuola v. Commissioner of Police of the Metropolis* [1992] 3 All E.R. 617 at 623e–j, *per* Bingham L.J.**

. . . Where a litigant asserts that documents are immune from production or disclosure on public interest grounds he is not (if the claim is well founded) claiming a right but observing a duty . . . This does not mean that in any case where a party holds a document in a class prima facie immune he is bound to persist in an assertion of immunity even where it is held that, on any weighing of the public interest, in withholding the document against the public interest in disclosure for the purpose of furthering the administration of justice, there is a clear balance in favour of the latter. But it does, I think, mean: (1) that public interest immunity cannot in any ordinary sense be waived, since, although one can waive rights, one cannot waive duties; (2) that, where a litigant holds documents in a class prima facie immune, he should (save perhaps in a very exceptional case) assert that the documents are immune and decline to disclose them, since the ultimate judge of where the balance of public interest lies is not him but the court . . .

The House of Lords took issue with this position in *ex parte Wiley*:

***R. v. Chief Constable of the West Midlands Police ex parte Wiley* [1994] 3 All E.R. 420 at 424e–j, *per* Lord Templeman**

It has been said that the holder of a confidential document for which public interest immunity may be claimed is under a duty to assert the claim, leaving the court to decide whether the claim is well founded. For my part I consider that when a document is known to be relevant and material, the holder of the document should voluntarily disclose it unless he is satisfied that disclosure will cause substantial harm. If the holder is in doubt he may refer the matter to the court. If the holder decides that a document should not be disclosed then that decision can be upheld or set aside by the judge. A rubber stamp approach to public interest immunity by the holder of a document is neither necessary nor appropriate.

[42] See Written Answer by the Attorney-General on 15th Decision 1993: H.C. Deb. Vol. c.636–7 15.12.1993.

[43] Allan T., "Public Interest Immunity and Minsters' Responsibilities" [1993] Crim.L.R. 600; Zuckerman A., "Public Interest Immunity — A Matter of Prime Judicial Responsibility" [1994] 57 MLR 703; Webb R. "Public Interest Immunity: The Demise of the Duty to Assert" [1995] Crim.L.R. 556.

Although *obiter,* this position would require the holders of sensitive material to come to an initial decision on the contents of a document as to whether to disclose it: they should not adopt a policy of, for example, never disclosing child care records in the absence of a court order.[44] This also allows prosecution authorities more latitude in the disclosure of unused material. It was a position mirrored in the report on the Matrix Churchill affair[45] in which Scott V.-C. recommended[46] that no claim should be put forward by a minister or other person unless they had reflected on the weight of the public interest factors involved and formed the opinion that disclosure would cause substantial harm.

Where an objection has been taken to disclosure on the grounds of public interest immunity, the pattern of events is as follows:

(1) the party who wishes to adduce the evidence must show that the documents are "likely to be necessary" under R.S.C., Ord. 24, r.13(1) either for disposing fairly of the cause or matter or for saving costs. Neither the party seeking disclosure nor the judge[47] see the documents at this point and in *Air Canada* Lord Fraser laid down a strict test before judicial inspection:

> . . . in order to persuade the court even to inspect documents for which public interest immunity is claimed, the party seeking disclosure ought at least to satisfy the court that the documents are very likely to contain material which would give substantial support to his contention on an issue which arises in the case, and that without them he might be 'deprived of the means of . . . proper presentation' of his case.[48]

The airlines in *Air Canada* failed this test since they were unable to show any fact or motive which might be in the privileged documents, which might be significant in the proceedings, and which were not revealed in other material. The rationale for imposing this evidential burden on the party seeking disclosure is to prevent fishing expeditions, but the party will have shown from the pleadings that there is substance to the cause of action. The appearance of the documents on the list for discovery also shows that the party resisting disclosure considers them "related to a matter in the case" under the *Peruvian Guano* rule. Litigants seeking to show that these documents are very likely to assist their case have a significant burden which they are ill-equipped to discharge. On the other hand it would be relatively simple task for the party resisting

[44] But see [1994] Fam. Law 513 at 515.

[45] Sir Richard Scott, *Report of the Inquiry into the Export of Defence Equipment and Dual Use Goods to Iraq and Related Prosecutions* (H.C.P. 1995–96 115).

[46] *ibid.* Vol. 4, para. K6.18 at 1790.

[47] The "judicial peep" suggested by Lord Edmund-Davies in *Burmah Oil supra* at 721g is disapproved of by Lord Fraser in *Air Canada supra* at 917j.

[48] *Air Canada supra* at 917d–f.

disclosure to show that the documents would not be of assistance to the other party. As Cross puts it, "There is some danger that the result of *Air Canada* will . . . be to claw back by the principles of discovery what *Conway v. Rimmer* achieved in liberalising the law of evidence."[49]

(2) if this burden is satisfied, under R.S.C., Ord., 24 r.13(2), it is for the judge to inspect the documents privately, to ensure that they are in a class which *prima facie* attracts public interest immunity, that proper consideration has been given by the person taking the objection and to determine whether the documents are in fact necessary for the disposition of the case.

(3) the final stage of this reasoning process is for the judge to decide whether the public interest in non-disclosure set out in the certificate outweighs the public interest in the efficacy and fairness of the proper administration of justice. But this balancing process should only take place after a proper case for disclosure has been made out. In *Burmah Oil*, Lord Wilberforce said:

> A claim for public interest immunity having been made, on manifestly solid grounds, it is necessary for those who seek to overcome it to demonstrate the existence of a counter-interest calling for disclosure of particular documents. When this is demonstrated, but only then, may the court proceed to a balancing process.[50]

The House agreed that the court should be persuaded that the documents contained material evidence before inspection. But after inspection, the court must engage in a balancing exercise:

Burmah Oil Co. Ltd v. Bank of England [1979] 3 All E.R. 700 at 734a–b, _per_ Lord Scarman

> . . . the balance which has to be struck between the public interest in the proper functioning of the public service (*i.e.* the executive arm of government) and the public interest in the administration of justice. Sometimes the public service reasons will be decisive of the issue; but they should never prevent the court from weighing them against the injury which would be suffered in the administration of justice if the document was not to be disclosed. And the likely injury to the cause of justice must also be assessed and weighed. Its weight will vary according to the nature of the proceedings in which disclosure is sought, the relevance of the documents and the degree of likelihood that the document will be of importance in the litigation. In striking the balance, the court may always, if it thinks necessary, itself inspect the documents.

Certainly the judge must consider the weight that the documents are likely to carry in the litigation as an important criterion,

[49] Tapper C., *Cross and Tapper on Evidence* (8th ed., 1995) 517.
[50] *Burmah Oil supra* at 708f–g.

whether their absence would mean a complete or partial denial of justice to the party concerned and the significance of the proceedings themselves. In *Campbell v. Tameside Metropolitan Borough Council*[51] a teacher had been assaulted by a pupil and sought disclosure of the local education authority's reports on that pupil to show that he should not have been allowed to be educated in an ordinary school:

> A judge conducting the balancing exercise needs to know whether the documents in question are of much or of little weight in the litigation, whether their absence will result in a complete or partial denial of justice to one or the other of the parties or perhaps to both, and what is the importance of the particular litigation to the parties and the public. All these are matters which should be considered if the court is to decide where the public interest lies . . .[52]

When public interest immunity is claimed in criminal proceedings ". . . touching or concerning liberty or conceivably on occasion life, the weight to be attached to the interests of justice is plainly very great indeed".[53]

The objection to disclosure of a document might not be to the contents on which the litigant wishes to rely, but to the publication of sensitive but subsidiary details such as the sources of the information which are not material. Partial disclosure, with names and other sensitive but irrelevant matters covered up is acceptable.[54]

Matters commonly covered by public interest immunity

Public interest immunity does not only cover the workings of central government but also local government, executive agencies, charities, professional organisations, and the police. This is not to imply that particular organisations attract immunity. It is the nature of the information they hold which attracts protection. The mere fact that that information is confidential is insufficient in itself; there has to be a more substantial public interest. Matters of national defence or economic policy are obvious examples. Another pervasive theme is crime detection when it concerns matters which, if public, would assist criminals or deter people from helping the police. Such information will be subject to public interest immunity. A further area where disclosure would be limited would involve the welfare of children. But the scope of public interest immunity is not constrained by precedent.

[51] [1982] 2 All E.R. 791.
[52] *ibid.* at 797f, *per* Ackner L.J.
[53] *R. v. Governor of Brixton Prison ex parte Osman (No. 1)* [1992] 1 All E.R. 108 at 116d, *per* Mann L.J.
[54] *Science Research Council v. Nasse* [1979] 3 All E.R. 673.

In *D. v. National Society for the Prevention of Cruelty to Children*[55] the plaintiff claimed damages after an officer of the NSPCC had falsely alleged that she had mistreated her child. The society acted on information given to it in confidence and the plaintiff sought discovery of documents which would disclose the identity of the informant. Although the decision (not to disclose the identity) rested on the well-established analogy with police informants, Lord Hailsham felt that the "categories of the public interest are not closed and must alter from time to time whether by restriction or extension as social conditions and social legislation develop." Lord Edmund-Davies summarised the position:

D. v. National Society for the Prevention of Cruelty to Children [1977] 1 All E.R. 589 at 618b–619d, _per_ Lord Edmund-Davies

(I) In civil proceedings a judge has no discretion, simply because what is contemplated is the disclosure of information which had passed between persons in a confidential relationship (other than that of lawyer and client), to direct a party to that relationship that he need not disclose that information even though its disclosure is (a) relevant to, and (b) necessary for the attainment of justice in the particular case. If (a) and (b) are established, the doctor or the priest must be directed to answer if, despite the strong dissuasion of the judge, the advocate persists in seeking disclosure. This is also true of all other confidential relationships . . .

(II) But where (I) a confidential relationship exists (other than that of lawyer and client) *and* (ii) disclosure would be in breach of some ethical or social value involving the public interest, the court has a discretion to uphold a refusal to disclose relevant evidence provided it considers that, on balance, the public interest would be better served by excluding such evidence.

(III) In conducting the necessary balancing operation between competing aspects of public interest, the presence (or absence) of involvement of the central government in the matter of disclosure is *not* conclusive either way, though in practice it may affect the cogency of the argument against disclosure . . . .

(IV) The sole touchstone is the public interest, and not whether the party from whom disclosure is sought was acting under a 'duty' — as opposed to merely exercising 'powers'. A party who acted under some duty may find it easier to establish that public interest was involved than one merely exercising powers, but that is another matter.

(V) The mere fact that relevant information was communicated in confidence does not necessarily mean that it need not be disclosed. But where the subject-matter is clearly of public interest, the *additional* fact (if such it be) that to break the seal of confidentiality would endanger that interest will in most (if not all) cases probably lead to the conclusion that disclosure should be withheld. And it is difficult to conceive of any judicial discretion to exclude relevant and necessary evidence save in respect of confidential information communicated in a confidential relationship.

(VI) The disclosure of all evidence relevant to the trial of an issue being at all times a matter of considerable public interest, the question to be determined is whether it is clearly demonstrated that in the particular case the public interest would nevertheless be better served by excluding evidence despite its relevance. If, on balance, the matter is left in doubt, disclosure should be ordered.

[55] [1977] 1 All E.R. 589.

Areas which attract public interest immunity are:

(1) **state interests:** where national defence[56] or diplomatic relations[57] are involved, the judges consider that ministers of the crown are in a better position to evaluate the overall public interest. "National" means the public interest of the U.K. (and possibly those of the European Union) but those requirements may be met if compelling disclosure of confidential information held by or concerning other states would affect relations between the U.K. and the other state. Another state, however, cannot claim public interest immunity on its own behalf.[58]

The court remains the final arbiter even in balancing vital state interests with the requirements of the proper administration of justice. Where the guilt or innocence of defendants is at stake, the court will often inspect documents which appear to deal with important economic and military matters, as was seen in the *Matrix Churchill*[59] affair. Other governmental interests arise, such as the formulation or execution of government policy at high level — both *Burmah Oil* and *Canada Air* involved economic and fiscal policy — which prima facie attract claims to public interest immunity but are not immune from judicial inspection.

(2) **administrative practices:** the history of public interest immunity has seen non-disclosure of more routine administrative information, both governmental and non-governmental. This was justified on the grounds that the proper functioning of public service required candour and openness from officials and from those who supplied information. Disclosure would inhibit this. The candour argument has been attacked but remains a factor, although the court would perhaps look at the specifics of the relationship and not accept (or at least give much weight) to the rationale as a general principle.

> The reasons given for protecting the secrecy of government at the level of policy-making are two. The first is the need for candour in the advice offered to Ministers; the second is that disclosure 'would create or fan ill-informed or captious public or political criticism'. Lord Reid in *Conway v. Rimmer* thought the second 'the most important reason'. Indeed he was inclined to discount the candour argument.
>
> I think both reasons are factors legitimately to be put into the balance which has to be struck between the public interest in the proper functioning of the public service (*i.e.* the executive arm of government) and the public interest in the administration of justice.[60]

[56] *Duncan v. Cammell Laird supra.*

[57] *R. v. Governor of Brixton Prison ex parte Osman (No. 1)* [1992] 1 All E.R. 108 at 115b where disclosure is resisted because of the prejudicial effect on the U.K.'s relations with Malaysia.

[58] *Buttes Gas & Oil Co v. Hammer (No. 3)* [1980] 3 All E.R. 475.

[59] Sir Richard Scott, *op. cit.*

[60] *Burmah Oil supra* at 733j–734a, *per* Lord Scarman.

All public interest does not have the same strength or importance. In *Campbell v. Tameside*, the claim was on the "candour" basis to which the Court of Appeal gave little weight in contrast to the significance of the reports on the violent disposition of the pupil involved.

There is a useful contrast of approach when the courts deal with private information held by public bodies. In *Norwich Pharmacal Co. v. Customs and Excise Commissioners*[61] the applicants owned the patent of a chemical compound "furazolidone". This chemical was being imported into the country in breach of the patent and the applicants sought the names of the importers from the commissioners, who claimed that the information was subject to public interest immunity. The House of Lords rejected this claim, feeling that disclosure would not impair the commissioners' functions and that the documents demanded were ordinary commercial records which were scarcely confidential and over which it was difficult to assert a right of privacy. At the same time, the House of Lords decision to order disclosure shows another aspect of access to information as it shows that litigants are able to demand the identity of a wrongdoer from a third party.[62]

In contrast in *Alfred Crompton Amusement Machines Ltd v. Customs and Excise Commissioners*[63] the company were in dispute with the commissioners over the company's liability for purchase tax. The commissioners objected to disclosure of a range of documents, both internal and with third parties, which had been used as a basis of the assessment. The House of Lords confirmed that confidentiality itself was not a basis for upholding a claim to public interest immunity:

Alfred Crompton Amusement Machines Ltd v. Customs and Excise Commissioners [1973] 2 All E.R. 1169 at 1184f–1185d, _per_ Lord Cross

'Confidentiality' is not a separate head of privilege, but it may be a very material consideration to bear in mind when privilege is claimed on the ground of public interest. What the court has to do is to weigh on the one hand the considerations which suggest that it is in the public interest that the documents in question should be disclosed and on the other hand those which suggest that it is in the public interest that they should not be disclosed and to balance one against the other. Plainly there is much to be said in favour of disclosure. The documents in question constitute an important part of the material on which the commissioners based their conclusion . . . On the other hand, there is much to be said against disclosure. The case is not, indeed, as strong as the case against disclosing

[61] [1973] 2 All E.R. 943.
[62] See also *Bankers Trust Co v. Shapira* [1980] 3 All E.R. 353.
[63] [1973] 2 All E.R. 1169.

> the name of an informer . . . Nevertheless, the case against disclosure is, to my mind, far stronger than it was in the *Norwich Pharmacal* case. There it was probable that all the importers whose names were disclosed were wrongdoers and the disclosure of the names of any, if there were any, who were innocent would not be likely to do them any harm at all. Here, on the other hand, one can well see that the third parties who have supplied this information to the commissioners because of the existence of their statutory powers would very much resent its disclosure by the commissioners to the appellants and that it is not at all fanciful . . . to say that the knowledge that the commissioners cannot keep such information secret may be harmful to the efficient working of the Act . . .

It is not the court's function to protect private information which is held in public hands — were such information still to reside with the individual, it would be obtainable by a litigant. The court must address the extent to which disclosure will impair the functioning of the public body. This would not be affected in the *Norwich Pharmacal* case where it appears the commissioners were merely recording everyday commercial documents and the third party documents emanated from wrongdoers, whereas in *Alfred Crompton* the third parties were innocent members of the public who would expect the information to be kept secret. But Lord Cross only felt that disclosure "may be harmful" and suggested, probably incorrectly, that where the competing interests were evenly balanced, the courts should uphold a claim to public interest immunity.

This seems a slender argument on which to base the suppression of information which is relevant to the fair disposition of the case. Elsewhere the courts have been more robust. In *Williams v. Home Office*[64] a prisoner challenged the Home Office's experimental "control units" for the long-term isolation and segregation of troublesome inmates. The department resisted disclosure for some 23 documents on the grounds of "candour" which McNeill J. rejected although he felt that he should take into account the factor that ". . . such disclosure would create or fan, ill-informed or captious public or political criticism".[65] Despite this opinion, he inspected the documents after treating the "rights of the citizen and the liberty of a prisoner" as the prevailing interest.

Non-disclosure is more likely when the public interest claimed is analogous to an established head. The non-disclosure of the identity of informers is often used, as in *D. v. National Society for the Prevention of Cruelty to Children*[66] where plaintiff was denied disclosure of the name of the person who had accused her of mistreating her children. This approach can also be seen in *Buckley v. Law Society (No. 2)*[67] where the plaintiff unsuccessfully sought

64 [1981] 1 All E.R. 1151.
65 *Conway v. Rimmer supra* at 888, *per* Lord Reid.
66 [1977] 1 All E.R. 589.
67 [1984] 1 W.L.R. 1101.

names of complainants whose complaints had led to an inquiry into a solicitor's conduct. The claim to immunity was upheld.

(3) **information given for the detection of crime:** it has long been a rule that no question may be asked nor answer given which would reveal the identity of a person who has given information for the detection of crime. In *Marks v. Beyfus* the plaintiffs sought damages for malicious prosecution and called upon the Director of Public Prosecutions to give the names of informants on whose information he had acted in bringing the prosecution.

Marks v. Beyfus (1890) 25 Q.B.D. 494 at 498, _per_ Lord Esher M.R.

> In the case of *Attorney-General v. Briant*,[68] Pollock C.B. . . . says '. . . that in a public prosecution a witness cannot be asked such questions as will disclose the informer, if he be a third person . . . and we think the principle of the rule applies where a witness is asked if he himself is the informer.' Now this rule . . . was founded on grounds of public policy, and if this prosecution was a public prosecution the rule attaches; I think it was a public prosecution and that the rule applies. I do not say it is a rule which can never be departed from; if . . . the disclosure of the name of the informant is necessary or right in order to show the prisoner's innocence, then one public policy is in conflict with another public policy, and that which says that an innocent man is not to be condemned when his innocence can be proved is the policy that must prevail. But, except in that case, this rule . . . is not a matter of discretion; it is a rule of law . . .

When such a conflict exists, the court will decide on the validity of a claim not to disclose information, whether by withholding documents or refusing to answer questions put in cross-examination. The process by which the court will inspect the relevant documents and balance the different public interests involved has been discussed earlier. That balance of interests will normally be exercised in favour of the accused in a criminal trial[69] unless the documents are of extreme sensitivity. *Keane* makes it clear that, even in relation to the identity of informants, the court must balance the public interest in protecting the informant (a weighty consideration) against the need to avoid miscarriages of justice. If the information may prove the defendant's innocence, "the balance comes down resoundingly in favour of disclosing it". The test is whether disclosure is necessary for the proper presentation of the defence case.[70] The court must continually review any decision in the light of developments during the case.[71]

[68] (1846) 15 M&W 169.

[69] *Ex parte Osman supra*; *R. v. Keane* (1994) 2 All E.R. 478 at 483g–484e, *per* Lord Taylor C.J.

[70] *R. v. Williams and Bellinfantie* [1988] Crim.L.R. 113: see 320, *et seq.*

[71] *R. v. Keane supra* at 484e–485c, *per* Lord Taylor C.J.

Public interest immunity is very significant in the rules concerning the disclosure of material by the prosecution.[72] The police may not wish to disclose to the defence such matters as the identity of informants, the location of surveillance posts, the fact of interception of communications, whether by telephone taps or other bugging devices, the development of new forensic techniques or computer files which may disclose trends in an investigation.

The rule was extended in *R. v. Rankine*[73] when, at the start of the trial, the prosecution asked for a ruling that police witnesses should not be asked questions as to the location of their observation post. The public interest was the need for the police to solicit co-operation of this nature which would be put at risk if members of the public realised that their identities would be revealed and that they might be at risk of reprisals. The Court of Appeal held that the reasons for the suppression of the names of informants applied with equal force to the identification of the premises used for surveillance and to the identification of the owner.

The prosecution should provide an evidential basis: if it is possible to show the difficulty faced by the police in getting co-operation and link that to the fear for the safety of occupiers and of informants, immunity from disclosure is routine unless the defence are able to show that the identity of the informant is necessary for the proper presentation of the defence. But the Court of Appeal's recognition that the fairness criterion embodied in section 78 of the Police and Criminal Evidence Act 1984 might potentially be used in excluding evidence, for example, that obtained by entrapment,[74] means that there is a greater likelihood that the identity of any informant will be material and liable to be disclosed.[75]

Similarly there should be an evidential basis for exclusion of the location of observation posts, since such information can be of importance in cross-examination. In *R. v. Johnson*[76] it was held that a senior officer should ascertain the attitude of the occupiers towards the disclosure of their address. If the occupiers wished to remain anonymous and were in fear of harassment, if not of physical violence, even where non-disclosure would restrict the defence, their identity should attract public interest immunity. *Blake v. DPP* suggests that this protection is available even where the offence is minor (indecency in a churchyard) and where there was no substantial evidential basis for the occupier's (undoubted) apprehension.

[72] See 316, *et seq.*
[73] [1986] 2 All E.R. 566.
[74] *R. v. Smurthwaite and Gill* [1994] 1 All E.R. 898.
[75] *R. v. Reilly* [1994] Crim.L.R. 279.
[76] [1989] 1 All E.R. 121; *R. v. Grimes* [1994] Crim.L.R. 213; *R. v. Hewitt and Davies* [1992] Crim.L.R. 650; *Blake v. DPP* [1993] Crim.L.R. 283.

These rules have not been extended to prevent evidence being given of police methods and techniques. In *R. v. Brown and Daley*[77] surveillance was from unmarked car. The officer in charge refused to disclose any information about the vehicles used. The judge allowed this information to be withheld but the convictions were quashed. Evidence of police methods was not necessarily covered by public interest immunity although the Court of Appeal conceded that sophisticated methods of investigation might lead to such claims being successfully invoked.

(4) **police complaints:** as discussed earlier, for many years there was a presumption of exclusion with regard to one class of documents, namely those related to inquiries into police misconduct under Pt. 9 of the Police and Criminal Evidence Act 1984,[78] based on the long-recognised refusal to disclose the names of informants to crime.[79] But such decisions as *Neilson v. Laugharne* had led to immunity from disclosure becoming almost automatic for documents coming into existence as a result of a police investigation. But this view was reconsidered and rejected by the House of Lords in *R. v. Chief Constable of the West Midlands Police ex parte Wiley*[80] holding that a class claim to public interest immunity did not attach generally in such circumstances. However:

> This does not, however, mean that public interest immunity can never apply to documents that come into existence in consequence of a police investigation into a complaint. There may be other reasons why because of the contents of a particular document it would be appropriate to extend immunity to that document . . .[81]

(5) **interception of communications:** under the Interception of Communications Act 1985, intercepts of communications by post or by means of a public telecommunication system may be authorised under section 2(1) by the warrant of the Home Secretary. Such warrants may be issued for the purpose of preventing and detecting serious crime. Section 9 imposes a prohibition on revealing in evidence the existence of such intercepts, whether authorised or not.

> 9.—(1) In any proceedings before any court or tribunal no evidence shall be adduced and no question in cross-examination shall be asked which (in either case) tends to suggest—
>
> (a) that an offence under section 1 above has been or is to be committed by any of the persons mentioned in subsection (2) below; or

[77] [1988] Crim.L.R. 239.
[78] Previously the Police Act 1964, s.49 and now replaced by the Police Act 1996, ss.65–68.
[79] *Marks v. Beyfus* (1890) 25 Q.B.D. 494; *D v. National Society for the Prevention of Cruelty to Children* [1977] 1 All E.R. 589.
[80] [1994] 3 All E.R. 420.
[81] *ibid.* at 446g, *per* Lord Woolf.

(b) that a warrant has been or is to be issued to any of those persons

(2) The persons referred to in subsection (1) above are—

(a) any person holding office under the Crown;

(b) the Post Office and any person engaged in the business of the Post Office; and

(c) any public telecommunications operator and any person engaged in the running of a public telecommunications system

In essence the accused is unable to ask questions in any circumstances as to whether the intercepts were authorised and who carried them out. This protects the Home Secretary's sources of knowledge and the methods of surveillance employed by the police (or other agency). The prosecution are under no duty to disclose the fact of such intercepts nor to reveal their contents. In *R. v. Preston*,[82] the defence sought to know the contents of the intercepted calls in the belief either that these would support the defence of duress or that nothing had been said in such calls to suggest that the defendant was party to the alleged conspiracy. Although the prosecution cannot be compelled to disclose the fact of an intercept, there may be occasions when the interests of justice demand that this should be done. However the contents should never be disclosed.[83]

Disclosure of the existence and product of other covert listening devices[84] follows the general principles regarding disclosure and public interest immunity. The existence of such devices might certainly attract a claim to public interest immunity and frequently will be the subject of an *ex parte* application by the prosecution under *R. v. Davis*.[85]

[82] [1993] 4 All E.R. 638. The prohibition under s.9 does not apply to interceptions made with the consent of the owner of the telephone — *R. v. Rasool*, *The Times*, February 17, 1997.

[83] *ibid.* at 672e, *per* Lord Mustill (but see headnote at 641e).

[84] Under Home Office Guidelines in 1984, these provide that only Chief Constables (and sometimes Assistant Chief Constables) may authorise such devices where there is an investigation of serious crime, normal methods are unlikely to succeed, there is good reason to believe that the use of the equipment would lead to an arrest or prevention of an act of terrorism and it is operationally feasible. It is only to be authorised in the most exceptional of cases.

[85] [1993] 2 All E.R. 643 at 647g–648a, *per* Lord Taylor C.J.

7

IMMUNITIES FROM TESTIFYING: PRIVATE PRIVILEGES AND CONFIDENTIAL INFORMATION

Private privilege, like public interest immunity, bars the court from access to certain kinds of information. There are two important categories: legal professional privilege[1] and the privilege against self-incrimination. Such privileges protect a private interest and, unlike public interest immunity, can be waived by the person to whom the privilege attaches or the privilege can be lost and the matter proved by secondary evidence.

Legal Professional Privilege

Lawyers, clients and, in some circumstances, third parties may validly claim not to answer questions or to supply information when those questions or that information relates to a lawyer/client relationship. The scope of the privilege arises under two heads:

(1) communications between a lawyer and the client which have the purpose of seeking or giving legal advice,
(2) communications between a lawyer and third parties or between the client and third parties which are made for the purposes of existing or contemplated legal proceedings.

The rationale for this privilege is grounded in the principle of a fair trial:

Zuckerman A., "Privilege and Public Interest" in Tapper C., *Crime, Proof and Punishment*. (1981) 248 at 262–263

Legal professional privilege is now well established and governed by fairly clear rules. It is not necessary for the present purposes to examine these rules, except to remark on the relation between this privilege and the principle of access to evidence. This privilege . . . exists, broadly speaking, in order to enable a party to legal proceedings to prepare his case adequately and to facilitate uninhibited access to legal advice. In an adversary system free and uninhibited access to professional legal advice is an essential corollary of the right to just and equal trial. In this sense

[1] Including "without prejudice" communications.

both this privilege and the principle of access to evidence have the same basic goal: promoting the efficacy of the legal procedure as a means of just determination of disputes. The conflict between the privilege and the principle is, therefore, confined within the basic goal of equal and just trial . . . Since the conflict . . . takes place within the confines of the administration of justice, a correct compromise of the conflict will promote the ends of the administration of justice rather than detract from them. It may be doubted whether the balance was correctly struck when extending legal professional privilege to communications made to the legal adviser for the purpose of obtaining advice on matters unconnected with pending or contemplated litigation, but the most recent trend in relation to this privilege is more cautious.

A statutory declaration of the common law is to be found in the Police and Criminal Evidence Act 1984, section 10 of which was said by the House of Lords in *Francis and Francis v. Central Criminal Court*[2] to be consistent with the common law position:

10.—(1) Subject to subsection (2) below, in this Act 'items subject to legal privilege' means —

(a) communications between a professional legal adviser and his client or any person representing his client made in connection with the giving of legal advice to the client;

(b) communications between a professional legal adviser and his client or any person representing his client or between such an adviser or his client or any such representative and any other person made in connection with or in contemplation of legal proceedings and for the purpose of such proceedings; and

(c) items enclosed with or referred to in such communications and made —

  (i) in connection with the giving of legal advice; or

  (ii) in connection with or in contemplation of legal proceedings and for the purposes of such proceedings,

when they are in the possession of a person who is entitled to possession of them.

(2) Items held with the intention of furthering a criminal purpose are not items subject to legal privilege.

Legal professional privilege is a privilege of the client, who is able in certain circumstances to prevent the lawyer or a third party from revealing confidential communications. As Zuckerman said in the passage above, "In an adversary system free and uninhibited access to professional legal advice is an essential corollary of the right to just and equal trial." The objective is to encourage candour between the lawyer and the client so as to enable the lawyer to represent the client effectively. Once the privilege has been waived by the client, the lawyer cannot refuse to disclose the information. In contrast, in France, the obligation is considered to be *"d'ordre publique"* so that, even where the client waives the privilege, the lawyer retains a discretion whether or not to disclose the contents of the communication.[3]

[2] [1988] 3 All E.R. 775 at 796g, *per* Lord Goff.

[3] *AM&S Europe Ltd v. E.C. Commission* [1983] 1 All E.R. 705 at 718c, *per* Advocate-General Warner.

An "absolute" privilege

The judicial "balancing of conflicting interests" which characterises public interest immunity has no place with legal professional privilege. It is not for the judge to decide if the client's interest in maintaining confidentiality is outweighed by the interests of the administration of justice. Until recently it was considered that the public interest in the accused's right to prove his or her innocence overrode the need for candour between lawyer and client. For example, in *R. v. Barton*[4] a defendant who was employed by a firm of solicitors was charged with fraud. He sought various documents which had come into existence as a result of the firm's probate work for clients. The firm alerted the clients and a claim to legal professional privilege was made and rejected:

R. v. Barton [1972] 2 All E.R. 1192 at 1194d–f, _per_ Caulfield J.

I think the correct principle is this, and I think that it must be restricted to these particular facts in a criminal trial, and the principle I am going to enunciate is not supported by any authority that has been cited to me; I am just working on what I conceive to be the rules of natural justice. If there are documents in the possession or control of a solicitor which, on production, help to further the defence of an accused man, then in my judgment no privilege attaches. I cannot conceive that our law would permit a solicitor or other person to screen from a jury information which, if disclosed to the jury, would perhaps enable a man either to establish his innocence or to resist an allegation made by the Crown.

This sweeping approach was modified in *R. v. Ataou*[5] above where the appellant was jointly charged with H and shared the same solicitor. H made a statement to the solicitor that the appellant was not involved but later changed his mind, pleaded guilty and gave prosecution evidence implicating the appellant. The appellant's counsel sought to examine H on this inconsistent statement but the trial judge held that the statement was privileged. The Court of Appeal held that there was a balancing act to be performed and held that it would be for the accused to show on the balance of probabilities that the accused's interest in seeking to breach the privilege outweighed that of the client in seeking to maintain it. Since H here no longer had an interest, the conviction was quashed:

R. v. Ataou [1988] 2 All E.R. 321 at 326g–h, _per_ French J.

When a communication was originally privileged and in criminal proceedings privilege is claimed against the defendant by the client concerned or his solicitor, it should be for the defendant to show on the balance of probabilities that the claim cannot be sustained. That might be done by demonstrating that there is no ground on which the client could any longer be regarded as having a recognisable interest

[4] [1972] 2 All E.R. 1192.
[5] [1988] 2 All E.R. 321.

in asserting the privilege. The judge must then decide whether the legitimate interest of the defendant in seeking to breach the privilege outweighs that of the client in seeking to maintain it.[6]

But both *Barton* and *Ataou* were overruled by the House of Lords in *R. v. Derby Magistrates' Court ex parte B.*[7] In 1978 the applicant was acquitted of murder, having made various statements admitting the killing but later retracting these and instead accusing his stepfather of the murder. In 1992 the stepfather was charged with murder and at the committal proceedings, the applicant was called as a witness for the Crown. Counsel for the stepfather sought to cross-examine him about instructions he had given to his solicitors in 1978 which were inconsistent with his statements implicating his stepfather. The applicant declined to waive his privilege and counsel applied under sections 4 and 5 of the Criminal Procedure Act 1865 to the magistrates for those instructions to be produced. The magistrates issued a witness summons under section 97 of the Magistrates' Court Act 1980, ordering the applicant to produce these documents on the grounds that they were likely to be material evidence and that the public interest in securing that all relevant information was before the court outweighed any interest protecting confidential communications between solicitor and client. Lord Taylor C.J. held that section 97 was not affected by the wide duty of disclosure on the prosecution under *R. v. Keane*[8] and furthermore, that if an order to produce a document or other evidence was a condition of the witness summons, that document or evidence must be admissible and not simply for use in cross-examination.[9] Section 97 was not a means of securing discovery in a magistrates' court. Under the provisions of the Criminal Procedure Act 1865, the appellant was unlikely to deny making the previous inconsistent statement. Lord Taylor reviewed the history of legal professional privilege and made important points as to its status:

R. v. Derby Magistrates' Court, ex parte B. [1995] 4 All E.R. 526 at 540j–542d, _per_ Lord Taylor C.J.

The principle which runs through all these cases, and many other cases which were cited, is that a man must be able to consult his lawyer in confidence, since otherwise he might hold back half the truth. The client must be sure that what he tells his lawyer in confidence will never be revealed without his consent. Legal professional privilege is thus much more than an ordinary rule of evidence, limited in its application to the facts of a particular case. It is a fundamental condition on which the administration of justice as a whole rests.

. . . [Counsel for the respondent] submitted that in other related areas of the law, privilege is less sacrosanct than it was. He points to the restrictions recently imposed on the right to silence, and the statutory exceptions to the privilege against self-incrimination in the fields of revenue and bankruptcy. But these examples only

[6] *ibid.* at 326g–h, *per* French J.
[7] [1995] 4 All E.R. 526.
[8] [1994] 2 All E.R. 478; see Chap. 10.
[9] *R. v. Cheltenham Justices ex parte Secretary of State for Trade* [1977] 1 All E.R. 460.

serve to illustrate the flaw in [counsel's] thesis. Nobody doubts that legal professional privilege could be modified, or even abrogated by statute, subject always to the objections that legal professional privilege is a fundamental human right protected by the European Convention for the Protection of Human Rights and Fundamental Freedoms[10] as to which we did not hear any argument. [Counsel's] difficulty is this: whatever inroads may have been made by Parliament in other areas, legal professional privilege is a field which Parliament has so far left untouched.

[The amicus curiae] acknowledged the importance of maintaining legal professional privilege as the general rule. But he submitted that the rule should not be absolute. There might be occasions, if only by way of rare exception, in which the rule should yield to some other consideration of even greater importance. He referred by analogy to the balancing exercise which is called for where documents are withheld on the ground of public interest immunity . . . But the drawback to that approach is that once any exception to the general rule is allowed, the client's confidence is necessarily lost. The solicitor, instead of being able to tell his client that anything which the client might say would never in any circumstances be revealed without his consent, would have to qualify his assurance. He would have to tell the client that his confidence might be broken if in some future case the court were to hold that he no longer had 'any recognisable interest' in asserting his privilege. One can see at once that the purpose of the privilege would thereby be undermined.

As for the analogy with public interest immunity, I accept that the various classes of case in which relevant evidence is excluded may . . . be regarded as forming part of a continuous spectrum. But it by no means follows that because a balancing exercise is called for in one class of case, it may also be allowed in another. Legal professional privilege and public interest immunity are as different in their origins as they are in their scope. Putting it another way, if a balancing exercise was ever required in the case of legal professional privilege, it was performed once and for all in the sixteenth century, and since then has applied across the board in every case, irrespective of the client's individual merits.

. . . it is not for the sake of the appellant alone that the privilege must be upheld. It is in the wider interests of all those hereafter who might otherwise be deterred from telling the whole truth to their solicitors. For this reason I am of the opinion that no exception should be allowed to the absolute nature of legal professional privilege, once established.

The width of this judgment is extraordinary. To hold that the court is never justified in undertaking a balancing exercise to compare the public interest in the lawyer/client privilege with the public interest in, for example, the liberty of an individual, seems unnecessarily wide and an approach that may well be regretted in hindsight. Lord Taylor called in aid the European Convention on Human Rights to justify the assertion that legal professional privilege is a fundamental condition on which the administration of justice rests. But Article 5 of the same convention asserts the right to liberty which is an equally fundamental concept. If a person's liberty is dependent upon the disclosure of communications between a third party and his or her lawyer, it seems bizarre to state that legal professional privilege must in all circumstances outweigh the injury that would occur if an innocent person received a lengthy prison sentence. The

[10] Rome, November 4, 1950; T.S. 71 (1953) (Cmd. 8969).

public's confidence in the rule of law and in the criminal justice system would surely be severely dented.

The European Court of Justice's position would appear to differ:

AM&S Europe Ltd v. E.C. Commission [1983] 1 All E.R. 705 at 721d–f, _per_ Advocate-General Warner

[The applicant] submitted that the right to confidential communication between lawyer and client was a fundamental human right. I do not think it is. There is no mention of it, as such, in the European Convention . . . or, seemingly, in the constitution of any member state; and your Lordships have already seen that, in England and France at least, it is acknowledged to be a right that can be overridden or modified by an appropriately worded statute . . . In my opinion it is a right that the laws of civilised countries generally recognise, a right not lightly to be denied, but not one so entrenched that, in the Community, the Council could never legislate to override or modify it.

Legal advice privilege

The first head of legal professional privilege concerns confidential communications passing between a client and his legal adviser. Such communications need not be given in evidence by the client nor can they be given in evidence by the client's legal adviser without the client's consent, as long as the communication was made in order to enable the client to obtain and the adviser to give legal advice:

Alfred Crompton Amusement Machines Ltd v. Commissioners of Customs and Excise (No. 2) [1972] 2 All E.R. 353 at 376e–h, _per_ Lord Denning M.R.

The law relating to discovery was developed by the Chancery courts in the first half of the 19th century. At that time nearly all legal advisers were in independent practice on their own account. Nowadays it is very different. Many barristers and solicitors are employed as legal advisers, whole time, by a single employer. Sometimes the employer is a great commercial concern. At other times it is a government department or local authority. It may even be the government itself, like the Treasury Solicitor and his staff. In every case these legal advisers do legal work for their employer and for no one else. They are paid, not by fees for each piece of work, but by a fixed annual salary . . . They are regarded by the law as in every respect in the same position as those who practice on their own account. . . . They must uphold the same standards of honour and of etiquette. They are subject to the same duties to their client and to the court. They must respect the same confidences. They and their clients have the same privileges.

Whether independent practitioners or salaried employees, it is qualified lawyers alone[11] who are covered by the privilege. This includes lawyers qualified in other jurisdictions.[12] Those not qualified, for example, workers

[11] The privilege can be extended by statute as it is , for example, to patent and trademark agents by the Copyright, Designs and Patents Act 1988, ss.280 and 284.

[12] *Great Atlantic Insurance Co v. Home Insurance Co* [1981] 2 All E.R. 485 where a memorandum from American legal advisers was undoubtedly privileged.

in a Citizens' Advice Bureau, would not be able to claim privilege, no matter how experienced or capable they were.[13]

The legal advice privilege was recognised in *Greenough v. Gaskell*[14] which extended privilege to communications where litigation was not contemplated.

> . . . the protection would be insufficient, if it only included communications more or less connected with judicial proceedings; for a person oftentimes requires the aid of professional advice upon the subject of his rights and his liabilities, with no reference to any particular litigation, and without any reference to litigation generally, than all human affairs have, in so far as every transaction may, by possibility, become the subject of judicial inquiry.[15]

Later decisions seemed to limit the scope of the privilege narrowly to the giving and taking of advice. In *Minter v. Priest*[16] Lord Atkin said:

> As to this it is necessary to avoid misapprehension lest the protection be too limited. It is, I think, apparent that if the communication passes for the purpose of getting legal advice, it must be deemed confidential. The protection, of course, attaches to the communications made by the solicitor as well as the client. If there the phrase is expanded to professional communications passing for the purpose of getting or giving professional advice, and it is understood that the profession is the legal profession, the nature of the protection is, I think, correctly defined.[17]

Recent authority suggests that the privilege is not limited to those communications that specifically give or seek advice but applies to a wide range of documents (letters, memoranda, notes) that are created in the course of a lawyer's relationship with his or her client. In *Balabel v. Air India*[18] an action was brought claiming specific performance of an agreement to grant a lease. The plaintiffs sought documents requested were all communications between the defendants and their solicitors, other than those seeking or giving legal advice, all working documents relating to the lease as well as internal communications of the defendants:

Balabel v. Air India [1988] 2 All E.R. 246 at 247g–255j, *per* Taylor L.J.

This case raises an important point concerning legal professional privilege. Broadly, the issue is whether such privilege extends only to communications seeking or conveying legal advice or to all that passes between solicitor and client on matters within the ordinary business of a solicitor . . .

It is common ground that the basic principle justifying legal professional privilege arises from the public interest requiring full and frank exchange of confidence

[13] The privilege did not cover communications to a legal aid officer working within in a prison — *R. v. Umoh* [1987] Crim. L.R. 258.
[14] (1833) [1824–31] All E.R. Rep. 767.
[15] *ibid.* at 770d–e, *per* Lord Brougham.
[16] [1930] All E.R. 431.
[17] *ibid.* at 440c.
[18] [1988] 2 All E.R. 246.

between solicitor and client to enable the latter to receive necessary legal advice. Originally it related only to communications where legal proceedings were in being or in contemplation. This was the rationale which distinguished the solicitor and client relationship from that between any other professional man and his client. There is no doubt that legal professional privilege now extends beyond legal advice in regard to litigation. But how far?

. . . Although originally confined to advice regarding litigation, the privilege was extended to non-litigious business. Nevertheless, despite that extension, the purpose and scope of the privilege is still to enable legal advice to be sought and given in confidence. In my judgment, therefore, the test is whether the communication or other document was made confidentially for the purpose of legal advice. Those purposes have to be construed broadly. Privilege obviously attaches to a document conveying legal advice from solicitor to client and to a specific request from the client for such advice. But it does not follow that all other communications lack privilege. In most solicitor and client relationships, especially where a transaction involves protracted dealings, advice may be required or appropriate on matters great or small at various stages. There will be a continuum of communications and meetings between the solicitor and client. The negotiations for a lease such as occurred in the present case are only one example. Where information is passed by the solicitor or client to the other as part of the continuum aimed at keeping both informed so that advice may be sought and given as required, privilege will attach. A letter from the client containing information may end with such words as 'please advise me what I should do'. But, even if it does not, there will usually be implied in the relationship an overall expectation that the solicitor will at each stage, whether asked specifically or not, tender appropriate advice. Moreover, legal advice is not confined to telling the client the law; it must include advice as to what should prudently and sensibly be done in the relevant legal context.

It may be that applying this test to any series of communications might isolate occasional letters or notes which could not be said to enjoy privilege. But to be disclosable such documents must be not only privilege-free but also material and relevant. Usually a letter which does no more than acknowledge receipt of a document or suggest a date for a meeting will be irrelevant and so non-disclosable. In effect, therefore, the 'purpose of legal advice' test will result in most communications between solicitor and client in, for example, a conveyancing transaction being exempt from disclosure, either because they are privileged or because they are immaterial or irrelevant.

. . . It follows from this analysis that those dicta in the decided cases which appear to extend privilege without limit to all solicitor and client communication on matters within the ordinary business of a solicitor and referable to that relationship are too wide. It may be that the broad terms used in the earlier cases reflect the restricted range of solicitor's activities at the time. Their role then would have been confined for the most part to that of lawyer and would not have extended to business adviser or man of affairs. To speak therefore of matters 'within the ordinary business of a solicitor' would in practice usually have meant the giving of advice and assistance of a specifically legal nature. But the range of assistance given by solicitors to their clients and of activities carried out on their behalf has greatly broadened in recent times and is still developing. Hence the need to re-examine the scope of legal professional privilege and keep it within justifiable bounds.

Those bounds were further considered in *Nederlandse Reassurantie Groep Holding NV v. Bacon and Woodrow*[19] in which the plaintiffs, a

[19] [1995] 1 All E.R. 976.

Dutch company, after consulting accountants, its banking and corporate finance advisers and its lawyers, took over other insurance companies. These companies proved to be over-exposed in the reinsurance market and the plaintiffs sought to recover damages from their non-legal advisers. The defendants argued that the lawyers gave advice of a general nature as to the commercial viability of the agreement and sought discovery of communications between the plaintiffs and their lawyers. The court held that *Balabel* had laid down that a solicitor's professional duty was not confined to giving advice on matters of law but could also relate to the commercial wisdom of entering into a given transaction in respect of which legal advice was also sought. In such a situation, all communications between the solicitor and the client relating to the transaction would be privileged, even though they did not give advice on matters of law or construction, provided that they were directly related to the performance by the solicitor of his or her professional duty as legal adviser.

Litigation privilege

The second head of legal professional privilege exists where the communications are made with reference to litigation that is actually taking place or is in the contemplation of the client. Between lawyer and client, such communications obviously come within the "legal advice" head of privilege but this "litigation" head also encompasses communications between the client and third parties or between the legal adviser and third parties. It also applies to "without prejudice" correspondence between opposing parties.

In the leading case of *Wheeler v. Le Marchant*[20] the Court of Appeal ordered the defendants to produce letters which had passed between the defendants' solicitors and a surveyor with regard to property, except for those which had been prepared after the conflict over the property had arisen:

Wheeler v. Le Marchant (1881) 50 L.J.Ch. 793 at 795–796, *per* Lord Jessel M.R.

. . . the principle is of a very limited character. It does not protect all confidential communications which a man must necessarily make in order to obtain advice, even when necessary for the protection of his life or of his honour, to say nothing of his fortune. There are many communications which must be made, because without them the ordinary business of life cannot be carried on, and yet they are not protected. As I have said in the course of argument, the communication made to a medical man, whose advice is sought by a patient . . . is not protected. Communications made to the priest in the confessional, on matters perhaps considered by the penitent to be more important even than the care of his life or his fortune, are not protected. Communications made to a friend with respect to matters of the most

[20] (1881) 50 L.J. Ch. 793.

delicate nature, on which advice is sought with respect to a man's honour or reputation, are not protected. Therefore it must not be supposed that there is any principle which says that every confidential communication which in order to carry on the ordinary business of life, must necessarily be made, is protected. The protection is of a very limited character. It is a protection in this country restricted to the obtaining of assistance of lawyers, as regards the conduct of litigation or the rights of property. It has never gone beyond the obtaining of legal advice and assistance; and all things reasonably necessary in the shape of communication to the legal advisers are protected from production or discovery, in order that that legal advice may be obtained safely and sufficiently . . .

The actual communication to the solicitor by the client is, of course, protected, and it is equally protected whether that communication is made by the client in person or by an agent on behalf of the client, and whether made to the solicitor in person or to a clerk or subordinate of the solicitor, who acts in his place and under his direction. Again, with the same view, the evidence obtained by the solicitor, or by his direction, or at his instance, even if obtained by the client, is protected if obtained after litigation has commenced or threatened, or with a view to the defence or prosecution of such litigation. So, again, it does not matter whether the advice is obtained from the solicitor as to a dealing which is not the subject of litigation. What is protected is the communication necessary to obtain legal advice. It must be a communication made to the solicitor in that character or for that purpose.

But what we are asked to protect here is this: the solicitor being consulted in a matter as to which no dispute has arisen, thinks he would like to know some further facts before giving his advice, and applies to a surveyor to tell him what the state of a given property is, or information of that character, and it is said that information given in answer to such application ought to be protected because it is desired or required by the solicitor in order to enable him the better to give legal advice. It appears to me that it is not only extending the rule beyond what has been previously laid down, but beyond what necessity warrants . . .

Litigation must be definitely in the contemplation of the parties. In *Alfred Crompton Amusement Machines Ltd v. Commissioners of Customs and Excise (No. 2)*[21] the company were in dispute with the commissioners over their liability for purchase tax. The commissioners objected to disclosure of a range of documents, both internal and with third parties, which had been used as a basis for the assessment. The commissioners were entitled to claim legal professional privilege for the communications with their own salaried legal advisers. But there were also documents received from third parties used to assess the market value of the machines in question:

Alfred Crompton Amusement Machines Ltd v. Commissioners of Customs and Excise (No. 2) [1973] 2 All E.R. 1169 at 1183f–1184c, _per_ Lord Cross

Here the two purposes for which the documents in question were obtained or came into existence were parts of a single wider purpose — namely, the ascertainment of the wholesale value in the manner prescribed by the Act. The first, and the sole immediate , purpose was to help the commissioners to fix what in their opinion was

[21] [1973] 2 All E.R. 1169.

the true value; the second purpose was to help the solicitor, if the commissioners' opinion was challenged, to prepare their case for arbitration. It was not — and hardly could have been — suggested that the mere fact that the commissioners would know in every case that their opinion might be challenged would itself enable them to claim that such documents as are in question here would be the subject of legal professional privilege whenever in fact their opinion was challenged. What is said to make them privileged in this case is the fact that the commissioners happened to expect that there would be an arbitration and called in the solicitor to 'hold their hands' in the early stages. But, even so, in this case just as much in cases in which no arbitration was in fact anticipated the commissioners had to form their own opinion as to value on the evidence available to them, including these documents, before any arbitration could take place. This feature of the case appears to me to . . . make it analogous to *Jones v. Great Central Railway Co. Ltd.*[22] There a member of a trade union who thought that he had been unjustly dismissed by his employers furnished the union authorities (as required by the rules) with information in writing as to the facts of the case as he saw them in order to satisfy them that it was proper for them to sanction the employment of a solicitor to conduct the case and also for use by the solicitor in the conduct of the action if the employment of a solicitor was sanctioned. This House held that the letters in question were not the subject of legal professional privilege because the union authorities had themselves to consider them and act on them before the solicitor was employed to conduct the case. So here the commissioners had to form their own opinion as to value before the solicitor would use the documents for the purpose of defending their opinion in the anticipated arbitration.

Here the documents in question came into existence because the commissioners were seeking to inform themselves about the value of the machines. There was an incidental purpose that the documents might be used by lawyers in later litigation. This secondary purpose was insufficient to attract legal professional privilege and this restrictive approach to the privilege was furthered in *Waugh v. British Rail.*[23] The widow of a train driver, killed in an accident, sued his employers and sought internal reports on the accident, made two days after the accident by two officers of British Rail. The early authorities such as *Ogden v. London Electric Railway Co*[24] suggested that such reports need not be disclosed if one of their purposes (even if that were subsidiary) was to inform the solicitor with a view to possible litigation. *Ogden* was distinguished in *Alfred Crompton* and the Australian High Court in *Grant v. Downs*[25] had adopted a very restrictive policy, allowing privilege to be claimed only where the document was produced wholly for the purpose of furthering the litigation. But in *Grant v. Downs*, Barwick C.J. preferred a test which allowed legal professional privilege whenever the "*dominant purpose*" of producing the document was to further the litigation, at the same time accepting that other, subsidiary, objectives need not destroy that privilege. It was this approach that the House of Lords adopted, although they held that the dominant

[22] [1910] A.C. 4.
[23] [1979] 2 All E.R. 1169.
[24] [1933] All E.R. Rep 896.
[25] (1976) 135 C.L.R. 674.

purpose of the accident report was not to assist in possible litigation but to inform British Rail about the cause of the accident with the aim of preventing any recurrence. As a result the reports were not privileged.

Waugh v. British Rail [1979] 2 All E.R. 1169 at 1181e–1183d, *per* Lord Edmund-Davies

It is for the party refusing disclosure to establish his right to refuse. It may well be that in some cases where that right has in the past been upheld the courts have failed to keep clear the distinction between (a) communications between client and legal adviser, and (b) communications between the client and third parties, made . . . 'for the purpose of obtaining information to be submitted to the client's professional legal advisers for the purpose of obtaining advice upon pending or contemplated litigation'. In cases falling within (a), privilege from disclosure attaches to communications for the purpose of obtaining legal advice and it is immaterial whether or not the possibility of litigation were even contemplated . . . But in cases falling within (b) the position is quite otherwise. Litigation, apprehended or actual, is its hallmark . . .

Preparation with a view to litigation, pending or anticipated, being thus the essential purpose which protects a communication from disclosure in such cases as the present, what in the last resort is the touchstone of the privilege? Is it sufficient that the prospect of litigation be merely one of the several purposes leading to the communication coming into being? And is that sufficient . . . despite the fact that there is also 'another and even more important purpose'? Is an appreciable purpose sufficient? Or does it have to be the main purpose? Or one of its main purposes . . .? Ought your Lordships to declare that privilege attaches only to material which . . . 'comes within the words "wholly or mainly" for the purpose of litigation'? Or should this House adopt the majority decision of the High Court of Australia in *Grant v. Downs* that legal professional privilege must be confined to documents brought into existence for the sole purpose of submission to legal advisers for advice or for use in legal proceedings? . . .

Justice is better served by candour than by suppression. For, as it was put in the *Grant v. Downs* majority judgment, 'privilege . . . detracts from the fairness of the trial by denying a party access to relevant documents or at least subjecting him to surprise'.

Adopting that approach, I would certainly deny a claim to privilege when litigation was merely one of several purposes of equal or similar importance intended to be served by the material sought to be withheld from disclosure, and a fortiori where it was merely a minor purpose. On the other hand, I consider that it would be going too far to adopt the '*sole* purpose' test applied by the majority in *Grant v. Downs*, which has been adopted in no United Kingdom decision nor, as far as we are aware, elsewhere in the Commonwealth. Its adoption would deny privilege even to material whose outstanding purpose is to serve litigation, simply because another and very minor purpose was also being served. But, inasmuch as the only basis of the claim to privilege in such cases as the present one is that the material in question was brought into existence for use in legal proceedings, it is surely right to insist that, before the claim is conceded or upheld, such a purpose must be shown to have played a paramount part. Which phrase or epithet should be selected to designate this is a matter of individual judgment . . . . I have finally come down in favour of the test propounded by Barwick C.J. in *Grant v. Downs* in the following words:

> . . . a document which was produced or brought into existence either with the dominant purpose of its author, or of the person or authority under whose

> direction, whether particular or general, it was produced or brought into existence, of using it or its contents in order to obtain legal advice or to conduct or aid in the conduct of litigation, at the time of its production in reasonable prospect, should be privileged and excluded from inspection . . .

Dominant purpose, then, in my judgment, should now be declared by this House to be the touchstone . . .

This test was applied in *Guinness Peat Properties Ltd v. Fitzroy Robinson.*[26] The plaintiffs, who were building developers, sued the architects of an office building which had developed a fault. The architects wrote to their insurers, enclosing a copy of the claim, other relevant memoranda and asking the insurers' opinion. Were these privileged? Even though the writer might have regarded the matter as "insurance", litigation was the underlying and dominant purpose of the insurers who insisted that a letter of notification be produced. This was with a view to legal advice about litigation that was a reasonable prospect. The court quoted Brightman L.J. in *Buttes Gas and Oil Co v. Hammer (No. 3)*:

> . . . if two parties with a common interest and a common solicitor exchange information for the dominant purpose of informing each other of the facts, or the issues, or advice received, or of obtaining legal advice in respect of contemplated or pending litigation, the documents or copies containing that information are privileged from production in the hands of each.[27]

The documents were therefore privileged.

Some general issues

(a) waiver: when privilege is based upon a private interest, the party to whom the privilege attaches has to assert it but also can waive it. Waiver can be express or it can be implied through disclosure. Parties need to exercise caution since, if privilege is waived for part of an otherwise privileged document, it is waived for the whole. In *Great Atlantic Insurance v. Home Insurance*[28] the plaintiffs received a memorandum from their U.S. attorneys relating to the litigation. The first two paragraphs of the memo related to discussions between the attorneys and third parties. In the course of discovery, the plaintiffs disclosed the first two paragraphs. Their solicitor intended to claim privilege for the remainder of the memo but failed to do so. At the trial, the plaintiffs' counsel read the first two paragraphs under the impression that it was complete as it stood. The defence asked for disclosure of the whole document and this was granted:

Great Atlantic Insurance v. Home Insurance [1981] 2 All E.R. 485 at 488j–492a, _per_ Templeman L.J.

In my judgment, the whole of the memorandum was privileged because it was a communication by the plaintiffs' American attorneys to the plaintiffs relating to a

26 [1987] 2 All E.R. 716.
27 [1980] 3 All E.R. 475 at 502.
28 [1981] 2 All E.R. 485.

matter . . . on which the American attorneys were instructed to act as legal advisers to the plaintiffs. The fact that the memorandum included an account of a conversation . . . which conversation was not privileged, does not alter the confidentiality attaching to the memorandum as a whole by virtue of the relationship between the American attorneys in their capacity as legal advisers and the plaintiffs in their capacity as clients of those legal advisers.

. . . The second question is whether, the whole of the memorandum being a privileged communication between legal adviser and client, the plaintiff may waive the privilege with regard to the first two paragraphs of the memorandum but assert privilege over the additional matter. In my judgment severance would be possible if the memorandum dealt with entirely different subject matters or different incidents and could in effect be divided into two separate memoranda each dealing with a separate subject matter . . .

Counsel for the plaintiffs argued that severance is permissible where the part disclosed is only an account of a discussion which in itself is not privileged. But, once it is decided that the memorandum deals with only one subject matter, it seems to me that it might be or appear dangerous or misleading to allow the plaintiffs to disclose part of the memorandum and assert privilege over the remainder. . . . In my judgment, the simplest, safest and most straightforward rule is that if a document is privileged then privilege must be asserted, if at all, to the whole document unless the document deals with separate subject matters so that the document can in effect be divided into two separate and distinct documents each of which is complete.

. . . The third question is whether privilege in respect of the memorandum . . . was in fact waived by or on behalf of the plaintiffs. Neither the plaintiffs nor any of the plaintiffs' legal advisers intended to waive any privilege. The plaintiffs' English solicitor intended to disclose the first two paragraphs of the memorandum which he wrongly but excusably considered must be disclosed. The plaintiffs' counsel, who read the memorandum in open court, did not know that the memorandum which he read was an incomplete part of a document. The plaintiffs in so far as they were in attendance by their directors and officers knew nothing of what was going on. The plaintiffs and all their legal advisers never intended to waive any privilege.

In interlocutory proceedings and before trial it is possible to allow a party who discloses a document or part of a document by mistake to correct the error in certain circumstances. Where a document has been disclosed as a result of misconduct by the defendants, against the will of the plaintiffs and in any event not by the deliberate act of the plaintiffs, then remedial action both before and during the trial may be possible. But in my judgment the plaintiffs deliberately chose to read part of a document which dealt with one subject matter to the trial judge, and must disclose the whole. The deliberate introduction by the plaintiffs of part of the memorandum into the trial record as a result of a mistake by the plaintiffs waives privilege with regard to the whole document. I can see no principle whereby the court could claim to exercise or could fairly and effectively exercise any discretion designed to put the clock back and to undo what has been done.

The issue of disclosure of part of a document resurfaced in *GE Capital Corporate Finance Group Ltd v. Bankers Trust*[29] in the context of discovery. Under R.S.C., Ord. 24, parties are obliged to discover those documents which relate to the matter in question. In this case, the plaintiff had blanked out certain irrelevant passages in some documents. The defendants sought to inspect the complete documents and submitted that the test was

[29] [1995] 2 All E.R. 993.

not whether the concealed part was relevant but whether it dealt with a separate subject matter. This, on the authority of *Great Atlantic Insurance*, was analogous with the test for the waiver of privilege. Hoffman L.J. disapproved of Templeman L.J.'s dicta that it might be dangerous to allow disclosure of part of a document and assertion of privilege over the remainder and that this was only possible where the document could be seen to deal with two different subject matters:

GE Capital Corporate Finance Group Ltd v. Bankers Trust [1995] 2 All E.R. 993 at 997d–998d, _per_ Hoffman L.J.

If this test is confined to the context in which it was applied, namely the case of a party who puts in evidence part of a privileged document, I would not in any way differ. But if (as certain dicta in the case suggest) it is extended to the discovery of parts of documents, I do not think that it can be reconciled with well-established principle. In my view, the test for whether on discovery part of a document can be withheld on grounds of irrelevance is simply whether that part is irrelevant. The test for whether part can be withheld on grounds of privilege is simply whether that part is privileged. There is no additional requirement that the part must deal with an entirely different subject matter from the rest.

. . . In the case of documents partly privileged, the dicta in the *Great Atlantic* case have caused some practical difficulty in the preparation of lists. Parties have been reluctant to disclose part of a document . . . and claim privilege for the rest . . . in case it should be said that because they relate to the same subject matter, privilege has been waived as to the whole . . . .I think that Seville J was right in *Bank of Nova Scotia v. Hellenic Mutual War Risks Association (Bermuda) Ltd, The Good Luck*[30] when he held that the disclosure of an unprivileged part of a document was not a waiver of privilege for the rest, even though both dealt with the same subject matter . . .

(b) the use of secondary evidence: when legal professional privilege is claimed, does it cover just the document or testimony that is the subject of that exclusion or can the contents be proved by some other means? Unlike public interest immunity, when private privilege is in issue, documents must be guarded carefully since if their contents become known, secondary evidence of those contents may be admissible.

In *Calcraft v. Guest*,[31] an action for trespass to a fishery, some documents about a previous action but involving the same rights, fell into the hands of the opposite party by accident. His lawyers took copies and returned the originals but sought to use the copies as evidence. The originals were still subject to privilege:

Calcraft v. Guest [1898] 1 Q.B. 759 at 761–762, _per_ Lindley M.R.

I take it that, as a general rule, one may say once privileged always privileged. I do not mean to say that privilege cannot be waived, but that the mere fact that

[30] [1992] 2 Lloyd's Rep. 540.
[31] [1898] 1 Q.B. 759.

documents used in previous litigation are held and have not been destroyed, does not amount to a waiver of the privilege . . . It appears that the appellant has obtained copies of some of these documents, and is in a position to give secondary evidence of them; and the question is whether he is entitled to do that. That appears to me to be covered by the authority of *Lloyd v. Mostyn*,[32] (where) Parke B. said, 'Where an attorney intrusted confidentially with a document communicates the contents or suffers another to take a copy, surely the secondary evidence so obtained may be produced. Suppose the instrument were even stolen, and a correct copy taken, would it not be reasonable to admit it?' The matter dropped there; but the other members of the court all concurred in that, which I take to be a distinct authority that secondary evidence in a case of this kind may be received.[33]

The means by which the documents come into the opposing party's hands may significantly affect any claim to privilege. In *ITC Film Distributors v. Video Exchange Ltd*,[34] one party brought documents into court which were the subject of legal privilege. The other party obtained them by underhand means and was prevented from using them. But the limits of this can be seen in *R. v. Tompkins*[35] when the defendant wrote a note to his counsel. This was accidentally dropped on the floor and was handed over to the prosecution who, not having acted improperly, were allowed to cross-examine the accused on the note's contents.

Calcraft v. Guest appears to be in conflict with the decision in *Lord Ashburton v. Pape*[36] in which case the defendant, an undischarged bankrupt, improperly obtained letters written by the plaintiff to his solicitor. He intended to use these in pending bankruptcy proceedings but the plaintiff was able to obtain an injunction to prevent this:

Lord Ashburton v. Pape [1913] 2 Ch. 469 at 473, *per* Cozens-Hardy M.R.

. . . The rule of evidence as explained in *Calcraft v. Guest*, merely amounts to this, that if a litigant wants to prove a particular document which by reason of privilege or some circumstance he cannot furnish by the production of the original, he may produce a copy as secondary evidence although that copy has been obtained by improper means, and even, it may be, by criminal means. The Court in such an action is not really trying the circumstances under which the document was produced. That is not an issue in the case and the Court simply says 'Here is a copy of a document which cannot be produced; it may have been stolen, it may have been picked up in the street, it may have improperly got into the possession of the person who proposes to produce it, but that is not a matter which the Court in the trial of the action can go into.' But that does not seem to me to have any bearing upon a case where the whole subject-matter of the action is the right to retain the originals or copies of certain documents which are privileged. It seems to me that, although Pape has had the good luck to obtain a copy of these documents which he

[32] (1842) 10 M.&W. 478.
[33] See *Re Brianmore Manufacturing* [1996] 3 All E.R. 132.
[34] [1982] 2 All E.R. 241.
[35] (1977) 67 Cr.App.R. 181 (although this outcome may be reconsidered in the light of the Police and Criminal Evidence Act 1984, s.78 which allows the judge to exclude evidence which would have an adverse effect on the fairness of the proceedings).
[36] [1913] 2 Ch. 469: upheld in *R. v. Cottrill* [1997] Crim.L.R. 56.

can produce without a breach of this injunction, there is no ground whatever in principle why we should decline to give the plaintiff the protection which in my view is his right as between him and Pape . . .

This suggests that a party is able to restrain an opponent making use of copies which have been wrongfully obtained. *Butler v. Board of Trade*[37] appears to extend this when Goff J. said, ". . . In the present case there was no impropriety on the part of the defendants in the way in which they received the copy, but that, in my judgment, is irrelevant because an innocent recipient of information conveyed in breach of confidence is liable to be restrained."

Difficulties have been perceived in reconciling these two decisions but it is principles of equity (rather than rules of privilege) that govern whether a litigant is able to make use of any secondary evidence of one's opponent's documents. In *Goddard v. Nationwide Building Society*,[38] a solicitor had acted for both house buyers and building society in a house purchase. The buyers sought to sue the building society for its surveyor's negligence. The defendants obtained a note of a conversation between one of the plaintiffs and the solicitor. Were the plaintiffs entitled to an injunction preventing use of this material?

Goddard v. Nationwide Building Society [1986] 3 All E.R. 264 at 270f–h, _per_ May L.J.

I confess that I do not find the decision in *Lord Ashburton v. Pape* logically satisfactory, depending as it does on the order in which applications are made in litigation. Nevertheless I think that it and *Calcraft v. Guest* are good authority for the following proposition. If a litigant has in his possession copies of documents to which legal professional privilege attaches, he may nevertheless use such copies as secondary evidence in his litigation; however, if he has not yet used the documents in that way, the mere fact that he intends to do so is no answer to a claim against him by the person in whom the privilege is vested for delivery up of the copies or to restrain him from disclosing or making use of any information contained in them.

Equitable jurisdiction through the means of injunctions is thus limiting the ambit of the rule in *Calcraft v. Guest*. But the jurisdiction cannot prevail over evidentiary rules generally. The law of evidence does not privilege confidential communications between a doctor and a patient and if a litigant sought to use these in some unauthorised fashion, equity would not restrain him or her:

> The equitable jurisdiction is well able to extend, for example, to the grant of an injunction to restrain the unauthorised disclosure of confidential communications between priest and penitent or doctor and patient. But those communications are not privileged in legal proceedings and I do not believe that equity would restrain a litigant who already had a record of such a communication in

[37] [1970] 3 All E.R. 593.
[38] [1986] 3 All E.R. 264.

his possession from using it for the purposes of his litigation. It cannot be the function of equity to accord a *de facto* privilege to communications in respect of which no privilege can be claimed. Equity follows the law.[39]

The *Goddard* approach was followed and extended in *Guinness Peat Properties v. Fitzroy Robinson Partnership*[40] where the developers of a building sued the architects after the building had developed faults. The defendant architects wrote to their insurers about the claim and expressing views on its merits. This letter was inadvertently disclosed to the plaintiffs who inspected it and took a copy. Usually the rule is that, once inspected, it is too late to claim privilege for a document. But the court has equitable powers to intervene since there had been an obvious error which the plaintiffs' solicitor must have realised and the defendant had acted promptly to seek relief:

Guinness Peat Properties v. Fitzroy Robinson Partnership [1987] 2 All E.R. 716 at 730–731, *per* Slade L.J.

In my judgment the relevant principles may be stated broadly as follows. (1) where solicitors for one party to litigation have, on discovery, mistakenly included a document for which they could properly have claimed privilege . . . to a list of documents without claiming privilege, the court will ordinarily permit them to amend the list under R.S.C., Ord. 20, r.8, at any time before inspection of the document has taken place . . . (2) However, once in such circumstances the other party has inspected the document in pursuance of the rights conferred on him by R.S.C., Ord 24, r.9, the general rule is that it is too late for the party who seeks to claim privilege to attempt to correct the mistake by applying for injunctive relief . . .

(3) If, however, in such a last-mentioned case the other party or his solicitor either (a) has procured inspection of the relevant document by fraud, or (b) on inspection, realises that he has been permitted to see the document only by reason of an obvious mistake, the court has the power to intervene for the protection of the mistaken party by the grant of an injunction in exercise of the equitable jurisdiction . . . Furthermore, in my view, it should ordinarily intervene in such cases, unless the case is one where the injunction can properly be refused on the general principles affecting the grant of a discretionary remedy, for example, on the ground of inordinate delay . . .[41]

This leaves open the question as to how the court should exercise its discretion. This was considered in:

Webster v. James Chapman & Co. [1989] 3 All E.R. 939 at 946h–947d, *per* Scott J.

If a document has been disclosed, be it by trickery, accident or otherwise, the benefit and protection of legal privilege will have been lost. Secondary evidence of

[39] *ibid.* at 271h–j, *per* Nourse LJ.
[40] [1987] 2 All E.R. 716 .
[41] See *IBM Corp v. Phoenix International (Computers) Ltd* [1995] 1 All E.R. 413.

the document will have come into the possession of the other side to the litigation. The question then will be what protection the court should provide given that the document which will have come into the possession of the other side will be confidential and that use of it will be unauthorised. If a document was obviously confidential and had been obtained by a trick or by fraud, it is not difficult to see that the balance would be struck in favour of the party entitled to the confidential document. If the document had come into the possession of the other side not through trick or fraud but due to a mistake or carelessness on the part of the party entitled to the document or by his advisers, the balance will be very different from the balance in a fraud case.

Suppose a case where the privileged document has come into the possession of the other side because of carelessness on the part of the party entitled to keep the document confidential and has been read by the other party, or by one of his legal advisers, without realising that a mistake has been made. In such a case the future conduct of the litigation by the other party would often be inhibited or made difficult were he to be required to shut out from his mind the contents of the document. It seems to me that it would be thoroughly unfair that the carelessness of one party should be allowed to put the other party at a disadvantage.

I do not think that this branch of the law is one where any firm rules as to how the balance should come down should be stated. It must be highly relevant to consider the manner in which the privileged document has come into the possession of the other side. It must be highly relevant to consider the issues in the action and the relevance of the document to those issues. It must be highly relevant to consider whether, under the Rules of the Supreme Court, the document ought in one way or another to have been disclosed anyway. All circumstances will have to be taken into account, as it seems to me, in deciding how the balance is to be struck.

So I do not accept the submission that in the present case I have no discretion . . .

Whatever the intrusion of equitable principles may be in civil proceedings to restrain the use of secondary evidence relating to privileged information, in criminal proceedings, it seems likely that the accused has no such rights. In *Butler v. Board of Trade*, Goff J. put it:

> In my judgment it would not be a right or permissible exercise of the equitable jurisdiction in confidence to make a declaration at the suit of the accused in a public prosecution in effect restraining the Crown from adducing admissible evidence relevant to the crime with which he is charged. It is not necessary for me to decide whether the same result would obtain in the case of a private prosecution, and I expressly leave that point open.[42]

(c) ownership and duration of the privilege: the term "legal professional privilege" is often judicially denounced as unfortunate since it is not a privilege that attaches to the legal profession but to the client. In *Wilson v. Rastall*[43] a witness wished to testify as to what he had learned whilst acting as the defendant's attorney. He was rebuked by Buller J.:

> . . . I strongly animadverted on his conduct, and would not suffer him to be examined; he had acquired his information during the time that he acted as attorney; and I thought that the privilege of not being examined to such points

[42] [1970] 3 All E.R. 593 at 599h–600a.
[43] (1792) [1775–1802] All E.R. Rep. 597.

> was the privilege of the party, . . . and not of the attorney: and that the privilege never ceased at any period of time. In such a case it is not sufficient to say that the cause is at an end; the mouth of such a person is shut for ever.[44]

"Once privileged, always privileged" was the maxim that decided the issue in *R. v. Derby Magistrates' Court ex parte B*[45] where the client had been acquitted of the murder of a young girl in 1978. He still asserted the privilege as a witness at his stepfather's trial for the same murder over a decade later. The House of Lords laid down the principle that once legal professional privilege attaches to a document, it attaches for all time and in all circumstances. Lord Taylor said, ". . . I am of the opinion that no exception should be allowed to the absolute nature of legal professional privilege, once established."[46] A narrower ground might well have sufficed to dispose of the issue. Despite the importance of the evidence to the defence, the client might still be seen to have a subsisting interest. This fact might be compared to the clients asserting privilege in *Barton*[47] or in *Ataou*,[48] neither of whom could be said to have any reasonable interest in continuing to assert their privilege.

Another complex problem emerges when a third party, not the client entitled to the privilege, seeks to rely on that privilege. In a New Zealand case, *R. v. Craig*,[49] that third party was the defendant who was accused of giving perjured evidence on behalf of a plaintiff in earlier proceedings. The prosecution sought to call the plaintiff's solicitor who had taken notes of Craig's evidence for the original hearing. The plaintiff in that case instructed his solicitor to claim privilege and the New Zealand Supreme Court held that the privilege did not last only for the original litigation. The court felt that there were limits to privilege but that the onus was on the prosecution to show that the client no longer had any reasonable interest in asserting the privilege. Decisions such as *Craig* can be reconciled with *Derby Magistrates* (and perhaps *Barton*) as those cases involved the client himself, and not a third party, asserting the privilege.

The third party can only avail himself or herself of the protection when there is some congruence of interest between the client and the third party In *Lee v. South West Thames Regional Health Authority*,[50] an infant plaintiff suffered brain damage while being transferred to and from hospitals administered by Hillingdon Health Authority in ambulances provided by the defendant Health Authority. Hillingdon obtained a report from the ambulance crew employed by South West Thames for the purpose of getting legal advice on their liability. The child's mother, seeking to find out what had happened, sought to compel the defendant to disclose the

[44] *ibid.* at 599i.
[45] [1995] 4 All E.R. 526.
[46] *ibid.* at 542d.
[47] [1972] 2 All E.R. 1192.
[48] [1988] 2 All E.R. 321.
[49] [1975] 1 N.Z.L.R. 597.
[50] [1985] 2 All E.R. 385.

memorandum in a preliminary action under section 33(2)(b) of the Supreme Court Act 1981. The Court of Appeal held that a third party was not generally entitled to rely on a defendant's privilege in relation to a document which came into existence for the purpose of enabling the defendant to obtain legal advice pending litigation unless there was some common interest between the defendant and the third party. In this case there was no common interest because, if the mother sued both authorities, their defences were likely to be of the "cut-throat" variety. But on the other hand, any actions against them arose out of the same incident, were likely to be tried together and this would not enable the document to be used against one defendant and not the other.

This decision must be distinguished from *Schneider v. Leigh*[51] where there was no common interest between the client and the third party. The plaintiff originally sued a company, Pedigree Stock, for personal injuries. The company arranged for the defendant doctor to examine him and report. This report was privileged but certain paragraphs of it were revealed to the plaintiff who decided to sue the doctor for libel and claimed disclosure of the full report. The defendant claimed it was subject to legal professional privilege:

Schneider v. Leigh [1955] 2 All E.R. 173 at 177c–g, _per_ Hodson L.J.

It is conceded by the defendant that the medical reports which form the basis of the libel action were brought into existence in contemplation of the action brought by the plaintiff against the company, and that privilege from production accordingly attaches to the company in the proceedings taken by the plaintiff against it. The question is whether the privilege from production extends beyond the company, so as to protect the defendant in separate proceedings brought against him, although the privilege is not his, but that of the company.

It is essential to bear in mind that the privilege is the privilege of the litigant, accorded to him in order that he may be protected in preparing his case, and not the privilege of his witnesses as such. The litigant can waive the privilege if he chooses, and if he does so the proofs of his witnesses can be shown to the opposing party without the witnesses having any ground for complaint. What is being sought here is, in effect, to extend the umbrella of the protection which the privilege gives the company to the defendant, who is, on the hypothesis that he is the author of the libel, to be looked at for the purpose of this application as a proposed witness on behalf of the company. In this capacity not only has he no privilege of his own, but he is under no duty to assert the rights of the company to resist the production of any documents.

I have emphasised that the privilege is the privilege of the company. This statement is subject to the qualification that the privilege enures for the benefit of successors in title to the party to an action, at any rate, where the relevant interest subsists . . .

The privilege attaches to the client who, according to Lord Taylor in *Derby Magistrates*, is entitled to play it as the ace of trumps at his or her

[51] [1955] 2 All E.R. 173.

discretion, even when the original litigation is at an end. A narrower reading of the authorities would suggest that, especially in criminal proceedings where the defence of an accused man is at stake, the privilege cannot be claimed where there are no reasonable grounds for the client having any recognisable interest in asserting it. The privilege can also be claimed by third parties but only where there is a clear congruence of interest between themselves and any client to whom the privilege attaches.

(d) the subject matter of the privilege: the privilege is about communications. It is not about facts. In *Brown v. Foster*[52] a lawyer attended a hearing on behalf of his client who was charged with embezzlement. The prosecution produced an accounts book in which the defendant was supposed to record money received. There was no entry for one particular transaction. Subsequently the book was again produced and miraculously an entry recording that transaction in the accused's handwriting was found. The defendant brought an action for malicious prosecution. The issue was whether the lawyer could be called as a witness to testify that, on the first production of the book, there was no entry:

> The counsel was called to state, not what he learned from his client, but whether a certain entry was then in that book. There is no breach of professional confidence in answering those questions. I agree that what passes between counsel and client ought not to be communicated and is not admissible in evidence, but with respect of matter which counsel sees with his eyes, he cannot refuse to answer.[53]

From this principle, where a defendant possesses documents which may be open to seizure by the police, these cannot be handed over to a solicitor for safekeeping and to secure immunity through privilege. In *R. v. Justice of the Peace for Peterborough ex parte Hicks*[54] the clients sent their solicitor a document, a forged power of attorney, to seek advice. A warrant was issued to search the solicitor's premises and seize the document under section 16 of the Forgery Act 1916:

> . . . the solicitor who holds the document in the right of his client and can assert in respect of its seizure no greater authority than the client himself or herself possesses. The client in this case would have possessed no lawful authority or excuse that would prevent the document's seizure. In my view the solicitor himself can be in no better position. The solicitor's authority or excuse in a case like this is the authority or excuse of the client.[55]

Similarly in *R. v. King*[56] the defendant forged an invoice which he hoped would support a possible defence and throw the blame on a third party.

[52] (1857) 1 H&N 736.
[53] *ibid., per* Pollock C.B.; cf *Bursill v. Tanner* (1885) 16 Q.B.D. 1 — a solicitor can be obliged to disclose the identity of his client.
[54] [1978] 1 All E.R. 225.
[55] *ibid.* at 228d–e, *per* Eveleigh J.
[56] [1983] 1 All E.R. 929.

This document was handed to the solicitor and then was forwarded to a handwriting expert to be compared with other documents which had been in possession of the Crown. The prosecution called the expert to produce the document which became an exhibit in the case.

> . . . the rule is that in the case of expert witnesses legal professional privilege attaches to confidential communications between the solicitor and the expert, but it does not attach to the chattels or documents on which the expert based his opinion, or to the independent opinion of the expert himself: see *Harmony Shipping Co v. Davis*.[57] The reasons for that are that there is no property in an expert witness any more than in any other witness and the court is entitled, in order to ascertain the truth, to have the actual facts which the expert has observed adduced before it in considering his opinion.[58]

Such a document was not privileged because it had not been produced for the purpose of the lawyer/client relationship. However the instructions to the expert and his report remained privileged. This can be distinguished from *R. v. R.*[59] where the accused was charged with rape and incest. An expert witness carried out DNA tests on a sample of the defendant's blood at the request of the defence.[60] At the trial, the scientist was called as a witness for the prosecution. The dispute centred on the fact that the expert's evidence was based on a blood sample which had been taken by the appellant's doctor. That sample was not produced in evidence and in all likelihood had been used up in the tests. But at common law and under section 10 of the Police and Criminal Evidence Act 1984 the sample was an item which could be subject to legal privilege because it was brought into existence (unlike the document in *King*) for the purposes of obtaining the expert's advice. Thus the sample was privileged as was any opinion which the expert had formed as a result of her tests on that sample.

(e) pre-existing documents: legal professional privilege protects documents (and other items as in *R*) which are brought into existence for the purpose of instructing a lawyer and obtaining his or her advice. Where a document existed before the litigation was contemplated but was obtained by the solicitor for the purposes of the litigation, this is not privileged from production. In *Ventouris v. Mountain*[61] the plaintiff claimed against the underwriters for the loss of a ship in an explosion. The defendants believed that the plaintiff had caused or connived at the loss of the ship and, as a

[57] [1979] 3 All E.R. 177.
[58] *King supra* at 931c–e, *per* Dunn L.J.
[59] [1994] 4 All E.R. 260.
[60] Under the Police and Criminal Evidence Act 1984, s.62, the police have no power to take an intimate sample without the consent of the accused. Refusal to give a sample is only sanctioned under subs. (10) by allowing the trier of fact to draw any necessary inference. Under s.63 non-intimate samples do not require consent under certain conditions and these can include mouth swabs and saliva as a result of the Criminal Justice and Public Order Act 1994, s.58.
[61] [1991] 3 All E.R. 472.

result of information supplied by the plaintiff's cousin, refused to pay. The plaintiff sought discovery of documents obtained by the defendants from the cousin:

Ventouris v. Mountain [1991] 3 All E.R. 472 at 475g–477f, _per_ Bingham L.J.

The doctrine of legal professional privilege is rooted in the public interest, which requires that hopeless and exaggerated claims and unsound and spurious defences be so far as possible discouraged, and civil disputes so far as possible settled without resort to judicial decision. To this end it is necessary that actual and potential litigants, be they claimants or respondents, should be free to unburden themselves without reserve to their legal advisers, and their legal advisers be free to give honest and candid advice on a sound factual basis, without fear that these communications may be relied on by an opposing party if the dispute comes before the court for decision. It is the protection of confidential communications between client and legal adviser which lies at the heart of legal professional privilege . . . Without the consent of the client, and in the absence of iniquity or dispute between client and solicitor, no inquiry may be made into or disclosure made of any instructions which the client gave the solicitor or any advice the solicitor gave the client . . .

Even confining oneself to the litigious field, it is however plain that legal professional privilege does not end there. Confidential communications between a party to litigation or his legal adviser and third parties for the purposes of the litigation are without doubt protected from production to the other party. So are documents prepared for the dominant purpose of submission to a legal adviser in connection with actual or anticipated litigation . . . The issue is how much further the privilege extends. The plaintiff argues that it does not extend to cover any original document, even if obtained by a party to litigation or his legal adviser for the purposes of the litigation, if the document did not come into existence for purposes of the litigation. The defendant argues that the privilege covers any original document obtained by a party to litigation or his legal adviser for purposes of the litigation whether or not the document came into existence for purposes of the litigation and (therefore) whether or not the document existed before the litigation was contemplated or commenced.

. . . Our system of civil procedure is founded on the rule that the interests of justice are best served if parties to litigation are obliged to disclose and produce for the other party's inspection all documents in their possession . . . [D]isclosure being generally regarded as beneficial, any exception has to be justified as serving the public interest which gives rise to the exception . . .

I begin with *Anderson v. Bank of British Columbia*[62] . . . James L.J. did, however, formulate the principle, much quoted since, 'that as you have no right to see your adversary's brief, you have no right to see that which comes into existence merely as materials for the brief'. The words I have emphasised make clear that he did not contemplate the extension of privilege to documents which were in existence before any question of litigation arose . . .

In *Southwark and Vauxhall Water Co v. Quick*[63] the plaintiff company sued its former engineer. Before the action documents were prepared to be laid before the company's solicitor for his advice, although there was some doubt whether all the documents were laid before him. The Court of Appeal held that if the documents came into existence merely for the purpose of being laid before the solicitor for his

[62] (1876) 2 Ch. D. 644.
[63] (1878) 3 Q.B.D. 315.

advice it made no difference whether they were prepared at his request or not and that if the documents were brought into existence for that purpose it made no difference whether they were in fact laid before him or not. While pre-existing documents (by which I mean documents in existence before there was any question of litigation) were not in issue, the rules as formulated would plainly not have covered them.

While pre-existing documents are not subject to legal professional privilege, it was suggested in *R. v. Inland Revenue ex parte Goldberg*[64] that where a copy of an existing document was made for the purpose of obtaining legal advice, that copy might be privileged even where the original document was not privileged. This was based on *The Palermo*[65] which was a collision action between two ships, the British-owned Rivoli and the foreign-owned Palermo. The Board of Trade took depositions from the crew of the Rivoli and allowed the solicitors for the Rivoli owners to take copies. They refused to allow the same latitude to the solicitors for the owners of the Palermo, the defendants, since no similar depositions had been made by that ship's crew. The defendants sought discovery of the plaintiffs' copies. This was refused:

> Here discovery is sought of copies of certain depositions and these were obtained for the purposes of this action, and as the phase is, 'to form part of the brief'. Therefore I think that they are privileged, and I shall not inquire for what purpose the original depositions were taken, since it is the copies of which discovery is sought, and which were obtained for the purposes I have stated.[66]

But this was doubted in *Chadwick v. Bowman*[67] in which Denman J. said:

> The originals of these documents would have been admissible in evidence against the defendant, and it seems to me that there is nothing in the circumstances under which the copies came into existence to render them privileged against inspection.[68]

This approach was certainly approved in *Ventouris v. Mountain* when Bingham L.J. said (albeit *obiter*):

> This does suggest a general rule that non-privileged documents do not, without more, acquire privilege simply because they are copied by a solicitor for purposes of an action. A non-privileged original document handed to a solicitor for purposes of an action and not copied would seem to be even more remote from any sustainable claim to privilege.[69]

However legal professional privilege may be available if there is a selection of pre-existing documents, not themselves privileged, but which

[64] [1988] 3 All E.R. 248.
[65] (1884) 9 P.D. 6.
[66] *ibid.* at 7–8, *per* Cotton L.J.
[67] (1886) 16 Q.B.D. 561.
[68] *ibid.* at 562.
[69] *Ventouris supra* at 480e–f.

have been copied or assembled by a solicitor and which, if disclosed, would be likely to betray the trend of legal advice. In *Lyell v. Kennedy (No. 3)*[70] the defendant objected to producing (*inter alia*) copies of entries in registers and public records and photographs of tombstones and houses on the grounds that these documents had been made by his solicitor for the purpose of the defence. In *Ventouris*, Bingham L.J. commented on this case:

Ventouris v. Mountain [1991] 3 All E.R. 472 at 479c–g, _per_ Bingham L.J.

The Court of Appeal (in *Lyall v. Kennedy*) upheld the claim to privilege. The ground of the decision is made clear by Cotton L.J. who relied on an earlier case, *Walsham v. Stainton*[71] in which Wood V.-C.—

> . . . protected the records and extracts from books which had been made by an accountant for the defendants, who had collected together a number of entries, because the extracts, when put together, showed the view which he and the solicitor of the defendants took of the particular fraud which they were there investigating, and the judge considered that to order the defendants to produce them would be not only giving production to the parties who were asking for production, but giving them a clue to the advice which had been given by the solicitor, and giving them the benefit of the professional opinion which had been formed by the solicitor and those who had acted in a professional capacity for the defendant.

. . . The ratio of the decision is, I think, that where the selection of documents which a solicitor has copied or assembled betrays the trend of the advice which he is giving the client the documents are privileged.

This approach was followed in *Dubai Bank Ltd v. Galadari (No 7)*.[72] Legal professional privilege extends to copies of client's pre-existing documents even if these are not in themselves privileged insofar as the selection tends to betray the advice given by the solicitor to the client.

(f) no "ambushing": while legal professional privilege enables a party to keep, for example, witness statements or reports from expert witnesses secret, it does not enable that party to "ambush" the opposition with them. In civil proceedings, R.S.C., Ord. 38, r.2A empowers the court to order a party to give written statements of the oral evidence on which that party is going to rely.

2A.—(2) At the summons for directions in an action commenced by writ the Court shall direct every party to serve on the other parties, within 14 weeks . . . of the hearing of the summons and on such terms as the Court may specify, written statements of the oral evidence which the party intends to adduce on any issues of fact to be decided at the trial.

[70] (1884) [1881–5] All E.R. Rep 814.
[71] (1863) 71 E.R. 357.
[72] [1992] 1 All E.R. 658.

If any party fails to do this and wishes to adduce evidence which has not been disclosed, he or she can only do so with the leave of the court:

2A.—(10) Where a party fails to comply with a direction for the exchange of witness statements he shall not be entitled to adduce evidence to which the direction related without the leave of the court.

Even where the party does disclose, under subsection (7)(b) the witness cannot testify to matters the substance of which is not in the written statement, unless there is the consent of the other parties or the leave of the court. There is no compulsory disclosure of privileged material but if a party wishes to rely on it, he or she has little choice.

In criminal cases, there is mutual disclosure under the provisions of the Criminal Procedure and Investigations Act 1996 although for many years the prosecution has been under an obligation not only to disclose prosecution evidence on which they would rely but also any unused material which might be of use to the defendant.[73]

Exceptions to legal professional privilege

There are three exceptions:

(a) proof of innocence: previously it was considered that the public interest in the liberty of the subject overrode legal professional privilege. In *R. v. Barton*[74] and *R. v. Ataou*[75] the court accepted that there was a balancing act to be performed and held that it would be for the accused to show on the balance of probabilities that the client no longer had a recognisable interest. However, as has been discussed earlier, both decisions were overruled by the House of Lords in *R. v. Derby Magistrates' Court ex parte B.*[76]

(b) communications to facilitate fraud: communications before a crime are not privileged if their purpose was to guide the commission of a crime. In *R. v. Cox and Railton*[77] the defendants sought the advice of a solicitor with reference to drawing up a bill of sale which was alleged to be fraudulent. The solicitor was compelled to disclose what had passed in the meeting:

R. v. Cox and Railton (1884) 15 Cox C.C. 611 at 613j, 620–621, _per_ Stephen J.

The conduct of . . . the solicitor appears to have been unobjectionable. He was consulted in the common course of business, and gave a proper opinion in good

[73] See 321, *et seq.*
[74] [1972] 2 All E.R. 1192.
[75] [1988] 2 All E.R. 321.
[76] [1995] 4 All E.R. 526.
[77] (1884) 15 Cox C.C. 611.

faith. The question therefore is, whether, if a client applies to a legal adviser for advice intended to facilitate or to guide the client in the commission of a crime or fraud, the legal adviser being ignorant of the purpose for which his advice is wanted, the communication between the two is privileged. We expressed our opinion at the end of the argument that no such privilege existed. If it did, the result would be that a man intending to commit treason or murder might safely take legal advice for the purpose of enabling himself to do so with impunity, and that the solicitor to whom the application was made would not be at liberty to give information against his client for the purpose of frustrating his criminal purpose . . .

We are greatly pressed with the argument that, speaking practically, the admission of any such exception to the privilege of legal advisers as that it is not to extend to communications made in furtherance of any criminal or fraudulent purpose would greatly diminish the value of that privilege. The privilege must, it was argued, be violated in order to ascertain whether it exists. The secret must be told in order to see whether it ought to be kept . . .

In each particular case the court must determine upon the facts actually given in evidence, or proposed to be given in evidence, whether it seems probable that the accused person may have consulted his legal adviser, not after the commission of the crime for the legitimate purpose of being defended, but before the commission of the crime, for the purpose of being guided or helped in committing it. We are far from saying that the question whether the advice was taken before or after the offence will always be decisive as to the admissibility of such evidence. Courts must in every instance judge for themselves on the special facts of each particular case, just as they must judge whether a witness deserves to be examined on the supposition that he is hostile or whether a dying declaration was made in the immediate prospect of death . . . Of course, the power in question ought to be used with the greatest care not to hamper prisoners in making their defence, and not to enable unscrupulous persons to acquire knowledge to which they have no right, and every precaution should be taken against compelling unnecessary disclosures.[78]

The limits of this rule can be seen in civil proceedings in *Crescent Farm (Sidcup) Sports Ltd v. Sterling Offices Ltd.*[79] The plaintiffs had originally sold land to the first defendants but with a right to buy it back if the defendants sold it within 20 years. The first defendants wished to sell it to the second defendants and, while appearing to negotiate a re-sale with the plaintiffs, sought counsel's opinion as to the validity of the pre-emption clause and in fact conveyed the land to the second defendants. The plaintiffs sought discovery of the relevant documents, including instructions to the defendants' solicitors. Goff J. held that the wide submission of the plaintiffs would endanger the whole basis of legal professional privilege. "Fraud" did not extend to every act or scheme which could give rise to a civil claim. Parties were entitled to seek legal advice as to their liability in contract and tort if they followed a particular course of action.

Where fraud is alleged, the party seeking disclosure must show a strong evidential basis for the allegation and a court will be slow to deprive a party of the protection of legal professional privilege on an interlocutory application.[80]

[78] *ibid.* at 613j, 620–621, *per* Stephen J.
[79] [1971] 3 All E.R. 1192.
[80] *Derby & Co Ltd v. Weldon (No. 7)* [1990] 3 All E.R. 161.

In criminal proceedings, the question as to the limits on privilege emerges in relation to police search warrants issued under Pt. 2 of the Police and Criminal Evidence Act 1984. Under section 8 warrants should not be issued to seize items subject to legal professional privilege, as defined in section 10. However under **section 10(2)**:

10.—(2) Items held with the intention of furthering a criminal purpose are not items subject to legal privilege.

This subsection was interpreted in *Francis & Francis v. Central Criminal Court*,[81] in which the police were investigating the affairs of a suspected drug trafficker. They believed that he was laundering the proceeds of the trafficking by purchasing property for various members of his family. The police applied for a warrant requiring the solicitor acting for one of the family to produce all files in their possession relating to a particular conveyance. Were these documents privileged? The question arose as to whether section 10(2) refers the the intention of the person holding the items (*i.e.* the solicitor) or whether it included the intention of any other person (*i.e.* the client or the alleged trafficker) irrespective of whether the solicitors holding the documents were party to that intention. The solicitors were ignorant of the source of the money and argued that the documents could not be "held with the intention of furthering a criminal purpose" as they did not have such an intention. On the subsidiary issue, the House agreed that a "criminal purpose" was not limited to "criminal offence". The bank robber salting away the proceeds of the robbery does not have "the intention of furthering a criminal offence" but does so with the intention of furthering his criminal purpose.[82]

On the central question, a minority, Lords Bridge and Oliver, adopted a literal interpretation of the statute and held that section 10(2) means that it is the holder of the documents (*i.e.* the solicitor) who must have the criminal purpose:

Francis & Francis v. Central Criminal Court [1988] 3 All E.R. 775 at 780d–f, _per_ Lord Bridge

My noble and learned friend Lord Griffiths gives the example: 'Ammunition held in the armoury with the intention of firing it at Bisley must be inspected'. Here the context is designed to demonstrate that the phrase 'held with the intention' cannot refer to the intention of the holder. But all this shows, with respect, is that the sentence is expressed in slipshod and ungrammatical English. To convey the writer's evident meaning accurately and grammatically it must read: 'Ammunition held in the armoury and intended to be fired at Bisley must be inspected'. This analysis may sound pedantic, but it is a basic rule of statutory construction that the draftsman is presumed to use the English language accurately and grammatically.

But the issue is not the construction of this subsection and thus the limits of police powers of search and seizure. The House of Lords is defining the

[81] [1988] 3 All E.R. 775.
[82] *ibid.* at 797j–798a, *per* Lord Goff.

scope of legal professional privilege, not simply for the purposes of section 10(2) but generally. The dissentients felt that their restrictive attitude was narrower than the common law expounded by Stephen J. in *Cox and Railton* when he talked of the privilege being overridden only where the client has conspired with the lawyer or deceived him. Even this latter ground requires the judge to exercise his discretion on the "special facts of each particular case" and seemingly does not encompass every straightforward situation of the client lying to his lawyer. Lord Bridge's concern was that the majority went beyond Stephen's statement of the common law, treating otherwise privileged communications between an innocent solicitor and an innocent client as losing their privilege by reference to the intention of some third party who has a criminal purpose to further.

The majority rejected this and felt that the subsection reflected the common law:

Francis & Francis v. Central Criminal Court op. cit. at 775a–h, *per* Lord Goff

. . . does the relevant intention have to be the intention of the person (*i.e.* in this example the solicitor) who has the items in his possession at the time when production of them is called for?

When one looks at the full meaning of the words, there is no compelling reason why the words should be so read. If documents are said to have come into the possession of a solicitor with the intention of furthering a criminal purpose, that intention could just as well be the intention of some person other than the solicitor, and in particular, the intention of his client. Furthermore, there are overwhelming reasons which favour that interpretation. First, the interpretation would reflect the common law position; and since in my opinion subsection (1) is intended to reflect the common law position, it would be most surprising if subsection (2) was not likewise intended to do so . . . Second, it would be equally surprising if, in the context of Pt. II of the 1984 Act, and its evident purpose, the legislature should have intended to restrict the effect of subsection (2), and therefore the power of the police in their efforts to detect crime, by confining subsection (2) (which is expressly directed towards a case where there is an intention to further a criminal purpose) only to those cases where the solicitor has an intention, and so extending legal privilege to protect the criminal. It is not to be forgotten that the privilege is the privilege of the client, not of the solicitor; and so it is to be expected that the privilege should be negatived where the client has the intention to further a criminal purpose, whether or not his intention is shared with his solicitor. Indeed, one of the most important points established in the leading case of *R. v. Cox and Railton* was that legal professional privilege does not exist where the client has such an intention, even though his intention is unknown to his solicitor; and it would surely be most extraordinary if section 10(2) was drafted with the intention of excluding that principle, thereby substantially extending the scope of the privilege to protect the dishonest client. Furthermore, the opposite conclusion would not merely lead to the remarkable result that two different versions of legal privilege would have to coexist, the common law version, which has long been entrenched in our law, and the statutory version encapsulated in section 10; but also that, in consequence, the extraordinary position would be reached that in certain circumstances the police would be prevented by legal privilege from calling for the production of certain documents although such documents, if obtained, would not be protected by legal privilege when placed in evidence before the court.

The majority's willingness to interpret the subsection broadly and treat it as reflecting the common law is defensible. But the criminal purpose in the case appears to be that of the drug trafficker and the House proceeded on the basis that both solicitor and client were innocent parties. The suggestion that the criminal intention of a third party, neither solicitor nor client, might defeat legal professional privilege seems dubious. Lord Oliver commented on the proposition that the interpretation reflected the common law:

> But this is, with respect, pure speculation. There is no, so far as I am aware, any authority in the common law dealing with the question whether a criminal intent on the part of a stranger to the relationship of solicitor and client destroys the privilege of the client. If, therefore, the subsection does indeed bear the meaning now sought to be ascribed to it by the respondent, it is breaking new ground and the legislative intent has to be gathered not from some supposed logical extension of the common law rule but from the words which Parliament has chosen to use.[83]

(c) statutory exclusion: legal professional privilege may be expressly or impliedly excluded. One example may be proceedings where the welfare of the child is the court's paramount consideration. In *Barking and Dagenham London Borough Council v. O.*[84] care proceedings were commenced by the local authority under the Children Act 1989. The mother sought not to disclose medical reports obtained by her solicitors. Although there was authority[85] that in wardship proceedings, legal professional privilege could be overridden, Douglas Brown J. held that the particular nature of the wardship jurisdiction had not been inherited by the Children Act jurisdiction. However in *Re R*[86] Thorpe J. declined to follow this lead:

> Legal professional privilege is a creature of case law and, where limitations by exception have seemed necessary, those limitations have equally been developed by case law. In my judgment, where the court considers the welfare of a child, the power that it holds, allied to its responsibility, enables it to override a legal professional privilege which is set up to preserve or enhance the adversarial position of one of the parties.
>
> For my part, I would wish to see case law go yet further and to make it plain that the legal representatives in possession of such material relevant to determination but contrary to the interests of their client, not only are unable to resist disclosure by reliance on legal professional privilege, but have a positive duty to disclose to the other parties and to the court.[87]

Statements Without Prejudice

In civil actions, negotiation and settlement by the parties is encouraged as opposed to them inevitably seeking recourse to a full trial. Lawyers talk

[83] *ibid.* at 793g–h, *per* Lord Oliver.
[84] [1993] 4 All E.R. 59.
[85] *Re A* [1991] 2 F.L.R. 473.
[86] [1993] 4 All E.R. 702.
[87] *ibid.* at 704j–705a.

and write to oposing lawyers, often making concessions and offers which would be damaging to their clients if they were revealed in court. Such communications do not in themselves attract legal professional privilege since they are between the parties or, more realistically, between their lawyers. But the risk of such statements being held against them is removed by treating them as "without prejudice" statements to which privilege attaches. In *Walker v. Wilsher*,[88] after the conclusion of an action, an application was made by the losing defendant to deprive the plaintiff of his costs on the grounds that the defendant had offered to settle the case before trial for the amount of damages finally accepted. This was proved by letters marked "without prejudice" which had been exchanged by the parties before the trial. The Court of Appeal held that these letters should not have been admitted:

> It is, I think, a good rule to say that nothing which is written or said without prejudice should be looked at without the consent of both parties, otherwise the whole object of the limitation would be destroyed. I am therefore of opinion that the learned judge should not have taken these matters into consideration in determining whether there was good cause, and as that was all that was before him on the point, if that is excluded, it follows that there was no good cause, and that the plaintiff should not have been deprived of his costs.[89]

As Lord Esher makes clear, the privilege is a joint privilege which can only be waived with the consent of both parties. It is a privilege that attaches to all forms of communication, oral as well as written. Nor need the term "without prejudice" be expressly used as the court will often infer that negotiations are without prejudice. The rule was explained in:

Rush and Tompkins Ltd v. Greater London Council [1988] 3 All E.R. 737 at 739h–740j, _per_ Lord Griffiths

The 'without prejudice' rule is a rule governing the admissibility of evidence and is founded upon the public policy of encouraging litigants to settle their differences rather than litigate them to a finish. It is nowhere more clearly expressed than in the judgment of Oliver L.J. in *Cutts v. Head*.[90]

> That the rule rests, at least in part, upon public policy is clear from many authorities, and the convenient starting point of the inquiry is the nature of the underlying policy. It is that parties should be encouraged so far as possible to settle their disputes without resort to litigation and should not be discouraged by the knowledge that anything that is said in the course of such negotiations (and that includes, of course, as much the failure to reply to an offer as an actual reply) may be used to their prejudice in the course of the proceedings . . . The public policy justification, in truth, essentially rests on the desirability of preventing statements or offers made in the course of negotiations for settlement being brought before the court of trial as admissions on the question of liability.

[88] (1889) 23 Q.B.D. 335.
[89] *ibid.* at 337, *per* Lord Esher M.R.
[90] [1984] Ch. 290 at 306.

The rule applies to exclude all negotiations genuinely aimed at settlement whether oral or in writing from being given in evidence. A competent solicitor will always head any negotiating correspondence 'without prejudice' to make clear beyond doubt that in the event of the negotiations being unsuccessful they are not to be referred to at the subsequent trial. However, the application of the rule is not dependent upon the use of the phrase 'without prejudice' and if it is clear from the surrounding circumstances that the parties were seeking to compromise the action, evidence of the content of those negotiations will, as a general rule, not be admissible at the trial and cannot be used to establish an admission or partial admission. I cannot therefore agree with the Court of Appeal that the problem in the present case should be resolved by a linguistic approach to the meaning of the phrase ' without prejudice'. I believe that the question has to be looked at more broadly and resolved by balancing two different public interests namely the public interest in promoting settlements and the public interest in full discovery between parties to litigation.

Nearly all the cases in which the scope of the 'without prejudice' rule has been considered, concern the admissibility of evidence at trial after negotiations have failed. In such circumstances no question of discovery arises because the parties are well aware of what passed between them in the negotiations. These cases show that the rule is not absolute and resort may be had to the 'without prejudice' material for a variety of reasons when the justice of the case requires it. It is unnecessary to make any deep examination of these authorities to resolve the present appeal but they all illustrate the underlying purpose of the rule which is to protect a litigant from being embarrassed by any admission made purely in an attempt to achieve a settlement. Thus the 'without prejudice' material will be admissible if the issue is whether or not the negotiations resulted in an agreed settlement,which is the point that Lindley L.J. was making in *Walker v. Wilsher* and which was applied in *Tomlin v. Standard Telephones and Cables Ltd.*[91] The court will not permit the phrase to be used to exclude an act of bankruptcy: see *In re Daintrey ex parte Holt*[92] nor to suppress a threat if an offer is not accepted: see *Kitcat v. Sharp.*[93] In certain circumstances the 'without prejudice' correspondence may be looked at to determine a question of costs after judgment has been given: see *Cutts v. Head.* There is also authority for the proposition that the admission of an 'independent fact' in no way connected with the merits of the cause is admissible even if made in the course of negotiations for a settlement. Thus an admission was in the handwriting of one of the parties was received in evidence in *Waldridge v. Kennison.*[94] I regard this as an exceptional case and it should not be allowed to whittle down the protection given to the parties to speak freely about all issues in the litigation both factual and legal when seeking compromise and, for the purpose of establishing a basis of compromise, admitting certain facts. If the compromise fails the admission of facts made for the purpose of the compromise should not be held against the maker of the admission and should therefore not be received in evidence . . .

Confidential Communications

Confidential communications may occur in many relationship whether with one's doctor, priest or therapist. There are different aspects of the protection of such communications:

[91] [1969] 1 3 All E.R. 201.
[92] [1893] 2 Q.B. 116.
[93] (1882) 48 L.T. 64.
[94] (1794) 1 Esp. 142.

(1) there is some immunity from search and seizure by the police. This immunity is provided under sections 9 and 11 of the Police and Criminal Evidence Act 1984 and relates to certain kinds of material such as personal records held in confidence, human tissue or tissue fluid, or journalistic material. The police may obtain access to such material by application to a circuit judge under Schedule 1 to the Act.[95]

(2) in evidential terms, the law does not recognise any privilege for confidential communications outside the sphere of legal professional privilege. In *Alfred Crompton Amusement Machine Ltd v. Customs and Excise Commissioners*[96] the House of Lords confirmed that confidentiality itself was not a basis for upholding a claim to public interest immunity:

> 'Confidentiality' is not a separate head of privilege, but it may be a very material consideration to bear in mind when privilege is claimed on the ground of public interest . . .[97]

Similarly confidentiality is not a basis for an assertion of a private privilege. Doctors and priests can be compelled to disclose communications received in the course of their work in court.

(3) in substantive terms, the law will protect confidential relationships and intervene to protect by injunction the voluntary disclosure of confidential matters.

(4) whereas the doctrine of public interest immunity will prevent the names of police informants from being revealed in civil proceedings and, in some cases, in criminal trials, common law will compel disclosure of the names of other informant. In *Norwich Pharmacal Co. v. Customs and Excise Commissioners*[98] the applicants owned the patent of a chemical compound "furazolidone". This chemical was being imported into the country in breach of the patent and the applicants sought the names of the importers from the commissioners. The House of Lords decision means to order disclosure that litigants are able to demand the identity of a wrongdoer from a third party even where that party is not involved in the wrong.[99] In *British Steel Corp v. Granada Television Ltd*[1] a television company received copies of secret documents from British Steel's files. These were then used in making a programme about a nationwide steel strike. British Steel applied for an order that Granada reveal the identity of their informant. The House of Lords held that journalists

[95] Lidstone K. and Palmer C., *Bevan and Lidstone's Investigation of Crime* (2nd ed., 1996) 153 *et seq.*
[96] [1973] 2 All E.R. 1169.
[97] *ibid.* at 1184f–1185d, *per* Lord Cross.
[98] [1973] 2 All E.R. 943.
[99] See also *Bankers Trust Co v. Shapira* [1980] 3 All E.R. 353.
[1] [1981] 1 All E.R. 417.

do not enjoy any immunity from the obligation to disclose. However it was recognised that there is a public interest in the free flow of information and in the protection of a source. Confidences bona fide given should not be breached unless it was necessary in the interests of justice:

British Steel Corp. v. Granada Television Ltd [1981] 1 All E.R. 417 at 459j–460a, _per_ Lord Wilberforce

Although, as I have said, the media, and journalists, have no immunity, it remains true that there may be an element of public interest in protecting the revelation of the source. This appears from the speeches in *Norwich Pharmacal* . . . The court ought not to compel confidences bona fide given to be breached unless necessary in the interests of justice . . . There is a public interest in the free flow of information, the strength of which will vary from case to case. In some cases it may be very weak; on others it may be very strong. The court must take this into account. How ought the discretion which the court undoubtedly has to be exercised? Sir Robert Megarry V.-C. considered this and exercised it in favour of BSC. I would, for myself, give somewhat greater weight to the public interest element involved in preserving, *qua* the relevant information, the confidence under which it was obtained than he did. But I think that even so the balance was strongly in BSC's favour. They suffered a grievous wrong, in which Granada themselves became involved, not innocently, but with active participation. To confine BSC to its remedy against Granada and to deny them the opportunity of a remedy against the source would be a significant denial of justice. Granada had on their side, and I recognise this, the public interest that people should be informed about the steel strike, of the attitude of BSC, and perhaps that of the government towards settling the strike. But there is no 'iniquity' here, no misconduct to be revealed. The courts . . . had to form their opinion whether the strong public interest in favour of doing justice and against denying it was outweighed by the perfectly real considerations that Granada put forward. I have reached the conclusion that it was not.

(5) there is now a statutory privilege under the Contempt of Court Act 1981:

10.—No court may require a person to disclose, nor is any person guilty of contempt of court for refusing to disclose, the source of information contained in a publication for which he is responsible, unless it be established to the satisfaction of the court that disclosure is necessary in the interests of justice or national security or for the prevention of disorder or crime.

In *Secretary of State for Defence v. Guardian Newspapers*[2] a copy of a classified document (about the arrival of cruise missiles at RAF Greenham Common) was leaked to *The Guardian* who published it. The Crown sought recovery of the photocopy in order to discover

[2] [1984] 3 All E.R. 601.

the identity of the informant. The House of Lords held that the protection afforded by section 10 applied in such circumstances and that the burden of showing that disclosure was necessary (and not merely expedient) rested on the party seeking that disclosure:

Secretary of State for Defence v. Guardian Newspapers [1984] 3 All E.R. 601 at 606e–607g, *per* Lord Diplock

The nature of the protection is the removal of compulsion to disclose in judicial proceedings the identity or nature of the source of any information contained in the publication, even though the disclosure would be relevant to the determination by the court of an issue in those particular proceedings; and the only reasonable inference is that the purpose of the protection is the same as that which underlay the discretion vested in the judge at common law to refuse to compel disclosure of sources of information, viz unless informers could be confident that their identity would not be revealed sources of information would dry up.

The words with which the section starts, before it comes to specifying any exceptions, impose a prohibition on the court itself that is perfectly general in its terms . . . This prohibition is in no way qualified by the nature of the judicial proceedings . . .

Again, what the court is prohibited from requiring is not described by reference to the form the requirement takes but by reference to its consequences, viz disclosure of the source of information. If compliance with the requirement, whatever form it takes, will, or is sought in order to enable, another party to the proceedings to identify the source by adding to the pieces already in the possession of that party the last piece to a jigsaw puzzle in which the identity of the source of information would remain concealed unless that last piece became available to put into position, the requirement will fall foul of the ban imposed by the general words with which the section starts . . .

So I turn next to the exceptions that the latter part of section 10 provides to the general ban on the court requiring disclosure of sources of information that is imposed by the opening words. There are only four interests, and each of these is specific, that are singled out for protection, viz, (a) justice, (b) national security, (c) prevention of disorder and (d) the prevention of crime.

The exceptions include no reference to 'the public interest' generally and I would add that in my view the expression 'justice', the interests of which are entitled to protection, is not used in a general sense as the antonym of 'injustice' but in the technical sense of the administration of justice in the course of legal proceedings in a court of law, or, by reason of the extended definition of 'court' in section 19 of the 1981 Act before a tribunal or body exercising the judicial power of the state.

The onus of proving that an order of the court which has or may have the consequences of disclosing the sources of information falls within any of the exceptions lies on the party by whom the order is sought. The words 'unless it be established to the satisfaction of the court' make it explicit and so serve to emphasise what otherwise might have been left to be inferred from the application of the general rule of statutory construction: the onus of establishing that he falls within an exception lies on the party who is seeking to rely on it. Again, the section uses the words 'necessary' by itself, instead of using the common statutory phrase 'necessary or expedient', to

> describe what must be established to the satisfaction of the court, which latter phrase gives to the judge a margin of discretion; expediency, however great, is not enough: section 10 requires actual necessity to be established; and whether it has or not is a question of fact that the judge has to find in favour of necessity as a condition precedent to his having any jurisdiction to order disclosure of sources of information.[3]

The Privilege against Self-incrimination

A witness may, if he or she so wishes, decline to answer a question where such answers might expose the witness[4] to subsequent criminal proceedings. In *Blunt v. Park Lane Hotel Ltd*[5] the plaintiff sued for slander based on an allegation that she had been guilty of adultery. The defendants were allowed to administer interrogatories to her to support their plea of justification as the old church courts' sanctions over sexual misconduct were now obsolete. As adultery was not a criminal offence, the witness could not claim the shelter of the privilege. Goddard L.J. explained the scope of the privilege:

> . . . the rule is that no one is bound to answer any question if the answer thereto would, in the opinion of the judge, have a tendency to expose the deponent to any criminal charge, penalty or forfeiture which the judge regards as reasonably likely to be preferred or sued for.

There must be reasonable grounds on which to apprehend a risk of such proceedings. In *R. v. Boyes*[6] the witness was handed a written pardon after declining to answer a question. He still declined to answer on the grounds that he might still be impeached by Parliament which was a process to which the pardon provided no bar. The court rejected the claim as there must be a real and appreciable risk. It is a privilege that applies in any legal proceedings and relates not only to oral testimony but also would permit a witness to refuse to produce documentary and real evidence.

The principle of access to evidence is displaced by the need for fairness to the accused and to minimise the risk that he or she will be convicted out of his or her own mouth. The instinct is that it is contrary to fairness to put witnesses in a position where they may be prosecuted if they answer, or punished in different ways, if they refuse to answer. This was accepted by the House of Lords in *AT & T Istel Ltd v. Tully*[7] who neverthless would restrict the scope of the privilege:

[3] See also *Re an inquiry under Companies Securities (Insider Dealing) Act 1985* [1988] 1 All E.R. 203; *Maxwell v. Pressdram Ltd* [1987] 1 All E.R. 656.
[4] Or spouse when the privilege is claimed in civil proceedings — Civil Evidence Act 1968, s.14(1)(b).
[5] [1942] 2 All E.R. 187.
[6] (1861) 30 L.J.Q.B. 301.
[7] [1992] 3 All E.R. 523.

***AT & T Istel Ltd v. Tully* [1992] 3 All E.R. 523 at 530a–c, *per* Lord Templeman**

. . . in my opinion, the privilege can only be justified on two grounds, first that it discourages the ill-treatment of a suspect and secondly that it discourages the production of dubious confessions. Neither of these considerations applies to the present appeal. It is difficult to see any reason why in civil proceedings the privilege against self-incrimination should be exercisable so as to enable a litigant to refuse relevant and even vital documents which are in his possession or power and which speak for themselves. And it is fanciful to suggest that an order on Mr Tully to say whether he has received Abbey's money and so what has happened to that money could result in his ill-treatment or in a dubious confession. I regard the privilege against self-incrimination exerciable in civil proceedings as an archaic and unjustifiable survival from the past when the court directs the production of relevant documents and requires the defendant to specify his dealings with the plaintiff's property or money.

Such a restrictive judicial attitude is mirrored in the numerous statutory exceptions which require persons to provide information which may be used as the basis for a criminal prosecution.[8] Examples are sections 434 and 436 of the Companies Act 1985 which require company officers to answer questions put by Board of Trade inspectors appointed to investigate fraud within the company; environmental legislation requires compulsory provision of water quality information by self-monitoring which can provide evidence for subsequent prosecutions. Section 2 of the Criminal Justice Act 1987 requires any person under investigation by the Serious Fraud Office to answer questions, produce documents and furnish information. The validity of such legislation has been questioned in *Saunders v. United Kingdom*.[9] The defendant was convicted of fraud on the basis of answers that he had been compelled to give in the course of investigations by inspectors from the Department of Trade. The Commission of Human Rights concluded that this infringed his freedom from self-incrimination and was in breach of the presumption of innocence and Article 6(2) of the European Convention on Human Rights. This is consistent with the approach of the European Court of Human Rights that any legal compulsion to produce incriminating evidence infringed the right of silence.[10] The European Court decided[11] that such evidence should not have been admitted, arguing that the public interest in combating fraud could not be invoked to justify the use of answers compulsorily obtained in a non-judicial investigation.[12]

[8] There are other statutes which compel the provision of information but where any statements made are inadmissible as evidence: Theft Act 1968, s.31(1); Criminal Damage Act 1971, s.9; Children Act 1989, s.98.

[9] The decision by the commission is reported in *The Independent*, September 30, 1994; the case was argued the full court in February 1996 — *The Times*, February 20, 1996.

[10] *Funke v. France* (1993) 16 E.H.R.R. 297.

[11] *The Times*, December 18, 1996.

[12] The case will not be referred to the Court of Appeal — *The Times*, February 1, 1997.

8

THE TESTIMONY OF WITNESSES: THEIR RELIABILITY, COMPETENCE AND COMPELLABILITY

THE PRIMACY OF ORAL EVIDENCE AND MODES OF PROOF

The trial system in England relies on the oral testimony of witnesses. Despite statutory inroads into this principle,[1] it is assumed that the evidence given by a witness present in court is superior to other forms of evidence. But the history of the use of evidence in our courts reveals no such early tradition:

Harding A., *A Social History of English Law* (1966) 126–128

The findings of the jury were the seeds of the trial as we know it today . . . The jury listened to no evidence in court, for it was called in only when pleading had arrived at a special issue of fact or the defendant asked for a decision on the general issue; and then it was expected to know the facts in dispute, rather than to decide upon them. The very simplicity of the jury as a method of settling cases often caused to be left to it both the functions of a group of witnesses providing facts and of a judge deciding questions of law. A number of different institutions seem to merge into each other: the twelve Anglo-Saxon oath-helpers, the 'jury' (its very name means 'sworn') which in some early instances seems to have been nominated jointly by the parties from their supporters, the 'suit' of supporters necessary in every claim, and sworn witnesses of the modern type. An early jury was sometimes composed of sworn groups from a number of villages, which provided the court with material for its decision: 'The eight men of Wormley being sworn say . . .'

. . . In practice the jury would usually not know the facts directly and would have to go to a man's house and ask him what he knew . . . But coroners, as part of their duty of recording the preliminaries of accusations, examined persons who could give information. A statute of 1554[2] made examination of criminals and the recording of it incumbent on coroners and J.P.s. A contemporary description of an Elizabethan criminal trial shows that the preliminary depositions were already being used as evidence in the trial, and that sworn witnesses for the prosecution carried on an altercation with the prisoner till the judges had heard enough.

The treatment of evidence was rudimentary: the criminal had no notice of those witnesses who would appear against him, and he was not allowed to arrange for

[1] Notably the admissibility of documentary hearsay under the Civil Evidence Act 1995 and the Criminal Justice Act 1988.

[2] 1 & 2 Ph. & M. c.13; see Langbein J., *Prosecuting Crime in the Renaissance* (1974).

any on his own behalf. The last condition was slowly modified in Elizabeth's reign, but at first the prisoner's witnesses could not be sworn . . . In any event, criminal trial was essentially still by jury and not by witnesses, as Chief Justice Coke often said, perhaps in dislike of the Crown's use of examination and bullied witnesses in political trials.

The chancellor's subpoena was the only way of enforcing the appearance of civil witnesses before 1563. Nevertheless throughout the middle ages witnesses to deeds and commecial transactions had appeared to sit with the jury when those deeds were in dispute. Here the witnesses were taking over some of the jury's original functions and forcing the jury into something like its modern position. Counsel became interested towards the end of the Middle Ages in assembling evidence to convince the jurymen: that is the modern way of presenting a case.[3] The change began in Chancery, for the chancellor, like the Roman Law judge, worked in his court without a jury, deciding issues on the evidence of deeds and witnesses. So, unlike his Common Law brethren, he had to evolve 'rules of evidence', to decide the relative weight of the different sorts of evidence and assess the reliability of witnesses. Only at this point, when it begins to be weighed in the balance, does a statement cease to be a verdict and becomes a piece of evidence at all.

In criminal cases, the rules remained rudimentary for centuries:

Harding A., *op. cit.* 274–275

The Trial of Treason Act (1696) was a turning point in the just regulation of criminal trials. The man accused of treason was to be given a copy of the indictment at least five days before arraignment; he was to have free access to counsel (whom the court would assign at the prisoner's request); And processes were allowed him to summon witnesses on his behalf, who would be sworn. He was not, however, to know the names of the witnesses against him; ordinary felons were not allowed counsel till 1837; and there were still few rules on the admissibility of evidence. The verbatim reports of the trial of John Donellan for murder, before Mr Justice Buller at Warwick assizes in 1781, shows well-developed methods of cross-examination, with objections to leading questions; but also a willingness to allow expert witnesses (physicians — it was a case of poisoning) to give decisive opinions on the whole question of guilt. The judge's summing up of the merely circumstantial evidence was weighted against the prisoner. Before the trial, the accused submitted a written defence which was read in court, for he could still not give evidence on oath — a grave disadvantage for a poor and ignorant man, unable to afford an elaborate defence.

Our legal culture has seen the emergence of the jury as the dominant form of trial and the emphasis placed upon the single self-contained hearing at which the facts and issues are decided. In a less literate world, it is not surprising to find the requirement that witnesses attend that hearing and testify orally. Some of the effects of the emphasis on the "day in court" and preference for oral testimony are:

- hearsay, *i.e.* statements from absent witnesses, is generally not admissible

[3] Hastings M., *The Court of Common Pleas in Fifteenth-Century England* (1971).

- witnesses are normally not permitted to give their testimony in advance of trial
- documentary evidence has remained suspect, requiring its provenance to be proved by oral testimony unless it belongs to a small class of public documents which are regarded as self-authenticating.[4] The second-class status of documents is seen especially in criminal proceedings in which a written statement is generally only admissible when the witness is unavailable to testify.[5] In civil proceedings, however, documents and documentary hearsay are now generally admissible.[6]

It has been argued[7] that this preference for oral testimony is a purely cultural one in the English-speaking world. The civil law systems in continental Europe display a marked preference for documentary evidence. As a German jurist puts it:

> Owing to the deficiencies of human observation and memory, and in view of the conscious or unconscious prejudice of the witnesses involves, a greater or lesser attitude of reserve [towards testimonial evidence] is called for. Testimonial evidence is therefore — apart from statements of the parties — the *least certain* means of proof. Generally speaking expert evidence, and above all documentary evidence, are to be preferred to it.[8]

Courts in civil law systems make extensive use of documents: in criminal proceedings, there will be pre-trial interviews with witnesses whose depositions will be their testimony at the trial proper:

Cooper J., "Criminal Investigations in France" 141 New L.J. (1991) 381

. . . police investigative powers are . . . far more limited in France than in this country and it is normal for the police to relinquish control of an investigation within one or two days of arrest, even in the most serious cases . . . [T]here is another method for investigating crime post arrest — a system under the direction of an examining magistrate, the *juge d'instruction* . . .

. . . All civil law systems are grounded in a philosophy of state responsibility and the French system is no exception. Thus, with an infallible Cartesian logic, it is axiomatic to the French system that the *juge d'instruction*, who is charged by the State with establishing the truth, should suffer no procedural or technical hindrance in investigating any matter that may be relevant to establishing guilt or innocence . . .

[4] Now under the Civil Evidence Act 1995, s.7 but see the simpler provisions for business documents under s.9 of the Act.
[5] Criminal Justice Act 1988, s.23 but note exceptions for business documents under s.24.
[6] Civil Evidence Act 1995.
[7] Spencer J. and Flin J., *The Evidence of Children — The Law and the Psychology* (2nd ed., 1993) Chap. 10; Spencer J., "Orality and the Evidence of Absent Witnesses" [1994] Crim.L.R. 628.
[8] Stein-Jonas, *Zivilprozessordnanz* (19th ed) Vol II 1572 cited in Honoré T., "The Primacy of Oral Evidence?" in Tapper C. (ed), *Crime, Proof and Punishment* (1981) 172 at 173.

A list of the powers of the *juge d'instruction* illustrates this point. They are very substantial. They include the power to interrogate the defendant anywhere, at any time; to interrogate any witness; to visit the scene of the crime with the defendant and any witness; to arrange identifications, or confrontations between accused and victim; to set up reconstructions of the crime to test evidence; and to investigate the social, economic and — if relevant — criminal background of the defendant and witnesses, and to draw inferences from such evidence. The investigation is not limited by time. And most significant of all, if the *juge* thinks there is a case to answer, he or she is obliged to pass on to the subsequent trial court a dossier which will contain all the relevant evidence on which the belief is grounded.

After such an investigation, the trial itself is a much shorter affair, dealing with the dossier prepared by the *juge d'instruction*, using witness depositions in a manner which would undoubtedly shorten common law trials but also revealing much information that would be inadmissible in a common law trial.

In civil proceedings in France, the preference for documentary evidence is even clearer. The French make documentary evidence a requirement in any matter involving 50 francs or above[9] and also make oral evidence inadmissible to contradict such a writing.[10] This contrast between common law and civil law, between oral and written traditions in evidence, can be exaggerated as the practices of differing systems often converge. But the distinction can be useful since, as Honoré argues, it demonstrates that a key characteristic of systems of evidence is the extent to which they control the mode of proof, that is, restricting how a matter may be proved in court. To give greater priority to either oral or to documentary evidence is such a controlling feature.[11] An ideal system of evidence would require a free system of proof so that all relevant evidence is admissible, leaving the probative value of the evidence, the weight, to be determined by the trier of fact. The traditional role of the jury in the common law has made such an open-ended approach impossible.

Evaluating Witness Testimony

There are many advantages in the triers of fact themselves listening to a witness:

- oral evidence is heard directly with no errors of transmission
- the evidence is given on oath and in a formal setting enhancing the likelihood that the witness will tell the truth
- the demeanour of the witness is in itself evidence from which the trier is able to assess the witness's credibility and therefore the weight to be given to the testimony

[9] Art. 1341 Code Civil, discussed in Honoré, *op. cit.* 172 at 181.
[10] Comparable to the "parol evidence" rule in common law.
[11] Honoré, *op. cit.* 172 at 181.

- that demeanour will be tested in cross-examination.

However, this presumes a rationality behind a trial, in the presentation of evidence and in the decision-making. Is this the case? Even when there is a contested trial, rational decisions can take a backseat to the high level of ritual in the formal procedures, dress and language which regulate the parties. On one level ritual contributes not only to the authority of the court but also to establishing the authoritative version of the events which is presented not merely in the courtroom but also for the consumption of the outside world. But the ritualism is an appeal which is less than rational, reinforcing a view of the courtroom as a reified rather than a human process. For example, one American sociologist[12] has suggested that the trial is a process of recasting the defendant, away from his own identity and into a stereotyped social role (as mugger, hooligan, drunk, or vagrant). The criminal trial becomes a degradation ceremony which reduces the defendant to a lower status and through him personifies broader patterns of social authority. Witnesses collude, voluntarily or not, in such a process.

Witnesses experience the courtroom as an imposed and imposing "world of authority"[13] with dominance and subordination clearly signposted. There is the deference shown by all the personnel towards the bench as well as those elements of "majesty": the elevated bench, private access to judge's "chambers" and the judge's throne-like chair. The geography of the court carries this on: in the dock, the defendant is raised but on a lesser level; there is a rail surround, not to stop an escape attempt but representative of captivity. The public are well to the back of the court, segregated so that we are allowed to observe but not to participate. Carlen suggests that the organisation of space is such as to impede communication, especially for those who are not part of the routine cast and who are unfamiliar with a courtroom. Distances are much greater than one would normally use for disclosure of private or traumatic incidents or indeed for effective intervention. Communication is through the lawyers and there is also the sense of a play being carefully stage-managed, again maintaining the sense of domination, of the inexorability of the law.

The language employed, with its technical vocabulary and flowery and archaic forms of address, again put the uninitiated at a disadvantage. The court insists upon precise technical words,[14] and any involvement by witnesses or the defendant is essentially passive, responding to questions. Indeed the mode of discourse in the courtroom involves either interrogation or monologue, both of which are extraordinary (and resented) when they occur in day-to-day conversation.[15] Even the intelligent and articulate

[12] Garfinkel, H., "The Trial as a Degradation Ceremony" 66 *American Journal of Sociology* (1956) 420.

[13] Carlen P., "Remedial Routines for the Maintenance of Control in Magistrates Courts" 1 *British Journal of Law and Society* (1974) 101.

[14] Carlen: *ibid.* 107.

[15] Atkinson J. M. and Drew P., *Order in Court* (1979).

witness is ill-equipped to deal on an equal basis. Defendants feel confused, alienated and by-passed so that even the practice of asking the defendant if he has anything to say before sentence is now delegated to the lawyer.

Through the ritual, the geography and the language, there is a high level of situational control by the court and the lawyers. "After all, they're near enough mates in the same play. They're the cast of the play, you're just the casual one-day actor. It's just another day's work to them".[16] This control is experienced by witnesses and defendants alike.

Do we over-estimate the quality of evidence put before juries and their ability to assess that evidence? Is too much weight is placed on identification, confession or eye-witness testimony? Witnesses' ability to assess the passage of time or speed, or to recall colours, events or statements varies considerably. Good powers of perception and recall are not related to the coherence and demeanour with which they present their testimony which are major factors in a jury's assessment of the reliability of a witness. Whether we believe or disbelieve what people tell us has as much to do with their abilities as story-tellers as with the truth of their story. Juries adopt unscientific standards to evaluate the probative quality of what is put before them.

Testimony and story-telling

We might think about the trial as story-telling. Narrative plays an important part in imposing order on our lives.[17] We see our own selves in terms of a biographical narrative, with the events of our lives moving in a connected flow, linked to some central theme. Similarly, narrative helps us to impose order on the external world. This can be done through imaginative fiction (and police and courtroom dramas are one of the most popular forms of these) as well through mechanisms in the non-fiction world, such as newspapers. Stories, of course, are the stuff of real courtroom interaction and it is the party that puts together the most credible narrative that often wins.

It is the lawyer who is responsible for the construction of a story, summoning witnesses to support the client's case and seeking to undermine the coherence of the opposition story by the cross-examination of their witnesses. Being called as a witness is an ordeal in itself[18] with the stress of testifying in addition to lost time from work and inadequate expenses. Once in the witness box, witnesses discover that they are not allowed to tell their own story or even to have an ordinary conversation. The techniques of witnesses examination are divorced from discourse in ordinary life which revolves around "turn-taking":

[16] Baldwin J. and McConville M., *Negotiated Justice* (1977) 85.
[17] Bennett W. and Feldman M., *Reconstructing Reality in the Courtroom* (1981).
[18] McBarnett D., *Conviction* (1983) 90 *et seq.*

> A central property of conversation appears to be that it is organised into single-speaker turns, with regular transitions between speakers. Participants take turns to talk, with one party at a time occupying a turn, then a next, then a next (though a 'next' can include a prior speaker) and so on until the end of the conversation.[19]

The order of speaking, the length of turns and what is said in a turn: all vary in everyday life and are not specified in advance. The more formal the situation, the more structured becomes the dialogue. Even in ordinary conversation, there are still unarticulated rules since we criticise those who dominate conversations, withdraw from them or who seek to interrogate ("I'm not here to be cross-examined!"). Compared to everyday life, the courtroom plays by a wholly different set of rules:

Atkinson J. M. and Drew P., *Order in Court* (1979) 61–62

. . . examination differs markedly from conversation in two major respects: in examination *turn order is fixed*, as is the *type of turn* which each speaker's talk constitutes. These features both arise from the fact that the talk in examination is restricted to two parties only, whose turns are pre-allocated (although a caveat to the term 'parties' will be mentioned in a moment). The way in which turn order and types of turn are fixed, can be summarised as follows:

1. The talk in examination is organised into series of 'question' and 'answer' pairs. Whatever else these utterances may be heard to do, and however else they might be characterised . . . speaker turns should be designed at least minimally as either questions or answers. This is in clear contrast to conversation, in which there is no guarantee that utterances can be treated as questions or answers, and in which even an utterance's interrogative syntactic structure does not assure its status as a question . . . .

2. But these two types of speaker turns are not randomly distributed between the participants. Crucially, only one party — the one conducting the examination, generally the counsel — has the right to ask questions. A consequence of that is that the other (examined) party's utterances are always produced in the sequential position of post-question, and should therefore be answers; this means that persons who are being examined may not exercise the option of selecting by, for instance, themselves asking the other party (*i.e.* the examiner) a question.

Such a move away from everyday conversation occurs in many situations: in the doctor's examining room, the conversation is likely to comprise questions and answers but the good doctor will allow the patient to tell the story in his or her own way. This raises the issue as to which method of eliciting information from a witness is the most effective:

Greer D., "Anything but the Truth? The Reliability of Testimony in Criminal Trials", 11 B.J.C. 131 (1971)

[This question] was the basis for a well-known experiment in 1924.[20] The usual sort of dramatic incident was staged during a lecture on legal psychology. The persons

[19] Atkinson J. M. and Drew P., *Order in Court* (1979) 36.
[20] Marston W., "Studies in Testimony" 15 *Journal of Crim. Law and Criminology* (1924) 5.

attending the lecture were all qualified lawyers and the incident contained a large number of details (over 100) of possible legal significance. None of those present had any intimation that an experiment was to be performed, and none was aware that a test was in progress until the incident had been concluded and the lecturer began to issue instructions for the recording of testimony.

Comparison of methods for eliciting testimony*

	Free narration per cent	Direct examination per cent	Cross-examination per cent
Completeness	23.2	31.2	28.7
Accuracy	94.05	83.2	75.7
Caution	—	40.1	51.8

* Average percentage scores of witnesses reporting an unexpected incident

[The table] shows the result of this experiment. 'Completeness' refers to the number of details given correctly in the reports. For example, the 'witnesses' testified correctly to an average of a little over 34 details in the 'free narration' part of their evidence. This was out of a possible total of 147, and represents a score of 23.2 per cent. Accuracy refers to the number of correct details given as compared with the total number of details included in the report. Thus the witnesses on free narration gave an average of 36 details in their report , and on average 34 of these were correct (94.05 per cent). 'Caution' compares the number of times the witnesses answered 'Don't Know' or failed to answer with the number of erroneous answers. The conclusions drawn by Marston from [this] were that

1. Free narration is less complete but more accurate than the other two methods: *i.e.* on free narration a witness will not give as many details, but those he does give are most likely to be correct.

2. Direct examination is both more complete and more accurate than cross-examination: *i.e.* on direct examination a witness will give more details than on cross-examination and these are also more likely to be correct.

3. Cross-examination shows greater caution than direct examination without any corresponding gain in either completeness or accuracy. It would appear to follow that added caution does an important, though hidden, work in redeeming cross-examination from a degree of inaccuracy which would render it almost wholly worthless: *i.e.* when a witness does not know the answer on cross-examination, he is as likely to answer erroneously as 'I don't know', but on direct examination he is more likely to answer erroneously than 'I don't know'.

These conclusions again are confirmed by later experiments . . .

Far from Wigmore's assertion that cross-examination is the "greatest legal engine ever invented for the discovery of truth", witnesses are confronted by techniques which both alienate and constrain the information that is elicited:

McBarnett D., *Conviction* (1983) 22–23

Evidence is not presented directly by witnesses, but indirectly in response to questions by counsel. The rules prohibit leading questions but the very framing of a question, whether leading or not, and the context in which it occurs, set parameters on what can be an acceptable answer. The witness is a respondent, 'he is there to answer questions, that is all' and the person who asks the questions is structurally very much in a position of control and quick to interrupt witnesses or warn them to confine themselves to the essential facts they are being asked about, or indeed merely to answer yes or no:

Prosecutor: [to victim]	Did you know him [the defendant] previously?
Witness:	Yes we had a scuffle the night before.
Prosecutor: [sharply]	Mr Sweeney, the question was very simple. Please answer yes or no. Don't volunteer anything. Understand?

The questions 'should be clear and unambiguous and as short as possible, each raising a single point' so particularising and abstracting the facts relevant for the case from the multiple possible facts of the incident. This style of presentation helps construct an idea of clear-cut proof, by filtering and controlling the information witnesses make available to the court, and so transforming what could emerge as an ambiguous welter of vying and uncertain perceptions into 'the facts of the case'.

Interrogation means not just filtering potential information but imposing order and meaning upon it by the sequence and context of questions asked — whatever meaning it may have had to the witness, control by questioning can impose the meaning of the questioner. The case thus takes on its own logic within the framework of the 'facts of the case', and any other issues mentioned, hinted at or unknown, lose any relevance to the meaning of the case that they may have had to the meaning of the incident. What is more the order and logic of a controlled case is much more visible than that in the welter of social reality, and therefore, arguably, the more persuasive in carrying its evidence along.[21]

But witnesses are not mere pawns. They and the lawyer co-operate to seek to convince the trier of fact of the truth of their story but the truth of the story does not guarantee belief or acceptance.

Stephenson G., *The Psychology of Criminal Justice* (1992) 137–138

Essentially this is because stories in court are a technique for ordering and presenting evidence, an activity that can be performed more or less skilfully, and which is dependent for its success on the quality of available evidence, something over which the story teller (defence or prosecution lawyer) may have little control. In addition, the hearers of the story may be overly impressed by who tells the story and how, rather than its effectiveness in accounting for the available evidence.

The importance of story structure to its acceptance by hearers was demonstrated in an experiment by Bennett and Feldman[22] in which student subjects were asked to tell true or false stories to the group of students. The listeners were asked to vote privately on the status of the stories as 'true' or 'false', and it was discovered that these judgements were totally unrelated to the actual truth value of the stories; a true story was as likely to receive a 'false' as a 'true' vote, and vice versa. Story length in words, and the number of actions it contained — straightforward

[21] The process of translation of the social into the legal is a central law job — Mansell W., Meteyard B. and Thomson A., *A Critical Introduction to Law* (1995) Chap. 5.
[22] *op. cit.*

measures of complexity — were also unrelated to truth judgements, as were the number and length of pauses — a measure of uncertainty. The important feature of the story to which listeners appeared to respond was the coherence of the story, as assessed by a measure that Bennett and Feldman termed 'structural ambiguity'. To be coherent, a story should have a central action to which various characters, objects and events ('elements') in the story should be clearly connected, either directly, or indirectly by virtue of their clear relation to other elements. The key feature here is the clarity of the relationships between elements and their linking to the central action. Bennett and Feldman found that the larger the proportion of ambiguous links in the story, the less likely it was to be believed. Structural ambiguity was the only measure which successfully predicted how listeners would vote: the less ambiguous a story, the more believers it would attract.

The relevance of this study to courtroom interaction is clear. Judges and juries will be impressed by, and tend to believe, that version of events and explanation of evidence whose elements are the more unambiguously related one to another and to the 'central action' which accounts for the known or alleged harm that has been done. In the adversarial system, it is in each side's interests so to distort its presentation of the evidence that its own story or version of events has the greater clarity and is therefore to be believed. Of course, structural ambiguity may be perceived in stories that are true, leading those whose stories may lack clarity through no fault of their own to become embittered and angry. Members of minority groups, for example, may find that their accounts of events are ill-received because the conventions of their social group which serve to clarify the actions in a story are not shared by the minority who sit in judgement upon them.

Thus we do not believe poor story-tellers since their narrative is often internally inconsistent, jumps from one point to another and does not link to central action. But whether we believe or disbelieve what people tell us is more related to their abilities as story-tellers than it is to the truth or otherwise of their story. Those who testify regularly probably acquire such skills in contrast to the "one-off" witness. The demeanour and coherence of a police officer or expert witness can lead the trier of fact to infer that they are more credible and that their accounts deserve greater weight. Similarly Stephenson suggests that class and gender are factors going to the "weight" of the evidence:

> The working class defendants were apparently consistently ill-at-ease, frequently switching linguistic styles in an anxious effort to please the judge. Middle class defendants were more consistently relaxed, adopting easy, flowing narrative styles — which they share with the judge — throughout the interaction. Their plausible stories were generally believed, and they received sympathetic treatment.[23]

The reliability of witnesses

Witnesses, especially in criminal cases, are often liable to be under pressure — from friends and relatives, lawyers, police or defendants. The frankness and quality of their testimony can always be affected. But how reliable is the neutral, honest and unpressured observer of an incident? There is an immense psychological research literature on this area.[24]

[23] *ibid.* at 150.

[24] Loftus E., *Eyewitness Testimony* (republished 1996); Lloyd-Bostock S. and Clifford B. (eds), *Evaluating Witness Evidence* (1983).

Greer D., "Anything but the Truth? The Reliability of Testimony in Criminal Trials", 11 B.J.C. 131 (1971)

The first common lawyer to take an interest in these developments appears to have been Wigmore. In 1905 he had conducted . . . a series of 'Testimonial and Verdict Experiments' which carried the 'reality experiment' a couple of stages further in legal relevance. The details of the dramatic incident — a quarrel between four of the students in his class — were agreed on beforehand and written down. The 'row' was then enacted during a lecture. An immediate adjournment took place to the law school courtroom. There, a jury of law students who had not witnessed the row was empanelled. Thirteen witnesses of the incident were arbitrarily selected and each was asked a series of nine questions about what had happened. The jurors then retired to consider the evidence and returned with their verdict — *i.e.* their version of the row. This version was then compared with the pre-arranged version and the following are some of the differences discovered:

1. The person found by the 'jury' to have made the first move did not in fact make it.
2. Several relevant 'facts' were not mentioned in the jury's version — *e.g.* that one of the participants had shouted 'That is an insult and I shall here resent it.'
3. The jury's version of another statement uttered during the incident differed from that actually made.

. . . On the whole, it seems, psychological theory in the field of perception is fairly well advanced. It is now generally recognised that there is an important distinction between 'actual' and 'perceived' characteristics of the environment . . . What a witness cognises perceptually is not necessarily an exact reproduction of the data presented and for legal purposes at any rate the most important finding in this area is that there can be a very considerable discrepancy between the two.

Many of the causes of this discrepancy are already well-known, *e.g.* the adverse effect on accuracy of testimony of poor lighting, long distance, short duration of exposure, etc. Less well-known factors influencing perception include emotion, interest, bias, prejudice or expectancy, on the part of the perceiver. . . .

One example of this is provided by Haward,[25] a psychologist who was called in by the defence in an English case where two men were charged with having committed an act of gross indecency in a public convenience. Complaints had been made to the police that the convenience was being used for indecent purposes and the accused were apprehended by two policemen who were keeping the convenience under secret observation. The defendants denied that any criminal acts had taken place. The psychologist reproduced the defence version of the facts (*i.e.* no criminal act) in a series of photographs and he showed these to twelve adults under different conditions of light, for varying lengths of time, and with reference to three different questions: in A, they were merely asked to say what they saw in the picture; in B, they were asked if they could see any crime being committed in any of the pictures; in C, they were told that some of the pictures actually portrayed criminal acts being committed and they were asked to identify the pictures concerned.

The result was that the number of errors increased considerably from A to B to C. In other words, the witnesses most frequently erred in asserting that a crime was being committed when they were led to expect to see this criminal behaviour. The

[25] Haward L., "The reliability of corroborated police evidence in a case flagrante delicto" 3 J. Forensic Science Soc. 71 (1963).

police, therefore, expecting to see an indecent act being committed might well have put an erroneous interpretation on innocent facts.

Research of this nature shows us that the accuracy of the honest witness cannot be assumed. Poor lighting, long distance and short duration are obviously factors that the trier of fact is likely to take into account. But there are many others which can run counter to about the instincts of the lay person and the judge:

(1) the heightened level of arousal experienced by a victim or witness to, for instance, a violent crime does not lead to any improved ability to perceive and recall details[26]:

> . . . subjects viewing a film will focus on a gun held by a customer in a restaurant, rather than (in the alternative version of the film) on a cheque in his hand. Identification of the suspect in a line-up, and the answers to a number of specific questions, were more accurate in the 'cheque' than in the 'gun' condition. In an ingenious and realistic simulation of the 'weapon effect', [researchers] enrolled students to participate in an experiment on sport-related activity and psychological well-being. The investigators demonstrated that having been approached by a white-coated female experimenter with a syringe, who then talked to them for 20 seconds before leaving, a student subject was very much more likely to misidentify foils[27] in a live identification parade than when the similarly white-coated female had approached them with a pen in her hand. The distraction caused by the syringe is similar . . . to the distraction that witnesses to a crime may experience by the weapon in the hand of the assailant.[28]

(2) police officers are probably no better than civilians at recalling details, especially in identifying faces. It appears to be difficult to train people to become better at recognising faces seen previously.

(3) perception and recall is related to age: children improve steadily up to the age of 14 and people deteriorate from late middle age onwards:

> . . . findings . . . showing that the number of people correctly identifying a (filmed) armed robber reduces from 51 per cent in 18–19 year olds to 25 per cent in 60–72 year olds, may in some circumstances be the kind of information which juries should be informed about.
>
> The young perform less well in eyewitness testimony research as much because of their inexperience as of their lesser capacity: the old, on the other hand, are to some extent victims of their long experience. Because of their greater experience, older persons are more likely to rely on (probably useful) stereotypes, and unconscious transference of experience from past situations. [Research] shows, for example, that older

[26] Deffenbacher K., "The Influence of Arousal on Reliability of Testimony" in Lloyd-Bostock (1983), *op. cit.*; there is a review of research in Stephenson (1992) *op. cit.* at 168.

[27] *i.e.* persons who are generally similar to the suspect.

[28] Stephenson (1992), *op. cit.* 169; this raises interesting questions about the assumptions behind the *res gestae* rule — see Chap. 17.

people are more likely than young adults to misidentify an innocent bystander at the scene of the assault when that bystander was 'criminal-looking' rather than 'inoffensive-looking'. Overall ability to pick out the culprit was also reduced in the older group, but the elderly had the advantage that they were generally more cautious than younger people, being less likely to make a selection in the first place than were younger people.

The most common accusation against children is that they are suggestible, meaning that it is relatively easy to confuse a child by asking highly suggestive or leading questions. Indeed it is probably the case that children can be led into inaccuracy by suggesting to them that they know the answer when in fact they do not . . .

The implication of this research is that we should strive to improve techniques of interviewing, rather than disallow children's testimony.[29]

(4) much of the literature has stressed that the criminal justice system needs guidance with regard to the limitations of identification evidence.[30] In particular it has concluded that cross-race eyewitness identifications are less accurate than same-race eyewitness identifications.[31]

Courts have not sought expert assistance in assessing the reliability of witnesses. In criminal cases, one major limitation on the testimony of expert witnesses is the *Turner* rule[32] that such witnesses should not express opinions on those matters which are within the competence of the jury.[33] The jurors are representatives of the community and are expected to understand how "normal" people behave and react. Expert evidence by psychologists is not admissible on such issues and only becomes admissible in dealing with the "abnormal" witness or abnormal circumstances which lie outside the experience of the jury.[34] In *R. v. Robinson*[35] the defendant was accused of indecent assault on a mentally retarded young woman. There was a *voire dire* at the start of the trial to determine whether the complainant was a competent witness in view of her retardation. The judge ruled that she was competent but at the trial proper admitted the evidence of an educational psychologist to the effect that the victim was a credible witness, not being suggestible or imaginative. On appeal Lord Taylor C.J. reviewed the state of the law:

[29] Stephenson (1992), *op. cit.* 165–166.
[30] Loftus (1996), *op. cit.*; Clifford B. and Bull R., *The Psychology of Person Identification* (1978).
[31] Lindsay R. and Wells G., "What do we really know about cross-race eyewitness identification?" in Lloyd-Bostock (1983) *op. cit.* 219.
[32] *R. v. Turner* [1975] 1 All E.R. 70.
[33] This does not apply in civil proceedings since under Civil Evidence Act 1972, s.3(1), ". . . where a person is called as a witness . . . his opinion on any relevant matter on which he is qualified to give expert evidence shall be admissible in evidence."
[34] *Toohey v. Metropolitan Police Comm.* [1965] A.C. 595.
[35] [1994] 3 All E.R. 346.

R. v. Robinson [1994] 3 All E.R. 346 at 350e–352b, *per* Lord Taylor C.J.

The locus classicus as to the admissibility of expert evidence to deal with a witness's state of mind or reliability is *R. v. Turner* where Lawton L.J. said . . .

> An expert's opinion is admissible to furnish the court with scientific information which is likely to be outside the experience and knowledge of a judge or jury. If on the proven facts a judge or jury can form their own conclusiuons without help then the opinion of an expert is unnecessary . . . The same reasoning applies to . . . admissibility on the issue of credibility. The jury had to decide what reliance they could put on the appellant's evidence. He had to be judged as someone who is not mentally disordered. This is what juries are empanelled to do. And the law assumes that they can perform their duties properly. The jury in this case did not need, and should not have been offered, the evidence of the psychiatrist to help them decide whether the appellant's evidence was truthful.[36]

. . . There have been cases where medical evidence has been ruled admissible to attack the reliability of a prosecution witness (*Toohey v. Metropolitan Police Commr*) or to cast doubt on the reliability of confessions by the defendant (*R. v. Raghip*[37] and *R. v. Ward*[38]) . . .

But . . . there is no case in which psychiatric or psychological evidence has been admitted to boost, bolster or enhance the evidence of a witness for the Crown or indeed of any witness. [Counsel for the appellant] submits that it is for the jury to assess the reliability and persuasiveness of witnesses and it cannot be right to allow evidence, however expert, to suggest to the jury that they should believe a witness of fact.

[Counsel for the appellant] drew our attention to a Canadian case, *R. v. Kyselka*[39] The headnote reads:

> In a rape trial, where the complainant was mentally retarded, the Crown called a psychiatrist who testified that a person of her mental classification, which was a mental age of 10-11 years, was likely to be a truthful witness because such a person would lack the imagination to fabricate. Held, that such evidence was inadmissible. While the credit of a witness may be impeached by the opposite party, a party cannot call witnesses to testify to the credibility or truth of his own witnesses.

Chief Justice Porter of Ontario said:

> There is no warrant or authority for such oath-helping as occurred in the circumstances of this case, reminiscent as it is of the method before the Norman Conquest by which a defendant in a civil suit or an accused person proved his case by calling witnesses to swear that the oath of the party was true.
>
> In our view the Crown cannot call a witness of fact and then, without more, call a psychologist or psychiatrist to give reasons why the jury should regard that witness as reliable.

Were the defence to attack the reliability of a witness on the ground of some mental abnormality outside the jury's experience, it would be open to

[36] *Turner supra* at 74.
[37] (1991) *The Times*, December 5.
[38] [1993] 2 All E.R. 577.
[39] (1962) 133 C.C.C. 103.

the Crown to call evidence in rebuttal. But, as Lord Taylor went on to say in *Robinson*,

> . . . great care would need to be taken to restrict the expert opinion to meeting the specific challenge and not to allow it to extend to 'oath-helping'.

In the light of such decisions, the prospects for the admissibility of psychological evidence on the general reliability of an eyewitness's account seem remote.[40] The problems surrounding witness reliability are exacerbated by the "law's delays". A witness may have made a statement relatively contemporaneously with the incident. But the trial may be many months, if not years, after the event. The common law's preference for oral testimony means that the truth of a person's testimony is assessed on the quality of their memory and on the performance in the witness box. Memory inevitably fades, although the decline is minimised when witnesses know that they are to be tested.[41] An equally important point is that we are all suggestible and information received after the event can interfere with accurate recall:

Loftus E. and Ketcham K., "The Malleability of Eyewitness Accounts" in Lloyd-Bostock (1983) *op. cit.* 159–160

> This extraordinary malleability of memory has been recently demonstrated . . . Consider a typical experiment in which college students were presented with a film of an automobile accident and immediately afterwards were asked a series of questions about the accident. Some of the questions were designed to present misleading information — that is, to suggest the existence of an object that did not in fact exist. Half the subjects were asked 'How fast was the white sports car going when it passed the barn while travelling along the country road?' In fact no barn existed. The remaining subjects were asked, 'How fast was the white sports car going while travelling along the country road?' Later all subjects were asked if they had seen a barn. When questioned again about the accident a week later, more than 17 per cent of those exposed to the false information about the barn said they had seen one. Apparently the assumption of a barn in the initial questioning caused many subjects to incorporate the non-existent barn into their recollections of the event.

It has been said that ". . . human memory is a fragile and elusive creature. It can be supplemented, partially restructured, or even completely altered by post-event inputs. It is susceptible to the power of a single word."[42]

[40] Under Federal Rules of Evidence, r.702, expert testimony is admissible where it will assist the finder of fact. However the leading appellate decision (*U.S. v. Amaral* (1973) 488 F. 2d 1148) stresses the discretion of the trial judge in deciding whether to admit such testimony — see Loftus E. "Expert testimony on the eyewitness' in Loftus E. and Wells G. (eds) *Eyewitness Testimony* (1984) 273.

[41] Egan D., Pittner M. and Goldstein A., "Eyewitness Identification — photographs v. live models" 1 *Law and Human Behaviour* 199 (1977).

[42] Loftus E. and Ketcham K., *op. cit.*

Despite such research, the earlier, potentially more reliable, witness statements are inadmissible to supplement the oral testimony.[43] The common law's technique for avoiding the worst effects of this was to allow witnesses in the witness box to 'refresh their memory' from contemporaneous statements.[44] But before taking the oath, witnesses are permitted to consult their statements prior to going into the witness box, even if this leads to the rather disreputable spectacle of witnesses frantically 'learning their lines' before entering the court.

> Testimony in the witness box becomes more a test of memory than of truthfulness if witnesses are deprived of the opportunity of checking their recollection beforehand by reference to statements or notes made at a time closer to the events in question . . . Refusal of access to statements would tend to create difficulties for honest witnesses but be likely to do little to hamper dishonest witnesses.[45]

This statement was approved in *R. v. Richardson*[46] in which prosecution witnesses in a burglary case were shown statements that had been made to the police 18 months earlier and a few weeks after the offences in question:

> Obviously it would be wrong if several witnesses were handed statements in circumstances which enabled one to compare with another what each had said. But there can be no general rule (which incidentally would be unenforceable, unlike the rule as to what can be done in the witness box) that witnesses may not before trial see the statements that they had made at some period reasonably close to the time of the event which is the subject of the trial. Indeed one can imagine many cases particularly those of a complex nature, where such a rule would militate very greatly against the interests of justice.[47]

Thus a pragmatic compromise is reached whereby a line is drawn at the witness box — the witness can review any statement prior to taking the oath but thereafter he or she must rely on memory.

Who can Testify? Who must Testify?

The general rule is that everyone is competent to give evidence; everyone can be compelled to attend court; everyone is under an obligation to disclose the truth.

[43] At least in criminal proceedings — in civil proceedings, this is common practice under the proviso to the Civil Evidence Act 1995, s.6(2); even in criminal cases, children's depositions can act as their evidence in chief in certain cases under the Criminal Justice Act 1988, s.32A.
[44] See 327, *et seq.*
[45] *Lau Pak Ngam v. R.* [1966] Crim.L.R. 443.
[46] [1971] 2 All E.R. 773.
[47] *ibid.* at 777, *per* Sachs L.J.; the sharp distinction between the "contemporaneous" statement (used in the witness box to refresh the memory) and the "not-so-contemporaneous" statement which is not permitted to be used in this way was significantly reduced in *R. v. Da Silva* [1990] 1 All E.R. 29.

(1) competence refers to a person's ability to testify. The law presumes that ordinary individuals are competent. When a person is not competent, they are barred from testifying. This happens mainly in cases of lack of age or where the prospective witness is mentally handicapped. A witness will testify either on oath or (in some cases[48]) unsworn.

(2) a person who is competent to testify can be compelled to testify:

- in civil cases a party may subpoena a person to attend court and testify. To refuse to attend court would put that person in contempt of court and liable to imprisonment.
- in trials on indictment, until 1996, witness orders to attend Crown Court could be made by the examining justices under the procedure laid down by section 1 of the Criminal Procedure (Attendance of Witnesses) Act 1965. This was repealed by section 65 of the Criminal Procedure and Investigations Act 1996. When brought into effect, this section, will mean that notification of witnesses to attend court will be achieved by administrative procedures.[49]

  The attendance of a reluctant witness can be secured by a witness summons under section 2 of the 1965 Act:[50]

> 2.—(1) This section applies where the Crown Court is satisfied that,
>
> (a) a person is likely to be able to give evidence likely to be material evidence, or produce any document or thing likely to be material evidence, for the purpose of any criminal proceedings before the Crown Court, and
> (b) the person will not voluntarily attend as a witness or will not voluntarily produce the document or thing.
>
> (2) In such a case the Crown Court shall . . . issue a summons (a witness summons) directed to the person concerned and requiring him to —
>
> (a) attend before the Crown Court at the time and place stated in the summons, and
> (b) give the evidence or produce the document or thing

Under the old procedure the summons was issued automatically. When brought into effect, this new procedure will

[48] Basically, children under 14 testify unsworn in criminal cases under the Criminal Justice Act 1991, s.52(1); in civil cases, children can testify unsworn under the Children Act 1989, s.96. For many years (from the passage of the Criminal Evidence Act 1898, s.1(h)) the defendant could make an unsworn statement from the dock but that right was removed by the Criminal Justice Act 1982, s.72.

[49] Hansard, H.L. Vol. 573, col. 969.

[50] As amended by the Criminal Procedure and Investigations Act 1996, s.66.

require an application that is timely, specific and with the grounds given for believing why the third party is able to give the evidence or produce the document.

Under section 3 of the Act, disobedience is an offence, punishable by a maximum of three months imprisonment. Also under section 67 of the 1996 Act, judges of the Crown Court have the power to issue arrest warrants for recalcitrant witnesses.

- for trials in magistrates' courts, witness summonses can be issued under Magistrates' Courts Act 1980

> 97.—(1) Where a justice of the peace . . . is satisfied that any person in England or Wales is likely to be able to give material evidence, or produce any document or thing likely to be material evidence, at the summary trial of an information or hearing of a complaint by a magistrates' court for that commission area and that person will not voluntarily attend as a witness or will not voluntarily produce the document or thing, the justice shall issue a summons directed to that person requiring him to attend before the court . . . to give evidence or to produce the document or thing . . .[51]

Similar provisions for committal proceedings are made in s.97A of the 1980 Act.[52] A witness order can be set aside if the evidence likely to be given is not material or inadmissible.[53]

(3) a person who is competent and compellable is under an obligation to disclose "the truth, the whole truth and nothing but the truth". They must answer honestly all questions put to them in the witness box under pain of committing perjury or being in contempt of court. The principle is that of the proper administration of justice and the rule of law requires that priority be given to securing information for the court over other interests of citizens. Some classes of witness may have a limited privilege not to answer certain questions: examples would be public interest immunity, legal professional privilege or the right against self-incrimination. These are discussed elsewhere.

Competence and the oath

It has been argued that originally, at common law, it was not only those prepared to take an oath on the Bible who were competent witnesses:

[51] As amended by the Criminal Procedure and Investigations Act 1996, s.51 and Sched. 1. para. 7.
[52] As inserted by the Criminal Procedure and Investigations Act 1996, Sched. 1, para. 8.
[53] *R. v. Derby Magistrates' Court* [1995] 4 All E.R. 526; cricketers will appreciate the decision in *R. v. Marylebone Justices ex p Gatting and Emburey* [1990] Crim.L.R. 578.

Spencer J. and Flin J., *The Evidence of Children—The Law and the Psychology* (2nd ed., 1993) 47

Originally there were rules forbidding certain persons to take oaths but no blanket rule against the acceptance of unsworn evidence and the courts would listen to unsworn evidence from those who were ineligible to be sworn. Thus defence witnesses were barred from taking oaths until 1702 and the defendant himself until the Criminal Evidence Act 1898: but both were permitted to make unsworn statements — an option the defendant retained until the Criminal Justice Act 1982. Similarly it seems that the courts would formerly listen to unsworn evidence from children who failed the competency examination. In his *History of the Pleas of the Crown*, Sir Matthew Hale (1609–76) wrote this:

> If the rape be committed upon a child under twelve years old, whether or how she may be admitted to give evidence may be considerable. It seems to me, that if it appear to the court, that she hath the sense and understanding that she knows and considers the obligation of an oath, tho she be under twelve years, she may be sworn . . . But if it be an infant of such tender years, that in point of discretion the court sees it unfit to swear her, yet I think she ought to be heard without oath to give the court information, tho singly of itself it ought not to move the jury to convict the offender . . .[54]

However in *R. v. Brasier*[55] the question arose as to whether the evidence of a child under seven years old was admissible on a charge of assault with intent to commit rape. It was held:

***R. v. Brasier* (1779) 1 Leach 199 at 200**

That no testimony whatever can be legally received except on oath and that an infant, though under the age of seven years, may be sworn in a criminal prosecution, provided such infant appears, on strict examination by the court, to possess a sufficient knowledge of the nature and consequences of an oath, for there is no precise or fixed rule as to the time within which infants are excluded from giving evidence, but the admissibility of their evidence depends upon the sense and reason they entertain of the danger and impiety of falsehood, which is to be collected from their answers to questions propounded to them by the court; but if they are found incompetent to take an oath, their evidence cannot be received.[56]

This test stressed the theological side of understanding the nature of the oath.[57] This was the case both for the mentally handicapped[58] and for children. A more secular approach emerged in *R. v. Hayes*[59] where the trial judge questioned the witness, a boy of twelve, about his religious instruction at school, whether he had been told about God and whether he had heard of God:

[54] The move to more restrictive practices, requiring testimony to be heard on oath began with *R. v. Brasier* (1779) 1 Leach 199.
[55] (1779) 1 Leach 199.
[56] The judgment was unanimous.
[57] For some entertaining accounts of the examination of child witnesses, Spencer J. and Flin J., *op. cit.* Chap. 4.
[58] *R. v. Hill* (1851) 2 Den. 254.
[59] [1977] 2 All E.R. 288.

R. v. Hayes [1977] 2 All E.R. 288 at 290j–291b, *per* Bridge L.J.

. . . the boy declaring that he is wholly ignorant of the existence of God does lend some force to the submission that if the essence of the sanction of the oath is a divine sanction, and if it is an awareness of that divine sanction which the court is looking for in a child of tender years, then here was a case where, on the face of it, that awareness was absent. The court is not convinced that that is really the essence of the court's duty in the difficult situation where the court has to determine whether a young person can or cannot properly be permitted to take an oath before giving evidence. It is unrealistic not to recognise that, in the present state of society, amongst the adult population the divine sanction of an oath is probably not generally recognised. The important consideration, we think, when a judge has to decide whether a child should properly be sworn, is whether the child has a sufficient appreciation of the solemnity of the occasion and the added responsibility to tell the truth, which is involved in taking an oath, over and above the duty to tell the truth which is an ordinary duty of normal social conduct.

This test, the ". . . appreciation of the solemnity of the occasion and the added responsibility to tell the truth", remains the common law test of competency to take the oath. This test no longer governs the competency of children. By statute, children under the age of fourteen now testify unsworn[60] and the criterion of competence has also changed:

A child's evidence shall be received unless it appears to the court that the child is incapable of intelligible testimony.[61]

But the *Hayes* test remains the yardstick for competency for the mentally handicapped. In *R. v. Bellamy*[62] the rape victim was mentally handicapped but although she understood the importance of telling the truth, her lack of belief in God led the judge to refuse to permit her to testify on oath and he required her to affirm. The Court of Appeal held that it is no longer necessary to investigate the theological understanding of a witness.

The requirement for witnesses to take an oath has historically affected the competence of both children and the mentally handicapped but now has less impact. Where a witness is competent to take the oath, this is administered according to section 1 of the Oaths Act 1978, section 1(3) of which permits an oath to be administered ". . . in any lawful manner" allowing a witness of any religious faith to take the oath. Section 5 permits agnostics and atheists to make a solemn affirmation. The primary purpose of the ceremony is to make the person aware of the solemnity of the occasion, of the legal requirement to tell the truth and of the possible penalties for perjury — thus under section 4(2) if an oath has been administered, the fact that the person has no religious belief does not affect the validity of the oath.

[60] Criminal Justice Act 1988, s.33A, as inserted by the Criminal Justice Act 1991, s.52(1).
[61] Criminal Justice Act 1988, s.33A(2A), as inserted by the Criminal Justice and Public Order Act 1994 Sched. 9, cl.33.
[62] (1985) 82 Cr.App.R. 222.

Competence: a matter for the judge

The question whether a witness is competent to testify is a matter for the judge alone. In *R. v. Deakin*[63] the victim was a woman with Downs Syndrome, indecently assaulted by a care assistant. At the competency hearing, the judge heard from the victim and also took expert testimony from two psychologists whose opinion was that she was capable of telling the truth. The appellant contended that this evidence should not have been heard in front of the jury who might well have been influenced by the experts' acceptance of the complainant's story. The Court of Appeal agreed, although applying the proviso and dismissing the appeal:

R. v. Deakin [1994] 4 All E.R. 769 at 774j–775d, *per* Farquharson L.J.

With diffidence we have come to the conclusion that in the circumstances of this case the evidence should have been heard in the absence of the jury for the following reasons.

1. Questions of admissibility of evidence are for the judge to decide.
2. If, after hearing the evidence and the submissions on the issue in the presence of the jury, the judge decides against admitting the evidence in question, the jury would have difficulty in excluding from their mind the evidence which the judge had ruled out. In the present case, this consideration was not significant as the prosecution would not have proceeded if the judge had decided not to admit the evidence of the complainant.
3. The rule, if it be a rule, that the jury should hear all the evidence given in a case does not here apply because at the time the evidence of the psychologists was given, the complainant was not a witness. It was, of course, only after hearing the evidence that the judge was able to rule on the complainant's competence to give evidence.
4. While acknowledging that it is right in law that questions relating to the competence of the witness in question should be answered by the witness himself in the presence of the jury, different considerations arise in relation to evidence given by 'third party' experts. In the former case, the jury may be assisted in deciding whether to accept the evidence of the complainant by observing the manner of his or her answers to the judge's questions. The evidence of the experts is in an altogether different category.
5. The jury would not be assisted in deciding the issue before them by hearing the expert evidence, which was concerned with the capacity of the complainant to tell the truth. As [counsel for the appellant] put it in argument, 'What good would it do?'

The Court of Appeal distinguished *R. v. Reynolds*[64] where the court held that an inquiry into the competence of a child should take place in the presence of the jury since it would enable the jury to assess the child's capacity for telling the truth. *Deakin* draws a sharper line between the question of competence which is a matter of admissibility for the judge and

[63] [1994] 4 All E.R. 769.

[64] [1950] 1 All E.R. 335; this was distinguished in the Australian case *Demirok v. R.* (1977) 137 C.L.R. 20 and the approach in *Deakin* has now been confirmed by the House of Lords in *R. v. Hampshire* [1995] 2 All E.R. 1019. This is discussed further in Chap. 2.

the question of weight which is within the competence of the jury. The problem was that the expert testimony that the complainant was capable of telling the truth was admissible on the first question but trespassed on the jury's preserve on the second point.[65]

Competence: some history

By the end of the eighteenth century, the categories of incompetent and disqualified witnesses were numerous. The rationale behind such exclusions has been expressed in two ways:

- the fear of manufactured evidence arising from the self-interests of the witness. This originally excluded the parties themselves, their spouses or people with other interests in the outcome of the proceedings
- the fear of evidence being unreliable due to the moral or other characteristics of the person giving evidence. Thus heathens, atheists, convicts, the mentally ill and children were treated as incompetent to testify.

Although initially there were a considerable number of categories of incompetent witnesses, these rapidly diminished in the nineteenth century:

(1) *non-Christians* were permitted to give evidence from the eighteenth century. In *Omychund v. Barker*[66] the witness held a belief in the "Governor of the Universe" and his evidence was receivable, having sworn an oath reflecting that belief. Atheists however had to wait until the Evidence (Further Amendment) Act 1869 before they became entitled to testify.
(2) *convicts* became finally competent by the Evidence Act 1843.
(3) *those with an interest* in the outcome of the proceedings were also made competent by the Evidence Act 1843.
(4) the *parties* in civil cases were recognised as competent witnesses by the Evidence Act 1851 (except for adultery and breach of promise cases where the parties were made competent by the Evidence (Further Amendment) Act 1869). The plaintiff or defendant could give evidence and also subpoena the other side (if that was tactically advisable!). Through this legislation, the spouses of parties also became competent and compellable.
(5) the *defendants* (and their spouses) in criminal cases have provided a longer lasting problem. At common law, the accused was incompetent as a witness as there was the fear that he or she might perjure

[65] Compare with *R. v. Robinson supra*.
[66] (1745) 1 Atk. 21.

himself or herself as a result of the personal interest in the proceedings but also the fear that the judiciary might compel the accused to incriminate himself or herself. A defendant could always make an unsworn statement from the dock. It was only with section 1 of the Criminal Evidence Act in 1898 that the accused became a competent witness for the defence in all criminal proceedings. The position of the accused as a witness[67] is discussed below.

(6) for the *accused's spouse*, the situation remained unclear after 1898. There was great reluctance to allow husbands or wives to give evidence against their spouse. The 1898 legislation permitted spouses to testify for the defence but whether a spouse was a competent witness for the prosecution remained obscure. At common law, the spouse was a competent witness in cases of personal violence or treason but even then was probably not a compellable witness. But this was resolved by section 80 of the Police and Criminal Evidence Act 1984 which made the spouse a competent witness in all criminal proceedings and a compellable witness in a small number of such cases. The position of the accused's wife or husband as a witness is discussed below.

The Defendant as Witness

In a criminal trial, it conceivable that the accused may be called as a witness for the prosecution, for the defence or for a co-accused.

As a witness for the prosecution

The common law rule is that the defendant in a criminal case is not a competent witness for the prosecution, even if he or she should wish to testify. This is only likely in a case where there are multiple defendants and one defendant cannot be called from the dock to give evidence on behalf of the prosecution against another defendant.[68] It is only if the defendant has ceased being a co-accused, in which case he or she becomes an ordinary person and may be competent and compellable for any party. This may occur:

(1) where the accused has pleaded guilty to all charges or where the accused has pleaded guilty to some charges and his or her plea of not guilty to the other charges has been accepted by the prosecution. A question which arises is whether the defendant should normally be sentenced after giving evidence. The position put forward in *R. v. Payne*[69] was that accomplices should be sentenced

[67] The issues surrounding the cross-examination of the accused are dealt with in Chap. 15.
[68] *R. v. Grant* [1944] 2 All E.R. 311.
[69] [1950] 1 All E.R. 102.

before giving evidence against their partners in crime. The obvious rationale is that the witness will no longer have any incentive to tailor evidence in favour of the prosecution in the hope of receiving a lighter sentence. This was reconsidered in *R. v. Palmer*[70] in which the accomplice was committed for trial separately and pleaded guilty. The accused opted for an old-style committal at which the accomplice testified. On appeal it was argued that it was improper for the Crown to have called the accomplice without his first having been sentenced. The Court of Appeal upheld the conviction, on the basis that modern sentencing practice had generally been not to sentence an accomplice until all the facts of the case had been heard, although it remained a matter of discretion for the trial judge.

(2) where the prosecution has successfully requested severance of the indictment. In *R. v. Pipe*,[71] the defendant was being prosecuted for theft and an accomplice who was to be tried separately for handling stolen goods, was called to testify. The court said that, as a rule of practice, in such circumstances, accomplices should not be called to testify unless the prosecution has agreed to discontinue the case against them. Obviously courts should be wary of witnesses with an interest in the outcome of the proceedings[72] but in *R. v. Turner*[73] it is suggested that whether an accomplice should be permitted to testify is ultimately a matter of discretion for the trial judge.

(3) where the accused has been acquitted through the prosecution offering no evidence or through the submission of a successful "no case to answer" plea at the close of the prosecution case or through a "*nolle prosequi*" being entered by the Attorney-General.

As a witness for the defence

The accused is a competent witness for the defence as a result of the Criminal Evidence Act 1898:

> 1.—Every person charged with an offence shall be a competent witness for the defence at every stage of the proceedings, whether the person charged is charged solely or jointly with any other person. Provided as follows:
>
> (a) A person so charged shall not be called as a witness in pursuance of this Act except on his own application . . .

". . . at every stage of the proceedings" includes committal, trial or *voire dire* or in mitigation of sentence. Having decided to testify, the accused

[70] (1993) 99 Cr.App.R. 83; [1994] Crim.L.R. 122; see also *R. v. Weekes* (1982) 74 Cr.App.R. 161.

[71] (1966) 51 Cr.App.R. 17.

[72] Especially since the mandatory corroboration warning in the case of accomplices is no longer necessary — see Chap. 9.

[73] (1975) 61 Cr.App.R. 67.

should give evidence before other defence witnesses in order to prevent his or her testimony being tailored to fit that of the the witnesses. This is provided for under section 79 of the Police and Criminal Evidence Act 1984, although the court has an unfettered discretion to depart from this procedure.

The free choice provided in proviso (a) as to whether to testify or to remain silent has been undermined by the Criminal Justice and Public Order Act 1994:

> 35.—(1) At the trial of any person who has attained the age of fourteen years for an offence, subsections (2) and (3) below apply unless —
>
> (a) the accused's guilt is not in issue; or
> (b) it appears to the court that the physical or mental condition of the accused makes it undesirable for him to give evidence;
>
> but subsection (2) below does not apply if, at the conclusion of the evidence for the prosecution, his legal representative informs the court that the accused will give evidence, or, where he is unrepresented, the court ascertains from him that he will give evidence.
>
> (2) Where this subsection applies, the court shall, at the conclusion of the evidence for the prosecution, satisfy itself (in the case of proceedings on indictment, in the presence of the jury) that the accused is aware that the stage has been reached at which evidence can be given for the defence and that he can, if he wishes, give evidence and that, if he chooses not to give evidence, or having been sworn, without good cause refuses to answer any question, it will be permissible for the court or jury to draw such inferences as appear proper from his failure to give evidence or his refusal, without good cause, to answer any question.
>
> (3) Where this subsection applies, the court or jury, in determining whether the accused is guilty of the offence charged, may draw such inferences as appear proper from the failure of the accused to give evidence or his refusal, without good cause, to answer any question.
>
> (4) This section does not render the accused compellable to give evidence on his own behalf, and he shall accordingly not be guilty of contempt of court by reason of a failure to do so.

This section applies where the prosecution have satisfied the court that there is a case to answer and a defendant declines to testify in his or her own defence. The judge, in the presence of the jury, is empowered to tell the defendant that the stage has been reached at which he or she can give evidence and to issue a warning that if he or she remain silent, that it will be permissible for the jury to draw whatever inferences appear to be proper.[74]

Having elected, willingly or not, to testify, the accused's position is analogous to any other witness. Once the accused has entered the witness box, he or she must answer all questions, even though they might incriminate him or her. This is made explicit under proviso (e) to section 1 of the Criminal Evidence Act 1898:

[74] The section is discussed in *R. v. Cowan* [1995] 4 All E.R. 939 and the issue of the right of silence is discussed further at 122, *et seq.*

1 . . . (a) A person charged and being a witness in pursuance of this Act may be asked any question in cross-examination notwithstanding that it would tend to criminate him as to the offence charged.

Nowadays under the Criminal Justice and Public Order Act 1994:

35.(2)— . . . it will be permissible for the court or jury to draw such inferences as appear proper from . . . his refusal, without good cause, to answer any question.'

It would not be not good cause to refuse to answer a question on the grounds that it may implicate him or her.

The defendant is subject to cross-examination and can be questioned about his or her involvement in the offence. Such cross-examination is not limited to matters dealt with in the examination in chief. In *R. v. Paul*[75] the accused limited himself to a statement admitting his own involvement but was cross-examined about his co-defendants' involvement. On appeal this was accepted as proper but it has been argued that this circumvents the policy which prevents the prosecution from calling co-accused to testify against each other.[76] The trial judge does have discretion to prevent such cross-examination and it has been suggested that in *Paul*, that discretion should have been exercised.[77]

In cross-examination, the major safeguards exist in relation to the accused's credibility since the prosecution is prevented from asking questions about the defendant's bad character under proviso (f) of section 1 of the Criminal Evidence Act 1898:

1. . . . (f) A person charged and called as a witness in pursuance of this Act shall not be asked, and if asked shall not be required to answer, any question tending to show that he has committed or been convicted of or been charged with any offence other than that wherewith he is then charged, or is of bad character.

There are exceptions[78] to this proviso which will be dealt with later.

When a defendant testifies, his evidence might well implicate a co-accused. In such circumstances, the testimony is like all other testimony and is evidence for all purposes.

> . . . while a statement made in the absence of the accused person by one of his co-defendants cannot be evidence against him, if the co-defendant goes into the witness box and gives evidence in the course of a joint trial, then what he says becomes evidence for all the purposes of the case including the purpose of being evidence against a co-defendant.[79]

The defendant is liable to cross-examination by a co-accused and in these circumstances, having given evidence against another person charged in the

[75] [1920] 2 K.B. 183.
[76] *R. v. Grant* [1944] 2 All E.R. 311.
[77] *Young v. H.M. Advocate* 1932 J.C. 63.
[78] see Chap. 15 — the exceptions include putting similar fact evidence to the accused; putting prior disreputable conduct to him or her where there has been an attack on prosecution witnesses; or where the defendant gives evidence against a co-accused.
[79] *R. v. Rudd* (1948) 32 Cr.App.R. 138 at 140, *per* Humphreys J.

same proceedings, can also be questioned about character.[80] Were an accused not to testify, counsel for a co-accused at common law can comment on such a failure.[81] Nowadays, under the Criminal Justice and Public Order Act 1994, the prosecution also has the right to comment on such a failure.

As a witness for a co-defendant

The accused is a competent but not compellable witness for a co-accused. Defendants are unlikely to give evidence for a co-accused where they have not given evidence on their own behalf, since they would open themselves up to cross-examination on their own involvement. However they might wish to do this in a *voire dire*, for example, where a co-accused is seeking a ruling on the admissibility of a confession. If a defendant has ceased to be a defendant, (for example, by pleading guilty or where there is a directed acquittal[82]), he or she becomes a competent and compellable witness.

The Spouse of the Defendant as Witness

At common law, the spouse of a party was not a competent witness. After 1853[83] this was no longer the case with civil proceedings but remained so in criminal proceedings until 1898 when the spouse became a competent and compellable witness for the defence as a result of section 1 of the Criminal Evidence Act. But the spouse was still generally not a competent witness for the prosecution,[84] subject to a range of common law[85] and statutory exceptions. The unsatisfactory state of the law was compounded with decisions such as *Hoskyn v. Metropolitan Police Commissioner*[86] in which the House of Lords held that, even where the husband was charged with an offence of violence against her, the wife, while a competent witness against the husband, was still not compellable.

Significant changes were brought about by section 80 of the Police and Criminal Evidence Act 1984. Husbands and wives are now like other witnesses, competent for the prosecution in any case and compellable in some. It is necessary to note that "husband or wife" is narrowly interpreted and limited to those who are *de iure* married to the defendant. In *R. v. Khan*[87] the witness, a woman, had gone through a Moslem ceremony of marriage with the accused who was already married to another woman under English law. The marriage was bigamous and void and the witness was not a spouse for the purposes of section 80.

[80] Criminal Evidence Act 1898, s.1(f)(iii).
[81] *R. v. Wickham* (1971) 55 Cr.App.R. 199.
[82] *R. v. Conti* (1973) 58 Cr.App.R. 387.
[83] Evidence (Further Amendment) Act 1853.
[84] *R. v. Deacon* [1973] 2 All E.R. 1145.
[85] Especially with cases of personal violence.
[86] [1979] A.C. 474.
[87] (1986) 84 Cr.App.R. 44.

80.—(1) In any proceedings[88] the wife or husband of the accused shall be competent to give evidence —

(a) subject to subsection (4) below, for the prosecution; and
(b) on behalf of the accused or any person jointly charged with the accused

(2) In any proceedings the wife or husband of the accused shall, subject to subsection (4) below, be compellable to give evidence on behalf of the accused.

(3) In any proceedings the wife or husband of the accused shall, subject to subsection (4) below, be compellable to give evidence for the prosecution or on behalf of any person jointly charged with the accused if and only if —

(a) the offence charged involves an assault on, or injury or a threat of injury to, the wife or husband of the accused or a person who was at the material time under the age of sixteen; or
(b) the offence charged is a sexual offence[89] alleged to have been committed in respect of the person who was at the material time under that age; or
(c) the offence charged consists of attempting or conspiring to commit, or of aiding, abetting, counselling, procuring or inciting the commission of, an offence falling within paragraph (a) or (b) above.

(4) Where an information or indictment charges a husband and his wife jointly with an offence neither spouse shall at the trial of the information or indictment be competent or compellable by virtue of subsection (1)(a), (2) or (3) above to give evidence in respect of that offence unless that spouse is not, or is no longer, liable to be convicted of that offence at the trial as a result of pleading guilty or for any other reason.

The provisions of the section are largely the result of the proposals of the Criminal Law Revision Committee.[90] The policy to treat a spouse, wherever possible, as any other witness was obvious as was the principle that the spouse should always be compellable on behalf of the accused. But the issues surrounding compellability for the prosecution were more complex:

Creighton P., "Spouse Competence and Compellability" [1990] Crim.L.R. 34 at 35

In general, the Committee accepted that a wife ought not to be compelled to testify against her husband. Compulsion could unnecessarily disrupt marital harmony and place the wife in the invidious position of having to incriminate her spouse. It was concluded, however, that, for certain offences against the person of the wife or children (aged under 16 years) of the household, the wife should be compellable, for otherwise these crimes would go unpunished, as in most cases there would be no other adult witnesses. Further, in offences against children of the household, the wife, although not charged, might have been guilty of some complicity and this might be reluctant to testify. These two factors, when combined with the serious nature of the offences, justified compellability; the seriousness of the offences was

[88] *i.e.* criminal proceedings (s.82(1)).
[89] As defined in s.80(7).
[90] Eleventh Report, *Evidence (General)* Cmnd. 4991 paras 143–157.

not in itself sufficient: 'The law has never made the seriousness of an offence by itself a ground for compellability, and we do not favour doing so now'.

The growing concern about sexual and physical abuse within the home was a motivating force behind the enactment of section 80. But the formal evidential rules on compellability have pulled in an opposite direction to prosecution policies. The Crown Prosecution Service have tended to discontinue prosecutions where the spouse is reluctant to testify.[91] However evidence from other jurisdictions suggest that a policy which pursues a prosecution regardless of the witness's reluctance to testify results in a reduction in the number of reported domestic assaults.[92] There are several strategies open to the CPS where a spouse is unwilling to testify:

(1) under section 80(3) the spouse may be compelled to testify under the threat of being held in contempt of court
(2) if the spouse is intimidated,[93] under section 23(3) of the Criminal Justice Act 1988, a written witness statement may be admissible if the spouse does not give evidence ". . . through fear or because he is being kept out of the way"[94]
(3) if the spouse has given evidence or a statement was adduced at committal proceedings, that statement may be admissible in the Crown Court under section 68 and Sched. 2 of the Criminal Procedure and Investigations Act 1996[95]
(4) having been called as a witness by the Crown, if the spouse refuses to answer questions, he or she can be treated as a hostile witness[96] under section 3 of the Criminal Procedure Act 1865. This can occur either when the spouse is a compellable witness under section 80(3) or where the offence is not a "compellable" offence but the spouse has chosen to take the oath but then has changed his or her mind. In *R. v. Pitt*[97] the husband was accused of violence to his baby daughter. His wife initially chose to testify but in the course of testimony, gave answers that led the prosecution to apply to treat her as a hostile witness. She was then cross-examined and her prior statements to the police, inconsistent with her evidence, were put to her. The appeal was on the basis that it was not correct to treat the wife, who was not a compellable witness, as hostile:

[91] Edwards S., "Compelling a Reluctant Spouse" (1989) 139 New L.J. 691.
[92] Torgbor S., "Police Intervention in Domestic Violence — A Comparative View" 19 Fam. Law 195 (1989).
[93] *R. v. Renshaw* [1989] Crim.L.R. 811 (decided prior to the passage of the Criminal Justice Act 1988, s. 23).
[94] See 566, *et seq.*
[95] *ibid.*
[96] See 348, *et seq.*
[97] [1982] 3 All E.R. 63.

R. v. Pitt [1982] 3 All E.R. 63 at 66b–d, *per* Peter Pain J.

Up to the point where she goes into the witness box, the wife has a choice: she may refuse to give evidence or waive her right of refusal. The waiver is effective only if made with full knowledge of her right to refuse. If she waives her right of refusal, she becomes an ordinary witness. She is by analogy in the same position as a witness who waives privilege, which would entitled him to refuse to answer questions on a certain topic.

In our view, in these circumstances, once the wife has started on her evidence, she must complete it. It is not open to her to retreat behind the barrier of non-compellability if she is asked questions that she does not wish to answer. Justice should not allow her to give evidence which might assist, or injure, her husband and then to escape from normal investigation.

It follows that if the nature of her evidence justifies it, an application may be made to treat her as a hostile witness . . .

The right to refuse to testify is not lost because a statement is made to the police or evidence is given at committal proceedings. The key point is taking the oath at trial but the Court of Appeal made it clear that it would be desirable for a judge to make it clear to a spouse that there is a right to refuse to testify and that a verdict may be upset if a spouse gives evidence without fully appreciating that there is such a right.

In enacting section 80, Parliament did not limit compellability to cases of domestic violence but extended the list of offences to include offences against children outside the family as well. This was on the grounds of the seriousness of the offences included but is open to the criticism that offences involving violence to people aged over sixteen are as serious and yet are not included. This is especially the case with crimes against the elderly. The principles involved in weighing "offence seriousness" against the significance of the spouse's evidence and the impact on the marriage mean that any approach involving listing offences is inevitably flawed:

Creighton P., "Spouse Competence and Compellability" [1990] Crim.L.R. 34 at 35

Considerations of this kind led to the enactment in the Australian State of Victoria of a provision[98] making the wife compellable against her husband in all cases, but conferring on the trial judge a discretion to exempt the wife from giving evidence, generally or in part, where the interest in obtaining the wife's evidence is outweighed by either or both the likely damage to the marital relationship and the harshness of compelling her to testify. The factors to be considered by the judge in exercising the discretion include the nature of the offence charged, the likely significance of the wife's evidence in the case, the state of the relationship between the spouses and the likely impact upon it of compelling her to testify.

In England at this time, the spouse is always competent for the prosecution but has a choice whether to testify or not, unless the offence falls under section 80(3). Zuckerman argues:

[98] Crimes Act 1958 s.400.

Zuckerman A., *The Principles of Criminal Evidence*, 290–292

When marriage was indissoluble, the souring of relations between spouses would have condemned them to living together in enmity for the rest of their lives or, alternatively, to separation without the prospect of establishing another family. However matrimonial morality and matrimonial policy have undergone radical transformation. If marital relations have deteriorated, the marriage can be brought to an end. Indeed, a very considerable proportion of marriages do in fact end in divorce. It is difficult to imagine that granting spouses immunity from having to testify against each other makes an appreciable contribution to the general stability of marriage in our community.

There are further considerations that weaken the justification based on marital harmony. If the wife is accorded a freedom to choose whether or not to testify, her accused husband will in many cases bring pressure to bear on her to refuse to testify when invited to do so by the prosecution . . .

Even where a spouse freely chooses to decline the prosecution's call to testify, the moral position of withholding information that may lead to the accused's conviction is highly ambivalent. One may perhaps be able to defend a failure to initiate a complaint but it could hardly be maintained that withholding incriminating evidence from the court, once the accused has been charged, is morally acceptable, especially where the offence is a grave one.

Zuckerman argues that there is a basic flaw in the rationale behind spousal privilege which has meant that the definition of its scope in section 80, although clear, is essentially haphazard. This point is supported by the fact that if it is repugnant to see a wife being compelled to testify against her husband, there are other levels of relationship to which the same argument would apply — a mother against her son, for example or unmarried couples. In Victoria, the Crimes Act 1958 gives discretion to the judge to exempt the parents or children of the accused from testifying.[99]

The current situation regarding the competence and compellability of the spouse of the accused is:

(a) for the prosecution

- the spouse is always competent but only compellable in the small range of offences under section 80(3)
- the spouse is not competent where the husband and wife are jointly charged with the same offence under section 80(4). However this appears to exclude those cases where they are being tried for related but different offences in the same proceedings
- where the accused is charged with multiple offences and the spouse is a compellable witness with regard to one of these, the better view would be that the spouse could only be compelled to answer questions in relation to that offence.

[99] Also see Israel Evidence Ordinance (New Version) (1971) cl.4.

(b) for the defence, the spouse is always competent and compellable[1] save for the situation under section 80(4) where they are jointly charged with the same offence. In such cases the spouse is still competent.

(c) for a co-accused, the spouse is always competent under section 80(1)(b) but is only compellable in the circumstances of section 80(3), even where this is necessary to prove the innocence of an accused. However this restrictive interpretation was dented to a certain extent in *R. v. Woolgar*[2] where the defendants, M and W, were charged in the same indictment but with different offences. M was convicted of assault and W of criminal damage. W had sought to call M's wife as to testify on his behalf but the trial judge held that the accused were "jointly charged" within section 80(1)(b) and, since neither was charged with an offence under section 80(3), the wife was not compellable. The Court of Appeal quashed the conviction, holding that M and W were not jointly charged with any single offence and as a result the wife was compellable, presumably as she would have been had there been separate trials.[3]

(d) failure to testify: where the spouse has the choice whether to testify or not, any failure to testify cannot be made the subject of comment by the prosecution under section 80(8):

80(8). The failure of the wife or husband of the accused to give evidence shall not be made the subject of any comment by the prosecution.

This restriction applies to the prosecution and not to any co-accused. This mirrored the position of the accused under proviso (b) of the Criminal Evidence Act 1898 until its repeal by the Criminal Justice and Public Order Act 1994, although this Act has not changed the position with regard to the spouse's "right to silence". The rationale for this restriction is ambiguous since marital harmony is not under threat from a spouse's refusal to testify and if it is possible to draw legitimate inferences from that refusal, there is little reason not to do so.

Former spouses as witnesses

Fortunately the old common law rules have now been superseded, at least in criminal proceedings. The problems can be seen in *R. v. Algar*[4] in which the defendant was charged with the forgery of his wife's signature on certain cheques. The cheques were drawn in 1947/48 and the marriage was

[1] Prior to the Police and Criminal Evidence Act 1984, s.80, the spouse was not a compellable witness for the accused — *R. v. Boal* [1964] 3 All E.R. 269.
[2] [1991] Crim.L.R. 545.
[3] Commentators have stressed that precedent would interpret "jointly charged" as "jointly indicted" — Creighton (1991) *op. cit.*; Smith J.C. in the commentary on *Woolgar supra.*
[4] [1954] 1 Q.B. 279.

annulled on the ground of the defendant's impotence in 1949. Despite the length of time since the annulment and the absence of any need to maintain "marital harmony", the wife was held to be incompetent to testify against the defendant since the marriage had been subsisting at the time of the offences.

By section 80(5) of the Police and Criminal Evidence Act 1984, the old rules have been abolished:

80(5). In any proceedings, a person who has been but is no longer married to the accused shall be competent and compellable to give evidence as if that person and the accused had never been married.

This refers only to criminal proceedings. ". . . no longer married" means divorce or annulment but not judicial separation or just non-cohabiting.[5] In those situations, these would be spouses and not former spouses.

But in civil proceedings, the old common law made both spouses and former spouses incompetent witnesses — former spouses were only incompetent witnesses with regard to matters that happened during the course of the marriage. The reforms of the nineteenth century[6] made the spouses competent but said nothing about former spouses. Therefore, however incongrously, *Monroe v. Twistleton*[7] remains good law. In that case the plaintiff sought to call the divorced wife of the defendant to prove a contract but as the matter at issue occurred in the course of the marriage, she was an incompetent witness. This position has not been changed by statute or by common law since that time.

[5] *Moss v. Moss* [1963] 2 All E.R. 829; *R. v. Mathias* [1989] Crim.L.R. 64.
[6] Evidence Amendment Act 1853 and Evidence (Further Amendment) Act 1869.
[7] (1802) Peake Add. Cas. 219.

9

THE TESTIMONY OF WITNESSES: THE NEED FOR SUPPORTIVE EVIDENCE

INTRODUCTION

One of the fundamental principles of justice is that the innocent must be protected from conviction and punishment. Miscarriages of justice in recent years have highlighted this. Following the release of the Guildford Four in October 1989, the Court of Appeal has quashed convictions in a number of highly publicised cases. Miscarriages of justice are not new and throughout its history, the criminal justice system has seen its fair share of disasters. At least Adolf Beck survived his imprisonment for fraud in 1907, having been wrongly identified by several victims. On release he was imprisoned a further time, again through misidentification. Timothy Evans, however, was executed in 1950 for murders committed by John Christie[1] and in 1962 James Hanratty was hanged for the A6 killing of Michael Gregsten.[2] Since 1989, the trickle of wrongful convictions has become a flood, with convictions quashed in cases such as the Birmingham Six,[3] Stefan Kiszko, Broadwater Farm, Judith Ward,[4] the Cardiff Three,[5] let alone those attributable to the activities of the West Midlands Serious Crime Squad.[6] Civil liberty organisations and TV programmes such as the BBC's *Rough Justice* have identified dozens of further cases where there is cause for doubting the propriety of the convictions. Inevitably the public have become aware that there are serious flaws in the criminal justice system.

Analysis of such miscarriages has revealed no single cause but shows that different elements of the system itself have at times been at fault: poor investigative procedures or oppressive interrogation by the police; failure to disclose evidence by the prosecution; the trial court's failure to assess properly the weight of evidence; the unwillingness of the Appeal Court and the Home Office to admit that things had gone wrong.

[1] Kennedy L., *Ten Rillington Place* (1961).
[2] Foot P., *Who Killed Hanratty?* (1971).
[3] Mullin C., *Error of Judgment* (1986).
[4] [1993] 2 All E.R. 577.
[5] *R. v. Paris* [1994] Crim.L.R. 361.
[6] Kaye T., *Unsafe and Unsatisfactory* (1991).

In the courtroom, the protection of the innocent necessarily involves rules for all defendants, innocent or not. These are the rules regarding not only the allocation of the burden of proof, which carries with it the presumption of innocence and the principles enunciated in *Woolmington v. DPP*,[7] but also the requirement for a sufficiency of reliable, relevant and admissible evidence. The formal guarantees of that sufficiency are the rules on the standard of proof in criminal proceedings, *i.e.*, that the weight of the evidence is such that the prosecution have proved their case beyond reasonable doubt. But the existence of miscarriages of justice show that judges and juries in serious cases involving murder and terrorist offences can wrongly evaluate the weight of the evidence. This can come about for various reasons:

Greer S., "Miscarriages of Criminal Justice Reconsidered" 57 M.L.R. (1994) 58 at 72–73

A 'mistaken' conviction occurs when the tribunal of fact honestly, and without impropriety, believes the prosecution evidence, either through misunderstanding the issues or because a defence which is in fact true seems to lack credibility. There are various sources of such convictions: vital evidence simply not coming to light, outside interference with vital witnesses resulting in either their failure to testify or perjured evidence at trial, mistaken or misleading directions by otherwise unbiased judges, joint trials in which an innocent defendant may be tarnished with the guilt of a co-defendant, mistaken identity, false confessions volunteered without police pressure, poor defence tactics, mistaken or deliberately false evidence by accomplices or other witnesses, and a failure on the part of jurors to understand the legal burden of proof or the issues involved in the trial. A jury or magistrate may be inclined to convict, for example, if presented with an entirely innocent but unconvincing defendant, who has had the opportunity to commit the offence, has been wrongly identified as the offender by a mistaken or dishonest witness, has no alibi and whose defence may amount to no more than a blank denial of the charge.

These risks have been recognised for many years and a variety of procedures have been developed in an attempt to deal with them, for example, the offence of perjury, the reliability tests which confessions must pass before being admitted in evidence, opportunities for the severance of trials, and the development of warnings about the dangers of relying upon uncorroborated accomplice evidence and about the care which must be taken with eyewitness testimony. But the adequacy of these arrangements needs constantly to be reviewed.

Supportive Evidence

One of the key checks on the quality of evidence has been the common law rules on the corroboration of certain categories of evidence. Any decision based on information from a single source must always be open to question and this is especially so in criminal proceedings where any verdict of guilty must be "beyond reasonable doubt". Logically it is difficult to exclude doubt by relying on a single witness and procedurally, fairness to a suspect demands more than accusation from one person.

[7] [1935] A.C. 462.

Stephens, Sir J., *General View of the Criminal Law* (1st ed.) 249

The circumstances may be such that there is no check on the witness and no power to obtain any further evidence on the subject. Under these circumstances juries may, and often do, acquit. They may very reasonably say we do not attach such credit to the oath of a single person of whom we know nothing, as to be willing to destroy another person on the strength of it.

Despite this, the rules requiring supporting evidence in English law are now few in number and the testimony of a single witness is sufficient on which to base a conviction or acquittal in criminal cases or a finding in a civil matter. There is no general rule that requires supporting evidence: that is, if there is evidence from Source A as to some fact in issue, there does not need to be further evidence from Source B that tends to confirm that fact. This can be contrasted to civil systems of law based on Roman Law where there is a general requirement of corroboration, although perhaps in practice, there is less difference.[8]

Tapper C., *Cross on Evidence* (7th ed., 1990) 224–225

The history of this subject is not without interest, for one of the great differences between the modern English law of evidence and that prescribed by the canon or civil law, which usually applied the maxim '*testis unus testis nullus*', consists in the absence of any general requirement of a plurality of witnesses. More than one oath helper was required when compurgation was among the standard methods of trial, so English law started with something like the requirements of a number of witnesses such as were demanded by the canon law under the influence of Roman law, although the compurgators were of course quite unlike the modern witness. The two systems diverged more or less completely when English jury trial began to assume its present form in the seventeenth century. Before that period, the jurors were themselves witnesses, rather than triers, of fact, so there was a sense in which it could be said that more than one witness was always necessary at a common law trial. It is of some significance that Coke maintained that more than one witness was necessary in proceedings without a jury as where the validity of challenges fell to be determined. When the jurors ceased to resemble the modern witness, some efforts to impose rules requiring two or more witnesses were made by statute; but provisions of this nature were never generalised, and they are now of no importance.

Common law and corroboration

The common law, while not developing a general rule requiring supporting evidence, did recognise that there were situations where the evidence of a single witness was not sufficient. This may be because of the nature of the witness (where there is a motive for lying or the court distrusts the intellectual faculties); the nature of the evidence (such as identification evidence); the gravity of the complaint. In such situations, the courts and the legislature evolved an ad hoc series of common law and statutory rules

[8] MacPhail I., "Safeguards in the Scottish Criminal Justice System" [1992] Crim.L.R. 144.

that required the judge and jury to consider whether there was supporting evidence. Formal rules developed as to what constituted sufficient supporting evidence which became technically known as *corroboration.* The rules about when and how corroboration was used were complex. Some of these still have limited relevance. These can be illustrated by examining the different categories of corroboration requirements:

(1) firstly are those situations where corroboration in the form of independent evidence was **required as a matter of law.** If there was no supporting evidence, the judge had to direct an acquittal or a finding for the other party. These situations are all statutory and in recent years the number has been steadily eroded by repeal, for instance:

   (a) in affiliation cases, section 17 of the Family Law Reform Act 1987 removed the requirement that corroboration of the mother's testimony was required before the defendant was adjudged the putative father

   (b) under section 38(1) of the Children and Young Persons Act 1933, the unsworn evidence of children required corroboration as a matter of law. This was dispensed with by section 34(1) of the Criminal Justice Act 1988

   (c) under sections 2, 3, 4, 22 and 23 of the Sexual Offences Act 1956, offences of procuring women for sex required corroboration. This was removed by section 33 of the Criminal Justice and Public Order Act 1994.

In all such cases, a warning to the jury might still be given as a matter of practice. This is considered below. The offences which still require the prosecution to adduce corroborative evidence are:

   (a) speeding offences, under the Road Traffic Regulation Act 1984.

> 89.—(2) A person prosecuted for such an offence shall not be liable to be convicted solely on the evidence of one witness to the effect that, in the opinion of the witness, the person prosecuted was driving the vehicle at a speed exceeding the specified limit.

These conditions are met, for example, by the police officer's observation of the car and a contemporaneous reading of a speedometer or other measuring device, or indeed by the opinions of two eyewitnesses.[9] In *Nicholas v. Penny*[10] it was

[9] *Brighty v. Pearson* [1938] 4 All E.R. 127.
[10] [1950] 2 All E.R. 89.

held that the section did not require testimony from two witnesses nor did it require evidence that the speedometer was accurate. Incidentally this latter point is another example of the rebuttable presumption that, in the absence of contrary evidence, mechanical devices are assumed to be operating properly.[11] In *Crossland v. DPP*,[12] the opinion of an expert witness who bases his opinion of speed on the indications at the scene of the accident such as skid marks and damage to the vehicle, does not require corroboration under section 89.

(b) perjury under the Perjury Act 1911:

> 13.—A person shall not be liable to be convicted of any offence against this Act, or of any offence declared by any other Act to be perjury or subornation of perjury, or to be punishable as perjury or subornation of perjury solely upon the evidence of one witness as to the falsity of any statement alleged to be false.

Perjury was originally an offence tried in Star Chamber, itself influenced by civil law methods of proof. In 1972, the Criminal Law Revision Committee recommended the retention of the corroboration requirement on the ground that if convictions for perjury were too easy, this might discourage witnesses from testifying.[13] However courts have put no great obstacles in the way of prosecutions for the offence:

> The meaning is this: it used sometimes to be said that there must be two witnesses; this was a delusion; the evidence of one witness and a confession may be enough, and the section has been drafted so as to make this clear. One witness can prove that the person charged swore to certain statements, but more than the evidence of one witness is required to prove that the statements were false.[14]

Evidence that the accused has confessed that his or her statement was false is evidence of its falsity. In *R. v. Peach*[15] the defendant made his confession in front of two witnesses and the Court of Appeal held that the requirements of section 13 were satisfied.

(c) treason under section 1 Treason Act 1795, although this is now of no practical importance.

(2) secondly came those situations where corroboration in the form of independent evidence was not itself required but where a **corroboration warning was required as a matter of law.** This required

[11] See Chap. 21 for further discussion of presumptions.
[12] [1988] 3 All E.R. 712.
[13] 11th Report (1972) Cmnd 4991 paras 178 and 190.
[14] *R. v. Threlfall* (1914) 10 Cr.App.R. 112 at 114.
[15] [1990] 2 All E.R. 966.

that the trier of fact had to be warned, as a matter of law, of the dangers of convicting on uncorroborated evidence. If no corroboration existed, the jury was still entitled to convict as long as they did so with full awareness of the dangers of that course of action and presumably having concluded that the witness whose testimony needed corroboration could be relied on. Thus the warning had to be properly worded:

R. v. Spencer [1986] 2 All E.R. 928 at 936e–f, _per_ Lord Ackner

. . . the rule of practice merely requires that the jury should be warned of the danger of relying on the sole evidence of an accomplice or of the complainant in the sexual case or on the evidence of a child. The warning to be sufficient must explain why it is dangerous so to act, since otherwise the warning will lack significance. The jury are, of course, told that, while as a general rule it is dangerous so to act, they are at liberty to do so if they feel sure that the uncorroborated witness is telling the truth.

If such a warning was not given, this would be good grounds for appeal and only if there were exceptional reasons for considering that no substantial miscarriage of justice had occurred would the proviso under section 2 of the Criminal Appeal Act 1968 be applied.[16]

There were three situations where a corroboration warning was required, explained by Lord Ackner in *Spencer*:

R. v. Spencer op. cit. at 937e–f

In the three established categories where the 'full warning' is obligatory, the inherent unreliability of the witness may well not be apparent to the jury. Hence the phrase often used in a summing up: it is the experience of the courts accumulated over many years etc. Complainants of sexual assaults do on occasions give false evidence for a variety of reasons, some of which may not have occurred to a jury. Accomplices may have hidden reasons for lying, and this possibility may again not be apparent to a jury. Children who, although old enough to understand the nature of an oath and thus competent to give sworn evidence, may yet be so young that their comprehension of events and of questions put to them, or their own powers of expression, may be imperfect. All this needs to be properly spelt out to the jury.

However this is now a category without content since legislation has removed any obligation on the judge to give a corroboration warning in any of these three cases:

(a) the old common law required a warning to be given with regard to the sworn testimony of children. The rules regarding

[16] *R. v. Trigg* [1963] 1 All E.R. 490. The proviso under s.2 of the Criminal Appeal Act 1968 was abolished by the Criminal Appeal Act 1995.

the need to corroborate the evidence of children rested on assumptions about a child's suggestibility, the powers of observation and memory, the predilections towards fantasy, the egocentricity and children's supposed evil nature. Their justification was attacked[17] and the calls for reform increased as studies showed that sexual abuse of children was far more widespread than previously believed[18] and that children's unreliability as witnesses was much less than previously accepted.[19] The old rules were removed by the Criminal Justice Act 1988:

> 34.—(2) Any requirement whereby at a trial on indictment it is obligatory for the court to give the jury a warning about convicting the accused on the uncorroborated evidence of a child is abrogated.

(b) perhaps more bizarrely, the common law singled out victims of sexual offences so that juries were warned that their evidence could be unreliable. Even recently, researchers found judges warning jurors "Experience has shown that people who allege sexual offences . . . tell false stories"[20] and asserting that such accusations are easy to make and difficult to disprove. Statistics tend to show otherwise: the majority of sexual assaults go unreported, indicating that victims find it difficult to make such allegations. Those which are reported rarely end in conviction. In 1992, 4,142 rapes were recorded by the police who also treated 75 per cent of these as cleared up and yet there were only 529 convictions in that year. The two assumptions are that there is a strong risk of false accusation and also that, especially with child victims, the jury will be strongly prejudiced against the accused. As Dennis argues, such assumptions have no real basis, "It is truly extraordinary to say that all female victims of sex crimes are presumed to be perjurers or fantasists unless the jury is convinced otherwise . . ."[21]

This "lingering insult to women" was finally removed with the Criminal Justice and Public Order Act 1994:

> 32.—(1) Any requirement whereby at a trial on indictment it is obligatory for a court to give the jury a warning about convicting the accused on the uncorroborated evidence of a person merely because that person is —

[17] Dennis I., "Corroboration Requirements Reconsidered" [1984] Crim.L.R. 316 at 329.
[18] Spencer J. and Flin J., *The Evidence of Children — The Law and the Psychology* (2nd ed., 1993) Chap. 1.
[19] Gertner, "The Unsworn Evidence of Children and Mutual Corroboration" (1978) 16 Osgoode Hall L.J. 495.
[20] Lees J. "Why Men Get Away with Rape" *The Guardian*, February 16, 1994, 9; older examples are given in Temkin J., *Rape and Legal Process* (1987) 135.
[21] Dennis, *op. cit.* at 326.

. . . (b) where the offence charged a sexual offence, the person in respect of whom it is alleged to have been committed
is hereby abrogated.

(c) less criticised was the rule that required a corroboration warning in the case of accomplices to the offence who were testifying on behalf of the prosecution:

Dennis I., "Corroboration Requirements Reconsidered" [1984] Crim.L.R. 316 at 322

It is argued that an accomplice may lie for a number of reasons. He may try to exculpate himself or minimise his own part in an offence by exaggerating or fabricating the role of the accused. He may act out of spite or revenge, as where he believes himself to have been informed against by the accused. He may be suspected of purchasing immunity from prosecution or a lesser charge or more favourable prospects of early release by ensuring the conviction of others. It is also argued that the risk of the accused being convicted on perjured evidence is increased by the accomplice's apparent plausibility. The latter will usually be familiar with at least some details of the offence and will be able to report them accurately.[22]

But it can be argued that an accomplice who incriminates himself or herself at the same time as incriminating the defendant is presumably more to be trusted. The substantive question that the court should be asking is about the witness's motives in giving evidence and whether those motives are such as to make the testimony unreliable and in need of supporting evidence. Even with accomplices, the trier of fact is dealing essentially with credibility. Are lies by accomplices any more difficult to detect than false allegations by other witnesses? A rigid rule which identifies one or more classes of potentially unreliable witnesses was indiscriminate and illogical and led to a legalistic approach to the issue of who was an accomplice.[23] The approach needed was one that gave more discretion to the trial judge who was in a position to assess potential unreliability on a more individual basis.[24] This recommendation was eventually followed in the Criminal Justice and Public Order Act 1994:

32.—(1) Any requirement whereby at a trial on indictment it is obligatory for a court to give the jury a warning about convicting the accused on the uncorroborated evidence of a person merely because that person is —

[22] [1973] 1 All E.R. 440 at 447d–e.
[23] *Davies v. DPP* [1954] 1 All E.R. 507.
[24] This was the approach favoured by the Criminal Law Revision Committee, Eleventh Report, *op. cit.* para. 183.

(a) an alleged accomplice of the accused
. . . is hereby abrogated

(3) the third situation is where a **corroboration warning is required as a matter of practice.** Here we are dealing with the discretion of the trial judge. Neither corroborative evidence itself nor a corroboration warning is required as a matter of law. On the facts of the particular case, it seems appropriate to warn the trier of fact of the dangers of convicting on uncorroborated evidence. If such a warning was not given, a conviction will not necessarily be quashed. Indeed recent decisions, such as *R. v. Makanjuola*[25] suggest that a full warning, explaining the nature of corroborative evidence, is no longer necessary. But currently the situations in which such a warning must be considered are:

(a) accomplices who testify in their own defence but who implicate a co-accused by their evidence

(b) matrimonial cases in which the court should warn itself explicitly about the dangers of acting on the uncorroborated evidence of a spouse, especially where sexual misconduct is alleged.

Ali v. Ali [1965] 3 All E.R. 480 at 484–5 _per_ Sir Jocelyn Simon P.

To sum up, then, our view of the authorities so far: (a) where a matrimonial offence is alleged, the court will look for corroboration of the complainant's evidence; (b) the court will normally, before finding a matrimonial offence proved, require such corroboration if, on the face of the complainant's own evidence, it is available; (c) these are not rules of law, but of practice only. They spring from the gravity of the consequences of the proof of a matrimonial offence; and because, we would add, experience has shown the risk of a miscarriage of justice in acting on the uncorroborated testimony of a spouse in this class of case; (d) it is, nevertheless, open to a court to act on the uncorroborated evidence of a spouse if it is in no doubt where the truth lies; . . .

(c) claims against a dead person's estate where warnings as a matter of practice are also advised.

(d) children's testimony where, although section 34 of the Criminal Justice Act 1988 has abrogated the need for obligatory warnings, the judge does have discretion to give a warning. But the full corroboration warning is no longer needed. In *R. v. Z.*[26] a six year old testified against her father accused of incest. The judge's direction to the jury was as follows:

[25] [1995] 3 All E.R. 730.
[26] [1990] 2 All E.R. 971.

R. *v.* Z. [1990] 2 All E.R. 971 at 975e–g, quoted by Lord Lane C.J.

As I have said, it is you who will decide whether the little girl you saw on video link firstly may have been a very wicked child, which she would be if she deliberately made a false allegation either at her mother's instigation or off her own bat, or secondly, she may have been living in a little child's world of make believe, believing that her allegation was true when really it was not, or believing it was true because her mother had implanted the thought in her mind when truly it was not, or thirdly, was a perfectly normal decent little child, telling us in her own way and using her own language what Daddy did to her. Those are your decisions and yours alone.[27]

This explicit caution but untainted with any mention of supporting (let alone corroborative) evidence, was approved by the Court of Appeal.

(e) a residual category when warnings should be issued where the testimony is tainted with improper motives. Lord Hailsham in *DPP v. Kilbourne*[28] said that a judge would be wise to warn about any principal witness where that witness has some purpose of his or her own to serve. But that warning need not be couched in terms of corroboration: in *R. v. Beck*[29] the appeal was based on the failure to warn the jury that it was dangerous to act on the uncorroborated evidence of witnesses who had purposes of their own to serve.

***R. v. Beck* [1982] 1 All E.R. 807 at 812f-j; 813h-j, *per* Ackner L.J.**

Merely because there is material to justify the suggestion that a witness is giving unfavourable evidence, for example, out of spite, ill-will, to level some old score, to obtain some financial advantage, cannot, counsel for the appellant concedes, in every case necessitate the accomplice warning, if there is no material to suggest that the witness may be an accomplice. But, submits counsel for the appellant, even though there is no material to suggest any involvement by the witness in the crime, if he has a 'substantial interest' of his own for giving false evidence, then the accomplice direction must be given. Where one draws the line, he submits is a question of degree, but once the boundary is crossed, the obligation to give the accomplice warning is not a matter of discretion. We cannot accept this contention. In many trials today, the burden on the trial judge of the summing up is a heavy one. It would be a totally unjustifiable addition

[27] See a similar approach in *R. v. Pryce* [1991] Crim.L.R. 379. This direction might usefully be considered in the light of the comments on judicial neutrality in summing up, discussed in Chap. 2.
[28] [1973] 1 All E.R. 440 at 447d–e.
[29] [1982] 1 All E.R. 807; also see *R. v. Prater* [1960] 1 All E.R. 298.

to require him, not only fairly to put before the jury the defence's contention that a witness is suspect, because he had an axe to grind, but also to evaluate the weight of the axe and oblige him, where the weight is 'substantial', to give an accomplice warning with the appropriate direction as to the meaning of corroboration together with the identification of the potential corroborative material.

. . . While we in no way wish to detract from the obligation on a judge to advise a jury to proceed with caution where there is material to suggest that a witness's evidence may be tainted with an improper motive, and the strength of that advice must vary according to the facts of the case, we cannot accept that there is any obligation to give the accomplice warning with all that entails, when it is common ground that there is no basis for suggesting that the witness is a participant or in any way involved in the crime the subject matter of the trial.

This approach was also apparent in *R. v. Spencer*[30] in which the defendants were nurses, charged under section 126 of the Mental Health Act 1959 with assaulting the witness-patients who were detained in Rampton, suffering from mental disorders and having committed serious offences themselves. The trial judge had warned the jury to approach the complainants' evidence with great caution but had not specifically directed them as to the dangers of convicting without corroboration. The House of Lords held that even if mental patients were analogous to the established categories for corroboration warnings, these categories were not to be extended:

R. v. Spencer [1986] 2 All E.R. 928 at 936j–937d, _per_ Lord Ackner

To create from them such a new category would clearly involve considerable problems of definition. What sort of patients, and patients with what sort of criminal records are to be included? The submission of the appellants, in essence, is that without use of the word 'danger', in any case analogous to those of the three established categories, and where the evidence of the only or principal witness relied on by the prosecution is inherently unreliable, such a warning must be inadequate. I cannot agree. It has been said, both in the Court of Appeal and in your Lordships' House, that the obligation to warn a jury does not involve some legalistic ritual to be automatically recited by the judge, or that some particular form of words or incantation has to be used and, if not used, the summing up is faulty and the conviction must be quashed. There is no magic formula which has to be used with regard to any warning which is given to juries. As this is no mere idle process it follows that there are no set words which must be adopted to express the warning. Rather must the good sense of the matter be expounded with clarity and in the setting of a particular case. The summing up should be tailored to suit the circumstances of the particular case.

[30] [1986] 2 All E.R. 928.

The problems of corroboration

As this survey reveals, the scope of corroboration requirements of whatever kind has decreased significantly. The assault on the corroboration rules occurred not because supportive evidence was undesirable. Rather it was because of the arbitrary and anomalous nature of the groups of witnesses and categories of evidence affected by it as well as the inflexibility and complexity of the rules themselves:[31]

(1) corroboration was never simply put to the jury as "supportive evidence". The common law required that it verified a material part of the testimony in need of corroboration and that it implicated the defendant. This was laid down in *R. v. Baskerville*[32] where Lord Reading said that corroborative evidence is evidence ". . . which confirms in some material particulars not only the evidence that the crime has been committed but also that the prisoner committed it." Thus in a rape case, medical evidence confirming that the victim had had sex at the time of the alleged rape would not corroborate her testimony alleging rape because, in itself, it does not confirm the identity of the man involved.

(2) corroborative evidence had to be relevant, admissible, credible and independent. This latter factor is an essential criterion for assessing the probative worth of any supporting evidence. The evidence should emanate from a source other than the original witness. Thus under the corroboration rules, the evidence could not be, for example, a recent complaint of a victim in a sexual assault case[33] although the visible distress of the victim, independently observed might be.[34] Similarly other prior consistent statements or contemporary notes admitted for the purpose of refreshing the memory[35] could not be seen as corroboration. Explaining such technicalities to the jury was never a simple task.

(3) equally complex was the rule that the testimony of a witness who required corroboration could not itself supply corroboration so that if there were a defendant and two accomplices involved in the same offence, the two accomplices could not corroborate each other.

(4) where there were several pieces of potentially corroborative evidence but the corroborative value of any single piece might be nil, the jury could be directed that the cumulative effect might be seen as constituting corroboration.[36]

[31] Law Commission, *Corroboration of Evidence in Criminal Trials* Cm. 1620 (1991); Birch D., "Corroboration: Goodbye to all that?" [1995] Crim.L.R. 524.

[32] [1916–17] All E.R. Rep 38.

[33] *R. v. Whitehead* [1929] 1 K.B. 99

[34] *R. v. Chauhan* (1981) 73 Cr.App.R. 232; *R. v. Redpath* (1962) 46 Cr.App.R. 319

[35] *R. v. Virgo* (1978) 67 Cr.App.R. 323.

[36] *R. v. Hills* (1987) 86 Cr.App.R. 26.

Corroboration rules appear to embody substantial safeguards. But a confused jury will rarely come to a just result. In *R. v. Hester*[37] Lord Diplock observed that the ". . . complicated formulae about the concept of corroboration and the respective functions of judge and jury are . . . unintelligible to the ordinary laymen". The Law Commission put it:

Law Commission, *Corroboration of Evidence in Criminal Trials*, Cm. 1620 (1991) para. 2.9

This complexity not only is the cause of unnecessary difficulties at trials but can also be positively detrimental to justice. The rules as to what evidence can and cannot count as corroborative are difficult and complex and the cause of many actual or alleged errors and of many appeals. The danger of injustice is increased by the irrational terms of the required direction itself. The judge is obliged to start by saying that it is dangerous to convict on the basis of certain evidence, but then to go on and tell the jury that it is possible for them to do exactly that. Those formulae can lead, according to the circumstances of the case, either to the placing of an unfair handicap on the prosecution or to confusion that may be positively detrimental to the accused. Far from protecting the accused, the rules, by requiring the jury to be given a complicated and technical discourse about the evidence to be corroborated , may 'have the contrary effect [on the jury] to a sensible warning couched in ordinary language directed to the facts of the particular case.

New solutions?

The need for corroboration or for a corroboration warning is now minimal. The question exists as to whether the judges will seek to fill this vacuum by developing corroboration warnings as a matter of practice in those areas formerly covered by the rules? The answer appears to be that, although warnings about the reliability of certain witnesses will continue to be given, such warnings will be couched in non-technical terms, will not mention corroboration nor necessarily refer to the need for supportive evidence. In *R. v. Makanjuola*[38] the defendant was convicted of an indecent assault on a young female fellow worker. On appeal it was argued that the trial judge should in his discretion have given a full direction in accordance with established corroboration rules regardless of section 32 of the Criminal Justice and Public Order Act 1994. The appellant suggested that the rationale for the old common law was that complainants in sexual offences may lie or fantasize for unascertainable reasons or for no reason at all, that this rationale had not evaporated overnight and the traditional warning should continue:

***R. v. Makanjuola* [1995] 3 All E.R. 730 at 731j–733g, *per* Lord Taylor C.J.**

If that were right, Parliament would have enacted section 32(1) in vain; practice would continue unchanged. It is clear that the judge does have a discretion to warn

[37] [1972] 2 All E.R. 1020.
[38] [1995] 3 All E.R. 730.

the jury if he thinks it necessary, but the use of the word 'merely' in the subsection shows that Parliament does not envisage such a warning being given just because a witness complains of a sexual offence or is an alleged accomplice.

It is further submitted that if the judge does decide a warning is necessary, he should give the jury the full old-style direction on corroboration. That means using the phrase 'dangerous to convict on uncorroborated evidence', explaining the meaning of corroboration, identifying what evidence under the old rules is capable of being corroboration, what evidence is not so capable, and the respective roles of the judge and jury in this bipartite quest . . . It was, in our judgment, partly to escape from this tortuous exercise, which juries must have found more bewildering than illuminating, that Parliament enacted s.32.

Given that the requirement of a corroboration direction is abrogated in the terms of section 32(1), we have been invited to give guidance as to the circumstances in which, as a matter of discretion, a judge ought in summing up to a jury to urge caution in regard to a particular witness and the terms in which that should be done. The circumstances and evidence in criminal cases are infinitely variable and it is impossible to categorise how a judge should deal with them. But it is clear that to carry on giving 'discretionary' warnings generally and in the same terms as were previously obligatory would be contrary to the policy and purpose of the 1994 Act . Whether, as a matter of discretion, a judge should give any warning and if so its strength and terms must depend upon the content and manner of the witness's evidence, the circumstances of the case and the issues raised. The judge will often consider that no special warning is required at all. Where, however, the witness has been shown to be unreliable, he or she may consider it necessary to urge caution. In a more extreme case, if the witness is shown to have lied, to have made previous false complaints, or to bear the defendant some grudge, a stronger warning may be thought appropriate and the judge may suggest it would be wise to look for some supporting material before acting on the impugned witness's evidence. We stress that these observations are merely illustrative of some, not all, of the factors which judges may take into account in measuring where a witness stands in the scale of reliability and what response they should make at that level in their directions to the jury. We also stress that judges are not required to conform to any formula and this court would be slow to interfere with the exercise of discretion by a trial judge who has the advantage of assessing the manner of a witness's evidence as well as its content.

To summarise:

1. Section 32(1) abrogates the requirement to give a corroboration direction in respect of an alleged accomplice or a complainant of a sexual offence simply because the witness falls into one of those categories.

2. It is a matter for the judge's discretion what, if any, warning he considers appropriate in respect of such a witness, as indeed in respect of any other witness in whatever type of case. Whether he chooses to give a warning and in what terms will depend on the circumstances of the case, the issues raised and the content and quality of the witness's evidence.

3. In some cases, it may be appropriate for the judge to warn the jury to exercise caution before acting upon the unsupported evidence of a witness. This will not be so simply because the witness is a complainant of a sexual offence nor will it necessarily be so because a witness is alleged to be an accomplice. There will need to be an evidential basis for suggesting that the evidence of the witness may be unreliable. An evidential basis does not include mere suggestions by cross-examining counsel.

4. If any question arises as to whether the judge should give a special warning in respect of a witness, it is desirable that the question be resolved by discussion with counsel in the absence of the jury before final speeches.

5. Where a judge does decide to give some warning in respect of a witness, it will be appropriate to do so as part of the judge's review of the evidence and his

comments as to how the jury should evaluate it rather than as a set-piece legal direction.

6. Where some warning is required, it will be for the judge to decide the strength and terms of the warning. It does not have to be invested with the whole florid regime of the old corroboration rules.

7. . . . .Attempts to re-impose the straitjacket of the old corroboration rules are strongly to be deprecated.

8. Finally, this court is disinclined to interfere with a trial judge's exercise of his discretion save in a case where that exercise is unreasonable in the *Wednesbury*[39] sense.

Makanjuola rejects any notion that warnings that were, before 1994, a matter of law should now routinely become a matter of practice. Indeed the judgment indicates that old-style corroboration directions will be restricted to those situations where statute requires it.

To summarise the current position:

- corroborative evidence is still required under certain statutes
- corroboration warnings are no longer required as a matter of law and will only be given very rarely as a matter of practice
- where there is an evidential basis showing that any witness in whatever sort of case may be unreliable, the trial judge in his or her discretion may warn the jury. This will not be in terms of corroboration but may be a simple caution or may in certain cases be expressed in stronger terms: the judge may suggest that the jury would be wise to look for some supportive evidence (*i.e.* material which is not dissimilar to corroboration but shorn of the complexities). Such material might well emanate from the source requiring support. For example, a rape victim's credibility might well be bolstered by her prompt complaint. Although such a complaint is admissible evidence, under the corroboration rules it did not amount to corroboration as, under the rigid interpretation of *Baskerville*, it was not independent. Under *Makanjuola*, the jury would be entitled to give the term "supportive evidence" a wider compass.

If the Court of Appeal's approach in *Makanjuola* is accepted, the problems surrounding corroboration should be in the past. Even those current warnings "as a matter of practice" are likely to be no longer phrased in terms of corroboration but subsumed within such general warnings to be given whenever there is an evidential basis for believing that a witness is unreliable. The judgment mentions some of the factors (where the witness holds a grudge or can be shown to have lied previously) affecting reliability but these relate to the individual witness.

[39] *Associated Provincial Picture Houses Ltd v. Wednesbury Corp.* [1947] 2 All E.R. 680.

But there remain categories of evidence, such as identification evidence and confessions, where there is an obvious need for supportive material. The possibility that a conviction can be based on an unsupported confession remains. Furthermore, although the dismantling of the corroboration rules is welcome, it should be emphasised that convictions which are based wholly or mainly on evidence from a single source will normally remain questionable. The "single source" was not a factor mentioned by the Court of Appeal in *Makanjuola* as a reason for a warning to the jury. This was possibly because this might be construed as an invitation to trial judges to reintroduce the "sexual complainants" rule by the back door since, all too often, such offences rely wholly or mainly on the evidence of the victim.

Supporting Evidence Issuing from the Accused

The actions and statements of the defendant are frequently used by the prosecution as a means of strengthening the Crown case. This technique has been facilitated by the passage of sections 34–37 of the Criminal Justice and Public Order Act 1994 which permits the trier of fact to draw relevant inferences either from certain aspects of the accused's silence in the face of police questions or from his or her failure to testify. But there are several other situations where the accused might unwittingly provide supporting evidence:

(1) support can obviously be derived from the accused's admissions, even where these do not confess to the whole offence. In *R. v. Dossi*[40] the charge was indecent assault on a child. The defendant testified, admitting some "innocent" fondling of the child. This enhanced the credibility of the child's story (and was treated as the corroboration which was at that time necessary)

(2) if the accused lies, this can also be treated as supportive. But lies are not necessarily indicative of guilt. In *R. v. Broadhurst*[41] Lord Devlin pointed out that there were many powerful motives for lying, both in and out of court, such as shame or terror or, as in *R. v. Richens*,[42] where the accused alleged that he had lied to the police to ensure both that his girlfriend had left the country and that his parents had a happy Christmas before he confessed. The courts have sought to warn the jury from leaping to the "natural" conclusion: in *R. v. Lucas*[43] an accomplice testified against the accused charged with importing drugs. The defendant gave evidence which was challenged as untrue. The trial judge suggested to the jury that corroboration could be found in the evidence of the defendant and that

[40] (1918) 13 Cr.App.R. 158.
[41] [1964] A.C. 441.
[42] [1993] 4 All E.R. 877.
[43] [1981] 2 All E.R. 1008.

if they rejected the accused's testimony, the consequent conclusion that she had lied to them could be corroborative of the accomplice's evidence. The Court of Appeal held that merely preferring the accomplice's testimony to that of the accused was not sufficient:

R. v. Lucas [1981] 2 All E.R. 1008 at 1011e–g, _per_ Lord Lane C.J.

To be capable of amounting to corroboration the lie told out of court must first of all be deliberate. Secondly it must relate to a material issue. Thirdly the motive for the lie must be a realisation of guilt and a fear of the truth. The jury should in appropriate cases be reminded that people sometimes lie, for example, in an attempt to bolster up a just cause, or out of shame or out of a wish to conceal disgraceful behaviour from their family. Fourthly the statement must be clearly shown to be a lie by evidence other than that of the accomplice who is to be corroborated, that is to say by admission or by evidence from an independent witness.

As a matter of good sense it is difficult to see why, subject to the same safeguards, lies proved to have been told in court by a defendant should not equally be capable of providing corroboration . . .

This approach was approved by the Court of Appeal in *R. v. Goodway*.[44] In the future, corroboration in the technical sense will have a very limited part to play. But lies by the accused, outside or inside the court, will still have an evidential function and a *Lucas* direction should be given whenever lies by the accused were relied upon:

- to undermine an alibi raised by the defence[45]
- where the trial judge considers it necessary to suggest that the jury look for some supporting evidence of a witness's testimony and draws the jury's attention to the accused's lies as evidence capable of providing such support
- where the prosecution relies on the lie as part of the Crown's case or where it might be used by the jury to support evidence of guilt.[46] In *R. v. Gordon*[47] the defence on a homicide charge was self-defence and the prosecution sought to undermine that by showing that the accused had originally lied about the possession of the murder weapon. While the denial was obviously a lie, it had little relevance to the plea of self-defence as there were a number of reasons why a person who has killed another might seek to extricate himself.

[44] [1993] 4 All E.R. 894.
[45] *R. v. Burge* [1996] Cr.App.R. 163.
[46] *Goodway supra.*
[47] *R. v. Gordon* [1995] Crim.L.R. 306.

The *Lucas/Goodway* warning is unnecessary where the purpose of proving the lie is merely to undermine the defendant's credibility.[48]

(3) under section 35 of the Criminal Justice and Public Order Act 1994 the accused's silence when called upon to testify will be used to enhance the cogency of the Crown case. The question arises as to what a "proper" inference might be. This was considered by the Court of Appeal in *R. v. Cowan*.[49]

R. v. Cowan [1995] 4 All E.R. 939 at 944e–945d, _per_ Lord Taylor C.J.

By way of guidance, a specimen direction has been suggested by the Judicial Studies Board in the following terms:

> 'The defendant has not given evidence. That is his right. But, as he has been told, the law is that you may draw such inferences as appear proper from his failure to do so. Failure to give evidence on its own cannot prove guilt but depending on the circumstances, you may hold his failure against him when deciding whether he is guilty. [There is evidence before you on the basis of which the defendant's advocate invites you not to hold it against the defendant that he has not given evidence before you namely . . . If you think that because of this evidence you should not hold it against the defendant that he has not given evidence, do not do so. But if the evidence he relies on presents no adequate explanation for his absence from the witness box then you may hold his failure to give evidence against him. You do not have to do so.] What proper inferences can you draw from the defendant's decision not to give evidence before you? If you conclude that there is a case for him to answer, you may think that the defendant would have gone into the witness box to give you an explanation for or an answer to the case against him. If the only sensible explanation for his decision not to give evidence is that he has no answer to the case against him, or none that could have stood up to cross-examination, then it would be open to you to hold against him his failure to give evidence. It is for you to decide whether it is fair to do so.'

We consider that the specimen direction is in general terms a sound guide. It may be necessary to adapt or add to it in the particular circumstances of an individual case. But there are certain essentials which we would highlight.

1. The judge will have told the jury that the burden of proof remains upon the prosecution throughout and what the required standard is.

2. It is necessary for the judge to make clear to the jury that the defendant is entitled to remain silent. That is his right and choice. The right of silence remains.

3. An inference from failure to give evidence cannot on its own prove guilt. That is expressly stated in section 38(3) of the Act.

4. Therefore, the jury must be satisfied that the prosecution have established a case to answer before drawing any inferences from silence. Of course, the judge must have thought so or the question whether the

[48] *R. v. Josephine Smith* [1995] Crim.L.R. 305.

[49] [1995] 4 All E.R. 939.

defendant was to give evidence would not have arisen. But the jury may not believe the witnesses whose evidence the judge considered sufficient to raise a prima facie case. It must therefore be made clear to them that they must find there to be a case to answer on the prosecution evidence before drawing an adverse inference from the defendant's silence.

5. If, despite any evidence relied upon to explain his silence or in the absence of any such evidence, the jury conclude the silence can only sensibly be attributed to the defendant's having no answer or none that would stand up to cross-examination, they may draw an adverse inference.

(4) failure to deny an accusation by a police officer was not corroborative[50] although there was some slight authority that an adverse inference might be drawn from silence in response to police questions where the defendant and the police were on equal terms.[51] That decision was not tested subsequent to the passage of the Police and Criminal Evidence Act 1984. But under the Criminal Justice and Public Order Act 1994 such silence can be used to strengthen the prosecution case: the failure to mention facts later relied on in one's defence under section 34 or the failure to explain marks, objects, substances or one's presence under sections 36 and 37.[52] In these cases the jury can be invited to draw appropriate inferences.

(5) at common law and away from the police station, there is authority that silence on accusation could be corroborative. In *R. v. Cramp*[53] the defendant was accused of administering a noxious thing with intent to induce a miscarriage. The defendant was silent when taxed by the woman's father with having given the drug to his daughter. Such a reaction is admissible.[54] Under the old law it could be corroborative and is also admissible today as part of the Crown case or as supportive of other evidence.

(6) at common law, a refusal to give a sample of hair to match with another hair found at the scene of the robbery was held to corroborate the evidence of an accomplice in *R. v. Smith*.[55] This is now dealt with under the Police and Criminal Evidence Act 1984 which deals with the refusal to give the appropriate consent to the taking of an intimate sample[56]:

62.—(10) Where the appropriate consent to the taking of an intimate sample from a person was refused without good cause, in any proceedings against that person for an offence —

[50] *R. v. Whitehead* [1929] 1 K.B. 99.
[51] *R. v. Chandler* [1976] 3 All E.R. 105.
[52] These are discussed further in Chap. 12.
[53] (1880) 14 Cox C.C. 390.
[54] As are all statements on accusation — *R. v. Sharp* [1988] 1 All E.R. 65.
[55] (1985) 81 Cr.App.R. 286.
[56] Non-intimate samples (hair, nail clippings) and fingerprints can be taken without consent under ss.61 and 63 of the Police and Criminal Evidence Act 1984; Easton S., "Bodily Samples and the Privilege Against Self-Incrimination" [1991] Crim.L.R. 18.

> . . . (b) the court or jury, in determining whether that person is guilty of the offence charged,
>
> may draw such inferences from the refusal as appear proper; [and the refusal may, on the basis of such inferences, be treated as, or as capable of amounting to, corroboration of any evidence against the person in relation to which the refusal is material][57]

(7) the previous conduct of the accused in certain circumstances may be adduced in evidence to establish that the accused had committed the offence. In the Rosemary West murder trial, the prosecution hypothesis was that the accused and her husband killed young women after violent sexual encounters. The Crown introduced evidence from other women who had been exposed to such encounters but had lived to testify. From this testimony about the Wests' predilections, the prosecution argued that the bodies found in Cromwell Street must also be the victims of such encounters. Such evidence is only admissible where it possesses significant probative weight and is known as "similar fact" testimony.[58]

Categories of Evidence Needing Support

When the problems of reliability of eyewitness evidence, discussed in the previous chapter, are linked to the fundamental tenets of the burden and standard of proof, this suggests that, in criminal proceedings, no conviction should be based wholly or mainly upon evidence from a single source. Recent legislation has gone in the opposite direction and shows that there is little possibility of establishing such a principle. But certain categories of evidence have been singled out as being less reliable than previously thought and as requiring, if not supportive evidence, at least a caution to the jury about convicting solely or mainly upon such evidence. The development of a direction advising caution has come about in relation to identification evidence. It is yet to emerge for confessions.

Identification evidence

Apart from the interrogation of suspects and the search of persons, vehicles and places for objects and traces as evidence of crime, the other main source of evidence for the police is the eyewitness, and one of the most obvious aspects of eyewitness testimony is the identification of suspects. As with the confession, identification is treated in court as possessing considerable probative weight; as with the confession, its probative value is overestimated. The opinion of a juror as to whether an eyewitness has made an accurate identification is critical and is often sufficient to decide the case

[57] The words following "proper" have been repealed by the Criminal Justice and Public Order Act 1994, Sched. 11.
[58] *R. v. P.* [1991] 3 All E.R. 337—this is discussed further in Chap. 14.

since, if the witness is correct, the defendant is guilty. Evidence of identification is direct evidence rather than circumstantial evidence and it is important to know how good people are at perception and recall, how good we are at assessing the accuracy of our own memory and what criteria we use in assessing others' eyewitness accounts.

Identification evidence can be very strong, especially when it is recognition evidence of a person already known to the witness. This is commonly the case with offences of personal violence. But the identification of strangers, perhaps glimpsed for a moment at the scene of a crime can be extremely weak, depending upon a range of factors which may not be taken into account at trial.[59] Unfortunately the jury's and the judge's perception of the weight of identification evidence is less likely to be affected by "scientific" factors (duration, range, visibility) than by the credence that is given to the witness (the witness's demeanour, the coherence of the testimony). The prejudicial effect of such testimony is strong since it is hard to doubt the impartial witness who clearly identifies the accused. Yet as psychological research has suggested, the odds on the witness being right are at best evens, odds which are difficult to square with proof "beyond reasonable doubt". In the notorious Sacco and Vanzetti case in the USA,[60] a prosecution witness claimed to have seen Sacco riding in a car which passed by her at a distance no closer than sixty feet and which she had in view for no more than the time it took for the car to travel fifty or sixty feet. Yet her identification was positive and detailed:

> Q. Can you describe him to these gentlemen here?
> A. Yes sir. He was a man that I should say was slightly taller than I am. He weighed possibly from 140 to 150 pounds. he was muscular — he was an active looking man. I noticed particularly the left hand was a good-sized hand, a hand that denoted strength or a shoulder that . . .
> Q. So that the hand you said you saw where?
> A. The left hand, that was placed . . . on the back of the front seat. He had a gray, what I thought was a shirt — had a grayish, like navy color, and the face was what we would call clear-cut, clean-cut face. Through here [indicating] was a little narrow, just a little narrow. The forehead was high. The hair was brushed back and it was between, I should think, two inches and two-and-one-half inches in length and had dark eyebrows, but the complexion was a white, a peculiar white that looked greenish.[61]

Whether this feat of perception and recall was psychologically possible is dubious. As Loftus says:

[59] Clifford B., "The Relevance of Psychological Investigation to Legal Issues in Testimony and Identification" [1979] Crim.L.R. 153; Jackson J., "The Insufficiency of Identification Evidence Based on Personal Impression" [1986] Crim.L.R. 203; Wells G. and Loftus E. (eds.), *Eyewitness Testimony* (1984).

[60] There is a summary in Loftus E., *Eyewitness Testimony* (1st ed., 1979) Chap. 1.

[61] Wall, P.M., *Eyewitness Identification of Criminal Cases* (1965), p. 20 cited in Loftus E., *Eyewitness Testimony* (1st ed., 1979) 19.

Loftus E., Eyewitness Testimony (1st ed., 1979) 50

When a witness sees a serious event such as a crime or traffic accident and then must recall it later, three major stages can be identified: the acquisition stage, the retention stage and the recall stage. In the acquisition stage, there are numerous factors that will affect the accuracy of the initial perception. Some of these factors, such as the amount of time the witness had to look at whatever is going to be remembered, are inherent in the situation itself. Other factors, such as the amount of stress a witness is experiencing, are inherent in the witness. Both event factors and witness factors can dramatically affect a witness's ability to perceive accurately.

It is not only a witness's powers of perception that can vary:

Loftus, *op. cit.* 108–109

The conditions prevailing at the time information is retrieved from memory are critically important in determining the accuracy and completeness of an eyewitness account. Some of the more important factors that operate during this stage are whether the retrieval environment is changed, what types of question are used to obtain information, how these questions are worded and who is asking them. Confidence in one's memory and the accuracy of that memory do not always go hand in hand; people are often confident and right, but they can also be confident and wrong . . .

Most people, including eyewitnesses, are motivated by a desire to be correct, to be observant, and to avoid looking foolish. People want to give an answer, to be helpful, and many will do this at the risk of being incorrect. People want to see crimes solved and justice done, and this desire may motivate them to volunteer more than is warranted by their meager memory. The line between valid retrieval and unconscious fabrication is easily crossed.

A juror's assessment of a witness is often related to factors, such as confidence, that do not necessarily predict accuracy:

Loftus, *op. cit.* 19

Jurors tended to believe witnesses who were highly confident more than those who had less confidence. This experiment leads to the conclusion that eyewitness testimony is likely to be believed by jurors particularly when it is offered with a high level of confidence, even though the accuracy of an eyewitness and the confidence of that witness may not be related to one another at all. All the evidence points rather strikingly to the conclusion that there is almost nothing more convincing than a live human being who takes the stand, points a finger at the defendant, and says 'That's the one!'

Where the identification evidence is simply corroborative of other testimony implicating the accused, there is less concern. But often the conviction is based wholly or mainly on such evidence. Figures in this area are hard to come by. The Devlin Report[62] suggested that in 1973, there

[62] *Report of Departmental Committee on Evidence of Identification in Criminal Cases* (1976) H.C.P. 338.

were 2,116 identity parades, resulting in identifications in 45 per cent. 850 people were prosecuted, of whom 82 per cent were convicted. But 347 people were prosecuted and 258 convicted solely or mainly on identification evidence. Naturally there have been many notorious cases of miscarriages of justice as a result of misidentification. The most famous of these was Adolf Beck in the early years of the century who was wrongly identified by 12 women.[63] The Devlin Committee itself was set up after the release of Luke Dougherty who was convicted of shoplifting.[64] Although Dougherty had been on a coach trip at the time and had a cast-iron alibi, he had only called two witnesses at his trial, his girlfriend and another friend who had previous convictions. The jury did not believe them and convicted. The initial appeal was rejected and it was only on a referral back to the Court of Appeal by the Home Secretary that additional alibi witnesses were heard.

The need for safeguards in the admission of identification evidence are obvious. These can exist either at the point of investigation (the manner in which the police gather identification evidence) or at the point of trial.

1. Safeguards at point of investigation

After the Devlin Report, some controls at the point of investigation were introduced, especially when the Home Office issued a 1978 circular to police forces tightening up procedures in identification parades. In 1981, the Report of the Royal Commission into Criminal Procedure called for such procedures to be made statutory[65] but instead the Codes of Practice introduced after the Police and Criminal Evidence Act 1984 included a Code on the identification of persons by police officers.[66] Under the Code there is a pecking order[67] of methods of identification which may be used:

- a parade
- a group identification
- a video film
- a confrontation

This is the order of preference and the police must consider each method in turn, although a parade is not needed, for example, if the suspect has

[63] There is a Report (Cmnd. 2315) of the Committee of Inquiry into the case ; Glanville Williams: "Evidence of Identification" [1976] Crim.L.R. 407 gives several other examples.
[64] Discussed in the Devlin Report, *supra*, Chap. 2.
[65] Royal Commission on Criminal Procedure (1981): *Report* (HMSO) Cmnd. 8092, para. 3.138.
[66] These much revised procedures are now contained in Code of Practice D under Police and Criminal Evidence Act 1984. The 3rd edition of the Codes came into force in April 1995 — see Wolchover D. and Heaton-Armstrong A., "Questioning and Identification: Changes under PACE '95" [1995] Crim.L.R. 356 at 367ff.
[67] *R. v. Ladlow* [1989] Crim.L.R. 219.

been clearly identified by witnesses at the scene,[68] if there is an accidental confrontation and identification[69] or where a witness is taken to a suspect's house.[70] However a prior identification by the witness does not rule out a subsequent parade. In *R. v. Brown*[71] the victim of a robbery toured the area in a police car immediately after the attack and picked out the defendant. No parade was held but the Court of Appeal felt that the Code was mandatory and that a parade was not necessarily otiose. Once a suspect is in a police station, Code D applies and the police cannot decide simply to dispense with a parade. In *Powell v. DPP*[72] a suspect was arrested and brought to the station where he was identified by a police officer who had witnessed the original incident. The Divisional Court held that the police were obliged to hold a parade.

(a) identity parades: a parade should be held where identification is disputed[73] and the suspect consents unless it is not practicable because of the unusual appearance of the suspect or for some other reason. It may also be held where the police feel it would be useful and the suspect consents.[74] It is only if a parade is not practicable or the suspect refuses to attend, that some other form of identification should be arranged.[75] Identity parades[76] have been in common use throughout this century. It was and remains a voluntary system and if the suspect chooses not to take part or to disrupt it (perhaps by refusing to wear some item of clothing or to speak certain words), there are no sanctions.[77] The arrangements for any form of identification must be conducted by a uniformed officer, inspector or above, not concerned with the case.[78] The suspect must be told of his rights not to participate and asked whether he wants a solicitor or friend present.[79] The parade has to be photographed or videoed.[80] Everything said or done should take place in the presence or hearing of the accused but

[68] *R. v. Rogers* [1993] Crim.L.R. 386; deliberately engineering a street confrontation prior to an identity parade will lead to the exclusion of the evidence — *R. v. Nagah* [1991] Crim.L.R. 55.

[69] *R. v. Long* [1991] Crim.L.R. 453.

[70] *e.g.* the facts in *Tobi v. Nicholas* [1987] Crim.L.R. 774 — although the police officer could not report what was said, the witness could have attested to the identification

[71] [1991] Crim.L.R. 368.

[72] [1992] R.T.R. 270.

[73] Even where the witnesses claims to be acquainted with the suspect and thus to recognise rather than to identify — *R. v. Conway* [1990] Crim.L.R. 402.

[74] Code D 2.3.

[75] Code D 2.6 — namely group identification but if that is impracticable, then video may be used and if that proves impossible, the last resort can be confrontation.

[76] Lidstone K. and Palmer C., *Bevan and Lidstone's The Investigation of Crime* (2nd ed., 1996) 430 *et seq.*

[77] Though there is some authority that the judge can comment on the fact that the suspect has refused to take part in a parade, drawing on analogy from *R. v. Robert William Smith* (1985) 81 Cr.App.R. 286. It would appear that in the U.S.A., the suspect can be forced to do this — *U.S. v. Wade* (1967) 388 U.S. 218.

[78] Code D 2.2.

[79] Code D 2.15 and Annex A to Code D, para. 1.

[80] *ibid.* para. 19.

where the witness is behind a screen, a representative of the suspect must be able to see and hear everything. If there is no such representative, everything relevant should be recorded on video.[81]

There should be a minimum of eight others on the parade.[82] The Code requires that these resemble the suspect as far as possible,[83] although the disclosure to the defence of the eyewitness's initial description suggests that the other members of the parade should resemble that description rather than the suspect, whenever there is a discrepancy between the two. The places are numbered and if the witness makes a positive identification, it is by number. The suspect is able to make objections to the arrangements and such objections should be met, if practicable. The suspect is allowed to stand where he likes and to change position. The 1995 requirement that the line-up be photographed or videoed means that the trier of fact will be in a position to assess the fairness of the composition of the parade for themselves.

Under the 1995 version of the Code, a record of the initial description given by the witness must be made before any other means of identification under the Code takes place.[84] This description is then disclosable to the defence prior to any subsequent trial.[85] The witness should not be shown or reminded of this description or shown photos or other descriptions prior to the parade and should be isolated from other witnesses.[86] A further source of error might be news coverage and this is recognised by the revised 1995 Code so that after the procedure, the witness is asked whether he or she has seen any video films or photographs that might have been released to the news media by the police. The witness should be encouraged to look at each member of the parade at least twice and to identify by number.[87] The witness can ask for particular clothing to be worn, gestures to be made or words to be spoken.

A failure to hold a parade or other improprieties in obtaining identification evidence and in observing the Code of Practice can lead to the identification evidence being excluded under section 78 of the Police and Criminal Evidence Act 1984 on the grounds that its inclusion will have an adverse effect on the fairness of the proceedings. Since the code is statutory, it is there to be observed and not varied at the will of the police.[88] In *R. v. Graham*[89] the accused agreed to attend a parade but none was arranged although it was practicable to do so. Since the jury should

[81] *ibid.* para. 7.
[82] *ibid.* para. 8 — a minimum of 12 is required if there are two suspects of similar appearance. Normally separate parades should be held for each suspect.
[83] Clifford B., "The Relevance of Psychological Investigation to Legal Issues in Testimony and Identification" [1979] Crim.L.R. 153.
[84] Code D 2.0.
[85] *R. v. Fergus* (1993) 98 Cr.App.R. 313.
[86] Code D Annex A, para. 12.
[87] *ibid.* paras. 14–15.
[88] *R. v. Quinn* [1995] Crim.L.R. 56.
[89] [1994] Crim.L.R. 212; *R. v. Conway* [1990] Crim.L.R. 402.

have been warned that the identification had taken place without a parade, the appeal was allowed. The courts place high value on the parades as providing persuasive evidence for the Crown and as being a substantial safeguard for the suspect. Even where the difficulties of holding parades are considerable, they may still be required. In *R. v. Ladlow*[90] there were 21 suspects and 11 witnesses so the police held confrontations having decided that 232 parades were impracticable. The evidence of identification was excluded. Similarly in *R. v. Gaynor*[91] the suspect asked for a parade to be held but the police decided (wrongly in the court's opinion) that it was impracticable. Difficulty in finding volunteers for a parade does not make it impracticable unless the suspect's appearance is the reason for that difficulty.[92]

(b) group identifications: if the suspect does not consent to a parade, if it is impracticable or if it is more satisfactory than a parade,[93] the police can arrange for a group identification[94] and can use their discretion to proceed even though the suspect does not consent.

A group identification takes place where the suspect is viewed by a witness amongst an informal group of people. The procedure may take place with the consent and co-operation of a suspect or covertly where a suspect has refused to co-operate with an identification parade or a group identification or has failed to attend. A group identification may also be arranged if the officer in charge of the investigation considers, whether because of fear on the part of the witness or for some other reason, that it is, in the circumstances, more satisfactory than a parade.[95]

The conditions under which a group identification takes place are detailed in a new Annex E to Code D. Many replicate the safeguards for identity parades so that the officer in charge must give notice to the suspect, *inter alia*, of its purpose, how it will be carried out, of the suspect's rights as well as warning him or her that a refusal to take part or any significant alteration of appearance can be given in evidence at trial.[96] Similarly any initial description by a witness must be recorded and officers who escort witnesses to the identification scene must not discuss the case or reveal whether any other witness has made an identification.[97] Again the witness is asked whether he or she has seen any video films or photographs that might have been released to the news media by the police.

The scene itself should be photographed or videoed where possible. The place where the group identification is held should be one where other people are passing by or waiting around informally so that the suspect can

[90] [1989] Crim.L.R. 219.
[91] [1988] Crim.L.R. 242.
[92] *R. v. Jamel* [1993] Crim.L.R. 52; *R. v. Campbell and Marshall* [1993] Crim.L.R. 47.
[93] Code D 2.7 suggests one reason might be fear on the part of the witness.
[94] Code D 2.7–2.9.
[95] Code D 2.7.
[96] Code D 2.15.
[97] Annex E, para. 15.

join them. The place for the identification should not be in a police station unless this is dictated by reasons of safety or security. Annex E gives examples of escalators, shopping centres or railway or bus stations. Such groups might be mobile (walking through a shopping mall) or stationary (in a bus queue). In either situation the suspect is allowed flexibility in joining the group or taking up position although unreasonable delay might be regarded as a refusal to co-operate. Anything done or said to or by the witness should be in the presence or hearing of the suspect's solicitor or friend. The witness should point out any person he thinks he saw at the earlier, relevant, occasion and if practicable, the officer in charge should arrange for a closer look and ask the witness if he or she can make a positive identification.[98]

It is possible for group identifications to be held covertly, without the suspect's consent. In such situations the identification necessarily takes place without the knowledge of the suspect who thus has no right to have a solicitor or friend present. The other provisions of Annex E should be adhered to.

(c) video identification: showing the witness a video of a suspect is a possibility where a parade or group identification is not possible or the police consider the video to be the most satisfactory course of action.[99] The police have discretion to proceed with this method of identification even if the suspect does not consent. In essence this is an identification parade conducted on video and the provisions of Annex B must be complied with. The film must include at least eight other people who, as far as possible, resemble the suspect. The film should be shown to the suspect and his or her lawyer before it is shown to any witness and any objections, if reasonable, should be addressed. The suspects' lawyer should be present at the showing of the film and in the absence of such a representative, the showing itself should be recorded on video. The provisions regarding the recording of initial descriptions as well as the prohibition of discussions between the witness and police officers or other witnesses remain the same as those with other methods of identification. Again the witness is asked whether he or she has seen any video films or photographs that might have been released to the news media by the police.

(d) confrontation: as a last resort, when no other method of identification is practicable, the suspect can be confronted by the witness.[1] Before the confrontation, the suspect and his or her lawyer is provided with details of the first description given by the witness to the police. Any material released to the media by the police should also be provided, if this is practicable. The confrontation will be in a police station, possibly in a

[98] *ibid.* paras. 21 and 27.
[99] Code D 2.10 and Annex B.
[1] The procedures are detailed in Annex C to the Code.

room equipped with a screen although this may only be used when a representative of the suspect is present or where the confrontation is recorded on video. The suspect shall be confronted by the witness who is asked "Is this the person?". Identification evidence obtained from a confrontation in the precincts of the trial court should not be admitted even when this takes place at the behest of the accused.[2] The dock identification, that is, an identification at the trial itself without any preceding method of identification, is normally not admissible.[3]

2. Safeguards at the trial

Safeguards at the point of trial relate to the conditions on the admissibility of identification evidence. There were a range of possible approaches canvassed by the Devlin Committee:

(1) that there should be no conviction based solely or mainly on identification evidence and supporting evidence, preferably emanating from an independent source and linking the accused to the crime, should be a requirement; or
(2) that the jury should be warned that conviction based solely or mainly on identification evidence is dangerous and that they should look for supporting evidence. It would not be a bar to conviction if none were found; or
(3) (the Devlin Report's preferred option) that there should be legislation for a special warning which explained to the jury that identification alone did not comprise probable cause for a conviction unless there were special circumstances, for instance, familiarity, where the accused was a member of a small group, one of whom had committed the crime or where the defendant had failed to counter evidence with his own story.

There was no legislation as a result of the Devlin Report. Instead the significant controls at the point of trial were introduced by the Court of Appeal's decision in *R. v. Turnbull*.[4] The court was against any rule which prevented convictions from being based on identification alone and argued that the crucial element was the quality of that identification:

***R. v. Turnbull* [1976] 3 All E.R. 549 at 551j–552e, *per* Lord Widgery C.J.**

First, whenever the case against an accused depends wholly or substantially on the correctness of one or more identifications of the accused which the defence allege to be mistaken, the judge should warn the jury of the special need for caution

[2] *R. v. Joseph* [1994] Crim.L.R. 48.
[3] *R. v. Eatough* [1989] Crim.L.R. 289; *R. v. Horsham Justices ex p. Bukhari* (1982) 74 Cr.App.R. 291.
[4] [1976] 3 All E.R. 549.

before convicting the accused in reliance on the correctness of the identification or identifications. In addition he should instruct them as to the reason for the need for such a warning and should make some reference to the possibility that a mistaken witness can be a convincing one and that a number of such witnesses can all be mistaken. Provided this is done in clear terms the judge need not use any particular form of words.

Secondly, the judge should direct the jury to examine closely the circumstances in which the identification by each witness came to be made. How long did the witness have the accused under observation? At what distance? In what light? Was the observation impeded in any way, as for example by passing traffic or a press of people? Had the witness ever seen the accused before? How often? If only occasionally, had he any special reason for remembering the act? How long elapsed between the original observation and the subsequent identification to the police? Was there any material discrepancy between the description of the accused given to the police by the witness when first seen by them and his actual appearance? If in any case, whether it is being dealt with summarily or on indictment, the prosecution have reason to believe that there is such a material discrepancy they should supply the accused or his legal advisers with particulars of the description the police were first given. In all cases if the accused asks to be given particulars of such descriptions, the prosecution should supply them. Finally, he should remind the jury of any specific weaknesses which had appeared in the identification evidence. Recognition may be more reliable than identification of a stranger; but, even when the witness is purporting to recognise someone whom he knows, the jury should be reminded that mistakes in recognition of close relatives and friends are sometimes made.

All these matters go to the quality of the identification evidence. If the quality is good and remains good at the close of the accused's case, the danger of a mistaken identification is lessened; but the poorer the quality, the greater the danger . . .

This judgment was one of the first nails in the coffin of corroboration. Lord Widgery considered that the jury could safely be left to assess the value of the identification evidence with a more general warning on the hazards of convicting wholly or mainly on such evidence accompanied by instructions to consider in detail the circumstances of the identification. To require corroboration would be an "affront to justice" in situations such as a kidnapping where the only significant evidence was the identification of the kidnapper by the victim.

The impact of *Turnbull* has been considerable. Where this warning is not given, the conviction will normally be quashed. Even where there is considerable other evidence, the Court of Appeal consider it prudent to issue a *Turnbull* direction. In *R. v. Andrews*[5] three white men attacked a black youth. The police witnessed the assault, two were arrested and the accused was found nearby after the incident acting in an aggressive fashion. The evidence against the accused, alleged to be the third man, was from the police, who described the third man as "extremely well-built" and dressed in jeans and a grey T-shirt. No identification direction was given by the trial judge and the conviction quashed by the Court of Appeal. But was this a *Turnbull* case? The Crown case was almost wholly circumstantial,

[5] [1993] Crim.L.R. 590.

based on the accused's association with the other two convicted men with whom he had been drinking that evening. Furthermore, one of those was his brother and all three had had an altercation with a black youth in the pub. Even without the testimony about identification, there was substantial evidence to link the accused to the assault.[6]

There are situations when a full *Turnbull* direction is not necessary. When the issue is not the accused's presence at the scene but whether it was the accused or another who committed the act, this has been considered to require less caution.[7] In *R. v. Slater*[8] there was an assault in a nightclub. The accused admitted to being present in the club and aware of the affray but denied being involved. The witness said that she had seen the man earlier and in the club witnessed him punch the victim. The judge did not give the full *Turnbull* direction but the Court of Appeal held that this was not a direction for all cases but only one where there is the possibility of mistaken identification, especially where the issue is whether the accused was present. When this is not in issue, as here, the direction is not automatic. It would be contrary to common sense to require a direction of this nature where the accused admits to being present and it is the conduct that is being disputed. In this particular case the defendant was of wholly unusual size, being very tall and large, and his companion (whom the witnesses distinguished) was shorter.

R. v. Slater [1995] Crim.L.R. 244, commentary by Prof. Birch at 245

[The judge] drew the jury's attention, at length and in the clearest terms, to all the factors pointing to the possibility that the prosecution witness had not seen what she claimed to have seen. Of these, by far the most potent was that she was giddy with drink and claimed the rest of the events that evening were 'a blur', although she claimed a clear recollection of the assault. There is a risk that, if the full *Turnbull* warning is given where it is not appropriate, the jury's attention will be distracted from such relevant considerations. Distraction is not in the interests of justice neither is it necessarily in the interests of the accused. A similar problem arose in relation to the corroboration of sexual complaints in *Chance*[9] where it was held to be distracting and potentially disadvantageous to the defence to give a warning geared to alerting the jury to the risk that a complaint has been fabricated in circumstances where it is common ground that an offence has occurred, and the only issue is whether the complainant has made a bona fide mistake in identifying the culprit.

Where there are a number of identification witnesses to a single incident, none of whose testimony would be sufficient on which to base a conviction, the standard of proof might be satisfied by cumulative identification.[10] A more problematic situation arises where the defendant is

[6] *ibid.* — commentary by Prof. Birch.

[7] *R. v. Oakwell* [1978] 1 All E.R. 1223.

[8] [1995] Crim.L.R. 244.

[9] [1988] 3 All E.R. 225.

[10] Analogous to the idea of "cumulative corroboration" in *R. v. Hills* (1988) 86 Cr.App.R. 26.

charged with several offences, to each of which there might be a single eye witness. If there was evidence which suggested that all the offences were the work of one person and that evidence relating to one charge was admissible on the other charges under the similar fact rules, testimony by one identification witness (not sufficient in itself) could be used to support the evidence of identification provided by another witness. Although in *R. v. McGranaghan*[11] the Court of Appeal suggested that ". . . an identification about which the jury are not sure cannot support another identification of which they are also not sure however similar the facts of the two offences may be", in *R. v. Downey*[12] the court pointed out that this proscribed using doubtful but cumulative identification evidence to establish that the offences had been committed by the same person. Once other evidence revealed that all the offences had been committed by one person, the identifications of that person might be used cumulatively.[13]

3. Identification and hearsay

The courts have sometimes appeared to take a relaxed attitude towards the use of hearsay in identification cases.[14] This was not originally the case. In *R. v. Gibson*[15] the prosecutor testified that, immediately after he had been struck by a stone, a passer-by pointed to the prisoner's door and said "The person who threw the stone went in there". This evidence was not objected to at trial but the conviction was quashed. Such identifications do not come within the *res gestae* exception. As Lord Normand said in:

Teper v. R. [1952] A.C. 480 at 488, *per* Lord Normand

There is yet another proposition which can be affirmed, viz that for identification purposes in a criminal trial the event with which the words sought to be proved must be so connected as to form part of the res gestae is the commission of the crime itself — the throwing of the stone, the striking of the blow, the setting fire to the building, or whatever the criminal act may be. Counsel for the Crown submitted that any relevant event or action may be accompanied by words which may have to be proved in order to bring out its true significance. There is a limited sense in which this is true, but it is not always true, and much depends on the use to be made of the evidence. In [*R. v. Christie*[16]] hearsay evidence of certain words uttered by a child, the victim of indecent assault, in the presence and hearing of the accused were held to be admissible in explanation of the demeanour of the accused in response to them. But the evidence was held inadmissible for the purpose of showing that the child identified the accused as his assailant. In the present case identification is the purpose for which the hearsay was introduced, and its admission goes far beyond anything that has been authorised by any reported case.

[11] [1995] 1 Cr.App.R. 559 at 572, *per* Glidewell L.J.
[12] [1995] 1 Cr.App.R. 547.
[13] *R. v. Barnes* [1996] Crim.L.R. 39; *R. v. Black* [1995] Crim.L.R. 640.
[14] See Chap. 16; this attitude also applies to the use of previous consistent statements in identification cases — see Chap. 10.
[15] (1887) 18 Q.B.D. 537.
[16] [1914] A.C. 545.

In both *Gibson* and *Teper*, the absent witness was in effect making an identification of the culprit. Recent authorities tend to suggest that such identifications can operate as an exception to hearsay. In *R. v. Osborne*; *R. v. Virtue*[17] two witnesses to an armed robbery picked out the accused in an identification parade but were unable to do so at the trial proper. A police officer was permitted to testify as to the conduct of the parade and as to whom the witnesses had identified on that parade. Lawton L.J. treated it as a question whether the officer was contradicting the evidence of the witnesses, and did not mention the difficult hearsay issue.

R. v. Osborne [1973] 1 All E.R. 649 at 657a–e, *per* Lawton L.J.

It was submitted that the admission of that evidence was contrary to a decision of the House of Lords in *R. v. Christie*.[18] This case has long been regarded as a difficult one to understand because the speeches of their Lordships were not directed to the same points; but this can be got from the speeches — evidence of identification other than identification in the witness box is admissible.

All that the Crown were seeking to do was to establish the fact of identification at the identity parade . . . This court can see no reason why that evidence should not have been admitted. The court is fortified in that view by a passage in the judgment of Sachs L.J. which appears in *R. v. Richardson*.[19] The case was a very different case from this one, but the principle enunciated by Sachs L.J. is applicable. He said,

> The courts, however, must take care not to deprive themselves by new artificial rules of practice of the best chances of learning the truth. The courts are under no compulsion unnecessarily to follow on a matter of practice the lure of the rules of logic in order to produce unreasonable results which would hinder the course of justice.[20]

It is pertinent to point out that in 1914 when the House of Lords came to consider *R. v. Christie* the modern practice of identity parades did not exist. The whole object of identity parades is for the protection of the suspect, and what happens at those parades is highly relevant to the establishment of the truth. It would be wrong in the judgment of this court, to set up artificial rules of evidence, which would hinder the administration of justice.

In *R. v. McCay*[21] the identification parade took place behind a two-way mirror, preventing those on the parade from seeing the witnesses. The witness picked out the accused by number but at the trial, having testified that he had made a positive identity, was unable to recall the number of the person he had identified. The officer in charge of the parade was permitted to testify to the fact of the identification. Russell L.J. approved of this, regarding the statement as one that accompanied and explained a relevant act:

[17] [1973] 1 All E.R. 649.
[18] [1914] A.C. 545.
[19] [1971] 2 All E.R. 773.
[20] *ibid.* at 777.
[21] [1991] 1 All E.R. 232.

R. v. McCay [1991] 1 All E.R. 232 at 234g–235c, *per* Russell L.J.

We are satisfied, however that the admissibility of the words 'It is number 8' can be fully justified, albeit spoken by the witness in the absence of the appellant, because the contemporary statement accompanied a relevant act and was necessary to explain that relevant act. The statement was not relevant as to the identity of the assailant, but it was relevant as to the identification of the suspect by the witness. Whether that identification assisted the jury was a matter for them. In asserting that the man whom the witness thought was the assailant was numbered 8 on the parade, Mr Beach was doing no more and no less than explaining his physical and intellectual activity in making the identification at the material time.

Counsel for the appellant was constrained to acknowledge that if the words 'It is number 8' had been accompanied by some physical touching of the appellant by Mr Beach (the normal procedure adopted in the old style identification parades) he could not have objected to Inspector Murfin giving evidence of what he had heard from the witness. The reason for this concession was that the words would then accompany a physical act, whereas no such physical act was part of the identification process employed in the present case. We consider this to be a distinction without a difference. In our judgment the procedure of looking at the suspect through the mirror, employing the physical activity of seeing coupled with the intellectual activity of recognising are together sufficient to amount to a relevant act in respect of which accompanying words are admissible. As Grove J. said long ago in *Howe v. Malkin*[22]

> . . . though you cannot give in evidence a declaration, *per* se, yet when there is an act accompanied by a statement which is so mixed up with it to become part of the res gestae, evidence of such statement may be given [in evidence]

In our view, whether the true analysis of the statement is that it was original evidence or whether it was admissible as an exception to the hearsay rule, the judge came to a proper decision.

Thus the identification is seen as an aspect of the *res gestae* exception to hearsay, but an aspect that has previously only been applied when the words accompany an ambiguous act. It is an interpretation which is "at odds with some respected authority".[23] However unsatisfactory the reasoning of such cases, the weight of recent authority suggests that statements made by witnesses attending identification parades are admissible. Other jurisdictions have specifically legislated for this situation. Under the U.S. Federal Rules of Evidence:

801.—A statement is not hearsay if —

(1) Prior statement by witness. The declarant testifies at the trial or hearing and is subject to cross-examination concerning the statement, and the statement is . . .

. . . (c) one of identification of a person made after perceiving the person;[24]

The hearsay issue also arises with any drawing or construction of the likeness of a suspect made according to the specifications of the witness.

[22] (1878) 40 L.T. 196.

[23] Comment on *McCay* by Birch in [1990] Crim.L.R. 338 at 341; on *res gestae*, see 549, *et seq*.

[24] Federal Rules of Evidence, r.801.

Nowadays this is likely to be produced using a computer graphics package. In *R. v. Cook*[25] the photofit itself was permitted in evidence. But why? If a witness had made a written or oral statement describing the characteristics of, say, an assailant, such a statement would not have been admissible in evidence either of its facts (since it is hearsay) nor as a prior consistent statement. Similarly a sketch produced by an artist following the directions of a witness is merely transforming words into images and must still be inadmissible. Watkins L.J. in *Cook* disagrees with this:

R. v. Cook [1987] 1 All E.R. 1049 at 1054c–j, *per* Watkins L.J.

The [hearsay] rule is said to apply not only to assertions made orally but to those made in writing or in conduct. Never so far as we know has it been held to apply to this comparatively modern form of evidence, namely the sketch made by the police officer to accord with the witness's recollection of a suspect's physical characteristics and mode of dress and the even more modern photofit compiled from an identical source. Both are manifestations of the seeing eye, translations of vision onto paper through the medium of a police officer's skill of drawing and composing which a witness does not possess. The police officer is merely doing what the witness could do if possessing the requisite skill. When drawing or composing he is akin to a camera, without, of course, being able to match in clarity the photograph of a person or scene which the camera automatically produces.

There is no doubt that a photograph taken, for example, of a suspect during the commission of an offence is admissible. In a bigamy case, namely *R. v. Tolson*,[26] Willes J. said,

> The photograph was admissible because it is only the visible representation of the image or impression made upon the minds of the witnesses by the sight of the person or the object it represents; and, therefore, is, in reality, only another species of the evidence which persons give of identity, when they speak merely from memory.

That ruling has never since been doubted and is applied with regularity to photographs including those taken nowadays automatically in banks during a robbery. Such photographs are invaluable aids to identification of criminals. It has never been suggested of them that they are subject to the rule against hearsay.

We regard the production of the sketch or photofit by a police officer making a graphic representation of a witness's memory as another form of the camera at work, albeit imperfectly and not produced contemporaneously with the material incident but soon or fairly soon afterwards. As we perceive it the photofit is not a statement in writing made in the absence of a defendant or anything resembling it in the sense that this very old rule against hearsay has ever been expressed to embrace. It is, we think, *sui generis*, that is to say, the only one of its kind. It is a thing apart, the admissibility to evidence of which would not be in breach of the hearsay rule.[27]

[25] [1987] 1 All E.R. 1049.

[26] (1864) 4 F&F 103 at 104.

[27] Authorities which support *Cook* are *R. v. Percy Smith* [1976] Crim.L.R. 511, *R. v. Okorodu* [1982] Crim.L.R. 747 and *R. v. Constantinou* [1989] Crim.L.R. 571; *R. v. O'Brien and Nicholson* [1982] Crim.L.R. 746 does not.

The court treated a photofit as direct evidence and thus admissible even if the eyewitness is unable to attend court. However the judgment conflates two different situations:

(1) photographs or video tapes taken at the scene of a crime by, say, a news cameraman or automatically by a security video are real evidence and admissible.[28]
(2) an image generated by an eye witness, whether they draw it themselves or through the medium of a police artist or a computer screen, is an assertion by a person and is not automatically created. As such, it is caught by the hearsay rule. Nor is it rescued by the *res gestae* exception.

The jury themselves can identify a defendant using a photograph or security video, although they may be warned of the perils of identification on such a basis.[29] Furthermore a witness who knows the identity of the person on the video can testify to this effect. This is illustrated in *Taylor v. Chief Constable of Cheshire*[30] in which a video was made of a shoplifter. Policemen were able to identify the accused from the video. Later the recording was erased by accident. The officers gave evidence of what they had seen on the video and Taylor was convicted. The video itself was direct evidence[31] and the court accepted the argument that there is no difference in principle between the evidence of witnesses who viewed the recording and those witnesses who claim to have seen the events by direct vision. Code D does not apply.

However there are reasons why this form of identification should be regulated in a similar fashion to parades or video identifications by eyewitnesses. In *R. v. Caldwell and Dixon*[32] the robbery of an off-licence was captured on video and evidence of identification was admitted from police officers who had viewed the videotape. It is only too easy for one officer to recognise an accused and mention it to a colleague who might see a likeness which had not previously occurred to him. This possibility was recognised by the Court of Appeal who felt that the Code D procedures should be adopted in such cases.

Confessions and supporting evidence

A confession by the defendant is direct evidence of guilt and common sense suggests that the trier of fact can rely upon it since people do not make statements against their own interests unless those statements are true. However experience over the past decade has shown that common sense is

[28] *The Statue of Liberty* [1968] 2 All E.R. 195.
[29] *R. v. Dodson and Williams* (1984) 79 Cr.App.R. 220; *R. v. Downey* [1995] Crim.L.R. 414.
[30] [1987] 1 All E.R. 225.
[31] *Kajala v. Noble* (1982) 75 Cr.App.R. 149.
[32] [1993] Crim.L.R. 862.

an unreliable guide. Under police interrogation, people have confessed to offences that they have not committed. Such admissions may be a result of police malpractice[33] or occur without any impropriety on the part of the questioners.[34] A central question for the Runciman Commission[35] was whether existing safeguards were adequate. As with identification evidence, such safeguards can be built in at the point of investigation or at the point of trial. At trial, the key issue is whether independent supporting evidence should be required for all cases resting solely or substantially on the defendant's confession.

Not only has experience revealed the risks of relying on unsupported admissions. Research has begun to explore the reasons for this phenomenon:

Royal Commission on Criminal Justice, *Report* (1993) Cm. 2263, para. 4.32

There is no way of establishing the frequency of false confessions: a retracted confession may nevertheless be true, and defendants who have made false confessions may have reasons of their own for adhering to them. However there is now a substantial body of research[36] which shows that there are four distinct categories of false confession:

(i) people who make confessions entirely voluntarily as a result of a morbid desire for publicity or notoriety; or to relieve feelings of guilt about a real or imagined previous transgression; or because they cannot distinguish between reality and fantasy;
(ii) a suspect may confess from a desire to protect someone else from interrogation and prosecution;
(iii) people may see a prospect of immediate advantage from confessing (for example,, an end to questioning or release from the police station), even though the long-term consequences are far worse (the resulting confessions are termed 'coerced-compliant' confessions); and
(iv) people may be persuaded temporarily by the interrogators that they really have done the act in question (the resulting confessions are termed 'coerced-internalised' confessions).

It is important therefore that the criminal justice system should contain effective safeguards against false confessions being believed.

Some jurisdictions[37] use corroboration as that safeguard:

Royal Commission on Criminal Justice, *op. cit.*, paras. 4.47–4.59

57. In Scotland, there is a general rule of evidence (to which there are a few minor statutory exceptions) that the accused's guilt cannot be established by the

[33] *R. v. Paris* [1994] Crim.L.R. 361.
[34] *R. v. Ward* [1993] 2 All E.R. 577.
[35] Royal Commission on Criminal Justice, *Report* (1993) Cm. 2263 paras. 4.56–4.87.
[36] Gudjonsson G., *The Psychology of Interrogations, Confessions and Testimony* (1992).
[37] Choo A., "Confessions and Corroboration: a Comparative Perspective" [1991] Crim.L.R. 867.

evidence of only one witness. There must be testimony incriminating the accused from two separate sources. This rule applies to all cases and not just those involving confession evidence. Applied to confession evidence, it means that no one who confesses to a crime, unless by a formal plea of guilty, can be convicted solely on his or her own confession. There must be evidence from some other source which supports the confession and incriminates the accused.

58. What amounts to corroboration of a confession varies from case to case. Something more than the confession itself is needed but what is required must depend on the circumstances of the case. As the Lord Justice-General said in the recent case of *Meredith and Lees*,[38]

> In some cases there may be ample evidence from other sources that the crime libelled has been committed. The remaining question will then be whether the accused committed it. A clear and unequivocal confession of guilt on his part may then require little more by way of evidence to corroborate it, if the admission is in terms which leave no room for doubt on this point and there is no reason to suspect that it was not freely made.

59. A further aspect of the Scottish rules of corroboration which was raised by many witnesses to the Commission was the 'special knowledge principle'. Confession evidence may be corroborated by facts which were mentioned by the accused in the course of the confession, which the accused would not have known if he or she had not been the perpetrator of the crime. For example, in *Manuel v. HMA*[39] the accused confessed to murdering a young woman and offered to point out to the police the separate places in a field where he had buried the victim and one of her shoes. His ability to do this was held to be corroborative. Doubts have, however, arisen about the width of this principle because the courts have held that 'special knowledge' does not necessarily mean 'sole knowledge'. It is, in other words, possible that facts mentioned in a confession may be held to corroborate that confession even though they were known to other people before the confession had been made. The passage of time between the date of the crime and the date of the confession is, however, relevant since the longer the delay the more likely it is 'that an accused person had acquired his knowledge of the detail not as a perpetrator of the crime or offence but as a recipient of the information from other sources'.[40]

An independent study suggested that 95 per cent of confession cases in fact had such supporting evidence:

Royal Commission, *op. cit.*, para. 4.69

In order to assess how many cases might be affected by a requirement for supporting evidence, the Home Office Research and Planning Unit examined at our request 2,210 recent cases from 13 CPS branch offices in 7 CPS areas. These were all magistrates' court cases. 30 (or less than 1.4 per cent) relied on confession evidence alone or on admissions that fell short of a confession. A more detailed study, also carried out at our request, by Michael McConville[41] examined the

[38] 1992 S.C.C.R. 459.
[39] 1958 J.C. 41.
[40] *McAvoy v. HMA* 1983 S.L.T. 16.
[41] McConville M., *Corroboration and Confessions: The Impact of a Rule Requiring that no Conviction be sustained on the Basis of Confession Evidence Alone* (Royal Commission on Criminal Justice Research Study No. 13, 1993). Corroboration is not a panacea against wrongful conviction — in the Birmingham Six case, there were confessions to the pub bombings and there was independent forensic evidence, later proved fatally flawed, that the defendants had handled explosives.

evidence available to the police in a sample of 524 cases. In 305 of these there was a confession. The study found that there were very few confession cases in which the police did not have other supporting evidence. In fact, the police and prosecution files showed that even the stricter *Baskerville* test of corroboration could have been satisfied in 87 per cent of such cases. In the remaining 13 per cent, corroborative evidence of this nature was not brought before the court but in close to half of these the police probably could, in McConville's view, have produced corroboration if the rule had required it. There were 15 confession cases (5 per cent) in which the author estimated that the *Baskerville* test could not have been satisfied, but in some of these the different Scottish rules might have been satisfied. McConville estimated that 14 convictions (5 per cent of confession cases) would probably have become acquittals because of the apparent lack of supporting evidence of any kind.

The argument against a rule requiring corroboration in essence is that it might lead to the acquittal (or non-prosecution) of people who are properly convicted on the basis of a confession and that it would require the police to devote more resources to investigation than is justified. The Runciman Commission also recognised the general trend in the law to move away from corroboration requirements. However, although three members of the Commission felt that there should never be a conviction based solely on a confession, the majority were satisfied with a recommendation that the judge in all cases should give a strong warning that care was needed before convicting on the basis of the confession alone,[42] explicitly referring to reasons why people might confess to crimes that they did not commit and, in suitable cases, referring to cases where persons were known to have confessed to crimes that they had not committed. The judge may also draw attention to any supporting evidence or lack of it, but explain that, having given full weight to the warning, the jury could convict even in the absence of supporting evidence. As yet Parliament has not legislated for such a warning nor has the Court of Appeal developed the common law, acting on analogy with *Turnbull*.

[42] *ibid.* para. 4.77 — such a development does not need legislation and has been implemented in the case of identification evidence by the Court of Appeal in *R. v. Turnbull* (1977) Q.B. 224 or in relation to sexual complainants in *R. v. Makanjuola* [1995] 3 All E.R. 730.

10

THE TESTIMONY OF WITNESSES: PRE-TRIAL DISCLOSURE AND EXAMINATION-IN-CHIEF

Providing Information Before the Trial

The centrepiece of adversarial trial is the day in court. But it is counter-productive for parties to conceal the information on which they intend to rely until the trial itself. Increasingly the efficiency and effectiveness of the courts depends upon parties revealing their hands to a greater or lesser extent before the issues come to trial:

Zuckerman A., "Privilege and Public Interest" in Tapper C. (ed.)., *Crime, Proof and Punishment* (1981) 248–250

It is a fundamental principle in the administration of justice that parties to litigation have a right to bring before the court all evidence relevant to their case and to call on others to produce such evidence as they may have. This right is derivative from the right to equal and just trial. Without it the efficacy of substantive rights would be much reduced and rendered uncertain. This principle — which may for convenience be termed the principle of unimpeded access to evidence — is therefore of cardinal constitutional significance and bears close relation to the constitutional right of unimpeded access to the courts of law generally . . .

In relation to a litigant's right of access to evidence the law draws a distinction between rights *inter partes* and rights as against third parties. As between the parties to pending proceedings the law provides machinery whereby the parties may, before the trial has begun, obtain from each other disclosure of information which is in each other's possession relating to the dispute. The main device is discovery whereby one party may obtain access to documents relating to matters in dispute which are in the other party's possession. The right to discovery of documents is not confined to documents which are admissible; it extends to documents containing information which may directly or indirectly enable the party to advance his own case or challenge that of his adversary, or which may lead to a train of inquiry which may have these consequences. This and other processes, such as interrogatories, are intended to enable the parties to appraise the strength of their respective cases and facilitate a good preparation for the trial. English law has recognised from an early time the importance of *inter partes* discovery for the promotion of just determination of disputes.

In addition to these pre-trial rights the parties may call on each other to give evidence and produce documents at the trial. As against third parties, ('mere witnesses'), the parties have a limited right of access to evidence. Their right extends only to the freedom to call on third parties — if need be by means of judicially-issued *subpoena ad testificandum* or *subpoena duces tecum* — to give evidence or produce documents admissible and relevant to matters in dispute.[1]

Such obligations in civil actions are to an extent mirrored in criminal proceedings where there are increasing duties of disclosure on both the prosecution and defence. In all actions, the parties' ability to surprise their opponents by not revealing the evidence on which they seek to rely or by concealing other material facts has become increasingly circumscribed.

Disclosure of Evidence in Civil Cases

Discovery of documents

Parties to civil proceedings are liable to reveal relevant documents. Under R.S.C., Ord. 24:

r 1.—(1) After the close of pleadings in an action begun by writ there shall be subject to and in accordance with the provisions of this Order, be discovery by the parties to the action of the documents which are or have been in their possession, custody prosecution power relating to the matters in question in the action.

(2) Nothing in this Order shall be taken as preventing the parties of an action agreeing to dispense with or limit the discovery of documents which they would otherwise be required to make to each other.

The document must be one which is disclosable within these rules:

Air Canada v. Secretary of State for Trade (No. 2) [1983] 1 All E.R. 910 at 921–922, _per_ Lord Edmund-Davies

My Lords, I proceed to state the obvious. Under our Supreme Court practice, discovery of documents between parties to an action with pleadings . . . is restricted to documents 'relating to the matters in question in the action' (R.S.C., Ord. 24, r.1(1)) and no order for their inspection by the other party or to the court may be made 'unless the Court is of the opinion that the order is necessary either for disposing fairly of the cause or matter or for saving costs' (R.S.C., Ord. 24, r.13(1)). It is common sense that the litigant seeking an order for discovery is interested, not in abstract justice, but in gaining support for the case he is presenting, and the sole task of the court is to decide whether he should get it. Applying that test, any document which, it is reasonable to suppose, contains information which may enable the party applying for discovery either to advance his own case or to damage that of his adversary, if it is a document which may fairly lead him to a train of inquiry which may have either of those two consequences, must be disclosed[2] . . . It is accordingly insufficient for a litigant to urge that the documents he seeks to inspect are relevant to the proceedings. For, although relevant, they may be of merely vestigial importance, or they may be of importance (great or small) only to his opponent's case. And to urge that, on principle, justice is most likely to be done

[1] The author is writing with reference only to civil proceedings.

[2] *Compagnie Financière et Commerciale du Pacifique v. Peruvian Guano Co* (1882) 11 Q.B.D. 55 at 63, *per* Brett L.J.

if free access is had to all relevant documents is pointless, for it carries no weight in our adversarial system of law.

Discovery depends on the honesty and diligence of the parties because withholding documents cannot necessarily be detected. Continental systems dispense with disclosure entirely. Lord Woolf's review of civil justice[3] recommended curtailing the categories for discovery of documents to those which are more directly significant and making extra disclosure dependent on a court order.[4]

The issue of discovery has been discussed further in relation to claims of privilege and public interest immunity.[5]

Exchange of statements

In civil proceedings the issues in a case are revealed by the initial pleadings but further information is also obtained by exchange of witness statements. This approach of "cards on the table" is achieved by R.S.C., Ord. 38:

> r.2A.—(2) At any stage in any cause or matter, the Court may, if it thinks fit for the purpose of disposing fairly and expeditiously of the cause or matter and saving costs, direct any party to serve on the other parties, on such terms as the Court shall think just, written statements of the oral evidence which the party intends to lead on any issues of fact to be decided at the trial.
>
> . . . (5) . . . (b) the Court may, on such terms as it thinks fit, direct that the statement served, or part of it, shall stand as the examination-in-chief of the witness or part of such evidence . . .

It is standard practice for witness statements to stand as evidence-in-chief of the relevant witness.[6]

In *Mercer v. Chief Constable of Lancashire*,[7] it was argued that an exception to such an exchange should be made in the case of jury trials but this was rejected and the normal rule is that there should be a simultaneous exchange of witness statements.

Mercer v. Chief Constable of Lancashire [1991] 2 All E.R. 504 at 508–509, *per* Lord Donaldson M.R.

Over the last quarter of a century there has been a sea change in legislative and judicial attitude towards the conduct of litigation, taking the form of increased positive case management by the judiciary and the adoption of procedures designed (a) to identify the real issues in dispute and (b) to enable each party to assess the relative strengths and weaknesses of his own and his opponent's case at the earliest

[3] Lord Woolf, *Access to Justice* (HMSO 1996).
[4] *ibid.* Chap. 12 para. 37ff.
[5] See Chaps. 6 and 7.
[6] As a result, witness statements are often elaborately over-drafted — see Woolf, *op. cit.* Chap. 12, para. 54ff.
[7] [1991] 2 All E.R. 504.

possible moment and well before any trial. Not only does this make for shorter trials and save costs, even more important it facilitates and encourages settlements. The most important change has been the requirement that, save in exceptional cases witness statements be exchanged prior to the trial.

A more proactive approach to case-management by the judiciary is one of Woolf's major themes and he has suggested that there should be a fundamental transfer in the responsibility for the management of civil litigation from litigants and their advisors to the courts.[8] This approach is also emerging in criminal trials which have never involved pre-trial process such written pleadings,[9] as occurs in civil cases. Pleadings reduce trial length by concentrating on those matters in dispute. Some magistrates courts have used pre-trial hearings[10] and a new system of preparatory hearings will be introduced for Crown Court trials as well as a result of Pt. 3 of the Criminal Procedure and Investigations Act 1996. These preparatory hearings are intended to identify the issues likely to be material in the trial, expediting the proceedings and assisting the judge's management of the trial, including the power to make rulings on the admissibility of evidence.[11]

Disclosure of Evidence in Criminal Cases[12]

Pre-1997 — disclosure by the prosecution

Full disclosure of prosecution information prior to trial is seen as an essential element in a fair trial.[13] In trials on indictment, the defendant is entitled to advance disclosure, not only of the evidence on which the prosecution are intending to rely but also of "unused material". In magistrates' courts, there is no obligation on the prosecution to disclose with regard to summary offences but there is a statutory obligation[14] in the case of triable-either-way offences which are being tried summarily. There is, of course, a general duty on the court to ensure a fair trial which would require the prosecution to produce all the material evidence.[15]

In Crown Court, it is the interpretation of 'unused material' that has been controversial. This was originally the subject of guidelines by the

[8] Woolf, *op. cit.* Section 2 generally and recommendation 1 at 299.
[9] One reason for this is that the plea of not guilty puts the entire prosecution case in issue. Criminal Justice Act 1967, s.10, provides for formal admissions but is rarely used.
[10] Baldwin J., *Pre-Trial Justice* (1985).
[11] Criminal Procedure and Investigations Act 1996, s.31.
[12] The following section is written on the basis that the Criminal Procedure and Investigations Act will be brought into operation in 1997 as planned.
[13] *R. v. Ward* [1993] 2 All E.R. 577; *R. v. Preston* [1993] 4 All E.R. 638; Art. 6 European Convention on Human Rights; Art. 14 International Covenant on Civil and Political Rights.
[14] Criminal Law Act 1977, s.48 and Magistrates Courts (Advance Information) Rules 1985 (S.I. 1985, No. 601).
[15] *R. v. Liverpool Crown Court ex parte Robinson* [1986] Crim.L.R. 622.

Attorney-General.[16] "Unused" material was information which had some bearing on the offence and the surrounding circumstances of the offence, such as witness statements not included in the committal bundles. Its importance is illustrated in *R. v. Taylor*[17] where a senior policeman did not mention to the prosecution that a witness identifying the defendants had made an earlier statement that one of the girls he had seen might have been black (neither defendant was) nor that the witness had claimed a reward. The officer withheld the information fearing that it would be disclosed to the defence.

Recently the boundaries of "unused material" has been the subject of active judicial debate. In 1991 Henry J, at the trial of Ernest Saunders,[18] ruled that "unused material" applied to almost all material collected during the course of an investigation and that whether it was "relevant" was not a matter for the prosecution. This ruling was upheld in *R. v. Maguire*[19] and *R. v. Ward*.[20] The prosecution had also to disclose any matters which might be held against prosecution witnesses, for example, police disciplinary hearings.[21] These developments were bitterly resented by the police and prosecution. It was not simply the quantity and inconvenience of the procedures but the nature of the information that they were being required to disclose. The argument was that they were faced with the dilemma of either having to disclose sensitive and confidential material, especially in relation to informants, or having to discontinue prosecution.

Before discussing recent developments in relation to prosecution disclosure, it is necessary to consider the position of the defence.

Pre-1997 — disclosure by the defence

There was never a common law obligation on the defendant to disclose the nature of the defence. It has been introduced in some circumstances by statute:

(1) for alibi defences by the Criminal Justice Act 1967 —

> 11.—(1) On a trial on indictment the defendant shall not without the leave of the court adduce evidence in support of an alibi unless, before the end of the prescribed period, he gives notice of particulars of the alibi.[22]

[16] Reported in (1982) 74 Cr.App.R. 302.

[17] (1993) 98 Cr.App.R. 133.

[18] A Serious Fraud Office prosecution arising out of the Guinness affair — see Royal Commission on Criminal Justice: *Report* Cm. 2263 (1993) para. 6.38ff.

[19] (1992) 94 Cr.App.R. 133.

[20] See *supra*.

[21] *R. v. Edwards* [1991] 2 All E.R. 266 — see *Edwards v. U.K.* (1992) 15 E.H.R.R. 417.

[22] The prescribed period is seven days after the end of any preliminary proceedings in magistrates' court.

(2) for expert evidence where section 81 of the Police and Criminal Evidence Act 1984 makes provision for the Crown Court Rules to specify conditions for the admission of expert evidence and under subsection (2) may specify the kind of evidence to which the rules apply.[23]

(3) for preparatory hearings in serious fraud cases where the judge may order the defendant to give the court and the prosecution a statement setting out in general terms the nature of the defence, indicating the principal matters on which issue is taken with the prosecution.[24]

The Runciman Commission,[25] while maintaining the defendant's right of silence at police station or trial, recommended that in all contested trials, the defence would have to indicate the substance of the defence or the fact that no evidence would be called:

Royal Commission on Criminal Justice: *Report* Cm. 2263 (1993) paras. 6.59–6.60

. . . we believe that there are powerful reasons for extending the obligations on the defence to provide advance disclosure. If all the parties had in advance an indication of what the defence would be, this would not only encourage earlier and better preparation of cases but might well result in the prosecution being dropped in the light of the defence disclosure, an earlier resolution through a plea of guilty, or the fixing of an earlier trial date. The length of the trial could also be more readily estimated, leading to a better use of the time both of the court and of those involved in the trial; and there would be kept to a minimum those cases where the defendant withholds his or her defence until the last possible moment in the hope of confusing the jury or evading investigation of a fabricated defence.

We do not, as we have said, believe that a requirement on the defence to disclose the substance of their case sooner rather than later infringes the right of defendants not to incriminate themselves. Where defendants advance a defence at trial it does not amount to an infringement of their privilege not to incriminate themselves if advance warning of the substance of such a defence has to be given. The matter is simply one of timing. We emphasise that under our proposals defendants may, if they so choose, still stay silent throughout the trial.

The arguments employed were pragmatic: defence disclosure would prevent the "ambush" defence; it would encourage better preparation as well as guilty pleas or prosecution discontinuances where appropriate; it would facilitate better estimates of length of trial and thus more efficient use of resources. Opposition to the proposal points to the lack of any evidence either of the widespread use of defence "ambushes"[26] or of the

[23] Crown Court (Advance Notice of Expert Evidence) Rules 1987 (S.I. 1987 No. 716).

[24] Criminal Justice Act 1987, s.9.

[25] Royal Commission on Criminal Justice, *op. cit.* para. 6.57ff (note of dissent by Professor Zander, 221–223); Glynn J., "Disclosure" [1993] Crim.L.R. 841.

[26] Zander M. and Henderson P., *Crown Court Study* (Royal Commission on Criminal Justice: Research Study No. 19, 1993) suggests that prosecution counsel see such ambushes in 7 per cent of case whereas for the C.P.S. and the police, the figures are 10 per cent and 23 per cent respectively. Counsel only considered them a serious problem in 3 per cent of cases.

effectiveness of defence disclosure.[27] However there are also issues of principle:

Royal Commission on Criminal Justice, ***op. cit.*** 221 — Note of Dissent by Professor Michael Zander, para. 2

The fundamental issue at stake is that the burden of proof lies throughout on the prosecution. Defence disclosure is designed to be helpful to the prosecution and, more generally, to the system. But it is not the job of the defendant to be helpful either to the prosecution or to the system. His task, if he chooses to put the prosecution to the proof, is simply to defend himself. Rules requiring advance disclosure of alibis and expert evidence are reasonably exceptions to this general principle. But, in my view, it is wrong to require the defendant to be helpful by giving advance notice of his defence and to penalise him by adverse comment if he fails to do so.

Obviously the shorter the notice that the prosecution have of a witness or item of evidence, the less able they are to counter it. But the principal function of a jury is to determine the truth, a difficult task amongst the rhetoric and emotion of the courtroom. They should be entitled both to an indictment which lays out an agenda of the issues to be decided and also to both parties putting forward their own evidence as to those issues and how they intend to answer the other's evidence. Concealment of evidence until a late stage by either side necessarily leads to the jury being unable to assess the weight or probative quality of such evidence.

Such principles of proof argue for joint disclosure. Scotland has operated such a practice for several years with little dissent.[28] But despite such principles, the practical disadvantages of applying disclosure to simple cases seem to outweigh the benefits. There are arguments for restricting such a reform to complex cases where there is a need for narrowing of the issues.

The Criminal Justice and Public Order Act 1994 adopts a less subtle approach. Section 34 is aimed at forcing disclosure of the defence by allowing a court to "draw such inferences as appear proper" from a failure to mention a relevant fact relied on in the defence when it might reasonably have been mentioned during police questioning. To that extent, section 34 is justified in allowing a jury to attach less weight to a defence which is only revealed at the trial and logically is correspondingly less credible. However at that stage a suspect will have had little opportunity to take legal advice or to consider the consequences of any decision.

But recently, two developments have significantly altered the law on disclosure.

[27] In serious fraud cases under Criminal Justice Act 1987, s.9, one study has shown that the system requiring a statement from the accused setting out the defence has proved largely ineffectual — Levi M., *The Investigation, Prosecution and Trial of Serious Fraud* (Royal Commission on Criminal Justice: Research Study No. 14, 1993).

[28] Glynn: *op. cit.* at 842.

Disclosure of confidential information

In many cases, the prosecution seek immunity from disclosure on the grounds of public interest immunity. Obtaining such immunity has been facilitated by the decisions *R. v. Keane*[29] and *R. v. Davis*[30] such material can now be placed before the court for a ruling on whether it should be disclosed without compromising its confidentiality. Under *Davis* and *Keane*, new procedures have developed to allow such material to be placed before the court for a ruling on whether it should be disclosed without compromising its confidentiality. Initially it is for the prosecution to take a view on the relevance of the material to the defence. Clearly they must err on the side of disclosing even matter of marginal relevance[31]:

R. v. Keane [1994] 2 All E.R. 478 at 484e–485a, *per* Lord Taylor C.J.

But how is it to be determined whether and to what extent the material which the Crown wishes to withhold may be of assistance to the defence?

First, it is for the prosecution to put before the court only those documents which it regards as material but wishes to withhold. As to what documents are 'material' we would adopt the test suggested by Jowitt J. in *R. v. Melvin and Dingle* (20 December 1993, unreported). The learned judge said:

> I would judge to be material in the realm of disclosure that which can be seen on a sensible appraisal by the prosecution: (1) to be relevant or possibly relevant to an issue in the case; (2) to raise or possibly raise a new issue whose existence is not apparent from the evidence the prosecution proposes to use; (3) to hold out a real (as opposed to fanciful) prospect of providing a lead on evidence which goes to (1) or (2).

As was pointed out later in that judgment, it is open to the defence to indicate to the prosecution a defence or an issue they propose to raise as to which material in the possession of the prosecution may be of assistance, and if that is done the prosecution may need to reconsider what should be disclosed.

We also wish, in passing to indorse the observations of the learned judge in that case as to the scope of the Crown's duty. It would be an abdication of that duty for the prosecution, out of an over-abundance of caution, simply to dump all its unused material into the court's lap and leave it to the judge to sort through it all regardless of its materiality to the issues present or potential. The prosecution must identify the documents and information which are material according to the criteria set out above. Having identified what is material, the prosecution should disclose it unless they wish to maintain that public interest immunity or other sensitivity justifies withholding some or all of it. Only that part which is both material in the estimation of the prosecution and sought to be withheld should be put before the court for its decision. If in an exceptional case the prosecution are in doubt about the materiality of some documents or information, the court may be asked to rule on that issue.

29 [1994] 2 All E.R. 478.
30 [1993] 2 All E.R. 643;.
31 *R. v. Winston Brown* [1995] 1 Cr. App. R 191 — an issue in the case must be construed broadly.

Normally such an application not to disclose would be in open court but this is not necessarily the case:

R. v. Davis [1993] 2 All E.R. 643 at 647g–648a, _per_ Lord Taylor C.J.

In our judgment, the proper approach is as follows. (1) In general, it is the duty of the prosecution to comply, voluntarily and without more, with the requirements in para. 2 of the Attorney General's guidelines. (2) If the prosecution wish to rely on public interest immunity or sensitivity to justify non-disclosure, then, whenever possible, which will be in most cases [the prosecution must give notice to the defence that they are applying for a ruling by the court, indicating at least the category of the material held and the defence must be given an opportunity of making representations.][32] (3) Where, however to disclose even the category of material would in effect be to reveal that which the Crown contends should not in the public interest be revealed, a different procedure will apply. The Crown should still notify the defence that an application to the court is to be made, but the category of material need not be specified and the application will be ex parte. If the court, on hearing the application, considers that the normal procedure under (2) above ought to have been followed, it will so order. If not, it will rule on the ex parte application. (4) It may be that, in a highly exceptional case, to reveal even the fact that an *ex parte* application is to be made, could 'let the cat out of the bag' so as to stultify the application. Such a case would be rare indeed, but we accept [the] contention that it could occur. In that even, the prosecution should apply to the court, *ex parte*, without giving notice to the defence. Again, if the court on hearing the application, decides that at least notice of the application should have been given to the defence or even that the normal inter partes procedure should have been adopted, it will so order.

Under (4), the prosecution can approach the court for an order for immunity from disclosure without informing the defence at all. These procedures, limiting the access of the defence to sensitive material, are not significantly affected by the Criminal Procedure and Investigations Act 1996. Where material has not been disclosed on the grounds of public interest immunity, an accused person can apply to the court for a review of this decision during the trial. Where the trial is in the Crown Court, there is a duty on the judge to keep the issue under review at all times without the need for an application.[33]

Disclosure under the Criminal Procedure and Investigations Act 1996[34]

The second major development is the impact of the Criminal Procedure and Investigations Act 1996. This was one of the consequences of the Runciman Commission.[35] The Commission saw practical problems in the sheer volume of material as well as the issue of principle concerning the disclosure of confidential and sensitive information. This was seen as

[32] The section in brackets adopts a formulation put to the court by the appellant.
[33] Criminal Procedure and Investigations Act 1996, ss.14 and 15.
[34] It is likely that these provisions will be brought into effect during 1997.
[35] Royal Commission on Criminal Justice, *op. cit.* para. 6.41ff.

particularly acute where informants or undercover police officers were involved. Runciman recommended a two-stage process.[36]

(1) primary disclosure which is automatic. The prosecution would be under a duty to supply the defence with copies of all material relevant to the offence, the offender and the circumstances of the case. Schedules of other information held by the police or other key participants such as expert scientific witnesses would be supplied at this point.

(2) secondary disclosure which takes place after the defence have disclosed their case. The defence would be obliged to establish the relevance of the material sought, relating it to their disclosed case. Where the parties disagree on this aspect, the court could rule, after weighing the potential importance of the material to the defence.

Under the Criminal Procedure and Investigations Act 1996, primary disclosure by the prosecution is ensured:

3.—(1) The prosecutor must —

(a) disclose to the accused any prosecution material which has not previously been disclosed to the accused and which in the prosecutor's opinion might undermine the case for the prosecution against the accused, or
(b) give to the accused a written statement that there is no material of a description mentioned in paragraph (a).

(2) For the purposes of this section prosecution material is material —

(a) which is in the prosecutor's possession, and came into his possession in connection with the case for the prosecution against the accused, or
(b) which, in pursuance of a code operative under Part II, he has inspected in connection with the case for the prosecution against the accused.

(3) Where material consists of information which has been recorded in any form the prosecutor discloses it for the purpose of this section —

(a) by securing that a copy is made of it and that the copy is given to the accused, or
(b) if in the prosecutor's opinion that is not practicable or not desirable, by allowing the accused to inspect it at a reasonable time and a reasonable place or by taking steps to secure that he is allowed to do so;

and a copy may be in such form as the prosecutor thinks fit and need not be in the same form as that in which the information has already been recorded.

(4) Where material consists of information which has not been recorded in any form the prosecutor discloses it for the purpose of this section by securing that it is recorded in such form as he thinks fit and —

[36] Royal Commission on Criminal Justice, *op. cit.* para. 6.50ff; for comments, see Glynn J. "Disclosure" (1993) Crim.L.R. 841.

(a) by securing that a copy is made of it and that the copy is given to the accused, or
(b) if in the prosecutor's opinion that is not practicable or not desirable, by allowing the accused to inspect it at a reasonable time and a reasonable place or by taking steps to seucre that he is allowed to do so;

(5) Where material does not consist of information the prosecutor discloses it for the purpose of this section by allowing the accused to inspect it at a reasonable time and a reasonable place or by taking steps to secure that he is allowed to do so.

(6) Material must not be disclosed under this section to the extent that the court, on an application by the prosecutor, concludes it is not in the public interest to disclose it and orders accordingly.

The Act then provides for disclosure by the accused in the form of a defence statement. In the case of proceedings in the Crown Court, this is compulsory. After the prosecution has complied with section 3:

5.—. . . (5) Where this section applies, the accused must give a defence statement to the court and the prosecutor.

(6) For the purposes of this section, a defence statement is a written statement —

(a) setting out in general terms the nature of the accused's defence,
(b) indicating the matters on which he takes issue with the prosecution, and
(c) setting out, in the case of each such matter, the reason why he takes issue with the prosecution.

Disclosure of the defence is not compulsory in the magistrates' court but the accused may give a defence statement to the prosecution and to the court on a voluntary basis.[37] Whether the disclosure is compulsory or voluntary, flaws in the defence statement can lead to adverse consequences for the accused:

11.—(1) This section applies where section 5 applies and the accused —

(a) fails to give a defence statement under that section,
(b) gives a defence statement under that section but does so after the end of the period which, by virtue of section 12, is the relevant period for section 5,
(c) sets out inconsistent defences in a defence statement given under section 5,
(d) at his trial puts forward a defence which is different from any defence set out in a defence statement given under section 5,
(e) at his trial adduces evidence in support of an alibi without having given particulars of the alibi in a defence statement given under section 5, or
(f) at his trial calls a witness to give evidence in support of an alibi without having complied with subsection (7)(a) or (b) of section 5 as regards the witness in giving a defence statement under that section.

(2) [This subsection makes similar provision for voluntary defence statements in the magistrates' court].

(3) Where this section applies —

[37] Criminal Procedure and Investigations Act 1996, s.6.

(a) the court, or, with the leave of the court, any other party may make such comment as appears appropriate;
(b) the court or jury may draw such inferences as appear proper in deciding whether the accused is guilty of the offence concerned.

However, where the accused has given a defence statement to the prosecution, the prosecutor is under a duty to make any additional disclosures that become necessary:

7.—(1) This section applies where the accused gives a defence statement under section 5 or 6.

(2) The prosecutor must —

(a) disclose to the accused any prosecution material which has not previously been disclosed to the accused and which might be reasonably expected to assist the accused's defence as disclosed by the defence statement given under section 5 or 6, or
(b) give to the accused a written statement that there is no material of a description mentioned in paragraph (a).

(3) For the purposes of this section prosecution material is material —

(a) which is in the prosecutor's possession, and came into his possession in connection with the case for the prosecution against the accused, or
(b) which, in pursuance of a code operative under Part II, he has inspected in connection with the case for the prosecution against the accused . . .

(5) Material must not be disclosed under this section to the extent that the court, on an application by the prosecutor, concludes it is not in the public interest to disclose it and orders accordingly.

The prosecutor remains under a continuing duty to keep under review the of question of whether there is prosecution material which might undermine the prosecution case and which has not been disclosed to the accused and, should such material exist, it should be disclosed to the accused as soon as reasonably practicable.[38]

Oral Testimony

Such developments in pre-trial disclosure emphasise openness in litigation, encouraging settlement in civil cases and guilty pleas or discontinuances in criminal proceedings. But where the action is contested, in criminal cases especially, adversarial trial still relies heavily upon oral testimony. By observing and listening to a witness, the trier of fact is believed to be able to assess the weight to be attached to the witness's evidence more effectively than by reading a written statement. This means that oral testimony is often given even where there is no dispute.

[38] Criminal Procedure and Investigations Act 1996, s.9.

In criminal proceedings, there are more circumstances where written statements are becoming admissible. For example,[39]

(1) a significant amount of evidence in magistrates' courts is given through the medium of agreed statements under section 9 of the Criminal Justice Act 1967.[40]
(2) formal admissions can also be adduced in any proceedings under section 10 of that Act although this is significantly under-used.
(3) where a written statement or deposition is admitted as evidence in committal proceedings before a magistrates' court, that statement can without further proof be read as evidence on the trial of the accused. This provision, under the Criminal Procedure and Investigations Act 1996,[41] allows uncontentious evidence to be read into the record, perhaps without cross-examination or the attendance of the witness, where there is no objection by the defendant.[42]
(4) under the Criminal Justice Act 1988, sections 23 and 24 in certain circumstances allow documentary hearsay to be admitted.

In civil proceedings, under the Civil Evidence Act 1995, hearsay evidence has become generally admissible where the witness is not present. Even where the witness is in court, which would normally mean that previous statements would not be admissible, a witness statement can be adopted as that witness's evidence in chief.[43]

Despite these derogations from the primacy of oral testimony and the principle of confrontation, the adversarial nature of the trial remains. But whether the "fight" theory is the best technique for a court to discover the facts in a case is dubious:

Frank J., *Courts on Trial* (1949) 80–82

. . . to have each side strive as hard as it can, in a keenly partisan spirit, to bring to the court's attention the evidence favorable to that side. Macaulay said that we obtain the fairest decision 'when two men argue, as unfairly as possible, on opposite side,' for then 'it is certain that no important consideration will altogether escape notice'

Unquestionably that view contains a core of good sense . . . But frequently the partisanship of the opposing lawyers blocks the uncovering of vital evidence or leads to a presentation of vital testimony in a way that distorts it.

This is perhaps most obvious in the handling of witnesses. Suppose a trial were fundamentally a truth-inquiry. Then, recognising the inherent fallibilities of

[39] These do not include specific provisions for the protection of child witnesses and victims, for example, under the Magistrates' Court Act 1980, s.103 and the Criminal Justice Act 1988, s.32A.
[40] See Chap. 18.
[41] s.68 and Sched. 2.
[42] See Chap. 18.
[43] Civil Evidence Act 1995, s.6.

witnesses, we would do all we could to remove the cause of their errors when testifying. Recognising also the importance of witnesses' demeanour as clues to their reliability, we would do our best to make sure that they testify in circumstances most conclusive to a revealing observation of that demeanour by the trial judge or jury. In our contentious trial practice, we do almost the exact opposite.

No business man, before deciding to build a new plant, no general before launching an attack, would think of obtaining information on which to base his judgment by putting his informants through the bewildering experience of witnesses at a trial . . .

In a book by Henry Taft (brother of Chief Justice Taft, and himself a distinguished lawyer) we are told: 'Counsel and court find it necessary through examination and instruction to induce a witness to abandon for an hour or two his habitual method of thought and expression, and conform to the rigid ceremonialism of court procedure. It is not strange that frequently truthful witnesses are . . . misunderstood, that they nervously react in such a way as to create the impression that they are either evading or intentionally falsifying. It is interesting to account for some of the things that witnesses do under such circumstances. An honest witness testifies on direct examination. He answers questions promptly and candidly and makes a good impression. On cross-examination, his attitude changes. He suspects that traps are being laid for him. He hesitates; he ponders the answer to a simple question; he seems to 'spar' for time by asking that questions be repeated; perhaps he protests that counsel is not fair; he may even appeal to the court for protection. Altogether the contrast with his attitude on direct examination is obvious; and he creates the impression that he is evading or withholding'. Yet on testimony thus elicited courts every day reach decisions affecting the lives and fortunes of citizens.

Examination-in-chief

Anonymity

After a witness has taken the oath or affirmed, he or she will be examined by the party calling him or her. Ordinarily the witness will be asked to state name and address. However victims of sexual offences[44] remain anonymous nor can children be identified.[45] At common law the judge has discretion to allow a witness to testify not to identify themselves in public. This has been commonplace in blackmail charges in order to encourage complainants to come forward but also has been used in sexual offences where witnesses who are or have been prostitutes have been referred to as "Miss X"[46] or where the witness has been a member of the security forces. Such anonymity may be enforced through section 11 of the Contempt of Court Act 1981. The Runciman Commission concluded that witnesses could find publicity a disincentive to giving evidence and that those who did not wish their addresses to be read out in court should be allowed to hand them into court.[47]

[44] Sexual Offences (Amendment) Act 1992 — witness anonymity is discussed at greater length at 375, *et seq.*
[45] Children and Young Persons Act 1933, s.39.
[46] *Shaw v. DPP* [1962] A.C. 220.
[47] Royal Commission on Criminal Justice, *op. cit.* para. 8.44.

Leading questions

One of the myths of adversarial trial is that the oral testimony of a physically-present witness, recollecting the relevant events, is the most reliable form of evidence. It is the witness's recollection that is important and thus the first "rule" for examining-in-chief is that counsel must not ask questions which either prompt the witness by suggesting the answer or which assume the existence of certain facts. These are known as "leading questions". This is not a cast-iron rule and it is possible to lead the witness on formal and introductory matters and where there is no dispute between the parties. Where one witness has testified to a particular fact, another witness may be asked, directly, whether that fact took place.[48]

The absurdity is that the witness will have given a statement to whichever party is calling him or her and that statement will have been given within a relatively short time of the events in question. The conditions under which these are generally taken are far from ideal: a statement made by a witness to the police is not regulated in the same manner, for example, as an interview with a suspect. Despite this, any statement is more likely to be reliable as evidence of the facts than the witness seeking to remember those events months, if not years, later. Counsel will be aware of the contents of the statement and there is great temptation to ensure that all the necessary facts emerge by leading questions rather than allowing the witness to recollect them freely.

Refreshing the memory before entering the witness box

This insistence on oral testimony can reduce a criminal trial[49] to a test of memory. Only a report by an expert witness[50] or, in some circumstances, a videotape of a child's testimony[51] can stand as the evidence-in-chief of that witness.[52] As a result, counsel are recommended to show their witnesses their statements *before* the witness goes into court to refresh the memory. A lawyer should not coach a witness nor should witnesses discuss their testimony at this point.

In *R. v. Richardson*,[53] shortly before testifying, the prosecution witnesses were given their statements to read although they were not allowed to take these into the witness box. These statements had been made to the police some weeks after the commission of the offences:

[48] *Courteen v. Touse* (1807) 1 Camp. 43.

[49] In civil proceedings, witness statements can be admissible as evidence in chief under the Civil Evidence Act 1995, s.6.

[50] Criminal Justice Act 1988, s.30.

[51] Criminal Justice Act 1988, s.32A (inserted by the Criminal Justice Act 1991, s.54).

[52] But the Criminal Procedure and Investigations Act 1996, s.68 and Sched. 2 may change this: see 566, *et seq.*

[53] [1971] 2 All E.R. 773.

R. v. Richardson [1971] 2 All E.R. 773 at 776j–777f, per Sachs L.J.

. . . it is however necessary to consider what should be the general approach of the court to there being shown in this way to witnesses their statements — which were not 'contemporaneous' within the meaning of that word as normally applied to documents used to refresh memory. First, it is to be observed that it is the practice of the courts not to allow a witness to refresh his memory in the witness box by reference to written statements unless made contemporaneously. Secondly . . . witnesses for the prosecution in criminal cases are normally (though not in all circumstances) entitled, if they so request, to copies of any statements taken from them by police officers. Thirdly, it is to be noted that witnesses for the defence are normally, as is known to be the practice, allowed to have copies of their statements and refresh their memories from them at any time up to the moment they go into the witness box — indeed counsel for the appellant was careful not to submit that there was anything wrong about that. Fourthly, no one has ever suggested that in civil proceedings witnesses may not see their statements up to the moment they go into the witness box. One has only to think for a moment of witnesses going into the box to deal with accidents which took place five or six years previously to conclude that it would be highly unreasonable if they were not allowed to see them. Is there then anything wrong in the witnesses in this case being offered an opportunity to see that which they were entitled to ask for and to be shown on request? In a case such as the present is justice more likely to be done if a witness may not see a statement made by him at a time very much closer to that of the incident?

Curiously enough, these questions are very bare of authority. Indeed the only case which has a direct bearing on this issue is one which was decided not in this country but on appeal in the Supreme Court of Hong Kong in 1966: *Lau Pak Ngam v. R.*,[54] which is compactly reported. In the view of each member of this court, it contains some sage observations, two of which are apt to be quoted. One of them is:

> Testimony in the witness box becomes more a test of memory than of truthfulness if witnesses are deprived of the opportunity of checking their recollection beforehand by reference to statements or notes made at a time closer to the events in question.

The other:

> Refusal of access to statements would tend to create difficulties for honest witnesses but be likely to do little to hamper dishonest witnesses.

With those views this court agrees.

Where a witness looks at a document outside the courtroom, if the prosecution is aware of that, they must inform the defence and allow the defence to see the document. In *Richardson*, the Court of Appeal held that the prosecution had a duty to disclose this fact to the defence.

It was considered that a line was drawn at the moment the witness entered the box but in *R. v. Da Silva*[55] the witness had already begun to

[54] [1966] Crim.L.R. 443.
[55] [1990] 1 All E.R. 29.

give evidence when the judge permitted him to leave the box to refresh his memory from a statement. The appellant submitted that the witness could either have read his statement before he entered the box or, if it were made contemporaneously, have refreshed his memory while testifying. However, having started to testify, there could not be a pause for reviewing a statement that was not made contemporaneously. The Court of Appeal disagreed:

R. v. Da Silva [1990] 1 All E.R. 29 at 33c–e, *per* Stuart-Smith L.J.

In our judgment, therefore, it should be open to the judge, in the exercise of his discretion and in the interests of justice, to permit a witness who has begun to give evidence to refresh his memory from a statement made near to the time of events in question, even though it does not come within the definition of contemporaneous, provided he is satisfied (1) that the witness indicates that he cannot now recall the details of events because of the lapse of time since they took place, (2) that he made a statement much nearer the time of the events and that the contents of the statement represented his recollection at the time he made it, (3) that he had not read the statement before coming into the witness box and (4) that he wished to have an opportunity to read the statement before he continued to give evidence.

We do not think that it matters whether the witness withdraws from the witness box and reads his statement, as he would do if he had had the opportunity before entering the witness box, or whether he reads it in the witness box. What is important is that, if the former course is adopted, no communication must be had with the witness, other than to see that he can read the statement in peace. Moreover, if either course is adopted, the statement must be removed from him when he comes to give his evidence and he should not be permitted to refer to it again, unlike a contemporaneous statement which may be used to refresh memory while giving evidence.

Refreshing the memory after entering the witness box

Once in the witness box, there is still one[56] means for witnesses to remind themselves of the events to which they will be testifying. While testifying, a witness is allowed to refer to any document, made at the time of the events by that witness. This is known as "refreshing the memory":

Newark M. and Samuels A., "Refreshing Memory" [1978] Crim.L.R. 408

Human memory is probably not as good as we believe. Generally contemporaneous notes made by a witness are likely to be fuller and more accurate than his memory at a trial many months after the incident. Moreover, contemporaneous notes, if referred to, may help to stimulate the memory to recall further facts not contained in the notes which would not otherwise have been recalled. It is therefore desirable that a court should allow use to be made of such notes. However, there are dangers involved. The notes may create a spurious impression of a vivid recollection. Inaccuracies in perception and memory become crystallised. The witness believes he

[56] In some other jurisdictions, witnesses have been hypnotised to improve their memory — Wrightman L., Willis C. and Saul K., *On the Witness Stand: Controversies in the Courtroom* (1987) Section 2.

remembers the incident but in truth only remembers his record of it. The testify of an untruthful witness is given enhanced credibility and he is able to tailor his evidence to fit in with his notes.

This is most commonly seen with police officers who, once sworn, produce and proceed to read from their notebooks. The problem is that notebooks and other such documents are hearsay and not admissible as evidence in their own right. Police witnesses are permitted to do this, not because they are constables, but because they have written up the notes at the time of the incident. As a result of this "contemporaneous recording", the witness can review the document in order to jog the memory. The witness then testifies and it is this oral testimony which is evidence and not the notebook.

This bizarre process is a "hearsay fiddle": an avoidance of the consequences of the hearsay rule more than an aid to recollection. This is illustrated in cases where the document does not stimulate the witness's present recollection at all but where the witness accepts that his past recollection must have been as recorded in the document. In *Maugham v. Hubbard*,[57] a witness was called to prove the receipt of money and was shown an unstamped acknowledgement of the receipt signed by himself. He had no recollection whatsoever of the transaction but swore that the receipt must be accurate and that he had received the money.

> In order to make the paper itself evidence of the receipt of the money it ought to have been stamped. The consequence of its not having been stamped might be that the party who paid the money, in event of the death of the person who recieved it, would lose his evidence of such payment. Here the witness, on seeing the entry signed by himself, said that he had no doubt that he had received the money. The paper itself was not used as evidence of the receipt of the money, but only to enable the witness to refresh his memory; and when he said that he had no doubt that he had received the money there was sufficient parol evidence to prove the payment.[58]

In *R. v. Kelsey*[59] the witness had dictated a car number plate to a police constable who wrote it down and repeated it back to the witness. The officer gave evidence that the note produced was the note the witness saw him make and as a result the witness was allowed to look at the notebook to "refresh his memory". In fact as the witness has no present recollection of the registration number, the notebook is the evidence, introduced through the medium of the witness.

In civil proceedings, these contortions are unnecessary as the note would be admissible evidence under the Civil Evidence Act 1995. Other jurisdictions also cut through this tangle. Under the U.S. Federal Rules of Evidence:

[57] (1828) 8 B & C 14; also *Topham v. McGregor* (1844) 1 Car. & Kir. 320 where the witness, having refreshed his memory, deposed to the state of the weather 14 years previously.
[58] *ibid.* at 16, *per* Lord Tenterden C.J.
[59] (1982) 74 Cr.App.R. 213 .

803.—A memorandum or record concerning a matter about which a witness had knowledge but now has insufficient recollection to enable the witness to testify fully and accurately, shown to have been made or adopted by the witness when the matter was fresh in the witness's memory and to reflect that knowledge correctly. If admitted, the memorandum or record may be read into evidence but may not itself be received as an exhibit unless offered by an adverse party.[60]

However in criminal proceedings, conditions have to be met before the witness can use the document as an aide-memoire while testifying:

(1) it is not necessary to show that the witness's memory is impaired. The request to refresh the memory can come from counsel nor is it too late to make such a request after a witness has departed from his statement.[61]

(2) the chief condition, before a witness can "refresh the memory", is contemporaneity. The document must have been made by the witness (or at least verified by him or her) at the time of the incident or soon after:

Newark M. and Samuels A., "Refreshing Memory" [1978] Crim.L.R. 408 at 409

. . . Wigmore believed that in the case of a present recollection revived it was an unnecessary requirement which had spilled over from cases of past recollection recorded. His point was that if the memory is truly revived it does not matter what triggers it off. But although the witness may genuinely believe that his memory is revived there is always the danger that he is deceiving himself. On the whole it seems better to insist on some degree of contemporaneity. However contemporaneity must be a flexible concept, a matter of fact and degree in the circumstances of each case.

The police officer who observes an incident and later in the station writes up the observations in a notebook can refer to that notebook. The requirement of contemporaneity is not strict and days if not weeks can pass between the incident and its recording in a document. While a delay of two weeks has not been fatal,[62] a gap of a month has led the trial judge to pause before giving leave for the witness to refresh his memory.[63]

(3) the document does not have to be written by the witness but it must be verified by him or her. Thus ships' logs, kept by the mate but later checked by the captain, can be used to refresh the captain's memory.[64] If a witness dictates a car number plate to a police constable who writes this down and repeats it back to the witness,

[60] Federal Rules of Evidence, r.803(5).
[61] Archbold, paras. 8.64–8.65.
[62] *R. v. Langton* (1876) 2 Q.B.D. 296.
[63] *R. v. Graham* [1973] Crim.L.R. 628.
[64] *Burrough v. Martin* (1809) 2 Camp. 112.

the witness can look at the notebook to refresh his memory, even though he did not look at it at the time:

R. v. Kelsey (1982) 74 Cr.App.R. 213 at 217, per Taylor J.

The question we have to decide is, therefore, whether witness A can verify a note he dictates to B only by reading it himself, or whether it is sufficient if the note is read back by B to A at the time of confirmation. In most cases we would expect the note to be read by A if it is made in his presence. But what of the instant case, or cases involving the blind or the illiterate? In our view, there is no magic in verifying by seeing as opposed to verifying by hearing. . . . What must be shown is that witness A has verified in the sense of satisfying himself whilst matters are fresh in his mind (1) that a record has been made and (2) that it is accurate. If A makes a 'contemporaneous' note himself or if A reads and adopts at the time a 'contemporaneous' note made by B, A may refresh his memory from it without need of another witness.

But there must be some form of verification. In *R. v. Eleftheriou*[65] customs officers investigating a VAT fraud were keeping observation on a fish and chip shop. One officer kept watch and said what was happening while the second officer wrote this down. Although both signed the document at the end of their shift, the observer did not read it through. The convictions were quashed as the record had not been verified.[66]

(4) nor does it matter that the note is a result of collaboration. In *R. v. Bass*,[67] the constables who interviewed the defendant denied making a joint note. But the Court of Appeal held that, even if they had collaborated, both could refresh their memory from it.

R. v. Bass [1953] 1 All E.R. 1064 at 1067, per Byrne J.

With regard to the second ground of appeal, the matter stood in this way. The officers' notes were almost identical. One officer made his notes after the appellant had been charged, and the other made his an hour later. Counsel for the appellant suggested to the officers in cross-examination that they had collaborated. They denied that suggestion. This court has observed that police officers nearly always deny that they have collaborated in the making of notes, and we cannot help wondering why they are the only class of society who do not collaborate in such a matter. It seems to us that nothing could be more natural prosecution proper, when two persons have been present in an interview with a third person, that they should afterwards make sure that they have a correct version of what was said. Collaboration would appear to be a better explanation of almost identical notes than the possession of a superhuman memory.[68]

[65] [1993] Crim.L.R. 947.

[66] In *R. v. Sekhon* (1986) 85 Cr.App.R. 19 the police observation log was verified. Note that such records might be admissible under the Criminal Justice Act 1988, s.24.

[67] [1953] 1 All E.R. 1064.

[68] Cited in Stephenson G., "Should collaborative testimony be permitted in courts of law?" [1990] Crim.L.R. 302.

Collaborative testimony increases accuracy and completeness as well as being administratively convenient. But it might also camouflage differences between witnesses, lead to the suppression of evidence and prevent effective cross-examination. This has been shown in experimental studies:

Stephenson G., "Should collaborative testimony be permitted in courts of law?" [1990] Crim.L.R. 302 at 313

The cost of these benefits is high. Much straightforward evidence that would have surfaced is excluded from group accounts. Group accounts are selective, conventional and devoid of descriptive and interpretative evidence. Moreover, groups are more or less unable to distinguish at all between answers which are correct and those about which individuals would express some doubt. Taking the formal objections one by one, it is clear that disagreement will, indeed, be camouflaged, and maybe just as importantly, individuals' recollections are not fully represented in a combined account. Evidence of all kinds — facts and wider-ranging observations- are excluded as groups compile a partial, conventional version of events. The extent to which hearsay is willingly included in collaborative accounts is unclear, especially since groups tend to be indiscriminately confident about all their answers. It appears that one person's confidence serves to generate confidence in others, or at least provides an excuse for belief in the veracity of the group decision.

(5) the document need not be the original and a copy of the original notes can be used. In *Topham v. Mcgregor*[69] the witness, a journalist, no longer had his copy but was entitled to refresh his memory from the 14-year-old newspaper in which that copy was printed.

The documents used for these purposes must be produced for the other party and for the jury[70] to inspect. This assists the jury in following the cross-examination and in assessing the witness's credibility. The opposition is allowed to cross-examine the witness on the relevant parts of the document, without making the document part of the evidence but if counsel chooses to examine on other parts of the document, the party calling the witness is entitled to require the cross-examiner to make the document evidence[71]:

Newark M. and Samuels A., "Refreshing Memory" [1978] Crim.L.R. 408 at 411

At first sight this looks like one of those rules that gets the law of evidence a bad name . . . The justification for the rule would seem to be this: When a cross-

[69] See *supra*.
[70] *Bass supra*.
[71] *R. v. Britton* [1987] 2 All E.R. 412 (where the defendant had made a note of the events, following his arrest for public order offences).

> examiner confines his cross-examination to the part of the document used by the witness to refresh his memory he is merely testing the genuine nature of the refreshment of the witness's memory or challenging the accuracy of the past recollection recorded and deposed to by the witness. But when he cross-examines on other parts of the document he is attempting to elicit testimony from the witness, or to discredit him by means of a document that is not before the jury as evidence in the case. The argument is that it would be wrong to allow the cross-examiner to make use of the document in a way quite unrelated to the testing of the refreshment of memory, and then to complain about being required to put the document in evidence.

But where the document is admitted, the jury may not use it as evidence of the facts but merely as evidence of the credibility of the witness. In *R. v. Virgo*,[72] the witness in a police corruption trial was Humphries, a man whose business interests involved Soho sex shops. He was permitted to use his diaries to "refresh his memory" as to dates of payments made to Virgo and was cross-examined extensively by the defence on other aspects of his diaries which unsurprisingly revealed his character to be far from unblemished. The diaries were admitted into evidence.

Humphries was an accomplice to the corruption whose evidence at that time required corroboration. The diaries could not be used for that purpose and could only go towards Humphries' credibility as a witness.

The rule against narrative — previous consistent statements[73]

A party cannot ask his or her own witness about earlier oral or written statements made by the witness which are consistent with current testimony. In *R. v. Roberts*,[74] the defendant was charged with murder. In his evidence, he wished to testify that it had been an accident and that, two days after the killing, he told his father that it had been an accident. He was not entitled to retail his statement to his father. As Humphreys J. remarked:

> It is because it does not assist the elucidation of the matters in dispute that the evidence is said to be inadmissible on the ground that it is irrelevant. It would not help the jury in this case in the least to be told that the appellant said to a number of persons, whom he saw while he was awaiting his trial, or on bail if he was on bail; that his defence was this, that or the other. The evidence asked to be admitted was tat the father had been told by his son that it was an accident. We think the evidence was properly refused[75]

At first this appears to be another illustration of the impact of the rule against hearsay. But the hearsay rule excludes statements so that they cannot be admitted as evidence of the facts contained within them. In this

[72] (1978) 67 Cr.App.R. 323.
[73] Gooderson R., "Previous Consistent Statements" (1968) 26 Cambridge L.J. 64.
[74] [1942] 1 All E.R. 187.
[75] *ibid.* at 191e–f.

situation, the witness wished to relate the prior statement, not as evidence of the facts, but as evidence of his own consistency and credibility. Despite this different purpose, such statements are still excluded. In *Corke v. Corke and Cooke*[76] the husband in a divorce action had gone to his wife's house at midnight and accused his wife and the lodger of having recently committed adultery. The wife telephoned the doctor, asking him to examine both herself and the lodger to show that there had been no recent intercourse. The doctor refused but at trial the court admitted evidence of the telephone conversation. On appeal, this evidence was treated as inadmissible:

Corke v. Corke and Cooke [1958] 1 All E.R. 224 at 235g–i, _per_ Sellars L.J.

In my view, not only is the evidence of what the wife did and said valueless and might indeed be misleading to the court, but it is not admissible. To what issue, it should be asked, does it go? It does nothing to prove the condition of either the female or male organ respectively of the parties alleged to be involved. It does nothing to disprove the intercourse the husband had alleged. The most that could be said is that the wife was showing a belief in her own story and adding some reason why the court should believe her. In this case I do not think the conduct and statement of the wife have that effect, but it is clear that a skilful witness might well embark on circumstantial matters to bolster up his or her story. Neville J.'s statement in *Jones v. South Eastern & Chatham Railway Co*[77] cited by my Lord, 'that you are not entitled to give evidence of statements on other occasions by the witness in confirmation of her testimony' neatly and accurately, in my opinion, states the law which is applicable to the question raised by the husband.

Whether or not this rule is strictly logical, it is one which keeps the evidence to the main issues in dispute and tends to avoid deception of the court by a resourceful witness . . .

The rationale for such an exclusion takes various forms:

- there is a danger of manufactured evidence to bolster the credibility of a witness
- such statements add little weight to a witness's testimony and are superfluous
- there is a danger of irrelevant side issues as to whether this prior statement was actually made.

There are several exceptions to this rule:

(1) prior consistent statements are admissible in civil proceedings ***under the Civil Evidence Act 1995***:

6.—(1) Subject as follows, the provisions of this Act as to hearsay evidence in civil proceedings apply equally (but with any necessary modifications) in relation to a previous statement made by a person called as a witness in the proceedings.

[76] [1958] 1 All E.R. 224.
[77] (1918) 87 L.J.K.B. 775.

(2) A party who has called or intends to call a person as a witness in civil proceedings may not in those proceedings adduce evidence of a previous statement made by that person, except —

(a) with the leave of the court, or

(b) for the purpose of rebutting a suggestion that his evidence has been fabricated.

A previous statement of a witness is only admissible as of right to rebut the suggestion that the witness's testimony has been fabricated under section 6(2)(b) and in all other cases, the leave of the court must be obtained before a previous statement is advanced in evidence.

(2) in criminal proceedings, the prior consistent statement may be used to rebut an ***allegation of recent fabrication***. This does not permit a witness to retail previous occasions on which the same story was told just because he or she has been attacked on cross-examination but only where counsel has accused the witness of recently inventing the story. In *R. v. Oyesiku*,[78] it was put to the defendant's wife that she had colluded with the defendant, charged with assault on a police officer, in making up the story that the police officer was the aggressor. The conviction was quashed after the judge did not allow the defence to show that the wife had made such a statement to the solicitor before she had even visited the defendant at the police station. Similarly in *R. v. Sekhon*[79] police officers kept observation on the defence, suspected of supplying drugs. The nature of the cross-examination involved a suggestion that the police had concocted the record and the observation log was admissible to rebut this suggestion.

(3) ***complaints made by victims of a sexual assault*** soon after the attack are admissible in support of the victim's testimony.[80] This exception is a relic from the rule that a woman should raise the hue and cry directly after an attack as a preliminary to an appeal of rape. A strong inference could be drawn from a failure to complain and the bare fact of the complaint could be given to rebut any such inference.[81] But it was not until 1896 that the details of the complaint could be given in evidence. In *R. v. Lillyman*[82] the employer of the victim was allowed to testify as to what the prosecutrix had told her about the attempted rape:

R. v. Lillyman [1896] 2 Q.B. 167 at 170–177, *per* Haskins J.

It is necessary in the first place to have a clear understanding as to the principles upon which evidence of such a complaint, not on oath, nor made

[78] (1971) 56 Cr.App.R. 240.

[79] (1986) Cr.App.R. 19.

[80] Temkin J., *Rape and Legal Process* (1987) 144 *et seq.*

[81] Cross suggests that the restriction to sexual offences is illogical and unhistorical since the hue and cry (and thus the "complaint" rule) applied to all appeals of felony: Tapper C., *Cross and Tapper on Evidence* (8th ed., 1995) 297.

[82] [1896] 2 Q.B. 167.

in the presence of the prisoner, nor forming part of the res gestae, can be admitted. It clearly is not admissible as evidence of the facts complained of; those facts must therefore be established, if at all, upon oath by the prosecutrix or other credible witness, and, strictly speaking, evidence by them ought to be given before evidence of the complaint is admitted. The complaint can only be used as evidence of the consistency of the conduct of the prosecutrix with the story told by her in the witness box, and as being inconsistent with her consent to that of which she complains.

In every one of the old textbooks, proof of complaint is treated as a most material element in the establishment of a charge of rape or other kindred charge . . . It is too late, therefore, to make serious objection to the admissibility of evidence of the fact that a complaint was made, provided it was made as speedily after the acts complained of as could reasonably be expected . . .

After very careful consideration we have arrived at the conclusion that we are bound by no authority to support the existing usage of limiting evidence of the complaint to the bare fact that a complaint was made . . .

The details are not evidence of the facts nor corroboration[83] of the victim's testimony but merely reinforce the victim's credibility. In *R. v. Wallwork*[84] a five year old was assaulted by her father and complained to her grandmother. The victim was not competent to give evidence but the grandmother was permitted to give details of the complaint. The testimony was wrongly admitted as the complaint cannot be used as evidence of the facts but only to bolster the credit given to the testimony of the victim. Since there was no such testimony, the evidence was inadmissible. But where consent is in issue, the fact that the complaint itself was made is evidence which negatives consent.

The key conditions for the complaint to be admitted are that it must be contemporaneous and spontaneous. In *R. v. Osborne*[85] the defendant was charged with indecent assault on a young girl. Another girl testified that she had left the victim with the accused shortly before the offence and on returning met her running home. She asked "Why are you going home? Why did you not wait?" and received a response which incriminated the accused. It was suggested that this was a conversation and not a complaint. The court explained the requirement of "spontaneity".

R. v. Osborne [1905] 1 K.B. 551 at 556–561, _per_ Ridley J.

It appears to us that the mere fact that the statement is made in answer to a question in such cases is not of itself sufficient to make it inadmissible as a complaint. Questions of a suggestive or leading character will, indeed, have that effect, and will render it inadmissible; but a question such as this, out

[83] Corroboration warnings are no longer mandatory for victims of sexual offences — Criminal Justice and Public Order Act 1994, s.32.
[84] (1958) 42 Cr.App.R. 153.
[85] [1905] 1 K.B. 551.

by the mother or other person, 'What is the matter?' or 'Why are you crying?' will not do so. These are natural questions which a person in charge will be likely to put. On the other hand, if she were asked 'Did So-and-so (naming the prisoner) assault you?' 'Did he do this and that to you?' then the result would be different, and the statement ought to be rejected. In each case the decision on the character of the question put, as well as other circumstances, such as the relationship of the questioner to the complainant, must be left to the discretion of the presiding judge. If the circumstances indicate that but for the questioning there probably would have been no voluntary complaint, the answer is inadmissible. If the question merely anticipates a statement which the complainant was about to make, it is not rendered inadmissible by the fact that the questioner happens to speak first . . .

We are, at the same time, not insensible of the great importance of carefully observing the proper limits within which such evidence should be given. It is only to cases of this kind that the authorities on which our judgment rests apply; and our judgment also is to them restricted. It applies only where there is a complaint not elicited by questions of a leading and inducing or intimidating character, and only when it is made at the first opportunity after the offence which reasonably offers itself. Within such bounds we think the evidence should be put before the jury; the judge being careful to inform the jury that the statement is not evidence of the facts complained of, and must not be regarded by them, if believed, as other than corroborative of the complainant's credibility, and, where consent is in issue, of the absence of consent.

The complaint must be made at the "first opportunity after the offence which reasonably offers itself". A victim need not complain to the first person encountered: in *R. v. Cummings*[86] the victim did not complain to a male supervisor in the camp but waited to speak to a woman friend the next morning. Whether the complaint was made expeditiously is a matter of fact for the judge.

The rule is restricted to sexual offences, including indecent assault on a male,[87] whether or not consent is in issue. It has not been extended to admitting other complaints, such as assault,[88] although logically it would fulfill the same purpose of revealing the victim's consistency.

Although the admissibility of a complaint seems to favour the victim of sexual assault over victims of other crimes, there is the other side of the coin as to whether any inference should be drawn from a failure to make such a complaint. In *Kilby v. R.*[89] the appellant, convicted of rape, argued to the Australian High Court that the jury should have been instructed that the absence of a complaint by the victim was evidence of consent:

Kilby v. R. (1973) 129 C.L.R. 460 at 472, _per_ Barwick C.J.

. . . the admissibility of that evidence in modern times can only be placed, in my opinion, upon the consistency of statement or conduct which it tends to

[86] [1948] 1 All E.R. 551.
[87] *R. v. Camelleri* [1922] 2 K.B. 122.
[88] *R. v. Jarvis and Jarvis* [1991] Crim.L.R. 374.
[89] (1973) 129 C.L.R. 460.

show, the evidence itself having no probative value as to any fact in contest but, merely and exceptionally constituting a buttress to the credit of the woman who has given evidence of having been subjected to the sexual offence. To understand the reasons for the admissibility and the use which can properly be made of the evidence of recent complaints is to deny the validity of the applicant's proposition that lack of complaint is probative of consent. I can see no ground in logic for saying that because evidence of complaint is admitted to show consistency in the story told by the woman, evidence of non-complaint is evidence of her consent to intercourse. In my opinion, quite apart from the fact that there may be many reasons why a complaint is not made, the want of a complaint does not found any inference of consent. It does tell against the consistency of the woman's account and accordingly is clearly relevant to her credibility in that respect . . .

As Temkin comments:

Temkin J., *Rape and Legal Process* (1987) 145–146

These cases suggest that old attitudes die hard. They reveal a total lack of understanding about rape victims and of knowledge about the rape trauma syndrome, for many perfectly genuine rape victims fail to report rape to a third party, either immediately or at all. In his study of 70 rape victims who did not report to the police, Paul Wilson[90] found that about 50 per cent never told anyone until they were interviewed for the study or had told someone weeks or months later in conjunction with a discussion on other matters . . . Victims decline to complain of rape for a variety of reasons. They may be too traumatised, too embarrassed, too scared of encountering a judgmental attitude, or too full of quite unjustified guilt feelings about what had occurred. The emphasis on the importance of recent complaint is therefore quite unjustified and it also presents yet another barrier to prosecution and conviction in rape cases. In England, Adler's Old Bailey study[91] confirmed that defending counsel may be relied upon to point out forcefully to the jury any delay in reporting. The judge may also refer to it. A significantly lower conviction rate was revealed in such cases.

The response to this problem in New South Wales has been to make it obligatory for the judge to warn the jury that absence of recent complaint does not necessarily betoken falsehood in the complainant. Under the Crimes Act 1900:

405B.—Where on the trial of a person for a prescribed sexual offence evidence is given or a question is asked of a witness which tends to suggest an absence of complaint in respect of the commission of the alleged offence by the person upon whom the offence is alleged to have been committed or to suggest delay by that person in making any such complaint, the Judge shall —

(a) give a warning to the jury to the effect that absence of complaint or delay in complaining does not necessarily indicate that the allegation that the offence was committed is false; and

[90] Wilson P., *The Other Side of Rape* (1978).
[91] Adler Z., *Rape on Trial* (1987).

(b) inform the jury that there may be good reasons why a victim of a sexual assault may hesitate in making, or may refrain from making, a complaint about the assault.[92]

However in *R. v. Davies*[93] the New South Wales Court of Criminal Appeal held that, alongside the warning required by section 405B, the jury should also be directed that delay in complaining can still be taken into account in assessing the credibility of the victim.

(4) crucially witnesses can generally testify to ***statements which are made by the accused on accusation***. In criminal proceedings, such statements can be made to a police officer or to the victim or other witness. They can consist of a denial of guilt, an admission or a mixture where an admission is accompanied by a justification or excuse for the conduct. There may be no statement at all but where the suspect remains silent upon accusation, that silence can be admissible and supportive evidence.[94] The accused can, of course, lie.[95]

(a) normally these are statements made by an accused to a police officer. Often it is an admission of some kind and is admissible as evidence of the facts it contains, although procedurally it must conform with sections 76 and 78 of the Police and Criminal Evidence Act 1984.[96] This exception does not just apply to incriminating statements. Everything said to the police is admissible evidence.[97] This includes not only inculpatory statements but also admissions that include exculpatory or self-serving statements. In *R. v. Duncan*,[98] the defendant, accused of strangling a woman, told the police that he had lost his temper when the victim teased him. There was thereby both an admission and perhaps some evidence either of lack of intent or of provocation. As we have seen, the admission is treated as evidence of the facts contained and the question arises whether the self-serving statement is to be treated in the same way or merely as supportive of the accused's credibility? The trial judge said that the exculpatory part of the statement was not evidence of facts but this was disapproved of by the Court of Appeal. This approach was supported by the House of Lords in *R. v. Sharp*[99] so that a mixed statement to the

[92] New South Wales, Crimes Act 1900, s.405B.
[93] (1985) 3 N.S.W.L.R. 276.
[94] *R. v. Cramp* (1880) 14 Cox C.C. 390.
[95] *R. v. Lucas* [1981] 2 All E.R. 1008 — discussed at 290, *et seq.*
[96] This is discussed at 43, *et seq.* and in Chap. 4.
[97] *R. v. Pearce* (1979) 69 Cr.App.R. 365 .
[98] (1981) 73 Cr.App.R. 359.
[99] [1988] 1 All E.R. 65 .

police is admissible as evidence of the facts it contains whether the statement is an admission or is self-serving:

R. v. Sharp [1988] 1 All E.R. 65 at 71e–g, *per* Lord Havers

My Lords, the weight of authority and common sense lead me to prefer the direction to the jury formulated in *R. v. Duncan* to an attempt to deal differently with the different parts of a mixed statement. How can a jury fairly evaluate the facts in the admission unless they can evaluate the facts in the excuse or explanation? It is only if the jury think the facts set out by way of excuse or explanation might be true that any doubt is cast on the admission and it is surely only because the excuse or explanation might be true that it is thought fair that it should be considered by the jury. I agree . . . that a jury will make little of a direction that attempts to draw a distinction between evidence which is evidence of facts and evidence in the same statement which whilst not being evidence of facts is nevertheless evidentiary material of which they may make use in evaluating evidence which is evidence of facts. One only has to write out the foregoing sentence to see the confusion it engenders.

However if the suspect's statement is simply exculpatory, it is still admissible. In *R. v. Storey*[1] the accused told the police that the cannabis found in her flat had been brought there by another against her will:

R. v. Storey (1968) 52 Cr.App.R. 334 at 337–338, *per* Widgery L.J.

The question which arises in this case is whether the fact that she gave shortly afterwards an explanation which , if true, would provide a completely innocent explanation is enough to produce a situation in which the learned judge's duty was to say that there was no case to answer . . . We think it right to recognise that a statement made by the accused to the police, although it always forms evidence in the case against him, is not in itself evidence of the truth of the facts stated. A statement made voluntarily by an accused person to the police is evidence in the trial because of its vital relevance as showing the reaction of the accused when first taxed with the incriminating facts. If, of course, the accused admits the offence, then as a matter of shorthand one says that the admission is proof of guilt, and, indeed, in the end it is. But the accused makes a statement which does not amount to an admission, the statement is not strictly evidence of the truth of what was said but is evidence of the reaction of the accused which forms part of the general picture to be considered by the jury at the trial.

Where the statement has less relevance, if it is made after long consideration and after legal advice, it may not be admissible.[2]

[1] (1968) 52 Cr.App.R. 334.
[2] *R. v. Newsome* (1980) 71 Cr.App.R. 325.

(b) if the accusation is not made by a police officer, the admissible fact is the reaction of the accused. In *R. v. Christie*[3] the defendant was accused of indecently assaulting a young boy. With his mother and a police officer, the boy went up to Christie and said "That's the man". Christie denied his guilt.

R. v. Christie [1914] A.C. 545 at 554, per Lord Atkinson

The rule of law undoubtedly is that a statement made in the presence of an accused person even upon an occasion which should be expected reasonably to call for some explanation or denial from him, is not evidence against him of the facts stated save so far as he accepts the statement so as to make it in effect his own. If he accepts the statement in part only, then to that extent alone does it become his statement. He may accept the statement by word or conduct, action or demeanour, and it is the function of the jury which tries the case to determine whether his words, action, conduct or demeanour at the time when the statement was made amounts to an acceptance of it in whole or in part. It by no means follows, I think, that a mere denial by the accused of the facts mentioned in the statement necessarily renders the statement inadmissible, because he may deny his statement in such a manner and under such circumstances as may lead a jury to disbelieve him, and constitute evidence from which an acknowledgement can be inferred by them.

If the accused makes an incriminating statement or response (*e.g.* lies or silence), this is admissible evidence of the facts, providing that the conditions of section 76 of the Police and Criminal Evidence Act 1984 have been satisfied. However, where there is no evidence that the accused has accepted any part of the accusation and where the response is wholly exculpatory, it appears that this would be regarded as a previous consistent statement and is thus inadmissible.

(5) witnesses can testify as to ***statements made on discovery of recently stolen or otherwise incriminating articles*** in the accused's possession. Where the only evidence is possession and the defendant offers no explanation, the jury is entitled to infer guilty knowledge.[4] Any statement on discovery, whether self-serving or not, is admissible as evidence.[5] There is authority that this applies even in a case of murder, where, for example, the defendant is discovered in possession of the murder weapon.[6]

(6) ***identification evidence***[7] is often treated exceptionally and so it is with previous consistent statements. When a witnesses identifies an

[3] [1914] A.C. 545.

[4] *R. v. Schama and Abramovitch* (1914) 11 Cr.App.R. 45.

[5] *R. v. Abraham* (1848) 3 Cox C.C. 430.

[6] *R. v. Muller* (1865) 4 F.&F. 383n — see Gooderson, *op. cit.* at 71.

[7] This will normally be subject to the regime of Code D of the Police and Criminal Evidence Act 1984 — the question of identification evidence is discussed at 294, *et seq.*

> accused in the course of the trial, evidence of a previous identification, normally at an identity parade, is admissible. This is not simply to add weight to the witness's consistency but the evidence of the previous identification is evidence in its own right. Where the identifying witness is unable to confirm the previous identification on oath, evidence of that identification can be given. In *R. v. Osbourne*,[8] the witness could not identify the defendant or remember that she had identified him previously at a parade. The police officer who had been in charge of the parade was permitted to testify to the fact of the identification. This was admitted despite a strong argument that such testimony was hearsay.

Also admissible are self-serving statements which are made as part of the ***res gestae***.[9] Everything which is part of and contemporaneous with the event itself can be rehearsed in court. In *R. v. Fowkes*[10] the accused was charged with murder. The son of the dead man was sitting in the room with his father and a policeman when a face appeared at a window and the fatal shot was fired. The son testified that he thought that the face was that of the accused but also that on seeing the face at the window, he shouted "There's Butcher". The policeman also testified as to what was said.

[8] [1973] Q.B. 678; *R. v. Christie* [1914] A.C. 545; *R. v. McCay* [1991] 1 All E.R. 232.
[9] This is discussed further at 541, *et seq*.
[10] *The Times*, March 8, 1856.

11

THE TESTIMONY OF WITNESSES: THE HOSTILE WITNESS AND CROSS-EXAMINATION

Impeaching Witnesses

Where a party is confronted with a witness who has given unfavourable evidence, they may seek to challenge the witness in various ways, suggesting:

- that the specific facts retailed to the court are incorrect and that the witness's powers of perception, memory and recall were faulty. Counsel can put leading questions, suggesting a contradictory account to that of the witness[1]
- that the witness has contradicted himself or herself in the past. Counsel can put previous inconsistent statements to the witness and, if necessary, prove them
- that the witness's general character means he or she is not to be believed. This might be general discreditable conduct or involve putting specific criminal convictions to the witness.

Such tactics, suggesting that a witness is not worthy of belief, are normally employed in the cross-examination of one's opponent's witnesses. But it is possible that a party calling a witness may find that the witness testifies in an unfavourable manner. In such a case, you are usually bound by the rule which prohibits impeaching one's own witness:

Newark M., "The Hostile Witness and the Adversary System" [1986] Crim.L.R. 441

It is clear that the origin of the rule against impeaching one's own witness lies in the development of the adversary system of trial. Certain rules follow from the notion of party responsibility for the collection and presentation of evidence. Others flow from the requirements of a well regulated contest under such conditions. The latter

[1] Always remembering that counsel's questions are not evidence.

group includes rules designed as a corrective to the wayward operation of such a system. But there is a difference between those rules that interfere with the free choice of the parties merely to preserve the true adversary character of the contest, and rules that are designed to subvert the system in some respect. Into the former character fall the rule against leading one's own witness, the rule against narrative, the regulation of refreshing memory. These rules are designed to preserve the oral character of the trial so as to make it a test of witness performance rather than a regurgitating of rehearsed statements. But the rule that prevents a party from discrediting his own witness seems to be part of the basic philosophy of the adversary trial and any exception to the rule must have the effect of undermining the adversary principle. The various rationale of the non-impeachment rule, that a party is bound by his own witness, that he guarantees his credibility, that he should not be allowed to blow hot and cold with his witness, while they emphasise adversarial responsibility in evidence presentation, seem to leave no room for the hostile witness exception. Nevertheless, attempts have been made to force the hostile witness exception into an adversary mould. So long as the treatment of the hostile witness was confined to a cross-examination to persuade the witness to tell the truth it was possible to accommodate the exception within adversary theory. The hostile witness is not open to the dangers of suggestion, so some of the ordinary rules of examination-in-chief can be relaxed. However, in criminal cases after 1865 when the impeachment of the hostile witness becomes possible, an adversary justification for such treatment must be sought in remedying some more serious dysfunctioning of the system. This is achieved by regarding testimony hostile witness as in reality the opponent's witness so that he may be treated much as though he were a witness for the other side.[2]

In the U.S.A., this rule has been abolished so that, under the Federal Rules of Evidence:

607.—The credibility of a witness may be attacked by any party, including the party calling the witness.[3]

The rationale for the American position is that the traditional rule against impeaching one's own witness is based on false premises. A party is not responsible for the presentation of evidence and thus does not hold out his or her witnesses as worthy of belief, since there is rarely a free choice in selecting them. Denial of the right to impeach leaves the party at the mercy of the witness and the adversary. If the impeachment is by prior statement, it is free from the dangers of hearsay. Despite this persuasive position, the English courts have eschewed this laissez-faire mentality and still regulate those situations where you may impeach your own witness.

The unfavourable witness

A witness may not give the testimony anticipated by the party who calls him or her. It may be actively hostile or just less favourable than was hoped for. The general rule is that counsel cannot question their own witness'

[2] This gives a useful account of the historical origins of the hostile witness rule.
[3] Federal Rules of Evidence, r.607.

character or credibility or produce prior statements which are inconsistent with the witness' testimony. In *Ewer v. Ambrose*[4] a defence witness called to prove the existence of a partnership, proved the contrary:

> I take the rule of law to be that, if a witness proves a case against the party calling him, the latter may show the truth by other witnesses. But it is undoubtedly true that, if a party calls a witness to prove a fact, he cannot, when he finds the witness proves the contrary, give general evidence to show that that witness is not to be believed on his oath, but he may show by other evidence that he is mistaken as to the fact which he is called upon to prove . . .[5]

There is nothing to stop a litigant from calling other witnesses to contradict the unfavourable testimony. As Littledale J. said in *Ewer v. Ambrose*:

> Where a witness is called by a party to prove his case and he disproves that case, I think the party is still at liberty to prove his case by other witnesses. It would be great hardship if the rule were otherwise, for if a party had four witnesses upon whom he relied to prove his case, it would be very hard that, by calling first the one who happened to disprove it, he should be deprived of the testimony of the other three . . . The order in which witnesses happen to be called ought not, therefore, to make any difference.

In civil proceedings, where unexpected and unfavourable testimony has been given (but the witness is not deemed hostile), a party may ask the leave of the court to introduce the witness's previous inconsistent statement under section 6(2)(a) of the Civil Evidence Act 1995.

> 6.—(1) Subject as follows, the provisions of this Act as to hearsay evidence in civil proceedings apply equally (but with any necessary modifications) in relation to a previous statement made by a person called as a witness in the proceedings.
> (2) A party who has called or intends to call a person as a witness in civil proceedings may not in those proceedings adduce evidence of a previous statement made by that person, except —
>
> (a) with the leave of the court . . .

This would certainly be possible where the witness has become senile.[6] In a criminal case, there is less flexibility but there are two possibilities under section 23 of the Criminal Justice Act 1988 where the witness's testimony is the result of illness or fear and as a result, a previous inconsistent statement may be admissible if it is contained in a document:

> 23.—(1) . . . statement made by a person in a document shall be admissible in criminal proceedings as evidence of any fact of which direct oral evidence by him would be admissible if —

[4] (1825) 3 B.&C. 746.
[5] *ibid.* at 750, *per* Holroyd J.
[6] *Harvey v. Smith-Wood* [1963] 2 All E.R. 127.

i) the requirements of one of the paragraphs of subsection (2) below are satisfied; or
ii) the requirements of subsection (3) below are satisfied.

(2) The requirements mentioned in subsection (1)(I) above are —

a) that the person who made the statement is dead or by reason of his bodily or mental condition unfit to attend as a witness;
. . . . . .

(3) The requirements mentioned in subsection (1)(ii) above are —

a) that the statement was made to a police officer or some other person charged with the duty of investigating offences or charging offenders; and
b) that the person who made it does not give oral evidence through fear or because he is being kept out of the way.

The first possibility under section 23(2)(a) is where the witness is "unfit to attend as a witness". This does not refer solely to the physical act of getting to court. In *R. v. Setz-Dempsey*[7] the witness came to court but, because of mental illness, was unable to recall the events. *Prima facie* the statement that he had previously made to the police was admissible.[8]

The second possibility under section 23(3) is where the witness does not give evidence "through fear or because he is being kept out of the way". These are to be read disjunctively. That is, the witness can be afraid or is possibly being kept out of the way, (as in *R. v. Acton Justices ex parte McMullen*[9]). Where the witness is intimidated and refuses to testify, section 23(3) clearly applies and the previous written statement is admissible in evidence in place of any oral testimony; but where a witness attends court, is sworn but testifies in a hostile or simply unfavourable manner, can it be said that the person ". . . does not give oral evidence . . ."? If not, the sensible course for the prosecution would be not to call the witness at all, in which case they could call section 23(3) in aid.[10] But in support of the policy which encourages oral testimony, it would be preferable to call the frightened witness and, if they fail to come up to proof, to regard them as "not having given oral evidence" through fear and thus allow the prosecution to introduce the witness statement.

The hostile witness

Where witnesses fail to reproduce their pre-trial accounts, in certain circumstances it is possible to impeach your own witness. If the witness is

[7] [1994] Crim.L.R. 123.
[8] Although the Court of Appeal held that it should have been excluded under the criteria for exercising judicial discretion under s.26.
[9] (1990) 92 Cr.App.R. 98.
[10] Munday R., "Hostile Witnesses and the Admission of Witness Statements under s.23 of the Criminal Justice Act 1988" [1991] Crim.L.R. 349.

not a compellable witness, it must be explained to them at the start and in the absence of the jury, that they have the right to refuse to testify but that if he or she chooses to give evidence, they will be treated as any other witness. In particular this might apply to the wife of the accused.[11]

(1) at common law, the judge has discretion, if the attitude and demeanour of the witness is hostile, to allow leading questions and to put any prior inconsistent statements to the witness. Prior to section 22 of the Common Law Procedure Act 1854,[12] it was undecided at common law whether these previous inconsistent statements could be proved as opposed merely to being put to the witness in cross-examination.

(2) by statute under section 3 of the Criminal Procedure Act 1865, if (in the opinion of the judge) the witness' "present testimony" should prove adverse, counsel can contradict by proving prior inconsistent statements, providing that these have first been put to the witness. Despite the name of the statute, section 3 applies equally to civil and criminal proceedings.

> 3.—A party producing a witness shall not be allowed to impeach his credit by general evidence of bad character, but he may, in case the witness shall, in the opinion of the judge, prove adverse, contradict him by other evidence, or, by leave of the judge, prove that he has at other times a statement inconsistent with his present testimony; but before such last-mentioned proof can be given the circumstances of the supposed statement, sufficient to designate the particular occasion must be mentioned to the witness, and he must be asked whether or not he has made such statement.

Neither common law nor statute exposes the hostile witness to the full panoply of the discrediting techniques used in cross-examination: in particular, counsel is not permitted to produce evidence of the witness's general bad character. Essentially a judge's ruling that a witness is hostile entitles a party to put previous inconsistent statements to that witness.

Another preliminary point is that the statute does not nullify the common law which gives latitude to the judge over the issue of mode of examination. In *R. v. Thompson*,[13] the defendant was accused of incest with his daughter. She had earlier given a statement to the police but at the trial, having been sworn, refused to answer questions. The judge gave permission for her to be treated as a hostile witness and eventually she agreed that her previous statements were true. It was argued on appeal that, since she had stayed silent, there was no "present testimony" to be inconsistent with these earlier statements and section 3 could not apply. The Court of Appeal held, regardless of s.3, that the common law gave the judge discretion as to what questions could be put to the witness[14]:

[11] *R. v. Pitt* [1982] 3 All E.R. 63.

[12] Superseded by the Criminal Procedure Act 1865, s.3 — see Newark, *op. cit.* 443–445.

[13] (1976) 64 Cr.App.R. 96.

[14] Had the witness denied making these earlier statements, they certainly could be proved under section 3. But it is a moot question whether they could have been proved at common law — see the authorities cited in Pattenden R., "The Hostile Witness" (1992) 56 *Journal of Criminal Law* 414 fn.5.

R. v. Thompson (1976) 64 Cr.App.R. 96 at 98–99, per Lord Parker C.J.

We do not find it necessary to express any view upon the section as applied to cases where there is an inconsistent statement. We think this matter must be dealt with by the provisions of the common law in regard to recalcitrant witnesses. Quite apart from what is said in section 3, the common law did recognise that pressure could be brought to bear upon witnesses who refused to co-operate and perform their duties. We have had the advantage of looking at one or two of the earlier cases . . .

The first is *Clarke v. Saffery*[15] . . . Best C.J. said 'there is no fixed rule which binds the counsel calling a witness to a particular mode of examining him. If a witness, by his conduct in the box, shows himself decidedly adverse, it is always in the discretion of the judge to allow a cross-examination'[16]

But who is hostile? Despite the use of the word "adverse" in the Criminal Procedure Act 1865, it is the same test for common law and statute. Prior to 1847, the prosecution was responsible for calling all necessary witnesses, whether for the Crown or for the defence and thus the threshold at which they could be treated as equivalent to defence witnesses was relatively low:

Newark M., "The Hostile Witness and the Adversary System" [1986] Crim.L.R. 441 at 445–446

The phrase 'hostile' was not universally applied prior to the Common Law Procedure Act 1854 to the kind of witness that might be cross-examined by the party calling him. Indeed section 22 refers to a witness proving 'adverse' and it is not until *Greenough v. Eccles*[17] that it is clearly established that this means something more than merely unfavourable. In *Greenough v. Eccles* we see the origin of the idea that it is manifest antipathy that is the hall-mark of the hostile witness. The trial judge, Cockburn C.J., had refused leave under section 22 on the basis that the witness had not proved adverse 'in the sense of showing a mind hostile to the party calling him'. On appeal Williams J. said that 'the Judge's discretion must be principally, if not wholly, guided by the witness's behaviour and language in the witness box (for the Judge can know nothing, judicially, of his earlier conduct)'. . . . This shifting of focus from treachery and surprise to manifest antipathy seems to be due to a number of reasons. A need is felt to distinguish sharply between the hostile and the merely unfavourable witness. The test must be applicable with the minimum of fuss, leaving a substantial discretion to the trial judge so that appellate courts will not be burdened with appeals on this issue.

Procedurally it is for the judge to determine whether a witness is hostile. Counsel should ensure that the answers received have not been the result of a mistake, perhaps may invite the witness to refresh his or her memory

[15] (1824) Ry&M 126.

[16] The comments about "recalcitrant" witnesses who "refuse to co-operate and perform their duties" scarcely seem apposite in talking about a 16-year-old girl, sexually abused by her father, no doubt interviewed in embarrassing detail and at length by the police and now called to testify to these matters in a public court.

[17] (1859) 5 C.B.N.S. 786.

but should not browbeat.[18] If there is no error, there should be an application in the absence of the jury. However if the witness is to be examined, this should be in the presence of the jury since it will give them a yardstick to assess what credit is, ultimately, to be given to the testimony.[19] It is generally agreed that the judge can look at any previous inconsistent statement.

Perhaps McBarnet's example (from a Scottish court) is, procedurally, more typical:

McBarnet D., *Conviction* (1983) 98

In another case where a victim of assault failed at first to identify the knife then to give clear evidence on what had been said during the attack, both prosecutor and judge made it clear they had ways and means of eliciting the information required:

Prosecutor:	Did he say anything?
Witness:	He might have. I couldn't make it out exactly.
Prosecutor:	Have you always said that?
Witness:	Yes.
Prosecutor:	What did you say to the police?
Witness:	Oh aye, he said he was going to get me or something.
Prosecutor:	Was it not more specific? I'm going to be talking to the policeman you spoke to that night you know, so let us be clear on what you are telling the court.
Judge:	Now, Mr S., you have at the moment made two contradictory statements. [Reading] 'I couldn't make it out' and 'he was going to get me or something'. If I think you are prevaricating — do you know what prevaricating means?
Witness:	It means, eh, saying something . . .
Judge:	[interrupting] It means avoiding a question. Now if I get the impression you are prevaricating then, believe me, I have powers to use. If you are going to answer, answer truthfully.

The prosecutor resumes with the now largely intimidated witness:

Prosecutor:	Did you tell the policeman you were not 100 per cent sure or did you give him two clear sentences?
Witness:	(pause) Yes. He said he had a knife for me. He said he'd use it through my heart.

Where the witness does not change his or her evidence to accord with the pre-trial account and is adjudged hostile, under section 3 the party affected can first put the previous inconsistent statements to the witness.

[18] The procedure is discussed in *R. v. Maw* [1994] Crim.L.R. 841.
[19] *R. v. Darby* [1989] Crim.L.R. 817.

The witness can adopt them as their oral testimony. If he or she refuses to do this, these statements can be proved. However the witness might still adhere to the original testimony. What is the evidential status of the previous inconsistent statements?

In civil proceedings, they are evidence of the facts they contain. But in criminal cases, they merely reduce the credibility of the witness who made them. In *R. v. White*[20] witnesses gave statements to the police implicating the accused in a public order offence but gave different testimony in court. Confronted with the prior statement, the witness insisted the sworn evidence was the correct version. The judge admitted the previous inconsistent statements and told the jury that they had to decide which story to believe. The conviction was quashed since the prior statement could only be introduced as casting doubt on the witness' credibility. It was not evidence of the accused's guilt.

In *R. v. Golder*[21] the accused was charged with theft of a watch. At trial a witness repudiated a deposition that she had made before the committing magistrates and the judge directed the jury that they could convict on the basis of the deposition:

> . . . while previous statements may be put to an adverse witness to destroy his credit and thus to render his evidence given at the trial negligible, they are not admissible evidence of the truth of the facts stated therein . . . In the judgment of this court, when a witness is shown to have made previous statements inconsistent with the evidence given by that witness at the trial, the jury should not merely be directed that the evidence given at the trial should be regarded as unreliable; they should also be directed that the previous statements whether sworn or unsworn, do not constitute evidence upon which they can act.[22]

The judge may properly invite the jury to disregard the testimony of the witness but this need not be the case as, for example, where a witness treated as hostile gives a sensible explanation of why he or she had deviated from what they said in the witness statement.[23]

Cross-Examination

Cross-examination is that stage in the trial which involves the questioning of the witnesses called by the other party. It is also one of the central techniques of adversarial advocacy.[24] The objectives of cross-examination are:

- to elicit facts favourable to your case which have not emerged

[20] (1922) 17 Cr.App.R. 59.
[21] [1960] 3 All E.R. 457.
[22] *ibid.* at 459a–i, *per* Lord Parker C.J. — although this case must be read in the light of the Criminal Procedure and Investigations Act 1996, s.68 and Sched 2.
[23] *R. v. Goodway* [1993] 4 All E.R. 894.
[24] Stone M., *Cross-Examination in Criminal Trials* (1988).

- to challenge and undermine adverse evidence given by the witness on behalf of your opponent.

All witnesses are liable to cross-examination unless they have been called either by mistake or merely to produce a document. Cross-examination is normally by counsel although the accused can conduct the defence in person. The only exception to this is under section 34A of the Criminal Justice Act 1988[25] which ensures that a defendant, who is accused of a sexual or violent offence against a child, cannot cross-examine that child in person, although such a cross-examination can be conducted by counsel. Adult victims of sexual assault can still be cross-examined by their assailants.[26] All other witnesses are liable to cross-examination by any party to the case or their counsel. In *R. v. Hilton*[27] the accused gave evidence in his own defence which did not adversely affect the position of his co-accused. The judge refused permission for the counsel for the co-accused to cross-examine him:

R. v. Hilton [1971] 3 All E.R. 541 at 543f–544f, *per* Fenton Atkinson L.J.

. . . counsel for one of two or more co-accused has for many years past invariably been allowed to cross-examine a co-accused who has given evidence whether or not such evidence was in any way adverse to his client . . . We are all quite satisfied that the practice to allow such cross-examination is well established in our courts and that it is necessary for justice to be done. This can be illustrated as follows. A and B are charged with an offence and are separately represented. A gives evidence in his own defence, making no mention of B. B's counsel knows that there is in fact important evidence that A can give in B's favour. If he cannot elicit the matter in cross-examination, he has no right to call A to give evidence a second time as A is not a compellable witness and may be unwilling for a number of reasons to give evidence for a second time. Clear though we believe the established practice to be, it is true . . . that the only authority supporting the right to cross-examine in such cases consists of dicta in the House of Lords in *Murdoch v. Taylor*[28] . . . . We agree entirely with the statement of the South African judge, Harcourt J., in the case of *The State v. Langa*[29] . . . when he said: 'An accused ought, if a fair trial is what is aimed at, to be at liberty to cross-examine a co-accused or any witness (not called by him) who may not have inculpted him in any way in order to establish facts which may tend to support the alibi'.

Where a witness gives evidence-in-chief but becomes unavailable for cross-examination, for example, through illness, the judge has discretion as to whether to order a new trial. In *R. v. Stretton*[30] the trial was allowed to continue after the witness had collapsed in the witness box after three-and-

[25] Inserted by Criminal Justice Act 1991, s.55(7).
[26] For example, the case of Ralston Edwards who questioned his victim for three days: *The Times*, August 23, 1996.
[27] [1971] 3 All E.R. 541.
[28] [1965] 1 All E.R. 406.
[29] 1963 (4) S.A. 941 at 945.
[30] (1986) 86 Cr.App.R. 7.

a-half hours of cross-examination. There was medical evidence that the witness would not be available for a new trial and the judge gave a clear warning about how they were to approach their task. The Court of Appeal upheld the conviction. Similarly in *R. v. Wyatt*[31] a seven-year-old girl became distressed and it was not possible to continue the cross-examination. The jury was fairly directed on the little girl's evidence and the conviction upheld.

In cross-examining, counsel is not restricted to matters that have been covered in examination-in-chief but is constrained by relevance, whether to the facts in issue or the witness's credit. The questioner is also limited by the rules of evidence: questions cannot be put to a witness which would elicit inadmissible evidence. In *R. v. Treacy*[32] the prosecution sought to introduce a confession allegedly made by the accused as part of their evidence-in-chief. The confession was deemed inadmissible. When the accused testified, the prosecution sought to cross-examine him. on the contents of the confession as a statement inconsistent with present testimony under section 4 of the Criminal Procedure Act 1865:

> In our view, a statement made by a prisoner is either admissible or it is not admissible. If it is admissible, the proper course for the prosecution is to prove it, give it in evidence, let the statement if it is in writing be made an exhibit, so that everybody knows what it is and everybody can inquire into it and do what they think right about it. If it is not admissible, nothing more ought to be heard of it, and it is quite a mistake to think that a document can be made admissible in evidence which is otherwise inadmissible simply because it is put to a person in cross-examination[33]

This is not a rule that binds a co-accused. In *R. v. Rowson*[34] the defendant made a statement which was ruled inadmissible but which was material to the defence of his co-accused. The co-accused sought to cross-examine the defendant and the Court of Appeal held that the exercise of judicial discretion should not be allowed to fetter a defendant in seeking to extract, by cross-examination, evidence of assistance to his own defence. But such examination goes to the defendant-witness's credibility and the jury must be warned about placing undue weight on it in considering the prosecution case.

In cross-examination, counsel is under a duty to challenge every part of the witness's testimony which runs counter to instructions, to put to the witness any allegations and any relevant matters. A failure to cross-examine any witness on any part of the testimony may be taken as an acceptance of that evidence.[35] In *Browne v. Dunn*,[36] witnesses in a libel matter were not

[31] [1990] Crim.L.R. 343.
[32] [1944] 2 All E.R. 229.
[33] *ibid.* at 236, *per* Humphreys J.
[34] [1985] 2 All E.R. 539.
[35] *R. v. Bircham* [1972] Crim.L.R. 430.
[36] (1894) 6 R. 67.

cross-examined on a relevant issue and it was held by the House of Lords that the jury could not be asked to disbelieve those witnesses:

Browne v. Dunn (1894) 6 R. 67, _per_ Lord Herschell L.C.

It seems to be absolutely essential to the proper conduct of a cause, that where it is intended to suggest that a witness is not speaking the truth on a particular point, to direct his attention to the fact by some questions put in cross-examination showing that the imputation is intended to be made, and not to take his evidence and pass it by as a matter altogether unchallenged, and then, when it is impossible for him to explain, as perhaps he might have been able to do if such questions had been put to him, the circumstances which it is suggested indicate that the story he tells ought not to be believed, to argue that he is a witness unworthy of credit . . .

Counsel may ask leading questions but this should not consist of questions such as "I suggest to you that . . .", "Do you ask the jury to believe that . . ." which are more in the nature of an invitation to argument than seeking answers to matters of fact. The true purpose of cross-examination is ". . . answers to questions of fact".[37]

It is the judge's duty to restrain unnecessary cross-examination. The Runciman Commission[38] revealed some concern about the treatment of witnesses and recommended that, in keeping with their wish to see judges take a more interventionist approach where necessary, judges should be particularly vigilant to check unfair and intimidatory cross-examination by counsel of witnesses who in the nature of the case are likely to be distressed or vulnerable. An example of this was seen in the case of Ralston Edwards[39] who subjected his rape victim to a series of very detailed and intimate questions over three days:

The Times, leader comment, August 23, 1996

A man who chooses to defend himself has a fool for his client — or so the lawyers like to say. Events this week in the Old Bailey demonstrate that folly can be the least of the iniquities when defendants dispense with professional representation. The decision by Ralston Edwards, convicted of rape yesterday, to conduct his own defence and cross-examine his victim forced a traumatised innocent woman through a second painful ordeal. There is understandable pressure to change the law to ensure that victims are protected from a repetition of these circumstances. It would be both dangerous and wrong if victims were deterred from coming forward by the prospect of such cross-examination and offenders thus remained at liberty.

Care must be taken, however, not to alter procedure in such a way as to deprive defendants of their historic and legitimate rights. The right of an accused man to speak in his own defence is entrenched in our legal tradition as indeed, until recently, was his right to remain silent and have no inference drawn. Debate in the past had concerned the right to representation . . . The idea that professional representation should move from being a right to a mandatory requirement in

[37] *R. v. Baldwin* (1925) 18 Cr.App.R. 175, *per* Lord Hewart at 178.
[38] Royal Commission on Criminal Justice: *Report* Cm. 2263 (1993), para. 8.43.
[39] *The Times*, August 23, 1996.

certain cases is a relatively recent innovation. Legislation passed in 1988 and amended in 1991 prevents the defendant cross-examining in person victims of violent offences under the age of 14 and victims of sexual offences under the age of 17. The ordeal inflicted by Ralston Edwards this week has inclined some to argue that women should be protected by the law which currently shields children.

It would be tempting, but probably wrong, to move quickly to change the law. There are other safeguards for victims which might wisely be deployed first, from screens in court to prevent eye-contact and more vigorous intervention from the judge to prevent questions which are gratuitous or irrelevant. It is already the case that the victim's previous sexual history should not be admitted as evidence. Judges should not feel they have to give those who defend themselves greater leeway because of their lack of legal knowledge if that freedom is abused to pursue a line of inquiry which is unnecessarily offensive or intimidatory.

Eroding the rights of defendants to choose how, and whom, to conduct their own defence, no matter how compelling the circumstances of any one case, could tilt the careful balance of the scales of justice. It is wrong in principle and could lead to unforeseen consequences in practice . . . There is a stronger case for reviewing the whole nature of the law on sexual offences. It is more than 20 years since the Heilbron Committee conducted the last such examination. Its efforts led to subsequent changes in the law which granted anonymity to rape victims and altered the rules of evidence. The Law Commission could, with profit, examine how victims might be better protected without damaging the position of defendants . . .

Counsel face judicial disapproval[40] and perhaps strong comment in the summing up where their conduct in cross-examination is challenged. For example, in *R. v. O'Neill*,[41] instructions were to challenge the police account of how the confessions came about, alleging assault on the defendants. In the event, the defendants exercised their right not to testify and thus the prosecution were not able to put their previous convictions to them under section 1(f)(ii) Criminal Evidence Act 1898. Lord Goddard commented:

> In this case a violent attack was made on the police. It was suggested that they had done improper things . . . The applicants had the opportunity of going into the box at the trial and explaining and supporting what they had instructed their counsel to say. They did not dare to go into the box and therefore counsel, who knew that they were not going into the box, ought not to have made these suggestions against the police . . . It is . . . entirely wrong to make such suggestions as were made in this case, namely that the police beat the prisoners until they made confessions, and then, when there is a chance for the prisoners to substantiate what has been said by going into the box, for counsel not to call them . . .[42]

Cross-examination: supporters and critics

Criticisms of cross-examination techniques and their effects in recent years have centred around the position of the child witness who has been

[40] Barristers are also subject to the *Code of Conduct for the Bar of England and Wales*.

[41] (1950) 34 Cr.App.R. 108.

[42] *ibid.* at 111, *per* Lord Goddard C.J. — with the benefit of forward vision and our knowledge of police conduct over the next 30 years, the court might have been more sympathetic to the defendants' dilemma.

sexually or physically abused.[43] But challenges to our system of questioning witnesses have a long history:

Anthony Trollope quoted in Frank J., *Courts on Trial* (1973) 83

One would naturally imagine that an undisturbed thread of clear evidence would be best obtained from a man whose position was made easy and whose mind was not harassed; but this is not the fact; to turn a witness to good account, he must be badgered this way and that till he is nearly mad; he must be made a laughing stock for the court; his very truths must be turned into falsehoods, so that he may be falsely shamed; he must be accused of all manner of villainy, threatened with all manner of punishment; he must be made to feel that he has no friend near him, that the world is all against him; he must be confounded till he forget his right hand from his left, till his mind is turned into chaos, and his heart into water; and then let him give his evidence. What will fall from his lips when in this wretched collapse must be of special value, for the best talents of practised forensic heroes are daily used to bring it about; and no member of the Humane Society interferes to protect the wretch. Some sorts of torture are as it were tacitly allowed even among humane people. Eels are skinned alive, and witnesses are sacrificed, and no one's blood curdles at the sight, no soft heart is sickened at the cruelty.

But cross-examination has powerful support. Indeed recently at least one civil law system has moved to a more adversarial system of trial,[44] trusting in Wigmore's view:

Wigmore, *Evidence* (revised ed., 1974) para. 1367

Not even the abuses, the mishandlings, and the puerilities which are so often associated with cross-examination have availed to nullify its value . . . It is beyond any doubt the greatest legal engine ever invented for the discovery of truth. However difficult it may be for the layman, the scientist, or the foreign jurist to appreciate its wonderful power, there has probably never been a moment's doubt upon this point in the mind of a lawyer of experience. He may, it is true, do more than he ought to do; he may "make the worse appear the better reason to perplex and dash maturest counsels" — may make the truth appear like falsehood. But this abuse of its power is able to be remedied by proper control. The fact of this unique and irresistible power remains, and is the reason for our faith in its merits . . . Cross-examination, not trial by jury, is the great and permanent contribution of the Anglo-American system of law to improved methods of trial procedure.

The major points of criticism of cross-examination as a technique are:[45]

(1) compared to other methods of eliciting testimony, cross-examination produces the largest number of errors, inducing greater

[43] Spencer J. and Flin J., *The Evidence of Children — The Law and Psychology* (2nd ed., 1993).
[44] Zander M., "From Inquisitorial to Adversarial — the Italian Experiment"(1991) 141 New L.J. 678.
[45] See Spencer J. and Flin J., *op. cit.* 270 *et seq.*

caution[46] without any gain in completeness.[47] Questions are not open-ended to enable witnesses to construct their own account, are frequently narrowly defined and take the witness along in small steps, permitting no deviation. Such deviation can be countered by warnings, repeating the question and demanding a proper answer. An alternative tactic is to present a comprehensive account ("I suggest to you that . . .") which obtains a blanket denial but provides little scope for countering on points of detail.

(2) distortion is also produced by putting leading questions to witnesses about peripheral matters ("What colour were his shoes?") and similarly confusion is induced by asking unconnected questions:

Brennan M. and R., *Strange Language* (1988) cited in Spencer J. and Flin J., *op. cit.* 274

In everyday interactions the unspoken conventions for changing topics of conversation are accepted. There is generally an obvious link between what has just been discussed and the new item of conversation on the agenda. It is common to hear people say '. . . speaking of such and such . . . did you read about . . . .have you seen . . .' If these cues are left out communication becomes disjointed and frustrated. Someone is inevitably left stranded by the privacy.

In court there is no provision within the language to establish these linkages. The cross-examiner jumps from topic to topic and the child witness is expected to keep pace. The juxtaposition of questions seems inexplicable as topics are jostled randomly. The effects of this are most critical when intimate details of the child's alleged sexual assault are questioned, and juxtaposed with general and more objective questions.

The technique of juxtaposing unrelated topics excludes the possibility of any transition time. Without this accommodation time, it is likely that the child will become disorientated, confused and unclear about the general line of questioning. The greater the frequency of these shifts from the personal to the objective, the greater the cumulative effect of the confusion will be.

(3) cross-examination is designed to put the witness in a state of stress, especially when in the course of testing the witness's sincerity, counsel is allowed to suggest that the witness is lying. This causes anger in adults and considerable distress in children.

The importance of putting the defence version of events to witnesses and to the court cannot be overstated. But that importance lies in procedural justice, the right of confrontation, and in preventing the evils that would

[46] Witness accounts under cross-examination are much more defensive than under direct examination, giving justifications for their conduct before they have been asked — see Atkinson M. and Drew P., *Order in Court* (1979) esp. Chap. 5 "Justifications and Excuses in Cross-examination".

[47] Greer D., "Anything but the Truth? The Reliability of Testimony in Criminal Trials" 11 Brit. Jour. Crim. 131 (1971); Luus E. and Wells G., "The Perceived Credibility of Child Eyewitnesses" in Dent H. and Flin R. (eds), *Children as Eyewitnesses* (1992).

follow from anonymous accusation. It can be argued that cross-examination and confrontation is not a means of getting to the truth:

Spencer J. and Flin J., *The Evidence of Children — The Law and Psychology* (2nd ed., 1993) 278–279

. . . when child witnesses are confronted with the defendant at a trial, quite often the effect is literally to scare them speechless. Of those who do succeed in giving evidence, many will be to some extent afraid, and . . . psychological research makes it plain that stress beyond a certain point makes it harder for witnesses to order their thoughts and produce accurate information from memory. Studies by Dent and Stephenson[48] shed some interesting light on the likely effect of confrontation on the accuracy of honest children's evidence. Children who had seen a workman enter their classroom were later asked to identify the man, some from a live parade, and others from slides. The children did significantly better from the slides than from the live parades, where a number showed significant signs of nervousness, and some refused to participate at all. Dent and Stephenson found a similar effect when the experiment was repeated using adults, but the effect of the suspect's presence was less marked . . .

If it is clear that confrontation makes it harder for honest witnesses to tell the truth, is there any validity in the common belief that it makes it more difficult for dishonest ones to lie? This could be so, at least in some cases. If a false accuser's conscience is already pricking, it is possible that the sight of the person he has wronged may give him the necessary psychological shove to return him to the path of righteousness. However we are unaware of any psychological research that suggests it is generally harder to tell unpleasant lies about someone in their presence than unpleasant truths. It may be that the notion that confrontation generally causes liars to retract is false; and if it is, psychology provides a possible explanation for the unfounded belief. Studies with mock juries have shown that people tend to think that confidence in a witness is a sure sign of truthfulness — although in fact it is anything but this. Confrontation will make many witnesses feel uncomfortable, and in this state they will seem unconfident. If lawyers and lay people are inclined to confuse confidence with truthfulness, the fact that confrontation makes some witnesses more unconfident than others might give rise to a false belief that confrontation enables the court to tell which witnesses are telling lies.

Previous inconsistent statements

Witnesses can be cross-examined on any relevant matter which either goes to the issue in front of the court or to the credibility of the witness. In particular prior statements which are inconsistent with the present testimony in chief can be put to the witness. Under the Criminal Procedure Act 1865:

4.—If a witness, upon cross-examination as to a former statement made by him relative to the subject matter of the indictment or proceeding, and inconsistent with his present testimony, does not distinctly admit that he has made such a statement, proof may be given that he did in fact make it; but before such proof can be given,

[48] Dent H. and Stephenson G., "Identification Evidence: Experimental Investigation of Factors Affecting the Reliability of Juvenile and Adult Witnesses" in Farrington D., Hawkins K. and Lloyd-Bostock S. (eds), *Psychology, Law and Legal Process* (1979).

the circumstances of the supposed statement, sufficient to designate the particular occasion, must be mentioned to the witness, and he must be asked whether or not he has made such statement.

It should be noted that:

(1) where a previous inconsistent statement made by the witness is proved, its evidentiary effect is on the credibility of the witness. It is not evidence of the facts contained.
(2) despite the name of the statute, this section applies to both criminal and civil proceedings. Nowadays in civil cases, previous inconsistent statements are admissible under section 1 of the Civil Evidence Act 1995 as evidence of their facts.[49]
(3) the section applies to all statements, however made and whether on oath or not.[50]
(4) where the statement is in writing, it is necessary to consider the provisions of section 5. As a result, section 4 is more apposite to oral statements.

Section 4 applies where the previous inconsistent statement relates to the subject matter of the proceeding. Where a witness' character is being questioned and he or she denies some discreditable act, does section 4 enable counsel to put to the witness a previous inconsistent statement admitting that act? Is character a matter "relative to the subject-matter of the indictment or proceeding"? The correct test of questions going only to credit was discussed in *R. v. Funderburk*[51] where the accused was charged with unlawful sexual intercourse with a 13-year-old girl. The girl and her mother had been lodgers with the defendant but had left after arguments. The defence was that the complainant was lying in support of her mother who bore the accused a grudge. The girl gave detailed accounts of sex with the defendant who sought to put to her in cross-examination that she had had sex with other men and that she was transposing those experiences to the appellant. The judge held that this was not material to the issue of whether she had had sex with the appellant. The Court of Appeal explored the relationship between questions in cross-examination which went to the witness's credibility and the function of section 4:

R. v. Funderburk [1990] 2 All E.R. 482 at 485h–491h, _per_ Henry J.

When one comes to cross-examination, questions in cross-examination equally have to be relevant to the issues before the court, and those issues of course include the credibility of the witness giving evidence as to those issues. But a practical

[49] However in civil proceedings, if such statements are adduced to attack the credibility of the witness, the provisions of the Criminal Procedure Act 1865, s.4 must be observed — Civil Evidence Act 1995, s.6(3)(b).
[50] *R. v. Hart* (1957) 42 Cr.App.R. 47.
[51] [1990] 2 All E.R. 482.

distinction must be drawn between questions going to an issue before the court and questions merely going either to the credibility of the witness or to facts that are merely collateral. Where questions go solely to the credibility of the witness or to collateral facts the general rule is that answers given to such questions are final and cannot be contradicted by rebutting evidence. this is because of the requirement to avoid multiplicity of issues in the overall interests of justice . . .

As far as the general test as to the limits of cross-examination as to credit, the *locus classicus* of that is to be found in Lawton J.'s judgment in *R. v. Sweet-Escott*.[52] There the witness was cross-examined as to his credit in relation to conviction 20 years ago. As a general test Lawton J., having found that the question should not have been allowed, said:

> What, then, is the principle upon which the judge should draw the line? It seems to me that it is this. Since the purpose of cross-examination as to credit is to show that the witness ought not to be believed on oath, the matters about which he is questioned must relate to his likely standing after cross-examination with the tribunal which is trying him or listening to his evidence.

. . . Was the trial judge right to apply the test set out in section 4 of that Act [dealing with the calling of evidence relating to the cross-examination] instead of the ordinary test set out in *R. v. Sweet-Escott* relating to questions going to the credibility of a witness? We see nothing in section 4 which would prevent a witness's previous statement inconsistent with his testimony before the judge being put to him to challenge his credibility even where the section did not allow the evidence of the making of the inconsistent statement to be given. So this court assumed in *R. v. Hart*[53]

The trial judge did not therefore have to go on to consider whether the 1865 Act would permit the disputed evidence to be called if the questions were put. In any event it would have been premature to do so before the reaction to such cross-examination were known and the application to call the disputed evidence made.

[Having considered the nature of the girl's evidence-in-chief] . . . it is submitted that this is not a challenge which goes merely to credit but that the disputed questions go directly to the issue and not merely to a collateral fact or, alternatively at least, in the words of section 4 of the 1865 Act, that her accounts of having lost her virginity on a previous occasion were statements 'inconsistent with [her] present testimony' made by her 'relative to the subject matter of the indictment'.

Questions on the victim's sexual history were not prohibited by the provisions of section 2 of the Sexual Offences (Amendment) Act 1976 which applies only in rape cases. In *Funderburk* the offence was unlawful sexual intercourse. But the court referred to *R. v. Viola*[54] and was concerned that the mischief which the 1976 statute sought to prevent should not be perpetuated in the context of other sexual offences and that courts should be concerned that cross-examination as to sexual history was not abused.

When the particular prior inconsistent statement is in writing, section 5 of the Criminal Procedure Act 1865 applies:

> 5.—A witness, may be cross-examined as to previous statements made by him in writing or reduced into writing relative to the subject matter of the indictment or

[52] (1971) 55 Cr.App.R. 316 at 320.
[53] (1957) 42 Cr.App.R. 47.
[54] [1982] 3 All E.R. 73.

proceeding, without such writing being shown to him; but if it is intended to contradict such witness by the writing, his attention must, before such contradictory proof can be given, be called to those parts of the writing which are to be used for the purpose of so contradicting him; provided always, that it shall be competent for the judge, at any time during the trial, to require the production of the writing for his inspection, and he may thereupon make such use of it for the purposes of the trial as he may think fit.

It should be noted that:

(1) as with section 4, where a previous inconsistent statement made by the witness in writing is proved, its evidentiary effect is on the credibility of the witness. It is not evidence of the facts contained.
(2) again in civil cases previous inconsistent statements in writing are admissible under section 1 of the Civil Evidence Act 1995 as evidence of their facts.[55]
(3) the writing does not initially need to be shown to the witness. If it is shown, it does not need to be put into evidence unless counsel wishes to use it to contradict a statement by the witness who by then will have had an opportunity to explain any contradiction. Counsel cannot state that the document does contradict the witness unless the document is put into evidence.[56]

Use of documents in cross-examination

There are two situations where documents may be used in cross-examination. The first is where the document emanates from the cross-examiner but has not been put into evidence. Where there is such a document, not made by the witness, and not admissible in evidence, counsel can ask the witness to look at it and whether he or she wishes to amend his or her answer.[57] If they accept the contents of the document, that becomes evidence. But the witness who refuses to accept those contents cannot be asked to read the document into evidence. In *R. v. Gillespie and Simpson*[58] the accused were charged with theft from the store of which they were employees. In cross-examining the accused, the prosecution handed them documents prepared by shopgirls which suggested that the defendants had accounted for less receipts than shown in these documents. The accused dissented from the contents but were still required to read them aloud and the judge referred to the documents in his summing up. The Court of Appeal regarded the documents as hearsay and their inadmissibility could not be avoided by putting them to the accused in cross-examination:

[55] However in civil proceedings, if such statements are adduced to attack the credibility of the witness, the provisions of s.4 of the Criminal Procedure Act 1865 must be observed — Civil Evidence Act 1995, s.6(3)(b).
[56] *R. v. Riley* (1866) 4 F&F 964.
[57] *R. v. Yousry* (1914) 11 Cr.App.R. 13 at 18, *per* Lord Coleridge.
[58] (1967) 51 Cr.App.R. 172.

> . . . if a document is produced to a witness and the witness is asked, 'Do you see what that document purports to record?' the witness may say 'I see it, I accept it as true' in which case the contents of the document become evidence; or he may say, 'I see what is there written, I do not accept it as true', whereupon that which is purported to be recorded in the document is not evidence against that person who has rejected the contents; it becomes what one might call non-evidence, the document itself being nothing but hearsay.[59]

The second situation is where the document does not emanate from the cross-examiner who calls on his adversary to produce it. The common law rule is that the cross-examiner is bound to put the document into evidence if required, even if it is otherwise inadmissible. In the divorce case of *Stroud v. Stroud*[60] the husband's counsel was cross-examining a doctor who was a witness for the wife. Counsel inspected medical reports by other doctors which were in the hands of the witness but which were inadmissible hearsay. The court held that documents were able to be put into evidence at the option of the wife. In civil proceedings, this rule is now obsolete as a result of the modern rules on discovery and the Civil Evidence Act 1995. There is no authority that it has ever been applied in a criminal case.

Cross-examination as to credit — finality of answers to collateral issues

Witnesses can be cross-examined on their credibility. This depends on the witness's knowledge of the facts, his or her disinterestedness, integrity and veracity. Counsel can explore their powers of perception and opportunities for observation, their reasons for remembering the incident and their quality of memory including, as we have seen, any prior inconsistent statements. The cross-examiner is also allowed to probe a witness's prejudices, prior disreputable conduct or criminal record and physical and mental disabilities. At all times counsel are expected to remain within the limits laid down by the Bar Council. The key is Sankey L.J.'s judgment in:

Hobbs v. C. T. Tinling & Co. Ltd [1929] 2 K.B. 1 at 50–51, *per* Sankey L.J.

The Court can always exercise its discretion to decide whether a question as to credit is one which the witness should be compelled to answer . . . In the exercise of its discretion the Court should have regard to the following considerations: (1) Such questions are proper if they are of such a nature that the truth of the imputation conveyed by them would seriously affect the opinion of the Court as to the credibility of the witness on the matter to which he testifies. (2) Such questions are improper if the imputation which they convey relates to matters so remote in time, or of such a character, that the truth of the imputation would not affect, or would affect in a slight degree, the opinion of the Court as to the credibility of the witness on the matter to which he testifies. (3) Such questions are improper if there

[59] *ibid.*
[60] [1963] 3 All E.R. 539.

is a great disproportion between the importance of the imputation made against the witness's character and the importance of his evidence.

This was explored further in *R. v. Edwards*,[61] a case involving the behaviour of police officers attached to the West Midlands Serious Crimes Squad.[62] A police witness can be cross-examined on any relevant convictions or disciplinary charges found against him. Should questions be permitted about complaints by members of the public, not yet adjudicated by the Police Complaints Authority, on discreditable conduct by officers of the same squad? Alternatively should questions be permitted on other cases in which the witness had given evidence which had resulted either in the acquittal of the defendant or the conviction being quashed on appeal? Lord Lane C.J. decided that it would not be proper to put questions to the witness on the subject of any outstanding criminal charges or PCA complaints. Nor could the witness be questioned about the allegedly discreditable conduct by other officers. But where previous acquittals or quashed convictions could be demonstrated to be based on disbelief in the police officer's testimony, it was proper that the jury were made aware of this fact. If the decision might mean no more than that the court or jury disbelieved some part of the prosecution case, it would not be proper to cross-examine the officer on this issue.[63]

There is thus a line to be drawn between those matters pertaining to credit which can be explored in cross-examination and those which cannot. There is another vital distinction between cross-examining on the facts relevant to issues which need to be decided in the case and cross-examining on facts that merely go to the witness's credit. These latter matters are known as collateral issues. This distinction between the issue in the case and matters collateral is difficult to draw but becomes important when counsel wants to introduce evidence in rebuttal of a witness's testimony. If the answers given concern the issues which the court has to decide, rebuttal is possible. But if it concerns a collateral issue, such as the credit of a witness, counsel is bound by the answer given by the witness and cannot call independent evidence to contradict. The rule is ". . . necessary to confine the ambit of the trial within its proper limits and to prevent the true issue from becoming submerged in a welter of detail."[64]

In *Att.-Gen. v. Hitchcock*,[65] the defendant was charged with unlawful use of a cistern. A witness testified that the cistern had been used. In cross-examination, the witness was asked and denied that he had been offered £20 by the Excise officers to testify to this effect. Was the witness bribed? Although this seems a central question, the defence were not permitted to contradict his denial by other independent evidence:

[61] [1991] 2 All E.R. 266.

[62] Kaye T., *Unsafe and Unsatisfactory* (1991) .

[63] *R. v. Thorne* (1977) 66 Cr.App.R. 6; *cf. R. v. Cooke* (1984) 84 Cr.App.R. 286.

[64] *Edwards supra* at 274c, *per* Lord Lane C.J.

[65] (1847) 1 Exch. 91.

Att.-Gen. v. Hitchcock (1847) 1 Exch. 91 at 99–101, *per* Pollock C.B.

. . . the test, whether an inquiry is collateral or not, is this: if the answer of a witness is a matter which you would be allowed on your part to prove in evidence — if it have such a connection with the issue, that you would be allowed to give it in evidence — then it is a matter on which you may contradict him. Or it may be as well put, or perhaps better, in the language of my Brother Alderson this morning, that, If you ask a witness whether he has not said so and so, and the matter he is supposed to have said would, if he had said it, contradict any other part of his testimony, then you may then call another witness to prove that he had said so . . . It must be connected with the issue as a matter capable of being distinctly given in evidence, or it must be so far connected with it as to be a matter which, if answered in a particular way, would would contradict part of the witness's testimony; and if it is neither the one or the other of these, it is collateral to, though in some sense it may be considered as connected with, the subject of the inquiry. A distinction should be observed between those matters which may be given in evidence by way of contradiction, as directly affecting the story of a witness touching the issue before the jury, and those matters which affect the motives, temper, character of the witness . . . It is certainly allowable to ask a witness in what manner he stands affected towards the opposite party in the cause, and whether he does not stand in such a relation to that person as is likely to affect him and prevent him from having an unprejudiced state of mind, and whether he has not used expressions importing that he would be revenged on some one, or that he would give such evidence as might dispose of the cause in one way or the other. If he denies that, you may give evidence as to what he has said, not with a view of having a direct effect on the issue, but to show what is the state of mind of that witness. But those cases, where you may show the condition of a witness, or his connection with either of the parties, are not to be confounded with other cases, where it is proposed to contradict a witness on some matter unconnected with the question at issue.

In this case it is admitted, that, with reference to the offering of a bribe, it could not originally have been proved that the offer of the bribe had been made to the witness to make a particular statement, the bribe not have been accepted by him. And the reason is, that it is totally irrelevant to the matter in issue, that some person should have thought fit to offer a bribe to the witness to give an untrue account of a transaction, and it is of no importance whatever, if that bribe was not accepted. It is no disparagement to a man that a bribe is offered to him . . .

Questions can be put to a witness which suggest that he or she may have been guilty of some discreditable behaviour. However, where those questions are irrelevant to any issue in the case, you cannot call other witnesses to contradict the answer given. This is the rule of the finality of answers to collateral issues.

This rule rests on our ability to distinguish between questions which go to the issue and questions which are collateral. This was considered in *R. v. Funderburk*[66] where the key question was whether the victim was still a virgin at the time of the alleged unlawful intercourse. Was this a collateral issue?:

R. v. Funderburk [1990] 2 All E.R. 482 at 491d–j, *per* Henry J.

We are disposed to agree with the editors of *Cross on Evidence*[67] that where the disputed issue is a sexual one between two persons in private the difference

[66] [1990] 2 All E.R. 482.
[67] (6th ed. 1985) 295.

between questions going to credit and questions going to the issue is reduced to vanishing point . . . The difficulty we have in applying that celebrated test (in *A.-G. v. Hitchcock*) is that it seems to us to be circular. If a fact is not collateral then clearly you can call evidence to contradict it, but the so-called test is silent on how you decide whether that fact is collateral. The utility of the test may lie in the fact that the answer is an instinctive one based on the prosecutor's and the court's sense of fair play rather than any philosophic or analytic process. Applying the test in argument before us, Morland J. put to counsel for the Crown the hypothetical question 'If the defence had medical evidence that this child was not a virgin before the date on which she gave her account of losing her virginity, would the defence be allowed to call such evidence?' On reflection, counsel accepted that they would be allowed to call such evidence, and we think that answer to the question not only right but inevitable. Otherwise there would be the danger that the jury would make their decision as to credit on an account of the original incident in which the most emotive, memorable and potentially persuasive fact was, to the knowledge of all in the case, false.

Zuckerman would also argue that this distinction between issue and credit is unfounded:

Zuckerman A., *The Principles of Criminal Evidence* (1989) 94 *et seq.*

Let us take the case in which the only issue is the offender's identity and the only evidence for the prosecution is W's testimony who claims to have observed the accused from thirty yards. The accused adduces evidence to show that W cannot see beyond ten yards. According to the rule we are discussing this evidence is inadmissible because it is only relevant to credit of the witness and to the issue of the commission of the offence. By contrast, if the accused calls evidence to show that he was a close friend of the victim, this evidence will be admissible because it is relevant to the issue; it makes it less probable that the accused would harm his friend. Yet the evidence of motive is far less significant in this case than W's ten-yard eyesight. It would not be irrational for the trier of fact both to believe that the accused was the victim's friend and to conclude that the accused committed an offence against the friend. But if the trier of fact believes that W could not have observed the offence, a conviction could not properly take place. It can hardly be maintained that evidence affecting credibility is as a general rule less important than evidence which impinges directly on the issue.

If our object is to arrive economically at factually correct conclusions, admissibility should depend on the degree to which evidence contributes towards this end. Since the distinction between relevance to credibility and relevance to issue does not reflect a divergence in probative force we should not allow it to govern admissibility.

The validity of the distinction between relevance to credibility and relevance to issue may be questioned at a more fundamental level. One fact is relevant to another when it renders the existence of the other more probable. The fact that the witness says: 'The man who committed the offence was the accused' is relevant because it renders more probable that the accused was the offender. However, W's testimony could have this effect only if it has some credibility. If the testimony has no credibility at all, for example, because it is the blabber of a madman, it is irrelevant. It follows that the connecting link between W's testimony and the conclusion based on it is credibility. In other words, the relevance of a witness's testimony is embedded in his credibility, actual or potential. Credibility is not something separate (a separate issue) which is somehow suspended between the witness's statement and the fact asserted therein. W's ten-yard eyesight does not pertain to something that is different from the relevance of W's testimony to the issue . . .

It is the probative weight of the collateral fact that is important. To what extent does the existence or non-existence of this fact affect a fact in issue? In *Hitchcock*, the mere fact that the witness was offered a bribe does not affect the probability that he observed the use of the cistern. However, if it was alleged that he accepted the bribe, that significantly affects those probabilities. In *Funderburk* the victim gave a compelling account of the loss of her virginity in the course of sex with the defendant. That fact made it more probable that the sex in fact took place. Evidence of her alleged sexual experience alters any assessment of that account and consequentially of the likelihood that intercourse, the central fact in issue, occurred. Rather than an artificial distinction between relevance to an issue or relevance to credibility, the test should be one that stresses probative weight and which allows the judge to decide whether the fact is one that renders the existence or non-existence of a fact in issue (or of a fact in itself relevant to a fact in issue) more or less probable. If the "collateral" fact materially affects those probabilities, not only should the question be asked but the party asking it should be permitted to adduce evidence in rebuttal.

Instead of developing such principles for the exercise of judicial discretion, the courts have created exceptions to the "finality rule" which permits evidence in rebuttal to be brought even on matters of credit:

(1) where a witness denies making a ***prior statement inconsistent with present testimony***. As has been discussed earlier, these can be proved under sections 4 and 5 of the Criminal Procedure Act 1865.
(2) where a witness ***denies previous convictions***,[68] these can be proved under section 6 of the Criminal Procedure Act 1865:

> 6.—A witness may be questioned as to whether he has been convicted of any felony or misdemeanour and upon being so questioned, if he either denies or does not admit the fact or refuses to answer, it shall be lawful for the cross-examining party to prove such convictions . . .

Generally any conviction can be put to a witness, even those which are spent under the Rehabilitation of Offenders Act 1974.[69] As discussed earlier, the judge does retain some control over the attacks that can be made on a witness's credibility.[70] Defendants who testify are normally protected from having their previous convictions revealed under section 1(f) of the Criminal Evidence Act 1898. However it must be remembered that defendants who choose to testify, put their own character at risk under section 1(f)(ii) of the

[68] Convicted persons only became competent to testify after the Evidence Act 1843.
[69] s.7(2)(a).
[70] *Sweet-Escott supra.*

Criminal Evidence Act 1898, should they attack prosecution witnesses by exploring their criminal past.

(3) where a witness ***denies bias***. In *Thomas v. David*[71] the witness denied that she was the mistress of the party calling her and it was held that evidence in rebuttal could be adduced. Usually when the witness is related to the party, it is unnecessary to bring out the potential bias but in R. v. *Mendy*[72] the wife was charged with assault and the husband was due to give evidence on her behalf. As witnesses in criminal cases are kept out of court before testifying, the husband got a man to take notes of other testimony before he himself went into the box. He denied this but, despite the fact that no-one seriously disputed that it was a wholly collateral matter, the prosecution were permitted to introduce witnesses in rebuttal. Similarly in *R. v. Phillips*[73] a father was accused of sexual abuse of his young daughters. His defence was that they had been schooled by their mother, repeating what she had told them to say. The girls denied this and the father was denied the opportunity of calling witnesses who were to testify that the daughters had admitted lying in previous criminal proceedings against their father for indecent assault. Although, on appeal, these questions were said to go, not to the credibility of the daughters but to the foundation of the defence, they do reveal animosity against a particular defendant.

Bias can be more insidious — in *R. v. Busby*[74] defence counsel cross-examined police officers with a view to showing that the accused had not made certain incriminating remarks and that one of the officers had threatened a potential defence witness. The officers denied this and the defence were not permitted to question this witness whether he had been threatened by the police officer. The Court of Appeal quashed the conviction, agreeing on the difficulty of deciding whether a question relates to facts that are collateral only but suggesting that here, if the evidence were true, it would indicate that the policeman was prepared to go to improper lengths to secure a conviction. In *R. v. Edwards*[75] it was held that *Busby* was an example of witnesses who were biased against a particular defendant in a particular case and that the decision did not create a broader exception in relation to the police misconduct generally. In *Edwards* itself, for example, the officers were questioned about other trials in which they had testified and which had ended in acquittals or convictions being quashed because of doubts about the officers' veracity. Such questions were permitted as they went to the officers' credibility but:

[71] (1836) 7 C.&P. 350 .
[72] (1976) 64 Cr.App.R. 4.
[73] (1936) 26 Cr.App.R. 17.
[74] (1982) 75 Cr.App.R. 79.
[75] *supra* at 274d–j, *per* Lord Lane C.J.

R. v. *Edwards* [1991] 2 All E.R. 266 at 278g–h, *per* Lord Lane C.J.

. . . There was in each case a sufficient connection between the evidence given by the police officers and the eventual outcome of the trial to entitle the defence to cross-examine the officers concerned about these matters upon the question of their credibility in the instant case.

That leaves the second question, namely whether it would have been proper to allow the defence to call evidence to contradict any answers given by the police officers in cross-examination, in the unlikely event of those officers giving answers unfavourable to the defence. In our judgment this questioning would have been as to credit alone, that is to say on a collateral issue. It would not have fallen within any exception to the general rule.

(4) where a witness ***denies that he or she is suffering from a mental or physical disability***. In *Toohey v. Commissioner of Metropolitan Police*,[76] the defendants were charged with assault with intent to rob. The defendants argued that the victim had been drinking and that they were trying to get him home when he became hysterical, alleging the accused were attacking him. A doctor examined the victim soon afterwards but, although he was allowed to testify whether the victim was drunk or hysterical, he was not allowed to give evidence as to whether drink would exacerbate hysteria or whether the victim was more prone than normal to hysteria. The House of Lords held that this had been wrongly excluded:

***Toohey v. Commissioner of Metropolitan Police* [1965] A.C. 595 at 608b–e, *per* Lord Pearce**

Human evidence shares the frailties of those who give it. It is subject to many cross-currents such as partiality, prejudice, self-interest and, above all, imagination and inaccuracy. Those are matters with which the jury, helped by cross-examination and common sense, must do their best. But when a witness through physical (in which I include mental) disease or abnormality is not capable of giving a true or reliable account to the jury, it must surely be allowable for medical science to reveal this vital hidden fact to them. If a witness purported to give evidence of something which he believed that he had seen at a distance of 50 yards, it must surely be possible to call the evidence of an oculist to the effect that the witness could not possibly see anything at a greater distance than 20 yards, or the evidence of a surgeon who had removed a cataract from which the witness was suffering at the material time and which prevented him from seeing what he thought he saw. So, too, must it be allowable to call medical evidence of mental illness which makes a witness incapable of giving reliable evidence, whether through the existence of delusions or otherwise.

This decision demonstrates that a party can introduce medical evidence which casts doubt upon a witness's credibility where that evidence goes to an issue which is beyond the knowledge and

[76] [1965] A.C. 595.

competence of the jury.[77] On this point it may be compared with *R. v. MacKenney*[78] where the defence were prevented from leading evidence from medical experts who had watched the chief prosecution witness and had formed the opinion that he was a psychopath very likely to be lying. Where a witness is capable of telling the truth (but may not be doing so) is a matter within the competence of the jury.

(5) where a witness has a ***reputation for untruthfulness***. In *R. v. Brown and Hedley*[79] the defence sought to call evidence to prove that the court should not believe the prosecution witnesses. The Court for Crown Cases Reserved held that this evidence should have been received and that it had been the practice for centuries to show that the general reputation of a witness was such that he or she could not be believed on oath. In *R. v. Richardson and Longman*[80] the trial judge permitted a witness to testify about the veracity of a prosecution witness but in a restricted fashion, limiting questions to whether the witness was aware of the prosecution witness's reputation for truthfulness and whether he would believe her on oath.

***R. v. Richardson and Longman* (1968) 52 Cr.App.R. 317 at 323, *per* Edmund-Davies L.J.**

1. A witness may be asked whether he has knowledge of the impugned witness's general reputation for veracity and whether (from such knowledge) he would believe the impugned witness's sworn testimony. 2. The witness called to impeach the credibility of another witness may also express his individual opinion (based upon personal knowledge) as to whether the latter is to be believed upon his oath, and is not confined to giving an opinion based merely on general reputation. 3. But whether his opinion as to the impugned witness's credibility be based simply upon the latter's general reputation for veracity or upon his personal knowledge, the witness cannot be permitted to indicate during his examination-in-chief the particular facts, circumstances or incidents which formed the basis of his opinion, although he may be cross-examined as to them . . .

The impeaching witness cannot, in evidence-in-chief, give detailed reasons for his belief, although these may be brought out in cross-examination.

Re-Examination

After cross-examination, a witness may be re-examined by the party initially calling him or her. The witness can be asked to explain any part of the cross-examination or about any new facts which may have emerged:

[77] *R. v. Turner* [1975] 1 All E.R. 70; see Chap. 20.
[78] (1981) 72 Cr.App.R. 78; affirmed (1983) 76 Cr.App.R. 271.
[79] (1867) 36 L.J.M.C. 59.
[80] (1968) 52 Cr.App.R. 317.

> I think counsel has a right, on re-examination, to ask all questions which may be proper to draw forth an explanation of the sense and meaning of the expressions used by the witness on cross-examination, if they be in themselves doubtful and also of the motive by which the witness was induced to use those expressions; but I think he has no right to go further, and to introduce new matters not suited to the purpose of explaining either the expressions or the motives of the witness.[81]

The purpose of re-examination is to limit any damage done during cross-examination: it is not the repetition of the evidence given originally. Counsel can only raise new matters with the leave of the judge. Leading questions cannot be asked and documents only used to the same extent that they could be in examination-in-chief. However inadmissible evidence may have become admissible: for example, a previous consistent statement by a witness may have been rendered admissible by an allegation of recent fabrication.

[81] *Queen Caroline's Case* (1820) 2 Brod. Bing. 284 at 297, *per* Lord Tenterden; see *Prince v. Samo* (1838) 7 L.J.Q.B. 123.

12

THE TESTIMONY OF WITNESSES: VULNERABLE WITNESSES

VICTIMS AND WITNESSES

Royal Commission on Criminal Justice: *Report* Cm. 2263 (1993) para. 5.44

The evidence of victims and other witnesses is crucial to the criminal justice process because prosecutions will founder, and guilty people thus escape justice, if victims and other witnesses are not prepared to make statements to the police and thereafter to give evidence. It is important therefore that everything possible is done to support and, where necessary, protect witnesses in what is often and unenviable role. We received a great deal of evidence that for witnesses to give evidence in a criminal trial is a daunting (and sometimes even dangerous) task and one that many come to regret having undertaken.

The Runciman Commission recommended:[1]

(1) improved communication so that victims were kept informed of progress.
(2) ensuring that the CPS ascertain the views of the victim,[2] especially in relation to bail decisions.[3] Cases where women have been the victims of violence or rape need particular care.
(3) meetings between CPS lawyers and victims and key witnesses before the trial: this would entail the abolition of the rule prohibiting counsel from interviewing witnesses (other than their own client or an expert witness) before the trial.
(4) adequate facilities at the court: this would involve segregated waiting areas[4] as well as consideration of reasonable waiting periods and possible appointment systems.[5]

[1] *ibid.* paras. 5.44–5.52; 8.36–8.47.
[2] *Code for Crown Prosecutors* (1994) for the factors affecting victim which affect the decision to prosecute; also see Ashworth A., *The Criminal Process* (1994) 183 *et seq.*
[3] Ashworth, *ibid.* 208 *et seq.*
[4] Fenwick H., "Rights of Victims in the Criminal Justice System: Rhetoric or Reality?" [1995] Crim.L.R. 843 at 849.
[5] In one study, 37 per cent of witnesses were not heard on the scheduled day — Fenwick, *supra* at 850.

(5) development of witness support schemes in all Crown Court centres to prevent witness intimidation.
(6) restrictions on publicity by allowing the witness to hand over their address rather than having it read out in court
(7) greater use of section 23(3) of the Criminal Justice Act 1988 to enable the use of witness statements to replace the oral evidence of witnesses who are too frightened to testify
(8) greater vigilance by judges to prevent unfair and intimidatory cross-examination and, where allegations are made about the victim in pleas in mitigation, for the judge to prohibit reporting of unsupported slurs.[6]

This chapter will consider two categories of vulnerable witnesses, namely victims of sexual assault and children. Other groups include witnesses with learning difficulties[7] and defendants who testify in their own defence.[8]

Victims of Sexual Offences

The physical and mental suffering of the victim of rape or other sexual assault is extreme. It is an experience which needs to be understood by the court when assessing aspects of their evidence, especially when considering the inferences that may properly be drawn from the timing of the complaint, their ability to confront their alleged attacker and the law's apparent willingness to disbelieve the victim of rape to an extent that occurs nowhere else.

Waddle J. and Parts M., "Rape Trauma Syndrome" Univ of Chicago Legal Forum (1989) 399

Researchers have divided Rape Trauma Syndrome (RTS) into two phases. The first phase of RTS is known as the acute phase. It is marked by extreme fear. The victim sometimes openly expresses this fear and sometimes controls her observable reactions and appears calm. Physical symptoms can include skeletal muscle tensions, sleep disturbances, and gastrointestinal and genitourinary problems. The second phase of RTS often begins two to three weeks after the attack. This is the period when the victim attempts to reorganise her life. Women during this phase often develop specific fears connected with the events of the rape. For example, women who were raped in open spaces may develop a fear of the outdoors while those raped at home may develop a fear of indoors. These phobia are often accompanied by nightmares involving specific incidents of the rape. Many women move during this phase, change telephone numbers or take other steps to hide their identity. During the second phase of RTS, many women change their sexual behavior and attitudes.

[6] A judge can now prevent the reporting of derogatory assertions under sections 58–61 of the Criminal Procedure and Investigations Act 1996.
[7] The problems for such witnesses are discussed in Sanders A. *et al.* "Witnesses with Learning Disabilities" (Home Office Research and Statistics Directorate: Research Findings No. 44, December 1996).
[8] The position of the accused as witness is discussed in Chap. 15.

. . . RTS can only be induced through a non-consensual sexual incident. There is, however, a related syndrome, Post-traumatic Stress Disorder (PTSD), which can be provoked by a number of traumatic incidents. Rare, traumatic incidents which can trigger the disorder include earthquakes, airplane crashes or torture.

. . . In *Pittsburgh Action Against Rape*[9] Judge Larsen described the unique nature of the trauma suffered by rape victims:

> The depth and range of emotional and psychological disturbance is not felt by the victims of most other crimes. Trauma is the natural consequence of any violent crime. However, many of the symptoms of RTS will not be experienced with any degree of regularity by victims of non-rape crimes. Little anguish over the role the non-rape victim might have played is likely (except, perhaps, for a feeling that one might have been careless or gullible). Rarely is a robbery, or even assault, victim traumatized over possible contributory behavior. Certainly no social rebuke is forthcoming for the usual non-rape victim — society will not look askance at that victim . . .

Rape is an experience that ". . . shakes the foundations of the lives of the victims. For many its effect is a long-term one, impairing their capacity for personal relationships, altering their behaviour and values and generating fear."[10] The legal system can only seek not to worsen this impact. However its record suggests that it fails to meet even this modest target: the investigation of the offence by the police has all too frequently turned into an investigation of the victim; in the courtroom, victims have had to confront their assailants, be subjected to cross-examination into the most intimate details of their lives and (until 1994) listen to the judge warn the jury that their word is not to be believed without independent supporting evidence.

Anonymity

The administration of justice should take place in open court and the accused has the right to see and know his or her accusers. Witnesses testify in the full glare of publicity. Few proceedings are heard *in camera*[11] and rarely are the press unable to report proceedings.[12] But judges at common law do have the power to grant anonymity to witnesses,[13] for example, in cases of blackmail victims, national security, police informants[14] or those who permit their premises to be used as police observation posts.[15] In *Att.-Gen. v. Leveller Magazine Ltd*[16] magistrates had allowed an army officer to

[9] 428 A2d 126.

[10] Young W., *Rape Study — A Discussion of Law and Practice* (1983) cited in Temkin J., *Rape and the Legal Process* (1987).

[11] One example is under Official Secrets Act 1920, s.8(4).

[12] Exceptions are the identification of children and young persons under the Children and Young Persons Act 1933, s.39 or committal proceedings, initially under the Criminal Justice Act 1967 but now the Magistrates' Courts Act 1980, s.8.

[13] For a recent general look at this topic, see Munday R. "Name Suppression" [1991] Crim.L.R. 680 and 753.

[14] *Rogers v. Home Secretary* [1973] A.C. 388.

[15] *R. v. Rankine* [1986] 2 All E.R. 566.

[16] [1979] 1 All E.R. 745.

be called "Colonel B." while testifying in committal proceedings for offences under the Official Secrets Acts. The defendant magazine published his name and were prosecuted for contempt of court:

> It is beyond doubt that a court has a wide inherent jurisdiction to control its own procedure. In certain circumstances it may decide to sit wholly or in part in camera. Or witnesses may be ordered to withdraw, 'lest they trim their evidence by hearing the evidence of others' (as Earl Loreburn put it in *Scott v. Scott*[17]). Or part of a criminal trial may be ordered to take place in the absence of the jury, such as during the hearing of legal submissions or during a 'trial within a trial' regarding the admissibility of an alleged confession. Or the court may direct that throughout the hearing in open court certain witnesses are to be referred to by letter or number only.[18]

But this common law power to grant anonymity is exercised only exceptionally. In *R. v. X., Y. and Z.*[19] Lord Lane said that, where there was a case for witholding the identity of a witness, the trial judge had a duty to see that justice was done, in the sense that the system operated fairly not only to the defendant but also to the prosecution and witnesses. Where a magistrate felt there was a real risk to the administration of justice because, for example, a witness feared for his or her safety if his or her identity were revealed, it was within the court's power not to disclose the identity. This balancing act has been affected by the passage of section 23(3) of the Criminal Justice Act 1988 which allows a court to admit the witness statement of a witness who is too frightened to give oral testimony. In such cases the defence would have no cross-examination at all and allowing the witness to testify behind a screen and/or to withhold his or her identity is a sensible compromise.

A measure of anonymity at large may be secured by a ruling that the name and address of a witness, although disclosed in court, should not be reported in the press. Within the courtroom, some protection may be achieved by use of a screen where the witness, although known to the accused, is unwilling to face him or her directly. The option of a television link is only available if the witness is outside the jurisdiction or is a child.[20] The use of screens is not restricted in this way. In *R. v. Lynch*[21] the 18-year-old victim of an indecent assault was sufficiently distressed for the judge to allow her to testify behind a screen and with a representative of Victim Support with her in the witness box. The Court of Appeal rejected the appellant's submission that this would have prejudiced the defendant in the eyes of the jury. The judge must warn the jury not to read anything into the use of the screens but the court saw little in the argument that screens were *per se* prejudicial to the accused.[22]

[17] [1913] A.C. 417 at 446.
[18] *Leveller Magazine supra* at 761a–c, *per* Lord Edmund-Davies — the appeal was allowed on other grounds.
[19] (1989) 91 Cr.App.R. 36.
[20] Criminal Justice Act 1988, s.32(1).
[21] [1993] Crim.L.R. 868.
[22] *R. v. Foster* [1995] Crim.L.R. 333.

A deeper intrusion into the right of confrontation involves not disclosing the identity of the witness at all. In *R. v. Watford Magistrates' Court ex parte Lenman*[23] a group of youths rampaged through a city centre, violently attacking people. The identities of the witnesses who identified the accused were withheld and at trial they were referred to by the names of colours, gave evidence behind screens and had their voices disguised. There is some risk of prejudice to the defence who were handicapped since they were restricted in cross-examination, unable to question the credibility of the witnesses, especially as to whether they had any personal animosity against the accused. In this case, this risk was minimised since there was ample supportive evidence. In *R. v. Taylor*[24] the Court of Appeal approved of the *Watford* decision and enumerated the factors to be considered in assessing the balance of fairness: were there real grounds for fear if the identity were disclosed? was the evidence sufficiently important to make it unfair on the prosecution to proceed without it? had the prosecution satisfied the court that the creditworthiness of the witness had been fully investigated? was the court satisfied that no undue prejudice was caused to the defendant?

This privilege was rarely, if ever, extended to complainants of rape. The problem facing the rape victim in particular was considered by the Heilbron Committee in 1975.[25] The insatiable desire of the press to report rape cases in full accentuated the problems for victims who might be subject to cross-examination on their past sexual history and find that this was blazoned across the tabloid press. The recommendations of the Heilbron Committee were partially implemented in section 4 of the Sexual Offences (Amendment) Act 1976. This provided anonymity for the victim but only after a person had been accused of rape. The structure set up by the 1976 Act was severely flawed.[26] The victim's anonymity only became protected from the moment of accusation: in 1986, in the Vicarage rape case, prior to the arrest of a number of accused, the press reported the site of the assault and photos of the victim which scarcely masked her identity. In 1988, section 158 of the Criminal Justice Act sought to improve this by protecting the victim's anonymity from the moment of allegation rather than accusation. Once the victim has reported the matter to the police, her identity should no longer be disclosed. Section 158(6) also met another criticism levelled at the 1976 legislation and removed the anonymity of the rape defendant. A further weakness was that the legislation excluded a whole range of forcible sexual acts which the law does not define as rape. In such cases, the victim's reluctance to report is often as great as in rape itself and the arguments for the victim's privacy are equally irresistible.[27]

[23] [1993] Crim.L.R. 388.

[24] [1995] Crim.L.R. 253.

[25] Advisory Group on the Law of Rape: *Report* Cmnd. 6352 (1975).

[26] The problems preceding the 1988 Criminal Justice Act and the 1992 Sexual Offences Act are cogently discussed in Temkin J. *op. cit.* 190–198.

[27] The Criminal Law Revision Committee argued against the extension of anonymity to such offences — Criminal Law Revision Committee 15th Report, *Sexual Offences* (Cmnd. 9213 1984) para. 2.92.

The Sexual Offences (Amendment) Act 1992 now extends the statutory anonymity of rape victims to other sexual offences. But we still readily accept the right of the press to publish the name and address and property lost of the burglary victim or of the victim of an ordinary, non-sexual assault.

Supportive testimony

English law does not normally require evidence from more than one source. However, as discussed earlier,[28] victims of sexual offences constituted an exception. Although juries were permitted to convict on the testimony of the victim, they were warned of the dangers of that course of conduct since such evidence could be unreliable. This was finally removed with the Criminal Justice and Public Order Act 1994:

32.—(1) Any requirement whereby at a trial on indictment it is obligatory for a court to give the jury a warning about convicting the accused on the uncorroborated evidence of a person merely because that person is —

(a) . . . or
(b) where the offence charged us a sexual offence, the person in respect of whom it is alleged to have been committed

is hereby abrogated.

The retreat from the technicalities of corroboration continues. Although judges will still need to warn juries about the testimony of suspect witnesses, such warnings will be framed in non-technical terms, using phrases such as "supportive evidence" rather than "corroboration". Such warnings will not automatically be delivered just because the trial involves a sexual offence. The fact that the witness falls into a particular category (child, victim of sexual assault or accomplice) will not necessarily trigger a warning. In:

R. v. Makanjuola [1995] 3 All E.R. 730 at 732g–j, *per* Lord Taylor

. . . The circumstances and evidence in criminal cases are infinitely variable and it is impossible to categorise how a judge should deal with them. But it is clear that to carry on giving 'discretionary' warnings generally and in the same terms as were previously obligatory would be contrary to the policy and purpose of the 1994 Act . Whether, as a matter of discretion, a judge should give any warning and if so its strength and terms must depend upon the content and manner of the witness's evidence, the circumstances of the case and the issues raised. The judge will often consider that no special warning is required at all. Where, however, the witness has been shown to be unreliable, he or she may consider it necessary to urge caution. In a more extreme case, if the witness is shown to have lied, to have made previous false complaints, or to bear the defendant some grudge, a stronger warning may be

[28] See 281, *et seq.*

thought appropriate and the judge may suggest it would be wise to look for some supporting material before acting on the impugned witness's evidence. We stress that these observations are merely illustrative of some, not all, of the factors which judges may take into account in measuring where a witness stands in the scale of reliability and what response they should make at that level in their directions to the jury. We also stress that judges are not required to conform to any formula . . .

Makanjuola rejects any notion that warnings that were, before 1994, a matter of law should now routinely become a matter of practice. Only where there is an evidential basis showing that any witness in whatever sort of case may be unreliable, the trial judge in his or her discretion may warn the jury. This will not be in terms of corroboration but may be a simple caution or may be stronger in that the judge may suggest that it would be wise to look for some supportive evidence.

Previous consistent statements

The rule against narrative is a prohibition on witnesses being asked about earlier oral or written statements that they have made which are consistent with current testimony. As discussed earlier,[29] one major exception to this rule has been that complaints made by the victim of a sexual assault soon after the attack are admissible in support of the victim's testimony.[30] Complaints were admitted as evidence since a strong inference might otherwise be drawn from a failure to complain and the fact of the complaint and its details can be given to rebut any such inference. The evidential effect of the admission of the previous consistent statement is on the credibility of the victim.[31] Although the complaint in itself is evidence of lack of consent, any details given in the complaint are not evidence of the facts. The key conditions for the complaint to be admitted are that it must be contemporaneous and spontaneous.[32] The rule applies to all sexual offences, including indecent assault on or rape of a male,[33] whether or not consent is in issue.

Although the admissibility of a complaint seems to favour the victim of sexual assault over victims of other crimes, there is the other side of the coin which suggests that an inference may be drawn from a failure to make such a complaint. To do so shows a lack of understanding about rape victims and of knowledge about the rape trauma syndrome, for many genuine rape victims fail to report rape to a third party, either immediately or at all.

[29] see 336, *et seq.*
[30] Temkin J., *op. cit.* 144ff.
[31] *R. v. Wallwork* (1958) 42 Cr.App.R. 153.
[32] *R. v. Osborne* [1905] 1 K.B. 551.
[33] *R. v. Camelleri* [1922] 2 K.B. 122.

Hearsay

However traumatised or intimidated, the victim of a sexual assault has physically to attend court to give oral evidence. The formal statement to the police is not admissible as evidence on the grounds that it is hearsay. There is one possibility to avoid a court appearance under the **Criminal Justice Act 1988**:

> s.23.—(1) . . . a statement made by a person in a document shall be admissible in criminal proceedings as evidence of any fact of which direct oral evidence by him would be admissible if —
>
> i) the requirements of one of the paragraphs of subsection (2) below are satisfied; or
> ii) the requirements of subsection (3) below are satisfied.
>
> (2) . . .
> (3) The requirements mentioned in subsection (1)(ii) above are —
>
> a) that the statement was made to a police officer or some other person charged with the duty of investigating offences or charging offenders; and
> b) that the person who made it does not give oral evidence through fear or because he is being kept out of the way.

This is discussed in more detail later.[34] Witness statements to the police are normally not admissible evidence, if the witness is available to testify. But it might be suggested that, even though the rape victim is available to testify, section 23(3) creates the possibility that her or his witness statement, although hearsay, can be used. This legislation was to deal with the general problem of intimidation of witnesses and allows statements to be admissible on the conditions that the statement was made to a person charged with investigating offences and that the maker of the statement is in fear or being kept "out of the way".

Obviously significant considerations of the balance of fairness arise here as the defendant is denied the right to cross-examine the victim. Equally the prosecution will be reluctant to lose the impact on the jury of the victim giving oral evidence. But confronting the alleged assailant in court will cause fear and may well cause the victim to withdraw. In such circumstances, section 23(3) is sufficiently widely drawn. It applies to any statement in a document which has been made in the course of a criminal investigation; there is no requirement that the accused has caused the fear or is keeping the witness out of the way; the "fear" is not necessarily

[34] See 566, *et seq.* — it should also be noted that under the Criminal Procedure and Investigations Act 1996, s.68 and Sched. 2, the victim's written statement given in evidence at the committal proceedings may be read as that person's evidence-in-chief at the trial proper. However, the victim would need to be available for cross-examination.

objective and based on reasonable grounds as long as it is genuine.[35] As such, it can operate as protection for the vulnerable witness, especially victims of sexual abuse and domestic violence.

Credibility and sexual history

Witnesses can be cross-examined on their credibility. Credibility does not refer solely to the witness's knowledge of the facts, his or her disinterestedness or integrity. Counsel is allowed to probe many aspects of the witness's character and prior conduct.[36] Particular problems arise within rape cases where victims have been freely cross-examined about their sexual history and where attempts to create rape shield laws have not been wholly effective.[37]

The common law rule was that the victim might be asked about sexual relationships with other men but that once an answer had been given, counsel had to accept it. This is the normal rule of finality of answers to collateral questions. In *R. v. Holmes*[38] the charge was indecent assault. The victim was asked whether she had had "connection" with another man. She denied it and the defence sought to call the man to rebut this. The judge disallowed the evidence and this was upheld in the Court for Crown Cases Reserved:

R. v. Holmes (1871) 12 Cox C.C. 137 at 143, _per_ Kelly C.B.

> On the trial of an indictment for rape, or an attempt to commit a rape, or for an indecent assault, which in effect may amount to an attempt to commit a rape, if the prosecutrix is asked whether she has not had connection with some other man named, and she denies it, we are clearly of the opinion that that man cannot be called to contradict her. The general principle is, that when a witness is cross-examined as to a collateral fact, the answer must be taken for better or worse, and the witness cannot be contradicted as to that by a third person. If the proposed evidence were receivable, the prosecutrix might be cross-examined as to the whole history of her life . . . There is no doubt the prosecutrix may be asked as to connection with the prisoner on a prosecution for rape . . .

As Kelly C.B. says,[39] if the victim denies earlier sex with the defendant, this can be rebutted. There the fact has a direct bearing on the question before the court, which involves the fact of consent or non-consent on the part of the prosecutrix. In *R. v. Riley*[40] the victim denied ". . . *previous voluntary connection* . . ." and the trial judge rejected the prisoner's evidence in rebuttal:

[35] *R. v. Acton Justices ex p. McMullen* (1990) 92 Cr.App.R. 98.
[36] Within certain limits — *Hobbs v. C. T. Tinling & Co. Ltd* [1929] 2 K.B. 1; see Chaps. 11 and 13.
[37] Temkin J., *op. cit.* 119ff.; Temkin J., "Sexual History Evidence — the Ravishment of Section 2" [1993] Crim.L.R. 3.
[38] (1871) 12 Cox C.C. 137.
[39] *ibid.*
[40] (1887) 16 Cox C.C. 191.

R. v. Riley (1887) 16 Cox C.C. 191 at 194, *per* Lord Coleridge C.J.

It appears to me clear that that such evidence was admissible. Now, it has been held over and over again, that where evidence is denied by the prosecutrix with regard to acts of connection committed by her with persons other than the prisoner, she cannot be contradicted. The rejection of such evidence is founded on good common sense, not only because it would put very cruel hardship on a prosecutrix; but also on the ground that the evidence does not go to the point in issue . . .

. . . but to reject evidence as to the particular person is another matter. Because not only does it render it more likely that she would or would not have consented, but it is evidence which goes to the very point in issue.

In addition the defence could introduce evidence in rebuttal of the victim's prostitution[41] or of other sexual acts going on at the same time as the alleged rape.[42]

The problem nowadays arises because of the definition of rape. Obviously the key fact in issue will be the mental state of the victim — did she consent? But it is not enough simply to prove lack of consent. As a result of the House of Lords' decision in *DPP v. Morgan*,[43] it is also necessary to show that the accused did not believe that his victim was consenting. The Crown bears the legal burden of proof that the accused intended to have non-consensual sex with the victim. The defendant does not bear even an evidential burden and, regardless of any evidence, is entitled to a direction from the judge to the jury that they must be sure that he possessed such an intention. As soon as the legal issue is defined in that way, the victim's prior sexual history may provide a basis for the accused's beliefs about consent and thus become relevant. For example, in *R. v. Bashir*,[44] the defence was that the victim was a prostitute and, if the defendant knew this, there was a greater possibility that he believed that the victim was consenting.

But the border between relevance to the issues and a question of credibility is very fine. *Cross* has put it:

Tapper C., *Cross and Tapper on Evidence* (8th ed., 1995) 341

Evidence is often effectively limited to that of the parties, and much is likely to depend upon the balance of credibility between them. This has important effects for the law of evidence since it is capable of reducing the difference between questions going to credit and questions going to the issue to vanishing point. If the only issue is consent and the only witness is the complainant, the conclusion that the complainant is not worthy of credit must be decisive of the issue. The difficulties caused by these factors are also present in relation to much of the evidence used to resolve them. If it is sought to prove consent by evidence that the complainant is sexually promiscuous, it is likely to be just as difficult for the defence to rebut her

[41] *R. v. Barker* (1829) 3 C&P 589.
[42] *R. v. Turner* [1944] 1 All E.R. 599.
[43] [1976] A.C. 182.
[44] [1969] 3 All E.R. 692.

denials of such promiscuity as it is for the prosecution to prove that she did not consent on the occasion in issue.

Morgan makes it difficult to maintain the distinction between questions which go to a fact in issue as opposed to those which go merely to credibility. Were the defence to bear an evidential burden on the issue of consent, any questions on the victim's sexual history could only be relevant where the defence was that the accused believed the victim was consenting. To establish this, there would have to be some evidence that the defendant possessed that belief. This would require the accused to testify and if he fails to do so, is there any evidence on which a jury could find a reasonable doubt that such a belief existed? If the accused were to bear such a burden, it might be argued that questions on sexual history should be contingent upon the defendant testifying. To an extent, this position has been approached by the passage of sections 34 and 35 of the Criminal Justice and Public Order Act 1994 so that if the defendant has failed to mention the victim's consent when questioned by the police or fails to testify at the trial, the jury can be invited to draw the relevant inference.

Yet the central problem is perhaps not a legal one, it is the law's disbelief in women's testimony. Kathy Mack has put it:

Mack K., "Continuing Barriers to Women's Credibility: A Feminist Perspective on the Proof Process" 4 *Criminal Law Forum* 327 (1993)

In the area of sexual assault, the dominant story in the law has been that propounded by Hale more than two and a half centuries ago. Rape is "an accusation easy to be made and hard to be proved, and harder to be defended by the party accused, tho' never so innocent".[45] This commitment to women's lack of credibility when testifying about rape, based on no evidence and indeed in the face of contrary evidence, has consistently been expressed in legal rules, in jury instructions, in appellate opinions, and in law treatises. This dominant legal story appears in many forms, but at its heart lies the assumption that women lie when talking about rape. One commentator[46] has noted that the myth of the lying woman is the most powerful myth in the tradition of rape law.

Mack surveys general problems facing women as witnesses: many features of women's language are associated with powerlessness, such as superlatives, intensifiers, fillers, hedges and politeness markers; women tend to be more hesitant even when certain, unlike men who are more likely to speak confidently even when unsure or wrong. The trier of fact gives greater weight to those who use a more powerful style of speech. But when women testify about sexual assault, other features emerge:

Mack, *op. cit.* 332–335

In fact, the common law developed a set of rules specifically to attack the credibility of women testifying in rape cases; these rules related to the expectation of a recent

[45] Sir Matthew Hale, *The History of the Pleas of the Crown* (1736), 634.
[46] Estrich S., "Palm Beach Stories" 11 Law & Phil. 5 at 11 (1992).

complaint, the relevance of sexual history, the requirement (mainly in the United States) of force or other forms of resistance, and the need for corroboration. The corroboration rules pertaining to women alleging rape contrasted sharply with the usual common law rule that the jury were entitled to convict on the unsupported testimony of one witness. The corroboration rules in rape cases ranged from a demand for corroboration of every material fact essential to constitute the crime to a judicial warning that it was unsafe to convict on the basis of a woman's uncorroborated testimony about rape (the usual rule in the United Kingdom and Australia).

The explicit basis of such rules was a belief in the untrustworthiness of women in general and their allegations of rape in particular. The Law Commission, summarizing the law of England and Wales in 1991, stated that the judge must explain to the jury why it was dangerous to convict only on the uncorroborated evidence of the complainant. The reason commonly given related to the putative nature of women and girls. Perhaps the most widely quoted version of this view was that articulated by Lord Justice Salmon:

> [H]uman experience has shown that . . . girls and women [in these courts] do sometimes tell an entirely false story which is very easy to fabricate, but extremely difficult to refute. Such stories are fabricated for all sorts of reasons, which I need not now enumerate, and sometimes for no reason at all.[47]

Besides reasons related to the likelihood of falseness in the woman's story, including the alleged ease of making unfounded allegations (and the ease of fabricating corroboration!), judicial explanations for requiring corroboration outlined the difficulty for a man to refute a false charge of rape, the likelihood of jury sympathy for the victim, and more detailed observations about qualities alleged to be significant in female psychology — neurosis, jealousy, spite, fantasy, and shame.

But the law's bias toward women went deeper than merely assuming that they are malicious and mendacious. It also regarded women as particularly adept at concealing these qualities, thus the need to warn jurors, based on some notion of the 'law's vast experience' or 'history'.

Some commentators took their distrust of women to fantastic extremes. John Henry Wigmore recommended that no rape case should go forward unless the victim had a psychiatric examination . . .

To subject any witness, let alone the victim of a serious assault, to questioning about intimate details of their private lives is at the very least humiliating for them and a major blemish on any legal system. To a certain extent such cross-examination is now regulated by section 2 of the Sexual Offences Act 1976. This statute was the result of the recommendations of the Heilbron Committee which recognised that sexual experiences ". . . are neither indicative of untruthfulness nor of a general willingness to consent."[48]

2.—(1) If at a trial any person is for the time being charged with a rape offence to which he pleads not guilty, then, except with the leave of the judge, no evidence and no question in cross-examination shall be adduced or asked at the trial, by or on behalf of any defendant at the trial, about any sexual experience of a complainant with a person other than that defendant.

[47] *R. v. Henry* (1968) 53 Cr.App.R. 150.
[48] Advisory Group on the Law of Rape, *Report* Cmnd. 6352 (1975), para. 131.

(2) The judge shall not give leave in pursuance if the preceding subsection for any evidence or question except on an application made to him in the absence of the jury by or on behalf of a defendant; and on such an application the judge shall give leave if and only if he is satisfied that it would be unfair to the defendant to refuse to allow the evidence to be adduced or the question to be asked.

This permits such cross-examination only with the leave of the judge and he or she should allow this where it would otherwise be 'unfair' on the defendant. This is designed to act as a 'rape shield' and does not apply to the cross-examination of victims of other sexual assaults. However, in *R. v. Funderburk*,[49] a case of unlawful sexual intercourse, Henry J. felt that the common law should take note of section 2 and the decision in *R. v. Viola*[50] and stated that the mischief which the Act sought to prevent should not be perpetuated in other contexts and that the trial judges should seek to ensure that cross-examination is not abused or extended unnecessarily.

Apart from its restriction to rape, the section only applies to the cross-examination of the complainant in relation to her[51] sexual experiences with men other than the accused. The victim's experiences with the accused are regarded as relevant to his belief in her consent. The fallacy of this argument is exposed by the removal of spousal immunity in rape.[52] As it is now recognised that a husband can rape his wife, it becomes apparent that consent to sex at one period in a woman's life does not imply consent at the time of the alleged rape. Nor, by itself, should previous consent be sufficient to found a belief that the victim is consenting at that time.

In *Viola*, the alleged rape occurred at midnight. The judge refused leave to cross-examine the complainant about whether she had had sex with two men in her flat on the afternoon and evening before the assault, whether on the morning after the assault there was a man in the complainant's flat "wearing nothing except a pair of slippers" and finally whether she had sex with her boyfriend on the day after the incident:

R. v. Viola [1982] All E.R. 73 at 76a–77h, *per* Lord Lane C.J.

It is, we think, apparent from [s.2], without more, that the first question which the judge must ask himself is this: are the questions proposed to be put relevant according to the ordinary common law rules of evidence and relevant to the case as it is being put. If they are not so relevant, that is the end of the matter . . .

The second matter which the judge must consider is this. If the questions are relevant, then whether they should be allowed or not will of course depend on the terms of s.2, which limits the admissibility of relevant evidence. That section has been the subject of judicial consideration first of all by May J. in *R. v. Lawrence*.[53] A passage, which is taken verbatim from the transcript of his decisions, reads:

[49] [1990] 2 All E.R. 482 at 487e.
[50] [1982] 3 All E.R. 73.
[51] Although the victim of rape can now be a man — Criminal Justice and Public Order Act 1994, s.142.
[52] *R. v. R.* [1992] 4 All E.R. 481.
[53] [1977] Crim.L.R. 492.

> The important part of the statute which I think needs construction are the words 'if and only if he [the judge] is satisfied that it would be unfair to that defendant to refuse to allow the evidence to be adduced or the question to be asked'. And, in my judgment, before a judge is satisfied or may be said to be satisfied that to refuse to allow a particular question or series of questions in cross-examination would be unfair to a defendant he must take the view that it is more likely than not that the particular question or line of cross-examination, if allowed, might reasonably lead the jury, properly directed in the summing-up, to take a different view of the complainant's evidence from that which they might take if the question or series of questions was or were not allowed.

... when one considers the purpose which lay behind the passing of the 1976 Act . . . it is clear that it was aimed primarily at protecting complainants from cross-examination as to credit, from questions which went merely to credit and no more. The result is that generally speaking . . . if the proposed questions merely seek to establish that the complainant has had sexual experience with other men to whom she was not married, so as to suggest that for that reason she ought not to be believed under oath, the judge will exclude the evidence. In the present climate of opinion a jury is unlikely to be influenced by such considerations, nor should it be influenced. In other words questions of this sort going simply to credit will seldom be allowed . . .

On the other hand, if the questions are relevant to an issue in the trial in the light of the way the case is being run, for instance relevant to the issue of consent, as opposed merely to credit, they are likely to be admitted, because to exclude a relevant question on an issue in the trial as the trial is being run will usually mean that the jury are being prevented from hearing something which, if they did hear it, might cause them to change their minds about the evidence given by the complainant . . .

Invariably, in this situation, . . . there is a grey area which exists between the two types of relevance, namely relevance to credit and relevance to an issue in the case. On one hand evidence of sexual promiscuity may be so strong or so closely contemporaneous in time to the event in issue as to come near to, or indeed to reach the border between mere credit and an issue in the case. Conversely, the relevance of the evidence to an issue in the case may be so slight as to lead the judge to the conclusion that he is far from satisfied that the exclusion of the evidence or the question from the consideration of the jury would be unfair to the defendant.

The Court of Appeal quashed the conviction, considering, probably justifiably, that the unusual facts in this case could have led the jury to take a different view of the victim's evidence and that the questions should have been put.

But the trend of appellate decisions does not recognise the need to protect the rape victim in the witness box and the impact of the rape shield legislation has been less than its protagonists would have hoped. In a study into the operation of section 2, Adler studied rape trials at the Old Bailey.[54] In 40 per cent of the cases, applications under section 2 were received and over 75 per cent of these were successful. This willingness of trial judges to grant applications is apparently matched (and presumably influenced) by that of the Court of Appeal which has consistently allowed appeals where

[54] Adler Z., "Rape — The Intention of Parliament and the Practice of the Courts" (1982) 45 M.L.R. 664.

the relevance of the sexual history evidence is marginal. In *R. v. Cleland*[55] the complainant had had an abortion before the rape which she had not mentioned in her police statement and another one after (and attributable to) the rape. The defendant applied to cross-examine in respect of the two abortions and evidence that she had menstruated after the rape. This was refused by the judge but the Court of Appeal ordered a retrial. None of these matters could be said to be relevant to the issue of consent or the defendant's beliefs. One may infer from the earlier abortion that the victim is sexually experienced but is it unfair to the defendant not to be allowed to mention it when it goes to no issue in the trial? If the complainant was lying about the later abortion being attributable to the rape, would a jury take a different attitude about the complainant's account of the circumstances of the rape itself? The Court of Appeal felt that it would and that this was a matter ". . . going to the heart of the complainants' credibility . . ."

The key issue is relevance: if the evidence is of negligible probative value, the cross-examination is unfair in compelling a vulnerable witness to submit intimate details to public gaze. If the evidence is directly relevant to an issue, it would be unfair on the defendant not to have this brought to the attention of the jury. In *Funderburk* the young girl gave a graphic account of her loss of virginity which occurred during sex with the defendant. It was essential to the defence to bring out the fact of her prior sexual experience which cast substantial doubt on her testimony. In *Viola* a rape victim was allegedly having sex within 24 hours of the incident. Any jury would be disturbed to be denied such information. But in *R. v. Brown*[56] or in *R. v. Bogie*[57] the defence is permitted to introduce evidence and cross-examine on the complainant's general promiscuity. In *R. v. S.M.S.*[58] and *R. v. Said*[59] applications were permitted to cross-examine complainants who were both 14 years old on their sexual past in case the jury might make wrong assumptions about as to their virginity. Temkin, in discussing these cases, comments:

Temkin J., "Sexual History Evidence — the Ravishment of Section 2" [1993] Crim.L.R. 3 at 5–6

Is a woman's sexual past ever relevant to whether she consented to this particular man on the occasion in question? Heilbron considered that such evidence was scarcely ever relevant but it is clear that the Court of Appeal today does not share this view and neither do some academic writers. The problem is that relevance is an insufficiently objective criterion. As L'Heureux-Dube J. stated in the Supreme Court of Canada's decision in *Seaboyer*[60]:

[55] [1995] Crim.L.R. 742.
[56] (1989) 89 Cr.App.R. 97.
[57] [1992] Crim.L.R. 301.
[58] [1992] Crim.L.R. 310.
[59] [1992] Crim.L.R. 433.
[60] *R. v. Seaboyer*; *R. v. Gayme* 83 D.L.R. (4th) 193.

> Regardless of the definition used, the content of any relevancy decision will be filled by the particular judge's experience, common sense and/or logic . . . There are certain areas of enquiry where experience, common sense and logic are informed by stereotype and myth . . . This area of the law [*i.e.* sexual history evidence] has been particularly prone to the utilization of stereotype in determinations of relevance.

Notably lacking from the discourse in *Viola* and later cases is any discussion of what might be described as the degree of relevance needed to qualify for admissibility in this context. It has been pointed out that evidence 'must not merely be remotely relevant, but proximately so. Again it must not unnecessarily complicate the case, or too much tend to confuse, mislead or tire . . . the jury, or withdraw their attention too much from the real issues of the case.'[61] Relevance is, as Hoffman has explained, 'a variable standard, the probative value of the evidence being balanced against the disadvantages of receiving it such as taking up a lot of time or causing confusion'[62] or, it might be added, causing undue prejudice which is likely to impede rather than assist the search for truth. These issues, so very pertinent where sexual history is concerned, might be thought to have merited some judicial consideration.[63]

> In too many cases, evidence is introduced to play on the jury's prejudices even though it has no relevance to the case. Section 2 as currently drafted is only a limited shield. All too frequently, the real issue in a rape trial is the character of the complainant. Yet there is a considerable public interest in encouraging people to report sexual offences and to testify. Victims and witnesses have a right to the protection of their own personal dignity and privacy. This has been recognised to some extent with children who have been the victims of sexual abuse — they are permitted to testify through TV links[64] so that the witness does not have to confront the assailant; in addition there can be video-recordings of interviews[65] played in lieu of direct examination. But the adversarial quality of the normal rape trial gives such overwhelming priority to the right of the accused to make a full defence that other, equally compelling, public interests are overlooked.[66]

The accused's sexual history

What the experience of the complainant demonstrates is "the double standard of sexual morality in its most virulent form". The jury is told about the victim's sexual past and may well take a different view of her evidence as a result. But the same jurors are prevented from learning of the

[61] Thayer, *A Preliminary Treatise on Evidence at Common Law* (1898), 516.
[62] Hoffman L., "Similar Facts After *Boardman*" (1975) 91 L.Q.R. 193 at 205.
[63] See also Adler Z., "The Relevance of Sexual History Evidence in Rape: Problems of Subjective Interpretation" [1985] Crim.L.R. 769.
[64] Criminal Justice Act 1988, s.32.
[65] Criminal Justice Act 1988, s.32A (introduced by the Criminal Justice Act 1991, s.54) following the recommendations of the Pigot Committee: *Report of the Advisory Group on Video-Recorded Evidence* (1989).
[66] *e.g.* the short and discursive treatment of such issues by Runciman — Royal Commission on Criminal Justice: *op. cit.* para. 8.36 *et seq.*

defendant's past sexual misdemeanours because of the prejudice that may result. An analogous situation is in murder trials where, to the relatives' distress, the character of the victim is often the defence target. For example, the victim can be painted as unbalanced and violent while the accused's own record of physical assault can remain a secret from the jury.

There are potential methods of placing the accused's own previous misconduct before the court, none of which provide much assistance for prosecution or victim:

(1) if the defence introduces evidence of the accused's own good character, the prosecution would be permitted to adduce evidence in rebuttal.[67]
(2) if previous misconduct (including convictions) so resembles the current charge that there is a compelling inference that, if the accused committed the previous acts, he must also have committed these acts, the prosecution can adduce evidence of that earlier misconduct.[68] This is known as the "similar facts" rule.
(3) if the defendant testifies, he is usually shielded from being cross-examined about convictions and other prior disreputable conduct by section 1(f) of the Criminal Evidence Act 1898. That shield is lost, under section 1(f)(ii) of the Act, by the defence casting "imputations" onto the character of the prosecution witnesses.

At first glance this latter provision appears to protect the rape victim from being questioned about her sexual experience. "Imputations" would seem to cover allegations of promiscuity or inchastity. Even more encouragingly, cases decided under section 1(f)(ii) suggest that the defence loses the shield even where the imputation is a necessary part of the defence. In *Selvey v. DPP*[69], the accused was charged with buggery. There was medical evidence which supported the victim's complaint. Selvey's defence was that the complainant had already committed buggery with another man on the same day which accounted for the doctor's evidence. The accused testified that the complainant had offered himself to the accused and when he refused, he had planted indecent photographs on him. The trial judge allowed the prosecution to question the accused on previous convictions for soliciting for a lewd and immoral purpose. The House of Lords held that section 1(f)(ii) was applicable even where the casting of such imputations is necessary to establish the defence.

The analogy between *Selvey* and the cross-examination of the victim in a rape trial seems compelling. Bizarrely there is a special interpretation of the statute for rape cases. In *Selvey*, Viscount Dilhorne said:

[67] *R. v. Rowton* (1865) Le & Ca 520; see 418, *et seq.*
[68] *R. v. P* [1991] 3 All E.R. 337; see Chap. 14.
[69] [1970] A.C. 304.

In rape cases the accused can allege consent without placing himself in peril of such cross-examination (*R. v. Sheean*[70]; *R. v. Turner*[71]). This may be because such cases are sui generis (per Devlin J. in *R. v. Cook*[72]), or on the ground that the issue is one raised by the prosecution.[73]

Lord Pearce distinguished rape cases as follows:

Selvey v. DPP [1970] A.C. 304 at 353c–354f, _per_ Lord Pearce

The other view would limit the literal meaning of the words. For it cannot, it is said, have been intended by Parliament to make a man liable to have his previous convictions revealed whenever the essence of his defence necessitates imputations on the character of the prosecutor. This revelation is always damaging and often fatal to a defence. The high-water mark of this argument is the ordinary case of rape. In this the vital issue (as a rule) is whether the woman consented. Consent (as a rule) involves imputations on her character. Therefore, in the ordinary case of rape, the accused cannot defend himself without letting in his previous convictions. The same argument extends in varying lesser degrees to many cases.

. . . The second part of the argument in favour of a construction more liberal to the accused is concerned with the words 'the conduct or nature of the defence'. One should, it can be argued, read conduct or nature as something superimposed on the essence of the defence itself . . . This argument has obvious force, particularly in a case of rape, where the allegation of consent is in truth no more than a mere traverse of the essential ingredient which the Crown have to prove, namely, want of consent. But the argument does not, and I think cannot, fairly stop short of contending that all matters which are relevant to the crime, that is, of rebutting evidence could be proved, are excluded from the words 'conduct or nature of the defence'.

The ratio of *Selvey* should apply equally to rape cases as to any other offence. Where the defence is that the victim consented (or the accused believed that she did), this should mean that the accused opens himself to cross-examination on his own record. To hold that the accused in rape cases can allege consent without risking such cross-examination, although this exception is established beyond doubt in *R. v. Turner*,[74] is no longer tolerable. The defendant in a rape trial would suffer no greater hardship than defendants accused of other crimes if required to consider the consequences of a particular line of defence. It is an exception that has magnified the problems surrounding the cross-examination of the victim on her sexual history. Such problems might be well overcome by the simple abrogation of the *Turner* rule.

[70] (1908) 21 Cox C.C. 561.
[71] [1944] K.B. 463.
[72] [1959] 2 Q.B. 340 at 347.
[73] *Selvey supra* at 339e.
[74] [1944] K.B. 463.

CHILD WITNESSES[75]

The imperatives of the adversarial trial (the formality of the trial, testifying in person, the hearsay rule, cross-examination) have their greatest impact on children. This became a matter of public concern in the 1980s as public awareness of the sexual and physical abuse of children increased, especially in the wake of the Cleveland scandal.[76] As a result there has been considerable legislation about and significant improvements in the the treatment of child witnesses.

Competence and oaths

Historically there was considerable suspicion of the quality of children's evidence:

Heydon D., *Evidence* (1st ed., 1984) 84

First, a child's powers of observation and memory are less reliable than an adult's. Secondly, children are prone to live in a make-believe world, so that they magnify incidents which happen to them or invent them completely. Thirdly, they are also very egocentric, so that details seemingly unrelated to their own world are quickly forgotten by them. Fourthly, because of their immaturity they are very suggestible and can be easily be influenced by adults and other children. One lying child may influence others to lie; anxious parents may take a child through a story again and again so that it becomes drilled in untruths. Most dangerously, a policeman taking a statement from a child may without ill will use leading questions so that the child tends to confuse what actually happened with the answer suggested implicitly by the question. A fifth danger is that children often have little notion of the duty to speak the truth, and they may fail to realise how important their evidence is in a case and how important it is for it to be accurate. Finally, children sometimes behave in a way evil beyond their years. They may consent to sexual offences against themselves and then deny consent. They may completely invent sexual offences. Some children know that the adult world regards such matters in a serious and peculiar way, and they enjoy investigating this mystery or revenging themselves by making false accusations.

This litany of the weaknesses of children's testimony has come under critical scrutiny.[77]

(1) a child's memory is different from that of an adult but not necessarily less reliable. There appear to be age differences in terms of the quantity of information freely recalled but not in the terms of the quality. There is some evidence that younger children forget

[75] A resounding critique of the law's treatment of child witnesses is to be found in Spencer J. and Flin J., *The Evidence of Children — The Law and the Psychology* (2nd ed., 1993).
[76] Department of Health and Social Security, *Report of the Inquiry into Child Abuse in Cleveland*, Cm. 412 (1987) [the Butler-Sloss report].
[77] Spencer J. and Flin J., *op. cit.* Chap. 11 — the following discussion draws heavily on this invaluable review of the research.

information faster than older children. Spencer and Flin conclude that the reliability of children's evidence depends crucially on how they are questioned but that if that is done properly, their evidence should be evaluated like that of any other witness.

Spencer J. and Flin J., *The Evidence of Children* (2nd. ed. 1993) 292

There are cases where a child's descriptive information has proved crucial for the apprehension of an assailant. A ten-year-old girl who had been abducted and sexually assaulted while walking home from school in Banff was abandoned in a desolate moorland culvert where her head was smashed with a boulder until, as she told the police, 'she fell asleep'. From hospital and with the help of a female detective, she was not only able to describe the man but provided precise details of an oil rig motif printed on his sweatshirt which was immediately published. She also gave an accuarate description of the vinyl on the rear seat of the man's car which proved to be the vital clue. The police were amazed at the quality of the information she supplied and her attacker (who had no previous convictions) was arrested on a North Sea oil rig within a week of the assault.

(2) the egocentricity of children can be looked at in two ways: as a moral weakness and as a cognitive weakness. Research suggests that the ability to make simple inferences about how other people think and feel develops in children who are about four or five. It is unclear whether this affects their ability to be truthful about events. Cognitively it is suggested that children do not take account of events unconnected with their own world and this may limit the quantity of peripheral information about an incident that a young child may remember. But we all pay more attention to events that affect us!

(3) one perennial theme is that children are suggestible and can easily be led.

Spencer J. and Flin J., *op. cit.* 306

In certain circumstances it appears that young children are susceptible to leading questions because the child bows to the superior social status of the adult and submissively complies with any suggestions that the interviewer appears to make. This can happen because the child is unfamiliar with the social rules of a formal interview and, in an attempt to make sense of the situation, is very sensitive to the cues given by the adult (including the adult's non-verbal behaviour). The child's aim may be to please the adult or to terminate the interview as quickly as possible, or the children may simply believe that the adult has superior knowledge and therefore must be correct. In our society, children are taught that adults know best, not to contradict adults, to be polite to strangers and that it is wiser to hazard a guess rather than to admit ignorance. This powerful constellation of social rules can make children compliant in all but the most carefully conducted interviews.

There is some indications that children are more resistant to (mis)leading questions when the events have personal significance for them. However Spencer and Flin argue that the key again appears to lie in the interviewing techniques employed.

(4) tradition has it that a child's imagination is so intense that there is an inability to tell the difference between fact and fantasy. Fantasy plays an important part in children's lives but they grasp the distinction between imagination and reality:

Spencer J. and Flin J., *op. cit.* 317–318

There is certainly no psychological research or medical case study material which suggests that children are in the habit of fantasising about the sort of incidents that might result in court proceedings: for example, observing road accidents or being indecently assaulted. Children's fantasies and play are characterised by their daily experience and personal knowledge, and unusual fantasies are seen by psychiatrists as highly suspicious: 'The cognitive and imaginative capacities of three-year-olds do not enable them to describe anal intercourse and spitting out ejaculate, for instance. Such detailed descriptions from small children, in the absence of other factors, should be seen as stemming from the reality of the past abuse rather than from the imagination'.[78] As a rule, young children have a very limited knowledge of sexual behaviour.

(5) as with women accusation's of rape, much energy has been spent to prove that children also falsely accuse men of sexual assault. The proportion of false allegations is probably less than 10 per cent[79] and frequently the accusations originate with other adults. False allegations in sexual offences are probably no more than false allegations of burglary, car theft or criminal damage. It would be futile to try to compare the truthfulness of children as opposed to adults but as the Pigot Committee said:

> We understand, however, that contrary to the traditional view, recent research shows that untruthful child witnesses are comparatively uncommon and that, like their adult counterparts, they act out of identifiable motives.[80]

Many of these myths are beginning to be seen as myths. But the common law took a more restricted view of the competence of children as witnesses. Before 1991, the position was:

[78] Vizard E. et al., "Interviewing Sexually Abused Children" 11 *Adoption and Fostering* 20 at 24 (1987).
[79] *ibid.* — see Table 11.1 at 326.
[80] Pigot Committee: *Report of the Advisory Group on Video-Recorded Evidence* (1989), para. 2.24.

(a) sworn testimony: the old common law test[81] of competence was based on a child's capacity to take the oath. In *R. v. Brasier*[82] the question arose as to whether the evidence of a child under seven years old was admissible on a charge of assault with intent to commit rape. If a child possessed a sufficient knowledge of the nature and consequences of an oath, their evidence could be admitted but if they were found incompetent to take an oath, their evidence was inadmissible. It was a test that stressed the theological side of understanding the nature of the oath.[83] A more secular approach emerged in *R. v. Hayes*[84] where the trial judge questioned the witness, a boy of twelve, about his religious instruction at school, whether he had been told about God and whether he had heard of God. The Court of Appeal held that the child needed to have ". . . appreciation of the solemnity of the occasion and the added responsibility to tell the truth". This remains the common law test of competency to take the oath and still affects, for example, the mentally handicapped.[85]

(b) unsworn testimony: in criminal proceedings, children were allowed under section 38(1) of the Children and Young Persons Act 1933 to testify unsworn provided that they understood "the duty of speaking the truth". Whether sworn or unsworn the testimony of children attracted additional requirements either for corroboration or for a warning to the jury about the dangers of convicting on the uncorroborated evidence of a child.

Both the common law and statutory positions, which had refused to recognise that children were competent to act as witnesses on the same basis as adults, have now been changed. Since 1991, the position is:

(a) criminal proceedings: the position for child witnesses is now regulated by s.33A of the Criminal Justice Act 1988:[86]

> 33A.—(1) A child's evidence in criminal proceedings shall be given unsworn.
> (2) A deposition of a child's unsworn evidence may be taken for the purposes of criminal proceedings as if that evidence had been given on oath.
> (2A) A child's evidence shall be received unless it appears to the court that the child is incapable of intelligible testimony.
> (3) In this section 'child' means a person under fourteen years of age.

The competence of the very youngest children is now tested by whether they are ". . . capable of intelligible testimony". The presumption is that

[81] See 258, *et seq.* for further discussion.
[82] (1779) 1 Leach 199.
[83] For some entertaining accounts of the examination of child witnesses, Spencer J. and Flin J., *op. cit.* 51.
[84] [1977] 2 All E.R. 288.
[85] *R. v. Deakin* [1994] 4 All E.R. 769.
[86] This section was inserted by the Criminal Justice Act 1991, s.52(1); s.2A was inserted by the Criminal Justice and Public Order Act 1994, s.168(1) and Sched. 9, para. 33.

they are and the court is under no obligation to inquire into a witness's competence unless there is some reason to doubt it. When the judge does consider it necessary to investigate a child's competence, he or she should do so in open court in the presence of the accused but not necessarily in the presence of the jury. The older view (that such an examination should be in front of the jury) had its origin in *R. v. Reynolds*[87] but the competency test itself and the procedure to be adopted was considered by the Court of Appeal in *R. v. Hampshire*[88] who considered that the jury's function was to assess the child's evidence, including its weight, from the evidence he or she gives on the facts of the case after the child has been found competent to give it. The exercise of determining competence is not a necessary aid to that function and it was not a material irregularity for the jury not be present.

There is no minimum age at which a child's evidence is assumed not to be intelligible. Previously it has been asserted that children under six were not competent even to give unsworn evidence. This was based on *R. v. Wallwork*[89] when Lord Goddard suggested that the jury could not attach any value to the evidence of a child aged five. This was overturned in *R. v. Z.*[90] which involved a six year old giving evidence of sexual abuse by her father. Lord Lane C.J. put it:

R. *v.* Z. [1990] 2 All E.R. 971 at 973d–f, *per* Lord Lane C.J.

Those criteria will inevitably vary widely from child to child, and may indeed vary according the the circumstances of the case, the nature of the case, and the nature of the evidence which the child is called on to give. Obviously the younger the child the more care the judge must take before he allows the evidence to be received. But the statute lays down no minimum age, and the matter accordingly remains in the discretion of the judge in each case. It may be very rarely that a five-year-old will satisfy the requirements of [the statute].[91] But nevertheless the discretion remains to be exercised judicially by the judge according to the well-known criteria for the exercise of judicial discretion.

Older children under the age of fourteen now testify unsworn. There is no discretion in the court to allow them to take the oath.

(b) civil proceedings: prior to 1989, there were no provisions for allowing children to testify unsworn. In 1989, the position in the civil courts was brought into line with the (as then) existing position in criminal proceedings so that children could testify unsworn provided they met the criteria for competence of children laid down by the Children Act 1989:

[87] [1950] 1 All E.R. 335.
[88] [1995] 2 All E.R. 1019 — for further discussion, see Chap. 8.
[89] (1958) 42 Cr.App.R. 153.
[90] [1990] 2 All E.R. 971.
[91] Lord Lane was alluding to the Children and Young Persons Act 1933, s.38(1) but his comments apply equally to the Criminal Justice Act 1988, s.33A(2A).

96.—(1) Subsection (2) applies where a child who is called as a witness in any civil proceedings does not, in the opinion of the court, understand the nature of an oath.

(2) The child's evidence may be heard by the court if, in its opinion —

(a) he understands that it is his duty to speak the truth; and
(b) he has sufficient understanding to justify his evidence being heard.

Compellability

A competent witness is a compellable witness. A child's attendance can be ensured by a formal order — a subpoena or witness summons. Failure to attend or to testify once sworn may be punishable as contempt of court. Other tactics may be used: in *R. v. Thompson*,[92] the father was charged with incest and one daughter was treated as a hostile witness while the other was detained overnight so that the next morning she agreed to testify! Conversely the court has a residual discretion at common law which may be used to permit a child not to give evidence. How that was to be exercised was considered by the Court of Appeal in *R. v. B County Council ex parte P.*[93] A father accused (but not convicted) of sexual abuse of his stepchildren and children, contested care proceedings brought by the local council and sought to compel his eldest stepdaughter to attend to testify. Under section 97 of the Magistrates' Court Act 1980 magistrates have to issue a witness summons when the person is likely to be able to give material evidence. Although the stepdaughter clearly would give such evidence, the magistrates rejected the father's request for a witness summons and relied on her hearsay statement.[94] Butler-Sloss L.J. supported this approach:

R. v. B. County Council, ex parte P. [1991] 2 All E.R. 65 at 71d–g, *per* Butler-Sloss L.J.

Research has shown the adverse effects upon some children of the requirement to give evidence in cases of sexual abuse. In cases of young children, such harm may well be inferred (see the report of the Advisory Group on Video Evidence, December 1989 (chairman Judge Pigot QC)). The introduction of the 1990 order[95] clearly envisages an alternative to oral evidence and cross-examination and to make it possible for children making allegations of, inter alia, sexual abuse to do so without the additional stress of a court hearing. The philosophy behind the Children Act would be thwarted by the ability of the alleged abuser himself being able to require the attendance of the child at court. A court should be very cautious in requiring the attendance of a child in these cases, reinforced as it must be by considerations as to how to deal with a refusal to give evidence after the issue of the summons.

[92] (1977) 64 Cr.App.R. 96.
[93] [1991] 2 All E.R. 65.
[94] Under the Children (Admissibility of Hearsay) Order 1990 (S.I. 1990, No. 143).
[95] *ibid.*

In my view, reading section 97 as a whole, if the juvenile court considers at the time of the application for a summons that, for reasons of welfare of the child, the child should not be called as a witness, then it would be inappropriate to issue the summons.

This decision cannot necessarily be limited to youth or family courts. Lord Donaldson M.R. argued that the applicant for a witness summons under section 97 has a prima facie right for the summons to be issued but:

> . . . a summons should not be issued under the section requiring a child or young person to attend court with a view to giving evidence, if the magistrate is satisfied that service of such a summons would itself be so inimical to the welfare of that child or young person as to outweigh the legitimate interest of the person seeking the summons to secure that the child or young person does so attend court. This is the consequence of the obligation to have regard to the welfare of the child or young person which is imposed upon every court by section 44(1) Children and Young Persons Act 1933 . . .[96]

Section 44 reads:

44.—Every court in dealing with a child or young person who is brought before it, either as . . . an offender or otherwise, shall have regard to the welfare of the child or young person.

In *ex parte P*, although there was a subsidiary reason not to issue the summons (namely that the father had no real intent to call the stepdaughter to testify), the dicta on the court's residual discretion are clear. Such reasoning based on section 44 must apply to any hearing in front of any court. A child will not be a compellable witness if testifying would have adverse effects on the child which would outweigh any legitimate interest of the party seeking to call the child to testify. The impact of such a conclusion on that party is softened by the admission of hearsay evidence in civil proceedings under the Civil Evidence Act 1995. In criminal cases, a child's witness statement may be admissible under section 23 of the Criminal Justice Act 1988 but only if the child's mental condition meant that he or she was unable to attend as a witness (under section 23(2)) or was frightened to do so (under section 23(3)). But if the child's statement has been admitted as evidence in committal proceedings, it may also be received into evidence in the trial proper.[97]

Hearsay — committal hearings

One important factor in creating stress for witnesses is the need to repeat the details of the offence to a range of different professionals: a child might need to tell parents or teachers, the police, social workers. Even at court, it

[96] *ex parte P supra* at 75c–e.
[97] Criminal Procedure and Investigations Act 1996, s.68 and Sched. 2.

might be necessary to go through the story twice: for serious offences, there is the system of committal proceedings before magistrates who will decide whether to commit the accused for trial.

Originally this meant that a child would have to give evidence not once but twice. However in 1967, there was the introduction of short-form committals reduced that possibility. The introduction of the transfer for trial arrangements will reduce that possibility still further. This was introduced initially for a small range of sexual and violent offences under the Criminal Justice Act 1991:

> 53.—(1) If a person has been charged with an offence to which section 32(2) of the 1988 Act (sexual offences and offences involving violence or cruelty) and the Director of Public Prosecutions is of the opinion —
>
> (a) that the evidence of the offence would be sufficient for the person charged to be committed for trial;
> (b) that a child who is alleged —
>   (i) to be a person against whom the offence was committed; or
>   (ii) to have witnessed the commission of the offence,
>
> will be called as a witness at the trial; and
> (c) that, for the purpose of avoiding any prejudice to the welfare of the child, the case should be taken over and proceeded with without delay by the Crown Court,
>
> a notice ('notice of transfer') certifying that opinion may be [given] by or on behalf of the Director [to] the magistrates' court in whose jurisdiction the offence has been charged.
>
> (2) A notice of transfer shall be [given] before the magistrates' court begins to inquire into the case as examining justices.
>
> (3) On the [giving] of a notice of transfer the functions of the magistrates' court shall cease in relation to the case . . .

While committal proceedings still exist,[98] there will still be instances where oral evidence will be called for at a full hearing. From 1963 it has been possible to replace a child's oral testimony with a written statement. These provisions are now consolidated under section 103 of the Magistrates' Court Act 1980.[99] The result of section 103 is that, for a wide range of violent and sexual offences specified in subsection (2), there is no need for a child to testify twice and their evidence can be given in written form in committal proceedings, even in the face of defence objections.

But the Criminal Procedure and Investigations Act 1996 has now brought in sweeping changes with regard to committal proceedings, transforming them into an even more formal process. When the Act is fully

[98] Under the Criminal Justice and Public Order Act 1994, s.44 and Sched. 4, committal proceedings were to be abolished and replaced with "transfer for trial" procedures but these reforms have now been abandoned by the Criminal Procedure and Investigations Act 1996, s.44.

[99] This is discussed in Chap. 18.

brought into effect, even where there is a long form committal with consideration of the evidence, the justices are entitled to admit and consider written statements as the basis for the committal.[1] Witnesses only have to appear at committal proceedings where they will not voluntarily make a written statement.[2]

Hearsay — videotaping evidence-in-chief

Taking the evidence of children in advance of the trial itself has been another objective of reformers. The stress experienced by all witnesses is particularly acute for children, remembering the often lengthy periods between committal and trial, the strain of re-living the events, confrontation with the defendant and the ordeal of cross-examination.

Spencer J. and Flin J., *op. cit.* 371–375

First the formality of the questioning procedure is likely to be unusual and potentially threatening for the child who may never have been interviewed in this way before. Barristers are skilled at projecting their voices and may stand some distance from the child when speaking, thus requiring the child to raise her voice in reply. The child may not fully understand the purpose of the trial[3] and having told her story several times already, the point of repeating it yet again may be far from clear. The aim of the cross-examination may be even more obscure, particularly if the child is directly accused of dishonesty, by statements such as 'I put it to you that you are not telling the truth.' It is interesting to note that 'Telling the truth but no one believing me' is regarded by children as one of life's most stressful occurrences. Yet in child sexual abuse prosecutions this is likely to be the principal line of attack during cross-examination . . .

Secondly, both the semantics and syntax of the language used in the court are likely to be at best unfamiliar to a child and at worst totally incomprehensible. Legal terminology (your lordship, objection, learned friend, recess, adjourn etc.) has the effect of accentuating formality but may also serve to baffle a child witness . . .

This highly structured interrogation is often accompanied by repeated requests to amplify certain answers, which can prevent the child recounting a series of events in what she remembers as their natural order . . . these interviewing techniques are not only difficult for children to comprehend, but they also maximise the chances of contaminating the child's memory. The various linguistic and behavioural tactics which can be used to constrain a witness's evidence, particularly during cross-examination, are obviously of enormous advantage to the defence in their attempt to discredit a hostile witness. American lawyers actually advise a comprehensive range of strategies for the deliberate manipulation of children's testimony during cross-examination.

Thirdly, irrespective of the child's level of comprehension, the experience of being examined in court can cause stress and be physically exhausting . . .

For many witnesses, the experience of being cross-examined is traumatic and adult witnesses have described it as a frustrating, humiliating and distressing ordeal

[1] Criminal Procedure and Investigations Act 1996, Sched. 1, para. 3.

[2] Magistrates' Court Act 1980, s.97A as inserted by the Criminal Procedure and Investigations Act 1996, Sched. 1, para. 8.

[3] Lack of knowledge is a stress-inducing factor at all stages of the criminal justice process.

. . . If mature and socially experienced adults who comprehend the meaning and purpose of the judicial process, can find their experience in the witness box to be distressing, one can only conjecture what it might feel like for a small child to be interviewed in this fashion.[4]

The Pigot Committee[5] argued that children should not be required to appear in court and that their testimony should consist of a videotape of an out-of-court hearing with an initial interview by a trained examiner and the opportunity for the defence to cross-examine. The videotapes would replace both examination-in-chief and cross-examination at the trial.

The reform introduced was much more limited. The background was that video-recordings of diagnostic interviews with neglected, ill-treated or abused children were being increasingly used in the 1980s, especially in Great Ormond Street Hospital. In policing as well, multi-agency teams, involving not only police officers but also local social services departments, were established to investigate complaints of child sexual abuse. In 1988 a Home Office circular[6] recommended the spread of such schemes and the increased use of taped interviews.[7] The potential of these tapes as evidence was obvious and s.32A[8] of the Criminal Justice Act 1988, in certain circumstances, made video recordings of testimony from child witnesses receivable as evidence.

The alleged offence must come within the provisions of section 32(2), embracing a range of sexual or violent crimes similar to those in section 103 of the Magistrates' Court Act 1980 above. In such cases, the videotape record of an interview between an adult and a child[9] is admissible at the trial as the child's evidence-in-chief, with the leave of the court. The court will not give leave if, *inter alia*, the the child witness is not available for cross-examination. These provisions merely remove the need for the examination-in-chief of a child. The child is still open to cross-examination with all its attendant distress.

One of the major advantages of taping an interview is that it can be done soon after any incident is reported. The court will be presented with an accurate and full account of the child's statements before time and repetition distorts them. The tape itself will speak to whether coaching or manipulation of the witness has taken place. Before any trial, the accused can be confronted with the tape, which could not occur with the child. There is some evidence that this generates more guilty pleas.[10] The key disadvantage is that the interview can be unfairly conducted and will have

[4] See Morgan J. and Zedner L. *Child Victims* (1992) Chap. 6.

[5] Pigot Committee: *Report of the Advisory Group on Video-Recorded Evidence* (1989); McEwan J. "In the Box or on the Box? The Pigot Report and Child Witnesses" [1990] Crim.L.R. 363.

[6] No. 52 of 1988.

[7] For more detail on these developments, Spencer J. and Flin J., *op. cit.* 169 *et seq.*

[8] Inserted by Criminal Justice Act 1991, s.54 — for text and further discussion, see 586, *et seq.*

[9] The age limits are laid down in s.32A(7).

[10] Spencer J. and Flin J., *op. cit.* 197.

a prejudicial effect on the jury. Indeed in *R. v. Rawlings*[11] the Court of Appeal accepted that the trial judge had the discretion to replay the tape to the jury if they requested it after retiring to consider their verdict. The judge should warn the jury against giving disproportionate weight to the evidence-in-chief of the complainant and should remind them of the cross-examination from his notes. But to counter the claim of unfairness, the Home Office have issued guidelines for good practice.[12] Breach of these are not automatically a ground for quashing a conviction.[13]

In civil proceedings, section 96(3) of the Children Act 1989 empowered the Lord Chancellor to make provision for the reception of hearsay from children. This has now been done by statutory instrument:

> 2.—In —
>
> (a) civil proceedings before the High Court or a county court; and
> (b) (i) family proceedings, and
> (ii) civil proceedings under the Child Support Act 1991 in a magistrates' court,
>
> evidence given in connection with the upbringing, maintenance or welfare of a child shall be admissible notwithstanding any rule of law relating to hearsay.[14]

The weight which is to be attached to such evidence was considered by the Court of Appeal in *R. v. B County Council ex parte P.*[15] The magistrates had relied on a child's hearsay statement. But how was that statement, untested by cross-examination, to be regarded? Butler-Sloss approved the observations of Neill L.J. in *Re W.*[16]:

> . . . hearsay evidence is admissible as a matter of law, but . . . this evidence and the use to which it is put has to be handled with the greatest care and in such a way that, unless the interests of the child make it necessary, the rules of natural justice and the rights of the parents are fully and properly observed.
>
> A court presented with hearsay evidence has to look at it anxiously and consider carefully the extent to which it can properly be relied upon. It is clear from the passage from the judgment of the stipendiary magistrate . . . he has that consideration well in mind.[17]

Videotaped interviews would be freely admissible as evidence in civil proceedings as a result of section 1 of the Civil Evidence Act 1995.

Protection in cross-examination and video-links

Protection for the child on cross-examination is limited. As with victims of sexual assault, a child witness is allowed to have someone sitting beside

[11] [1995] 1 All E.R. 580.
[12] Memorandum of Good Practice on Video Recorded Inteviews with Child Witnesses for Criminal Proceedings (1992).
[13] *R. v. Dunphy* (1994) 98 Cr.App.R. 393.
[14] Children (Admissibility of Hearsay) Order 1993 (S.I. 1993. No. 621) — but possibly redundant as a result of Civil Evidence Act 1995, s.1.
[15] [1991] 2 All E.R. 65.
[16] [1990] 1 F.L.R. 203 at 227.
[17] *ex parte P supra* at 72h–j.

him or her in the witness box. In *R. v. Smith*[18] a social worker consoled the complainant, who was aged 12, when she broke down in tears during her testimony in a rape case. Such assistance is not a material irregularity, although the person should talk as little as possible. The judge should reduce the strain on child witnesses without prejudicing the interests of the defendant.

In addition the defendant should never cross-examine the child himself. This recommendation of the Pigot Committee[19] was put into force by section 57(1) of the Criminal Justice Act 1991, inserting section 34A into the Criminal Justice Act 1988:

> 34A.—(1) No person who is charged with an offence to which section 32(2) above applies shall cross-examine in person any witnesses who —
>
> (a) is alleged —
>   (i) to be a person against whom the offence was committed; or
>   (ii) to have witnessed the commission of the offence; and
>
> (b) is a child, or is to be cross-examined following the admission under s.32A above of a video recording of testimony from him.

This prohibition applies only to a range of violent and sexual offences similar to those in section 103 of the Magistrates' Court Act 1980 above and which the child witnessed or of which he or she was a victim.

Further stress factors for the child witness are the layout, formality and ceremony of the courtroom as well as the confrontation with the accused. The use of screens has been discussed earlier. In addition, live video links are possible under section 32 of the Criminal Justice Act 1988[20]:

> 32.—(1) A person other than the accused may give evidence through a live television link . . . if —
>
> (a) the witness is outside the United Kingdom; or
>
> (b) the witness is a child, or is to be cross-examined following the admission under section 32A below of a video recording of testimony from him, and the offence is one to which subsection (2) applies,
>
> but evidence may not be so given without the leave of the court

These provisions take away much of the distress from being physically in the courtroom while enabling the jury to judge the child's demeanour while giving evidence. A child no longer need be confronted by the alleged assailant. However this is restricted to a range of violent and sexual offences, detailed in subsection (2), similar to those in section 103 of the Magistrates' Court Act 1980 above. This restriction is difficult to understand since the rationale relates to the welfare of the child witness and this

18 [1994] Crim.L.R. 458.
19 *op. cit.* para. 12.30.
20 As amended by the Criminal Justice Act 1991.

might apply equally to a child who witnesses a car theft as to one who sees an assault.[21]

Supportive evidence

This issue is now of historical interest. Until the late 1980s, there were technical corroboration requirements surrounding children's testimony in criminal[22] proceedings:

(1) if the child gave evidence unsworn, corroboration was needed in the form of other independent evidence implicating the accused in a material particular. Without this corroborative evidence, there could be no conviction. If the accusation related to sexual abuse of a very young child, such evidence would rarely be available.
(2) if the child gave sworn testimony, corroborative evidence itself was not required but there had to be a corroboration warning. The jury had to be told of the dangers of convicting on the basis of uncorroborated evidence and would be pointed in the direction of any potentially corroborating material. Confusingly they were also told that, even if no corroboration was present, they could still convict.

This confusing state of the law has been clarified. As a result of section 52 of the Criminal Justice Act 1991, (which is incorporated in Criminal Justice Act 1988 as section 33A), a child under 14 testifies unsworn and there is no need to draw any distinction between two different categories of evidence. Furthermore:

(1) there is no statutory requirement for corroboration of unsworn testimony as section 38 of the Children and Young Persons Act 1933 has been repealed
(2) the common law requirement for a corroboration warning was removed by section 34(2) of the Criminal Justice Act 1988:

> 34.—(2) Any requirement whereby at a trial on indictment it is obligatory for the court to give the jury a warning about convicting the accused on the uncorroborated evidence of a child is abrogated [in relation to cases where such a warning is required by reason only that the evidence is the evidence of a child].

This provision meant that for some years, juries were still warned, not because the witness was a child, but because the child was the victim of a sexual assault. However the need for such warnings were

[21] For an evaluation of video links, see Spencer J. and Flin J., *op. cit.* 101 *et seq.*; Davies G. and Noon E., *An Evaluation of the Live Link for Child Witnesses* (1991).
[22] There are no requirements for civil proceedings.

dispensed with by section 32 of the Criminal Justice and Public Order Act 1994. This in turn meant that the words in brackets in section 34(2) were redundant and these are also repealed.

As a result of these changes, corroboration warnings are unlikely to be given in the case of a child witness. But judges will need to warn juries about the testimony of unreliable witnesses and these may include young children. The fact that the witness was a young child would not automatically mean that a warning would be given. There must be an evidential basis for believing the child to be unreliable. In addition any warning will be couched in non-technical terms, inviting the jury to look for "supportive evidence" and not "corroboration". The Court of Appeal has discussed these issues in relation to victims of sexual assault in *R. v. Makanjuola*.[23]

R. v. Makanjuola [1995] 3 All E.R. 730, per Lord Taylor

. . . Whether, as a matter of discretion, a judge should give any warning and if so its strength and terms must depend upon the content and manner of the witness's evidence, the circumstances of the case and the issues raised. The judge will often consider that no special warning is required at all. Where, however, the witness has been shown to be unreliable, he or she may consider it necessary to urge caution. In a more extreme case, if the witness is shown to have lied, to have made previous false complaints, or to bear the defendant some grudge, a stronger warning may be thought appropriate and the judge may suggest it would be wise to look for some supporting material before acting on the impugned witness's evidence . . .

Routine warnings about the dangers of convicting on a child's testimony should be a thing of the past.

[23] [1995] 3 All E.R. 730.

13

CHARACTER EVIDENCE

The Relevance of Character in Civil Proceedings

Issues of character would appear to have no place in a civil action. Whether a party is of unblemished reputation or has a criminal record would on first glance have no relevance to any issue that might arise. But such issues can emerge in three ways in the course of civil proceedings:

(a) character as a fact in issue:

Defamation is the most obvious example where the character of the plaintiff is a fact in issue. If the plaintiff is suing as a result of being accused of being a fraud, evidence of convictions for dishonesty would be admissible. Equally in *Cornwell v. Myskow*[1] the plaintiff, an actress, sued over newspaper comment about her ability and the quality of her performance in a show. Evidence of her ability and reputation at the time of the publication may be adduced by the plaintiff. Such evidence can also go to the quantum of damages. In *Scott v. Sampson*[2] the plaintiff, a journalist, sued after the defendant alleged that he had obtained money by threatening to publish damaging stories and had abused his position as a drama critic and journalist to extort money. The trial judge refused to receive evidence firstly of the plaintiff's character, secondly of rumours to the same effect as the alleged libel and thirdly of specific acts of misconduct:

Scott v. Sampson (1882) 8 Q.B.D. 491 at 503–505, *per* Cave J.

. . . it seems most material that the jury who have to award damages should know, if the fact is so, that he is a man of no reputation . . . To enable the jury to estimate the probable quantum of injury sustained, a knowledge of the party's previous character is not only material, but seems to be absolutely essential . . .

As to the second head of evidence, or evidence of rumours and suspicions to the same effect as the defamatory matter complained of, it would seem that upon principle such evidence is not admissible, as only indirectly tending to affect the

[1] [1987] 2 All E.R. 504.
[2] (1882) 8 Q.B.D. 491.

plaintiff's reputation. If these rumours and suspicions have, in fact, affected the plaintiff's reputation, that may be proved by general evidence of reputation. If they have not affected it, they are not relevant to the issue . . . . Unlike evidence of general reputation, it is particularly difficult for the plaintiff to meet and rebut such evidence; for all those who know him best can say is that they have not heard anything of these rumours. Moreover, it may be that it is the defendant who himself has started them . . .

As to the third head, or evidence of facts and circumstances tending to show the disposition of the plaintiff, both principle and authority seem equally against its admission. At the most it tends to prove not that the plaintiff has not, but that he ought not to have, a good reputation, and to admit evidence of this kind is, in effect, to throw upon the plaintiff the difficulty of showing a uniform propriety of conduct during his whole life . . .

(b) character as relevant to a fact in issue

Evidence of the character of the parties in civil proceedings is normally irrelevant. In *Att.-Gen. v. Bowman*,[3] there was a civil suit for keeping false weights. The defendant sought to adduce evidence of good character but this was deemed inadmissible as it was not relevant to the issue as to whether he had used false weights on this occasion. But where the prior acts are of such a nature that those acts possess some probative weight and tend to show that the defendant is more likely to have committed the act complained of, such evidence may be admissible under the similar fact rules.[4]

(c) character as to credit

Any witness in civil proceedings, whether a party to the proceedings or not, is liable to cross-examination as to credit. The party asking the question will normally be bound by the answer received as the rule about the finality of answers to collateral questions[5] applies (as do the exceptions to the rule):

Hobbs v. Tinling & Co Ltd [1929] 2 K.B. 1 at 18–19, *per* Scrutton L.J.

. . . When a witness has given evidence material to the issues . . . you can cross-examine him on matters not directly material to the case in order to ask the jury to infer from his answers that he is not worthy of belief, not a credible person, and therefore that they should not accept his answers on questions material to the case as true. This is cross-examination as to his credibility, commonly called cross-examination to credit. But as it is on matters not directly material to the case, the party cross-examining is not allowed to call evidence-in-chief to contradict his answers. To permit this would involve the court in an interminable series of controversies not directly material to the case on alleged facts of which the witness had no notice when he came into court, and which he or the party calling him

[3] (1791) 2 Bos & Pul. 532n.
[4] This is discussed in Chap. 14.
[5] See 343, *et seq.*

might not be prepared without notice to meet. This rule, which has been established by cases in which the party cross-examining has desired to call rebutting evidence-in-chief, has been expressed in various ways . . . But this does not go to the extent contended for by the appellant's counsel that the jury must believe the answers given by the witness. No case has been found where such a contention has been put forward, and if the jury, hearing the answers given by the witness, do not believe him they are entitled to do so, and to use the view thus obtained as to his credibility in rejecting answers given by him on matters material to the case. But rejecting his denials, does not prove the fact he denies, of which there is, and can be, no other evidence. It only destroys his credibility in respect of other evidence . . .

The Relevance of Character in Criminal Proceedings

Does the character of the defendant, whether churchgoer or sinner, help us as to whether he or she committed an offence? At first sight such information seems irrelevant: the fact that the accused has committed several previous burglaries does not make it more probable that he or she has committed the specific burglary with which he or she is now charged. On reflection, it has some, limited, relevance, as a defendant with such a record is more likely to have committed this offence than another person with no background in housebreaking. We still exclude any information about prior convictions and prior bad character, not because it is irrelevant, but more on the ground that it will prejudice the trier of fact and that such revelations before convictions are grossly unfair. This is the case in most common law jurisdictions. After sentence, of course, prior convictions are relevant to the issue of sentence.

If the rationale is one of fairness and not of irrelevance, this helps to acquit the common law of a charge of inconsistency. If prior bad character is irrelevant, so should prior good character. But the vicar charged with misappropriating the Sunday collection is allowed to introduce character witnesses as part of the defence and is entitled to a direction from the judge that this is not simply relevant to credibility but also to guilt.[6]

The truth is that character has some relevance (the persistent burglar is more likely to re-offend and the vicar less likely to steal) but bad character especially is accorded much more weight than that relevance warrants. As such its prejudicial effect outweighs its probative value and the jury, with little experience in assessing such matters, should be prevented from hearing about previous convictions. As far as good character is concerned, prejudice is not a problem and the evidence can be admitted, although judges frequently suggest that such testimony is of limited worth.

A brief review of the use of previous convictions in the rest of Europe shows considerable diversity:

[6] *R. v. Vye* [1993] 2 All E.R. 241.

Osner N., Quinn A. and Crown G., *Criminal Justice Systems in Other Jurisdictions* (Royal Commission on Criminal Justice, 1993)

Belgium:
Judges will have before them the accused's prior convictions. There are no specific rules about the admissibility of previous convictions. The dossier will contain the police record mentioning the previous convictions. The prosecutor may refer to them. It is up to the judge to determine the weight of this evidence.

Denmark:
The legal judge has the accused's previous convictions before him or her, but the lay judges and the jury do not. Prior convictions are generally only of relevance after conviction for sentencing. They are not normally admissible in evidence during the trial as evidence of guilt unless there is a striking similarity between the facts of the cases.

France:
The trial judges have before them during the trial the prior convictions, together with all the facts concerning the background and personal life history of the accused. All these facts are made known to the whole court before it reaches its judgment.

Germany:
The judges will have the accused's previous convictions before them during the trial. As a rule, prior convictions are only relevant in determining the scale of penalty.

Italy:
Trial judges must have before them prior convictions of the accused during the trial. They count as evidence of the accused's character, and are usable to ascertain his or her responsibility and to determine the sentence.

Netherlands:
The accused's criminal record will be in the dossier which the court will see. However, the record is relevant only when determining sentence and not guilt.

Spain:
Judges have the accused's prior convictions before them during trial, but they are generally only relevant in sentencing.

Sweden:
The court has access to the accused's prior convictions. If the offence is such that a sanction other than a fine can be expected or if special cause otherwise warrants, reference can be made during the hearing to the penalties to which the accused person has previously been sentenced.

Other jurisdictions use such information more freely not merely because they employ an investigative mode of trial but also because they place more emphasis on the professionally trained judge rather than on a lay jury. The latter are assumed to be more likely to pre-judge a case on the basis of an accused's prior convictions than the former.

But even during the common law trial, it has not been feasible to treat the biography of the accused as a blank sheet. Evidence relating to the accused's character can be admitted in several contexts:

(a) as part of the prosecution case:

- bad character which needs to be proved by the prosecution as an element of the offence
- prior offences which the prosecution alleges are evidence that the accused has committed the offence charged. Although the principle is that a person should only be tried for the crime charged, if a person has acted in a dramatically similar way previously, it can be argued that this tends to make it more likely that they have acted in the same manner this time. This is known as the "similar fact" rule. The prejudice aroused when a jury hears of previous crimes is considerable and there is a difficult juggling act for the judge who must decide whether the probative weight of the previous actions exceeds the prejudicial effect.[7]

(b) as part of prosecution rebuttal of the defence case:

- where the defence case contains evidence of good character suggesting that he or she is not the sort of person likely to commit such an offence, the prosecution might rebut this by adducing evidence of the defendant's bad character.

(c) as part of the defence case:

- good character as evidence for the defence that the accused is not the sort of person likely to commit such an offence.

(d) through cross-examination of the accused:

- if the accused decides to testify, the problem of previous discreditable acts arises again. A normal witness can be cross-examined as to credit. But this would be very prejudicial for the defendant. When the defendant was made a competent witness on his or her own behalf by the Criminal Evidence Act 1898, section 1(f) provided a shield which protected the accused from such questions. There are situations when that shield can be lost such as where the accused alleges good character, gives evidence against a fellow defendant or attacks the character of prosecution witnesses.[8]

The first and last of these are dealt with in succeeding chapters. This chapter considers the impact of evidence of the accused's good character and the ability of the prosecution to rebut this.

[7] See Chap. 14.
[8] See Chap. 15.

The accused's good character

A defendant can adduce evidence of his own good character, either by testifying himself or through witnesses. In *R. v. Rowton*, the defendant was charged with indecent assault and was permitted to introduce such evidence of good reputation:

R. v. Rowton (1865) 34 L.J.M.C. 57 at 60–61, *per* Cockburn C.J.

. . . Now, in determining this, it becomes necessary in the first instance, to consider what is the meaning of evidence of character. It is laid down in the books that a prisoner is entitled to give evidence as to his general character. What does that mean? Does it mean evidence as to his reputation amongst those to whom his conduct and position are known, or does it mean evidence of disposition? I think it means evidence of reputation only . . . No one ever heard of a question put deliberately to a witness called on behalf of a prisoner as to the prisoner's disposition of mind; the way, and the only way the law allows of your getting at the disposition and tendency of his mind, is by evidence as to his general character found upon the knowledge of those who know anything about him and his general conduct. Now, that is the sense in which I find the word "character" used and applied in all the books of the text-writers of authority upon the subject of evidence . . .

No one pretends that, according to the present practice, examination can be made as to a specific fact, though every one would agree that evidence of one fact of honesty or dishonesty, as the case might be, would weigh infinitely more than the opinions of a man's friends or neighbours as to his general character. The truth is, this part of our law is an anomaly. Although, logically speaking, it is quite clear that an antecedent bad character would form quite as reasonable a ground for the presumption and probability of guilt, as previous good character lays the foundation for the presumption of innocence, yet the prosecution cannot go into evidence as to the prisoner's bad character. The allowing evidence of a prisoner's good character to be given has grown from a desire to administer the law with mercy, as far as possible . . .

When we come to consider the question of what, in the strict interpretation of the law, is the limit of such evidence, I must say that, In my judgment, it must be restrained to this: the evidence must be of the man's general reputation, and not the individual opinion of the witness . . . The witness who acknowledged that he knew nothing of the general character, and had no opportunity of knowing it in the sense of reputation, would not be allowed to give an opinion as to a man's character in the more limited sense of his disposition.

The law still insists that in examination-in-chief a witness may only speak to general reputation. But this can just be the form of words in which the question is asked or answered. Opinions about individuals vary widely, there is no realistic way of assessing any generality of opinion and witnesses are often generalising from their own opinions. Testimony cannot extend to detailing specific creditable acts which at least would give some credibility to such an opinion. Nor can a witness be asked as to the accused's disposition, for example, whether or not he or she was a violent person who might be likely to commit the offence charged. But a witness to character can be cross-examined about particular matters.[9]

[9] *R. v. Winfield* [1939] 4 All E.R. 164.

In *R. v. Redgrave*,[10] the appellant was charged with persistently importuning for an immoral purpose contrary to section 32 of the Sexual Offences Act 1956. He sought to tender detailed evidence of documents and photos of his heterosexual relationships in order to rebut the inference from his conduct, as observed by police officers, that he had been making homosexual approaches. The judge ruled the evidence inadmissible. The appellant appealed on the ground, *inter alia*, that the judge had erred. It was held, dismissing the appeal, that an accused could call evidence to show that he did not commit the acts alleged against him but (save in special circumstances) he could not, by reference to particular facts, call evidence that he was of a particular disposition that made it unlikely that he had committed the offence. Although disposition to commit the kind of offence was relevant, the accused could go no further than to call evidence that by way of general reputation he was not the kind of young man who would behave in the way charged. It might seem hard that he could not call other evidence but it was in the public interest generally that evidence should be so limited.

In *Rowton*, Cockburn C.J. talked of ". . . a desire to administer the law with mercy, as far as possible . . .", suggesting that evidence of character and disposition are, at best, evidence going to the credibility of the accused's denials. Such evidence is seen as collateral, a side-issue to the focus of the court on the direct questions as to whether the accused committed the acts alleged. But how valid is this distinction between testimony going to the issues and testimony merely going to credibility?

Zuckerman A., *The Principles of Criminal Evidence* (1989) 94–95

. . . the justification of the present rule rests on the supposition that evidence which merely tends to discredit a witness makes, on the whole, insufficient probative contribution to warrant its reception.

. . . If our object is to arrive economically at factually correct conclusions, admissibility should depend on the degree to which evidence contributes towards this end. Since the distinction between relevance to credibility and relevance to issue does not reflect a divergence in probative force we should not allow it to govern admissibility.

The validity of the distinction between relevance to credibility and relevance to issue may also be questioned at a more fundamental level. One fact is relevant to another when it renders the existence of the other more probable. The fact that the witness says: 'The man who committed the offence was the accused' is relevant because it renders it more probable that the accused was the offender. However, W's testimony could have this effect only if it has some credibility. If the testimony has no credibility at all, for example, because it is the blabber of a madman, it is irrelevant. It follows that the connecting link between W's testimony and the conclusion based on it is credibility. In other words, the relevance of a witness's testimony is embedded in his credibility, actual or potential.

Such an analysis also goes to good character — specific acts and disposition such as Redgrave's sexual orientation can have probative force. Furthermore:

[10] (1981) 74 Cr.App.R. 10.

McEwan J., *Evidence and the Adversarial Process* (1991), 154–155

. . . it is nonsense to argue that evidence of heterosexuality, however established, has something to do with credibility on oath. Redgrave was not asking the court to believe what he said in the witness-box because he was really a heterosexual. He was suggesting that his sexual proclivities made it unlikely that he would approach men in a public lavatory. The fact is that 'character' evidence is a broad category, at times relating to honesty and at others to very different attributes. A defendant might suggest that he has a gentle disposition incompatible with the violent offences alleged. He might wish to establish lifelong patriotism in order to suggest that he would not betray his country. He might even argue that as a committed homosexual he is an unlikely rapist. None of these arguments has anything to do with credibility as a witness; whether or not he gives evidence has absolutely no effect on its relevance. The proper direction to the jury must therefore depend on the purpose for which the evidence is admitted, rather than some ex post facto categorization by the judge. It would be absurd . . . to demand that if the accused gives evidence of these matters he or she should do so by way of establishing his or her own reputation, and he or she should not be dependent on the generosity of judges to get it in. The Court of Appeal thought that Redgrave's trial judge 'might, as an indulgence', have allowed evidence of marriage or a relationship with one girl. It would be better simply to acknowledge, as Continental courts do, that it is irrational to try an individual without knowing what sort of person he or she is. The chop-logic characteristic of the cases on the significance of cross-examination on the accused's criminal record or general bad character proves this.

Not only is the accused permitted to introduce evidence of good character, he or she is also entitled to a direction as to the effect of that evidence.[11] The purpose of such testimony appears primarily to go to the credibility of the accused who has testified, giving his or her denials more weight.[12] However, whether or not the defendant has testified, he or she is entitled to a direction that good character is an indicator of innocence. In *R. v. Vye*,[13] the defendant appealed against a rape conviction on the grounds that the direction to the jury was inadequate. Lord Taylor said:

R. v. Vye [1993] 3 All E.R. 241 at 243h–248g, *per* Lord Taylor

. . . At one time these issues would not have been regarded even as arguable in this court.

The trial judge was understood to have a broad discretion to comment on the defendant's good character or not as he thought fit. The principle applied by this court was that the judge had no obligation to give directions on good character or even to remind the jury of it (see *R. v. Aberg*,[14] and *R. v. Smith*[15]).

Since about 1989, however, there has been a dramatic change. This court has been inundated with appeals based upon the judge's alleged misdirection or failure to give any direction to the jury about good character . . .

[11] *R. v. Berrada* (1989) 91 Cr.App.R. 131.
[12] In medieval England the accused could escape liability by such means through compurgation — producing sufficient neighbours to swear to your honesty and credibility.
[13] [1993] 3 All E.R. 241.
[14] [1948] 1 All E.R. 601.
[15] [1971] Crim.L.R. 531.

Before considering the authorities, it is helpful to say something of the historical background. The defendant was entitled to adduce evidence of his good character long before the law treated him as a competent witness in his own defence. Such evidence was allowed —

> 'to be submitted to the jury, to induce them to say whether they think it likely that a person with such a character would have committed the offence.' (See *R. v. Stannard*[16].)

Once the defendant became able to give evidence, a further consideration in regard to good character was introduced. Thus in *R. v. Bellis*[17] that consideration was encapsulated by Widgery J. as follows:

> 'Although there is . . . no formal or standard direction in these terms, this court does take the view that possession of a good character is primarily a matter which goes to credibility . . .

In *R. v. Bryant*[18] the defendant, a man of good character, elected not to give evidence. In his direction to the jury the judge appeared to suggest that good character was relevant only to credibility. In this court that approach was said to be 'too restrictive'. Good character was relevant 'primarily to the issue of credibility'. Nevertheless, juries 'should' be directed that it was capable of general significance of the kind suggested in the passage quoted from *R. v. Stannard* . . .

. . . in *R. v. Berrada*[19] this court considered, amongst other grounds, an alleged misdirection about good character. The defendant had given evidence. Waterhouse J. giving the judgment of the court, said:

> 'In the judgment of this Court, the appellant was entitled to have put to the jury from the judge herself a correct direction about the relevance of his previous good character to his credibility. This is a conventional direction and it is regrettable that it did not appear in the summing-up in this case. It would have been proper also (but was not obligatory) for the judge to refer to the fact that the previous good character of the appellant might be thought by them to be one relevant factor when they were considering whether he was the kind of man who was likely to have behaved in the way that the prosecution alleged . . . We have no doubt, however, that the modern practice is that, if good character is raised by a defendant, it should be dealt with in the summing-up. Moreover, when it is dealt with, the direction should be fair and balanced, stressing its relevance primarily to a defendant's credibility.'[20]

That decision, therefore, confirmed that, whatever the position may have been previously it is now an established principle that, where the defendant of good character has given evidence, it is no longer sufficient for the judge to comment in general terms. He is required to direct the jury about the relevance of good character to the credibility of the defendant. Conventionally this has come to be described as the 'first limb' of a character direction. The passage quoted also stated that the judge was entitled, but not obliged, to refer to the possible relevance of good character to the question whether the defendant was likely to have behaved as alleged by the Crown. That (in effect the *Stannard* direction) is the 'second limb'.

[16] (1837) 7 C&P 673 at 675.
[17] [1966] 1 All E.R. 552.
[18] [1978] 2 All E.R. 689.
[19] (1989) 91 Cr.App.R. 131.
[20] *ibid.* at 134.

Leaving aside cases involving more than one defendant where one is of good character and one is not, virtually all the numerous decisions since *R. v. Berrada* have reiterated that the first limb direction is necessary whenever the defendant has given evidence. This has been held to be so even when, on his own admission, he has told lies in interview with the police (see *R. v. Kabariti*[21]).

Accordingly, we turn to the three problems which seem presently to be unresolved on the authorities. They are (a) whether a 'first limb' direction needs to be given in a case where the defendant does not give evidence but has made statements to the police or others, (b) whether the 'second limb' direction should now be regarded as discretionary or obligatory and (c) what course the judge should take in a joint trial where one defendant is of good character but another is not.

(a) Defendant of good character not giving evidence

. . . In our judgment, when the defendant has not given evidence at trial but relies on exculpatory statements made to the police or others, the judge should direct the jury to have regard to the defendant's good character when considering the credibility of those statements. He will, of course, be entitled to make observations about the way the jury should approach such exculpatory statements in contrast to evidence given on oath (see *R. v. Duncan*[22]), but when the jury is considering the truthfulness of any such statements, it would be logical for them to take good character into account, just as they would in regard to a defendant's evidence.

Clearly if a defendant of good character does not give evidence and has given no pre-trial answers or statements, no issue as to his credibility arises and a first limb direction is not required.

(b) The 'second limb' direction

The relevant authorities as to the judge's duty with regard to the 'second limb' are confusing. On a number of occasions it has been said that the second limb direction is 'discretionary' or 'not obligatory'. This was expressly stated in the passage quoted from *R. v. Berrada* and also appears in *R. v. Thanki*[23] and *R. v. Bainbridge*.[24] Nevertheless, despite these repeated statements, in a number of recent cases this court has held omission of such a direction to be inappropriate . . . In *R. v. Marr*,[25] which concerned a relatively minor indecent assault on a woman in a public street in daylight, such a direction 'should have [been] mentioned'. In *R. v. Cohen*,[26] a case concerning serious dishonesty by a defendant aged over 60, this court said such a direction was 'not vital' but was 'in a case of this nature . . . appropriate'.

. . . we have been unable to discern any principle or consistent pattern as to when a second limb direction should be given and when it need not. Neither the nature of the crime, its gravity, the age of the defendant, whether he is merely of no previous convictions or of positively good character nor the nature of the defence would seem to have provided clear guidance . . .

. . . At one extreme there is the case of an employee who has been entrusted with large sums of money over many years by his employer and, having carried out his duties impeccably, is finally charged with stealing from the till. There a second limb

[21] (1990) 92 Cr.App.R. 362.
[22] (1981) 73 Cr.App.R. 359.
[23] (1990) 93 Cr.App.R. 12.
[24] (1991) 93 Cr.App.R. 32.
[25] (1989) 90 Cr.App.R. 154 at 157.
[26] (1990) 91 Cr.App.R. 125 at 131.

direction is obviously relevant and necessary. At the other extreme is a case such as *R. v. Richens*[27] where the defendant, charged with murder, admits manslaughter. It might be thought that in such a case a second limb direction would be little help to the jury . . .

. . . It cannot be satisfactory for uncertainty to persist so that judges do not known whether this court, proceeding on a case by case basis, will hold that a 'second limb' direction should or should not have been given. Our conclusion is that such a direction should be given where the defendant is of good character.

Does the need for a second limb direction still exist when the defendant has not given evidence? . . . We can see no logical ground for distinguishing . . . .between cases where the defendant has given evidence and cases where he has not.

Having stated the general rule, however, we recognise it must be for the trial judge in each case to decide how he tailors his direction to the particular circumstances. he would probably wish to indicate, as is commonly done, that good character cannot amount to a defence. In cases such as that of the long serving employee . . . he may wish to emphasise the 'second limb' direction more than in the average case. By contrast, he may wish in a case such as the murder/ manslaughter example given above, to stress the very limited help the jury may feel they can get from the absence of propensity to violence in the defendant's history. Provided the judge indicates to the jury the two respects in which good character may be relevant, *i.e.* credibility and propensity, this court will be slow to criticise any qualifying remarks he may make based on the facts of the individual case.

c) Two or more defendants of good and bad character

This situation clearly creates difficulties for the trial judge in summing up. Lord Lane C.J. in *R. v. Gibson*[28] put the matter thus:

> There may be very difficult problems facing a judge in dealing with cases of character where one of the participants in this sort of offence is of good character and the other is not, because by stressing the good character of the one he may be doing two things: first of all highlighting the bad character of the other and secondly, by reason of highlighting the bad character of the other, reflecting that bad character on to the good character of the first offender..
>
> It may be that when there are two defendants, one of good character and the other not of good character, it will be advisable for the judge to say very little, if anything, about the character of the defendant who has no previous convictions. If that is the judge's view, it will be prudent for him, in the absence of the jury, to indicate to counsel that that is what is in his mind, namely to make no reference about character at all, and to explain to counsel the reasons for it. That will enable counsel not only to address the judge on the point but also, if necessary, to make such reference to character as counsel may think fit in the case of his individual client in the course of his speech to the jury. It seems to us that that is the proper way in circumstances such as these, which may provide very great difficulty for the judge to balance fairness in respect of each of the defendants

. . . [this] suggestion . . . involves a number of undesirable features and possible results. First the defendant is entitled . . . to a direction from the judge in regard to his good character. For the direction to be left to counsel without indorsement by the judge would be to devalue that factor . . . Secondly, it cannot be desirable for

[27] [1993] 4 All E.R. 877.
[28] (1991) 93 Cr.App.R. 9 at 1 1–12.

the content of the summing up to be determined by whether counsel insists on a particular direction or not. It should be for the judge to decide what directions to give. Further should the jury seek directions . . . the judge could not abstain from assisting them . . . Again it would seem undesirable that there should be negotiations . . . over the content of the summing up . . .

. . . we conclude that the solution suggested in *Gibson* is not satisfactory . . . In our judgment a defendant of good character is entitled to have the judge direct the jury even if he is jointly tried with a defendant B of bad character. This leaves the question as to what, if anything, the judge should say about the latter. In some cases the judge may think it best to grasp the nettle in his summing up and tell the jury that they must try the case on the evidence, that there has been no evidence about B's character, that they must not speculate and must not take the absence of information as to B's character as evidence against B. In other cases the judge may, however, think it best to say nothing . . .

To summarise . . . 1) A direction as to the relevance of his good character to a defendant's credibility is to be given where he has testified or made pre-trial answers or statements. 2) A direction as to the relevance of his good character to the likelihood of his having committed the offence charged is to be given, whether or not he has testified, or made pre-trial answers or statements. 3) Where defendant A of good character is jointly charged with defendant B of bad character, 1) and 2) still apply.

But what constitutes "good character"? *Vye* is concerned with the scope of a judge's directions to the jury, not only when there is positive evidence of good character but also the usual case of the defendant with no previous convictions. The difficulties of applying these principles where there is positive evidence of misconduct is shown in *R. v. Aziz*[29] where the respondents were charged with evasion of income tax and VAT. At the trial the first defendant did not testify but relied on statements given to the investigating officers, in the course of which he made significant admissions but also exculpatory claims. The second and third defendants did testify, denying the offences charged but admitting previously making false mortgage applications, false tax returns and lying in interview. All three relied on their lack of previous convictions. The Court of Appeal certified the following question for the consideration of the House of Lords:

> Whether directions in accordance with *R. v. Vye* must be given in all cases in which a defendant has adduced evidence of previous good character, and if not, in what circumstances must such directions be given?

Lord Steyn responded:

R. v. Aziz [1995] 3 All E.R. 149 at 157j–158g, _per_ Lord Steyn

The certified question, although phrased in very general terms, was intended to raise the problem whether a defendant without any previous convictions may 'lose' his good character by reason of other criminal behaviour. It is a question which was not directly before the Court of Appeal in *R. v. Vye*. It is a complex problem. It is

[29] [1995] 3 All E.R. 149.

also an area in which generalisations are hazardous. Acknowledging that a wide spectrum of cases must be kept in mind, the problem can be illustrated with a commonplace example. A middle-aged man is charged with theft from his employers. He has no previous convictions. But during the trial it emerges, through cross-examination on behalf of a co-defendant, that the defendant has made dishonest claims on insurance companies over a number of years. What directions about good character, if any, must the judge give?

. . . A good starting point is that a judge should never be compelled to give meaningless or absurd directions. And cases occur from time to time where a defendant, who has no previous convictions, is shown beyond doubt to have been guilty of serious criminal behaviour similar to the offence charged in the indictment. A sensible criminal justice system should not compel a judge to go through the charade of giving directions in accordance with *R. v. Vye* in a case where the defendant's claim to good character is spurious. I would therefore hold that a trial judge has a residual discretion to decline to give any character directions in the case of a defendant without previous convictions if the judge considers it an insult to common sense to give directions in accordance with *R. v. Vye*. I am reinforced in thinking that this is the right conclusion by the fact that after *R. v. Vye* the Court of Appeal . . . ruled that such a residual discretion exists: see *R. v. H*[30] and *R. v. Zoppola-Barraza*.[31]

That brings me to the nature of the discretion. Discretions range from open-textured discretionary powers to narrowly circumscribed discretionary powers. The residual discretion of a trial judge to dispense with character directions in respect of a defendant of good character is of the more limited variety. Prima facie the directions must be given. And the judge will often be able to place a fair and balanced picture before the jury by giving directions in accordance with *R. v. Vye* and then adding words of qualification concerning other proved or possible criminal conduct of the defendant which emerged during the trial. On the other hand, if it would make no sense to give character directions in accordance with *R. v. Vye*, the judge may in his discretion dispense with them . . .

The accused's bad character

The prosecution are generally prohibited from mentioning the accused's bad character or prior convictions.[32]

> It is undoubtedly not competent for the prosecution to adduce evidence tending to show that the accused has been guilty of criminal acts other than those covered by the indictment, for the purpose of leading to the conclusion that the accused is a person likely from his criminal conduct or character to have committed the offence for which he is being tried.[33]

But this is not an absolute ban. Bad character might be brought out:

- when it is an element in the offence charged

[30] [1994] Crim.L.R. 205.
[31] [1994] Crim.L.R. 833.
[32] It can emerge by accident — Munday R., "Irregular Disclosure of Evidence of Bad Character" [1990] Crim.L.R. 92.
[33] *Makin v. Attorney-General for New South Wales* [1894] A.C. 57 at 65, *per* Lord Herschell.

- when the prosecution are entitled to rebut defence testimony about the accused's good character
- when previous criminal acts tend to show that the accused committed the offence charged[34]
- in cross-examination, when the accused has lost the "shield".[35]

The last two points are discussed in the following chapters.

(a) Bad Character as an Element of the Offence

Bad character, in the shape of a previous conviction, can be an element of another offence. In such circumstances, this conviction can be proved. Obvious example are the offence of driving while disqualified under section 103 of the Road Traffic Act 1988 or that of possessing firearms being a person sentenced to three years or more years imprisonment contrary to section 21 of the Firearms Act 1968. In pleas of *autrefois convict*, it may be the defendant who pleads the prior conviction.

(b) Rebuttal of "good character"

In *Rowton*, after the accused had put his own character into issue, the prosecution were able to call witnesses as to his reputation, one of which, when asked as to the defendant's general reputation for decency and morality of conduct, answered:

> I know nothing of the neighbourhood's opinion, because I was only a boy at school when I knew him; but my opinion, and the opinion of my brothers, who were also pupils of his, is that his character is that of a man capable of the grossest indecency and the most flagrant immorality.[36]

Was this admissible? Such evidence is restricted to reputation and not to specific discreditable acts. Cockburn C.J. held:

R. v. Rowton (1865) 34 L.J.M.C. 57 at 62, *per* Cockburn C.J.

. . . within what limits must the evidence be confined which is adduced in rebutting evidence to meet the evidence which the prisoner has brought forward? I think that that evidence must be of the same character and kept within the same limits: that while the prisoner can give evidence of general good character, so the evidence called to rebut it must be evidence of the same general description, showing that the evidence which has been given to establish a good reputation is not true, because the man's general reputation is bad.

. . . The witness, it seems, disclaims all knowledge as to the general reputation of the accused; what he says is this: 'I know nothing of the neighbourhood's opinion.'

[34] This is the similar fact rule discussed in Chap. 14.
[35] Cross-examination of the accused is discussed in Chap. 15.
[36] (1865) 34 L.J.M.C. 57 at 60.

I take the witness in this expression to mean to say, 'I know nothing of the opinion of those with whom the man has in the ordinary occupations of life been brought immediately into contact. I knew him, and so did two brothers of mine when we were at school, and in my opinion his disposition (for in that sense the word 'character' is used by the witness) — 'in my opinion his disposition is such that he is capable of committing the class of offences with which he is charged' I am strongly of opinion that that answer was not admissible in evidence . . .

The prosecution are only entitled to adduce rebutting evidence when the accused puts good character into issue by advancing evidence. In *R. v. Butterwasser*[37] the accused cross-examined the prosecution witnesses on their bad character. Lord Goddard C.J. held:

R. v. Butterwasser [1948] 1 K.B. 4 at 6–7, *per* Lord Goddard C.J.

When it became clear that the appellant's counsel, after having attacked the witnesses for the prosecution, was not going to call the appellant, the prosecution sought and were allowed to give evidence-in-chief of the prisoner's bad character. A police officer was called who testified to the prisoner's previous convictions and general character. In the opinion of the court, that was a course which cannot possibly be allowed as the law is at present . . . It is, of course, permissible, where a prisoner takes advantage of the Criminal Evidence Act 1898 which made prisoners competent witnesses on their trial in all cases, and goes into the witness box and attacks the witnesses for the prosecution, to cross-examine him with regard to convictions and matters of character . . . But it is admitted that there is no authority, and I do not see on what principle it could be said, that if a man does not go into the box and put his own character in issue, he can have evidence given against him of previous bad character when all that he has done is to attack the witnesses for the prosecution. The reason is that by attacking the witnesses for the prosecution and suggesting that they are unreliable, he is not putting his character in issue; he is putting their character in issue. And the reason why, if he gives evidence, he can be cross-examined if he has attacked the witness for the prosecution is that the statute says he can.

As we shall see, there is a difference between what the prosecution are entitled to do in adducing evidence-in-chief or in rebuttal and what they are entitled to do in cross-examining the accused.

	Defendant advances own good character	Defendant attacks prosecution witness's character
Prosecution can lead evidence-in-chief or rebut on accused's character	Yes — under common law	No — not permitted at common law and no statutory exception
Prosecution can cross-examine accused on character	Yes — under Criminal Evidence Act 1898, s.1(f)(ii)	Yes — under Criminal Evidence Act 1898, s.1(f)(ii)

[37] [1948] 1 K.B. 4.

In *Butterwasser*, the accused's previous convictions could have been put to him if he had testified[38] but he did not do so and there is no common law rule which permits the prosecution to counter defence imputations against prosecution witnesses by advancing evidence of the defendant's bad character.

Once the accused's character is in issue,[39] every aspect of that character is included. In *R. v. Winfield*,[40] the charge was indecent assault and the accused led evidence of his sexual propriety. But the prosecution were permitted to counter this by cross-examining on the defendant's previous convictions for dishonesty. Humphreys J. put it:

> . . . there is no such thing known to our procedure as putting half a prisoner's character in issue and leaving out the other half. A man is not entitled to say, "Well, I may have a bad character as a dishonest rogue, but at all evetnts nobody has ever said that I have acted indecently towards women!" That cannot be done. If a man who is accused chooses to put his character in issue, he must take the consequences.[41]

There are problems here:

(1) is this a common law rule or an interpretation of the Criminal Evidence Act 1898 section 1(f)(ii)? It is not clear whether the character witness or Winfield himself (or both) was asked about the convictions. But it would be absurd to restrict the class of questions which could be asked of a character witness as opposed to those which could be put to the accused.

(2) in the nineteenth century, evidence of good character and any consequent rebuttal testimony was expected to be relevant to the charge. But this approach became increasingly honoured in the breach, especially as character evidence was seen as going to credibility as well as to issues of guilt or innocence. The *Winfield* rule follows this trend, allowing rebuttal evidence simply to have prejudicial effect.

(3) the *Winfield* rule emphasises the absurdity of the *Rowton* rule since it is permissible to cross-examine about specific acts (including previous convictions) while examination-in-chief is limited to general good reputation.

The co-accused's bad character

Cut-throat defences which involve laying sole responsibility for a crime at the door of an accomplice are a commonplace in joint trials. The Privy

[38] Criminal Evidence Act 1898, s.1(f)(ii).
[39] Character cannot be put into issue "accidentally" by witnesses blurting out their good opinion of the accused — *R. v. Gadbury* (1838) 8 C&P 676; *R. v. Redd* [1923] 1 K.B. 104.
[40] [1939] 4 All E.R. 164.
[41] *ibid.* at 165a–c.

Council in *Lowery v. R*[42] treated evidence from a psychologist of the sadistic and aggressive disposition of a co-accused as admissible at the instance of an accused, even though such evidence could not have been introduced by the Crown. Courts in Victoria have said that a judge can exclude character evidence tendered by an accused which has little probative force and is prejudicial to a co-accused.[43] Such an exercise of discretion will, it has been said, be rare. Indeed the existence of such a discretion runs directly counter to statements in numerous English cases[44] which have stressed the right of an accused to establish his innocence by relevant evidence regardless of the impact on other defendants.[45]

There are three situations where an accused might wish to adduce evidence against a co-defendant:

(1) where the co-accused has made an incriminating statement to the police that the prosecution cannot or do not rely upon.
(2) where the co-accused has displayed a particular propensity that makes it more likely that he or she committed the offence charged.
(3) where the co-accused possesses prior convictions or generally a bad character.

Incriminating statements

Where there is an incriminating statement by a co-accused which is relevant to the defendant's case, the defence may introduce it either by evidence-in-chief or through cross-examination. But, if the admission is inadmissible for the prosecution, then it is also inadmissible, insofar as adducing evidence-in-chief is concerned, for the defence. This is the case. for example, where the confession is caught by the provisions of section 76 of the Police and Criminal Evidence Act 1984.

However, under section 78 of that Act, the situation might be different so that, if the situation were to arise in which the co-accused sought to adduce a confession after the court had exercised its section 78 discretion against the prosecution, the result would presumably be that, as the exclusionary discretion clearly only applies to prosecution evidence, the co-accused would be free to introduce the evidence. In *R. v. Campbell and Williams*[46] there was a robbery in which C and W got out of car driven by B, approached the victim, punched him and took two rings. B was charged with handling which she denied, alleging that the rings had been given to her by C and she had no idea that they were stolen. In her defence, she was

[42] [1974] A.C. 85.
[43] *Darrington* (1980) 1 A.Crim.R. 124, 162 (Vic.F.C.).
[44] *R. v. Allen* [1965] 2 Q.B. 295; *R. v. Neale* (1977) 65 Cr.App.R. 304; *R. v. Bracewell* (1978) 68 Cr.App.R. 44; *R. v. Rowson* [1985] 2 All E.R. 539.
[45] Pattenden R., "Character of Victims and Third Parties in Criminal Proceedings" [1986] Crim.L.R. 367 at 370.
[46] [1993] Crim.L.R. 448.

permitted to introduce a tape-recording made by her father in which C admitted getting out of the car, fighting with the victim and giving the rings to B. This was relevant to B's case, supporting her statement to the police. Where defendants are being tried together, the jury are entitled to take into account the strength of the case against one defendant in considering whether it weakened the case against another. One defendant was entitled to add to the strength of the case against a co-defendant with evidence admissible against a co-defendant if it assisted the defendant's own case.

But even where the co-accused's confession is inadmissible, any other defendant (although not the prosecution) can cross-examine the co-accused on that statement. This is despite the dicta in *R. v. Treacey*[47] where it was said:

> If it is admissible, the proper course for the prosecution is to prove it, give it in evidence, let the statement if it is in writing be made an exhibit, so that everybody knows what it is and everybody can inquire into it and do what they think right about it. If it is not admissible, nothing more ought to be heard of it, and it is quite a mistake to think that a document can be made admissible in evidence which is otherwise inadmissible simply because it is put to a person in cross-examination.[48]

This was said in the context of the prosecution seeking to cross-examine the accused on a confession which had already been ruled inadmissible as part of the Crown's evidence-in-chief. Different considerations apply where defendants are jointly accused. In *R. v. Rowson*,[49] the Rowson brothers and Keating were convicted of causing grievous bodily harm. The key issue was Keating's statement to the police that he had hit the victim with the wood. This admission was ruled inadmissible for the prosecution. Could Rowsons' counsel cross-examine put the admission to Keating in cross-examination?

R. v. Rowson [1985] 2 All E.R. 539 at 542g–543g, *per* Goff L.J.

We have come to the conclusion that the judge should have permitted counsel for the Rowsons to put Keating's previous statement to him, unfettered by the conditions which he imposed. The statement was plainly relevant, in the sense that it went to the credibility to be attached to evidence given by Keating on a material issue, for, . . ., the statement constituted a previous inconsistent statement by Keating relating to the question whether Keating had had the piece of wood in his possession at the relevant time . . .

In forming this conclusion, we have been assisted by guidance from the speech delivered by Lord Donovan in *Murdoch v. Taylor*[50] . . . That case was concerned with a different question, viz cross-examination by a co-accused in a case falling within proviso (f)(iii) to section 1 of the Criminal Evidence Act 1898. That

[47] *R. v. Treacey* [1944] 2 All E.R. 229.
[48] *ibid.* at 236, *per* Humphreys J.
[49] [1985] 2 All E.R. 539.
[50] [1965] A.C. 574.

provision authorises cross-examination of an accused tending to show that he is of bad character, when he has given evidence against another person charged in the same proceedings. Lord Donovan recognised that, if the prosecution sought to avail itself of proviso (f)(iii), the court might, in the exercise of its discretion to ensure a fair trial, rule that a prosecutor should not proceed with this line of cross-examination; but he considered that the court did not have the same power to prevent such questioning by a co-accused. He said . . .

> . . . but when it is the co-accused who seeks to exercise the right conferred by proviso (f)(iii) different considerations come into play. he seeks to defend himself; to say . . . that the man who is giving evidence against him is unworthy of belief; and to support that assertion by proof of bad character. The right to do this cannot, in my opinion, be fettered in any way.[51]

It is, of course, true that the present case is not identical with that which Lord Donovan considered in *Murdoch v. Taylor.* He was there concerned with the provision of a particular statute whereas in the present case there is no applicable statute which governs the situation. But we observe that proviso (f)(iii) simply creates an exception to a rule which precludes a certain line of questioning; in that form it simply prevents a line of questioning from being excluded, thus leaving it to the courts to decide, as they have done, whether or not the judge at any particular trial should or should not be free to exercise his discretion to rule that certain evidence should be excluded on the ground that its prejudicial value outweighs its evidential value. In *Murdoch v. Taylor* the House of Lords concluded that the exercise of that discretion should not be allowed to fetter a defendant in seeking to extract, by cross-examination, admissible evidence of assistance to his own defence . . . .

We wish to add that in *Murdoch v. Taylor* Lord Donovan gave an indication of the guidance which a judge might be expected to give to the jury if evidence of a defendant's previous convictions was elicited by a co-accused in cross examination. he said:

> . . . his counsel or the judge or both would explain to the jury just how it was that accused No. 1 was able to force the revelation of No. 2's record. the judge would probably go on to exhort the jury not to let that revelation sway their minds and to consider the case against No. 2 primarily on the basis of the other evidence.[52]

We think that, if following our decision in this case, evidence of an otherwise inadmissible previous statement of a defendant were to be elicited in cross-examination by a co-accused in a case such as the present, the judge should likewise briefly explain the position to the jury, and, having regard to the circumstances in which the previous statement was made, he would be able to discourage the jury from placing weight on that statement in considering the prosecution case against the defendant who made the statement.

This decision was approved by the Privy Council in *Lui-Mei Lin v. R*[53] which held that the right to cross-examine a witness was unfettered. Relevance was the only limit to that right. The jury should be told not to

[51] *ibid.* at 593.
[52] *ibid.* at 594.
[53] [1989] 1 All E.R. 359.

use the excluded statement as evidence against the co-accused and to be aware that its only relevance was to test the credibility of the evidence that the witness had given. In the case, the appellant was one of several defendants jointly charged with forgery offences. One of the accused had made an incriminating statement which the trial judge ruled was inadmissible. That defendant testified in his own defence and his evidence differed in a number of respects from what had been said in the excluded statement. The appellant's counsel sought to cross-examine on the basis that the oral testimony was false and wished to put the excluded statement to the witness as a prior inconsistent statement. The trial judge refused to admit the statement but the Privy Council allowed the appeal:

***Lui-Mei Lin v. R.* [1989] 1 All E.R. 359 at 361h–363d, *per* Lord Roskill**

(Lord Roskill cited Devlin J. in *R. v. Miller*[54])

> The fundamental principle, equally applicable to any question that is asked by the defence as to any question that is asked by the prosecution, is that it is not normally relevant to inquire into a man's previous character, and, particularly, to ask questions which tend to show that he has previously committed some criminal offence. it is not relevant because the fact that he has committed an offence on one occasion does not in any way show that he is likely to commit an offence on any subsequent occasion. Accordingly, such questions are, in general, inadmissible, not primarily for the reasons that they are prejudicial, but because they are irrelevant. There is, however, this difference in the application of the principle. In the case of the prosecution, a question of this sort maybe relevant and at the same time be prejudicial, and, if the court is of the opinion that the prejudicial effect outweighs its relevance, then it has the power, and, indeed, the duty, to exclude the question. Therefore counsel for the prosecution rarely asks such a question. No such limitation applies to a question asked by counsel for the defence. his duty is to adduce any evidence which is relevant to his own case and assists his client, whether or not it prejudices anyone else.[55]

. . . Ever since section 5 of the Criminal Procedure Act 1865 . . . it has been permissible in every criminal . . . trial to cross-examine a witness as to any previous inconsistent statement made by him in writing or reduced into writing subject, where the inconsistent statement is said to be in writing, to his attention first being called to those parts of any writing which were to be used in order to contradict him. The only limit on the right of a co-accused to cross-examine another accused in these circumstances is . . . relevancy. If one co-accused has given evidence incriminating another it must be relevant for the latter to show, if he can, that the former has on some other occasion given inconsistent evidence and thus is unworthy of belief.

Counsel . . . also argued . . . that *R. v. Rowson* was wrongly decided and should not be followed. With respect, their Lordships disagree . . . .Their Lordships respectfully agree with the distinction which the Court of Appeal drew in *R. v. Rowson* between *R. v. Treacey* and *R. v. Rice*[56] on the one hand and the case then

[54] [1952] 2 All E.R. 667.
[55] *ibid.* at 668–669.
[56] [1963] 1 All E.R. 832.

before that court where it was, as already stated, counsel for the co-accused who sought to cross-examine another co-accused on his excluded statement. When Humphreys J. said in *R. v. Treacey* that 'nothing more ought to be heard of it' he clearly meant that nothing more ought to be heard of the excluded statement, as between the prosecution and the defendant. The judge plainly did not have in mind the possibility of a co-accused subsequently seeking to make use of the excluded statement, for in that case there was no co-accused..

. . . to allow a co-accused complete freedom to cross examine on an excluded statement could give rise to difficult questions how far, if at all, a trial judge should explain to a jury why it was that they were suddenly hearing of this statement and perhaps even seeing it for the first time at a comparatively late stage of the trial . . . the trial judge should warn the jury that they must not use the statement in any way as evidence in support of the prosecution's case and that its only relevance is to test the credibility of the evidence which the maker of the statement has given against his co-accused . . .

It was also suggested . . . that if cross-examination on the excluded statement were to be permitted, the trial judge might have to carry out what was described as a balancing exercise, balancing the interests of the maker of the statement against the interests of the co-accused on whose behalf it was sought to cross-examine before deciding whether or not to permit the proposed cross-examination. Their Lordships disagree. In their view the right to cross-examine is . . . unfettered, the only limit being relevancy. If the statement contains irrelevant matter the trial judge would no doubt insist that that irrelevant matter should not be referred to . . .

It is unlikely that a wholly satisfactory solution is possible:

(I1) as between prosecution and accused A, the prosecution cannot rely upon an excluded statement nor can they cross-examine on it. But indirectly the Crown benefits if A is cross-examined upon the statement by co-accused B. Although the jury are warned that the statement is only introduced as a measure of A's credibility, it would be naive to believe that they would not also take account of the statement's content.

(2) as between A and B, the authorities favour fairness to B who is entitled to emphasise A's inconsistency of testimony even at the cost of considerable prejudice to A's case.

Particular propensity

Another tactic of the "cut-throat" defence is to suggest that one's co-accused possesses a particular trait of character that makes it more likely that he or she committed the offence. In *Miller*, one defendant alleged that the offences had been committed by a co-accused and to that end sought to ask a prosecution witness whether or not it was true that the offences stopped when that accused had been in prison and re-started after his release. Although the prosecution would be barred from such a line of questioning, Devlin J. held that questioning by a co-accused was only limited by considerations of relevance.

In *Lowery v. R*,[57] the two accused, L and K, attacked and sadistically killed a 15 year old girl. K's defence was that the killing was the work of L, that he (K) had been under the influence of drugs and that, although he had seen L strangling the girl, he had been helpless to stop him. He wished to introduce testimony from a psychologist who had examined both defendants. The psychologist's expert opinion was that L possessed a sadistic and aggressive disposition. L's defence was that K had committed the killing. He (L) had driven to the spot as he believed that K wished to have sex with the victim. Only later did he follow them and found K assaulting the girl. L also called evidence as to his own reputation with a view to showing that his disposition made him unlikely to have committed such a crime. In this context the Privy Council agreed that the psychologist's testimony was admissible:

Lowery v. R. [1973] 3 All E.R. 662 at 668–671, *per* Lord Morris

. . . It was said that the evidence was not relevant to any issue and was of no probative value in considering the guilt of the accused; that evidence of the psychological condition of an accused person as tending to prove his guilt ought never to be introduced either by the prosecution or by the defence of a co-accused person; that the evidence whether adduced by prosecution or by defence ought to have been excluded as a matter of law because its introduction would merely show disposition; that the evidence did not fall within any of the exceptions denoted in *Makin v. Attorney-General for New South Wales* . . .

. . . The questions arise whether the evidence was (a) relevant and (b) admissible: not all evidence that is relevant is admissible because its prejudicial effect heavily overbalances its probative value and as a matter of fairness or of public policy a court will not allow the prosecution to call such evidence . . . [Lord Morris summarises the psychologist's conclusions on the psychological make-up of L and K].

In all these circumstances it was necessary on behalf of K to call all relevant and admissible evidence which would exonerate K and throw responsibility entirely on L. If in imaginary circumstances similar to those of this case it was apparent that one of the accused was a man of great physical strength whereas the other was a weakling it could hardly be doubted that in forming an opinion as to the probabilities it would be relevant to have the disparity between the two in mind. Physical characteristics may often be of considerable relevance: see *Toohey v. Metropolitan Police Commissioner*.[58] The scientific evidence . . . was not related to crime or criminal tendencies: it was scientific evidence as to the respective personalities of the two accused . . .[59]

The admissibility of expert psychiatric testimony is often controversial. *Lowery* must be considered in the context of the *Turner* rule.[60] It is also regarded as influenced by its own particular facts. Later authority suggests that a defendant can only lead evidence of propensity when the co-accused

[57] [1973] 3 All E.R. 662.
[58] [1965] 1 All E.R. 506.
[59] *Lowery supra* at 668–671, *per* Lord Morris.
[60] See 624, *et seq.*

has raised the issue, as with *Lowery*. In *R. v. Bracewell*,[61] B and L were accused of killing an old man whose home they were burgling. Both blamed the other and B wished to cross-examine L's lover on L's propensity for violence. The Court of Appeal upheld the trial judge's rejection of this line of questioning at this point. Later in the trial, L did deny that he was violent and B's counsel could, had he chosen to, at that point have questioned L on his violent conduct towards his mistress.

The authorities suggest that a defendant can introduce evidence of a co-accused's disposition:

(1) when that evidence is clearly relevant to the defendant's case as in *Miller*, the defendant can lead evidence or cross-examine on the issue without waiting for the co-accused to put character into issue. The only limit is that of relevance and the trial court should not use its discretion to balance the probative weight against the prejudicial effect
(2) when that evidence is less obviously relevant to the defendant's case as in *Bracewell*, it requires that the character of the co-accused be put into issue at which point it can be rebutted.

General bad character

Following from this it is clear that an accused cannot lead evidence on a co-accused's general bad character simply because it would not be relevant. Where the line of questioning is relevant, as in *Miller*, it is clearly admissible. The position would be the same with cross-examination. Where the line of questioning is not relevant to the case in itself, questions revealing the bad character of the co-accused may still be possible but only if the co-accused has thrown away the shield provided by section 1(f) of the Criminal Evidence Act 1898.[62]

[61] [1979] Crim.L.R. 111; (1978) 68 Cr.App.R. 44.
[62] See 464, *et seq.*

14

SIMILAR FACT EVIDENCE

Introduction

The general rule is that parties in legal proceedings are prohibited at common law from introducing evidence of their opponent's bad character or disposition. 'Bad character' encompasses not merely previous convictions but also other disreputable actions. Such evidence has little probative weight but is highly prejudicial and this must be guarded against, especially In criminal trials before a jury. At the same time, the jury's view of a potentially weak prosecution case can be significantly altered by such evidence. In the case below, a tragic accident takes on a very different appearance.

In *R. v. Smith*,[1] in 1915 the defendant was tried for the murder in July 1912 of Beatrice Mundy by drowning her in the bath. He had been through a bigamous form of marriage with her in 1910 and she believed herself to be his wife. After her death, Smith "married" Alice Burnham in November 1913. She died in the same manner in December that year. On December 17th 1914, he "married" Margaret Lofty — she died, also in her bath, on December 18th! Although only charged with one murder, the prosecution were allowed to advance evidence that the second and third "wives" had died in identical circumstances: all the "brides" were in the bath, had apparently slipped backwards, hit their heads on the taps and died through drowning. Smith had benefited from all three wills. Smith's unlucky marital history is clearly relevant to the offence charged because the defence claimed that Beatrice's death was an accident. The evidence of the fate of Alice and of Margaret made that claim look not just less likely but incredible.

> And then comes in the purpose and the only purpose for which you are allowed to consider the evidence as to the other deaths. If you find an accident which benefits a person and you find that the person has been sufficiently fortunate to have that accident happen to him a number of times, benefiting him each time, you draw a very strong, frequently irresistible inference, that the occurrence of so many accidents benefiting him is such a coincidence that it cannot have happened unless it was design.[2]

[1] (1915) 11 Cr.App.R. 229; Humphreys, Sir Travers, *A Book of Trials* (Pan 1955) 82–86.
[2] *Smith supra* at 233 — the words of the trial judge, Scrutton J. to the jury quoted at the appeal.

This demonstrates that the general prohibition on introducing evidence of your opponent's bad character is modified when that previous behaviour is sufficiently relevant. The consistencies and patterns in people's behaviour mean that in some circumstances the court is justified in treating previous conduct as a factor in deciding whether a person has committed this particular act.

There are obvious dangers in allowing such evidence, especially in criminal cases. The problem is that as soon as, for example, the evidence of the other "brides in the bath" was introduced, the jury inevitably paid less (if any) attention to the evidence as to the offence charged. Such testimony about an accused's previous offences is highly prejudicial in the sense that the trier of fact pre-judges the issue: it appears that Smith has killed before and therefore must have killed again. The proof of the previous offences detracts attention from the proof of guilt of this offence and tends to undermine the standard of proof required. Thus the court must be satisfied that the probative weight is so strong that it will compensate for any breakdown in the jury's logical processes and that the prejudice will be balanced by the overwhelming relevance of such evidence. This is demonstrated in *Smith* where inference that Smith had killed the three women was irresistible. But the circumstances in which such evidence is used are not always so conclusive.

Such evidence is known as "similar fact" evidence. This phrase is not helpful[3] since we are dealing here with one of the main exclusionary rules that a party cannot normally advance evidence of an opponent's disposition. The "similar fact" category is one of the main exceptions to this rule. But to treat it as a category suggests a coherence that, as will be seen, is illusory.[4]

The Makin Principle

At its most basic level, similar fact evidence is merely an illustration of the general principles regarding the admissibility of evidence. There are just two elements to be considered regarding its admission: relevance and probative weight. The first of these was considered in *Makin v. Attorney-General for New South Wales*[5] in which the defendants were tried for the murder of a baby. The couple had accepted a child from its mother, alleging that they would adopt and care for it on payment of a small sum of money. A baby's body was found buried in the garden and the accused were charged with the murder. The prosecution sought to adduce evidence from other mothers that the couple had received their children on the same basis. They also were allowed to show that thirteen other such bodies had been found in gardens of three other houses occupied by the defendants.

[3] Tapper C., *Cross and Tapper on Evidence* (8th ed., 1995) 361.
[4] The area has been reviewed in the Law Commission Consultation Paper No. 141 on *Previous Misconduct*. For comment, see Roberts P., "All the Usual Suspects" [1997] Crim.L.R. 75; McEwan J., "Law Commission Dodges the Nettles" [1997] Crim.L.R. 93.
[5] [1894] A.C. 57.

As with the brides in the bath, this evidence showed that the Makins had probably committed murders other than the one with which they were charged. The relevance of such evidence was that it tended to rebut any defence of accident or natural causes. Lord Herschell delivered the judgment of the Privy Council:

***Makin v. Attorney-General for New South Wales* [1894] A.C. 57 at 65, *per* Lord Herschell**

In their Lordships' opinion the principles which must govern the decision of the case are clear, though the application of them is by no means free from difficulty. It is undoubtedly not competent for the prosecution to adduce evidence tending to show that the accused has been guilty of criminal acts other than those covered by the indictment for the purpose of leading to the conclusion that the accused is a person likely from his criminal conduct or character to have committed the offence for which he is being tried. On the other hand, the mere fact that the evidence adduced tends to show the commission of other crimes does not render it inadmissible if it be relevant to an issue before the jury and it may be so relevant if it bears upon the question whether the acts alleged to constitute the crime charged in the indictment were designed or accidental or to rebut a defence which would have been otherwise open to the accused.

There are two legs to the *Makin* principle:

(1) the general rule is that evidence of the accused's disposition *simpliciter* is inadmissible: in *R. v. Brown*,[6] the defendants were charged with shopbreaking and the prosecution sought to show that one of the accused had broken into a shop five days previously, during the lunch hour and using a skeleton key. All of these were characteristics of the alleged offence but the evidence was excluded. Simply being a shopbreaker is not evidence of committing a particular offence.

(2) but this does not mean that evidence of the commission of crimes other than the one charged is always inadmissible. Such evidence can be introduced where it is relevant to an issue before the jury: for example, where it shows a particular modus operandi or abnormal propensity as in *R. v. Straffen*[7] where the accused had been committed to Broadmoor after being found unfit to plead to a charge of manually strangling two small girls. He escaped and was at large for four hours. During that time, another young girl, Linda Bowyer, was strangled. The defendant admitted being in the neighbourhood and that he had seen her. On trial for the third killing, evidence of the other murders was admitted:

[6] (1963) 47 Cr.App.R. 204.

[7] [1952] 2 Q.B. 911.

R. v. *Straffen* [1952] 2 Q.B. 911 at 916–917, *per* Slade J.

> Abnormal propensity is a means of identification . . . It is an abnormal propensity to strangle young girls and to do so without any apparent motive, without any attempt at sexual interference, and to leave their bodies where they can be seen and where, presumably, their deaths would be detected. In the judgment of the court, that evidence was admissible because it tended to identify the person who murdered Linda Bowyer with the person who confessed in his statements to having murdered the other two girls a year before, in exactly similar circumstances.

Lord Herschell's judgment in *Makin* is justly famous for the clarity with which these basic principles are explained but is perhaps limited in other ways:

Zuckerman A., *The Principles of Criminal Evidence* (1989), 242

If deviation from the principle that the accused is tried only for the offence charged and nothing else is common,[8] we cannot expect to find strict compliance with the principle when it comes to the admissibility of evidence. Looked at from this point of view Lord Herschell's famous dictum appears in a new light. It expresses neither an antithesis between kinds of relevance nor one between degrees of relevance but a tension between an ideal and reality. The exclusionary part reflects the aspiration that the accused be tried only for the offence charged, while the inclusionary part accepts that this cannot always be achieved. Much of the dissatisfaction with the rule concerning similar-fact evidence, whether it be the *Makin* or the *Boardman* version, is caused by unduly high expectations. Judges have protested too much about the importance of the principle of exclusion and, as a consequence, their record on admissibility has been found wanting and has prompted a continual search for fresh and better rules. But when it comes to practice, admissibility is determined by the same imprecise judicial instincts about acceptable and unacceptable prejudice that determine the result in other areas, where no pretence of a rule is maintained.

Is Zuckerman unduly hard on Lord Herschell? The judgment is very clear that evidence of character and disposition is to be excluded. Although the sense of the common person might regard criminal record as relevant to guilt, that sense is a "*faux ami*" since, although attractive, the record's relevance is so limited that it will lead us as often to wrong conclusions as to right. It is only when that relevance is of a higher order that the evidence becomes admissible.

But what order of relevance is enough? It should be where the probative weight is so strong that any prejudice to the accused is simply part of the background. The *Makin* judgment does not consider that issue, simply because, as with *Smith*, it does not arise. The evidence of thirteen other little corpses makes the conclusion that the couple killed the baby who was

[8] *ibid.*, 234 *et seq.* where Zuckerman argues that through joinder of trials, cross-examination of the accused on his or her record and through pre-trial publicity, the defendant's record is often disclosed.

the subject of the charge so irresistible that any question of prejudice to the accused becomes redundant. Thus we might add a third leg:

(3) even though evidence of the commission of other crimes is relevant to an issue before the jury, it is only admissible where its probative force outweighs the prejudice generated by such evidence.

Relevance versus prejudice

As Zuckerman notes, judges have historically had more success identifying the relevance that similar facts might possess than they have in isolating the quality of the prejudice engendered. Courts have consistently admitted deeply prejudicial testimony especially in cases involving what the courts regarded as sexual deviancy. In *R. v. Thompson*[9] the defendant was accused of gross indecency with two boys. He did not deny that the offences had taken place, just that he was not the person. However, the offender, whoever he was, had made a second rendezvous with the boys and they had taken the police to the place. On that occasion, the defendant met the boys and gave them money. He was arrested without any further offence taking place. The prosecution were allowed to use evidence that the accused had two powder puffs on him on arrest and that he had indecent photographs of boys in his flat. The House of Lords upheld the conviction on the basis that the accused's sexuality could be seen as confirming the boys' identification of him as the offender:

R. v. Thompson [1918] A.C. 221 at 232–235, *per* Lord Sumner

. . . No one doubts that it does not prove a man guilty of a particular crime to show that he is the kind of man who would commit a crime, or that he is generally disposed to crime and even to a particular crime; but, sometimes for one reason, sometimes for another, evidence is admissible, notwithstanding that its general character is to show that the accused had in him the makings of a criminal, for example, in proving guilty knowledge, or intent, or system, or in rebutting an appearance of innocence which, unexplained, the facts might wear. In cases of coining, uttering, procuring abortion, demanding by menaces, false pretences, and sundry species of frauds such evidence is constantly and properly admitted. Before an issue can be said to be raised, which would permit the introduction of such evidence so obviously prejudicial to the accused, it must have been raised in substance if not in so many words, and the issue so raised must be one to which the prejudicial evidence is relevant. The mere theory that a plea of not guilty puts everything material in issue is not enough for this purpose. The prosecution cannot credit the accused with fancy defences in order to rebut them at the outset with some damning piece of prejudice . . . In the present case, even before the justices, it became clear that the accused made one case, and one case only, and so it has been throughout. He said that he was not the man.

As was admitted, there was a stronger case for the admissibility of the powder puffs than of the photographs. I think the powder puffs were clearly admissible.

[9] [1918] A.C. 221.

The criminal made an appointment with the boys for the following Monday, and to the place of that appointment at the appointed time there came the appellant, equipped with articles recognised by the courts as 'used for the carrying out of their design' by persons of the class to which the criminal belonged. They are direct evidence that the appellant was keeping the criminal's appointment and was the same man . . .

The photographs thus became the turning point of the case. The principles on which the admissibility of evidence of identification rest are in no need of restatement . . . All lawyers recognise, as part of their professional premisses, that there is all the difference in the world between evidence proving that the accused is a bad man and evidence proving that he is the man . . . . There must be something to connect the circumstance tendered in evidence, not only with the accused, but with his participation in the crime. It is this something which is expressed in the judgment under appeal in the words 'ordinary men do not keep indecent photographs of naked boys in their possession. Men who commit the offences charged do . . . The man who did the acts on March 16 was a man who would be likely to have such photographs in his possession. The man arrested on the 19th in fact had such photographs in his possession at his rooms'. As applied to the facts of the case I think the meaning of the above passage may be restated more fully as follows: The actual criminal made an appointment to meet the same boys at the same time and place three days later and presumably for the same purpose. This tends to show that his act was not an isolated act, but was an incident in the habitual gratification of a particular propensity. The appellant, as his possession of the photographs tends to show, is a person with the same propensity. Indeed, he went to the place of appointment with some of the outfit, and he had the rest of it at home. The evidence tends to attach to the accused a peculiarity which, though not purely physical, I think may be recognised as properly bearing that name. Experience tends to show that these offences against nature connote an inversion of normal characteristics which, while demanding punishment as offending against social morality, also partake of the nature of an abnormal physical property. A thief, a cheat, a coiner or housebreaker is only a particular specimen of the genus rogue and, though no doubt each tends to keep to his own line of business, they all alike possess the by no means extraordinary mental characteristic that they propose somehow to get their living dishonestly. So common a characteristic is not a recognisable mark of the individual. Persons, however, who commit the offences now under consideration seek the habitual gratification of a particular perverted lust which not only takes them out of the class of ordinary men gone wrong but stamps them with a hallmark of a special and extraordinary class as much as if they carried on their bodies some physical peculiarity. So expanded and understood, I accept the passage which I have quoted above, and think that the photographs, found as they were and after a short interval of time, tend to show that the accused has this recognisable propensity, which it was shown was also the propensity of the criminal of March 16. It was accordingly admissible evidence of his identity with that criminal . . .

There were two items of evidence in dispute:

(1) the boys identify Thompson as the man who assaulted them. He is in possession of powder puffs which, presumably, the boys testified as being used in the course of the offence. These are unusual items for males to carry and their existence tends strongly to support their identification of Thompson, just as discovering lock-picking equipment on a suspected burglar. However the powder puffs also suggest that Thompson is homosexual, inevitably prejudicial in the

eyes of an all-male, middle class jury. But the corroboration of the identification is so strong as to set that prejudice to one side.

(2) the photos are weaker evidence to support the identification. But they suggest that the accused is a paedophile — for the jury as well as for Lord Sumner, this creates the irresistible and fallacious inference that the accused assaulted the young boys. Admitting the photos creates a wholly illegitimate and overwhelming prejudice against the accused who must require ". . . the habitual gratification of a particular perverted lust . . ." and must therefore be guilty. In the case of his hypothetical burglar, would Lord Sumner have regarded the discovery in the accused's house of property stolen in other burglaries as admissible?

Lord Sumner's judgment demonstrates the focus on identifying relevance at the expense of an abject failure to recognise the prejudice engendered in his own mind as well as in the minds of the jury. Homophobia of this nature is again seen in *R. v. Sims*[10] where the accused was charged on counts of buggery and indecent assault against several men. He applied for severance of the trials but this was refused since the evidence relating to one complaint was admissible on the other charges. Lord Goddard's opinion was that:

R. v. Sims [1946] K.B. 531 at 540, per Lord Goddard

. . . Sodomy is a crime in a special category . . . On this account, in regard to this crime we think that the repetition of the acts is in itself a specific feature connecting the accused with the crime and that evidence of this kind is admissible to show the nature of the act done by the accused. The probative force of all the acts together is much greater than one alone; for, whereas the jury might think one man might be telling an untruth, three or four are hardly likely to tell the same untruth unless they were conspiring together.[11]

Such a notion was rejected by Lord Wilberforce in *DPP v. Boardman*,[12]

> We can dispose at once of the suggestion that there is a special rule or principle applicable to sexual, or to homosexual, offences . . . Evidence that an offence of a sexual character was committed by A against B cannot be supported by evidence that an offence of a sexual character was committed by A against C, or against C, D and E.
>
> If the evidence is to be received, then it must be on some general principle not confined to sexual offences . . .

But the law reports feature many such cases. One reason for this is that there is an absence of independent evidence in sexual assaults of all types and prosecutions need to rely heavily on the victim's account. Characteristically the prosecution seeks to strengthen this by adducing evidence of

[10] [1946] K.B. 531.
[11] *cf* heterosexual indecent assault in *R. v. Roy* [1992] Crim.L.R. 185.
[12] [1974] 3 All E.R. 887.

other offences. This can be seen in *Boardman* itself as well as in cases such as *R. v. P.*,[13] *R. v. W.*[14] and *R. v. H.*[15] The latter three have all involved sexual abuse of children within the family. The indictments have all contained multiple charges and the impact on the jury of these must have been highly prejudicial. In such cases the quality of a decision in any single case must have been adversely affected and this must summon up the possibility of the conviction of an innocent person. But there are difficult social choices here since the sexual abuse of children has been recognised as a major social problem for a decade[16] and failures to convict abusers can be viewed equally as miscarriages of justice which bring the criminal justice system into disrepute. Relaxing the rules of evidence (in this case, the similar fact rules) ensures convictions but it has to be recognised that it does so at the expense of reducing the standard of proof.

Categories of relevance and proof of knowledge

Historically the quality of Lord Herschell's logic was diminished as the *Makin* question "Is the evidence of propensity relevant to an issue in the case?" was reduced to formal categories where relevance was assumed to exist:

(1) where the previous acts revealed a propensity to commit acts in a specific manner, a ***modus operandi***, as in *R. v. Straffen*.[17]
(2) where that propensity supports ***evidence of identity***, for example by showing the accused to be a member of a particular class or group as in *R. v. Thompson*.[18]
(3) where evidence of previous similar acts would rebut a ***defence of accident*** as in *R. v. Smith*.[19]
(4) where the evidence would rebut a ***defence of innocent association***. In *R. v. Ball*,[20] the accused were brother and sister charged with incest. The House of Lords held that evidence that the sister had a child by the brother before the passage of the Punishment of Incest Act 1908 was admissible.

The primary question from *Makin* must be 'Why is the previous conduct relevant?' and although formal categories provide a guide, they can never be an exclusive answer to such a question. One example of this is the question of "knowledge". Did the accused "know" a particular fact or

[13] [1991] 3 All E.R. 337.
[14] [1994] 2 All E.R. 872.
[15] [1995] 2 All E.R. 865.
[16] Butler-Sloss, Lord Justice, *Report of the Inquiry into Child Abuse in Cleveland* (1987) Cm. 413.
[17] [1952] 2 Q.B. 911.
[18] [1918] A.C. 221.
[19] (1915) 11 Cr.App.R. 229.
[20] (1911) A.C. 47.

circumstance: were the goods stolen? was the substance an illegal drug? Previous convictions are obviously relevant to the issue of what the accused knew. But there are other considerations. An illustration would be the doctrine of *doli incapax* that a child under 14 is rebuttably presumed not to understand the distinction between right and wrong and that the prosecution is responsible for adducing evidence to rebut that presumption. In *R. v. A., R. v. B.*,[21] the central issue was whether the child's prior convictions could be used in that way. In that case, Lord Widgery said:

R. v. A., R. v. B., [1979] 3 All E.R. 460 at 462, *per* Lord Widgery

The judge in clear terms was taking the view that where the presumption applies the prosecution can seek to remove the effect of the presumption and to call evidence to that effect. A moment's thought will make it clear that this is so. If the presumption is allowed to stand and the prosecution did not call evidence to rebut it, then, at the close of the prosecution case, there would be a ruling that there was no case to answer. It seems to us, as it seemed to the judge below, that to guard against that ridiculous result one must accept the fact that the prosecution can call relevant evidence which is relevant on the issue of the young man's capacity to know good from evil.

A moment's further thought reveals a problem because where a child pleads "not guilty", there are two issues: firstly whether he or she has committed the offence and secondly whether he or she understood that what they were doing was wrong. While a previous conviction might be relevant and admissible on the latter point, it may be irrelevant, prejudicial and inadmissible on the primary issue. The choice appears to be between admitting the evidence and risking injustice to the accused or excluding it and ensuring injustice to the prosecution. This point was taken by Lord Lowry[22]:

C. v. DPP [1995] 2 All E.R. 43 at 58, *per* Lord Lowry

. . . Assuming that the previous convictions were allowed to be put in evidence but were not admissible under the similar facts rule, it would clearly have been in vain for the judge to tell the jury to disregard them when considering the primary issue but then to take account of then if they had to decide the 'knowledge' issue. [Lord Lowry then quoted Lord Widgery's observations in *R. v. A., R. v. B.*]

The cases cited in *R. v. A., R. v. B.* were concerned with evidence of the defendant's general background and, so far as the above passage deals with that kind of evidence, I freely concur in what was said. But I do not think it right (assuming that to be the position) to admit non-similar fact evidence which would be inadmissible on issue 1 for the purpose of proving the prosecution's case on issue 2. If the prosecution's case must sometimes fail because some or all of the probative evidence cannot be given, that is not a unique situation and it must be borne with fortitude in the interests of fairness to the accused. To hold a split trial, dividing

[21] [1979] 3 All E.R. 460.

[22] The primary issue in the case was the House of Lords' refusal to uphold the Divisional Court's decision that the doctrine of *doli incapax* was no longer law. See further 692, *et seq.*

issues 1 and 2, would not be practicable and such a procedure would soon conduce to the inference at an early stage of the trial that evidence of previous convictions will be tendered if issue 1 is decided against the accused. I hope your Lordships will forgive me for devoting some time to the previous convictions argument, which appears to me to involve a general principle and to be something which will concern trial judges for so long as they have to cope with the *doli incapax* doctrine.

The common law is restrictive in admitting evidence of the accused's knowledge, albeit relevant, if there is a danger of the jury drawing an inference to the defendant's prejudice from it. This protective approach has proved less robust in the interpretation of statutes. Under the Theft Act 1968:

27.—(3) Where a person is being proceeded against for handling stolen goods (. . .) then at any stage of the proceedings, if evidence has been given of his having or arranging to have in his possession the goods the subject of the charge, or of his undertaking or assisting in, or arranging to undertake or assist in, their retention, removal, disposal or realisation, the following evidence shall be admissible for the purpose of proving that he knew or believed the goods to be stolen goods: —

a) evidence that he has had in his possession, or has undertaken or assisted in the retention, removal, disposal or realisation of, stolen goods from any theft taking place not earlier than twelve months before the offence charged; and
b) . . . evidence that he has within the five years preceding the date of the offence charged been convicted of theft or of handling stolen goods.

Munday has commented:

Munday R., "Handling the Evidential Exception" [1988] Crim L.R. 345 at 347–354

The courts have always accepted that the admission of evidence of disposition under section 27(3) of the Theft Act 1968 represents an attempt by the legislature to surmount the particular difficulty of proving guilty knowledge on the part of handlers. However, the highly exceptional nature of the provision has also persuaded courts to pursue what might be termed a policy of damage limitation in a bid to minimise what they conceive to be the potentially harmful effects of the provision. Thus, in order to avoid any risk of its being misapplied in relation to other offences, in *Davies*[23] the Court of Appeal made clear that the relevant provision of the Larceny Act 1916 should only apply where the indictment contained no other charge than handling — a refinement subsequently ratified by the legislature in the Theft Act. In such ways, it could be proclaimed that, whilst giving effect to Parliament's literal intention, the courts were nevertheless circumscribing this rather shocking exception to the civilised principles governing character evidence elaborated at common law by the judges. Well-meaning though the objective may appear, its consequence has been to strip this area of the law of its few remaining legal bearings. Recent decisions on section 27(3) illustrate the perplexity: whether to restrict a legislative provision and deprive it of clear meaning or to give it a full reading and run unconditionally counter to hallowed canons of the common law.

[23] [1953] 1 Q.B. 489.

. . . In the recent case of *Fowler*,[24] a defendant was charged with eight counts of handling, but the prosecution also introduced in evidence the defendant's previous conviction for handling stolen goods on an earlier occasion. the Court of Appeal, taking the customary view that section 27(3) is a clear derogation from normal evidentiary principles and thus to be "construed literally and favourably towards an accused person", held that the trial judge had been wrong to allow the Crown to introduce not merely the fact that the defendant had a previous conviction under paragraph (b) but also a description of the goods and the date of their receipt. Since such information might markedly deepen the potential for prejudice and thereby serve to overbear all other evidence. Watkins L.J. held that the Crown was only entitled to relate the fact of the previous conviction.

Such an interpretation will not occasion surprise. Moreover, there is some force in the court's contention that the more details of the offence the prosecution wishes to adduce, the greater prejudice to the accused this evidence of general disposition is likely to occasion. However, such a posture merely accentuates the oddity of the statutory provision under consideration,divorcing it further from the mainstream of evidentiary thinking. It is instructive to compare the English Court of Appeal's argument in *Fowler* with the very different reasoning employed by the New Zealand appellate court in *Brosnam*[25] when it was called upon to construe the equivalent provision of section 43 of the Larceny Act. The New Zealand Court held that evidence admissible under the statute was,

> . . . not limited to a mere record of the conviction, but may include the relevant surrounding circumstances, such as the nature of the previous offence, the property which was the subject thereof, and the name of the owner. The intention of the section is to prove guilty knowledge from the similarity of the events . . .

In short, the Commonwealth court sought to make sense of the provision by assimilating it more closely into the principles of similar fact evidence. the English courts have preferred to treat the entire subsection as introducing a new denomination of highly prejudicial and practically unassessable character evidence. The result of such a stance has been a marked reluctance on the part of English courts to admit such evidence at all.

. . . as things stand, section 27(3) endures, an object of practically unique curiosity, eccentric in conception, irresolute in its development, erratic of application, its adverse influence only contained by bold judicial contrivance.

Fowler is disapproved of in *R. v. Hacker*[26] when the accused was charged with handling a stolen car, namely a Ford Escort RS Turbo. The prosecution sought to prove guilty knowledge under section 27(3) by adducing evidence of a previous handling conviction. The problem was that the prosecution wished not merely to show the fact of conviction but also that the previous offence was also for handling a Ford Escort RS Turbo. The Houses of Lords held that section 27 must be read alongside section 73(2) of the Police and Criminal Evidence Act 1984 which states that where a conviction is admissible in evidence, the certificate shall give

[24] (1987) 86 Cr.App.R. 219.
[25] [1951] N.Z.L.R. 1030.
[26] [1995] 1 All E.R. 45.

"the substance and effect (omitting the formal parts) of the indictment and of the conviction". Lord Slynn held that the particulars of the motor car were "of the substance of the indictment". He quoted the judgment of the Court of Appeal:

> One of the troubles that the decision [in *Fowler*] can potentially give rise to is this. If the only evidence that can go in is the bare evidence of handling stolen goods, then what will happen if the jury indicate that they wish to know what goods were stolen? They might, quite sensibly, take the point that if it was a handling of a stolen motor car it might be very different from handling of half a pound of sugar. However, that is a matter on the authorities as they presently stand either for the legislator or for a higher court than this.[27]

The jury are entitled to know facts which it is necessary for them to know. But, even where such facts are admissible, the trial judge has a discretion to exclude the evidence where the prejudicial effect outweighs the probative value, either at common law or under section 78 of the Police and Criminal Evidence Act 1984. In *Hacker* the trial judge warned the jury, both as to the fact that the conviction was admissible only as to the accused's knowledge and also to the fact that they were not entitled to convict just because he had previous convictions.

As these examples of guilty knowledge show, where the previous misconduct is directly relevant to a specific element of the prosecution case, the evidence is admissible even though it reveals the accused's bad character. In *R. v. Ollis*,[28] the defendant was acquitted of obtaining by false pretences when a cheque he gave the victim was dishonoured, his defence being that he thought the cheque would be honoured. The accused was then tried on another indictment on similar counts of obtaining money on cheques which were dishonoured. The prosecution called the first victim to prove guilty knowledge and the admission of this evidence was upheld on appeal. A recent example is *R. v. Caceres-Moreira*[29] where the accused was charged with importation of cocaine and a previous incident was admitted as going to the issue of the defendant's knowledge that the parcel contained drugs.[30]

Similar fact evidence is a useful and justifiable means of proving knowledge. There are greater difficulties where the evidence is introduced on the basis that such conduct has taken place in the past and therefore the conduct alleged in the indictment must also have occurred. Relevance is more difficult to demonstrate and the old approach merely led to artificiality: do the facts conform to a technical category?

[27] *ibid.* at 51h–j.
[28] [1900] 2 Q.B. 758.
[29] [1995] Crim.L.R. 489.
[30] This is discussed further at 666.

Boardman and "Striking Similarity"

The House of Lords in *DPP v. Boardman*[31] rejected the earlier category approach and their judgment seemed to herald a return to a simpler approach, based on a judicial discretion which required the judge to consider the balance of the prejudicial and probative effects of the evidence. In the case, the accused was a headmaster of a boarding school for boys, charged with sexual offences on separate occasions on two pupils. The similarities in the accounts by the two pupils were striking but the defence was that the boys were lying and that the incidents never occurred. Were the accounts given by each boy admissible on the charge relating to the other boy? The House of Lords upheld the trial judge's decision to admit the evidence. Evidence of similar facts may be admitted if the judge views its probative force in relation to an issue in the trial as outweighing its prejudicial effect. The strength of the probative force lies in its striking similarity and where that similarity is inexplicable on the basis of coincidence or concoction:

DPP v. Boardman [1974] 3 All E.R. 887 at 896b–898f, *per* Lord Wilberforce

My Lords, the question for decision in this appeal is whether, on a charge against the appellant of buggery with one boy, evidence was admissible that the appellant had incited another boy to buggery, and vice versa. The judge ruled that, in the particular circumstances of this case, the evidence was admissible. We have to decide whether this ruling was correct; for reasons which other of your Lordships have given, we cannot answer the question certified in the terms in which it is stated. Whether in the field of sexual conduct or otherwise, there is no general or automatic answer to be given to the question whether evidence of facts similar to those the subject of a particular charge ought to be admitted. In each case it is necessary to estimate (i) whether, and if so how strongly, the evidence as to other facts tends to support, *i.e.* to make more credible, the evidence given as to the fact in question, (ii) whether such evidence, if given, is likely to be prejudicial to the accused. Both these elements involve questions of degree.

It falls to the judge, in the first place by way of preliminary ruling, and indeed on an application for separate trials if such is made (. . .) to estimate the respective and relative weight of these two factors and only to allow the evidence to be put before the jury if he is satisfied that the answer to the first question is clearly positive, and, on the assumption, which is likely, that the second question must be similarly answered, that on a combination of the two the interests of justice clearly require that the evidence be admitted.

Questions of this kind arise in a number of different contexts and have, correspondingly, to be resolved in different ways. I think that it is desirable to confine ourselves to the present set of facts, and to situations of a similar character. In my understanding we are not here concerned with cases of "system" or "underlying unity" (*cf Moorov v. H.M. Advocate*[32]), words whose vagueness is liable to result in their misapplication, nor with a case involving proof of identity, or an

[31] [1974] 3 All E.R. 887.
[32] [1930] J.C. 68.

alibi, nor, even, is this a case where the evidence is adduced to rebut a particular defence. It is sometimes said that evidence of "similar facts" may be called to rebut a defence of innocent association, a proposition which I regard with suspicion since it seems a specious manner of outflanking the exclusionary rule. But we need not consider the validity or scope of this proposition. The Court of Appeal dealt with the case on the basis, submitted by the appellant's counsel, that no defence of innocent association was set up; in my opinion we should take the same course.

This is simply a case where evidence of facts similar in character to those forming the subject of the charge is sought to be given in support of the evidence on that charge. Though the case was one in which separate charges relating to different complainants were tried jointly, the principle must be the same as would arise if there were only one charge relating to one complainant. If the appellant were being tried on a charge relating to S, could the prosecution call H as a witness to give evidence about facts relating to H? The judge should apply just as strict a rule in the one case as in the other. If, as I believe, the general rule is that such evidence cannot be allowed, it requires exceptional circumstances to justify the admission. This House should not, in my opinion, encourage erosion of the general rule.

We can dispose at once of the suggestion that there is a special rule or principle applicable to sexual, or to homosexual, offences . . . Evidence that an offence of a sexual character was committed by A against B cannot be supported by evidence that an offence of a sexual character was committed by A against C, or against C, D and E.

The question certified suggest that the contrary may be true if the offences take a "particular form". I do not know what this means: all sexual activity has some form or other and the varieties are not unlimited: how particular must it be for a special rule to apply? The general salutary rule of exclusion must not be eroded through so vague an epithet. The danger of it being so is indeed well shown in the present case for the judge excluded the (similar fact) evidence of one boy because it showed "normal" homosexual acts while admitting the (similar fact) evidence of another boy because the homosexual acts assumed a different, and, in his view, "abnormal" pattern. Distinctions such as this, rightly called fine distinctions by the judge, lend an unattractive unreality to the law.

If the evidence was to be received, then it must be on some general principle not confined to sexual offences. There are obvious difficulties in the way of formulating any such rule in such a manner as, on the one hand, to enable clear guidance to be given to juries, and, on the other hand, to avoid undue rigidity.

The prevailing formulation is to be found in the judgment of the Court of Criminal Appeal in *R. v. Sims* where it was said,

> The evidence of each man was that the accused invited him into the house and there committed the acts charged. The acts they describe bear a striking similarity. That is a special feature sufficient in itself to justify the admissibility of the evidence; . . . The probative force of all the acts together is much greater than one alone; for, whereas the jury might think that one man might be telling an untruth, three or four are hardly likely to tell the same untruth unless they were conspiring together. If there is nothing to suggest a conspiracy their evidence would seem to be overwhelming.

Sims has not received universal approbation or uniform commentary, but I think that it must be taken that this passage has received at least the general approval of this House in *R. v. Kilbourne*.[33] For my part, since the statement is evidently related to the facts of that particular case, I should deprecate its literal use in other cases. It

[33] [1973] A.C. 529.

is certainly neither clear nor comprehensive. A suitable adaptation, and, if necessary, expansion, should be allowed to judges in order to suit the facts involved. The basic principle must be that the admission of similar fact evidence (of the kind now in question) is exceptional and requires a strong degree of probative force. This probative force is derived, if at all, from the circumstance that the facts testified to by several witnesses bear to each other such a striking similarity that they must, when judged by experience and common sense, either all be true, or have arisen from a cause common to the witnesses or from pure coincidence. the jury may, therefore, properly be asked to judge whether the right conclusion is that all are true, so that each story is supported by the other(s).

I use the words "a cause common to the witnesses" to include not only (as in *R. v. Sims*) the possibility that the witnesses may have invented a story in concert but also the possibility that a similar story may have arisen by a process of infection from media of publicity or simply from fashion. In the sexual field, and in others, this may be a real possibility: something much more is needed if this evidence is to be allowed. This is well illustrated by *R. v. Kilbourne* where the judge excluded "intra group" evidence because of the possibility, as it appeared to him, of collaboration between boys who knew each other well. This is, in my respectful opinion, the right course rather than to admit the evidence unless a case of collaboration or concoction is made out.

If this test is to be applied fairly, much depends in the first place upon the experience and common sense of the judge. As was said by Lord Simon in *R. v. Kilbourne*, in judging whether one fact is probative of another, experience plays as large a place as logic. And in matters of experience it is for the judge to keep close to current mores. What is striking in one age is normal in another: the perversions of yesterday may be the routine or the fashion of tomorrow. The ultimate test has to be applied by the jury using similar qualities of experience and common sense after a fair presentation of the dangers either way of admission or of rejection. Finally, whether the judge has properly used and stated the ingredients of experience and common sense may be reviewed by the Court of Appeal.

The present case is, to my mind, right on the border-line. There were only two relevant witnesses, S and H. The striking similarity as presented to the jury was and was only the active character of the sexual performance to which the accused was said to have invited the complainants. In relation to the incident which was the subject of the second charge, the language used by the boy was not specific: the "similarity" was derived from an earlier incident in connection with which the boy used a verb connoting an active role. I agree with, I think, all your Lordships in thinking that all of this, relating not very specifically to the one striking element, common to two boys only, is , if sufficient, only just sufficient. Perhaps other similarities could have been found in the accused's approaches to the boys (I do not myself find them particularly striking) but the judge did not rest upon them or direct the jury as to their "similarity". I do not think that these ought now to be relied upon. The dilution of the "striking" fact by more prosaic details might have weakened the impact upon the jury rather than strengthened it. The judge dealt properly and fairly with the possibility of a conspiracy between the boys.

These matters lie largely within the field of the judge's discretion, and of the jury's task; the Court of Appeal has reviewed the whole matter in a careful judgment. I do not think that there is anything which justifies the interference of this House. But I confess to some fear that the case, if regarded as an example, may be setting the standard of "striking similarity" too low.

A common theme from the judgments in *Boardman* was that the similar fact evidence should possess a "unique or striking similarity" to the offence charged. How does this test relate to the issues faced by a court in deciding whether to admit similar fact evidence? Those issues are firstly the evidence's relevance to an issue and secondly whether the evidence's probative weight (or degree of relevance) is sufficient to overcome its prejudicial effect:

probative force: the "striking similarity" between the offence charged and the "other" act leads to the conclusion that the two acts were committed by the same person. If both victims identify the accused as that person, then, in the absence of any evidence suggesting collusion or coincidence, the similar fact evidence is relevant since it makes it more likely that the defendant is guilty.

prejudice: laying other accusations not in the indictment at the door of the accused invariably creates prejudice in the mind of the jury. The "striking similarity" test also provides a guideline for the level of probative weight which is required to overcome that prejudice. Revealing the accused's sexual proclivities must lead to preconceptions in the mind of the jury. For the prosecution to demonstrate that those proclivities are also unusual and that it would be most unlikely for another to share them gives the evidence enough probative force to nullify that prejudice. Having said that, the facts in *Boardman* clearly only just reach that level — their Lordships are far from convinced that the accused's desire to play the passive sexual role is that unusual; additionally the boys are at the same school and collusion could scarcely be ruled out.

The "striking similarity" test addresses both these issues but overall it can be argued that *Boardman* has had both good and bad effects:

(1) prior to *Boardman*, firstly "relevance" was a matter of whether the similar fact evidence conformed to artificial categories. *Boardman* moved away from this technical approach; secondly too little attention was given to whether the probative force of the evidence was sufficient to overcome the prejudicial effect. 'Striking similarity' was a constructive guideline.

(2) subsequent to *Boardman*, firstly the judgment conflates the issues of relevance and probative force which should be kept analytically separate; secondly subsequent courts have become fixated by the phrase, "striking similarity", seeing it as the only test for relevance or probative weight whereas similar fact evidence may be not at all striking and yet relevant. This can be seen in factual situations such as that in *R. v. Roy*[34] where a doctor was accused of indecent assault on a number of patients. There was nothing "striking" about the accounts nor were there any bizarre elements. But aggregated, the stories had considerable probative weight, rebutting any suggestion that these assaults might have been bona fide medical examinations. Finally and pragmatically the criterion of "striking similarity" has proved less than easy to apply[35]

[34] [1992] Crim.L.R. 185; *R. v. Laidman and Agnew* [1992] Crim.L.R. 428 .

[35] *R. v. Novac* (1976) 65 Cr.App.R. 107; *R. v. Johannsen* (1977) 65 Cr.App.R. 101; *R. v. Tricoglus* (1976) 65 Cr.App.R. 16; *R. v. Barrington* [1981] 1 WLR 419.

R. v. P. and the retreat from "striking similarity"

The House of Lords addressed these issues in *R. v. P*[36] where the defendant was accused of incest with and rape of his two daughters. There was evidence that he had engaged in incest over a long period, using force and threatening both girls unless they kept silent. He had paid for abortions for both. At trial, he applied for the counts relating to each daughter to be tried separately. The judge refused, holding that the testimony of one daughter was admissible evidence on charges involving the other. The Court of Appeal quashed the conviction on the grounds that there was no feature of striking similarity. The House of Lords restored the conviction and held that the test of admissibility was whether the evidence was relevant and had probative value which outweighed its prejudicial effect. It was not necessary to single out "striking similarity" as an essential element, though in some cases where identity was in issue, a "signature" might be looked for.

R. v. P. [1991] 3 All E.R. 337 at 340e–348f, *per* Lord Mackay L.C.

It is apparent that the particular difficulty which arose in this case is the development of the authorities in this area of the law requiring some feature of similarity beyond what has been described as the paederast's or incestuous father's stock-in-trade before one victim's evidence can be properly admitted upon the trial of another that inhibited the Court of Appeal from deciding as otherwise it would have done. The question in this appeal therefore is whether this development is a sound one or not. (Lord Mackay reviewed the judgments in *Makin* and *Boardman*)

As this matter has been left in *Boardman* I am of the opinion that it is not appropriate to single out 'striking similarity' as an essential element in every case in allowing evidence of an offence against one victim to be heard in connection with an allegation against another. Obviously, in cases where the identity of the offender is in issue, evidence of a character sufficiently special reasonably to identify the perpetrator is required . . .

From all that was said by the House in *Boardman* I would deduce the essential features of evidence which is to be admitted is that its probative force in support of the allegation that an accused person committed a crime is sufficiently great to make it just to admit the evidence, notwithstanding that it is prejudicial to the accused in tending to show that he was guilty of another crime. Such probative force may be derived from striking similarities in the evidence about the manner in which the crime was committed and the authorities provide illustrations of that, of which *Straffen* and *Smith* provide notable examples. But restricting the circumstances in which there is sufficient probative force to overcome prejudice of evidence relating to another crime to cases in which there is some striking similarity between them is to restrict the operation of the principle in a way which gives too much effect to a particular manner of stating it, and is not justified in principle. Hume in his work *Commentaries on the Law of Scotland Respecting Crimes*,[37] said long ago:

[36] [1991] 3 All E.R. 337.
[37] (4th ed. 1844) Vol. 2, p. 384.

> . . . the aptitude and coherence of the several circumstances often as fully confirm the truth of the story, as if all the witnesses were deponing to the same facts.

Once the principle is recognised, that what has to be assessed is the probative force of the evidence in question, the infinite variety of circumstances in which the question arises demonstrates that there is no single manner in which this can be achieved. Whether the evidence has sufficient probative value to outweigh its prejudicial effect must in each case be a question of degree.

The view that some feature of similarity beyond what has been described as the paederast's or incestuous father's stock-in-trade before one victim's evidence can be properly admitted upon the trial of another seems to have been stated for the first time in those terms in *R. v. Inder*.[38] Although that case also contains a reference to a warning not too attach too much importance to Lord Salmon's vivid phrase 'uniquely or strikingly similar' I think in the context this is what has occurred. This trend has been followed in later cases, for example, *R. v. Clarke*,[39] *R. v. Tudor*[40] and particularly *R. v. Brooks*.[41] In so far as these decisions required, as an essential feature, a similarity beyond the stock-in-trade I consider they fall to be overruled.

In the present case the evidence of both girls describes a prolonged course of conduct in relation to each of them. In relation to each of them force was used. There was a general domination of the girls with threats against them unless they observed silence and a domination of the wife which inhibited her intervention. The accused seemed to have an obsession for keeping the girls to himself, for himself. The younger took on the role of the elder daughter when the elder daughter left home. There was also evidence that the accused was involved in regard to payment for the abortions in respect of both girls. In my view these circumstances taken together gave strong probative force to the evidence of each of the girls in relation to the incidents involving the other, and was certainly sufficient to make it just to admit that evidence, notwithstanding its prejudicial effect. This was clearly the view taken by the Court of Appeal and they would have given effect to it were it not for the line of authority in the Court of Appeal to which I have referred.

The approach which I have suggested is in accordance with the law of Scotland as described in *Moorov v. HM Advocate* and the cases which followed it . . . .Although there is a difference between the law of Scotland, which requires corroboration generally in criminal cases, and the law of England, which does not, the principles which determine whether one piece of evidence can corroborate another are the same as those which determine whether evidence in relation to one offence is admissible in respect of another. The law of New Zealand, to which we were referred, also shows, in my opinion, a similar development. The latest of the cases from New Zealand to which we were referred is the decision of the Court of Appeal in *R. v. Huijser*.[42] The crux of the judgment is set out succinctly:[43]

> In essence the argument for the appellant is that the evidence in question is no more than evidence of propensity. On the other hand the argument for the Crown is in essence, to quote from the written submission by Mr Burston based on *Hsi En Feng*'s case[44] ". . . after hearing the four women in this case, the jury

[38] (1977) 67 Cr.App.R. 143.
[39] (1977) 67 Cr.App.R. 398.
[40] July 18, 1988 (unreported).
[41] (1990) 92 Cr.App.R. 36.
[42] [1988] 1 N.Z.L.R. 577.
[43] *ibid.* at 578.
[44] [1985] 1 N.Z.L.R. 222.

> would be entitled to take the view that the appellant was operating his business in such a way as to create and take advantage of opportunity for sexual contact, not necessary for business purposes, with relatively young women shop employees. it would be contrary to the requirements of justice to deny the jury the advantage of the full picture." Weighing the arguments and considering the depositions, we have concluded that the judge, in his conclusion, and the Crown are right. This is not a case like the more borderline one of *R. v. McLean*[45] where this court held the prejudicial effect clearly outweighed probative value. The evidence, if accepted, shows a practice established over a considerable number of years by the accused of subjecting women employees to minor sexual assaults and harassment during the course of their working relationships with him. It indicates a constant or continual attitude by him.

When a question of the kind raised in this case arises I consider that the judge must first decide whether there is material upon which the jury would be entitled to conclude that the evidence of one victim, about what occurred to that victim, is so related to the evidence given by another victim, about what happened to that other victim, that the evidence of the first victim provides strong enough support for the evidence of the second victim to make it just to admit it, notwithstanding the prejudicial effect of admitting the evidence. This relationship, from which support is derived, may take many forms and while these forms may include 'striking similarity' in the manner in which the crime is committed, consisting of unusual characteristics in its execution the necessary relationship is by no means confined to such circumstances. Relationships in time and circumstances other than these may well be important relationships in this connection. Where the identity of the perpetrator is in issue, and evidence of this kind is important in that connection, obviously something in the nature of what has been called in the course of argument a signature or other special feature will be necessary. To transpose this requirement to other situations where the question is whether a crime has been committed, rather than who did commit it, is to impose an unnecessary and improper restriction upon the application of the principle.

For the reasons which I have given, I am of the opinion that there was sufficient connection between the circumstances spoken of by the two girls in the present case for their evidence mutually to support each other, that the appeal should be allowed, and the conviction restored.

I would answer the first question posed by the Court of Appeal[46] by saying that the evidence referred to is admissible if the similarity is sufficiently strong, or there is other sufficient relationship between the events described in the evidence of the other young children of the family, and the abuse charged, that the evidence if accepted, would so strongly support the truth of that charge that it is fair to admit it, notwithstanding its prejudicial effect. It follows that the answer to the second question[47] is No, provided there is a relationship between the offences of the kind I have just described.

Lord Mackay is clear that it is "not appropriate" to single out "striking similarity" as an essential element. This judgment reflects the principles

[45] [1978] 2 N.Z.L.R. 358.

[46] "Where a father or step-father is charged with sexually abusing a young daughter of the family, is evidence that he also similarly abused other young children of the family admissible (assuming there to be no collusion) in support of such a charge in the absence of other 'striking similarities'?".

[47] "Where a defendant is charged with sexual offences against more than one child or young person, is it necessary in the absence of 'striking similarities' for the charges to be tried separately?"

propounded by Lord Wilberforce in *Boardman* while at the same time casting off the straitjacket of "striking similarity". Relevance depends on the issue which needs to be decided. Smith[48] suggests three scenarios where the evidence may attain that degree of cogency:

(1) where the evidence shows that the crime was committed by the accused.
(2) where the evidence shows that the witness was speaking the truth: in *Roy*, while one patient might be disbelieved, it is hard not to believe in the defendant's guilt when there are nine unconnected complaints of indecency during medical examinations.
(3) where the evidence identifies the defendant as the criminal: in *P.*, Lord Mackay considered that in cases where similar fact evidence is used to prove identity, something in the nature of a hallmark is required. This can lead to unnecessary distinctions as can be seen in *R. v. Johnson*[49] and *R. v. Downey*.[50]

The degree of relevance of one victim's account to that of the other is provided by the circumstances and relationships. This may take many forms. But the probative force must be of such a degree that it is "just to admit the evidence" despite the prejudicial effect. However in both *Boardman* and *P*, their Lordships give considerable attention to the issue of relevance but the nature of the prejudice generated gets short shrift. It was emphasised by Lord Wilberforce in *Boardman* that where there is evidence of similar conduct on other occasions, those stories must derive from a common cause, which can be collusion, coincidence or the fact that the witnesses are all telling the truth. Whatever the degree of probative force that the evidence possesses, a court must be able to rule out collusion or coincidence.

Collusion and contamination

In *R. v. Ananthanarayanan*[51] there were four complaints, all from nurses at different establishments, complaining of indecent assaults by the defendant, a consultant psychiatrist. The complaints were all made at the same time, prompted by a common source in the local social services department who had sought out potential complainants. The relevance of the evidence lay in the fact that it tended to show that the witnesses were speaking the truth unless there was collusion.

[48] Smith J.C., *Criminal Evidence* (1995), 137 *et seq.*
[49] [1995] Crim.L.R. 53.
[50] [1995] Crim.L.R. 414.
[51] [1994] 2 All E.R. 847; applied in *R. v. Ryder* [1994] 2 All E.R. 859.

R. v. Ananthanarayanan [1994] 2 All E.R. 847 at 851j–858c, per Laws J.

. . . The question is whether the judge's direction to the jury as to what is meant by 'contamination' in a context such as this was correct. He said:

> . . . go on to ask yourselves, "Are we sure that the evidence of all the women is free from . . . contamination", by which I mean that you are sure that they have not put their heads together to make false allegations or to exaggerate allegations or to put a sinister connotation on an incident which does not deserve a sinister connotation or they have been influenced by hearing of other people's allegations or they have been influenced by the suggestion by some third person, such as a person carrying out the preliminary investigation in this case. You have to be satisfied that all these women are independent witnesses when they make these allegations.

Had the judge only directed the jury that the possibility of contamination could be excluded, if they were sure that the witnesses had not conspired to give false evidence, that, we think, would have been a misdirection. The reason is that for the evidence of one complainant to be admissible as corroborative of the evidence of another it is a necessary condition that each be truly independent of the other; and a witness's account may be infected by what another complainant has said without there being even a suspicion of a deliberate intention to tell a false story. One witness may be unconsciously influenced by what she has heard from another: she may adopt details of which she has been told as if they were details of what had happened to her, and may do it in all innocence, and so it is not enough to direct the jury that they must negative perjury or conspiracy to perjure. But the judge did not limit his direction in that way . . .

His (the appellant's counsel) proposed . . . reasons why we should hold that the judge ought not to have directed the jury that the evidence of the women was capable of offering mutual corroboration. The first was that on the facts there was a real risk that any one of the complainant's accounts might have been 'contaminated' by any other . . .

In our judgment these circumstances give rise, at least, to a real possibility that the complaints which ultimately emerged and which formed the basis of the prosecution case before the jury, were not truly independent one of another. The fact that some of them may have been prompted obviously suggests this . . .

Given the judge's direction as to what would constitute contamination of one witness's evidence by that of another cannot itself be impeached, the true question here is whether he should have left the possibility of mutual corroboration to the jury at all . . .

. . . The question starkly raised in this case is whether it is for the judge or the jury to decide whether the risk exists. That being so, one can see at once that the answer depends upon a correct analysis of their respective roles. Elementarily it is always the judge's function to decide what evidence is admissible before the jury, and the jury's function to decide what facts to find on the evidence. In principle, therefore, where a question of admissibility depends on the resolution of an issue of fact, it is for the judge to resolve it.

(Having reviewed the authorities, Laws J. continued)

In *R. v. Johannsen*,[52] which was also a sexual case, Lawton L.J., having cited from *Kilbourne*[53] and *Boardman*, said this, If the defendant alleges, as in this case, that there is a real chance that the alleged victims conspired to give false evidence, how

[52] (1977) 65 Cr.App.R. 101.
[53] *DPP v. Kilbourne* [1973] 1 All E.R. 440.

is [the judge] to determine that issue? . . . How is any conflict to be resolved? The answer must surely be — by the jury. This has long been the practice of the Courts. Judges know of the possibility. That is why it is common practice to direct juries about it . . .

There is, however, one aspect of *Johannsen* from which we would respectfully depart. It consists of Lawton L.J.'s remarks to the effect that the question of whether evidence of this kind should be left to the jury is a matter for judicial discretion. We have already explained that the risk of contamination in potentially corroborative evidence goes to the admissibility of that evidence. Questions of admissibility are not matters for the discretion of the judge, since by definition the existence of a true discretion means that the judge may in principle lawfully decide the point either way. But if evidence is inadmissible, nothing is more obvious than that the judge cannot properly admit it. If a trial judge concludes that a real risk of contamination exists in circumstances of the kind raised by this case, he possesses no discretion to admit it . . .

The Court of Appeal held that where there is a real risk of contamination, the evidence must be excluded. If the judge feels that there is a possible risk, the evidence can be left to the jury who should be directed that if they feel it is a substantial risk, then they should not treat the evidence as corroborative. To decide whether the risk exists or not warrants a holding of a *voire dire*. This cannot be on the basis of a bare assertion by the defence at the start of a case but it is a factor to be borne in mind by the trial judge throughout the prosecution case.[54]

The ruling in *Ananthanarayanan* carried a serious risk of rendering the ruling in *P.* ineffective since there must always be a real risk of contamination between siblings living under the same roof. It was reconsidered by the House of Lords in *R. v. H.*[55] which involved a defendant accused of sexual offences carried out against his adopted daughter and stepdaughter between 1987 and 1989. The complaints were made in 1992, after confiding in the appellant's wife. Russell L.J. reviewed the decision of Laws J. in *Ananthanarayanan* and said:

_R. v. H._ [1994] 2 All E.R. 881 at 886b–887a, _per_ Russell L.J.

For our part we pause and venture to suggest that in the passage cited from *Ananthanarayanan* the court was confusing the admissibility of evidence with the quality of evidence, that is, the role that the evidence, once admitted, plays in the jury's deliberations. If there is a risk of contamination the evidence cannot be used as corroboration. it does not necesssarily follow that the evidence becomes wholly inadmissible as is the case when the judge excludes evidence because of breaches of the code made under the provisions of the Police and Criminal Evidence Act 1984. In our judgment the two situations are quite different and the one is not an analogy of the other.

In our judgment and experience, in almost every case where two or more daughters are living under the same roof and complain of molestation by their

[54] *R. v. W* [1994] 2 All E.R. 872.
[55] [1994] 2 All E.R. 881.

father it is virtually inevitable that at some stage the daughters will have talked between themselves and usually with their mother. Whether this contaminates their evidence is very much a fact-finding process. Active collaboration will invariably be denied. there may be extreme cases where the judge concludes, having seen and heard the witnesses, that collaboration has taken place, and in such a case he may exercise his powers to stop the trial and direct an acquittal on *Galbraith* principles[56] or abort the trial and sever the indictment. But these exceptional cases apart, we take the view that a jury, having seen and heard the witnesses, should form its own assessment of the dangers and, provided it receives the warnings and directions to be found in the summing up of Tucker J. in the instant case, the jury can properly decide whether the evidence of one complainant corroborates the evidence of another. In our view, to deny the jury the responsibility of this fact-finding exercise is to usurp the function of the jury and we do not believe that the long line of authority to which reference was made in *Ananthanarayanan* was ever intended to assert the contrary . . .

. . . The judge is not deciding a question of admissibility when he considers whether evidence can be used as corroboration. The evidence of the individual complainant remains admissible even if it is contaminated. Contamination goes not to admissibility but to the part to be played by the evidence after it is admitted. The proper role of the evidence, once admitted, can be left to the jury, who will receive appropriate directions from the judge. It must depend, in our judgment, upon the degree of contamination.

For the prosecution, the admission of similar fact evidence is often important to strengthen an evidentially weak case. The cases express a valid principle, namely that if evidence is relevant to a fact in issue, it should be admitted. But while relevance can be demonstrated by logical steps, there are no objective criteria for determining the probative weight, let alone the prejudicial effect, of evidence of previous criminal conduct. As long as the trial judge addresses his or her mind to the balance between proof and prejudice, the appellate court will not interfere with any conclusion. Without guiding criteria, the admission of similar fact evidence becomes a lottery and abrogates the principle is that it is unfair that an accused should be answerable at a trial for anything other than the offence charged. The admission of such evidence also infringes the concept of treating like cases alike because an accused with a criminal record will be treated differently from an accused without a record. The need is for the courts take a less relaxed attitude to identifying and combating prejudice.

Similar Fact Evidence in Civil Proceedings

Similar principles apply to the admission of similar fact evidence in civil cases, although there is not the emphasis on the protection of the accused from prejudice that is found in criminal cases. The key factors are again relevance and the probative force. In *Mood Music Publishing v. De Wolfe Publishing Ltd*[57] the plaintiffs owned the copyright of a musical work. The defendants supplied a musical work for use in a television play. The

[56] *R. v. Galbraith* [1981] 1 W.L.R. 1039.
[57] [1976] 1 All E.R. 763.

plaintiffs complained that the work infringed their copyright. The defendants conceded that the works were similar but argued that this was coincidence. The plaintiffs sought to adduce evidence, some of which was obtained by a trap engineered by the plaintiff, that the defendants had reproduced other musical works that were subject to copyright:

Mood Music Publishing v. De Wolfe Publishing Ltd [1976] 1 All E.R. 763 at 766c–h, _per_ Lord Denning M.R.

The admissibility of evidence as to 'similar facts' has been much considered in the criminal law. Some of them have reached the highest tribunal . . . The criminal courts have been very careful not to admit such evidence unless its probative value is so strong that it should be received in the interests of justice: and its admission will not operate unfairly to the accused. In civil cases the courts will admit evidence of similar facts if it is logically probative, that is it is logically relevant in determining the matter which is in issue; provided that it is not oppressive or unfair to the other side; and also that the other side has fair notice of it and is able to deal with it.

The matter in issue in the present case is whether the resemblances . . . are mere coincidences or are due to copying. on that issue it is very relevant to know that there are these other cases of musical works which are undoubtedly the subject of copyright, but yet the defendants have produced musical works bearing a close resemblance to them. Whereas it might be due to mere coincidence in one case, it is very unlikely that there would be coincidences in four cases. It is rather like *R. v. Sims* where it was said 'The probative force of all the acts together is much greater than one alone'. So the probative force of four resemblances together is much better than one alone.

It seems to me the judge was right . . . I would dismiss the appeal.

15

THE ACCUSED AS WITNESS

Introduction

The problems which emerge when the defendant testifies did not arise until 1898. Before that time, he or she was not a competent witness but became one under the Criminal Evidence Act 1898:

1.—Every person charged with an offence shall be a competent witness for the defence at every stage of the proceedings, whether the person so charged is charged solely or jointly with any other person. Provided as follows:

a) A person so charged shall not be called as a witness in pursuance of the Act except on his own application;

b) The failure of any person charged with an offence to give evidence shall not be the subject of any comment by the prosecution;[1]

[c) and d) repealed]

e) A person charged and being a witness in pursuance of this Act may be asked any question in cross-examination notwithstanding that it would tend to criminate him as to the offence charged;

f) A person charged and called as a witness in pursuance of this Act shall not be asked, and if asked shall not be required to answer, any question tending to show that he has committed or been convicted of or been charged with any offence other than that wherewith he is then charged, or is of bad character, unless: —
   i) the proof that he has committed or been convicted of such other offence is admissible evidence to show that he is guilty of the offence wherewith he is then charged; or
   ii) he has personally or by his advocate asked questions of the witnesses for the prosecution with a view to establish his own good character, or has given evidence of his own good character, or the nature or conduct of the defence is such as to involve imputations on the character of the prosecutor or the witnesses for the prosecution; or
   iii) he has given evidence against any other person charged in the same proceedings.

[1] This proviso has now been repealed by the Criminal Justice and Public Order Act 1994, s.168 and Sched. 11. The position is now governed by ss.34–37 of that Act.

The Sword and the Shield — section 1(e) and section 1(f)

As a result of the passage of the Criminal Evidence Act 1898, defence counsel could examine the defendant for the first time. Evidence-in-chief poses no problems but real difficulties arise in cross-examination. What questions could the accused be made to answer? What constraints were to be imposed on the prosecution? There are two basic problems:

(1) should the accused be allowed to rely upon the privilege against self-incrimination?[2] The position for witnesses generally is as follows:

Blunt v. Park Lane Hotel [1942] 2 K.B. 253 at 257, _per_ Goddard L.J.

> The rule is that no-one is bound to answer any question if the answer thereto would, in the opinion of the judge, have a tendency to expose [him or her] to any criminal charge, penalty or forfeiture which the judge regards as reasonably likely to be preferred or sued for.

Were the accused able to take advantage of this privilege, any testimony that he or she gave would be merely an exculpatory account which could not be challenged by the prosecution. But under section 1(e) of the Act, prosecuting counsel is given a sword and is able to ask the defendant any question

> "notwithstanding that it would tend to criminate him as to the offence charged".

(2) should the prosecution be permitted the normal right to attack the credibility of any witness appearing for the defence, by asking questions about prior convictions or bad character generally?

Were this permissible, evidence on the accused's criminal record would be admitted which would be deeply prejudicial but may have little probative value. A shield against this was erected by s. 1(f) which forbids questions in cross-examination

> ". . . tending to show that he has committed or been convicted of or been charged with any offence other than that wherewith he is then charged or is of bad character . . ."

This enabled the accused to testify about the offence, be cross-examined about his or her participation while keeping any murky past a secret. As we shall see, it is only under certain circumstances, such as raising the issue of one's own good character or attacking

[2] This privilege is discussed at 239, *et seq.*

the character of prosecution witnesses, that the prosecution would be entitled to inquire into that disreputable past.

The structure of section 1 seems unproblematic at this point: proviso (e) allows questioning on any directly relevant issue; proviso (f) forbids questioning which simply goes to the defendant's credibility since this is only indirectly relevant and is also prejudicial. But this clear distinction does not always exist. The sections can be mutually contradictory since a question which reveals a previous conviction can still be relevant to a fact in issue and thus can tend to incriminate. Such a question may be admissible within section 1(e) while at the same time the fact that it shows that the accused has committed another offence makes it inadmissible under section 1(f).

This contradiction asks questions about the relationship between section 1(e) and section 1(f). Which paragraph is to be treated as predominant: if the question is relevant under section 1(e), are we to ignore the fact that it reveals prior crimes? if the question reveals a previous offence, is it to be excluded regardless of its relevance?

This problem was directly put to the House of Lords in *Jones v. DPP*.[3] The accused was charged with murder and rape of a young girl guide. Previously he had been convicted of the rape of another young girl. The rape conviction was not proved as part of the prosecution case. At his trial for murder, he gave an account of his movements which involved his being with a prostitute and having had a long conversation with his wife when he returned home. This alibi corresponded very closely with the account that he had given in the previous rape trial. In the course of giving evidence Jones made reference to having previously been in trouble with the police.

Could he be questioned about these suspiciously similar alibis with a view to showing that the proferred alibi was false? The paradox is that section 1(e) permitted the question since it tended to show that his account was false but that section 1(f) prohibited it since it revealed a previous conviction. Lord Reid said:

Jones v. DPP [1962] A.C. 635 at 662–666, *per* Lord Reid

It is well established that the 1898 Act has no application to evidence given by any person other than the accused: where it was competent before that Act for a witness to prove or refer to a previous conviction of the accused, that is still competent. What the Act does is to alter the old rules as regards the accused. It might merely have provided that the accused should be a competent witness; then the ordinary rules would have applied to him. But it goes on to afford to him protection which the ordinary rules would not give him: it expressly prohibits certain kinds of question being put to him. That must mean questions which would be competent and relevant under the ordinary rules, because there was no need to prohibit any question which would in any event have been excluded by the ordinary

[3] [1962] A.C. 635.

rules. So what must now be considered is what kinds of question, which would have been competent and relevant under the ordinary rules of evidence, does the Act prohibit . . .

The questions prohibited are those which 'tend to show' certain things. Does this mean tend to prove or tend to suggest? . . . In my judgment, 'tends to show' means tends to suggest to the jury. But the crucial point in the present case is whether the questions are to be considered in isolation or whether they are to be considered in light of all that had gone before them at the trial. If the questions or line of questioning has to be considered in isolation I think that the questions with which this appeal is concerned would tend to show at least that the accused had previously been charged with an offence. The jury would be likely to jump to that conclusion, if this was the first they had heard of the matter. But I do not think that the questions ought to be considered in isolation. If the test is the effect the questions would be likely to have on the minds of the jury that necessarily implies that one must have regard to what the jury had already heard. If the jury already knew that the accused had been charged with an offence, a question inferring that he had been charged would add nothing and it would be absurd to prohibit it. If the obvious purpose of this provision is to protect the accused from possible prejudice, as I think it is, then 'show' must mean 'reveal', because it is only a revelation of something new which could cause such prejudice.

. . . I am of the opinion that this appeal should be dismissed on the ground that these questions were not prohibited because they did not 'tend to show' any of the matters specified in proviso (f).

But in case it should be thought that some of the views which I have expressed are not in accord with what was said by Lord Simon in *Stirland v. DPP*,[4] I must say something about that case. That was a case where the accused had put his character in issue and the questions which it was held ought not to have been put to him in cross-examination dealt with an occasion when a former employer had questioned him about a suspected forgery. But the case did not turn on proviso (f) because the second exception in the proviso was satisfied by the accused having given evidence of his good character and there the proviso was excluded.

Lord Simon did, however, state six rules which should govern cross-examination to credit of an accused person. First he set out proviso (f). Then comes the rule which gives rise to the difficulty: '2. He may, however, be cross-examined as to any of the evidence he has given in chief, including statements concerning his good record, with a view to testing his veracity or accuracy or to showing that he is not to be believed on his oath.' Applied to a case where the accused has put his character in issue I think that is correct, because then proviso (f) does not apply. But I do not think that Lord Simon can have meant it to apply in its general form to a case where proviso (f) does operate because earlier in his speech he said: 'This House has laid it down in *Maxwell v. DPP*[5] that, while paragraph (f) of this section absolutely prohibits any question of the kind there indicated being put to the accused in the witness box unless one or other of the conditions (i), (ii) or (iii) is satisfied, it does not follow that such questions are in all circumstances justified whenever one or other of the conditions is fulfilled'. Thus he recognised the absolute character of the prohibition except where one or other of the conditions is satisfied, so he cannot have intended to say that there is another case, not covered by the conditions, where the proviso also does not apply, namely, where questions are put with a view to testing the veracity of the accused's evidence in chief. but if he did mean that it was certainly obiter and I would not agree with it. It would in effect be legislating by adding a fourth condition to proviso (f). The Attorney-General refused to take this point and I think he was perfectly right.

[4] [1944] A.C. 315.
[5] [1935] A.C. 309.

It is said that the views which I have expressed involve overruling two decisions of the Court of Criminal Appeal, *R. v. Chitson*[6] and *R. v. Kennaway*.[7] I do not think so. I think the decisions were right but the reasons given for them were not. In the former case the accused was charged with having had carnal knowledge of a girl aged 14. Giving evidence, she said that the accused told her that he had previously done the same thing to another girl, who, she said, was under 16. No objection was taken to this evidence, I assume rightly. So before the accused gave evidence the jury already knew that he was alleged to have committed another offence. If the views which I have already expressed are right, cross-examining the accused about this matter disclosed nothing new to them and therefore did not offend against the prohibition in proviso (f). But the judgment of the court was not based on that ground: it was said that although the questions tended to prove that the accused was of bad character they also tend to show that he was guilty of the offence with which he was charged. For the reasons which I have given I do not think that that is sufficient to avoid the prohibition in proviso (f).

R. v. Kennaway was a prosecution for forgery. Accomplices giving evidence for the prosecution described the fraudulent scheme of which the forgery was a part and related a conversation with the accused in which he stated to them that some years earlier he had forged another will in pursuance of a similar scheme. Then in cross-examination the accused was asked a number of questions about this other forgery. Those questions were held to have been properly put to him. here, again, these questions disclosed nothing new to the jury and I can see no valid objection to them. But again that was not the ground of the court's decision. Their ground of decision was similar to that in *Chitson*'s case, and I need not repeat what I have said about that case . . .

Lord Denning took a different approach:

Jones op. cit. at 666–671, *per* Lord Denning

My Lords, much of the discussion before your Lordships was directed to the effect of section 1(f) of the Criminal Evidence Act 1898: and, if that were the sole paragraph for consideration, I should have thought that counsel for the Crown ought not to have asked the questions he did . . . But I do not think it rests on section 1(f). In my judgment, the questions were admissible under section 1(e), which says that a person charged 'may be asked any question in cross-examination notwithstanding that it would tend to criminate him as to the offence charged'. As to this subsection, Viscount Sankey LC speaking for all in this House in *Maxwell*'s case, said that under section 1(e) 'a witness may be cross-examined in respect of the offence charged, and cannot refuse to answer questions directly relevant to the offence on the ground that they tend to incriminate him: thus if he denies the offence, he may be cross-examined to refute the denial.' I would add that, if he gives an explanation in an attempt to exculpate himself, he may be cross-examined to refute his explanation. And nonetheless so because it tends incidentally to show that he had previously been charged with another offence . . .

The situation is precisely covered by the second proposition in *Stirland*'s case where Viscount Simon LC in this House, with the assent of all present, said that, notwithstanding the prohibition in section 1(f), the accused man, ". . . may, however, be cross-examined as to any of the evidence he has given in chief, including statements concerning his good record . . .' and including, I would add,

[6] [1909] 2 K.B. 945.
[7] [1917] 1 K.B. 25.

any explanation offered by him '. . . with a view to testing his veracity or accuracy or showing that he is not to be believed on his oath.'

It is noteworthy that everyone at the trial of Jones acted on this view of the law. No one suggested that the questions were absolutely prohibited. All that was suggested was that it was a matter of discretion. And that is, I think, the true position. the judge was entitled in his discretion to exclude them if he thought they were so prejudicial as to outweigh their probative value. It was his discretion, not that of the prosecution. He did not exclude them but permitted them to be asked. They were, therefore, properly put.

In conclusion I would say that I view with concern the suggestion that the reasoning in *R. v. Chitson* and *R. v. Kennaway* was wrong and that what Viscount Simon LC said in *Stirland*'s case is no longer a safe guide. Those cases have governed the practice in our criminal courts for years: and the result has been wholly beneficial. It is not, in my opinion, right to resort now to a literal reading of the Act so as to displace them . . .

Although the dismissal of the appeal was unanimous, there was a significant split over the relationship between provisos (e) and (f):

(1) the majority opinion was that proviso (f) was predominant and prohibited any question ". . . tending to show that [the accused] has committed or been convicted of or been charged with any offence other than that wherewith he is then charged, or is of bad character". If the question revealed such offences, then it could not be asked even if it were relevant and tended to incriminate under proviso (e).

(2) the minority (Lords Denning and Devlin) took the broader view that the line of questioning was permissible under proviso (e) because the answers would tend to persuade the jury that the alibi which Jones was advancing was false. The questions were seeking to incriminate the defendant as to the offence charged.

There are differences of principle here: the minority approach has logical weight, believing that if the answer to a question would have direct probative force, it is admissible and any shield for the accused was secondary to probative value; the majority take a "due process" position, giving priority to the protection afforded by proviso (f) and construing proviso (e) narrowly to permit questioning only facts which immediately relate to the offence charged. This liberal position is undermined by the strict interpretation given to the phrase "tending to show". Since the defendant had mentioned "being in trouble with the police", the prosecution were not "revealing" prior offences and thus their questions were permissible. But this interpretation is highly technical and the protection afforded to the accused easily avoided. The defendant had not revealed any specific prior offence — "in trouble with the police" can mean anything. But the subsequent questioning about a previous alibi must have made the seriousness of the previous incident apparent to the jury. As Lord Denning said in *Jones*:

It is one thing to confess to having been in trouble before. It is quite another to have it emphasised against you with devastating detail. Before these questions were asked by the Crown, all that the jury knew was that at some unspecified time in the near or distant past, this man had been in trouble with the police. After the questions were asked, the jury knew, in addition, that he had very recently been in trouble for an offence on a Friday night which was of so sensational a character that it featured in a newspaper on the following Sunday — in these respects closely similar to the present offence — and that he had been charged in a court of law with that offence.[8]

The literal approach of the majority was mirrored in *R. v. Anderson*[9] where the defendant was charged with conspiracy to cause explosions at the Conservative Party Conference at Brighton in 1984. She had been arrested at a Glasgow flat with others where there were considerable amounts of incriminating evidence. She testified that she knew nothing of any conspiracy but had come over from Northern Ireland to smuggle escapees from the Maze prison through Scotland to Denmark. She was to play the innocent female escort to hoodwink immigration. At trial the prosecution obtained permission to question her on the fact that she was "wanted" by the Northern Irish police. The prosecution did not elicit the reason why she was wanted but they had been "ambushed" by the direction the defence had taken and wished to show that it was unlikely that the accused would be chosen as "innocent" escort. Such a line of questioning was directly relevant to an issue in the case and was admissible under section 1(e) but at the same time the questions showed the accused was of bad character as she was suspected of having committed another criminal offence. Section 1(f) prohibited such questions. Lord Lane C.J. held:

R. v. Anderson [1988] 2 All E.R. 549 at 555b–556g, *per* Lord Lane C.J.

[Having reviewed the facts in *Jones*] The majority supported the view that para. (e) is subordinate to and governed by para. (f)(i). Lord Reid's view was that the words of para. (e) have two possible interpretations . . . They could, first of all, mean 'tend to convince or persuade a jury that he (the defendant) is guilty' or, second, 'tend to connect him (the defendant) with the commission of the offence charged.' If they have the first meaning, the broader meaning, that, in Lord Reid's view, produces the insoluble conflict with para. (f) which we mentioned . . . . If, on the other hand, they have the second meaning, the narrower meaning, there is no such conflict because para. (f) could then apply to questions which tend to persuade a jury that the defendant is guilty. That, of course, leaves the residual problem which is not easy to answer, namely, how close the connection must be with the offence to bring it within the narrower meaning of para. (e).

. . . In the present case there was, in the question, a clear tendency to show that Martina Anderson had committed an offence other than that with which she was charged; obviously so because otherwise she would not be 'wanted' by the police. So in the light of the decision in *Jones v. DPP* the question would be admissible in

[8] *ibid.* at 667.
[9] [1988] 2 All E.R. 549.

any of the following circumstances, that is applying the reasoning which we have attempted to set out as explained by the House of Lords: first of all, if there was no tendency to reveal the commission of an offence as in *Jones v. DPP*, for example, because the commission of an offence had already (properly) been made known to the jury; second, if the proof of the commission tended to connect the defendant with the offence charged; and, third, if the defendant had given evidence of her own good character.

. . . As to the tendency to reveal, Anderson had already revealed that it was likely that she had committed a number of offences in respect of any one of which she might well have been 'wanted' by the police. There was probably a conspiracy to assist the escape of a prisoner, probably forgery of documents, probably conspiracy to forge, possession of firearms and so on, as already set out when we detailed the evidence which she gave before the jury. Thus it was already revealed that she had committed offences, although it might be that she was not yet 'wanted' by the police in respect of them. The jury already knew, therefore, that she had committed a number of offences, and the fact that she was 'wanted' by the police in respect of an unspecified offence, and therefore was probably guilty of committing an unspecified offence, was not, on the reasoning in *Jones v. DPP*, in the view of this court, a revelation to the jury.

As to the second point: does evidence which tends to destroy the defendant's innocent explanation of prima facie damning circumstances, connect the defendant with the crime so as to come within Lord Reid's analysis of the meaning of para. (e)? We are inclined to think it may, but we prefer to base our conclusion primarily on the fact that the appellant had already revealed that she had committed crimes.

There is however a different approach which is perhaps less artificial than the reasoning in *Jones v. DPP*, if we may say so.

Section 1 of the 1898 Act did nothing to alter the pre-existing law regarding what evidence the prosecution were entitled to adduce in order to prove their case . . .

The extent of that pre-existing law had been examined only four years previously in *Makin v. Att.-Gen. for New South Wales*. Lord Herschell L.C. said,[10]

> It is undoubtedly not competent for the prosecution to adduce evidence tending to show that the accused has been guilty of criminal acts other than those covered by the indictment for the purpose of leading to the conclusion that the accused is a person likely from his criminal conduct or character to have committed the offence for which he is being tried. On the other hand, the mere fact that the evidence adduced tends to show the commission of other crimes does not render it inadmissible if it be relevant to an issue before the jury and it may be so relevant if it bears upon the question whether the acts alleged to constitute the crime charged in the indictment were designed or accidental or to rebut a defence which would have been otherwise open to the accused.

Thus, if the prosecution know that a particular defence is going to be advanced, they may (subject to the judge's discretion) call evidence to rebut it as part of their own substantive case even if that tends to show the commission of other crimes. The defendant can plainly then be cross-examined about the matter. If the prosecution do not know of the defence in advance, then they may call evidence to rebut it and the defendant can be recalled, if that is desired, to deal with the rebutting evidence. The judge in the present case, wisely, the evidence not being in dispute, allowed that somewhat laborious process to be short-circuited. The result however was just as much in accordance with authority and the 1898 Act as if the procedure had been carried out *in extenso*.

[10] [1894] A.C. 57 at 64.

Lord Lane follows *Jones*, cataloguing a long list of offences which the accused had implicitly testified to having committed. She had already revealed her bad character and consequently the prosecution's questions about "being wanted by the police" did not "*tend to show*" that bad character afresh. Unlike *Jones*, the prosecution's line of questioning was not about the offences about which Anderson testified but about the fact that she was "wanted" by the police in Northern Ireland for an unspecified offence. The prosecution tactics were to suggest that the accused was not an ephemeral player in the IRA but a more central player, unlikely to be involved in relatively mundane operations such as assisting escapees. Again the court does not analyse the prejudice engendered by such questions.

But more significant is Lord Lane's alternative approach through *Makin* principles. Common law permits the prosecution to introduce any evidence which relevant and probative (whether directly or indirectly). Lord Herschell said:

> . . . the mere fact that the evidence adduced tends to show the commission of other crimes does not render it inadmissible if it be relevant to an issue before the jury.

In relation to the prosecution evidence-in-chief, this is a position that has become more substantial after the House of Lord's decision in *P.*[11] which lays down that, as long as the probative force outweighs the prejudicial effect, evidence is admissible despite the fact that it reveals previous disreputable or criminal conduct. What Lord Lane is suggesting in *Anderson* is that this common law position also applies in relation to the cross-examination of the accused, preserved by section 1(f)(i),[12]:

> the proof that he has committed or been convicted of such other offence is admissible evidence to show that he is guilty of the offence wherewith he is then charged;

In other words, the purpose of section 1(f) is to prevent the questioning of the defendant on matters that go merely to credit. The fact that evidence tends to show other crimes does not make it inadmissible if it is relevant to a matter before jury. The prosecution are entitled to advance evidence-in-chief as long as the probative weight is sufficient to outweigh any prejudicial effect. This is shown in *Jones* where it is difficult to argue that the defence should be permitted to advance a complicated exculpatory story without the jury being made aware that the same story had been used before.

The difficulty here is that the accused is at a considerable disadvantage by having leading questions (such as "It's true, isn't it, that the police in

[11] [1991] 3 All E.R. 337.

[12] This assumes that proviso (e) should be interpreted as simply excluding any right the accused might claim against self-incrimination.

Northern Ireland wish to interview you?") advanced in cross-examination, without prior argument and without foundation being laid by the prosecution. Procedurally it would be better if the prosecution advanced their own witnesses who could then be cross-examined by the defence.[13] Although this would initially disadvantage the prosecution, the relevant facts could still be laid before the jury and the judge may recall the defendant so that he or she could be cross-examined on the issue.

Dropping the shield

The defendant who chooses to testify can be questioned about any matter that is probative and relevant, subject to judicial discretion to disallow questions that are more prejudicial than probative. But the defendant is protected by section 1(f) from being questioned about extraneous matters of character that go solely to credit and have no bearing on any issue in the case. However this protection can be lost or thrown away under the exceptions to section 1(f).

Whether the shield is lost at any time is a matter for the judge. In *Maxwell v. DPP*,[14] the accused was charged with manslaughter arising out of the death of a woman on whom it was alleged an illegal abortion had been performed. He was cross-examined about a previous occasion when he was charged, although not convicted, in similar circumstances. The House of Lords held that the common law rules of relevance applied even where the exceptions to section 1(f) had been satisfied:

Maxwell v. DPP [1935] A.C. 309 at 316–320, *per* Viscount Sankey

. . . It must first of all be stated that it has been admitted throughout that the prisoner in saying that he had lived a good, clean, moral life had put his character in issue and had in the words of proviso (f)(ii) 'given evidence of his good character'. The first question here is, What consequences follow from that?

This involves the proper construction of section 1(f) . . . It was clear that if you allowed a prisoner to go into the witness-box, it was impossible to allow him to be treated as an ordinary witness. Had that been permitted, a prisoner who went into the box to give evidence on oath could have been asked about any previous conviction, with the result that an old offender would seldom, if ever, have been acquitted. This would have offended against one of the most deeply rooted and jealously guarded principles of our criminal law . . .

Some middle way, therefore, had to be discovered, and the result was that a certain amount of protection was accorded to a prisoner who gave evidence on his own behalf. As it has been expressed, he was presented with a shield. Apart, however, from this protection, he was placed in the position of an ordinary witness in an ordinary civil case. The laws of evidence were not otherwise altered by the Criminal Evidence Act 1898, and the prisoner who was a witness in his own case could not be asked questions which were irrelevant or had nothing to do with the

[13] In *R. v. Cokar* [1960] 2 All E.R. 175 the prosecution were not allowed to advance similar fact evidence in cross-examination — a proper foundation had to be laid.
[14] [1935] A.C. 309.

issue which the court was endeavouring to decide. As has already been pointed out, the prisoner in the present case threw away his shield and, therefore, the learned counsel for the prosecution was entitled to ask him, and he could be required to answer, any question tending to show that he had committed or been convicted of or been charged with an offence, but subject to the consideration that the question asked him must be one which was relevant and admissible in the case of an ordinary witness. The Act does not in terms say that in any case a prisoner may be asked or required to answer questions falling within proviso (f), or impose any such affirmative or absolute burden upon him. I think this conclusion is confirmed by a study of the words of the statute. In section 1, proviso (e), it has been enacted that a witness may be cross-examined in respect of the offence charged, and cannot refuse to answer questions directly relevant to the offence on the ground that they tend to incriminate him: thus if he denies the offence, he may be cross-examined to refute the denial. These are matters directly relevant to the charge on which he is being tried. Proviso (f), however, is dealing with matters outside and not directly relevant to the particular offence charged; such matters, to be admissible at all, must in general fall under two main classes: one is the class of evidence which goes to show not that the prisoner did the acts charged, but that, if he did those acts, he did them as part of a system or intentionally, so as to refute a defence that if he did them he did them innocently or inadvertently . . .

The other main class is where it is sought to show that the prisoner is not a person to be believed on his oath, which is generally attempted by what is call cross-examination to credit. Closely allied with this latter type of question is the rule that, if the prisoner by himself or his witnesses seek to give evidence of his own good character, for the purpose of showing that it is unlikely that he committed the offence charged, he raises by way of defence an issue as to his good character, so that he may fairly be cross-examined on that issue, just as any witness called by him to prove his good character may be cross-examined to show the contrary. All these matters are dealt with in proviso (f). The substantive part of that proviso is negative in form and as such is universal and is absolute unless the exceptions come into play. Then come the three exceptions: but it does not follow that when the absolute prohibition is superseded by a permission, that the permission is as absolute as the prohibition. When it is sought to justify a question it must not only be brought within the terms of the permission, but also must be capable of justification according to the general rules of evidence and in particular must satisfy the test of relevance . . . But it seems clear that the mere fact of a charge cannot in general be evidence of bad character or be regarded otherwise than as a misfortune. It seemed to be contended on behalf of the respondent that a charge was *per se* such evidence that the man charged, even though acquitted, must thereafter remain under a cloud, however innocent. I find it impossible to accept any such view. The mere fact that a man has been charged with an offence is no proof that he committed the offence. Such a fact is, therefore, irrelevant; it neither goes to show that the prisoner did the acts for which he is actually being tried nor does it go to his credibility as a witness. Such questions must, therefore, be excluded on the principle which is fundamental in the law of evidence as conceived in this country, especially in criminal cases, because if allowed, they are likely to lead the minds of the jury astray into false issues; not merely do they tend to introduce suspicion as if it were evidence, but they tend to distract the jury from the true issue — namely, whether the prisoner in fact committed the offence on which he is actually standing his trial. It is of the utmost importance for a fair trial that the evidence should be prima facie limited to matters relating to the transaction which forms the subject of the indictment and that any departure from these matters should be strictly confined.[15]

[15] His belief that to be charged is a "misfortune" can be contrasted with *Anderson* where Lord Lane said ". . . the fact that she was 'wanted' by the police in respect of an unspecified offence, and thefore was *probably guilty* of committing an unspecified offence . . ." However the question in *Anderson* related to the unlikelihood that the accused could front as an "innocent escort" and not to her credibility as a witness which was the issue in *Maxwell*.

Even when the shield is lost, any cross-examination must be relevant either to issues in the case or to the accused's credibility. Simply being charged is no proof that a person has been convicted and is not relevant to the question of credibility. Such a rule must apply to all witnesses who are being cross-examined and not just the accused. The general rule is that the accused cannot be examined as to credit unless:

(a) the first exception
This is contained in section 1(f)(i) and allows the accused to be asked questions about other offences where such evidence would be admissible at common law or statute.

This is not an illustration of the accused throwing away the shield but of losing it. The main example would be that of similar facts evidence where the previous misconduct is relevant to an issue in the case. The implications of this have been discussed above with relation to *Jones* and *Anderson*. In addition there are several situations where the accused can be questioned about previous convictions as a result of statutes such as section 27(3) Theft Act 1968.[16]

(b) the second exception, first limb
This provides, under section 1(f)(ii), that the shield is lost by the defendant seeking to establish his or her own good character.

A simple assertion of innocence is not putting your character into issue, requiring positive evidence of good character. Prior to 1898, where an accused sought to establish his or her own good character, the prosecution could both cross-examine any character witness and also introduce evidence in rebuttal. After 1898, the accused could testify and the first part of section 1(f)(ii) merely extends that common law to include the cross-examination of the accused. In *R. v. Samuel*,[17] the accused testified as to the occasions on which he had returned lost property and was then properly cross-examined on his theft convictions.

The purpose of such questioning is obviously to attack the accused's credibility as a witness but can it also be relevant to the probability of the accused having committed the offence charged? If Samuel's assertions of honesty had gone uncontroverted, he would have been entitled to rely upon a judge's direction to the effect that an honest man is less likely to have committed these offences.[18] Once good character has been raised and refuted, are the jury entitled to conclude that a dishonest person is more likely to commit such crimes? In *Samuel*, Lord Goddard J. said:

> It is very difficult to see how it is permissible to cross-examine a prisoner with regard to convictions, for instance, if he is a thief, and he is cross-examined on previous convictions of larceny, the jury is not, in effect, being asked to say: 'The

[16] See 438, *et seq*.
[17] (1956) 40 Cr.App.R. 8.
[18] *R. v. Vye* [1993] 2 All E.R. 241 — see 412, *et seq*.

> prisoner is just the sort of man who would commit these crimes and therefore it is highly probable that he did.' In theory, at any rate, what the jury is being asked to do is to reject the prisoner's evidence . . .[19]

Cross-examination about the accused's character goes to credibility. As has been seen in *Maxwell*, any line of questioning must be relevant to that credibility. However the cross-examination can be broad-ranging since the character is indivisible. In *Stirland v. R.*,[20] the defendant was accused of forgery and testified as to his own good character and good employment record. He was cross-examined as to suspicions about forgery that had been voiced by that previous employer, questioning that was deemed inadmissible by the House of Lords:

Stirland v. R. [1944] A.C. 315 at 323–327, *per* Viscount Simon

When the appellant denied that he had ever been 'charged' he may fairly be understood to use the word in the sense it bears in the statute, and to mean that he had never previously been brought before a criminal court. Questions as to whether his previous employer had suspected him of forgery were not therefore any challenge to the veracity of what he had said . . .

It is most undesirable that the rules which should govern cross-examination to credit of an accused person in the witness-box should be complicated by refined distinctions . . . The following propositions seem to cover the ground. . . .

(1) The accused in the witness-box may not be asked any question 'tending to show that he had committed or been convicted of or been charged with any offence other than that wherewith he is then charged or is of bad character' unless one of the three conditions laid down in section 1(f) of the Act of 1898 is fulfilled.

(2) He may, however, be cross-examined as to any of the evidence he has given in chief, including statements as to his own good record, with a view to testing his veracity or accuracy or to showing he is not to be believed on his oath.

(3) An accused who puts his character in issue must be regarded as putting the whole of his past record in issue. He cannot assert his good character in certain respects without exposing himself to inquiry as to the rest of his record so far as this tends to disprove a claim for good character.

(4) An accused is not to be regarded as depriving himself of the protection of the section because the proper conduct of his defence necessitates the making of injurious reflections on the prosecutor or his witnesses.[21]

(5) It is no disproof of good character that a man has been suspected or accused of a previous crime. Such questions as 'Were you suspected?' or 'Were you accused?' are inadmissible because they are irrelevant to the issue of character and can only be asked if the accused has sworn expressly to the contrary.

(6) The fact that a question put to the accused is irrelevant is in itself no reason for quashing a conviction, though it should have been disallowed by the judge.

Stirland appears to restrict the decision in *Maxwell* to its own facts. It is not relevant to cross-examine the accused about mere suspicions or even accusations but it is relevant to credibility to question him or her about

[19] *Samuel supra* at 12.
[20] [1944] A.C. 315.
[21] This proposition must be considered in the light of *Selvey v. DPP* [1968] 2 All E.R. 497, discussed *infra* at 469, *et seq.*

previous convictions[22] even where those offences are wholly dissimilar to the current charges such as an accused, charged with theft, who asserts honest conduct in the past, only to have a previous conviction for violence put to him. This has not only little relevance to the issue of the defendant's credibility but is also prejudicial and the judge has discretion to exclude questions where the prejudicial effect outweights the probative value.

(c) the second exception, second limb

This provides, under section 1(f)(ii), that the shield is lost by the defence casting imputations onto the character of the prosecution witnesses.

Mere denials of guilt, which imply that the prosecution witnesses are lying, are not enough. If the nature or character of the defence involves making allegations about the conduct or character of the prosecutor or the prosecution witnesses,[23] the defendant's shield is lost and he or she can be cross-examined about character and previous convictions. The problems lie in deciding what is an "imputation"? Clear examples might might include the defence putting prior convictions, sexual peccadillos or other character defects to the witness. A frequent scenario will be an attack on the police in charge of the investigation or interrogation, suggesting violent or manipulative conduct or simply that the police witnesses are lying. It is this latter category where the boundary between the proper and improper presentation of a defence can prove difficult.[24] In *R. v. Jones*,[25] Lord Hewart said that it was one thing for the defendant merely to deny making a confession but quite another matter to allege that it was a deliberate and elaborate police concoction. In *R. v. Britzman*[26] the Court of Appeal were considering a burglary conviction. The accused had been arrested on May 29, denying guilt and refusing to make statement. He remained in custody during May 30, still asserting innocence. However on June 1 (pre-Police and Criminal Evidence Act 1984) the police officers said that there had been a long interview, recorded in their notebooks which contained comments from the accused from which the jury might infer guilt. One officer testified that he had heard the accused shouting to one another whilst in their cells, again making statements that were highly suggestive of guilt ("Look, we've only got to sweat this out. They can't keep us here forever. That old bird won't pick us out. Just keep your mouth shut. We'll be OK"). The accused denied that the June 1st interview or the shouting between the cells had taken place. They were cross-examined on their previous convictions and the Court of Appeal upheld this decision:

[22] The prior conduct need not be evidenced by a conviction — in *R. v. Marsh* [1994] Crim.L.R. 52 the findings of a rugby disciplinary tribunal could be put to a rugby player charged with causing GBH and who had put his good character into issue.

[23] This does not include those not involved in the proceedings — police officers who are not testifying or an attack on the character of the murder victim.

[24] *R. v. Tanner* (1977) 66 Cr.App.R. 56; *R. v. Nelson* (1978) 68 Cr.App.R. 12.

[25] (1923) 17 Cr.App.R. 117.

[26] [1983] 1 All E.R. 369.

R. v. Britzman [1983] 1 All E.R. 369 at 372a–374c, *per* Lawton L.J.

. . . Any denial that the conversation had taken place at all necessarily meant by implication that the police officers had given false evidence which they had made up in order to get the appellants convicted. On the facts of this case there could be no question of mistake, misunderstanding or confusion . . .

A defence to a criminal charge which suggests that prosecution witnesses have deliberately made up false evidence in order to secure a conviction must involve imputations on the characters of those witnesses with the consequence that the trial judge may, in the exercise of his discretion, allow prosecuting counsel to cross-examine the defendant about offences of which he has been convicted. In our judgment this is what Parliament intended should happen in most cases. When allegations of the fabrication of evidence are made against prosecution witnesses, as they often are these days, juries are entitled to know about the characters of those making them.

The duty of the judge in such cases to exercise a discretion whether to allow prosecuting counsel to cross-examine a defendant about previous convictions puts defending counsel in a difficulty because some judges . . . .will exercise their discretion in favour of the defendant if either he or his counsel avoids making specific allegations of misconduct . . . With such judges a suggestion that a witness is mistaken or had misunderstood usually attracts a favourable exercise of discretion.

. . . [The trial judge] would have none of this delicate forensic language. When prosecuting counsel applied for leave to cross-examine . . . he ruled that the could do so. He gave a reasoned ruling, the essence of which is contained in the following passage:

> In my judgment, the delicacy with which cross-examination was conducted on behalf of this defendant cannot hide the basic commonsense position, which is this; there is no room for error or mistake; it must be clear to the jury that the only real issue for their consideration, although, I repeat, it has never been so put to these police officers, that the only real issue for their consideration is whether the statements were made, or in the case of the conversation between the two defendants whether the conversation took place; or whether these officers have made them up. There is simply no other possibility.

Counsel for Britzman submitted that this ruling was wrong because the defence amounted in reality to no more than a denial of the charge . . .

In our judgment the nature and conduct of the defence did involve imputations on the characters of the three officers . . . This opinion is in accord with two decisions of this court, namely *R. v. Tanner*[27] and *R. v. McGee and Cassidy*.[28] In *Tanner*, . . . Browne L.J. said:

> In some cases the distinction may be a very narrow one, but that it exists in principle is clear. the decision whether a case is on one side of the line or the other must depend on the facts of each particular case. In our judgment, the nature and conduct of the defence in the present case did involve imputations on the character of the police officers. This was not a case of a denial of a single answer, nor was there any suggestion or possibility of mistake or misunderstanding. The appellant was denying not only his admission, nut in the case of each

[27] (1977) 66 Cr.App.R. 56.
[28] (1979) 70 Cr.App.R. 247.

> interview a series of subsequent important answers attributed to him by the police . . .
>
> In deciding as we have, we have not overlooked the potentiality of unfairness to defendants with previous convictions which a rigid application of section 1(f)(ii) of the 1898 Act would cause and the difficulties in advising and deciding tactics which defending counsel have. No doubt it was appreciation of the potentiality of unfairness to defendants which led the House of Lords in *Selvey*[29] to reject the Crown's submission in that case that judges had no discretion to refuse leave to cross-examine about previous convictions.
>
> We hope that it will be helpful for both judges and counsel if we set out some guidelines for the exercise of discretion in favour of defendants. First, it should be used if there is nothing more than a denial, however emphatic or offensively made, of an act or even a short series of acts amounting to one incident or in what was said to have been a short interview . . . The position would be different however if there were a denial of evidence of a long period of detailed observation extending over hours and just as in this case and in *Tanner*, where there were denials of long conversations.
>
> Second, cross-examination should only be allowed if the judge is sure that there is no possibility of mistake, misunderstanding or confusion and that the jury will inevitably have to decide whether the prosecution witnesses have fabricated evidence. Defendants sometimes make wild allegations when giving evidence. Allowance should be made for the strain of being in the witness box and the exaggerated use of language which sometimes results from such strain or lack of education or mental instability. Particularly care should be used when a defendant is led into making allegations during cross-examination. The defendant who, during cross-examination, is driven to explaining away the evidence by saying it has been made up or planted on him usually convicts himself without having his previous convictions brought out. Finally there is no need for the prosecution to rely on section 1(f)(ii) if the evidence against a defendant is overwhelming . . .

The effect of *Britzman* is that, if there is a denial of a short interview, the presumption is in favour of the defendant. But if the accused denies a long conversation, makes wild allegations or used unrestrained language and the judge was sure that there is no possibility of mistake or confusion, cross-examination under section 1(f)(ii) is permissible. Judges should not rely on section 1(f)(ii) where the other evidence was overwhelming. But perhaps there is an equally strong case for the judge using his discretion to disallow cross-examination on credit when the evidence against a defendant is marginal?

One significant point is that the defence loses the shield even where the imputation is a necessary part of the defence.[30] In *Stirland*, Viscount Simon said:

> An accused is not to be regarded as depriving himself of the protection of the section because the proper conduct of his defence necessitates the making of injurious reflections on the prosecutor or his witnesses.[31]

[29] [1968] 2 All E.R. 497.

[30] The Law Commission (Consultation Paper 141) has proposed that the accused should only lose the shield where the imputations relate to the witness's conduct in the incident in question.

[31] *Stirland supra* at 327.

But in *Selvey v. DPP*,[32] the accused was charged with buggery. There was medical evidence which supported the victim's complaint. Selvey's defence was that the complainant had already had sex with another man. The House of Lords held that section 1(f)(ii) was applicable even where the casting of such imputations is necessary to establish the defence:

Selvey v. DPP [1968] 2 All E.R. 497 at 521a–522h, *per* Lord Pearce

My Lords, ever since the Criminal Evidence Act 1898 came into force there has been difficulty and argument about the application of the words in section 1(f)(ii) 'the nature or conduct of the defence is such as to involve imputations on the character of the prosecutor or the witnesses for the prosecution.'

Two main views have been put forward. One view adopts the literal meaning of the words. The prosecutor is cross-examined to show that he has fabricated the charge for improper reasons. That involves imputations on his character. Therefore, it lets in the previous convictions of the accused. The practical justification for this view is the 'tit for tat' argument. If the accused is seeking to cast discredit on the prosecution, then the prosecution should be allowed to do likewise. If the accused is seeking to persuade the jury that the prosecutor behaved like a knave, then the jury should know the character of the man who makes these accusations, so that it may judge fairly between them instead of being in the dark as to one of them.

The other view would limit the literal meaning of the words. For it cannot, it is said, have been intended by Parliament to make a man liable to have his previous convictions revealed whenever the essence of his defence necessitates imputations on the character of the prosecutor. This revelation is always damaging and often fatal to a defence. The high-water mark of this argument is the ordinary case of rape. In this the vital issue (as a rule) is whether the woman consented. Consent (as a rule) involves imputations on her character. Therefore, in the ordinary case of rape, the accused cannot defend himself without letting in his previous convictions. The same argument extends in varying lesser degrees to many cases.

The argument in favour of a construction more liberal to the accused is supported in two ways. First it is said that character is used in the sense in which it was used in *R. v. Rowton*[33] where the full court ruled that evidence of good character must be limited solely to general reputation and not to a man's actual disposition . . .

. . . It might be justifiable to consider whether 'character' means in the context solely general reputation, if a reassessment could lead to any clarification of the problem. But in my opinion it leads nowhere. For I cannot accept the proposition that to accuse a person of a particular knavery does not involve imputations on his general reputation. The words 'involve' and 'imputations' are wide. It would be playing with words to say that the allegation of really discreditable matters does not involve imputations on his general reputation, if only as showing how erroneous that reputation must be. The argument is, however, a valuable reminder that the Act is intending serious and not trivial imputations.

The second part of the argument in favour of a construction more liberal to the accused is concerned with the words 'the conduct or nature of the defence'. One should, it can be argued, read conduct or nature as something superimposed on the essence of the defence itself. In *O'Hara v. H.M. Advocate*[34] the learned Lord Justice-Clerk (Lord Thomson), after a careful review of the English cases, construed

[32] [1968] 2 All E.R. 497.
[33] (1865) Le & Ca 520.
[34] [1948] J.C. 90.

'conduct' as meaning the actual handling of the case by the accused or his advocate. He found difficulty with 'nature' but said:

> But the more general considerations which I have mentioned persuade me to the view that 'nature' is to be read, not as meaning something which is inherent in the defence, but as referable to the mechanism of the defence; nature being the strategy of the defence and conduct the tactics.

This argument has obvious force, particularly in a case of rape, where the allegation of consent is in truth no more than a mere traverse of the essential ingredient which the Crown have to prove, namely, want of consent. But the argument does not, and I think cannot, fairly stop short of contending that all matters which are relevant to the crime, that is, of which rebutting evidence could be proved, are excluded from the words 'conduct or nature of the defence'.

To take the present case as an example, the evidence having established physical signs on the victim of the alleged offence, his admission that he had previously committed it with somebody else was relevant. So, too, was his admission that he had been paid £1 for it, since, when the conversation was relevant, it could not be right to bowdlerise it. And, therefore, it is said, the putting of the allegation in cross-examination and the evidence given by the accused was an essentially relevant part of the defence and therefore was not within the words, 'the nature or conduct of the defence'. If Mr Jeremy Hutchison's forceful argument on the proper construction of the subsection is right, the story told by the accused did not let in the conviction.

So large a gloss upon the words is not easy to justify, even if one were convinced that it necessarily produced a fair and proper result which Parliament intended. But there are two sides to the matter. So liberal a shield for an accused is in many cases unfair to a prosecution.

The proposition that the accused loses the shield even where the line of questioning is a necessary part of the defence is well illustrated in *R. v. Bishop*[35] where the accused had been the tenant of a room in a house belonging to Mr Price. He only stayed there for 12 days before leaving and Mr Price complained that his bedroom door had been forced and after-shave and money taken. Bishop was charged with burglary. Not only had he left precipitously, the after shave was found in his room. Worse, Bishop's fingerprints were found in Price's bedroom. Bishop's explanation was that, during his brief stay, he had had a homosexual affair with Price. Price vehemently denied this. The prosecution sought and were allowed to cross-examine about Bishop's previous convictions. The conviction was upheld since the allegation of homosexual relations between Mr Price and the appellant was an imputation on Mr Price's character and it was not material that the imputation had been made, not to blacken the name of the witness but to explain the presence of the accused's fingerprints at the scene of the crime.

Had the occupant been a woman and the allegation one of a heterosexual affair, would the result have been different? One major exception to

[35] (1975) Q.B. 274.

this rule lies in the area of rape to which the logic of *Selvey* and *Bishop* would seem to apply. Where the defence is that the victim consented, this should theoretically mean that the accused opens himself to cross-examination on his own record. Yet the House of Lords in *Selvey* held that the accused in rape cases can allege consent without risking such cross-examination, either because rape is *sui generis*[36] or on the ground that the issue is one raised by the prosecution. In *Selvey* Lord Pearce said:

> The second part of the argument in favour of a construction more liberal to the accused is concerned with the words 'the conduct or nature of the defence'. One should, it can be argued, read conduct or nature as something superimposed on the essence of the defence itself . . . This argument has obvious force, particularly in a case of rape, where the allegation of consent is in truth no more than a mere traverse of the essential ingredient which the Crown have to prove, namely, want of consent. But the argument does not, and I think cannot, fairly stop short of contending that all matters which are relevant to the crime, that is, of which rebutting evidence could be proved, are excluded from the words 'conduct or nature of the defence'[37]

This exception, although established beyond doubt,[38] raises difficult problems:

(1) there is no justification for treating rape as an offence *sui generis*: the rape defendant would suffer no greater hardship than defendants accused of other crimes if required to consider the consequences of a particular line of defence.
(2) Lord Pearce's comment that the issue of consent is one on which the prosecution bears the burden of proof is one that might equally be made about *Bishop* where the Crown were obliged to prove that the defendant was a trespasser. A more general point is that the incidence of the burden of proof on a particular issue is irrelevant to the question of the conduct of the accused's defence.
(3) even if Lord Pearce were correct, as a result of *DPP v. Morgan*,[39] the issue is rarely that of the victim's consent but of the accused's belief in her consent. The accused should bear an evidential burden here just as if he were raising a defence of duress or self-defence and equally should bear the consequences of raising a specific line of defence.

This exception in the case of rape has magnified the problems surrounding the use of the victim's sexual history in cross-examination[40] which would be easily overcome by the abrogation of the *Turner* rule.

[36] *R. v. Cook* [1959] 2 Q.B. 340 at 347, *per* Devlin J.
[37] *Selvey supra* at 522c–f.
[38] *R. v. Turner* [1944] K.B. 463.
[39] [1976] A.C. 182.
[40] Sexual Offences (Amendment) Act 1976, s.2; *supra* 381, *et seq.*

When cross-examination is permitted under section 1(f)(ii), it goes to the credibility of the accused:[41]

(1) a failure to warn the jury that the evidence elicited only goes to the credibility of the defendant and not to his or her guilt may result in the quashing of any conviction.
(2) the prosecution can bring out the fact of any prior conviction but not question the accused on the details of such a conviction. In *R. v. Khan*,[42] the appellant was tried for, *inter alia*, assault on a police officer. His defence was that the police had lied and the prosecution was permitted to cross-examine on a previous conviction for assault on a police officer, eliciting the details of the previous incident with obvious similarities between the present and previous cases, showing that the accused was predisposed to violence, bad language and other conduct alleged against him. The conviction was quashed because these details should not be referred to as a matter of course but only where they are relevant to issues of credit. Details such as *modus operandi* should only be admitted where they would be admissible as similar-fact evidence.[43]
(3) the judge possesses an exclusionary discretion where there is a risk that the jury will believe that the cross-examination will go not to credit but to the probability that the accused committed the offence.[44] Where the accused's previous convictions bear a close resemblance to the offence charged, it is possible that the judge will disallow the examination. In *R. v. Watts*,[45] the charge was indecent assault and the accused alleged that the admission had been fabricated. The prosecution were allowed to cross-examine on previous convictions for indecent assault on young girls. The conviction was quashed since the risk of prejudice was too great.

These issues were reviewed in *R. v. Powell*[46] in which the defendant was charged with living off immoral earnings. Police officers testified as to the fact that they had observed prostitutes using his premises and giving him money. The defence was that the police evidence was a total fabrication. The defendant also gave evidence of his own good character. The Crown sought to question him on convictions in 1969 and 1984 on charges of allowing his premises to be used for the purpose of prostitution. The judge permitted this although he gave a clear direction on the significance of this to the jury. On appeal counsel submitted that this was a wrong exercise of judicial discretion. Lord Lane C.J. referred to *Watts* and continued:

[41] *R. v. France* [1979] Crim.L.R. 48.
[42] [1991] Crim.L.R. 51.
[43] *R. v. Duncalf* [1979] 2 All E.R. 1116.
[44] *Maxwell v. DPP* [1935] A.C. 309.
[45] [1983] 3 All E.R. 101.
[46] [1986] 1 All E.R. 193.

R. v. Powell [1986] 1 All E.R. 193 at 196c–198g, per Lord Lane C.J.

In *R. v. Watts* the circumstances were somewhat special, and it may be that the decision would have been the same even if we had had the speeches of their Lordships in *Selvey v. DPP* in mind.

The same cannot be said of *R. v. Braithwaite, R. v. John*.[47] The facts in that case were these. The police saw two youths in Oxford Street jostle a woman and steal her purse. They chased and arrested the youths. The defence at trial was that the policemen had fabricated their evidence: they had not seen what they said. The judge gave leave to cross-examine the youths as to their convictions. Each of them had to admit a number of convictions for offences closely resembling that with which they were charged.

In allowing the appeal the judgment of the court referred to the decision in *R. v. Watts* and to Viscount Sankey LC's observations in *Maxwell v. DPP*, and went on:

> . . . in the light of those records, it seems to us that a jury might think that these two young men had a specific disposition to snatch bags from the person as much as Mr Watts could be said to have a specific disposition to indecently assault females. In those circumstances, as in *R. v. Watts*, it would have been extremely difficult, if not practically impossible, for the jury to have done what the judge had suggested, namely to use those convictions to judge the respective credibility of the appellants and the police officer, but not as evidence that they had committed the offence charged . . .

[Lord Lane then reviewed the facts of *Selvey* and continued]

Thus the judge (in *Selvey*) was permitting evidence to go before the jury which was at least as prejudicial to the defendant as that which was admitted in *R. v. Watts* and in *R. v. Braithwaite, R. v. John*.

. . . The results of their Lordships' opinions in *Selvey v. DPP* in so far as they are relevant to the instant case were analysed by another division of the court in *R. v. Burke*.[48] We respectfully agree with the judgment in that case delivered by Ackner LJ, and cannot improve on his analysis which was as follows . . .

> 1. The trial judge must weigh the prejudicial effect of the questions against the damage done by the attack on the prosecution's witnesses and must generally exercise his discretion so as to secure a trial that is fair both to the prosecution and the defence (thus approving the observations of Devlin J . . . in *R. v. Cook*[49]).
>
> 2. Cases must occur in which it would be unjust to admit evidence of a character gravely prejudicial to the accused, even though there may be some tenuous grounds for holding it technically admissible (thus approving the observations made by Lord du Parcq . . . in *Noor Mohammed v. R.*[50] Thus although the position is established in law, still the putting of the questions as to character of the accused person may be fraught with results which immeasurably outweigh the result of questions put by the defence and which make a fair trial of the accused almost impossible (thus approving the observations of Singleton J. in *R. v. Jenkins*[51]).

[47] November 24, 1983 (unreported).
[48] (1985) 82 Cr.App.R. 156.
[49] [1959] 2 All E.R. 97.
[50] [1949] 1 All E.R. 365 at 370.
[51] (1945) 31 Cr.App.R. 1 at 15.

3. In the ordinary and normal case the trial judge may feel that if the credit of the prosecutor or his witnesses has been attacked it is only fair that the jury should have before them material on which they can form their judgment whether the accused person is any more worthy to be believed than those he has attacked. It is obviously unfair that the jury should be left in the dark about an accused's character if the conduct of the defence has attacked the character of the prosecutor or the witnesses for the prosecution within the meaning of the section . . .

4. In order to see if the conviction should be quashed, it is not enough that the court thinks it would have exercised its discretion differently. the court will not interfere with the exercise of a discretion by a judge below unless he has erred in principle or there is no material on which he could properly have arrived at his decision (see, *per* Viscount Dilhorne in *Selvey v. DPP*[52] . . .)

. . . In the light of all these considerations, it is clear that in *R. v. Braithwaite*, *R. v. John* and possibly to a lesser extent in *R. v. Watts*, the court fell into error. First we interfered too lightly with the exercise of the judge's discretion . . . Second we overlooked the 'tit for tat' principle . . . at the same time paying too much attention . . . to the question whether the previous offences did or did not involve dishonesty in the ordinary sense of that word. We further suggested that care should be taken to conceal from the jury that previous convictions of the prisoner were of a similar nature to the offence being charged. We have said enough about . . . *Selvey v. DPP* and the facts of that case to show that those views were wrong.

. . . In short, if there is a deliberate attack being made on the conduct of a prosecution witness calculated to discredit him wholly, if there is a real issue about the conduct of an important witness which the jury will have to settle in order to reach their verdict, the judge is entitled to let the jury know the previous convictions of the man who is making the attack. The fact that the defendant's convictions are not for offences of dishonesty, the fact that they are for offences bearing a close resemblance to the offences charged, are matters for the judge to take into consideration when exercising his discretion, but they certainly do not oblige the judge to disallow the proposed cross-examination.

Comparably, in *R. v. McLeod*,[53] the defendant was charged with armed robbery and was cross-examined on a series of previous convictions which brought out a range of similarities with the immediate offence. The Court of Appeal again upheld the conviction. There was nothing improper in such cross-examination although it was undesirable that it should be prolonged or extensive.

(d) the third exception

This exception is contained in section 1(f)(iii) whereby the shield is lost where the accused has given evidence against any other person charged in the same proceedings.

The leading case is *Murdoch v. Taylor*[54] where Murdoch, who had a criminal record, was tried for handling stolen goods jointly with Lynch, who had no previous convictions. Lynch testified, implicating Murdoch.

[52] [1970] A.C. 304 at 342.
[53] [1994] 3 All E.R. 254.
[54] [1965] A.C. 574.

Murdoch testified under cross-examination that the box containing the stolen property had been in Lynch's possession. Counsel for Lynch then cross-examined Murdoch on his previous convictions:

Murdoch v. Taylor [1965] A.C. 574 at 592f–594d, *per* Lord Donovan

On the question of discretion, I agree with the Court of Criminal Appeal that a trial judge has no discretion whether to allow an accused person to be cross-examined as to his past criminal offences once he has given evidence against his co-accused. Proviso (f)(iii) in terms confers no such discretion and, in my opinion, none can be implied. It is true that in relation to proviso (f)(ii) such a discretion does exist; that is to say, in the cases where the accused has attempted to establish his own good character or where the nature or conduct of the defence is such as to involve imputations on the character of the prosecutor or of a witness for the prosecution.

But in these cases it will normally, if not invariably, be the prosecution which will want to bring out the accused's bad character — not some co-accused; and in such cases it seems to me quite proper that the court should retain some control of the matter. For its duty is to secure a fair trial and the prejudicial value of evidence establishing the accused's bad character may at times wholly outweigh the value of such evidence as tending to show that he was guilty of the crime alleged.

These considerations lead me to the view that if, in any given case (which I think would be rare), the prosecution sought to avail itself of the provisions of proviso (f)(iii) then here, again, the court should keep control of the matter in the like way. Otherwise, if two accused gave evidence one against the other, but neither wished to cross-examine as to character, the prosecution could step in as of right and reveal the criminal records of both, if both possessed them. I cannot think that Parliament in the Act of 1898 ever intended such an unfair procedure. So far as concerns the prosecution, therefore, the matter should be one for the exercise of the judge's discretion, as it is in the case of proviso (f)(ii). But when it is the co-accused who seeks to exercise the right conferred by proviso (f)(iii) different considerations come into play. He seeks to defend himself; to say to the jury that the man who is giving evidence against him is unworthy of belief; and to support that assertion by proof of bad character. The right to do this cannot, in my opinion, be fettered in any way.

Finally, it is said that the decision in *R. v. Stannard*,[55] if upheld, will make it impossible for a person to defend himself at all effectively if he has a criminal record and is charged jointly with some other person. If he knows that the other person is guilty, and if in the witness box he speaks the truth, then he is liable to have his criminal past disclosed with fatal results.

This would, indeed, be a melancholy result, but I do not think the prospect is so gloomy. To test the matter, let me assume the case of two accused each charged with the same offence — No 1 in fact being guilty but having no criminal record, No 2 being in fact innocent but having such a record. No 1 has nothing to lose by going into the witness box and accusing No 2 of the crime; No 2 quite truthfully in his evidence accuses No 1, whereupon the past criminal record of No 2 is disclosed to the jury by or on behalf of No 1. It is said that No 2 would have practically no hope of avoiding a conviction — hence the argument for an over-riding discretion in the judge, although this would not necessarily cure the situation.

But in the case supposed, what would the position be in practice? In the first place, if No 2 were in fact innocent, it would be in the highest degree unlikely that he would be found relying simply on his own denial. There would almost invariably be some evidence to support his defence. In the second place, his counsel or the

[55] [1964] 1 All E.R. 34.

judge or both would explain to the jury just how it was that accused No 1 was able to force the revelation of No 2's record. The judge would probably go on to exhort the jury not to let that revelation sway their minds and to consider the case against No. 2 primarily on the basis of the other evidence. The assistant recorder in the present case indeed went further and told the jury to ignore Murdoch's past altogether. It would be a very unusual jury which, in these circumstances, did not require cogent proof of guilt before convicting . . .

Lord Donovan stresses:

- it does not matter whether the evidence is given in chief or under cross-examination
- the issue is the effect on the jury. It does not require hostile intent on part of the co-accused.
- "giving evidence against" encompasses more than mere denial of something said by the co-accused, requiring either support of the prosecution case or undermining the co-accused's defence.

In *R. v. Bruce*,[56] the two accused were charged with robbery. The first admitted the plan to rob but denied taking part in its execution. The second denied any plan to rob at all. The first defendant cross-examined the second on his previous convictions. The second defendant's conviction was quashed. Although he had contradicted his co-defendant's evidence, he had not given evidence against him. In *R. v. Varley*[57] the appellant was jointly charged with Dibble with offences of robbery and possession of a firearm. The appellant initially admitted his part in the robbery but at trial denied that he had participated at all. Dibble's defence was that he had been forced to take part by Varley and he testified to this:

R. v. Varley [1982] 2 All E.R. 519 at 521c–522g, *per* Kilner Brown J.

Now was Dibble's evidence 'against' the appellant? Clearly it was. Was the appellant's evidence 'against' Dibble? That is what this appeal is all about. Fortunately, in the interests of justice, the jury learned about Dibble's criminal history because he was cross-examined about his convictions. The jury rejected his defence of duress . . .

The trial reached the stage of cross-examination of Varley by counsel on behalf of Dibble when, knowing the nature of Dibble's case, he applied for leave to put questions as to Varley's previous convictions on the basis that his evidence was evidence against Dibble . . .

The operation [of proviso (f)(iii)] seems to have given rise to no difficulty and no detailed analysis for over 60 years. No doubt, as Lord Pearce indicated in his speech in *Murdoch v. Taylor* 'the practice and the general view of bench and bar alike was that a judge had discretion whether to give leave to cross-examine under section 1(f)(iii)' and, in difficult cases where it was not easy to determine whether the

[56] [1975] 3 All E.R. 277.
[57] [1982] 2 All E.R. 519.

evidence could be categorised as 'against' or where the questioning could well be unduly prejudicial, a judge would decline to rule that the proposed questions could be put. But this discretionary power was removed from trial judges by the Court of Criminal Appeal in *R. v. Ellis*[58] when it was decided that cross-examination of a co-defendant who had given evidence against a person jointly charged with him was a matter of right and not od discretion.

The decision was approved in *Murdoch*'s case. This decision created difficult problems in practice because either to establish or to destroy this right involved, in many cases, an acute analysis of whether or not the evidence which had been given was 'against' the other party charged . . .

. . . What was the nature of the guidance in *R. v. Stannard*[59]? It was this, approved by Lord Donovan in *Murdoch*'s case ' . . . 'evidence against' means evidence which supports the prosecution in a material respect or which undermines the defence of the co-accused.' There are three reported cases in the Court of Appeal, Criminal Division , in which this interpretation has been considered and to which we were referred. They are *R. v. Davis*,[60] *R. v. Bruce*[61] and *R. v. Hatton*.[62] Now putting all the reported cases together, are there established principles which might serve as guidance . . . ? (1) If it is established that a person jointly charged has given evidence against the co-defendant that defendant has a right to cross-examine the other as to previous convictions and the trial judge has no discretion to refuse an application. (2) Such evidence may be given either in chief or during cross-examination. (3) It has to be objectively decided whether the evidence either supports the prosecution in a material respect or which undermines the defence of the co-accused. A hostile intent is irrelevant. (4) If consideration has to be given to the undermining of the other's defence care must be taken to see that the evidence clearly undermines the defence. Inconvenience to or inconsistency with the other's defence is not of itself sufficient. (5) Mere denial of participation in a joint venture is not of itself sufficient to rank as evidence against a co-defendant. For the proviso to apply, such denial must lead to the conclusion that if the witness did not participate then it must have been the other who did. (6) Where the one defendant asserts or in due course would assert one view of the joint venture which is directly contradicted by the other such contradiction may be evidence against the co-defendant.

We apply these principles to the facts of this case and particularly the latter two. Here was Dibble going to say, as he did, that he took part in the joint venture because he was forced to do so by Varley. The appellant, Varley, was saying that he was not a participant and had not gone with Dibble and had not forced Dibble to go. His evidence therefore was against Dibble because it amounted to saying that not only was Dibble telling lies but that Dibble would be left as a participant on his own and not acting under duress. In our view, the judge was right to rule that cross-examination as to previous convictions was permissible.

Tarred with the Same Brush — Police and Criminal Evidence Act 1984, s.74

The old common law rule in *Hollington v. Hewthorn*[63] created difficulties in criminal proceedings. This rule stated that parties were not permitted to

[58] [1961] 2 All E.R. 928.
[59] [1964] 1 All E.R. 34.
[60] [1975] 1 All E.R. 233.
[61] [1975] 3 All E.R. 277.
[62] (1976) 64 Cr.App.R. 88.
[63] [1943] K.B. 587.

use convictions in previous cases as evidence of the facts on which those convictions were based. The case itself was a negligence action between two drivers where the Court of Appeal held that the plaintiff was not entitled to use the prior conviction of the defendant for careless driving as evidence of the defendant's negligence. In criminal trials, this meant that the prosecution[64] would need to prove the facts anew even in related trials. The absurdity of this is shown in *R. v. Spinks*,[65] the principal offender had stabbed the victim and had been convicted of GBH. Spinks was now being tried as an accomplice and it was held that prosecution could not use the principal's conviction as evidence that the offence had been convicted.

This position was changed by the Police and Criminal Evidence Act 1984:

> 74.—(1) In any proceedings the fact that a person other than the accused has been convicted of an offence by or before any court in the United Kingdom or by a Service Court outside the United Kingdom shall be admissible in evidence for the purpose of proving, where to do so is relevant to any issue in those proceedings, that that person committed that offence, whether or not any other evidence of his having committed that offence is given.

A conviction is admissible where it is relevant to an issue in the case. If there is conflict about the correctness of the conviction, the burden of proving it incorrect lies on, normally, the defendant.[66]

But when is the conviction of a person other than the accused "relevant" to an "issue"? In *R. v. Robertson*, *R. v. Golder*,[67] the charge involved in one case was conspiracy to burgle and evidence of convictions for burglaries carried out by Robertson's alleged co-conspirators was permitted; in the other case Golder was charged with robbery and the convictions of his alleged partners was given in evidence against him. The burden of proving the convictions wrong would normally rest on the defence.

The prejudicial effect of proving convictions is obvious and the problem is one of fairness. Even where the conviction is admissible under section 74, it may be excluded under section 78 since it would have an adverse effect on the fairness of the proceedings.[68] In *R. v. Mattison*[69] the accused was charged with indecency with another person who was similarly charged with indecency with the accused. The other person pleaded guilty but the defendant pleaded not guilty. The conviction was quashed after the other person's conviction was admitted into evidence.[70]

[64] This would normally be the case although s.74 applies equally to the defence.
[65] [1982] 1 All E.R. 587; *R. v. Hassan* (1970) 1 Q.B. 423.
[66] Police and Criminal Evidence Act 1984, s.74(2) — for the defendant the standard of (dis)proof would be on the balance of probabilities.
[67] [1987] 3 All E.R. 231.
[68] *R. v. O'Connor* (1986) 85 Cr.App.R. 298.
[69] [1990] Crim.L.R. 117; see also *R. v. Turner* [1991] Crim.L.R. 57.
[70] The implications of section 74 are discussed further at 681, *et seq*.

16

THE RULE AGAINST HEARSAY — ITS SCOPE AND RATIONALE

The Common Law Rule

The major concept in studying evidence is that of hearsay and its associated rule which prevents adducing hearsay statements as evidence. The classic statement of the rule was formulated by Cross:

> an assertion other than one made by a person while giving oral evidence in the proceedings is inadmissible as evidence of any fact asserted.[1]

Despite considerable criticism from judges, academics[2] and other sources,[3] the rule remains stubbornly in force.[4] Lord Normand's comments in *Teper* remain appropriate:

> The rule against admission of hearsay evidence is fundamental. It is not the best evidence and it is not delivered on oath. The truthfulness and accuracy of the person whose words are spoken to by another witness cannot be tested by cross-examination and the light which his demeanour would throw on his testimony is lost.[5]

Witnesses are expected to testify from their own knowledge or belief. They are not expected to testify as to what they think others might know or believe. They thus give evidence of what they themselves perceived: what they saw, felt, tasted or heard. A witness cannot testify about another's perceptions. Were the court seeking to establish the accused's

[1] Tapper C., *Cross and Tapper on Evidence* (8th ed., 1995) 46. This formula was approved by the House of Lords in *R. v. Sharp* [1988] 1 All E.R. 65 at 68b–c.

[2] Guest S., "The Scope of the Hearsay Rule" 101 L.Q.R. (1985) 355; Ashworth A. and Pattenden R., "Reliability. Hearsay Evidence and the English Criminal Trial" 102 LQR (1986) 292; Birch D., "Hearsay-logic and Hearsay-fiddles: *Blastland* revisited" in Smith P. (Ed.), *Essays in Honour of J. C. Smith* (1987) 24; Pattenden R., "Conceptual Versus Pragmatic Approaches to Hearsay" 56 M.L.R. [1993] 138.

[3] *Evidence in Criminal Proceedings: Hearsay and Related Topics* (Law Commission Consultation Paper No. 138, 1995).

[4] *R. v. Kearley* [1992] 2 All E.R. 345, although the scope of the rule is now largely limited to criminal trials as a result of the Civil Evidence Acts 1968 and 1995.

[5] [1952] 2 All E.R. 447 at 449.

presence at the scene of the crime and a witness were permitted to say, "My husband told me that he saw the defendant at the scene", in the absence of the husband as a witness, the court could not investigate the probative value of that identification. The court would be able to inquire whether the husband spoke those actual words because that is within the wife's own perceptions. But the court could not explore other factors such as the circumstances in which the identification was made or the husband's credibility as a witness. To that extent the court cannot assess whether the contents of the statement ("the accused was there") are likely to be true. Thus the wife's testimony is hearsay and is not admissible evidence to prove the fact that the defendant was at the scene. If the prosecution wishes to prove that, they have to call the husband to testify to that effect.

Of course the prosecution is seeking to rely on the wife's evidence because the husband is not available. The hearsay rule is mainly about excluding the evidence of absent witnesses. But the rule does not only apply to repeating other people's statements. Witnesses cannot testify as to what they themselves said prior to the court proceedings. In the example above, were the husband to testify that "I told my wife that I saw the defendant at the scene", this would also not be admissible as evidence that the defendant was there. The fact that the witness told his wife does not prove anything about the defendant's whereabouts. If the witness has already testified that he saw the accused at the place, it does show the witness's consistency but there are considerable limitations on introducing such prior consistent statements.[6]

Any out-of-court statement is excluded:

- whether it is sworn or unsworn
- whether the person making the statement is a witness or not
- whether the statement is oral or in writing or by conduct
- whether the statement expressly asserts a fact or does so only by implication.

The common law rule against hearsay is very broad, its rationale seemingly unclear to the judiciary and its boundaries indefinite.[7] Additionally there is a range of common law and statutory exceptions, permitting the reception of hearsay evidence in particular circumstances. But the common law rule remains a rule of exclusion and the judge has no discretion to admit a hearsay statement simply on the grounds that, as evidence, it is relevant, reliable and probative.

[6] See 334, *et seq.*
[7] *Woodhouse v. Hall* (1980) 72 Cr.App.R. 39.

Out-of-court Assertions

In what forms can assertions be made?

(a) oral statements: the oral statement is the most common example of hearsay. In *Sparks v. R.*[8] a young girl who had been indecently assaulted told her mother that her attacker was "a coloured boy". The defendant was white but the mother was not permitted to testify as to what her daughter (who was too young to be a witness) had said. In *Jones v. Metcalfe*[9] the witness reported a lorry number involved in an incident to a police officer. The witness was later unable to recollect that number but the officer could not testify as to what the witness had said as that was inadmissible hearsay.

(b) written statements: the classic case here is *Myers v. DPP*[10] where the defendant bought wrecked cars for their registration certificates. He would then steal a similar car and alter it to fit the details in the document. He would sell the disguised stolen car along with the genuine log book of the wrecked car. The prosecution sought to show that the cars and registration documents did not match up by reference to the engine block numbers and introduced microfilm evidence kept by the manufacturer, showing that this block number did not belong in a car of this registration date. The microfilm was prepared from cards which were themselves prepared by workers on the assembly line. Lord Reid in the House of Lords held that the microfilm was inadmissible since it contained the out-of-court assertions by unidentified workers:

Myers v. DPP [1964] 2 All E.R. 877 at 886b–887h, *per* Lord Reid

It is not disputed before your Lordships that to admit these records is to admit hearsay. They only tend to prove that a particular car bore a particular number when it was assembled if the jury were entitled to infer that the entries were accurate, at least in the main; and the entries on the cards were assertions by the unidentifiable men who made them that they had entered numbers which they had seen on the cars. Counsel for the respondents were unable to adduce any reported case or any textbook as direct authority for their submission. Only four reasons for their submission were put forward. It was said that evidence of this kind is in practice admitted at least at the Central Criminal Court. Then it was argued that a judge has a discretion to admit such evidence. Then the reasons given in the Court of Criminal Appeal were relied on. And lastly it was said with truth that common sense rebels against the rejection of this evidence.

At the trial counsel for the prosecution sought to support the existing practice of admitting such records, if produced by the persons in charge of them, by arguing that they were not adduced to prove the truth of the recorded particulars but only to prove that they were records kept in the normal course of business. Counsel for

[8] [1964] A.C. 964.
[9] [1967] 3 All E.R. 205.
[10] [1964] 2 All E.R. 877.

the accused then asked the very pertinent question — if they were not intended to prove the truth of the entries, what were they intended to prove? I ask what the jury would infer from them: obviously that they were probably true records. If they were not capable of supporting an inference that they were probably true records, then I do not see what probative value they could have, and their admission was bound to mislead the jury.

The first reason given by the Court of Criminal Appeal for sustaining the admission of the records was that, although the records might not be evidence standing by themselves, they could be used to corroborate the evidence of other witnesses. I regret to say that I have great difficulty in understanding that . . . Unless the jury were entitled to regard them as probably true records they afforded no corroboration at all. If the jury were entitled so to regard them, I can see no reason why they should only become admissible evidence after some witnesses have identified the cars for different reasons . . .

At the end of their judgment, the Court of Criminal Appeal gave a different reason. 'In our view the admission of such evidence does not infringe the hearsay rule because its probative value does not depend upon the credit of an unidentified person but rather on the circumstances in which the record is maintained and the inherent probability that it will be correct rather than incorrect.' That, if I may say so, is undeniable as a matter of common sense. But can it be reconciled with the existing law? I need not discuss the question on general lines because I think that this ground is quite inconsistent with the established rule regarding public records. Public records are prima facie evidence of the fact which they contain but it is quite clear that a record is not a public record within the scope of that rule unless it is open to inspection by at least a section of the public. Unless we are to alter that rule how can we possibly say that a private record not open to public inspection can be prima facie evidence of the truth of its contents? I would agree that it is quite unreasonable to refuse to accept as prima facie evidence a record obviously well kept by public officers and proved never to have been discovered to contain a wrong entry though frequently consulted by officials, merely because it is not open to inspection. But that is settled law. This seems to me to be a good example of the wide repercussions which would follow if we accepted the judgment of the Court of Criminal Appeal. I must therefore regretfully decline to accept this reason as correct in law.

In argument, the Solicitor-General maintained that, although the general rule may be against the admission of private records to prove the truth of entries in them, the trial judge has a discretion to admit a record in a particular case if satisfied that it is trustworthy and that justice requires its admission. That appears to me to be contrary to the whole framework of the existing law. It is true that a judge has a discretion to exclude legally admissible evidence if justice so requires, but it is a very different thing to say that he has a discretion to admit legally inadmissible evidence. The whole development of the exceptions to the hearsay rule is based on the determination of certain classes of evidence as admissible or inadmissible and not on the apparent credibility of particular evidence tendered. No matter how cogent particular evidence may seem to be, unless it comes within a class which is admissible, it is excluded. Half a dozen witnesses may offer to prove that they heard two men of high character who cannot now be found discuss in detail the fact now in issue and agree on a credible account of it, but that evidence would not be admitted although it might be by far the best evidence available.

It was admitted in argument before your Lordships that not every private record would be admissible. If challenged it would be necessary to prove in some way that it had proved to be reliable, before the judge would allow it to be put before the jury. And I think that some such limitation must be implicit in the last reason given by the Court of Criminal Appeal. I see no objection to a judge having a discretion of this kind though it might be awkward in a civil case; but it appears to me to be an innovation on the existing law which decides inadmissibility by categories and not by apparent trustworthiness . . .

The House of Lords recognised the absurdity of their position but felt strongly that it was for the legislature to reform the law and create new exceptions. Parliament dealt with the problem of documentary hearsay with the Criminal Evidence Act 1965 which created an exception for trade and business records. This was later extended by section 68 of the Police and Criminal Evidence Act 1984 and now by sections 23 and 24 of the Criminal Justice Act 1988.[11] Such records have all been admissible in civil proceedings since the Civil Evidence Act 1968.

Myers has been regularly followed in such cases as *Patel v. Comptroller of Customs*[12] where the appellant was convicted of making a false declaration to customs, having stated that the bags of seed were originally from India. The prosecution sought to prove that the seed originated in Morocco and adduced evidence that the bags were stamped with "Produce of Morocco". The Privy Council, following *Myers* held that these words were hearsay and inadmissible. Unlike *Myers*, there was no evidence that the writing was at all reliable, there being no testimony as to how or by whom the bags were marked.

(c) statements by conduct: statements can also be made by actions. Wearing a Chelsea Football Club scarf indicates that you are a club supporter and, applying the hearsay rule technically, testimony that the accused was wearing such a scarf would not be admitted if the purpose of the testimony is to prove that he or she was a Chelsea fan.

In *Chandrasekera v. R.*,[13] the victim had her throat cut. At the trial, evidence was admitted that she was unable to speak as a result of her injuries but had indicated that it was the defendant who had committed the act. This was an intentional assertion on the victim's part and as such was hearsay.[14] A similar situation arose in *R. v. Gibson*[15] where the victim was injured by a stone. The victim testified that, shortly after the attack, an unidentified woman had pointed to a house and said that the person who had thrown the stone had gone in there. The testimony was excluded and the conviction was quashed.

Justifications

The hearsay rule has come under significant academic and judicial criticism. Even where the evidence can be shown to be reliable and even when that evidence is necessary for the defence,[16] it is still excluded. It is a rule that can produce results that are wholly contrary to common sense. In *Sparks*, a three year old girl was indecently assaulted. She told her mother

[11] See Chap. 18.
[12] [1965] 3 All E.R. 593.
[13] [1936] 3 All E.R. 865.
[14] The evidence was admitted for other reasons, namely a statutory exception in Ceylon law.
[15] (1887) 18 Q.B.D. 537.
[16] *R. v. Harry* (1988) 86 Cr.App.R. 105.

that the assailant was coloured. The defendant was white but the child was too young to testify and the mother was not permitted to say what the child had said. On appeal to the Privy Council, Lord Morris said:

Sparks v. R. [1964] A.C. 964 at 978, _per_ Lord Morris

The mother would clearly be giving hearsay evidence if she were permitted to state what her girl had said to her. It becomes necessary, therefore, to examine the contentions which have been advanced in support of the admissibility of the evidence. It was said that 'it was manifestly unjust for the jury to be left throughout the whole trial with the impression that the child could not give any clue to the identity of her assailant'. The cause of justice is, however, best served by adherence to rules which have long been recognised and settled. If the girl made a remark to her mother (not in the presence of the appellant) to the effect that it was the appellant who had assaulted her and if the girl was not to be a witness at the trial, evidence as to what she said would be the merest hearsay. In such circumstances it would be the defence who would wish to challenge a contention, if advanced, that it would be 'manifestly unjust' for the jury not to know that the girl had given a clue to the identity of her assailant.

The conviction in *Sparks* was overturned on other grounds but what can justify a rule of evidence that would have produced such palpable injustice? The reasons advanced for excluding hearsay are essentially twofold: either the testimony is unreliable or its admission is unfair.

Unreliability

A traditional plank for the rule's proponents is the unreliability of hearsay. This can take a number of forms:

(1) the probative value of a hearsay statement is evidentially inferior as it is not the "best evidence".[17] But often hearsay is not only the best evidence, it is the only evidence and yet is excluded because of the hearsay rule: if a witness to a traffic accident repeats a car number to a constable, that constable cannot prove that number if the witness did not inspect it at the time.[18]

(2) admitting hearsay evidence encourages parties to manufacture evidence[19]

(3) the trier of fact is denied the opportunity to judge the demeanour of the witness. This has been described as " . . . the inestimable advantage — the one great advantage to which those who uphold

[17] This is related to but is not the same as the "best evidence rule' which states that there is ". . . but one general rule of evidence, the best that the nature of the of the case will admit" *Omychund v. Barker* (1744) 1 Atk. 21.

[18] *Jones v. Metcalfe* [1967] 3 All E.R. 205.

[19] Criminal Law Revision Committee, *Evidence* (11th Report, 1972) Cmnd. 4991, para. 229; Law Commission, *Evidence in Criminal Proceedings: Hearsay and Related Topics* (Consultation Paper No. 138, 1995), para. 6.8.

the system of trial by jury always point — of the opportunity of not only seeing the witnesses who give evidence and hearing what they have to say, but also of observing their demeanour in the witness-box."[20] But psychological research suggests that our ability to judge character or to spot the liar is less than we would suppose.[21] Often it is the quality of the story-telling that is being judged, not the quality of the story-teller.[22]

(4) the trier of fact is denied the opportunity to judge the demeanour of the witness under cross-examination:

Zuckerman A., *The Principles of Criminal Evidence* (1989) 180–181

A hearsay statement may be flawed in four principal respects. First, the person whose statement is reported, the declarant, may have wrongly perceived the event in question. This can occur because of some defect in the declarant's sense of perception or for some other reason. Secondly, the declarant's memory may have been faulty or inaccurate when he made the statement. Thirdly, he may have lied or deliberately distorted the event. Fourthly the declarant's statement may have been misunderstood by the witness now reporting it. Since meaning is so dependent on context, nuance and shared cultural background, the scope for misunderstanding is substantial.

All of these risks, save the fourth, are also present when the person who observed the facts testifies in court. There is, however, one fundamental difference: when a witness is in court, the opponent is able to cross-examine him in order to investigate his powers of perception, test his memory, and appraise his veracity, thus enabling the trier of fact to determine the probative value of the testimony according to the witness's performance in the witness-box. It is the unavailability of a hearsay declarant for cross-examination which constitutes the central reason for the exclusion of hearsay statements. It is said that in the absence of cross-examination of the declarant jurors are likely to overestimate the probative significance of his hearsay statement.

This argument cannot be dismissed altogether. On introspection most of us will admit to undue susceptibility to hearsay especially when the hearsay appears to confirm a belief we already hold or a prejudice to which we are predisposed.

Attitudes vary widely as to the value of cross-examination as a mechanism for discovering truth. For Wigmore, it was the ". . . greatest legal engine ever invented for the discovery of truth", whereas others see it as a means for making an honest witness seem at best confused and at worst a liar.[23]

[20] *R. v. Collins* (1938) 26 Cr.App.R. 177 at 182, *per* Humphreys J.

[21] Wellborn O. G., "Demeanor" Cornell LR (1991) 1075; Blumenthal J.A., "A Wipe of the Hands, A Lick of the Lips: The Validity of Deameanor Evidence in Assessing Witness Credibility" 72 Neb. L.R. (1993) 1157; Law Commission, *supra* paras. 6.22 ff.

[22] Bennett W. and Feldman M., *Reconstructing Reality in the Courtroom* (1981).

[23] See 357, *et seq.*

(5) juries are unqualified in assessing the probative value of hearsay evidence as opposed to direct evidence. But already in criminal cases, juries follow complex directions on issues of doctrine, for example, the relationship between foresight and intention[24] or the concept of dishonesty.[25] Assessing the relative weight of items of evidence is no more complex. Furthermore documentary hearsay is now admissible under the conditions laid down in sections 23 and 24 of the Criminal Justice Act 1988 and juries are directed as to its weight relative to non-hearsay testimony.[26] Jurors would not be required to undertake any different intellectual exercise, were oral hearsay to become admissible evidence.

But even where there is no reason to doubt the reliability of the evidence and therefore, on the basis of a rationale of unreliability, no reason to exclude, the evidence will still be excluded. Were "reliability" the true rationale for the exclusion of hearsay, we would require, not a *rule* of exclusion, but judicial discretion. But the exclusion of hearsay evidence is based on a rule, an idea that was firmly put by Lord Morris in *Sparks*:

> If it is said that hearsay evidence should freely be admitted and that there should be concentration in any particular case upon deciding as to its value or weight it is sufficient to say that our law has not been evolved upon such lines but is firmly based upon the view that it is wiser and better that hearsay should be excluded save in certain well-defined and rather exceptional circumstances.[27]

Unfairness to the parties

The other rationale for the exclusion of hearsay is that hearsay evidence is unsatisfactory not simply because of its unreliability, nor because the witness is not subject to cross-examination. The use of hearsay also means that the trial itself can be stigmatised as unfair and an abuse of due process.

One of the hallmarks of totalitarian societies is the anonymous accusation based on rumour.[28] While medieval England might have been content to hang a man who was a "notorious thief", modern legal values require specificity both as to what acts of theft have been committed and as to those who witnessed it. The latter must be identified and not anonymous and must be confronted publicly with their accusation. It is this notion of fairness which lies behind the hearsay rule and is expressed in several human rights documents:

[24] *R. v. Nedrick* [1986] 3 All E.R. 1.
[25] *R. v. Ghosh* [1982] 2 All E.R. 689.
[26] *R. v. Cole* [1990] 2 All E.R. 108.
[27] *Sparks supra* at 978.
[28] However this practice is still to be found in Western European jurisdictions where police officers are able to testify that X, who is not named, saw the accused commit the offence. Such testimony is admitted — Andersen J., "The Anonymity of Witnesses — a Danish Development" [1985] Crim.L.R. 363.

In all criminal prosecutions, the accused shall enjoy the right to a speedy and public trial, by an impartial jury of the state and district wherein the crime shall have been committed, which district shall have been previously ascertained by law, and to be informed of the nature and cause of the accusation; to be confronted with the witnesses against him; to have compulsory process for obtaining witnesses in his favour, and to have the assistance of counsel for his defence.[29]

The right to confront one's accusers is linked to the rule excluding hearsay. Giving of evidence in public is regarded as a key component of justice and evidence which is given anonymously, secretly or at one remove is inevitably tainted with unfairness. In England, the lack of entrenched constitutional rights results in such issues being camouflaged in other concepts, in this case that of hearsay. This can mean that the issue of fairness is confused with that of probative worth. To what extent is hearsay an aspect of procedural due process?

Federal Rules of Evidence (1993), Commentary at 107–109

Until very recently decisions invoking the confrontation clause of the Sixth Amendment were surprisingly few, a fact probably explainable by the former inapplicability of the clause to the states and by the hearsay rule's occupancy of much the same ground. The pattern which emerges from the earlier cases invoking the clause is substantially that of the hearsay rule applied to criminal cases: an accused is entitled to have the witnesses against him testify under oath in the presence of himself and trier subject to cross-examination; yet considerations of public policy and necessity require the recognition of such exceptions as dying declarations and former testimony of unavailable witnesses.[30]

Beginning with *Snyder v. Massachusetts*[31] the Court began to speak of confrontation as an aspect of procedural due process, thus extending its applicability to state cases and to federal cases other than criminal. The language of *Snyder* was that of an elastic concept of hearsay . . . Ascertaining the constitutional dimensions of the confrontation-hearsay aggregate against the background of these cases is a matter of some difficulty yet the general pattern is at least not inconsistent with that of the hearsay rule.

In 1965 the confrontation clause was held applicable to the states: *Pointer v. Texas*.[32] Prosecution use of former testimony given at a preliminary hearing where petitioner was not represented by counsel was a violation of the clause. The same result would have followed under conventional hearsay doctrine read in the light of a constitutional right to counsel and nothing in the opinion suggests any difference in essential outline between the hearsay rule and the right of confrontation. In the companion case of *Douglas v. Alabama*[33] however the result reached by applying the confrontation clause is one reached less readily via the hearsay rule. A confession implicating petitioner was put before the jury by reading it to the witness in portions and asking if he made that statement. The witness refused to answer on grounds of self-incrimination. The result, said the Court, was to deny cross-

[29] Amendment VI to the U.S. Constitution.
[30] *Mattox v. United States* 156 U.S. 237 (1895); *Motes v. United States* 178 U.S. 458 (1900); *Delaney v. United States* 263 U.S. 586 (1924).
[31] 291 U.S. 97 (1934).
[32] 380 U.S. 400 (1965).
[33] 380 U.S. 415 (1965).

examination and hence confrontation. True, it could broadly be said that the confession was a hearsay statement which for all practical purposes was put in evidence. Yet a more easily accepted explanation of the opinion is that its real thrust was in the direction of curbing undesirable prosecutorial behavior rather than merely applying rules of exclusion and that the confrontation clause was the means selected to achieve this end. . . .

The pattern suggested in *Douglas* was developed further and more distinctly in a pair of cases at the end of the 1966 term. *United States v. Wade*[34] and *Gilbert v. California*[35] hinged upon practices followed in identifying accused persons before trial. This pretrial identification was said to be so decisive an aspect of the case that accused was entitled to have counsel present; a pretrial identification made in the absence of counsel was not itself receivable in evidence and in addition might fatally infect a courtroom identification. The presence of counsel at the earlier identification was described as a necessary prerequisite for a meaningful confrontation at trial. *Wade* involved no evidence of the fact of a prior identification and hence was not susceptible of being decided on hearsay grounds. In *Gilbert* witnesses did testify to an earlier identification readily classifiable as hearsay under a fairly strict view of what constitutes hearsay. The Court however carefully avoided basing the decision on the hearsay ground choosing confrontation instead . . .

Under the earlier cases the confrontation clause may have been little more than a constitutional embodiment of the hearsay rule, even including traditional exceptions but with some room for expanding them along similar lines. But under the recent cases the impact of the clause clearly extends beyond the confines of the hearsay rule. These considerations have led the Advisory Committee to conclude that a hearsay rule can function usefully as an adjunct to the confrontation right in constitutional areas and independently in nonconstitutional areas.

This link between the hearsay rule and procedural justice is also reflected in Article 6 of the European Convention on Human Rights and Fundamental Freedoms:

6.—(3) Everyone charged with a criminal offence has the following minimum rights:

(d) to examine or have examined witnesses against him and to obtain the attendance and examination of witnesses on his behalf under the same conditions as witnesses against him;

It is this paragraph which impinges on the operation of the hearsay rule and which underlines an accused's right to be protected from anonymous accusation:

Osborne C., "Hearsay and the Court of Human Rights" [1993] Crim.L.R. 255 at 261–263

There is now a very substantial body of case law on this provision, which has been held to be a rule of central importance to the concept of a fair trial.

. . . Article 6(3)(d), however, is essentially a rule to do with admissibility rather than weight. Prima facie Article 6(3)(d) imposes a strict rule against the use of

[34] 388 U.S. 218 (1967).
[35] 388 U.S. 263 (1967).

hearsay evidence by the prosecution. This is because if one has the right to 'examine or have examined' witnesses against one, then that on the face of it requires the witness to be present in court for cross-examination. Three matters need to be considered to arrive at a full understanding of the Article, namely:

1. What is meant by 'witness against' and does that phrase apply to absent persons whose statements are tendered in evidence?
2. What is meant by 'examine or have examined' and would it, for example, suffice that the 'examination should be by the judge rather than one's own counsel?
3. Is it sufficient if that examination of witnesses takes place at some preliminary stage rather than in the 'public hearing' which is guaranteed by Article 6(1)?

The strongest view is that Article 6(3)(d) prohibits the prosecution from adducing hearsay evidence. Unsurprisingly, the Commission and Court have lately tended to shrink from so strict an interpretation, although the reasoning in the relevant cases must be scrutinised carefully.

The two leading cases are those of *Unterpertinger* and *Kostovski*. In *Unterpertinger v. Austria*[36] the issue concerned the admissibility of hearsay statements admitted at Unterpertinger's trial. He was charged with causing actual bodily harm to his stepdaughter and wife. His defence was in part self-defence, and in part exaggeration of the incident. A report was prepared by the Austrian police including statements by the accused, two victims and a doctor. Under Article 152 of the Austrian Code of Criminal Procedure members of an accused's family are not compellable. The accused's wife attended a preliminary investigation and gave evidence of the assaults to a judge. However at the trial proper both victims refused to testify. The Court thereupon caused the record of Frau Unterpertinger's interview with the investigating judge to be read out. Further, under the Austrian Code of Criminal Procedure the investigation file was read out in court and this included, amongst other things, police reports of the incident, the accused's criminal record and various witness statements. Thereafter the accused was convicted and his subsequent appeal dismissed. Unterpertinger then applied to the European Commission on the grounds that the acceptance of written evidence of interviews with the judge and the police infringed Article (1) and Article (6)(3)(d), contending that his inability to have the alleged victims cross-examined was in breach of the Convention. The Court concluded that whilst there were other documents which the Court had before it to assist it to arrive at the truth, including the accused's criminal record and the accused's own testimony, the conviction must have been substantially based on the statements made by the victims to the police and therefore that there was a breach of the Article. Somewhat mysteriously the Court added that 'in itself the reading out of statements in this way cannot be regarded as being inconsistent with Article 6 . . . but the use made of the statements as evidence must nevertheless comply with the rights of the defence.' The meaning of this additional phrase is opaque unless it simply means that the reading out of the evidence is in order (*i.e.* that examination-in-chief may be dispensed with) providing there is also an opportunity for cross-examination, *i.e.* that the witness must be present.

A similar result occurred in *Kostovski v. Netherlands*.[37] The accused was convicted of armed robbery, the conviction being based to a decisive extent on reports of statements by two anonymous witnesses interviewed in the absence of the accused and counsel for the accused by police, and in one case by an examining magistrate at an earlier stage. The Court stressed that it was not its task to express a

[36] Case 1985/87/134.
[37] Case 10/1988/154/208.

view on whether statements were correctly admitted and assessed by the court of trial but to ascertain whether the proceedings as a whole, including the way in which evidence was taken and the defence rights were honoured, was fair. The Court held that in principle all the evidence had to be produced in the presence of the accused at a public hearing with a view to cross-examination, although statements obtained at a pre-trial stage could be used as evidence 'provided the rights of the defence were respected'. As a rule, however, those rights would require that the accused have at some stage a proper opportunity to challenge and question a witness against him. In the present case that opportunity had not been provided and the witnesses therefore had at no stage been cross-examined, directly or indirectly. There were further difficulties in that the prosecution witnesses' identity had been withheld, thus rendering it difficult for the accused to demonstrate prejudice, hostility or unreliability. Notwithstanding the possibility of intimidation of witnesses in serious cases, there was a need to balance the use of anonymous statements with the interests of the accused and the present conviction was held to be irreconcilable with the guarantee in Article 6.

If the exclusion of hearsay in criminal cases is an instance of the principle of fairness guaranteeing a fair trial, the rule's primary objective must be the protection of the defendant who is most at risk from anonymous accusation by the state. But this does not mean that the defence must also be prevented from adducing hearsay evidence. The prosecution (and the community they represent) should be protected from 'dirty tricks' by the accused but, as long as there is due notice, the State possess the resources to ensure that the prosecution will not be improperly prejudiced by hearsay introduced on behalf of the defence.

If the principle of a "fair trial" is accepted as the rationale for excluding hearsay evidence, this probably requires amendment to the rigid application of the rule as far as defendants are concerned. Such decisions as *R. v. Blastland*[38] have led to the argument that the principle of procedural justice requires an inclusionary discretion for hearsay statements on behalf of the accused:

Allen T., "Implied Assertions as Hearsay" 142 New L.J. (1992) 1194

An inclusionary discretion, to be exercised, like its exclusionary counterpart, only in favour of the defence, should apply to all evidence whose rejection, on technical grounds, may do real injustice. Express, as well as implied, hearsay assertions should clearly be admitted in exceptional cases. Few people, surely, would wish to defend the decision in *Sparks* . . .

The Criminal Law Revision Committee,[39] which proposed significant modifications to the hearsay rule, rejected the idea of a general inclusionary discretion. The Committee thought that in practice hearsay would be freely allowed for the defence but rarely for the prosecution. The idea that hearsay evidence of the kind excluded in *Sparks* should be admitted was also rejected on the basis of the principle 'that any evidence admissible for the defence must also be admissible for the prosecution'.

[38] [1985] 2 All E.R. 1095 — a confession to the murder by a third party was excluded; *R. v. Turner* [1975] 1 All E.R. 70; *R. v. Harry* (1986) 86 Cr.App.R. 105; *R. v. Beckford and Daley* [1991] Crim.L.R. 833.

[39] 11th Report, Cmnd. 4991 (1972).

However, the Committee seemed to overlook the distinction between rule and discretion. The equality between prosecution and defence, as regards admissibility of evidence, is already sharply undermined by the existing exclusionary discretion.

Moreover, in a footnote the Committee acknowledged that there was 'a case in principle for wider admissibility of evidence on behalf of the defence than on behalf of the prosecution.'

Although formally consistent with both majority and minority speeches in *Kearley*, the decision in *Blastland* may be thought to strengthen the case for reform . . . Although the exclusion of both pieces of evidence — M's confession and his knowledge of the crime — may be defended individually (as a matter of logic), the result was to deprive the jury of information which might properly have left them with an entirely reasonable doubt about the defendant's guilt. In many cases, a third party's confession should no doubt be dismissed as a distraction of little significance. But fairness cannot be ensured without a power to admit such evidence in an appropriate case. Where the context and circumstances of a third party's confession can be fully and accurately related . . . and where other evidence would appear to lend it some credence, it should sometimes be brought to the attention of the jury. The rules governing hearsay and relevance, while independent in theory, can in practice conspire to cause grave injustice to the defendant. In such circumstances, the exercise of an inclusionary discretion would seem to provide an essential safeguard.

. . . In *Kearley*, Lords Bridge and Oliver held fast to Lord Reid's opinion, in *Myers*, that only systematic legislative reform was feasible. While the judges' reluctance to modify the formal rules of evidence may be understood, it is however important to stress that there should be no barrier to wider exercise of the court's discretion. Exercise of an inclusionary discretion may reasonably be thought to be an integral feature of the principal constitutional function of the trial judge — to ensure the defendant receives a fair trial. In that context, the distinction between exclusionary and inclusionary discretions is somewhat arbitrary. In *Sang*,[40] Lord Scarman concluded that the various forms of the exclusionary discretion were all instances of a general discretion founded on the right to a fair trial; and also that the demands of fairness inevitably depended on all the circumstances of particular cases.

Lord Scarman's denial that the 'principle of fairness' was 'susceptible to categorisation and classification' — even in the context of exclusionary discretion — reflected the importance of allowing the judge to depart from the rules when their application would cause injustice in particular cases. There is an ineradicable tension between formal legality and substantive equity — between legal rule and judicial discretion — which we cannot finally (or safely) resolve except in the circumstances of particular cases. Even if the rules of evidence should generally be altered by formal legislation alone, the judge's discretion should be invoked at common law whenever it is necessary to prevent injustice. All relevant evidence — even hearsay, express or implied — should be admitted in support of the defence where the interests of justice plainly support it.

The U.S. Supreme Court has held that the exclusion of evidence of confessions made by a third party, in accordance with ordinary rules of evidence, deprived the defendant of a fair trial.[41] . . . It cannot be accepted that the right to a fair trial is any less fundamental in Britain than in the U.S. - could Parliament abolish the right to a fair trial? — and similar consequences must surely follow. As the Supreme Court said, '. . . where constitutional rights directly affecting the ascertainment of guilt are implicated, the hearsay rule may not be applied mechanically to defeat the ends of justice'.

[40] [1980] A.C. 402 at 453–457.
[41] *Chambers v. Mississippi* 410 U.S. 295 (1973).

Presenting the testimony of an absent witness through the medium of another witness means that the triers of fact are being asked to accept information at face value, the quality of which they have no means to evaluate. But it is not simply a matter of reliability — indeed perhaps reliability should not be regarded as a relevant factor? Fairness requires that defendants should not face anonymous accusation and be unable to confront witnesses against them. It is this uneasy amalgam of probative significance and procedural fairness that underlies the existence of the hearsay rule.

The Scope of Hearsay

There are two conceptual issues which are critical to any discussion of the scope of the rule. The Cross formulation is:

> an assertion other than one made by a person while giving oral evidence in the proceedings is inadmissible as evidence of any fact asserted

(1) the first issue is what may be termed the "purpose rule". The formula suggests that a statement "is inadmissible as evidence of any fact asserted". This requires us to identify the purpose for which the statement is being introduced. If the statement is introduced for a purpose other than that of proving the truth of the facts contained in it, the statement may be admissible. For example, where a witness's truthfulness has been doubted, a prior consistent statement may be introduced, not as evidence of the facts that the statement contains but as evidence that the witness is consistent and therefore more likely to be truthful and credible.[42] Another example of this can be seen where the witness testifies that the defendant had stated that there were pink elephants in the road. Although the witness is repeating another's words, such a statement is not hearsay because it is introduced, not as evidence that the elephants existed but that the defendant was drunk or mad.[43]

(2) the second issue centres around the word "assertion". Does the hearsay rule only exclude those statements in which the declarant[44] expressly and intentionally asserted a fact or does it also strike out those statements where the fact is asserted unintentionally and by implication? In *R. v. Kearley*[45] the police raided a house searching for drugs. Drugs were found but not in sufficient quantities that any trier of fact would be justified in concluding that there was any intent to supply. The prosecution sought to rely on the testimony of

[42] *R. v. Oyesiku* (1971) 56 Cr.App.R. 240.
[43] *Ratten v. R* [1971] 3 All E.R. 801.
[44] "Declarant" — the absent witness who made the original statement which one of the parties seeks to adduce in evidence.
[45] [1992] 2 All E.R. 345.

police officers who had taken various phone calls from anonymous callers. These callers had spoken in terms which suggested that the accused was their drug supplier, although they had not expressly stated that he was a dealer. The House of Lords ruled that such 'implied assertions' were also excluded by the hearsay rule.

Other jurisdictions are more restrictive, only excluding those statements which intentionally assert a fact. Under the Federal Rules of Evidence:

> 801.—A statement is (1) an oral or written assertion or (2) nonverbal conduct of a person if it is intended by the person as an assertion.[46]

This is also the case under the Evidence Act 1995 in Australia:

> 59.—(1) Evidence of a previous representation made by a person is not admissible to prove the existence of a fact that the person intended to assert by the representation.

These two issues define the boundaries of hearsay and will be examined in more detail.

The Scope of the Hearsay Rule — Hearsay or Original Evidence?

Cross's definition of hearsay was that any assertion other than one made by a person while giving oral evidence in the proceedings was inadmissible as evidence of any fact asserted. The key element here is that a statement will only be treated as hearsay if the party adducing it intends to rely on the truth of its contents.

It becomes essential to isolate what fact you are seeking to prove by adducing the statement. Only then is it possible to identify the purpose of introducing the statement. Thus in a case of careless driving, where the car also failed to stop, the prosecution must show that it was the accused's car. There is a witness, now disappeared, who saw the registration number and repeated it to the police officer. The officer attempts to testify to that and obviously wishes the court to rely on the truth of the assertion that the number was that of a car belonging to the accused. As such the assertion is inadmissible hearsay. But were the witness to be charged with obstruction of a police officer on the grounds that he had deliberately given a false registration number, the officer could quite properly recount the statement. In these circumstances, the prosecution would not be relying on the truth of the statement but the fact that it was a lie. The court would not be interested in the perceptions of the declarant but only in whether these words were in fact spoken and the police officer's testimony is admitted for that purpose. This is illustrated in *R. v. Chapman*[47] when the defendant was

[46] Federal Rules of Evidence, r.801.
[47] [1969] 2 All E.R. 321.

charged under the Road Safety Act 1967 with drunk driving. Section 2(2)(b) of the Act provided that a hospital patient should not provide a breath specimen if the doctor objected. A breath test had been administered to the defendant while in hospital. The constable gave evidence that the doctor had not objected. On appeal, the appellant contended that the prosecution should have called the doctor to prove that there was no objection. The conviction was affirmed as this was not a hearsay statement — the fact which needed to be proved was that no objection to a breath test had been made. If there had been no objection, the proper procedure was followed and the appellant had no grounds for appeal. The constable testified that there had been no objection. Whether the doctor spoke the truth or not was immaterial.

This can be compared to words of offer and acceptance in a breach of contract action where there is testimony that words of acceptance were spoken. This is not hearsay. It is evidence that such a statement was made. It is irrelevant whether the declarant means to accept the offer or not since he may have altered his legal position just by speaking these words. Whether in law it amounts to an acceptance will depend on whether a reasonable person would have construed them as accepting the offer.

It is a very fine line between statements which contravene the hearsay rule and those statements which courts regard as original evidence. Although fine, it is a distinct line which the courts neglect at their peril.[48]

We might consider two categories:

(a) the very existence of a statement may be a fact in issue in a case:

Illustrations of this are:

(1) if the accused is charged with obtaining by deception, evidence that a false representation was made is essential. It is not hearsay because the prosecution are not relying on the statement's truth. Indeed they must prove its falsity.

(2) in an action for defamation, the plaintiff must prove that the defamatory words were uttered. It is not hearsay because the plaintiff is not relying on their truth but simply the fact that the words were spoken or written. Often the plaintiff is seeking to show that the words are untrue.

(3) in breach of contract, the plaintiff might well wish to rely on the words of acceptance spoken by the defendant. He or she must show that the words were uttered and that a reasonable person would have understood them to mean the acceptance of the offer.

[48] In *Kearley*, the majority in the House of Lords focus solely upon the category of implied assertions and fail to recognise the argument that the statements may be admissible to prove the use of the premises, a fact which is itself of circumstantial relevance to proving the accused's intent to supply.

This important point is illustrated by *Subramaniam v. Public Prosecutor.*[49] The defendant was accused of being in unlawful possession of ammunition. His defence was that he was acting under duress and he sought to testify that he had been threatened by terrorists. The trial judge excluded the evidence of the threats as hearsay but the conviction was quashed on appeal. The issue before the court was whether the defendant believed that he would be killed if he refused to carry out the terrorists' orders. To establish that belief and thus the defence of duress, there must be evidence that threatening words were spoken. It was not relevant whether those words were true or not — the issue was whether the defendant believed them:

Subramaniam v. Public Prosecutor [1956] 1 W.L.R. 965 at 970, per Mr. L. M. D. De Silva

In ruling out peremptorily the evidence of conversation between the terrorist and the appellant the trial judge was in error. Evidence of a statement made to a witness by a person who is not himself called as a witness may or may not be hearsay. It is hearsay and inadmissible when the object of the evidence is to establish the truth of what is contained in the statement. It is not hearsay and is admissible when it is proposed to establish by the evidence, not the truth of the statement, but the fact that it was made. The fact that the statement was made, quite apart from its truth, is frequently relevant in considering the mental state and conduct thereafter of the witness or of some other person in whose presence the statement was made. In the case before their Lordships statements could have been made to the appellant by the terrorists, which, whether true or not, if they had been believed by the appellant, might reasonably have induced in him an apprehension of instant death if he failed to conform to their wishes.

In the rest of the evidence given by the appellant statements made to him by the terrorists appear now and again to have been permitted, probably inadvertently, to go in. But, a complete, or substantially complete, version according to the appellant of what was said to him by the terrorists and by him to them has been shut out. This version, if believed, could and might have afforded cogent evidence of duress brought to bear upon the appellant. Its admission would also have meant that the complete story of the appellant would have been before the trial judge and assessors and enabled them more effectively to have come to a correct conclusion as to the truth or otherwise of the appellant's story . . .

In *Subramaniam* the court is not interested in perceptions of the terrorist but in the perceptions of the witness in the courtroom. The accused can testify whether a threat was made and whether he believed that it would be carried out. Such testimony can be evaluated by the court and thus the statements are original evidence and not hearsay.

(b) the statement itself might not be a legally constitutive fact but may be relevant to such a fact:

In *Subramaniam* the existence of the statement might also be analysed, not as a fact in issue in establishing the defence but as a fact relevant to a fact

[49] [1956] 1 W.L.R. 965.

in issue. In other words, the existence of the statement was evidence from which the jury might conclude that the accused believed himself to be under threat. As long as the issue remains the existence of the statement rather than the truth of its contents, the testimony is not hearsay.

A more complex case but raising the same questions is *Woodhouse v. Hall*[50] where the defendant was charged with managing a brothel contrary to section 33 of the Sexual Offences Act 1956. Plainclothes officers kept observation on the building and also entered as customers for a massage. They alleged that they had been offered masturbation by the masseuses working there. Could the officers testify that the offers had been made? The justices excluded the evidence as hearsay but the Divisional Court held these statements were operative words. Why? The prosecution had to prove that the use of the premises amounted to a brothel. The officers could not have testified to statements by customers or by the employees that "This is a brothel". Obviously evidence of their own eyes as to sexual activity would have been admissible. But in addition a brothel is a place where offers of sexual services are made and accepted. The words of offer and acceptance are a statement which is relevant to the fact in issue, namely the use to which the premises are being put.

A similar answer is to be found in cases such as *Davidson v. Quirke*[51] in which the accused was charged with using premises for the purposes of betting and evidence was given by police officers of a number of phone calls to the premises from people seeking to place bets:

Davidson v. Quirke [1923] N.Z.L.R. 552 at 555–557, _per_ Salmond J.

If the testimony of the police officers was limited to the mere fact that on the day in question a large number of persons rang up the appellant's house within the space of an hour and twenty-five minutes, all evidence as to the contents of the communications being excluded, such testimony would prove merely that the premises were being used for a business of some kind, but would fall short of proving that they were being used for the business of betting. I am of opinion that, notwithstanding the general rule which excludes evidence of statements, the contents of those telephone messages as received and testified to by the police officers are legally admissible in evidence. This is an illustration of the principle that, notwithstanding the rule against hearsay, where the purpose or meaning of an act done is relevant, evidence of contemporaneous declarations accompanying and explaining the act is admissible in proof of such purpose or meaning . . . since the act of numerous strangers in using the appellant's telephone for the purpose of betting is relevant to the issue, the statements made by them at the same time are admissible as explaining their actions and showing the purpose of them.

Talking about "verbal acts" might not be helpful as it might be questioned whether the court requires any explanation of the acts of the callers. What the callers believed or purposed is not in issue. The fact in

[50] (1980) 72 Cr.App.R. 39.
[51] [1923] N.Z.L.R. 552.

issue for the prosecution is the "use of the premises", as a brothel or a bookies. But were this proscribed use to be entertainment, evidence that singing was heard would surely be admissible and nobody would suggest that it was necessary to call the singer as a witness. Similarly a statement such as "£5 on Fighting Scot on the nose" is admissible not because of its truth or falsity (it has none) nor because of the implied belief of the declarant that the receiver of the call is a bookmaker. The statement is admitted as evidence which tends to prove that these are premises where bets are made.

Is the admission into evidence of these statements fair in terms of the accused's "right of confrontation"? Are the accused in all these cases being convicted on the testimony of absent witnesses? To take the example of "using premises for the purpose of entertainment", if a witness testified as to someone singing, it is the correct witness who is testifying and who can be cross-examined on their perceptions. The singer, were he or she to testify, would merely add more or less weight. This is the situation with the phone calls in *Davidson v. Quirke* and *Woodhouse v. Hall* as the accused is able to cross-examine the witness as to whether these statements were made or not. This is the same question that would be put to the declarant, were he or she present. It is not the declarant's perceptions that are in issue but whether a particular form of words were used.[52]

Many commentators would argue that such an analysis is simply an artificial technique from escaping from the logical consequences of the hearsay rule, another "hearsay fiddle" comparable to a witness "refresh the memory":

Zuckerman A., *The Principles of Criminal Evidence* (1989) 195–197

It is therefore said that [words of offer and acceptance] are proved as original evidence and are not adduced as evidence of anything other than the fact that they were made.

However, admissibility if such words has been extended beyond statements with independent legal consequences to cover statements that explain or qualify some act that they accompany. On a charge of running an illegal betting shop it has been held, in the Commonwealth and the United States, that it is admissible to adduce evidence that, while the police were raiding the premises, telephones calls were received in which unidentified callers tried to place bets. However, decisions to admit such evidence ignore the fact that by dialling a telephone number one is addressing oneself to the intended recipient of the call. The act of dialling is a mechanical equivalent of a verbal address. There cannot be a difference between

[52] Although I argue that admission of such statements is within the principles of a fair trial, there are other policy considerations. The Police and Criminal Evidence Act 1984 and its Codes of Practice sought to remove police "verbals" from the courtroom — *i.e.* unverified police accounts of what the accused said. The argument above might well be attacked on the grounds that it would encourage a new species of verbals — *i.e.* unverified police accounts of what unidentified witnesses said. In my defence, I might say that a police officer would have to be well-versed in the intricacies of hearsay versus original evidence to succeed in such manoeuvres.

saying 'Look here, Mr Bookie, I wish to place a bet on Lucifer' and dialling Mr Bookie's number and then saying 'I wish to place a bet on Lucifer'.

The theory of operative words was taken to its logical conclusion in *Woodhouse v. Hall* where the requirement for a mechanical act was dispensed with . . . If we ask ourselves how the court is to infer the fact in issue from the fact that the statements were made, the answer must be: by reasoning that, when the women made the said statements, they intended to offer themselves to clients as part of the services provided by the establishment. Yet this is the very reasoning that the hearsay rule forbids; it forbids adducing out-of-court statements as proof of facts stated therein, whether expressly or, as here, by implication. Recently the Court of Appeal seems to have accepted that an infringement of the rule is involved in these situations.[53]

The methodology just described illustrates a fairly common tendency in this area. A certain type of statement is taken to be reliable. To avoid exclusion the court searches for a convenient tag which may be given to this type of evidence so that it may pass for something other than hearsay. To fulfil its function the tag or label must be associated with admissible evidence. Hence the usefulness of notions such as 'operative words' and 'circumstantial evidence directly relevant to the issue'. Once the label is attached to a piece of evidence, the inhibiting effect of the hearsay rule disappears as if by magic.

This might be countered by the argument that it is essential to identify the fact in issue (or the fact relevant to a fact in issue) that the statements are relevant to. Once that fact is identified as the use of the premises, as in *Woodhouse v. Hall*, it becomes a question of whether offers of sexual services were or were not being made. What the women may or may not have intended and their implicit beliefs are, on this argument, irrelevant.

Zuckerman places emphasis not on the express words but on the implications that can be drawn from the women's statements. The obvious inference to be drawn was their knowledge that the establishment operated as a brothel. Thus the same statement could be said to perform two different functions:

(1) the mere existence of the words is admissible and relevant evidence tending to prove the use to which the premises are put
(2) the statements reveal an implied knowledge of the women as to the function of the establishment and that knowledge is hearsay and inadmissible.

Is it justifiable for a court to direct a jury that the words spoken are admissible but that the beliefs of the witness are not? In *Kearley*,[54] Lord Browne-Wilkinson says:

. . . But the fact that his action (viz asking for drugs or queuing for coffee) is capable of raising an inadmissible inference of irrelevant fact does not mean that

[53] *R. v. Harry* [1988] 86 Cr. App.R 105 although it might be said that the use of statements was to identify H's co-accused as the supplier and, by negative inference, to exculpate H. Here the court is being asked to rely on the truth of the assertion.
[54] [1992] 2 All E.R. 345.

evidence of that action cannot be admitted with a view to proving a relevant fact.[55]

However in the Court of Appeal in the same case, Lloyd L.J. observed:

> We have been assuming that the words had a dual purpose, first, to show the commercial supply of drugs from the premises, and, secondly, to show that the appellant was the supplier. But in truth there is no distinction. It was all part and parcel of the same purpose. If the evidence was admissible to prove the first purpose, it was admissible to prove the second. Any attempt to draw a line between the two would, we think, be indefensible.[56]

Another example of such a dual statement is in *Ratten*.[57] The defendant was convicted of murdering his wife. She was shot at about 1.20 p.m. The defence was that the accused was cleaning his gun and it went off accidentally. The central issue was the "accidental" nature of the shooting. The defendant testified and the prosecution sought to introduce evidence in rebuttal that in the minutes before the shooting, the telephonist at the local exchange had taken a call from that number and from a woman who sobbed and whose voice had sounded hysterical and that the caller had said, "Get me the police, please." Was this evidence hearsay?

Ratten v. R. [1971] 3 All E.R. 801 at 805–806, _per_ Lord Wilberforce

The mere fact that evidence of a witness includes evidence as to words spoken by another person who is not called is no objection to its admissibility. Words spoken are facts just as much as any other action by a human being. If the speaking of the words is a relevant fact, a witness may give evidence that they were spoken. A question of hearsay only arises when the words spoken are relied on 'testimonially', *i.e.* as establishing some fact narrated by the words. Authority is hardly needed for this proposition . . . (Lord Wilberforce quotes from *Subramaniam supra*).

A fuller statement of the same principle is provided by Dean Wigmore in his work on Evidence (para. 1766). He emphasises, as their Lordships would emphasise, that the test of admissibility . . . is relevance to an issue.

The evidence, relating to the act of telephoning by the deceased was, in their Lordships' view, factual and relevant. It can be analysed into the following elements.

(1) At about 1.15 pm the number Echuca 1494 rang. I plugged into that number.
(2) I opened the speak key and said number please.
(3) A female voice answered.
(4) That voice was hysterical and sobbed.
(5) The voice said 'Get me the police, please'.

The factual items numbered (1)–(3) were relevant in order to show that, contrary to the evidence of the appellant, a call was made, only some three to five minutes

[55] *ibid.* at 384h.
[56] *ibid* at 377–378 quoted by Lord Oliver.
[57] [1971] 3 All E.R. 801.

before the fatal shooting, by a woman. It not being suggested that there was anybody in the house other than the appellant, his wife and small children, this woman, the caller, could only have been the deceased. Items (4) and (5) were relevant as possibly showing (if the jury thought fit to draw the inference) that the deceased woman was at this time in a state of emotion or fear . . . They were relevant and necessary evidence in order to explain and complete the fact of the call being made. A telephone call is a composite act, made up of manual operations together with the utterance of words . . . To confine the evidence to the first would be to deprive the act of most of its significance. The act had content when it was known that the call was made in a state of emotion. The knowledge that the caller desired the police to be called, helped to indicate the nature of the emotion — anxiety or fear at an existing or impending emergency. It was a matter for the jury to decide what light (if any) this evidence, in the absence of any explanation from the appellant, who was in the house, threw on what situation was occurring or developing at the time.

If, then, this evidence had been presented in this way, as evidence purely of relevant facts, its admissibility could hardly have been plausibly challenged. But the appellant submits that in fact this was not so. It is said that the evidence was tendered and admitted as evidence by the deceased that she was being attacked by the appellant, and that it was, so far, hearsay evidence, being put forward as evidence of the truth of facts asserted by his statement. It is claimed that the learned chief justice so presented the evidence to the jury and that, therefore, its admissibility, as hearsay, may be challenged.

Their Lordships, as already stated, do not consider that there is any hearsay element in the evidence . . .

The prosecution needed to establish as a fact that the victim was in fear and hysterical. This was relevant since it made the defence of accident less credible. The operator's opinion of Mrs Ratten's state of mind, based on non-verbal indications such as the caller sobbing or sounding panicky, is clearly admissible.[58] But is the operator allowed to repeat the words used? Lord Wilberforce suggests that the words are "... relevant and necessary evidence in order to explain and complete the fact of the call being made". This is another illustration of the judges' fondness for the "verbal act" approach.[59] Although the fact that the call was made (which had been denied by the appellant in testifying) was relevant to the weight to be put on the appellant's evidence, this stress on the "verbal act" is a distraction from the essential fact to be proved, the state of the victim's mind.

Are the victim's words non-hearsay evidence of her state of mind? Can a witness testify that the victim shouted "Help me!"? If so, the evidence was admissible as the telephonist could testify not only that a call had been made from that number and that the wife was apparently very upset but also the words that made up the statement. It is not the truth of the statement that is the relevant factor. But again the victim's statement can be analysed not simply as revealing her state of mind but as asserting a fact, in this case, "My husband's trying to kill me". If so, as discussed below,

[58] If it is an opinion, it is one which does not call for specialist knowledge and where the non-expert witness would find it difficult to separate fact from inference; see 641, *et seq.*

[59] The weaknesses of such an approach as part of the res gestae exception are discussed in 549, *et seq.*

this is hearsay since the court is being asked to rely on the truth of the statement and it is only admissible if an exception such as *res gestae* applies.[60]

In summary, the facts in *Ratten* can be analysed in two, equally valid, ways:

(1) the purpose of adducing the statement is to establish the wife's state of mind. From that fact it is permissible to infer that all was not well in the Ratten household that day and therefore that it was less likely that the gun went off by accident. The wife's state of mind is simply circumstantial evidence of the accused's *mens rea*.

(2) alternatively, the purpose is to establish the accused's *mens rea* directly from the assertion implied in the wife's statement, "He's trying to kill me!". This infringes the hearsay rule.

Where there are competing analyses of this sort, directing the jury not to draw the latter inference but to use the testimony to establish her state of mind as the relevant fact and to draw the necessary inferences from that fact seems both practical and logically justified.

This discussion leads to another issue: Mrs Ratten did not intend to say "My husband's trying to kill me" but it is an assertion that can be implied from her statement "Get me the police, please". The second issue in discussing the scope of the hearsay rule is whether such implied assertions are covered by the rule.

The Scope of the Hearsay Rule — Implied Assertions

This fine line between hearsay and original evidence is further complicated when there are assertions of fact that are not expressly or intentionally made by the declarant. The classic case,[61] *Wright v. Tatham*,[62] concerned a will in which the testator, John Marsden, had left a substantial amount of property to his steward, Wright. Tatham, heir at law and entitled on intestacy, challenged the will, asserting the mental incompetence of the testator. Those parties seeking to uphold the will and asserting John Marsden's competence, sought to introduce evidence of letters written to the testator. Had the writers of these letters been called as witnesses, they could have testified as to their opinion of Marsden's sanity. In their place, the court had the letters which did not expressly state that the testator was sane and would clearly have been inadmissible hearsay had they done so. But the inference that could be drawn from reading the letters was that the letter writers regarded the testator as in full possession of his mental faculties. Was such an implied assertion admissible?

[60] See 541, *et seq.*
[61] Although described by the editor of Cross as "old and unsatisfactory".
[62] (1837) 7 Ad. & El. 313.

Wright v. Tatham (1837) 7 Ad. & El. 313 at 384–389, _per_ Parke B.

. . . Each of the three letters, no doubt, indicates that in the opinion of the writer the testator was a rational person. He is spoken of in respectful terms in all. Mr Ellershaw describes him as possessing hospitality and benevolent politeness; and Mr Marton addresses him as competent to do business to the limited extent to which his letter calls upon him to act; and there is no question but that, if any one of those writers had been living, his evidence, founded on personal observation, that the testator possessed the qualities would be admissible on this issue. But the point to be determined is, whether these letters are admissible as proof that he did possess these qualities? I am of the opinion that, according to the established principles of the law of evidence, the letters are all inadmissible for such a purpose . . . .

But the question is, whether the contents of these letters are evidence of the fact to be proved upon this issue — that is, the actual existence of the qualities which the testator is, in those letters, by implication, stated to possess; and those letters may be considered in this respect to be on the same footing as if they had contained a direct and positive statement that he was competent. For this purpose they are mere hearsay evidence, statements of the writers, not on oath, of the truth of the matter in question, with this addition, that they have acted upon the statements on the faith of their being true, by their sending the letters to the testator. That the so acting cannot give a sufficient sanction for the truth of the statement is perfectly plain; for it is clear that, if the same statements had been made by parol or in writing to a third person, that would have been insufficient; and this is conceded by the learned counsel for the plaintiff in error . . .

Many other instances of a similar nature, by way of illustration were suggested by the learned counsel for the defendant in error . . . [the testator's] election, in his absence, to some high and responsible office; the conduct of a physician who permitted a will to be executed by a sick testator; the conduct of a deceased captain on a vessel, embarked in it with his family; all these, when deliberately considered are, with reference to the matter in issue in each case, mere instances of hearsay evidence, mere statements, not on oath, but implied in or vouched by the actual conduct of persons by whose acts the litigant parties are not to be bound. The conclusion at which I have arrived is, that proof of a particular fact, which is not itself a matter in issue, but which is relevant only as implying a statement or opinion of a third person on the matter in issue, is inadmissible in all cases where such a statement or opinion not on oath would itself be inadmissible; and, therefore, in this case the letters which are offered only to prove the competence of the testator, that is the truth of the implied statements therein contained, were properly rejected, as the mere statements or opinions of the writer would certainly have been inadmissible . . .

The letters were excluded as hearsay. The old common law embodied a strict rule of exclusion, both for express and implied assertions. Parke B. gave the example of the ship's captain who is seen to examine a ship thoroughly before embarking on it with his family and setting off on a voyage. The ship disappears, presumably sunk and litigation follows on the cause of the disappearance. Was the captain's conduct a statement that in his opinion the ship was seaworthy? Obviously this was the case and perhaps it was the more reliable because it was unintentional and thus there was less likelihood that it was manufactured. But Parke B. still treated it as hearsay. The party adversely affected by the captain's assertion could never cross-examine him on what facts or perceptions led him to the conclusion that the ship was seaworthy. That inability to question exists whether the witness expressly states an opinion or simply implies it through conduct.

How is this to be distinguished from *Ratten*?

(1) in *Ratten*, the evidence goes to establish the victim's emotional state, that of high anxiety, which tends to rebut the accused's testimony that the shooting was accidental. As long as the court treats the caller's mental state as the relevant fact and not any assertion by the caller, it is the telephone operator's testimony that is of importance for the trier of fact.
(2) in *Wright v. Tatham*, the evidence goes to establish a belief of the absent witness and it is the *content of that belief* that is relied upon to establish the fact of Marsden's sanity. In this case it is the assertion of the letter-writer that is in issue and which cannot be tested in court.

Despite such efforts at reconciliation of the authorities, the recent cases such as *Ratten* and *Woodhouse v. Hall* suggested that a more relaxed attitude was emerging to the exclusion of hearsay. The result in both cases (if not the reasoning) meant that the statements were admitted and that the parties were able to rely, not upon the direct meaning of the words ("Get me the police" or "Would you like hand relief") but on the very clear implication that those words contained ("I am in fear of my husband" or "This is a brothel").

There was also strong academic support: Cross[63] argued that the rationale for hearsay only covered the intentional direct assertion of fact and that there was neither doctrinal nor policy reasons to include the implied assertion. There was support also from other jurisdictions, especially the U.S.A. where implied assertions are excluded from the scope of the hearsay rule. Under the Federal Rules of Evidence:

801.—. . . (1) an oral or written assertion or (2) non-verbal conduct of a person if it is intended by the person as an assertion.[64]

Cross bases his discussion around the awkward case of *R. v. Rice*[65]:

Tapper C., *Cross and Tapper on Evidence* (8th ed., 1995) 572–573

R. v. Rice was also a car fraud case. It was relevant to establish that Rice flew from London to Manchester on a particular day. The prosecution proposed to do so by putting in evidence a used ticket for the relevant flight bearing Rice's name. It was

[63] Tapper C., *Cross and Tapper on Evidence* (8th ed., 1995) 583 *et seq.*
[64] Federal Rules of Evidence, r.801.
[65] [1963] 1 All E.R. 832.

perhaps unfortunate from the point of view of the prosecution that the ticket was for two seats, and it was also part of the case that the second seat had not been occupied by the man whose name appeared on it. Nevertheless the Recorder and the Court of Criminal Appeal agreed in holding that the ticket, having been produced from the repository of tickets used on that particular flight, could be admitted as circumstantial evidence from which the jury could draw what inference it chose. The Recorder was quite explicit in rejecting any suggestion that this breached the hearsay rule. This result can be supported only by taking an extremely strict view of what amounts to an assertion. If an assertion is defined in this context as words primarily intended to assert a state of fact, it is possible to contend that the names of the passengers inscribed on an airline ticket are not primarily intended to assert anything. The whole ticket is primarily intended to be used as a valid warrant for travelling on an aeroplane. As such it may be permissible to treat it as a piece of real evidence, and to allow it to be proved as one of the circumstances of the case from which the jury is entitled to make common-sense inferences. It is indeed difficult, on the facts of *Rice*, even to identify the maker of an assertion, or what precisely the assertion was. It is far from inconceivable that the clerk writing the ticket simply asked whose name should be inserted. It would then have been different if the prosecution had sought to tender a list of passengers compiled by the airline as a result of the scrutiny of the used tickets. Then the document would have been intended to assert the identities of the passengers, and the author of the assertion would have been the official who compiled the list. That quite different situation was the one which occurred in *Myers*, which may explain why the majority there made so little attempt to discredit the decision in *Rice*, even though it had been the cornerstone of the argument which had succeeded in the Court of Criminal Appeal.

It is readily conceded that the line between that which is primarily intended to assert, and that which is not, will often be difficult to draw,[66] and that opinions might legitimately differ as to where in relation to it the facts of *Rice* ought to be placed. In many cases intention may properly be inferred from the external and objective manifestations normally taken to signify intention. It is nevertheless contended that concentration upon the presence of an intention to assert provides the most defensible watershed between hearsay and non-hearsay both as a matter of logical coherence and of practical common sense.

But is this level of analysis necessary to explain *Rice*? The ticket is adduced as evidence that the defendant was at a particular place at a particular time. There are many sorts of evidence that might link the accused in this way, including fingerprints and security videos. There might also be the accused's own possessions — what is the evidential status of a credit card bearing the accused's name found at the scene of the crime? Or a firearm registered in his or her name? In *R. v. Lydon*,[67] the accused was convicted of robbery. The gun, allegedly used in the robbery, had been abandoned by the robbers but was found and beside it were two pieces of paper, bearing the words "Sean Rules" and "Sean Rules 85". The accused's first name was Sean:

[66] This point is not so readily conceded by the advisory committee on the U.S. Federal Rules of Evidence who suggest that it involves no greater difficulty than many other preliminary questions of fact — *Federal Rules of Evidence* (1994) Commentary at 111.
[67] (1987) 85 Cr.App.R. 221.

Comment on *Lydon* by Birch in [1987] Crim.L.R. 407 at 408–409

What of admissibility? The Court of Appeal overcomes the hearsay objection by confining the rule to assertions put in evidence in order to establish the truth of the fact asserted. In this they are to be commended, for the question whether a statement constitutes an assertion is seldom referred to judicially, and yet the view of many academics is that 'concentration upon the presence of an intention to assert provides the most defensible watershed between hearsay and non-hearsay . . .' What was written on the paper was clearly not tendered in order to show that Sean 'ruled' anything, but rather to support the inference that the writer was likely to have been someone by the name of Sean. This is certainly a ground of distinction between the present case and cases of 'identifying marks' such as the inscription 'Produce of Morocco' on bags of coriander which was held to be hearsay evidence of the place of origin in *Patel v. Comptroller of Customs* for in that case reliance was sought to be placed on the very fact asserted by the identifying label. Similarly in *R. v. Romeo*[68] Cox J. regarded an assertion of ownership on the flyleaf of a booklet as hearsay evidence of the facts stated. The trouble is that it may lead us to the conclusion that, whereas 'Sean rules' scratched onto the barrel of a gun might be acceptable non-hearsay evidence of Sean's connection with the gun, 'Property of Sean' similarly etched would fail the test. One possible way of resolving the difficulty without depriving a jury of the evidence provided in the first example is to regard identifying marks as exempt from the hearsay rule too; a theory favoured by Wigmore. But such exemption could only really be justified because of the strength of the inference which could be drawn from the statement. As Wigmore would have in (quoting the case of *People v. Hill*[69] in which it was held that the discovery of a bunch of keys bearing D's name was 'doubtful' evidence):

> . . . this case shows how different a man a judge is when reasoning about his own affairs at home as opposed to reasoning in the judicial straitjacket: suppose he had forbidden a certain young man to court his daughter and then one morning found on the parlour floor by the sofa a bunch of keys with the tabooed young man's name; would he hold that 'there was some doubt whether the evidence was properly admitted'?

Clearly he would not, but if challenged in an English court to explain why evidence which he regards as cogent in his everyday affairs must be excluded in judicial proceedings, the judge needs look no further than *Myers* . . .

Given that the function of identifying marks is to assert identity, then where that identity is a matter in issue it is difficult to extract such marks from the ambit of the rule . . . Such fine distinctions do the hearsay rule no credit. It is not unknown for incompetent burglars to leave a variety of personal belongings at the scene of their crimes: many investigating officers and prosecutors have a story or two of finding cheque books or cards, keys, wallets, envelopes with D's address on them etc. If the admissibility of such items is really conditioned by such factors as whether the maker of an identifying mark on the object intended to assert the ownership of it, the point at which the line is to be drawn will (apart from being unclear in the extreme) have little to do with reliability. It is time for a complete re-think of the hearsay rule . . .

In cases of identifying marks, the prosecution seeks to show that an object belongs to the accused as a basis for establishing, for example, the

[68] (1982) 30 S.A.S.R. 243 at 267.
[69] (1910) 198 N.Y. 64.

accused's presence at the scene of a crime. If we take as an example, an envelope addressed to the accused, found at the scene. The prosecution might claim that it was dropped by the defendant at the time of the crime. The objection based on the confrontation principle is essentially, "says who?", suggesting that the court would be relying on an assertion by the writer of the address. But is this so?

(1) were a fingerprint found on the envelope, that would be real evidence, directly linking the accused to the object. Objects with a person's print will have been in that person's possession.[70] The only relevant witness is the forensic scientist.
(2) the same argument can be advanced in relation to the address label on the envelope. Calling the letter-writer as a witness is a futile exercise[71] — they can testify to writing the address and posting the letter but neither of these facts are relevant. The relevant fact is that an opened envelope addressed to a particular person is likely to have been in that person's possession. It has nothing to do with hearsay and the only relevant witness is the finder.

This approach works if the fact that you are seeking to establish is that of possession which in itself is a circumstantially relevant fact from which other more directly related facts may flow. The key issue is to identify the fact which needs to be proved and ask whether the evidence establishing this fact relies on the perceptions of an absent witness. Does this work with *Rice*? The fact needing to be established is that Rice was on the plane. Testimony from the ticket seller that he or she wrote the name 'Rice' on the ticket is neither here nor there. The real question (staying in the vernacular) is not "says who?" but "so what?" The existence of a ticket in this particular name is on the margins of admissibility, not because of hearsay but because it lacks sufficient probative weight.

This might be compared to *R. v. McIntosh*[72] where the accused was charged with being concerned in the importation of cocaine. The Crown sought to rely on a piece of paper, authorship unknown, concealed in a chimney with calculations of the price and weight of a quantity of drugs. It was found in the house that the defendant had been jointly occupying. The Court of Appeal held that the document did not offend the hearsay rule. Why? It might be argued that the prosecution needed to show that the accused was interested in the buying and selling of drugs. The existence of a document detailing prices and quantities prima facie supports the inference that the defendant was interested in the information. From that

[70] An example of the convoluted thinking induced in otherwise rational people by the hearsay rule might be the fingerprint left at the scene by the criminal as a gesture of defiance to the police. Is this an intentional assertion "I was here. Come and get me"? If so, are all other fingerprints unintentional, implied, assertions and thus excluded in accordance with *Kearley*?
[71] Nowadays the "sender" is often a computer which prints address labels.
[72] [1992] Crim.L.R. 651.

the jury might infer intent to supply or import. It is irrelevant who wrote down the information.[73] A parallel might be with charge of conspiracy to cause explosions. Possession of books on bomb-making would be admissible evidence. The authorship of the books may be of interest to the police but it is of no relevance at the trial.

Rice, *Lydon* and *MacIntosh* should either not be discussed as hearsay cases at all or be used as examples of the "purpose" element in the Cross formula. If that is correct, they do not illustrate the criticism that the hearsay rule is too wide because it embraces such implied assertions and we need to look elsewhere for the justification of restricting the ambit of the rule.

In *U.S. v. Zenni*,[74] another prosecution for illegal bookmaking, District Judge Bertelsman outlines the criticisms of the old rule:

U.S. v. Zenni [1980] 492 F. Supp. 464

The common law rule that implied assertions were subject to hearsay treatment was criticised by respected commentators for several reasons. A leading work on the Federal Rules of Evidence, referring to the hotly debated question whether an implied assertion stands on better ground with respect to the hearsay rule than an express assertion, states: "By the time the federal rules were drafted, a number of eminent scholars and revisers had concluded that it does. Two principal arguments were usually expressed for removing implied assertions from the scope of the hearsay rule. First, when a person acts in a way consistent with a belief but without intending by his act to communicate that belief, one of the principal reasons for the hearsay rule — to exclude declarations whose veracity cannot be tested by cross-examination — does not apply, because the defendant's sincerity is not then involved. In the second place, the underlying belief is in some cases self-verifying: 'There is frequently a guarantee of trustworthiness of the inference to be drawn . . . because the actor has based his actions on the correctness of his belief, *i.e.* his actions speak louder than words.' "[75] In a frequently cited article[76] the following analysis appears: "But ought the hearsay rule be deemed applicable to evidence of conduct? As McCormick has observed[77] the problem 'has only once received any adequate discussion in any decided case' *i.e.* in *Wright v. Tatham*, . . . And even in that case the court did not pursue its inquiry beyond the point of concluding that evidence of an 'implied' assertion must necessarily be excluded wherever evidence of an 'express' assertion would be inadmissible. But as has been pointed out more than once (although I find no judicial recognition of the difference), the 'implied' assertion is, from the hearsay standpoint, not nearly so vulnerable as an express assertion of the fact which the evidence is offered to establish. This is on the assumption that the conduct was 'nonassertive'; that the passers-by had their umbrellas up for the sake of keeping dry, not for the purpose of telling anyone it was raining; that the truck driver started up for the sake of resuming his journey,

[73] As with *Rice*, the problem here is to establish a link between the document and the accused who had only been resident in the house a short time. Without this the document is not relevant.

[74] [1980] 492 F. Supp. 464.

[75] *Weinstein's Evidence*, para. 801(a)[01] at 801–55.

[76] Falknor, "The 'Hear-Say' Rule as a 'See-Do' Rule: Evidence of Conduct" (1961) 33 *Rocky Mountain L.R.* 133 at 136.

[77] *Handbook on the Law of Evidence* (1st ed. 1954) 229.

not for the purpose of telling anyone that the light had changed; that the vicar wrote the letter to the testator for the purpose of settling the dispute with the latter, rather than with any idea of expressing an opinion of the testator's sanity. And in the typical 'conduct as hearsay' case this assumption will be quite justifiable. On this assumption, it is clear that evidence of conduct must be taken as freed from at least one of the hearsay dangers, *i.e.* mendacity. A man does not lie to himself. Put otherwise, if in doing what he does a man has no intention of asserting the existence or non-existence of a fact, it would appear that the trustworthiness of evidence of this conduct is the same whether he is an egregious liar or a paragon of veracity. Accordingly, the usual judicial disposition to equate the 'implied' to the 'express' assertion is very questionable."

The argument being advanced for the exclusion of implied assertions from the operation of the hearsay rule is one based on the lack of any need to question the witness's sincerity and on a corresponding reliability. But just because the witness treats a "fact" as "to be taken for granted" and acts accordingly, this is no guarantee of other forms of unreliability. It is not the witness's sincerity but his or her perceptions and powers of judgment that need to come under scrutiny. Moreover, as has been argued, the primary principle in support of the hearsay rule is that of the fair trial which requires that every party, let alone an accused person, should be able to confront every witness on whose perceptions the opposing party relies.

Despite the criticism, the rigidity of the old common law position was reasserted by the House of Lords decision in *Kearley*.[78] The Dorset police raided a flat occupied by the appellant, his wife and one other person. In the course of the raid they recovered a relatively small quantity of amphetamine and while on the premises the police answered the phone and encountered visitors many requesting drugs from "Chippie", the appellant's nickname. Since the actual amount of drugs and money discovered in the flat were not enough to raise an irresistible presumption that the accused was in possession of the drugs "with intent to supply", the prosecution sought to rely on the testimony of police officers who had heard these requests. The appeal raised two issues. The first of these was whether a telephone caller's belief that the accused was a drug supplier was at all relevant to proving an intent to supply and secondly, if it were relevant, was it excluded by the hearsay rule?

The majority regarded the evidence as irrelevant and inadmissible on that basis but, assuming its relevance, would have excluded it as hearsay. Lord Oliver said:

R. v. Kearley [1992] 2 All E.R. 345 at 370–371, _per_ Lord Oliver

The first inquiry must be: is it relevant evidence? For nothing that is not relevant is admissible. 'Relevant' cannot, I think, be better defined that in art. 1 of *Stephen's Digest of the Law of Evidence*,[79] that is to say that the word means that —

[78] [1992] 2 All E.R. 345 — see also *R. v. Harry* (1988) 86 Cr.App.R. 105.
[79] 12th ed., 1936 at 4.

> Any two facts to which it is applied are so related to each other that according to the common course of events one either taken by itself or in connection with other facts proves or renders probable the past, present or future existence or non-existence of the other.

To put it, perhaps more succinctly, a fact to be relevant must be probative, and if one asks whether the fact that a large number of persons called at the premises seeking to purchase from 'Chippie' renders probable the existence of a person at the premises called 'Chippie' who is willing to supply drugs, the answer can, I think, only be in the affirmative. But the difficulty here is that it is only the combination of the facts (a) that persons called, (b) that they asked for 'Chippie' and (c) that they requested drugs which renders the evidence relevant. The mere fact that people telephoned or called, in itself, is irrelevant, for it neither proves nor renders probable any other fact. In order to render evidence of the calls relevant and therefore admissible there has to be added the additional element of what the callers said, and it is here that the difficulty arises. What was said — in each case a request for drugs — is, of course probative of the state of mind of the caller. But the state of mind of the caller is not the fact in issue and is, in itself, irrelevant, for it is not probative of anything other than its own existence. It becomes relevant only if and so far as the existence of other facts can be inferred from it. So far as concerns anything in issue at the trial, what the caller said and the state of mind which that fact evinces becomes relevant and probative of the fact in issue (namely the intent of the appellant) only if, or because, (i) what was said amounts to a statement, by necessary implication, that the appellant has in the past supplied drugs to the speaker (as in two cases in which requests were made for 'the usual') or (ii) it imports the belief or opinion of the speaker that the appellant has drugs and is willing to supply them. And here, as it seems to me, we are directly up against the hearsay rule which forms one of the major established exceptions to the admissibility of relevant evidence. Clearly if, at the trial, the prosecution had sought to adduce evidence from a witness to the effect that the appellant had, in the past, supplied him with quantities of drugs, that evidence would have been both relevant and admissible; but equally clearly, if it had been sought to introduce the evidence of a police constable to the effect that a person not called as a witness had told him, in a conversation in a public house, that the appellant had supplied drugs, that would have been inadmissible hearsay evidence and so objectionable. It cannot, it is cogently argued, make any difference that exactly the same evidence is introduced in an indirect way by way of evidence from a witness that he has overheard a request by some other person for 'the usual', from which the jury is asked to infer that which cannot be proved by evidence of that other person's direct assertion. Equally if, at the trial, the prosecution had sought to adduce evidence from a witness not that drugs had been supplied but that it was his opinion or belief that drugs had been or would be supplied, that evidence would be inadmissible as amounting to no more than a statement of belief or opinion unsupported by facts upon which the belief is grounded. A fortiori, it is argued, that same inadmissible belief or opinion cannot be introduced by inference from the reported statements of someone who is not even called as a witness. Thus, it is said, in seeking to introduce the evidence of the police officers of what the callers said, the Crown faces the difficulty that it has to contend that by combining two inadmissible items of evidence — that is to say, the evidence of the calls (which are, standing alone, inadmissible because irrelevant) and the evidence of what was said by the callers (which might be relevant but is inadmissible because hearsay) — it can produce a single item of admissible evidence.

The impermissibility of such a course rests upon a well-established principle expounded in the context of civil proceedings some 150 years ago in *Wright v. Doe d. Tatham* . . .

Lord Ackner said:

***Kearley*, *op. cit.* at 362–363, *per* Lord Ackner**

Each of those requests was, of course, evidence of the state of mind of the person making the request. He wished to be supplied with drugs and thought that the appellant would so supply him . . . But the state of mind of the person making the request was not an issue at the trial; accordingly the evidence of his request was irrelevant and therefore inadmissible. If the prosecution had sought to call any of the persons who had made such requests, merely to give evidence of the making of the request, in order to establish their appetite for drugs and their belief that such appetite would be satisfied by the appellant, such evidence could not have been properly admitted. Indeed [counsel] for the Crown essentially conceded this. The evidence of the requests were, she submits, not being tendered in order to establish that the person making the request believed that the appellant was a supplier of drugs. She accepted that the state of mind of the person or persons making the request was irrelevant. That must include not only his or their beliefs but his or their appetites for the drug, the 'potential market' referred to by my noble and learned friend Lord Browne-Wilkinson in his speech . . . [Counsel for the Crown] maintained that the evidence of the request for drugs to be supplied by the appellant tended to show that the premises at which the request was made were being used as a source of supply of drugs and that the supplier (*i.e.* that the person who had been supplying the drugs) was the appellant.

The certified question[80] confines itself to a single request. [Counsel for the Crown] accepts that a single request would not provide evidence either that the premises were being used as a source of supply of drugs or that the appellant was the supplier. It could only be evidence of the state of mind of the person making the request. I can see no basis in logic or principle for validly contending that an additional request or requests would fundamentally alter the situation. The request or requests, in the terms which I have described, and which were so referred to by the learned judge in his summing up, contain neither an express nor an implied assertion that the person making the inquiry has either obtained drugs from the premises or from the appellant in the past, or has been told by the appellant (or his duly authorised agent) that he, the appellant, would satisfy his requirements (the 'potential market') for drugs if he phoned or called at the premises. Indeed the request or requests do not contain any factual assertion. They ask a question of the appellant: will you supply me with drugs? — thus by inference suggesting that they believed the appellant would supply what they requested.

Thus my reply to the certified question would simply be as follows. An oral request or requests for drugs to be supplied by the defendant, not spoken in his presence or in his hearing, could only be evidence of the state of mind of the person or persons making the request, and since his or their state of mind was not a relevant issue at the trial, evidence of such a request or requests, however given, would be irrelevant and therefore inadmissible.

The House as a whole acceded to the argument that, regardless of hearsay issues, the evidence of the callers' opinions was irrelevant to

[80] The question was "Whether evidence may be adduced at a trial of words spoken (namely a request for drugs to be supplied by the defendant) not spoken in the presence or hearing of the defendant, by a person not called as a witness, for the purpose not of establishing the truth of any fact narrated by the words, but of inviting the jury to draw an inference from the fact that the words were spoken (namely that the defendant was a supplier of drugs)".

proving the accused's intent. Initially this is attractive especially when dealing with a single caller whose opinion would have so little probative weight as to make it inadmissible. But when the reasoning is extended to a significant number of callers, the argument that their opinions are irrelevant is more difficult to follow: the fact that I believe that you possess a particular characteristic, makes it more likely that you have such a characteristic. A single person's belief has little probative weight but nevertheless it has some. When many witnesses are willing to testify that you possess that characteristic, not only is such testimony relevant but it has much more weight.

But for the minority, the existence of the callers proved a different fact. While the caller's beliefs might be irrelevant to the issue of the accused's *mens rea*, the very existence of such a demand showed that the premises were being used to supply drugs. The analogy drawn was with the witness who testified that she had seen a queue. Such evidence would be relevant as it indicated that there was a market for the goods or services alleged to be on offer:

Kearley, _op. cit._ at 383–384, _per_ Lord Browne-Wilkinson (dissenting)

On that basis, [counsel for the appellant] submitted that such belief of third parties was irrelevant and inadmissible in deciding the intent of the accused. I accept that the opinions or beliefs of the callers were irrelevant and as such inadmissible. But in my judgment the calls prove more than the opinions or beliefs of the callers.

The evidence was, in my judgment, relevant because it showed that there were people resorting to the premises for the purposes of obtaining drugs from Chippie. Although evidence of the existence of such would-be buyers is not, by itself, conclusive, the existence of a substantial body of potential customers provides some evidence which a jury could take into account in deciding whether the accused had an intent to supply. The existence of a contemporaneous potential market to buy drugs from Chippie, by itself, shows that there was an opportunity for the accused to supply drugs.

In order to eliminate, for the purpose of considering relevance only, the complication that the purpose of the callers can only be demonstrated by the words that the callers use, I will seek to demonstrate the position by reference to a case where no such recourse is necessary. Suppose a shop which has a sole proprietor and sells only coffee. Say the issue is whether the proprietor had an intent to supply coffee. On a particular day there was a long queue of persons at the door of the shop waiting for it to open. Evidence of the existence of the queue would surely be admissible towards proving an intent to supply. The presence of potential purchasers is circumstantial evidence from which a jury can draw the inference that the shopkeeper was going to supply coffee. There can be no supply without persons to whom supply is made: if the existence of such persons is shown, that provides evidence of the opportunity for supply.

[Counsel for the appellant] submitted . . . that on analysis the only effect of such evidence is to prove a belief in the minds of members of the queue that the shopkeeper will supply coffee. But although that is one of the matters which may be inferred from the existence of the queue, in my judgment it is not the only matter which can be inferred. The existence of the queue is a fact from which a jury could draw any one or more of a number of inferences, viz: (1) the existence of potential buyers of coffee on that day from the shop; (2) the belief of the members of the queue that the proprietors will sell coffee; (3) the fact that some at least of the members of the queue are running short of coffee; (4) the opinion of at least some of the members of the queue that the proprietor sells good coffee etc. Inferences (3) and (4) are wholly irrelevant to the issue. Inference (2), though bearing on the issue, is irrelevant because it is mere belief. But the existence of irrelevant inferences which could be drawn does not mean that the evidence is not probative in support of inference (1), although a judge would no doubt be careful as the judge was in this case to caution the jury against drawing the wrong inferences.

In my view [counsel for the appellant]'s analysis seeks to eliminate the probative fact (that people were seeking to buy drugs) by concentrating on the reasons why they were seeking to buy drugs. The reasons for a third party doing an act will, normally, be irrelevant and inadmissible. Any action involving human activity necessarily implies that the human being had reasons and beliefs on which his action was based. But the fact that his action (viz asking for drugs or queuing for coffee) is capable of raising an inadmissible inference of irrelevant fact does not mean that evidence of that action cannot be admitted with a view to proving a relevant fact.

In my view therefore the fact that there were a number of people seeking to buy drugs was legally relevant and admissible as showing that there was a market to which the accused could sell, even though such evidence was also capable of giving rise to an impermissible secondary inference, viz that the callers believed Chippie supplied drugs. If the callers themselves had given evidence at the trial and said only that on the relevant day they had made a call for the purpose of obtaining drugs from Chippie, I can see no ground on which such evidence could have been excluded as being irrelevant.

Kearley is of considerable interest for its discussion of relevance and of the purpose for which the statements were adduced. If the dissenting arguments are accepted, it is not about hearsay at all since the purpose of introducing the statements is not to rely on the truth of their contents.

But the central importance of *Kearley* lies in its affirmation that implied assertions still come within the hearsay rule. If the statements of the callers are understood as meaning "Chippie is a drug dealer" and such beliefs are accepted as relevant, it remains an out-of-court assertion by a person not called as a witness and subject to the hearsay rule. The majority in *Kearley* considered the argument that the rule itself is restricted to express and intentional assertions but adopted the *Wright v. Tatham* position. The hearsay rule excludes a police officer testifying that he or she had answered the phone and had heard the caller had said "Hey, that Kearley's dealing drugs again". Logically the rule must also exclude implied assertions to the same effect:

Kearley, _op. cit._ at 363–364, _per_ Lord Ackner

Such being the law, [counsel for the Crown] frankly concedes that if the inquirer had said in the course of making his request, 'I would like my usual supply of amphetamine at the price which I paid you last week' or words to that effect, then, although the inquirer could have been called to give evidence of the fact that he had in the past purchased from the appellant his requirements of amphetamine[81] and

[81] This would be giving evidence of bad character and could presumably only be admitted on the basis that it constituted similar fact evidence.

had made his call at the appellant's house for a further supply on the occasion when he met and spoke to the police, the hearsay rule prevents the prosecution from calling police officers to recount the conversation which I have described. This is for the simple reason that the request made in the form set out above contains an express assertion that the premises at which the request was being made were being used as a source of supply of drugs and the supplier was the appellant.

If, contrary to the view which I have expressed above, the simple request or requests for drugs to be supplied by the appellant, as recounted by the police, contains in substance, but only by implication, the same assertion, then I can find neither authority nor principle to suggest that the hearsay rule should not be equally applicable and exclude such evidence. What is sought to be done is to use the oral assertion, even though it may be an implied assertion, as evidence of the truth of the proposition asserted. That the proposition is asserted by way of necessary implication rather than expressly, cannot, to my mind, make any difference.

Although as a matter of policy, there are reasons to restrict the scope of the hearsay rule, Lord Ackner points out that reliance on an implied assertion is the same as reliance on an express assertion. The argument that the implied assertion is more reliable may well be correct but, as we have seen, reliability is not the touchstone for the exclusion of hearsay. Above all it is fairness — just as Kearley could not confront the absent witness who said expressly "Chippie deals drugs" nor can he confront the absentee who has merely said "Chippie, let's have the usual".

To summarise: for the majority in *Kearley*, the caller's statements establish only the callers' beliefs which have no relevance to any fact in issue. The jury is not entitled to draw inferences regarding the intent of the accused to supply drugs from such beliefs, firstly because the beliefs are not relevant but secondly because the callers' statements involve implied assertions and these are caught by the hearsay rule.

statements → declarant's state of mind → accused's mens rea

For the minority in *Kearley*, the statements establish the use to which the premises are being put, namely as a market for drugs. For this purpose the statements are relevant and admissible. Equally, when introduced for that purpose, the statements are not hearsay. Establishing the existence of a market for drugs has circumstantial relevance because the jury is entitled to infer that somebody on the premises is intending to supply drugs and that person may be the accused.

statements → use of the premises → existence of a supplier → accused's mens rea

The Scope of the Hearsay Rule — Mechanical Devices

Statements produced by mechanical devices are normally original rather than hearsay evidence. The videotape on which there is a visual record of an event is original evidence of that incident. A printout which details a computer's analysis of the composition of a compound is evidence of the constitution of that compound.[82] If the evidence is original, the jury can draw conclusions from the thing itself. Thus in *The Statue of Liberty*[83] a film record of a radar screen showed the course of two ships before a collision in the Thames. This was admitted as real evidence:

***The Statue of Liberty* [1968] 2 All E.R. 195 at 196g–h, *per* Sir Jocelyn Simon P.**

If tape-recordings are admissible, it seems that a photograph of radar reception is equally admissible — or indeed any other type of photograph. It would be an absurd distinction that a photograph should be admissible if the camera were operated manually by a photographer, but not if it were operated by a trip or clock mechanism. Similarly, if evidence of weather conditions were relevant, the law would affront common sense if it were to say that those could be proved by a person who looked at a barometer from time to time, but not by producing a barograph record. So, too, with other types of mechanical recordings. Again, cards from clocking-in-and-out machines are frequently admitted in accident cases. The law is now bound to take cognizance of the fact that mechanical means replace human effort.

Here the assertion is a statement by a machine automatically tracking the ships. It is not a hearsay statement which must be by a person. Where a machine is being used to collect, process and output information without any human input (apart from the original building and programming of the machine), the output is original evidence.[84]

In *R. v. Wood*[85] the question was the origin of certain metals — were those found in the possession of the appellant the same as those which had been stolen? The chemical composition of the metals was achieved by computer calculation and the printout was adduced in evidence. Was it hearsay? The headnote reads:

> . . . the computer in the instant case had been used as a calculator — it was described as a tool and did not contribute its own knowledge and was properly treated as a piece of real evidence, the actual proof of which depended on the testimony of the witnesses; thus, the answers produced by the computer were in principle admissible at common law and were properly proved[86]

In *Castle v. Cross*,[87] the defendant breathed several times into an Intoximeter, a machine for measuring the alcohol level in blood. It

[82] *R. v. Wood* (1982) 76 Cr.App.R. 23.
[83] [1968] 2 All E.R. 195 — the case was decided before the Civil Evidence Act 1968 allowed the admission of much hearsay evidence in civil proceedings.
[84] This formulation might well cast doubt on the example of the "clocking-in-and-out machine" given by Sir Jocelyn Simon P. — this is surely no different to the worker writing down the times of arrival and departure on a card. This in turn must be distinguished from machines that can recognise a palmprint or thumbprint!
[85] (1983) 76 Cr.App.R. 23.
[86] *ibid.* at 23–24.
[87] [1985] 1 All E.R. 87.

produced a printout which stated that the machine had not received a sufficient sample in order to carry out an analysis. It was held by the Divisional Court that this printout was admissible evidence against the accused on a charge of failing to supply a breath specimen. In *Sophocleous v Ringer*,[88] a scientist gave evidence of analyses of a blood sample by gas chromatography to decide on blood alcohol level, again carried out by computer. The Divisional Court held that the scientist, as an expert witness, was merely using the computer as a tool and was entitled to refresh her memory from the computer figures. But surely the print-out was itself admissible as real evidence, regardless of the scientists's evidence?

The scientist should be able to produce the printout or to testify as to what it contained. This is also illustrated in *Taylor v. Chief Constable of Cheshire*[89] in which a video was made of a shoplifter. Policemen were able to identify the accused from the video. Later the recording was erased by accident. The officers gave evidence of what they had seen on the video and Taylor was convicted. The video itself was direct evidence and the witnesses testified as to what they had seen on the video with their own eyes.

Courts initially struggled with this distinction. In *R. v. Pettigrew*[90] new banknotes were found in the possession of the burglar. A Bank of England computer recorded the serial numbers of £5 notes so that the notes could be traced to a particular branch and hence to the victim. On the analysis above, such a list is not hearsay although the court considered otherwise as the document was only admitted on the basis of an exception to hearsay found in section 1(1)(a) of the Criminal Evidence Act 1965.

But in *R. v. Neville*[91] the evidence adduced was the itemised record by a phone company of the calls made from a mobile phone which the court accepted as original evidence and this was confirmed by the House of Lords' judgment in *R. v. Shepherd*[92] where the evidence involved the use of computerised checkouts using bar codes to identify the item being bought. The till roll showed no trace of the unique barcode on the items alleged to have been stolen by the accused. This was original evidence that the item had not been paid for.[93]

In all of these cases, the information is generated by the machine. This must be distinguished from information originally coming from a person but being stored in the machine. The printout from a word-processing programme remains hearsay as do statements on audio-tape. For example, in *Kearley*, if the phone calls had been tape-recorded, this would make no

[88] [1987] Crim.L.R. 422.
[89] [1987] 1 All E.R. 225.
[90] (1980) 71 Cr.App.R. 39.
[91] [1991] Crim.L.R. 288; *R. v. Spiby* [1991] Crim.L.R. 199.
[92] [1993] 1 All E.R. 225.
[93] The other problem faced by the courts in these cases was whether the conditions laid down by Police and Criminal Evidence Act 1984, s.69 for the admissibility of computer-generated documents applied — see 559, *et seq*.

difference to their admissibility. Only if such statements are otherwise admissible (for example, a taped record of a police interview) is the tape-recording admissible. For example, in *Li Shu-ling v. R.*[94] the defendant confessed and later took part in a videotaped re-enactment of the offence. Such an enactment by the accused was clearly hearsay by conduct[95] but it was also an admission and as such is admissible. The Privy Council held that a re-enactment in words during interrogation was admissible and there was no reason in principle why re-enactment on film was not equally admissible.[96]

More of a problem exists with cases which involve a photofit, drawing or construction of the likeness of a suspect made to the specifications of the witness as in *R. v. Cook.*[97] In that case, the photofit itself was admitted in evidence. But why? Had a witness made a written statement describing an assailant, such a statement would not have been admissible either of its facts (since it is hearsay) nor as a prior consistent statement. Similarly a sketch produced by an artist following the directions of a witness is merely transforming words into images and must still be inadmissible. Watkins L.J. disagreed with this analysis:

R. v. Cook [1987] 1 All E.R. 1049 at 1054, *per* Watkins L.J.

The [hearsay] rule is said to apply not only to assertions made orally but to those made in writing or in conduct. Never so far as we know has it been held to apply to this comparatively modern form of evidence, namely the sketch made by the police officer to accord with the witness's recollection of a suspect's physical characteristics and mode of dress and the even more modern photofit compiled from an identical source. Both are manifestations of the seeing eye, translations of vision onto paper through the medium of a police officer's skill of drawing and composing which a witness does not possess. The police officer is merely doing what the witness could do if possessing the requisite skill. When drawing or composing he is akin to a camera, without, of course, being able to match in clarity the photograph of a person or scene which the camera automatically produces.

There is no doubt that a photograph taken, for example, of a suspect during the commission of an offence is admissible. In a bigamy case, namely *R. v. Tolson*,[98] Willes J. said:

> The photograph was admissible because it is only the visible representation of the image or impression made upon the minds of the witnesses by the sight of the person or the object it represents; and, therefore, is, in reality, only another species of the evidence which persons give of identity, when they speak merely from memory.

That ruling has never since been doubted and is applied with regulairty to photographs including those taken nowadays automatically in banks during a

[94] [1988] 3 All E.R. 138.
[95] As it was in *R. v. Quinn, R. v. Bloom* [1961] 3 All E.R. 88.
[96] Such re-enactments are admissible in Australia (*R. v. Lowery and King* [1972] V.L.R. 554), Canada (*R. v. Tookey and Stephenson* (1981)) 58 C.C.C. 2d 421) and in the U.S.A. (*People v. Dabb* (1948) 32 Cal. 2d. 491).
[97] [1987] 1 All E.R. 1049.
[98] (1864) 4 F.&F. 103 at 104.

robbery. Such photographs are invaluable aids to identification of criminals. It has never been suggested of them that they are subject to the rule against hearsay.

We regard the production of the sketch or photofit by a police officer making a graphic representation of a witness's memory as another form of the camera at work, albeit imperfectly and not produced contemporaneously with the material incident but soon or fairly soon afterwards. As we perceive it the photofit is not a statement in writing made in the absence of a defendant or anything resembling it in the sense that this very old rule against hearsay has ever been expressed to embrace. It is, we think, sui generis, that is to say, the only one of its kind. It is a thing apart, the admissibility to evidence of which would not be in breach of the hearsay rule.[99]

The court treated a photofit as direct evidence and thus admissible even if the eyewitness is unable to attend court.

Hearsay Problems

"Negative" hearsay

Sometimes documents (and other testimony) are introduced to prove a negative. Thus in *R. v. Patel*,[1] the defendant was accused of breaching the Immigration Acts by assisting illegal immigrants. It was necessary to prove the status of the alleged illegal immigrant and evidence of the Home Office records was introduced which showed that the person was not entitled to a certificate of registration. Following *Myers*, the conviction was quashed. This can be contrasted with the decision in *R. v. Shone*[2] where the accused was charged with theft of three car-springs from a warehouse. The warehouse records were introduced to show that, although the receipt of the springs had been entered, there was no record of these springs having been removed. The inference to be drawn was that they had been removed without authority. The Court of Appeal upheld the conviction, suggesting that the evidence:

> . . . was not hearsay but evidence from which the jury were entitled to draw the inference . . . that all three springs were stolen. If there had been one spring found in the appellant's possession, which was traceable to [the warehouse], the absence of a record of sale or legitimate disposal would have been evidentially relatively insignificant . . . the absence of such a record in respect of all three springs . . . was overwhelming.[3]

But why was this "not hearsay"? The overwhelming weight and reliability of the evidence is irrelevant to this question. Were a club secretary

[99] Authorities which support *Cook* are *R. v. Percy Smith* [1976] Crim.L.R. 511, *R. v. Okorodu* [1982] Crim.L.R. 747 and *R. v. Constantinou* [1989] Crim.L.R. 571; *R. v. O'Brien and Nicholson* [1982] Crim.L.R. 746 does not. This is discussed further at 307, *et seq.*

[1] [1981] 3 All E.R. 94.

[2] (1983) 76 Cr.App.R. 72 (although the facts in this case and *Patel* would now be covered by the Criminal Justice Act 1988, s.24).

[3] *ibid.* at 76, *per* Leonard J.

to compile minutes of a committee meeting, detailing those present, such minutes would be hearsay if relied upon to prove that those mentioned were present. Logically one cannot distinguish the situation where you seek to prove that someone was not present because they were not mentioned. Other jurisdictions regard this as hearsay and have specifically legislated for its inclusion. Under the Federal Rules of Evidence:

803.—The following are not excluded by the hearsay rule, even though the declarant is available as a witness:

(6) Records of regularly conducted activity. A memorandum, report, record, or data compilation, in any form, of acts, events, conditions, opinions, or diagnoses, made at or near the time by, or from information transmitted by, a person with knowledge, if kept in the course of a regularly conducted business activity . . .

(7) Absence of entry in records kept in accordance with the provisions of paragraph (6). Evidence that a matter is not included in the memoranda reports, records, or data compilations, . . . to prove the non-occurrence or non-existence of the matter, if the matter was of a kind of which a memorandum, report, record, or data compilation was regularly made and preserved, unless the sources of information or other circumstances indicate lack of trustworthiness.[4]

Such an approach can also be seen in New South Wales under section 14CH of the Evidence Act 1898 which makes negative hearsay admissible, a provision which assumes that, at common law, it is hearsay.

Identification

In cases such as *Gibson*[5] the absent witness was in effect making an identification of the culprit. Recent authorities tend to suggest that such identifications can operate as an exception to hearsay. In *R. v. Osborne and Virtue*[6] two witnesses to an armed robbery picked out the accused in an identification parade but were unable to do so at the trial proper. A police officer was permitted to testify as to the conduct of the parade and as to whom the witnesses had identified on that parade. Lawton L.J. treats it as a question whether the officer was contradicting the evidence of the witnesses and does not advert to the difficult hearsay issue. In *R. v. McCay*[7] the identification parade took place behind a two-way mirror, preventing those on the parade from seeing the witnesses. The witness picked out the accused by number but at the trial, having testified that he had made a positive ID, was unable to recall the number of the person he had identified. The officer in charge of the parade was then permitted to testify to the fact of the identification. Russell L.J. approved of this, regarding the statement as one that accompanied and explained a relevant act, an aspect of the *res gestae* exception to hearsay,[8] but one that has previously only

[4] Federal Rules of Evidence, r.803.
[5] (1887) Q.B.D. 537, discussed *supra* 303.
[6] [1973] 1 All E.R. 649.
[7] [1991] 1 All E.R. 232.
[8] See *Howe v. Malkin* (1878) 40 L.T. 196.

been applied when the words accompany an ambiguous act. It is an interpretation which is "at odds with some respected authority".[9]

However unsatisfactory the reasoning of such cases, the weight of recent authority suggests that statements made by witnesses attending identification parades are admissible. Other jurisdictions have specifically legislated for this situation. Under the Federal Rules of Evidence:

801.—(d) Statements which are not hearsay.
A statement is not hearsay if —
(1) Prior statement by witness. The declarant testifies at the trial or hearing and is subject to cross-examination concerning the statement, and the statement is . . .

(c) one of identification of a person made after perceiving the person;[10]

Third party confessions

A further problem exists with the question of the admissibility of third party confessions as in *R. v. Blastland*[11] The defendant was accused of sexual assault and murder. Part of his defence was that, although he had sex with the victim, he had left him unharmed and that another person, M, had later killed him. M made a statement confessing to the killing which was later retracted. The statement itself was not admissible and the accused also was prevented from proving that M had told other people of the murder in circumstances indicating that M knew of the killing before the body was found. Neither piece of evidence was admissible.

R. v. Blastland [1985] 2 All E.R. 1095 at 1099–1100, *per* Lord Bridge

It is, of course, elementary that statements made to a witness by a third party are not excluded by the hearsay rule when they are put in evidence solely to prove the state of mind either of the maker of the statement or the person to whom it was made. What a person said or heard said may well be the best and most direct evidence of that person's state of mind. This principle can only apply, however, when the state of mind evidenced by the statement is either itself directly in issue at the trial or is of direct and immediate relevance to an issue which arises at the trial. It is at this point, as it seems to me, that the argument for the appellant breaks down. The issue at the trial of the appellant was whether it was proved that the appellant had buggered and murdered Karl Fletcher. Mark's knowledge that Karl had been murdered was neither itself in issue, nor was it, *per* se, of any relevance to the issue. What was relevant was not the fact of Mark's knowledge but how he had come by that knowledge. He might have done so in a number of ways, but the two most obvious possibilities were either that he had witnessed the commission of the murder by the appellant or that he had committed it himself. The statements which it was sought to prove that Mark had made, indicating his knowledge of the murder, provided no rational basis whatever on which the jury could be invited to

[9] Comment on *McCay* by Birch in [1990] Crim.L.R. 338 at 341; for further discussion on identification issues, see 304, *et seq.*
[10] Federal Rules of Evidence, r.801.
[11] [1985] 2 All E.R. 1095: see also *R. v. Turner* (1975) 61 Cr.App.R. 67.

draw an inference as to the source of that knowledge. To do so would have been mere speculation. Thus, to allow this evidence of what Mark said to be put before the jury as supporting the conclusion that he, rather than the appellant, may have been the murderer seems to me, in the light of the principles on which the exclusion of hearsay depends, to be open to still graver objection than allowing evidence that he had directly admitted the crime. If the latter is excluded as evidence to which no probative value can safely be attributed, the same objection applies a *fortiori* to the admission of the former.

Under the U.S. Federal Rules of Evidence, third party confessions are admissible when corroborated by other evidence indicating the accused's guilt:

804.—Hearsay Exceptions; Declarant Unavailable

(b) Hearsay exceptions.

The following are not excluded by the hearsay rule if the declarant is unavailable as a witness:

(3) Statement against interest. A statement which was at the time of its making so far contrary to the declarant's pecuniary or proprietary interest, or so far tended to subject the declarant to civil or criminal liability, or to render invalid a claim by the declarant against another, that a reasonable person in the declarant's position would not have made the statement unless believing it to be true. A statement tending to expose the declarant to criminal liability and offered to exculpate the accused is not admissible unless corroborating circumstances clearly indicate the trustworthiness of the statement.[12]

This provision ensures the reliability of a third party confession by requiring "corroborating circumstances" but it also recognises the importance of including all evidence which might exculpate the accused. This can be contrasted with the position taken by the House of Lords in *Blastland* that the statement provides "no rational basis" from which to infer the source of the declarant's knowledge.

[12] Federal Rules of Evidence, r.804.

17

COMMON LAW EXCEPTIONS TO HEARSAY

Introduction

The breadth of the hearsay rule itself is matched by the number and variety of the exceptions to the rule. Many exceptions to the hearsay rule are based in common law. The major common law exceptions are:

(1) *admissions*: a statement made by a party, adverse to his or her own case, is admissible as evidence of the truth of what it contains. This was especially significant in relation to confessions made by defendants in criminal cases.
(2) *statements in public documents*.
(3) *statements by deceased persons*.[1]
(4) *res gestae*: if a statement is made spontaneously as an intrinsic part of the action or event, that statement is admissible as evidence of the truth of what it contains.

These have been amended by statute and other, highly significant, exceptions have been introduced:

(1) under the *Civil Evidence Act 1995*, evidence can no longer be excluded in civil proceedings on the basis that it is hearsay.
(2) in criminal proceedings, admissions against interest (*i.e. confessions*) are wholly governed by section 76 of the Police and Criminal Evidence Act 1984. In civil proceedings admissions will normally be admissible by virtue of the Civil Evidence Act 1995.
(3) *documentary hearsay in criminal proceedings* is now often admissible under the Criminal Justice Acts 1988 and 1991.

The standard rationale for these exceptions, whether statutory or common law, is that the evidence in these categories is more reliable and

[1] Only where these are against interest, in the course of a duty, as to pedigree or as to public rights or in the settled and hopeless expectation of death. Statements by murder victims are not automatically admissible.

probative than other types of hearsay statement. But, as has been suggested, fairness is a more convincing rationale than reliability as the core criterion for the exclusion of hearsay. The confusion between the different rationales for the hearsay rule perhaps explains the pragmatism which seemingly underlies the piecemeal nature of the exceptions to the rule.

Firstly, it may be useful to look at the exceptions schematically:

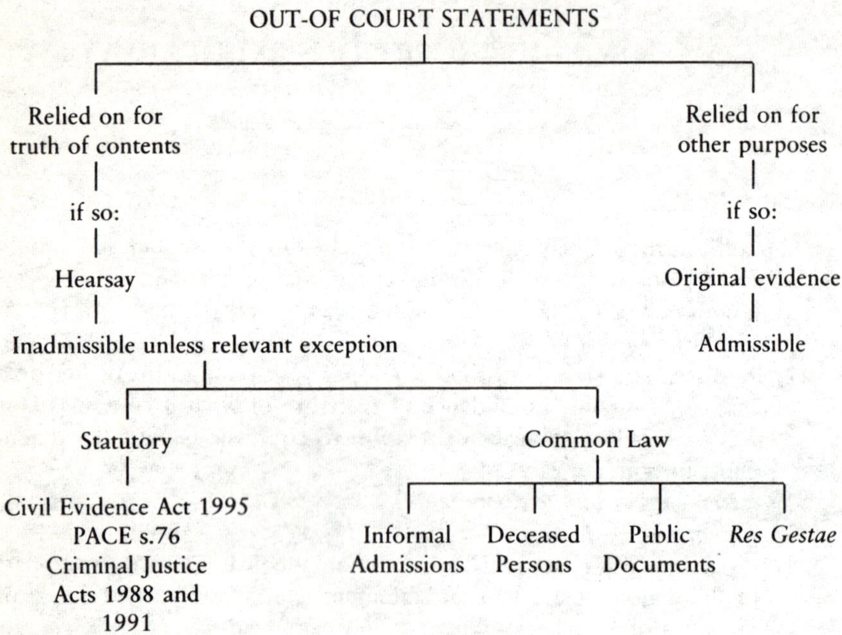

This chapter will only discuss exceptions at common law.

Informal Admissions

Admissions are representations of fact, made in words or by conduct, by a party or another, adverse to his or her own case. At common law such statements are admissible as evidence of the truth of what they contain. The rationale of this rule is that the statement is likely to be reliable as a party is unlikely to make statements against his or her own interests but the theoretical basis for admissions is still debated:

Scott I., "Reception in Evidence of Unreliable Admissions" [1981] Crim.L.R. 285 at 286–287

Professor Wigmore took the view that admissions are not hearsay because they are not affirmative proof but operate only destructively to shake the admitting party's case just as prior inconsistent statements of a witness may be introduced to shake his testimony.[2] Professor Morgan strongly advanced the view[3] that admissions could

[2] *Wigmore on Evidence* (1904), para. 1048.
[3] Morgan, "Admissions as an Exception to the Hearsay Rule" 30 Yale L.J. 355 (1921).

be received for the purpose of proving the truth of their contents (that is, as affirmative evidence) and this opinion has prevailed in the United States.

There is no question that, in England, evidence of relevant admissions may be received . . . The acceptance . . . of the Morgan approach to admissions may be seen, as it operates in criminal cases, as yet another illustration of the subtle ways in which the rules of evidence may be developed in a manner which weakens the impact of rules relating to the allocation of the burdens of proof and the various manifestations of the privilege against self-incrimination.

Although the 'admissions exception' to the hearsay rule is now well-established on both sides of the Atlantic, in both civil and criminal cases, attempts to construct a satisfactory theory or doctrinal basis for it have produced considerable disagreement amongst judges and legal writers. And it seems that this controversy, together with the uncertainties which necessarily existed before the exception became universally accepted and which have tended to linger in the minds of lawyers, has created doubts about the precise legal rules which govern the circumstances in which admissions may be received and the evidential weight to be given to them. It has been said that admissions are an anomalous exception to the hearsay rule because this exception admits statements 'that do not in theory carry some special guarantee of reliability or provide some extra test of [the] declarant's credibility'.[4] On the other hand it has been argued that, though hearsay, the reception of informal admissions is justified by the fact that the person against whom an admission is introduced, being a party to the proceedings and interested in weakening the effect of the statement, may deny it or explain it in court. Further, it has been said that admissions will usually be against the party's interest when made and therefore more likely to be true because citizens do not lightly make statements that tend to be self-disserving . . .

Professor Morgan thought it was fruitless to search for a satisfactory explanation of the admissions exception based on factors that gave special reliability to admissions sufficient to allay our usual fears about hearsay. He preferred to say that the explanation for the exception lay in 'the adversary theory of litigation' and thought it 'too obvious for comment' that a party whose statements are offered against him is in no position to object, as he may be when other forms of admissible hearsay are offered against him, that he did not have an opportunity to cross-examine the declarant or that the statement was not made on oath. Therefore admissions are free from the main objections to hearsay testimony. Professor Morgan put his point more strikingly when he wrote[5] that a party can hardly say 'that he is unworthy of credence save when speaking under sanction of oath'.

In English law, the whole statement is admissible as proof of its contents. The major effect of such a statement is to admit a fact which is against the interest of the declarant. But the statement might also include some material which advances the declarant's case. Under the rule in *R. v. Sharp*[6] the whole statement is put into evidence, including the self-serving aspects.

Informal admissions must be distinguished from formal admissions which may be made to save an opposing party time and trouble. The facts in a formal admission need not be proved and evidence to contradict them is not admissible:

[4] Lempert and Salzburg, *A Modern Approach to Evidence* (1976) 365.
[5] Morgan, *Basic Problems of Evidence* (1962) 266.
[6] [1988] 1 All E.R. 65.

(1) in civil cases, a fact may be formally admitted in a variety of ways[7] including in response to a notice to admit facts under R.S.C., Ord 27, r.2.
(2) in criminal cases, parties can make formal admissions under the conditions laid down in section 10 of the Criminal Justice Act 1967. Normally such an admission will be in writing but it can be made orally by counsel in court.[8]

In contrast to this, informal admissions are not conclusive and parties can lead evidence to rebut them. In criminal cases, the common law is no longer relevant as the conditions for the admissibility of confessions are laid down by section 76 of the Police and Criminal Evidence Act 1984.[9] In civil matters, the old common law rules on admissions were retained under section 9 of the Civil Evidence Act 1968 which preserved several common law exceptions to the hearsay rule. The passage of the Civil Evidence Act 1995 did not alter the position as far as several of the exceptions were concerned and these are preserved by section 7(2) of the 1995 Act. But the Law Commission considered that admissions should be treated differently:

Law Commission, *The Hearsay Rule in Civil Proceedings* (Cm. 2321, 1993)

4.33.—So far as the notice and weighting provisions are concerned, adverse admissions are in a different category from the other exceptions and it is clearly necessary that the same provisions need to apply to these as apply to other hearsay statements. By contrast, in the case of published works dealing with matters of a public nature, and public documents and records, it will be rare for the weight to be attached to such evidence to be a matter for debate. Moreover, we are preserving the common law rules concerning public registers, and it is not our policy to add procedural burdens where none exist at present. We have therefore concluded that the notice and weighting provisions should not apply to these cases.

Consequently under the 1995 Act, informal admissions were to be treated no differently from other hearsay statements:

7.—(1) The common law rule effectively preserved by section 9(1) and (2)(a) of the Civil Evidence Act 1968 (admissibility of admissions adverse to a party) is superseded by the provisions of this Act.

Informal admissions are now admissible as a result of section 1(1) of the Act which provides that evidence shall not be excluded on the grounds that it is hearsay. Furthermore they are only admissible as a result of section 1 as the common law basis of admissibility has been removed.

Whether a statement constitutes an informal admission is no longer of any relevance in civil proceedings but aspects of the common law might

[7] There is a list in Keane A., *The Modern Law of Evidence* (4th ed., 1996), 611.
[8] *R. v. Lewis* [1989] Crim.L.R. 61.
[9] See Chap. 4.

still be applicable in criminal proceedings. Under section 82 of the Police and Criminal Evidence Act 1984, a confession ". . . includes any statement wholly or partly adverse to the person who made it, whether made to a person in authority or not and whether made in words or otherwise". This can include representations by words or conduct, express or implied. This is illustrated by *Moriarty v. London Chatham and Dover Railway*[10] when the conduct of the plaintiff was held to constitute an admission. He sued a railway company for personal injury and sought to suborn witnesses who had not been present at the accident to give evidence on his behalf. Evidence of this was regarded as admissible as it indicated that the plaintiff was aware of the falsity of his claim. Lush J. said that:

> . . . this species of evidence is receivable as an admission by the party that the case he is putting forward is not the true one. It was an admission by conduct and receivable on that ground . . .[11]

More difficult are inferences which are drawn from silence or from a party's reactions when taxed outside the court with an allegation of some sort. The statements and the response are both admissible as is shown in *R. v. Christie*[12] where the defendant was charged with the indecent assault of a small boy. The boy testified and identified the defendant. However the boy's mother was also allowed to testify that she and the boy went up to the accused and the boy had said "That is the man" and described the assault. Christie had said "I am innocent". The House of Lords admitted the mother's testimony as to the allegation and Christie's response[13]:

R. v. Christie [1914] A.C. 545 at 554, *per* Lord Atkinson

. . . the rule of law undoubtedly is that a statement made in the presence of an accused person, even upon an occasion which would be expected reasonably to call for some explanation or denial from him, is not evidence against him of the facts stated save so far as he accepts the statement, so as to make it, in effect, his own. If he accepts the statement in part only, then to that extent alone does it become his statement. He may accept the statement by word or conduct, action or demeanour, and it is the function of the jury that tries the case to determine whether his words, action, conduct or demeanour at the time when a statement was made amounts to an acceptance of it in whole or in part. It by no means follows, I think, that a mere denial by the accused of the facts mentioned in the statement necessarily renders the statement inadmissible, because he may deny the statement in such a manner and under such circumstances as may lead a jury to disbelieve him, and constitute evidence from which an acknowledgement may be inferred by them.

Of course, if at the end of the case the presiding judge should be of opinion that no evidence has been given upon which the jury could reasonably find that the accused had accepted the statement so as to make it in whole or in part his own, the

[10] (1870) L.R. 5 Q.B. 314.
[11] *ibid.* at 323.
[12] [1914] A.C. 545.
[13] They did not admit testimony as to the boy's description of the assault — this would have been a prior consistent statement.

judge can instruct the jury to disregard the statement entirely. It is said that, despite this direction, grave injustice might be done to the accused, inasmuch as the jury, having once heard the statement, could not, or would not, rid their mind of it. It is, therefore, in the application of the rule that the difficulty arises. The question then is this: Is it to be taken as a rule of law that such a statement is not to be admitted in evidence until a foundation has been laid for its admission by proof of facts from which, in the opinion of the presiding judge, a jury might reasonably draw the inference that the accused had so accepted the statement as to make it in whole or in part his own, or is it to be laid down that the prosecutor is entitled to give the statement in evidence in the first instance, leaving it for the presiding judge, in case no such evidence as the above-mentioned should be ultimately produced, to tell the jury to disregard the statement altogether.

In my view the former is not a rule of law, but it is, I think, a rule which, in the interest of justice, it might be most prudent and proper to follow as a rule of practice . . .[14]

In civil cases, reactions such as this would still be admissible under the 1995 Act. This is demonstrated in *Bessela v. Stern*[15] in which the defendant was sued for breach of a promise to marry.[16] There was testimony that he stayed silent when taxed by the plaintiff: "You always promised to marry me. Why have you changed your mind?" Silence was accepted as an admission. The complaint was in the presence of the defendant and a response might reasonably have been expected. This can be contrasted with *Wiedemann v. Walpole*[17] where the defendant's failure to answer a letter taxing him with his failure to wed the plaintiff was held not to be an admission by him:

> . . . silence upon the receipt of a letter cannot be taken as evidence of admission of the truth of its contents unless there are some circumstances in the case which would render it probable that the person receiving the letter, who dissented from the statements, would answer it and deny them . . .[18]

In criminal proceedings, the weight to be attached to a confession will be assessed by the tribunal of fact according to factors such as the circumstances in which it was made, its contents and its consistency with other evidence. In civil cases, section 4 of the 1995 Act mentions specific considerations to be taken into account.[19] But other factors may come into play, *e.g.* admissions might be made by persons without personal knowledge of the facts and such statements might be admissible under section 1 of the Act. Where an admission is made which is not based on the personal knowledge of the speaker, it has limited evidential value but is admissible. Precedent suggests that the 'personal knowledge' rule affects

[14] *Christie supra* at 554, *per* Lord Atkinson. In criminal cases the effect of *Christie* is expressly preserved by the Criminal Justice and Public Order Act 1994, s.34(5).
[15] (1877) 46 L.J.C.P. 467.
[16] Such actions were abolished by the Law Reform (Miscellaneous Provisions) Act 1970, s.1.
[17] [1891] 60 L.J.Q.B. 762.
[18] *ibid.* at 764, *per* Bowen L.J.
[19] These are discussed in 601, *et seq.*

the probative worth of an admission rather than its admissibility. In *Comptroller of Customs v. Western Electric Co. Ltd*,[20] there was an admission that the goods were made in the United States. This was based upon the markings on the goods, markings which were themselves inadmissible hearsay. The admission was of no more value than the information on which it was based. If the admission is based on personal experience, its evidential value is enhanced. In *Bird v. Adams*,[21] the defendant was charged with possession of drugs. He admitted that he had 15 tablets of LSD. At the trial the issue arose as to whether there was any evidence of the nature of the tablets. The Divisional Court held that the defendant's past experience and conduct were such that the admission was at least prima facie evidence of its truth. Lord Widgery said:

> If a man admits possession of a substance which he says is a dangerous drug, if he admits it in circumstances like the present where he also admits he has been peddling the drug, it is of course possible that the item in question was not a specific drug at all but the admission in these circumstances is not an admission of some fact about which the admitter knows nothing.[22]

Such an approach fits well within the framework of the 1995 Act and this would also apply in the case of vicarious admissions. At common law, admissions did not need to be made by the party to the proceedings so long as the person who makes the admission was in some form of privity with the party. However in civil proceedings, even if there is no privity and the admission is made by some other person, that statement might still be admitted under the general exception created by the 1968 and 1995 legislation. The weight that is attached to such a statement may well be greater when one or more of the following factors are present:

where privity exists: predecessors in title, partners,[23] trustees might all be seen to be in "privity" with the party. There is no exhaustive definition but it requires some identity of interest in the property or obligation.

where there is express or implied authority: in *Williams v. Innes*,[24] the defendants were executors of an estate and referred the plaintiff to a third party for information concerning the estate. It was held that they were bound by the statements of the third party.

[20] [1966] A.C. 367.
[21] [1972] Crim.L.R. 174.
[22] See discussion in Scott, *op. cit.* at 292 and the related question of whether an admission to handling stolen goods is evidence that the goods are in fact stolen — see *R. v. Hulbert* (1979) 69 Cr. App. R. 243; *R. v. Overington* [1978] Crim.L.R. 692; *R. v. McDonald* [1980] Crim.L.R. 242.
[23] This is given statutory effect by the Partnership Act 1890, s.15.
[24] (1808) 1 Camp. 364.

"If a man refers another upon any particular business to a third person, he is bound by what this third person says or does concerning it, as much as if that had been said or done by himself"[25]

where the relationship is that of principal and agent: where an agent is acting within the scope of his or her authority and makes an admission, this can be seen to have greater probative value in evidence against the principal if the agency existed at the time of the admission;[26] the agent was authorised to make the statement;[27] the statement was made in the course of employment;[28] and the statement was made to a third party and not to the principal.

The major exception to this rule about the admissibility of vicarious admissions is there is no privity between spouses or between parents and children just because of their familial relationship. But if the wife made an admission concerning the joint ownership of the family home, that would be admissible against the husband.

Statements in Public Documents

In civil proceedings, the common law nature of this exception to the hearsay rule was overtaken by section 9 of the Civil Evidence Act 1968:

9.—(1) In any civil proceedings a statement which, if this Part of this Act had not been passed, would by virtue of any rule of law mentioned in subsection (2) below have been admissible as evidence of any fact stated therein shall be admissible as evidence of that fact by virtue of this subsection.

This in turn has been superseded by Civil Evidence Act 1995:

7.—(2) The common law rules effectively preserved by section 9(1) and (2)(b) to (d) of the Civil Evidence Act 1968, that is, any rule law whereby in civil proceedings —

(b) public documents (for example, public registers and returns made under public authority with respect to matters of public interest) are admissible as evidence of facts stated therein; or
(c) records (for example, the records of certain courts, treaties, Crown grants, pardons and commissions) are admissible as evidence of facts stated therein

shall continue to have effect.

If admissible at common law, in civil proceedings, public documents are now admissible by virtue of s.7. Documents not covered by section 9 will

[25] *ibid.* at 365, *per* Lord Ellenborough C.J.
[26] *Peto v. Hague* (1804) 5 Esp 134 — Lord Ellenborough said that what an agent said about former transactions (prior to his becoming an agent) would not be admissible evidence against his master.
[27] *Kirkstall Brewery v. Furness Rly* (1874) 43 L.J.Q.B. 142.
[28] *Burr v. Ware Rural District Council* [1939] 2 All E.R. 688.

be admissible by virtue of section 1 of the 1995 Act but will need to comply with the notice and weighting provisions of the Act.

In criminal cases, public documents are admissible at common law. They may also be admissible under statute, in particular under ssection 23 and 24 of the Criminal Justice Act 1988. The criteria of the common law are still relevant. If the document:

- is made and preserved for public use;
- has its entries made promptly and by person acting under a strict duty to inquire into the circumstances recorded;
- is open to public inspection;

such a document[29] is admissible evidence of the facts contained in it. Foreign as well as British public records are within this rule but whatever the provenance, the conditions above must be adhered to. In *Sturla v. Freccia*[30] a report of a public committee in Genoa, a foreign state, was deemed inadmissible:

Sturla v. Freccia (1880) 5 App. Cas. 623 at 642–647, _per_ Lord Blackburn

It is an established rule of law that public documents are admitted for certain purposes. What a public document is, within that sense, is of course the great point which we have now to consider . . . the principle, upon which it goes is, that there should be a public inquiry, and a public document, made by a public officer. I do not think that 'public' there is to be taken in the sense of meaning the whole world. I think an entry in the books of a manor is public in the sense that it concerns all the people interested in the manor. And an entry probably in a corporation book concerning a corporate matter, or something in which all the corporation are concerned, would be 'public' within that sense. But it must be a public document, and it must be made by a public officer. I understand a public document there to mean a document that is made for the purpose of the public making use of it, and being able to refer to it. It is meant to be where there is a judicial, or quasi-judicial, duty to inquire, as might be said to be the case with the bishop acting under the writs issued by the Crown. That may be said to be quasi-judicial. He is acting for the public when that is done; but I think the very object of it must be that it should be made for the purpose of being kept public, so that the persons concerned in it may have access to it afterwards . . . Can the document in this case be said to come within that class of cases? I think it impossible to look at it in this way. There is not the slightest evidence, or the least circumstance, to lead me to the conclusion that it was ever intended that this private and confidential report should be seen by anyone interested in it. It was meant for private information, to guide the discretion of the Government. It was not, like the bishop's return of the first-fruits, for public information, to be kept in the office and to be seen by all in the diocese who might be concerned when there came to be any litigation.

[29] There is an interesting historical note in Carter P., *Cases on Evidence* (2nd ed., 1990) 332 with examples of public documents. A further list of examples is given in Keane A., *The Modern Law of Evidence* (4th ed., 1996) 240–241.

[30] (1880) 5 App. Cas. 623.

In many public offices, there is a duty to record accurately but officials have neither the time nor resources to inquire into the correctness of the information being recorded. In *R. v. Halpin*,[31] the defendant was charged with conspiracy to defraud a local council by making false claims for work allegedly done by a limited company. The Crown sought to prove that at the relevant time the accused and his wife were the sole shareholders in that company by adducing extracts from the annual returns of the company filed at the Companies Registry. Obviously the official had no personal knowledge of the facts being recorded. On appeal, Lane L.J. held that the judge was correct to admit the document and that the duty could be divided between the provider of the information and the officer with the statutory duty to record:

R. v. Halpin [1975] Q.B. 907 at 915, _per_ Geoffrey Lane L.J.

The common law as expressed in the earlier cases which have been cited were plainly designed to apply to an uncomplicated community where those charged with keeping registers would, more often than not, be personally acquainted with the people whose affairs they were recording and the vicar, as already indicated, would probably himself have officiated at the baptism, marriage or burial which he later recorded in the presence of the churchwarden on the register before putting it back in the coffers. But the common law should move with the times and should recognise the fact that the official charged with recording matters of public import can no longer in this highly complicated world, as like as not, have personal knowledge of their accuracy.

What has happened now is that the function originally performed by one man has had to be shared between two: the first having the knowledge and the statutory duty to record that knowledge and forward it to the registrar, the second having the duty to preserve that document and to show it to members of the public under proper conditions as required.

Works of Reference

At common law, authoritative works of reference were admissible to prove the facts (of a public nature[32]) contained or to allow the court to take judicial notice of such facts. This exception still applies in criminal cases and was put on a statutory basis for civil proceedings by section 9 of the Civil Evidence Act 1968:

9.—(1) In any civil proceedings a statement which, if this Part of this Act had not been passed, would by virtue of any rule of law mentioned in subsection (2) below have been admissible as evidence of any fact stated therein shall be admissible as evidence of that fact by virtue of this subsection.

This is now governed by the Civil Evidence Act 1995:

7.—(2) The common law rules effectively preserved by section 9(1) and (2)(b) to (d) of the Civil Evidence Act 1968, that is, any rule law whereby in civil proceedings —

[31] [1975] Q.B. 907.
[32] *Read v. Bishop of Lincoln* [1892] A.C. 644.

(a) published works dealing with matters of a public nature (for example, histories, scientific works, dictionaries and maps) are admissible as evidence of facts of a public nature stated in them.

Statements by Deceased Persons

At common law only certain categories of statements by people now dead were admissible as exceptions to hearsay:

(1) in criminal proceedings, all of those discussed below are admissible.[33] If the statement is in writing, different considerations may also need to be considered under sections 23 and 24 of the Criminal Justice Act 1988.
(2) in civil proceedings, these statements will normally be admissible under section 1 of the Civil Evidence Act 1995. Where they are not capable of being admitted under those sections and it involves an issue of pedigree or public and general rights, section 7(3) of that Act may be relevant.

Declarations against interest

In criminal proceedings, written or oral statements made by a person now dead which, when made, were known by the declarant to be against his or her pecuniary or proprietary interests, are admissible evidence of the facts contained. The principle is that people are less likely knowingly to lie about matters that affect their pockets, although it has been said "Men lie for so many reasons and some for no reason at all and some tell the truth without thinking or even in spite of thinking about their pockets".[34] Extraordinarily this exception and its rationale does not extend to declarations against penal interest: confessions to a crime by a now dead person remain inadmissible although it would seem that (in the eigthteenth century at least) the prospect of being hanged if one admitted one's part in a crime would seem an even more effective indicator of reliability.

A modern example of this "semi-defunct" rule is *R. v. Rogers*.[35] In this case the accused was arrested leaving a house in Balham carrying cocaine and almost £2,000. In the house were found heroin and firearms. He was charged with possession of drugs with intent to supply. His defence was that a man named Law was the dealer and that his possession was for personal use. Law was now dead but before his death had told his wife:

a) "that there were a number of guys after him for the money for the heroin that the police had found . . ."

[33] Although some (*e.g.* statements as to pedigree) are scarcely relevant.
[34] Hamilton L.J. in *Ward v. H S Pitt & Co* [1913] 2 K.B. 130 at 138.
[35] [1995] Crim.L.R. 148.

b) ". . . he had been supplying [R] with heroin for his personal use . . ."
c) ". . . [R] didn't know about the guns and heroin stored . . ."

These statements were oral hearsay and inadmissible as *R. v. Blastland*[36] has held that there is no special rule attaching to third party confession to crime. Could Rogers escape the consequences of *Blastland* by treating Law's statements as a declaration against interest? The Crown contended that the exception did not apply in criminal cases:

R. v. Rogers [1995] Crim.L.R. 148 at 149–150

. . . the exception did apply, despite the lack of authorities in criminal cases applying it. The common law rules of evidence were the same in civil and criminal cases, and there was no logical reason to limit the exception to the former . . . Its application was conditional on four factors: (i) the deceased must have had a peculiar means of knowledge of the facts stated in the declaration. Here, Law had personal knowledge. (ii) The interest against which the declaration was made must be either pecuniary or proprietary,[37] (iii) must relate to a present and not a future obligation, (iv) and the declarant must know it is against his interests.

Only [statement (a) above] could possibly be against his pecuniary interest. The judge was correct in his view that it was not an acknowledgement that he owed money. To say one was being chased for money, was not an acknowledgement that one owed it. To say one was being sued did not amount to acknowledging an obligation unless one acknowledged the he owed the money. It was possible to provide a reason why Law might say he was being chased because the police had taken the heroin, even though he was not then presently under any obligation to pay for it. If he did owe money, he had the drugs on credit. There was no acknowledgement that the sum was due, and they might be chasing him because they had lost the drugs.

As to the lack of any legal or moral obligation, all that was necessary was that the declaration should be against the pecuniary interest of the maker. The acknowledgement of an obligation, even if not enforceable save by criminal fraternity strong-arm tactics, was still against his pecuniary interest. The rationale of the exception was that a man would not say something against his pecuniary interest unless it was true. Public policy did not enter into the question of admissibility of evidence, so it was beside the point that this transaction was against public policy and against public policy for the courts to give effect to such transactions . . .

Appellate counsel submitted that the rest of the statement was admissible because if the declaration itself was admissible, that let in collateral evidence[38].

In *The Churchwardens, Overseers and Guardians of the Parish of Birmingham*,[39] Cockburn C.J. said that it had been held that the deceased's declaration might be received also to prove collateral facts stated in it, at all events, so far as related to facts not foreign to it, and might be taken to have formed a substantial part of it.

It was only in so far as the collateral matters were necessary to explain the nature of the transaction in question that they were admissible. The heroin to which Law was referring was that seized by the police. Nothing more needs to be said about it

[36] *R. v. Blastland* [1985] 2 All E.R. 1095.
[37] *The Sussex Peerage Case* (1844) 11 Cl. & Fin. 85.
[38] *Higham v. Ridgway* (1808) 10 East 109.
[39] (1861) 1 B&S 763.

to identify it. If he had said that R had known about it and the guns, the Crown could not have sought to put this admission in and what was alleged to be a collateral statement.

As to proprietary interest, to say, as Law had done, that the heroin was his was not a declaration against such an interest. Contrariwise, it was asserting a proprietary interest.

Appellate counsel accepted that if only the first sentence was admissible, that took the matter no further. For those reasons, and for the additional reasons that the latter part of the statement was not in any event admissible as being collateral to the alleged statement against interest, the judge was right to exclude evidence of what Law had told his wife.

The appeal in *Rogers* is seeking to escape from the rule regarding the inadmissibility of oral third party confessions. Had Law scribbled a note to his wife instead of speaking to her, his statements might well have been admissible under section 23 of the Criminal Justice Act 1988.[40] However accidentally, the case illuminates the issues surrounding declarations against interest:

(1) the declarant must have personal knowledge of the facts.

(2) the interest must be either a pecuniary or proprietary one. The statement by a deceased landholder that, for example, the land was subject to an easement would be admissible. In *Peaceable d. Uncle v. Watson*,[41] Mansfield C.J. said:

> . . . Possession is prima facie evidence of seisin in fee simple; the declaration of the possessor that he is tenant to another makes most strongly, therefore, against his own interest, and consequently is admissible . . .[42]

The declaration must be against immediate pecuniary interests: in *Lloyd v. Powell Duffryn Steam Coal Co. Ltd*[43] there was a claim for workmen's compensation on behalf of an illegitimate child born after the death of the putative father. The issue was whether the statements of the father that he was the father of the child and intended to marry the mother were admissible evidence of paternity. Lord Atkinson said that to treat the statements made by the deceased as statements against pecuniary interest was ". . . wholly to mistake their true nature and significance." Perhaps his Lordship was unaware of the cost of bringing up children!

(3) declarations against penal interest (*i.e.* that make the speaker liable to punishment) do not come within the scope of this exception. In the *Sussex Peerage Case*[44] a deceased clergyman made a statement to

[40] As Birch notes (*ibid.* at 150), this might leave the court a problem under section 26 as to whether admitting such a note would be in the interests of justice.

[41] (1811) 4 Taunt. 16.

[42] *ibid.* at 17.

[43] [1914] A.C. 733.

[44] (1844) 11 Cl. & Finn. 85.

his son about a marriage at which he had officiated. Such a statement would have been evidence that the marriage had taken place. It also opened up the possibility of prosecuting the clergyman under the Royal Marriage Act 1772. The House of Lords held that only those declarations by deceased persons which were against their pecuniary or proprietary interests were admissible.[45] This has been followed in South Australia[46] and by the Supreme Court in the United States in *Donnelly v. United States*,[47] although there reform has come about through r.804(3) of the Federal Rules of Evidence which makes such statements admissible if there are corroborating circumstances.

Canada followed a different route in *R. v. O'Brien*[48] in which O'Brien and Jensen were jointly charged with supplying drugs. Jensen fled while O'Brien was convicted. Later Jensen returned and admitted to O'Brien's counsel that he had committed the act alone. However he died before any re-trial. The Canadian Supreme Court said:

R. v. O'Brien [1978] 1 S.C.R. 591, *per* Dickson J.

The distinction [between proprietary and penal interest] is arbitrary and tenuous. There is little or no reason why declarations against penal interest and those against pecuniary or proprietary interest should not stand on the same footing. A person is as likely to speak the truth in a matter affecting his liberty as in a matter affecting his pocketbook. For these reasons and the ever-present possibility that a rule of absolute prohibition could lead to grave injustice, I would hold that, in a proper case, a declaration against penal interest is admissible, according to the law of Canada; the rule as to absolute exclusion of declarations against penal interest established in the *Sussex Peerage* case should not be followed. There is a further point. Can it be said that Jensen's declarations . . . qualifies as a declaration against penal interest? . . . To be admissible there must be a realisation by the declarant that the statement may well be used against him. That is the very thing Jensen wished to avoid. He had no intention of furnishing evidence against himself. His obvious desire was not to create damaging evidence, detrimental to his penal interest. Yet, that is the very basis upon which the admissibility of extra-judicial declarations of penal interest rests. In my opinion the statement . . . failed to meet the requirement for admissibility.[49]

(4) the declaration must relate to a present and not a future obligation.
(5) the declarant must know it is against his interests. In the *Sussex Peerage Case* it is far from clear that the clergyman was aware of the dangers to which he was exposing himself.

[45] *R. v. Turner* (1975) 61 Cr App R 78; *R. v. Blastland supra*; *R. v. Rogers* [1995] Crim.L.R. 148.
[46] *Re Van Beelen's Case* (1974) 9 S.A.S.R. 163.
[47] 228 U.S. 243 (1913) although with Holmes J. dissenting.
[48] [1978] 1 S.C.R. 591.
[49] See also *R. v. Pelletier* (1978) 38 C.C.C. (2d) 515 (Ont.) *Lucier v. R* [1982] 1 S.C.R. 28.

(6) the statement may be admitted to prove a matter collateral to the content of the statement. In *Taylor v. Witham*,[50] there was an action to recover a loan. The problem was how to prove the debt as the lender had now died. But he had left an entry in an account book showing that the borrower had paid three months interest and in the same entry the loan itself was mentioned. The receipt for payment of interest was a declaration against interest and the whole entry was admitted to allow the loan itself to be proved.

In *Rogers*, the appellant wished to adduce Law's statement about being "chased for the money" so that the other statements could be admitted as collateral to this. Even had Law's initial statement been accepted as a declaration against interest, before the subsequent statements could be admitted, it would be necessary to show that in some way they explained the nature of the initial statement. The two parts "I'm being chased for the money" and "I supplied Rogers" have no logical connection. This can be compared to *Taylor v. Witham* where the initial admissible statement '£20 interest paid' is explained by the subsequent statement "£2,000 loan owing".

Declarations in course of a duty

In criminal proceedings, written or oral statements made by a person now dead but which were made under a duty to report or record his or her acts are admissible evidence of the facts which relate to that duty. If the record is written, there is an alternative channel of admissibility under sections 23 and 24 of the Criminal Justice Act 1988. In civil proceedings any such records, written or oral, will be admitted as a consequence of section 1 of the Civil Evidence Act 1995.

The exception rests again on the enhanced reliability of such records since an employee who failed in his or her duty would be likely to be dismissed for incompetent record keeping. This is supported by the requirement of contemporaneity.[51] But necessity of admitting such evidence is also involved since the record might be the only evidence of the employee's acts. The criteria for admitting such declarations are:

(1) there must be a duty owed to another.
(2) the record must relate to the exact scope of the duty. In *Smith v. Blakey* a clerk's record of a transaction was deemed inadmissible and Lord Blackburn said:

> . . . It is an essential fact to render such an entry admissible, that not only should it have been made in the due discharge of the business about which

[50] (1876) 3 Ch.D. 605.
[51] Lord Blackburn saw this as the essence of the exception — *Smith v. Blakey* (1867) L.R. 2 Q.B. 326.

the person is employed, but the duty must be to do the very thing to which the entry relates, and then to make a report of record of it.[52]

In *Chambers v. Bernasconi*,[53] it was necessary to prove the location where an arrest took place. The arresting constable had left a record of the fact of arrest, the time and date and the place. However it was his duty to record only the first two of these and not the location. This was excluded. As this case also shows, the only statement admissible is that which relates to the duty: in a record, an entry of marginal relevance may be admissible while others of greater relevance are not. Unlike the situation with declarations against interest, collateral facts cannot be proved as the whole record is not admissible.

Both these aspects are illustrated in *R. v. McGuire*,[54] where the accused was charged with arson of his own hotel in order to claim the insurance money. A Home Office Scientific Officer inspected the site and his report contained an opinion as to the seat of the fire, an opinion which would have been favourable to the accused. The officer died before trial. The Court of Appeal upheld the decision to reject that part of the report that contained conclusions. Only that part referring to his observations, measurements etc was admissible as this related directly to his duty. The officer's opinion could not be included as a collateral matter despite its obvious link to the facts reported. However this exclusion would not have prevented another expert testifying and using the original report as the basis of his opinion.

(3) the record must be made contemporaneously. In *The Henry Coxon*,[55] the litigation concerned a collision at sea and this was recorded by the (now deceased) first mate, two days after the event. The log was excluded and the standard appears strict.[56]

(4) the record must relate to the acts undertaken by the declarant and not by others. In *The Henry Coxon*, the first mate referred not only to his own acts but those of the crew and the manoeuvres of the other ship involved. Phillimore J. said that entries could only be admitted when they relate to acts done by the deceased and not by third parties.

The statement should also relate to acts done and not to future acts — in *Rowlands v. De Vecchi*,[57] the clerk made a note of the letters which were to be posted. This was rejected as evidence that a particular letter had in fact been posted. However against this is the

[52] See *supra* at 332.
[53] (1834) 3 L.J. Ex. 373.
[54] (1985) 81 Cr. App. R. 323.
[55] (1878) 3 P.D. 156.
[56] This might be compared with the flexible time limits which apply when a document is simply being used to refresh the witness's memory — *R. v. Da Silva* [1990] 1 All E.R. 29.
[57] (1882) 1 Cab. & El. 10.

unsatisfactory[58] (and first instance) case of *R. v. Buckley*[59] where the defendant was charged with the killing of a policeman. The officer had earlier announced his intention of watching the defendant's movements on the night in question. This statement of intent was admitted as evidence that the officer had in fact done this. It might be argued that the prejudicial effect is much greater than any probative value. The statement only goes to prove the victim's intent and not to prove what the defendant did.

(5) the declarant must have no motive to lie. Again in *The Henry Coxon* it was apparent that the mate had every reason to misrepresent the facts in order to negative any charge of negligence which might be made as a result of the collision.

Dying declarations

This is a much more limited exception than this phrase implies. In *R. v. Woodcock*,[60] the defendant was tried for the murder of his wife. Before she died, she made a statement on oath to a magistrate. She said nothing about her impending death but the court were clearly satisfied that she knew she was going to die:

R. v. Woodcock (1789) 1 Leach 500 at 502–504, *per* Eyre C.B.

. . . The general principle on which the species of evidence is admitted is, that they are declarations made in extremity, when the party is at the point of death, and when every hope of this world is gone; when every motive to falsehood is silenced, and the mind is induced by the most powerful considerations to speak the truth; a situation so solemn and so awful is considered by law as creating an obligation equal to that which is imposed by a positive oath administered in a court of justice. But a difficulty also arises with respect to these declarations; for it has not appeared, and it seems impossible to find out, whether the deceased herself apprehended that she was in such a state of mortality as would inevitably oblige her soon to answer before her Maker for the truth or falsehood of her assertions . . ., however, my judgment is, that in as much as she was mortally wounded, and was in a condition which rendered almost immediate death inevitable; as she was thought by every person about her to be dying, though it was difficult to get from her particular explanations as to what she thought of herself and her situation; her declarations, made under these circumstances, ought to be considered by a jury as being made under the impression of her approaching dissolution; for, resigned as she appeared to be, she must have felt the hand of death, and must have considered herself a dying woman . . .Declarations so made are certainly entitled to credit; they ought therefore to be received in evidence; but the degree of credit to which they are entitled must always be a matter for the sober consideration of the jury, under all the circumstances of the case . . .

[58] It is equally unsatisfactory if considered as part of the *res gestae*.
[59] (1873) 13 Cox C.C. 293.
[60] (1789) 1 Leach 500.

This justification has been attacked by commentators on many grounds, not least on the basis that a victim of a serious assault, believing that they are about to die, is likely to be in a highly emotional and probably confused state, a state, moreover, where theological concerns have less significance than in previous centuries. Indeed it has been suggested that motives such as a desire to protect relatives or close friends or to pay off old scores may be as significant. But the exception is of little practical importance nowadays, probably because of the expanded scope of the *res gestae* rule.[61] The conditions for admissibility are:

(1) that the exception only concerns victims in murder or manslaughter cases. To exclude dying declarations in other cases, for example in cases of robbery or rape, is difficult to justify. In *R. v. Mead*[62] the accused was convicted of perjury. He obtained a re-trial but before that shot the deceased who had been a witness at the original perjury trial. The dying declaration about the perjury was excluded:

> . . . evidence of this description is only admissible where the death of the deceased is the subject of the charge, and the circumstances of the death the subject of the dying declaration.[63]

(2) that the victim must be in a settled and hopeless expectation of death. Despite *Woodcock*, evidence of that belief is essential. In *R. v. Perry*,[64] the victim was a woman who had undergone an illegal abortion. Lord Alverstone put it:

> . . . the declarant must be under a 'settled hopeless' expectation of death'. 'Immediate death' must be construed in the sense of death impending, not on the instant but within a very, very short distance indeed. In other words, the test is whether all hope of life has been abandoned so that the person making the statement thinks that death must follow . . .[65]

It must be an unqualified belief and any hope in a miracle, however unreasonable, will exclude the statement. Thus the words of a victim who amended her statement from "with no hope of my recovery" to "with no hope at present of my recovery" were excluded.[66]

(3) that the victim would have been a competent witness. In *R. v. Pike*,[67] the victim was a four-year-old child. What she said shortly before her death was not admissible evidence against the accused. This restriction now would only apply to very young children and the mentally handicapped.

[61] *R. v. Andrews* [1987] 1 All E.R. 513, discussed at 541, *et seq.*
[62] (1824) 2 B. & C. 605.
[63] *ibid.* at 608, *per* Abbott C.J.
[64] [1909] 2 K.B. 697.
[65] *ibid.* at 701.
[66] *R. v. Jenkins* (1869) L.R. 1 C.C.R. 187.
[67] (1829) 3 C. & P. 598.

(4) that the statement must relate to the cause of death. But the whole statement is admissible even where the statement was partly favourable to the accused as in *R. v. Scaife*[68] where the victim said the defendant ". . . would not have struck me but I provoked him to it."

Declarations as to pedigree

Technically the common law exception to hearsay admitting statements pertaining to a family's pedigree is still available in criminal proceedings, although some imagination is needed to devise cases where it might be used.

In civil proceedings, these types of statement will normally be admitted as a result of section 1 of the Civil Evidence Act 1995. Where they are not capable of being admitted under those sections, section 7(3) of that Act may be relevant:

> 7.—(3) The common law rules effectively preserved by section 9(3) and (4) of the Civil Evidence Act 1968, that is, any rule of law whereby in civil proceedings —
>
> . . . (b) evidence of reputation or family tradition is admissible —
>
> (i) for the purpose of proving or disproving pedigree or the existence of a marriage, or . . .
>
> shall continue to have effect in so far as they authorise the court to treat such evidence as proving or disproving that matter.
>
> Where any such rule applies, reputation or family tradition shall be treated for the purposes of this Act as a fact and not as a statement or multiplicity of statements about the matter in question.

The significance of the final proviso is that strict application of the notice and weighing provisions of the 1995 Act would otherwise have been impossible.[69] The common law permits a multiplicity of hearsay handed down through the family. In *Goodright d. Stevens v. Moss*,[70] the issue was a person's legitimacy. Declarations of the dead parents that the child was born before the marriage were admissible:

> An entry in a father's family Bible, an inscription on a tombstone, a pedigree hung up in the family mansion, are all good evidence. So too the declarations of parents in their lifetime . . .[71]

In such circumstances it is necessary to observe the common law preconditions:

[68] (1836) 2 Lewin 150, *per* Lord Coleridge C.J.
[69] Law Commission, *op. cit.* para. 4.34.
[70] (1777) 2 Cowp. 591.
[71] *ibid.* at 594, *per* Lord Mansfield C.J.

- that the declaration relates to an issue of pedigree: for example, a declaration as to a date of birth would not necessarily be a question of pedigree which is the subject of family relationships[72]
- that the declarant is related by blood or marriage to the person whose pedigree is in issue[73]
- that the declaration was made before the dispute in question arose.[74]

Declarations as to public and general rights

At common law evidence of reputation was admissible to prove public and general[75] rights. Technically this exception to hearsay is still available in criminal proceedings, although it can have no practical application.

The preconditions at common law are:

- that the declaration should have been made before the dispute arose
- that the declaration should concern the reputed existence of the right

In civil proceedings, these statements will normally be admissible as a consequence of section 1 of the Civil Evidence Act 1995. Where they are not capable of being admitted under those sections, section 7(3) of that Act may be relevant:

> 7.—(3) The common law rules effectively preserved by section 9(3) and (4) of the Civil Evidence Act 1968, that is, any rule of law whereby in civil proceedings —
>
> (b) evidence of reputation or family tradition is admissible —
> (ii) for the purpose of proving or disproving the existence of a any public or general right or of identifying any person or thing,
>
> shall continue to have effect in so far as they authorise the court to treat such evidence as proving or disproving that matter.
>
> Where any such rule applies, reputation or family tradition shall be treated for the purposes of this Act as a fact and not as a statement or multiplicity of statements about the matter in question.

Testators' declarations about their wills

A testator's statement about the contents of his or her will is admissible evidence of the facts. In *Sugden v. Lord St Leonards*[76] the will went missing

[72] *Haines v. Guthrie* (1884) 53 L.J.Q.B. 521.
[73] *Johnson v. Lawson* (1824) 2 Bing. 86.
[74] *Butler v. Mountgarret (Viscount)* (1859) 7 H.L. Cas. 633.
[75] Public rights are those common to everyone (a highway, for example) whereas general rights are those available to a considerable class — for example, all those belonging to a particular parish.
[76] (1876) 1 P.D. 154.

and the daughter, who had been constantly consulted about the contents, wrote out the entire will from memory. Her account was corroborated to some extent by other papers and by the testator's statements about the will to others.

Res Gestae

Alongside admissions, the major exception at common law was that which glories in the name of *res gestae*. Litigation often concerns a key event, especially in criminal law where, for example, the court can be dealing with an act of violence which takes only moments. It would be absurd for witnesses only to testify as to what they saw and not as to what they heard as such words are often the key to understanding the incident. Although the speaker might not be a witness, the evidence is seen as more reliable as the statement is made spontaneously as an intrinsic part of the action or event. In such cases, that statement is admissible as evidence of the truth of what it contains. All acts and statements which are part of the whole event are admissible and this exception overrides all other exclusionary rules. The critical question is what is "part of the action" as opposed to statements preceding or subsequent to the event?

This is an important rule in criminal proceedings, although detested by commentators,[77] perhaps because the principles have never been comprehensively or clearly enunciated in precedent. But in civil proceedings, it was not an exception that was preserved by the Civil Evidence Acts of either 1968 or 1995. Such statements will nowadays be admitted as a result of section 1 of the 1995 Act.[78]

Historically the rule was strictly applied and the critical elements were that the statement had to be spontaneous and contemporaneous with the events. These elements were often seen as technical rules. *R. v. Bedingfield*[79] was a case where the defendant was charged with murder by cutting the victim's throat. The defence was one of suicide. There was evidence that the accused was in a room with the victim who emerged with her throat cut and said, "Oh dear, Aunt, see what Bedingfield has done to me!" The evidence of that statement was held inadmissible because it occurred after the throat cutting and the *'res'* had been completed. As will be seen, such a strict approach to contemporaneity has long since disappeared.

The broad scope of the exception means that all acts and statements which are part of the whole event are admissible — the *res gestae* rule overrides all exclusionary rules. In *R. v. Ellis*,[80] the defendant was charged

[77] Heydon gives a selection of abuse — "damnably pretended doctrine" (Pollock); "The marvellous capacity of a Latin phrase to serve as a substitute for reasoning . . ." (Morgan) — Heydon J., *Evidence* (3rd ed., 1991) 349.
[78] Although see the obscure final paragraph of Lord Ackner's judgment in *R. v. Andrews* [1987] 1 All E.R. 513 at 521.
[79] (1879) 14 Cox C.C. 341.
[80] (1826) 6 B.&C. 145.

with stealing certain marked coins from a till. Evidence was given that he was seen taking money from the till and was also caught in possession of these marked coins as well as other money, presumably also from the till. This evidence tended to show that the defendant was guilty of other crimes other than the one with which he was charged and such evidence is normally inadmissible but as it was part of the whole event of "taking", it was admitted.

The inclusionary effect of *res gestae* has been to soften the effect of sundry exclusionary rules such as the similar fact rule. In *O'Leary v. R*,[81] at the end of a day-long drunken orgy at a logging camp in Australia, the victim was killed. The actions of the accused throughout the day, including assaults on others, were admitted as evidence since ". . . a connected series of events occurred which should be considered as one transaction".[82] The greatest impact is seen in relation to the hearsay rule as in *Manchester Brewery Co. v. Coombs*[83] when a brewery sued a publican for the latter's breach of an undertaking to buy all his beer from the brewery. The defence was that the beer supplied was not of acceptable quality and part of the evidence concerned complaints from customers who had not been called as witnesses. Statements from absent witnesses such as "This beer is bad" introduced to prove the poor quality of the beer are obviously hearsay but as Farwell J. said:

> . . . Counsel can certainly ask as to the facts — Did the customer order beer? Did he finish it? What did he do with it? If the matter is left there with the answer that he tasted and left it or threw it away, the judge cannot avoid drawing an inference, and the cross-examining counsel is driven to ask for some explanation. It is simpler, therefore, to allow the statement of the customer of the reason for his conduct to be given in chief.'[84]

Such examples raise problems as to the scope of this exception. It has been suggested that the *res gestae* rule lacks "plausible logical analysis" and thus any form of classification is likely to be more expedient than principled.[85] Cross has isolated four different situations where *res gestae* might apply. These are not exclusive categories and often can cover the same territory.

Statements by participants or observers to events

In *Teper v. R.*[86] the defendant was charged with the arson of a shop belonging to his wife. A police officer testified that he heard a woman say

[81] (1946) 73 C.L.R. 566.
[82] *ibid.* at 577, *per* Dixon J.
[83] (1900) 82 L.T. 347.
[84] *ibid.* at 349.
[85] Morgan, "A Suggested Classification of Utterances Admissible as Res Gestae" 31 Yale L.J. 299 (1922).
[86] [1952] A.C. 480.

to a passing motorist, "Your place burning and you going away from the fire". The officer also testified that the driver resembled the accused. It was introduced to rebut a defence of alibi. But the alleged identification took place nearly 30 minutes after the fire started. Lord Normand said:

Teper v. R. [1952] A.C. 480 at 486–488, *per* Lord Normand

The rule against the admission of hearsay is fundamental. It is not the best evidence and it is not delivered on oath. The truthfulness and accuracy of the person whose words are spoken to by another witness cannot be tested by cross-examination, and the light which his demeanour would throw on his testimony is lost. Nevertheless, the rule admits of certain carefully safeguarded and limited exceptions, one of which is that the words may be proved when they form part of the *res gestae*. [This exception] appears to rest ultimately on two propositions — that human utterance is both a fact and a means of communication, and that human action may be so interwoven with words that the significance of the action cannot be understood without the correlative words and the dissociation of the words from the action would impede the discovery of truth. But the judicial application of these two propositions, which do not always combine harmoniously, have never been precisely formulated as a general principles. Their Lordships will not attempt to arrive at a general formula, nor is it necessary to review all of the considerable number of cases cited in the argument. This, at least, may be said, that it is essential that the words sought to be proved by hearsay should be, if not absolutely contemporaneous with the action or event, at least so clearly associated with it, in time, place and circumstance, that they are part of the thing being done, and so an item of real evidence and not merely a reported statement . . . How slight a separation of time and place may suffice to make hearsay evidence of the words spoken incompetent is well illustrated . . . In [*O'Hara v. Central Scottish Motor Traction Co Ltd*[87]], a civil action, the event was an injury to a passenger brought about by the sudden swerve of the omnibus in which she was travelling. The driver of the omnibus said in his evidence that he was forced to swerve by a pedestrian who hurried across his path. Hearsay evidence of what was said by the man on the pavement at the scene of the accident as soon as the injured party had been attended to was held to be admissible in corroboration of the driver's evidence. But what was said twelve minutes later and away from the scene by the same man was held not to be part of the *res gestae* . . . In *R. v. Gibson*[88] the prosecutor gave evidence in a criminal trial that, immediately after he was struck by a stone, a woman going past, pointing to the prisoner's door, said: "The person who threw the stone went in there." This evidence was not objected to at the trial, but it was admitted by counsel for the prosecution in a Case Reserved that the evidence was incompetent. The conviction was quashed, and from their judgments it is clear that the learned judges who took part in the decision were far from questioning the correctness of counsel's admission. In *Gibson*'s case the words were closely associated in time and place with the event, the assault. But they were not directly connected with that event itself. They were not words spontaneously forced from the woman by the sight of the assault but were prompted by the sight of a man quitting the scene of an assault and they were spoken for purpose of helping to bring him to justice . . .

There is yet another proposition which can be affirmed, viz that for identification purposes in a criminal trial the event with which the words sought to be proved

[87] 1941 S.C. 363.
[88] (1887) 18 Q.B.D. 537.

must be so connected as to form part of the *res gestae* is the commission of the crime itself — the throwing of the stone, the striking of the blow, the setting fire to the building, or whatever the criminal act may be. Counsel for the Crown submitted that any relevant event or action may be accompanied by words which may have to be proved in order to bring out its true significance. There is a limited sense in which this is true, but it is not always true, and much depends on the use to be made of the evidence. In [*R. v. Christie*[89]] hearsay evidence of certain words uttered by a child, the victim of indecent assault, in the presence and hearing of the accused were held to be admissible in explanation of the demeanour of the accused in response to them. But the evidence was held inadmissible for the purpose of showing that the child identified the accused as his assailant. In the present case identification is the purpose for which the hearsay was introduced, and its admission goes far beyond anything that has been authorised by any reported case.

The strict criteria in *Teper* were relaxed in *Ratten v. R*,[90] in which the telephone operator took a call from the house at 1.15 p.m. It was made by an hysterical woman, the accused's wife, asking for the police. By 1.20 p.m the wife was dead. As discussed in the previous chapter, the statement "Get me the police, please" could be interpreted in two ways:

(1) as containing an inference, namely "My husband is attacking me". This would be an implied assertion and nowadays would be inadmissible as hearsay,[91]
(2) not as hearsay at all but as direct evidence of the speaker's state of mind.

There is also a third option:

(3) regardless of whether the statement was hearsay or direct evidence, as part of the *res gestae*.

The strict *Bedingfield* approach to contemporaneity would have undoubtedly led to the exclusion of the evidence. But the Privy Council held that the statement was made under the overwhelming pressure of the situation and thus admissible as an exception to hearsay. Lord Wilberforce said that the approach was not purely technical in the sense of lapse of time or change of venue. Although these were factors, they were not decisive. The judge must be satisfied that the statement was made in circumstances of spontaneity or of involvement so that the possibility of concoction could be disregarded:

Lord Wilberforce firstly argues that the statement is not hearsay but original evidence and continues:

[89] [1914] A.C. 545.
[90] [1971] 3 All E.R. 801.
[91] *R. v. Kearley* [1992] 2 All E.R. 345.

Ratten v. R. [1971] 3 All E.R. 801 at 806b–809e, *per* Lord Wilberforce

. . . If then, this evidence had been presented in this way, as evidence purely of relevant facts, its admissibility could hardly have been plausibly challenged. But the appellant submits that in fact this was not so. It is said that the evidence was tendered and admitted as evidence of an assertion by the deceased that she was being attacked by the accused, and that it was, so far, hearsay evidence, being put forward as evidence of the truth of facts asserted by his statement. It is claimed that the Chief Justice so presented the evidence to the jury and that, therefore, its admissibility, as hearsay, may be challenged.

Their Lordships, as already stated, do not consider that there is any hearsay element in the evidence, nor in their opinion was it so presented by the trial judge, but they think it right to deal with the appellant's submission on the assumption that there is: *i.e.* that the words said to have been used involve an assertion of the truth of some facts stated in them and that they may have been so understood by the jury. The Crown defended the admissibility of the words as part of the *res gestae*, a contention which led to the citation of numerous authorities.

The expression '*res gestae*' like many Latin phrases, is often used to cover situations insufficiently analysed in clear English terms. In the context of the law of evidence it may be used in at least three different ways:

1. When a situation of fact (*e.g.* a killing) is being considered, the question may arise when does the situation begin and when does it end. It may be arbitrary and artificial to confine the evidence to the firing of the gun or the insertion of the knife, without knowing in a broader sense what was happening. Thus in *O'Leary v. R.*[92] evidence was admitted of assaults, prior to the killing, committed by the accused during what was said to be a continuous orgy. As Dixon J. said[93]:

> Without evidence of what, during that time, was done by those men who took any significant part in the matter and especially evidence of the behaviour of the prisoner, the transaction of which the alleged murder formed an integral part could not be truly understood and, isolated from it, could only be presented as an unreal and not very intelligible event.

2. The evidence may be concerned with spoken words as such (apart from the truth of what they convey). The words are then themselves the res gestae or part of the *res gestae*, *i.e.* are the relevant facts or part of them.

3. A hearsay statement is made either by the victim of an attack or by a bystander — indicating directly or indirectly the identity of the attacker. The admissibility of the statement is then said to depend on whether it was made as part of the *res gestae*. A classical instance of this is the much debated case of *R. v. Bedingfield* and there are other instances of its application in reported cases. These tend to apply different standards, and some of them carry less than conviction. The reason, why this is so, is that concentration tends to be focused upon the opaque or at least imprecise Latin phrase rather than upon the basic reason for excluding the type of evidence which this group of cases is concerned with. There is no doubt what this reason is: it is twofold, the first is that there may be uncertainty as to the exact words used because of their transmission through the evidence of another person than the speaker. The second is because of the risk of concoction of false evidence by persons who have been victims of assault or accident. The first matter goes to weight. The person testifying to the words used is liable to cross-examination: the accused person (as he could not at the time when earlier reported cases were

[92] (1946) 73 C.L.R. 566.
[93] *ibid.* at 577.

decided) can give his own account if different. There is no such difference in kind or substance between evidence of what was said and evidence of what was done (for example, between evidence of what the victim said as to an attack and evidence that he (or she) was seen in a terrified state or was heard to shriek) as to require a total rejection of one and admission of the other.

The possibility of concoction, or fabrication, where it exists, is on the other hand an entirely valid reason for exclusion, and is probably the real test which judges in fact apply. In their Lordships' opinion this should be recognised and applied directly as the relevant test: the test should be not the uncertain one whether the making of the statement was in some sense part of the event or transaction. This may often be difficult to establish: such external matters as the time which elapses between the events and the speaking of the words (or vice versa), and differences in location being relevant factors but not, taken by themselves, decisive criteria. As regards statements made after the event it must be for the judge, by preliminary ruling, to satisfy himself that the statement was so clearly made in circumstances of spontaneity or involvement in the event that the possibility of concoction can be disregarded. Conversely, if he considers that the statement was made by way of narrative of a detached prior event so that the speaker was so disengaged from it as to be able to construct or adapt his account, he should exclude it. And the same must in principle be true of statements made before the event. The test should be not the uncertain one, whether the making of the statement should be regarded as part of the event or transaction. This may often be difficult to show. But if the drama, leading up to the climax, has commenced and assumed such intensity and pressure that the utterance can be safely regarded as a true reflection of what was unrolling or actually happening, it ought to be received. The expression '*res gestae*' may conveniently sum up these criteria, but the reality of them must always be kept in mind: it is this that lies behind the best reasoned of the judges' rulings.

A few illustrations may be given. One of the earliest and as often happens also the clearest, is that of Holt C.J. at *nisi prius* in *Thompson v. Trevanion*.[94] He allowed that 'what the wife said immediate upon the hurt received, and before that she had time to device or contrive anything for her own advantage' might be given in evidence . . .

In Australia, a leading authority is *Adelaide Chemical and Fertiliser Co. Ltd. v. Carlyle*[95] . . . Dixon J. with some caution reaches the conclusion that although English law, in the general view of lawyers, admits statements only as parts or details of a transaction not yet complete, while in America, greater recognition is given to the guarantee of truth provided by the spontaneity and the lack of time to devise or contrive, yet English decisions do show some reliance on the greater trustworthiness of statements made at once without reflection . . . The authorities show that there is ample support for the principle that hearsay evidence may be admitted if the statement providing it is made in such conditions (always being those of approximate but not exact contemporaneity) or involvement or pressure as to exclude the possibility of concoction or distortion to the advantage of the maker or the disadvantage of the accused.

. . . In the present case, in their Lordships' judgment, here was ample evidence of the close and intimate connection between the statement ascribed to the deceased and the shooting which occurred very shortly afterwards. They were closely associated in place and time. The way in which the statement came to be made (in a call for the police) and the tone of voice used, showed intrinsically that the statement was being forced from the deceased by an overwhelming pressure of contemporary event. It carried its own stamp of spontaneity and this was endorsed

[94] (1693) Skin. 402.
[95] (1940) 64 C.R. 5.4.

by the proved time sequence and the proved proximity of the deceased to the accused with his gun. Even on the assumption that there was an element of hearsay in the words used, they were safely admitted. The jury was, additionally, directed with great care as to the use to which they might be put. On all counts, therefore, their Lordships can find no error of law in the admission of the evidence . . .

Lord Wilberforce's judgment was accepted by the House of Lords in *R. v. Andrews*[96] where the victim was attacked and stabbed in his own flat by two men. One pleaded guilty to manslaughter and testified against Andrews. As his testimony was that of an accomplice, corroborating evidence was required. Andrews' possession of the victim's video, his lies to the police and the existence of forensic evidence made it a strong case. But the Crown also sought to use the victim's statements, after he had crawled to the neighbouring flat, at which point he identified his attackers. In the House of Lords, Lord Ackner quoted at length from *Ratten* and continued:

R. v. Andrews [1987] 1 All E.R. 513 at 519–521, *per* Lord Ackner

[*Ratten*] had previously been applied in *R. v. Nye and Loan*[97] by the Court of Appeal, where the victim of a criminal assault, which had occurred within a few yards of a police station, in a statement to police officers made within minutes of the assault, identified the defendant as the man who had hit him in the face. Lawton L.J. in giving the judgment of the court put, as he described it, a gloss on Lord Wilberforce's test by adding as an additional factor to be taken into consideration 'was there any real possibility of error?' I will return to this particular point later. In *R. v. Turnbull*[98] the Court of Appeal again applied the *Ratten* approach, where a man who had been mortally wounded staggered into the bar of a public house and in answer to questions put to him in the bar and in the ambulance on the wat to hospital he was understood to say that 'Ronnie Tommo' had done it. He died half an hour later in hospital. The victim had a Scottish accent and had consumed a great quantity of alcohol and the name 'Ronnie Tommo' was said to constitute his attempt to name the appellant. There have been two further decisions of the Court of Appeal in 1986 which have followed *Ratten*'s case. *R. v. Boyle*[99] involved the theft of a grandfather clock from an old lady to whose home the appellant had obtained access by a false representation. When he took away the clock she came out of the house with a piece of paper in her hand and when asked by a neighbour 'what is happening' she said 'I am coming for his address'. This statement was admitted to support the victim's account that the removal of the clock was against her will and to negative the defence that it was being taken away by the defendant with her consent, to have it repaired. I, for myself, would doubt whether this evidence was hearsay evidence. A clear issue in the case was the state of mind of the victim in relation to the removal of her clock. Her statement in the circumstances, as the car drove off, was evidence from which the jury could infer that she was not consenting to the clock being taken away. *R. v. O'Shea*[1] is a clearer case. The appellant was charged with burglary and manslaughter. The prosecution case against the appellant was that he went to a second floor flat and while he was

[96] [1987] 1 All E.R. 513.
[97] (1978) 66 Cr.App.R. 252.
[98] (1985) 80 Cr.App.R. 104.
[99] March 6, 1986 (unreported).
[1] July 24, 1986 (unreported).

battering down the door, the occupier of the flat, who was 79 years of age, attempted to escape through the window, slipped and fell some 20 feet and sustained bruising to his heart, which resulted in his death a week later. The statement made by the deceased to two passers-by an hour or so later, when they found him lying where he had fallen, that he had tried to get out of his flat because he was frightened that two robbers who were trying to break down his door would kill him and that he had therefore jumped from the window to escape, was admitted, as was a similar statement which he made to two police officers less than 20 minutes later.

Counsel for the appellant submitted, first, that there is no such exception to the rule against the admission of hearsay evidence as that said to be covered by the *res gestae* doctrine. Having regard to the authorities there is no substance in this proposition. Second he submitted that a hearsay statement cannot be admitted under the doctrine if made after the criminal act or acts charged have ceased. He contended that the hearsay statement must form part of the criminal act for which the accused is being tried. He relied strongly on *R. v. Bedingfield* . . . [That] exclamation was not admittedby Cockburn C.J. because 'It was something stated by her after it was all over, whatever it was, and after the act was completed'. Counsel for the appellant submits that the decision in *Ratten*'s case involved an extension of the existing hearsay rule and so was in conflict with the ruling of the majority in your Lordships' House in *Myers v. DPP*[2] that it is now too late to add a further exception to the rule against hearsay otherwise than by legislation. This submission is not assisted by the fact that both Lord Reid and Lord Hodgson, who were party to the majority decision in the *Myers* case, were also members of the Board in the *Ratten* case.

I do not accept that the principles identified by Lord Wilberforce involved any extension to the exception to the hearsay rule. Lord Wilberforce clarified the basis of the *res gestae* exception and isolated the matters which the trial judge, by preliminary ruling, must satisfy himself before admitting the statement. I respectfully accept the accuracy and the value of this clarification. Thus it must, of course, follow that *R. v. Bedingfield* would not be so decided today. Indeed, there could, as Lord Wilberforce observed, hardly be a case where the words uttered carried more clearly the mark of spontaneity and intense involvement.

The trial judge

My Lords, may I therefore summarise the position which confronts the trial judge when faced in a criminal case with an application under the *res gestae* doctrine to admit evidence of statements, with a view to establishing the truth of some fact thus narrated, such evidence being truly categorised as 'hearsay evidence'.

1) The primary question which the judge must ask himself is: can the possibility of concoction or distortion be disregarded?

2) To answer that question the judge must first consider the circumstances in which the particular statement was made, in order to satisfy himself that the event was so unusual or startling or dramatic as to dominate the thoughts of the victim, so that his utterance was an instinctive reaction to that event, thus giving no real opportunity for reasoned reflection. In such a situation the judge would be entitled to conclude that the involvement or the pressure of the event would exclude the possibility of concoction or distortion, providing that the statement was made in conditions of approximate but not exact contemporaneity.

3) In order for the statement to be sufficiently 'spontaneous' it must be so closely associated with the event which has excited the statement that it can fairly stated

[2] [1964] 2 All E.R. 881.

that the mind of the declarant was still dominated by the event. Thus the judge must be satisfied that the event which provided the trigger mechanism for the statement was still operative. The fact that the statement was made in answer to a question is but one factor to consider under this heading.

4) Quite apart from the time factor, there may be special features in the case, which relate to the possibility of concoction or distortion. In this instant appeal the defence relied on evidence to support the contention that the deceased had a motive of his own to fabricate or concoct, namely a malice which resided in him against [the accomplice] and the appellant because, so he believed, [the accomplice] had attacked and damaged his house and was accompanied by the appellant, who ran away, on a previous occasion. The judge must be satisfied that the circumstances were such that, having regard to the special feature of malice, there was no possibility of any concoction or distortion to the advantage of the maker or the disadvantage of the accused.

5) As to the possibility of error in the facts narrated in the statement, if only the ordinary fallibility of human recollection is relied on, this goes to the weight to be attached to and not the admissibility of the statement and is therefore a matter for the jury. However here again there may be special features that may give rise to the possibility of error. In the instant case there was evidence that the deceased had drunk to excess, well over double the permitted limit for driving a motor car. Another example would be where the identification was made in circumstances of particular difficulty or where the declarant suffered from defective eyesight. In such circumstances the trial judge must consider whether he can exclude the possibility of error.

. . . Where the trial judge has properly directed himself as to the correct approach to the evidence and there is material to entitle him to reach the conclusions which he did reach, then his decision is final, in the sense that it will not be interefered with on appeal . . .

The reported cases mainly deal with identification of the accused: *Ratten* and *Andrews* derogate from Lord Normand's strictures in *Teper* that the words should be connected with the criminal act itself. But the Court of Appeal decisions in *Nye and Loan*, *Turnbull* and *R. v. Carnall*[3] as well as the Privy Council in *Mills v. R*[4] all treat *Andrews* as authoritative. But the *res gestae* doctrine cannot be used as an excuse for failing to call a witness who should have been called. In *Tobi v. Nicholas*,[5] the accused was convicted of drink driving and failing to stop after an accident. He was identified when, 20 minutes after the accident, a police constable took the other driver to the defendant's home nearby where a damaged car was parked. When the defendant answered the door, the witness said "That's the guy". This was not admissible.

Statements accompanying relevant acts

Where a statement is made by a person performing an act and the statement contributes to an understanding of the action, the statement is admissible to prove the truth of its contents. The required conditions are:

[3] [1995] Crim.L.R. 944.
[4] [1995] Crim.L.R. 884.
[5] [1987] Crim.L.R. 774.

(1) that the statement relates to the act in question
(2) that it is more or less contemporaneous with the act —

> "... a contemporaneous declaration may be admissible as part of a transaction, but an act done cannot be varied or qualified by insulated declarations made at a later time."[6]

(3) that it is made by the person who is performing the act. In *Howe v. Malkin*[7] the issue was the position of a boundary. During the plaintiff's father's lifetime, work had been carried out on the land by builders and the plaintiff sought to prove statements made by his father at that time. Even though the builders' actions might be said to be vicariously those of the person who employed them, this evidence was rejected. Grove J. said:

Howe v. Malkin (1878) 40 L.T. 196, _per_ Grove J.

> It appears to me that the evidence was properly rejected; no act was shown to have been done by the plaintiff's father at the time of making the alleged statement, so that the declaration was by one person, and the accompanying act by another. That does not appear to me to come within the rule. The rule is that, though you cannot give in evidence a declaration, *per se*, yet when there is an act accompanied by a statement which is so mixed up with it as to become part of the *res gestae*, evidence of such statements may be given. The statements here do not come fairly within that rule.

The scope of this exception is potentially very broad. What must be the nature of an act to justify the statements accompanying it being admitted as evidence? One approach would be to require that the act itself possesses sufficient probative value to be relevant and admissible evidence before the statements are introduced to enhance that weight. But the authorities seek to expand these limits. In *Davidson v. Quirke*[8] the accused was charged with using premises for the purposes of betting and evidence was given by police officers of a number of phone calls to the premises from people seeking to place bets:

Davidson v. Quirke [1923] N.Z.L.R. 552 at 556, _per_ Salmond J.

If the testimony of the police officers was limited to the mere fact that on the day in question a large number of persons rang up the appellant's house within the space of an hour and twenty-five minutes, all evidence as to the contents of the communications being excluded, such testimony would prove merely that the premises were being used for a business of some kind, but would fall short of proving that they were being used for the business of betting. I am of opinion that, notwithstanding the general rule which excludes evidence of statements, the

[6] *Peacock v. Harris* (1836) 5 Ad & El 449 at 454, *per* Lord Denman.
[7] (1878) 40 L.T. 196.
[8] [1923] N.Z.L.R. 552.

contents of those telephone messages as received and testified to by the police officers are legally admissible in evidence. This is an illustration of the principle that, notwithstanding the rule against hearsay, where the purpose or meaning of an act done is relevant, evidence of contemporaneous declarations accompanying and explaining the act is admissible in proof of such purpose or meaning . . . since the act of numerous strangers in using the appellant's telephone for the purpose of betting is relevant to the issue, the statements made by them at the same time are admissible as explaining their actions and showing the purpose of them.

In *McGregor v. Stokes*[9] the facts were similar to *Davidson v. Quirke*. Herring C.J. put it:

McGregor v. Stokes [1952] V.L.R. 347 at 350–351, _per_ Herring C.J.

What the caller had to say in each case was an utterance that accompanied his act of calling, and also explained his purpose in calling. Without the words his act taken as a whole was incomplete. The fact that he has called on the telephone by itself tells you no more than that he has made the call and the making of the call unexplained is an equivocal act. Till you know what he has to say, you cannot tell whether he has rung up to ask the occupant about a dog or to invite him to dinner or what his purpose was. And so it is in the case of many things we do that our acts are partly conducted and partly utterance. A man walks into a shop for example, but the significance of his visit cannot be ascertained until he states his business. The learned author of Wigmore on Evidence has this to say about utterances that form a verbal part of an act:- 'A second kind of situation in which utterances are not offered testimonially arises when the utterance accompanies conduct to which it is desired to attach some legal effect. The conduct or act has intrinsically no definite significance, or only an ambiguous one, and its whole purport or tenor is to be more precisely ascertained by considering the words accompanying it. The utterance thus enters merely as a verbal part of the act, or, in common phrase, a 'verbal act' . . .

These authorities were used by Lord Browne-Wilkinson in *Kearley*[10] to suggest that the statements of the telephone callers were admissible as "verbal acts":

> One of the classic examples of evidence which does not fall within the hearsay rule is a statement by a third party accompanying and explaining his acts, sometimes called verbal acts. Such evidence is admitted not to prove the truth of what the third party said but to explain the acts of the third party.[11]

Were this analysis accepted, the hearsay rule would cease to exist since the "acts" of making a telephone call or calling at a house would suffice to permit the statements explaining the act to be given in evidence. This must be contrasted to the *Manchester Brewery* case where the acts were those of customers leaving their beer, tasted but unfinished. Unlike the callers in *Kearley*, these acts, even if left unexplained, would still be sufficiently relevant to be admissible in evidence.[12]

[9] [1952] V.L.R. 347.
[10] [1992] 2 All E.R. 345.
[11] *ibid.* at 386.
[12] Unless, of course, it were argued that such conduct contained implied assertions ("This beer is bad") so as to be excluded under the majority ruling in *Kearley*.

This "verbal act" analysis has also been applied to certain identification parade cases: in *R. v. McCay*,[13] the defendant was convicted of wounding with intent, the assault taking place in a pub. The licensee attended an identification parade and picked out the appellant sitting in position number eight. At the trial the witness testified as to the fact of identification but could not remember which position the appellant had occupied. The police inspector in charge of the parade testified that the appellant had occupied position number eight and that the witness had said to him "It is number eight". The Court of Appeal held that the police officer's testimony was admissible:

R. v. McCay [1991] 1 All E.R. 232 at 234–235, *per* Russell L.J.

We are satisfied, however, that the admissibility of the words . . . can be fully justified, albeit spoken by the witness in the absence of the appellant, because the contemporary statement accompanied a relevant act and was necessary to explain that relevant act. The statement was not relevant as to the identity of the assailant, but it was relevant to the identification of the suspect by the witness. Whether that identification assisted the jury was a matter for them. In asserting that the man whom the witness thought was the assailant was numbered 8 on the parade, [the witness] was doing no more and no less than explaining his physical and intellectual activity in making the identification at the material time.

Counsel for the appellant was constrained to acknowledge that if the words 'It is number eight' had been accompanied by some physical touching of the appellant by [the witness] . . . he could not object to [the police inspector] giving evidence of what he heard from the witness. The reason for this concession was that the words would then accompany a physical act, whereas no such physical act was part of the identification process employed in the instant case. We consider this to be a distinction without a difference. In our judgment the procedure of looking at the suspect through the mirror, employing the physical activity of seeing coupled with the intellectual activity of recognising are together sufficient to amount to a relevant act in respect of which accompanying words are admissible.

This is surely misconceived as this "physical activity" of seeing is not a relevant act for the purposes of this exception. Separated from the statement, the "act" of looking at the parade is irrelevant and would not be adduced but for the statement. It can be compared to a more straightforward hearsay situation where a witness observes a car number plate, recognises the relevant letters and numbers and says to a police officer within a short space of time "It was ABC 123". Suggesting that the officer could testify as to what was said because it was a statement accompanying a relevant act of "observing a number plate" would be patently absurd. The decision in *McCay* is also contrary to the authorities in *Christie*[14] and *Teper*.[15] However, although it is artificial to apply the *res gestae* doctrine to the facts in *McCay*, no unfairness is being done to the defendant in that

[13] [1991] 1 All E.R. 232.
[14] [1914] A.C. 545.
[15] [1952] A.C. 480.

case. The witness has testified that he indeed made an identification,[16] although now he cannot remember who it was. Allowing the officer to testify as to the position is justifiable because this is a matter within his knowledge and on which the officer can be examined. Equally the identifying witness is present in court, available to be questioned by the accused. Considered in this way, no problem of hearsay or of *res gestae* arises.[17]

Statements concerning physical sensation

Where a person makes a statement about their contemporaneous physical feelings, that statement is admissible evidence of that fact, although not of the causes of such feelings. Declarations of hunger by a child may be admissible in a case involving child neglect.[18] But statements by a child to a teacher and a foster parent about sexual abuse by a close family relative are not admissible, although presumably certain aspects of such statements may well come within this aspect of the rule. Although such aspects may be admissible as to the fact of abuse, they have no probative weight as to the identity of the abuser.[19]

Pain,[20] disgust,[21] fear[22] — all may be proved under this exception. But the admissibility is limited to the physical sensation itself and cannot be used collaterally to prove, for example, the cause of such feelings. In *R. v. Gloster*,[23] the deceased was the victim of an illegal abortion. The prosecution sought to introduce statements by the deceased not only as to how she was feeling but as to the fact of the abortion and as to who had performed it. Charles J. held that the "admissible statements were to be confined to contemporaneous symptoms". The authorities show that "contemporaneous" is to be interpreted to include the recent past: "I felt poorly after that meal my husband cooked yesterday".

Statements concerning the maker's state of mind

Statements detailing a physical sensation are analogous to those detailing an emotion or a belief. Indeed these categories obviously overlap. Is a feeling of disgust a physical feeling or a state of mind? This category admits statements which reveal the speaker's emotions,[24] knowledge, beliefs[25] or

[16] Unlike the witnesses in *R. v. Osborne and Virtue* [1973] 1 All E.R. 649.
[17] *Alexander v. R* (1981) 34 ALR 289; comment by Birch in [1990] Crim.L.R. 338 at 340–341.
[18] *R. v. Conde* (1867) 10 Cox C.C. 547.
[19] *Re K.* (1989) 139 New L.J. 864.
[20] *Aveson v. Lord Kinnaird* (1805) 6 East 188; *Gilbey v. Great Western Railway Co.* (1910) 102 L.T. 202.
[21] *R. v. Gott* (1922) 16 Cr.App.R. 87.
[22] *R. v. Vincent* (1840) 9 C. & P. 275.
[23] (1888) 16 Cox C.C. 471.
[24] Such as fear (*Neil v. North Antrim Magistrates' Court* [1992] 4 All E.R. 846 at 854) or marital affection (*Trelawney v. Coleman* (1817) 1 B. & Ald. 90).
[25] See statements admitted to prove political opinion — *R. v. Tooke* (1794) 25 State Tr. 344.

intentions. Lies or delusions do not come under this heading since these are provable as original, non-hearsay, evidence since the statements would not be relied on for the truth of their contents but for the reverse!

Ratten again provides a useful example. Even were the wife's plea for help not spontaneous (and as such admissible under the first category of *res gestae)*, her agitation and fear were in themselves relevant facts since they tend to disprove the defence argument of accident. Not only her tone of voice but also her words could be adduced as evidence of that state of mind. But are we dealing with an exception to hearsay or with original evidence here?[26] If the state of mind (or a physical sensation) is a fact relevant to a fact in issue, are statements which reveal that emotion, pain, etc being relied on for their truth or because they are in themselves the manifestation of that inner state?

The statement is adduced to prove the state of mind. In handling stolen goods, the Crown must show that the accused "knew or believed" the goods to be stolen. Were the defendant to answer the question "Where did the goods come from?" "Oh, they fell off the back of a lorry", this would be admissible to prove his or her belief that the goods were stolen. This must be distinguished from the burden of proof on the Crown to show that the goods were in fact stolen and the statement could not be used for that purpose.[27] In *Thomas v. Connell*,[28] it was alleged that a bankrupt made a payment to one creditor in order to defraud others. It was necessary to show that he was aware of his financial state at that time in order to prove the fraud. While the statement he made at the time of the payment was admissible to show his knowledge, that statement could not be used to prove the fact of insolvency itself.

The issue is whether the state of mind is relevant. In *Blastland*[29] the accused was charged with the murder of a young boy. The defence was that another person, Mark, was the killer (who later confessed to the killing but withdrew the confession). Mark had shown knowledge about the murder before the discovery of the body and had been in a very agitated state at that time. Under this exception, Mark's statements are admissible to prove his knowledge of the killing but the House of Lords held that Mark's state of mind was not relevant:

> . . . statements made to a witness by a third party are not excluded by the hearsay rule when they are put in evidence solely to prove the state of mind either of the maker of the statement or the person to whom it was made. What a person said or heard said may well be the best and most direct evidence of that person's state of mind. This principle can only apply, however, when the state of mind evidenced by the statement is either itself directly in issue at the trial or is of direct and immediate relevance to the issues which arise at the trial.[30]

[26] Carter P., "Hearsay: Whether and Whither?" (1993) L.Q.R. 573 at 585.
[27] *R. v. Hulbert* (1979) 69 Cr. App. R. 243; *R. v. Overington* [1978] Crim.L.R. 692; *R. v. McDonald* [1980] Crim.L.R. 242.
[28] (1838) 3 M. & W. 267.
[29] [1985] 2 All E.R. 1095.
[30] *ibid.* at 1099, *per* Lord Bridge.

Their Lordships felt that there were many different ways that Mark could have come by his knowledge and that admitting the statement would give rise to collateral issues. But the key fact in issue was whether Blastland caused the death of the victim. Mark's early knowledge of the killing was a circumstance which rendered that conclusion less probable and thus was relevant under normal rules.

In criminal law, the prosecution always bears the burden of proving mens rea. Although intent is often inferred from the offence itself, statements by the accused that they intend to commit an offence are admissible. In *R. v. Moghal*[31] the defendant was jointly accused of murder with his lover, S. She was tried separately and acquitted. His defence was that he was a terrified spectator and it was accepted by the Court of Appeal that a tape-recorded statement made six months previously by S to the effect that she intended to kill the victim was admissible. Not only are such statements admissible but such a declaration can be used as evidence that she still possessed the intent to kill six months later.[32]

It is more controversial whether it is justifiable to infer from a declaration of intent that the intended action was in fact carried out. In *R. v. Buckley*,[33] a first instance case, the accused was charged with the murder of a police officer. The victim had told his superior officer that he had heard that Buckley was "at his old game of thieving again" and that "he intended to watch his movements that night". The statement was admitted as evidence, not merely of the officer's state of mind but from which the inference could be drawn that the officer in fact acted in this way and thus provided opportunity and motive for the accused. As such, the state of mind becomes relevant to an issue and furthermore any inferences possess greater weight because the statement was made by the police officer to a senior officer in the course of his duty.

No such obligation existed in *R. v. Wainwright*.[34] The statement by the victim of a killing that she was going to pay a social visit the accused's premises was held by Cockburn C.J. to be inadmissible:

> It was no part of the act of leaving, but only an incidental remark. It was only a statement of intention which may or may not have been carried out. She would have gone away under any circumstance[35]

A similar conclusion was reached in *R. v. Thomson*[36] the defendant was charged with procuring an abortion on a woman who had subsequently died. The defence was that the victim operated on herself and sought to introduce a witness to testify that the victim had stated that she intended to

[31] (1977) 65 Cr.App.R. 56.
[32] Or indeed, a month earlier — *Re Fletcher, Reading v. Fletcher* [1917] 1 Ch. 339.
[33] (1873) 13 Cox C.C. 293.
[34] (1875) 13 Cox C.C. 171.
[35] *ibid.* at 172.
[36] [1912] 3 K.B. 19.

operate on herself and a later statement that she had indeed carried out the operation. The later statement was more clearly hearsay but both were excluded.

These authorities suggest, however weakly, that declarations of intention, while evidence of mens rea, cannot be used as evidence that the act was actually performed. The opposite is the case in Australia where in *Walton v. R*,[37] a husband was charged with the murder of his wife and a witness was permitted to testify that the victim received a phone call and announced that she was going to meet her husband in the town centre. Similarly in *Mutual Life Insurance v. Hillmon*[38] the insurance company contested a claim on a life insurance policy taken out on the life of Hillmon. A body had been found in Colorado, alleged to be Hillmon. The insurers sought to introduce letters written by one Walters which stated his intention of accompanying Hillmon on the trip. The U.S. Supreme Court admitted the letters as evidence of Walters' intentions, from which, presumably, the jury might draw appropriate inferences.

[37] (1989) 84 A.L.R. 59.
[38] (1892) 145 U.S. 284.

18

STATUTORY EXCEPTIONS TO HEARSAY IN CRIMINAL PROCEEDINGS: THE CRIMINAL JUSTICE ACT 1988 AND OTHER ANIMALS

DOCUMENTARY HEARSAY IN CRIMINAL CASES — A BRIEF HISTORY

Myers v. DPP[1] highlighted the difficulties of using documents, especially business records, as evidence in a criminal prosecution. Such documents were frequently hearsay, as in *Myers*, because the person whose responsibility it was to keep the records invariably relied on information from other people — the information from the shop floor was documented in a series of stages before being archived in the Austin motor company's records. Despite the multiple hearsay involved, the quality of the information recorded remained high since everything was done within the course of employment by workers whose jobs would be at risk if they performed these tasks incompetently. Lord Reid recognised the reliability of the evidence and the need for reform:

Myers v. DPP [1965] A.C. 1001 at 1023d–1024a, *per* Lord Reid

At the end of their judgment, the Court of Criminal Appeal gave a different reason. 'In our view the admission of such evidence does not infringe the hearsay rule because its probative value does not depend upon the credit of an unidentified person but rather on the circumstances in which the record is maintained and the inherent probability that it will be correct rather than incorrect.' That, if I may say so, is undeniable as a matter of common sense. But can it be reconciled with the existing law? I need not discuss the question on general lines because I think that this ground is quite inconsistent with the established rule regarding public records. Public records are prima facie evidence of the fact which they contain but it is quite clear that a record is not a public record within the scope of that rule unless it is open to inspection by at least a section of the public. Unless we are to alter that rule how can we possibly say that a private record not open to public inspection can be prima facie evidence of the truth of its contents? I would agree that it is quite unreasonable to refuse to accept as prima facie evidence a record obviously well

[1] [1965] A.C. 1001.

kept by public officers and proved never to have been discovered to contain a wrong entry though frequently consulted by officials, merely because it is not open to inspection. But that is settled law. This seems to me to be a good example of the wide repercussions which would follow if we accepted the judgment of the Court of Criminal Appeal. I must therefore regretfully decline to accept this reason as correct in law.

Although the Civil Evidence Acts of 1968 and 1995 have introduced a comprehensive code in relation to adducing hearsay evidence in civil proceedings, reform of the hearsay rule in criminal procedure has been piecemeal. Initially this was through section 1 of the Criminal Evidence Act 1965 which went some way towards overturning the effect of *Myers*: documentary records compiled within a trade or a business were admissible, so long as they were based on information supplied by people with direct knowledge and those people were unavailable or could not be expected to give evidence. This was restrictively interpreted: a car's registration document was not evidence of the engine number[2] nor was a Home Office record evidence of legal immigrant status.[3]

The Eleventh Report of the Criminal Law Revision Committee[4] in 1972 failed to lead to wholesale revisions of criminal evidence. But the Police and Criminal Evidence Act 1984, following certain of the committee's recommendations, repealed section 1 of the Criminal Evidence Act 1965 and replaced and extended the exception through sections 68 and 69. Under section 68, the document had to form part of a record compiled by a person under a duty to compile it and the information must have been supplied directly by a person with personal knowledge or to that person by someone else with personal knowledge or to such people by others acting under a duty to record the information. The person with personal knowledge must be unavailable for one of the reasons given in section 68(2).

Section 68 removed the "business or trade" limitation, ensuring a wider range of admissible documents but still only applied to records: the limits can be seen in *R. v. Cunningham*[5] where the accused was charged with smuggling drugs from Swaziland and sought to rely on statements taken from witnesses in Swaziland who were unable to attend the trial. But such proofs were only admissible under section 68 if they formed part of a record and so the conviction was upheld. Section 68 has now itself been repealed by sections 23 and 24 of the Criminal Justice Act 1988. Before discussing the scope of these provisions, it is necessary to consider the impact of section 69 of the Police and Criminal Evidence Act 1984 which laid down conditions for the admissibility of documents produced by computers.

[2] *R. v. Sealby* [1965] 1 All E.R. 701; reversed 109 S.J. 512.
[3] *R. v. Patel* [1981] 3 All E.R. 94.
[4] Cmnd. 4991 (1972).
[5] [1989] Crim.L.R. 435; *cf. R. v. Iqbal* [1990] 3 All E.R. 787.

Documents Produced by Computer

The draftsmen of the 1984 legislation recognised that documents of all kinds were increasingly produced by computer and s.69, which is still operative, laid down the requirements for the admissibility of computer records in criminal proceedings[6]:

> 69.—(1) In any proceedings, a statement in a document produced by a computer shall not be admissible as evidence of any fact stated therein unless it is shown —
>
> a) that there are no reasonable grounds for believing that the statement is inaccurate because of improper use of the computer;
>
> b) that at all material times the computer was operating properly, or if not, that any respect in which it was not operating properly or was out of operation was not such as to affect the production of the document or the accuracy of its contents; and
>
> c) that any relevant conditions specified in rules of court under subsection (2) below are satisfied.
>
> (2) Provision may be made by rules of court requiring that in any proceedings where it is desired to give a statement in evidence by virtue of this section such information concerning the statement as may be required by the rules shall be provided in such form and at such time as may be so required.

The conditions in section 69 can be satisfied by a certificate from "a person in a responsible position in relation to the operation of the computer" that the computer was properly used and in proper working order and the original supplier of the information must not be available to give evidence.[7] Evidence of the proper working of the computer can also be given orally by a wider range of witnesses.[8]

Section 69 applies whether the computer records are characterised as either original or hearsay evidence. Obviously business records are often hearsay documents but when the computer is used as a purely mechanical apparatus, the output might well be original evidence. For example, in *R. v. Neville*[9] the evidence adduced was the itemised record made by a phone company of the calls made from a mobile phone. This document was produced automatically by the company's computer system and was accepted as original evidence.

For several years, it was suggested that such original evidence was unaffected by section 69 which was considered to affect only hearsay documents. In *R. v. Harper and Minors*[10] the Court of Appeal said that

[6] The Civil Evidence Act 1968, s.5 had prescribed detailed safeguards with regard to the use of computer-produced documents in civil proceedings. This section was repealed by Civil Evidence Act 1995 and not replaced.

[7] Police and Criminal Evidence Act 1984, Sched. 3, para. 8.

[8] *R. v. Shepherd* [1993] 1 All E.R. 225 at 231b.

[9] [1991] Crim.L.R. 288; *R. v. Spiby* [1991] Crim.L.R. 199.

[10] [1989] 2 All E.R. 208.

section 69 did not provide a self-contained code of admissibility but merely laid down additional requirements for the admissibility of a computer record which had already passed the hurdle of section 68. The misconceptions in this judgment were criticised[11] and were corrected by the House of Lords in *Shepherd*. The case involved computerised checkouts which read bar codes on the item being purchased to recognise the item being bought, to identify the price and to generate a till roll. The evidence against the alleged shoplifter was that the till roll showed no trace of the items found in her possession. The provenance of the till rolls was explained to the court by the store detective who described the operations, had collected all the till rolls and examined them without finding any trace of the relevant items. The court was faced with the questions, firstly, whether section 69 was relevant and, secondly, whether the detective's testimony satisfied the conditions of the section:

R. v. Shepherd [1993] 1 All E.R. 225 at 228–231, *per* Lord Griffiths

The object of section 69 of the Act is clear enough. It requires anyone who wishes to introduce computer evidence to produce evidence that will establish that it is safe to rely on the documents produced by the computer. This is an affirmative duty emphatically stated in subsection (1) . . . Such a duty cannot be discharged without evidence by the application of the presumption that the computer is working correctly expressed in the maxim *omnia praesumuntur rite esse acta* as appears to be suggested in some of these cases. Nor does it make any difference whether the computer document has been produced with or without the input of information provided by the human mind and thus may or may not be hearsay. If the document produced by the computer is hearsay it will be necessary to comply with the provisions of section 24 of the Criminal Justice Act 1988, the successor to section 68 of the Police and Criminal Evidence Act 1985, before the document can be admitted as evidence and it will also be necessary to comply with the provisions of section 69 of the 1984 Act. I see no warrant for an interpretation of the 1984 Act which limits the operation of section 69 to cases that fall within section 68 of that Act or section 24 of the Criminal Justice Act 1988. This, however, was the construction of the 1984 Act adopted by the Court of Appeal in *R. v. Minors*, *R. v. Harper* . . . The court then gave as its reason for confining the operation of section 69 to cases falling within section 68 the fact that in *R. v. Ewing*[12] a computer print-out of an appellant's bank account was held admissible under section 1 Criminal Evidence Act 1965 which was the forerunner of section 68 of the 1984 Act from which the court drew the inference that Parliament must have intended section 69 to apply only to computer documents falling within the meaning of s.68. I cannot accept this reasoning. When *R. v. Ewing* was decided the safeguards later introduced by section 69 had not yet been enacted and I see no reason to suppose that because of the decision in *R. v. Ewing* Parliament intended the language of section 69 which is in general terms to be read in a restricted sense. It is surely every bit as important that a document produced by a computer and tendered as proof of guilt should be reliable whether or not it contains hearsay.

The principal argument for the appellant starts with the proposition that the store detective was not 'a person occupying a responsible position in relation to the

[11] *ibid.* — commentary by Birch.
[12] [1983] 2 All E.R. 645.

operation of the computer' within the meaning of para. 8(d) of Sch 3 and therefore was not qualified to sign a certificate for the purpose of providing proof of the matters contained in section 69(1). This I accept. Although the store detective understood the operation of the computer and could speak of its reliability she had no responsibility for its operation.

I cannot however accept the next step in the appellant's argument, which is that oral evidence is only acceptable if given by a person who is qualified to sign the certificate . . .

Documents produced by computers are an increasingly common feature of all business and more and more people are becoming familiar with their uses and operation. Computers vary immensely in their complexity and in the operations they perform. The nature of the evidence to discharge the burden of showing that there has been no improper use of the computer and that it was operating properly will inevitably vary from case to case. The evidence must be tailored to suit the needs of the case. I suspect that it will very rarely be necessary to call an expert and that in the vast majority of cases it will be possible to discharge the burden by calling a witness who is familiar with the operation of the computer in the sense of knowing what the computer is required to do and who can say that it is doing it properly.

The store detective's testimony was admissible as it related to the proper functioning of the computer at the time of the offence and satisfied the requirements of section 69(1). In *East and West Transport Ltd v. DPP*[13] evidence was given of proper functioning of a computerised weighbridge some months before the crime. This did not satisfy the conditions. Even relatively trivial matters can render the evidence inadmissible under section 69: in *McKeown v. DPP*[14] the malfunctioning of the clock on a Lion Intoximeter was sufficient to infringe section 69(1)(b).

Whether the section 69 safeguards are still necessary is doubtful. There seems little reason not to rely on the presumption that a machine is functioning properly in the absence of any evidence to the contrary. The Law Commission in its report on hearsay in civil proceedings found it difficult to distinguish between a map produced by radar (as in the *Statue of Liberty*[15]) and computer-generated documents. There is little reason for having different regimes for proving such documents.[16] As a result the Civil Evidence Act 1995 contains no special provisions for computerised records which are dealt with similarly to other records.

Criminal Justice Act 1988, Section 23 — First-hand Documentary Hearsay

Section 68 of the Police and Criminal Evidence Act 1984 survived only a short time. The Roskill Committee on fraud trials recognised the need for wider admissibility of documentary evidence in such cases and Pt. 2 of the

[13] [1995] Crim.L.R. 642.
[14] [1995] Crim.L.R. 69.
[15] [1968] 2 All E.R. 195.
[16] Law Commission, *The Hearsay Rule in Civil Proceedings* (1993 Law Comm. 216) Cm. 2321 para. 3.20.

Criminal Justice Act 1988 went some way towards meeting that need. For the first time, section 23 provides a general exception to the hearsay rule in criminal proceedings allowing for first-hand documentary hearsay to be admissible:

23.—(1) Subject —

a) to subsection (4) below

b) to paragraph 1A of Schedule 2 to the Criminal Appeal Act 1968 (evidence given orally at original trial to be given orally at retrial); and

c) to section 69 of the Police and Criminal Evidence Act 1984 (evidence from computer records),

a statement made by a person in a document shall be admissible in criminal proceedings as evidence of any fact of which direct oral evidence by him would be admissible if —

i) the requirements of one of the paragraphs of subsection (2) below are satisfied; or
ii) the requirements of subsection (3) below are satisfied.

(2) The requirements mentioned in subsection (1)(i) above are —

a) that the person who made the statement is dead or by reason of his bodily or mental condition unfit to attend as a witness;
b) that —
   i) the person who made the statement is outside the United Kingdom; and
   ii) it is not reasonably practicable to secure his attendance; or

c) that all reasonable steps have been taken to find the person who made the statement, but that he cannot be found.

(3) The requirements mentioned in subsection (1)(ii) above are —

a) that the statement was made to a police officer or some other person charged with the duty of investigating offences or charging offenders; and

b) that the person who made it does not give oral evidence through fear or because he is being kept out of the way.

(4) Subsection (1) above does not render admissible a confession made by an accused person that would not be admissible under section 76 of the Police and Criminal Evidence Act 1984.

The following points should be noted:

(1) this is *a general exception to the hearsay rule*. It is not limited to a particular class of documents or makers of documents. As long as the maker of the document is unavailable to give oral evidence in one of the ways specified in subsections (2) or (3), the document itself can be admitted as evidence of its contents.

(2) the statement can be made in *any document* but in this section, there is no restriction about documents created in the course of a trade or business and thus 'document' can encompass not just records, business letters but all forms of maps, plans, discs, tapes, films, diaries, shopping lists.[17]

(3) *proof of contents* of the document are facilitated under the provisions of s.27:

> 27.—Where a statement contained in a document is admissible as evidence in criminal proceedings, it may be proved —
>
> a) by the production of that document; or
> b) (whether or not that document is still in existence) by the production of a copy of that document, or of the material part of it,
>
> authenticated in such manner as the court may approve; and it is immaterial for the purposes of this subsection how many removes there are between a copy and the original,

(4) there is a *broad definition of a "statement"*, namely any representation of fact whether made in words or otherwise. The statement must be made by a person. Normally the absent witness will have written the document but as long as it has been verified by him or her, it remains their statement. Often these authenticated statements will be made to police officers: in *R. v. McGillivray*,[18] the victim of an arson attack made a statement to the police in hospital. It was read back to him in the presence of a nurse and he agreed that it was accurate. But he was in no state to sign the document. The Court of Appeal upheld the decision to admit it under s.23. The fact that the document was authenticated orally presents no problem. However the deceased never saw the document and thus the authentication was itself apparently based on hearsay.[19] This might be contrasted with *Re D.*[20] which concerned wardship proceedings in which maternal grandparents sought custody of a child from the father. The mother, now deceased, had had an interview with her solicitor concerning a divorce. The notes of that interview, although containing statements by the mother about violence in the family, were not verified by her and were they to be tendered in a criminal case would not constitute "*a statement by a person in a document*" for the purposes of s.23.

[17] See 147, *et seq.* for a discussion on what constitutes a document.
[18] (1992) 97 Cr.App.R. 232.
[19] *Cf. R. v. Chapman* [1969] 2 All E.R. 321 where the repetition of the doctor's statement that he had no objection to administering a breath test was not hearsay. In this case, the court is interested in the words of authentication, *i.e.* the fact that the statement was made. See a similar situation with documents used to refresh memory, see *R. v. Kelsey* (1982) 74 Cr.App.R. 213.
[20] [1986] 2 FLR 189.

(5) the statement *must be tendered as evidence of fact*. Statements of opinion are not admissible under section 23 even if the absent witness would have been allowed to testify in this way. However section 30 does allow for expert reports to be admissible (with the leave of the court) as evidence, whether or not the person making the report attends to give oral evidence.

(6) the *documents do not constitute corroboration*. Documents admissible under section 23 (or section 24) are evidence of their contents but are not, under paragraph 2 of Schedule 2 of the 1988 Act, capable of corroborating the original evidence of the maker of the statement.[21]

(7) the section is *limited to direct hearsay*. The only contents of the document which are admissible are those statements of which the absent witness could have given direct oral evidence. Normally witnesses cannot testify to hearsay. There are situations where this is possible (*res gestae* would be an example) and Birch suggests that section 23 allows any statement of which the person creating the document could have given evidence, thus including statements made by a third party which would have been admissible under another exception to hearsay.[22]

(8) *section 23 only cures the vice of hearsay*. The statement is admissible as evidence of any fact of which direct oral evidence would be admissible. The provision does not permit other exclusionary rules to be bypassed by reducing the offending information (for example, evidence about the accused's character or antecedents) to writing. A further example would be the incompetent witness whose statement does not become admissible because it is written down and signed. In *H. v. H.*[23] the statements of a five-year-old to a social worker did not become admissible simply because they were written down.

(9) *the Act does not impose additional conditions* on already admissible evidence. Under section 28(1)(a), section 23 and its preconditions do not prejudice the admissibility of hearsay statements that might be admissible in some other way, *e.g.* under the common law exceptions to hearsay, confessions under section 76 of the Police and Criminal Evidence Act 1984 or documents admissible under other statutory exceptions. Similarly, under section 28(1)(b) the court's discretion to exclude evidence is not fettered by these provisions:

> 28.—(1) Nothing in this Part of the Act shall prejudice —
>
> (a) the admissibility of a statement not made by a person while giving oral evidence which is admissible otherwise than by virtue of this Part of this Act; or

[21] Such a provision seems redundant since at common law, corroboration must emanate from an independent source. Also there will only be a few cases under s.24 (and none under s.23) where a document will be admitted AND the maker of the statement attends to testify.

[22] See correspondence in [1989] Crim.L.R. 603.

[23] [1989] 3 All E.R. 740.

(b) any power of a court to exclude at its discretion a statement admissible by virtue of this Part of this Act.

Under section 23, documentary hearsay is admissible under certain conditions, the key ones being those which relate to the unavailability of the witness. There are three possibilities[24] under subsection (2) and a further one under subsection (3).

under section 23(2):

(1) where the maker of the statement is *dead or mentally or physically unfit* to attend as a witness. In *R. v. Setz-Dempsey*[25] the witness identified the accused but later became mentally disordered and, although he could physically attend court, could not give coherent testimony. It was held that section 23 applied to the capacity of the witness to give evidence and not simply the physical act of getting to court.

(2) where the maker of the statement is *outside the U.K.*[26] and it is not reasonably practicable to secure his or her attendance. Efforts must be made to secure attendance and the court will not assume that it is 'not reasonably practicable' from the sole fact that the witness is abroad. In *R. v. Bray*[27] the prosecution only realised at the date of trial that the witness was abroad and had been away seven months. They were not permitted to call section 23 in aid of their incompetence. It is similar for the defence: in *R. v. Mattey and Queeley*[28] the defence wished to rely on written statements from a couple living in France. One of the accused testified that the witnesses had recently found new jobs and would find the cost of travel difficult. There was no evidence of any formal efforts to secure the witnesses' attendance. Even on the lower burden of proof for the defence (on the balance of probabilities), the application was rejected. However the subsection talks of an inability to "secure" attendance and should the court obstruct the introduction of documentary evidence if there is evidence that witnesses outside the jurisdiction are unwilling, for good reason or not, to attend court?

(3) where reasonable steps have been taken but the *maker of the statement cannot be found*. But the witness cannot be anonymous and that a party seeking to rely on a document must satisfy the court as to the identity of the person before it will be admitted.

[24] These are more limited than the Police and Criminal Evidence Act 1984, s.68 which mentioned the possibilities of the maker of the statement not being able to recollect or not being able to be identified, although these might be now brought under section 23(2)(a) or (c).
[25] [1994] Crim.L.R. 123.
[26] This means physically outside — it does not include a diplomat resident in the U.K. (*R. v. Jimenez-Paez* [1993] 98 Cr.App.R. 239.
[27] [1988] Crim.L.R. 829.
[28] [1995] Crim.L.R. 308.

under section 23(3):
even where the maker of the statement is available, section 23(3) creates a more controversial situation where documentary hearsay can be used. This is to deal with the intimidation of witnesses. Their statements can be admissible where those statements were made to a person charged with investigating offences and where *the maker of the statement is in fear or being kept "out of the way"*.

This has to be compared with section 13(3) of the Criminal Justice Act 1925 which provided:

> 13.—(3) Where any person has been committed for trial for any offence, the deposition of any person taken before the examining justices may, if the conditions hereinafter set out are satisfied, without further proof be read as evidence on the trial of that person, whether for that offence or for any other offence arising out of the same transaction, or set of circumstances, as that offence.
>
> The conditions hereinbefore referred to are the following:
>
> a) The deposition must be a deposition either . . . of a witness who is proved at the trial by the oath of a credible witness to be dead or insane, or so ill as not to be able to travel, or to be kept out of the way by means of the procurement of the accused or on his behalf;

This provision has been cited in full for purposes of comparison. It was repealed and replaced by section 68 and Schedule 2 of the Criminal Procedure and Investigations Act 1996. This Schedule provides:

> 1.—(1) Sub-paragraph (2) applies if —
>
> (a) a written statement has been admitted in evidence in proceedings before a magistrates' court inquiring into an offence as examining justices,
>
> (b) in those proceedings a person has been committed for trial,
>
> (c) . . .
>
> (d) the statement purports to be signed by a justice of the peace, and
>
> (e) sub-paragraph (3) does not prevent sub-paragraph (2) applying.
>
> (2) Where this sub-paragraph applies the statement may without further proof be read as evidence on the trial of the accused, whether for the offence for which he was committed for trial or for any other offence arising out of the same transaction or set of circumstances.
>
> (3) Sub-paragraph (2) does not apply if —
>
> (a) it is proved that the statement was not signed by the justice by whom it purports to have been signed,
>
> (b) the court of trial at its discretion orders that sub-paragraph (2) shall not apply, or
>
> (c) a party to the proceedings objects to sub-paragraph (2) applying.
>
> (4) If a party to the proceedings objects to sub-paragraph (2) applying the court of trial may order that the objection shall have no effect if the court considers it to be in the interests of justice so to order.

Both the 1925 and 1996 Acts deal with evidence given before magistrates at committal proceedings. The 1996 legislation is broader than section 13(3). It still requires that the statements are admitted as part of the committal proceedings before a magistrates' court . But it does not require that the witness's absence is caused by the accused and the judge would be able to take into account a range of reasons for the witness's absence. Further, a literal reading of the section suggests that the witness need not even be absent and that the statement might be read as the witness's evidence-in-chief. It is a matter of judicial discretion if such a statement is to be admitted but that discretion exists even where a party to the proceedings objects to the introduction of the written statement.

This can be contrasted with the history of the 1925 legislation which reveals a restrictive interpretation. In *R. v. O'Loughlin*[29] two witnesses were scared and unwilling to testify. The prosecution at the Central Criminal Court argued unsuccessfully that their depositions should be admitted under section 13(3). This was rejected revealing the limitations of the provision: firstly, although threats were made to the witnesses, there was no evidence that they were by the accused or those acting on his behalf, even though the threats obviously emanated from people with the accused's interests at heart. This would not be relevant under s.68. Secondly section 13 said that the deposition "may be read", vesting a discretion in the court which must be read alongside section 78 of the Police and Criminal Evidence Act 1984. This would allow the judge to refuse to admit evidence where its admission would be adverse to the fairness of the proceedings. In any section 13 application,[30] the jury would not see the witnesses or hear them cross-examined. The significance of that has to be measured by the nature of the evidence in the deposition. If it is the sole or critical evidence against the accused, the inability to cross-examine may well be crucial. If the deposition is long and detailed with many contested points, that might be another factor. The same considerations of fairness would apply with a section 68 application:

R. v. O'Loughlin [1988] 3 All E.R. 431 at 437d–h, *per* Kenneth Jones J.

. . . how could a jury exercise its judgment to decide that the contents of those depositions were true and accurate? How could they ever become sure in their minds that the evidence should be accepted? It seems that it would be well-nigh impossible for counsel to present any arguments to the jury and, indeed, it is difficult to envisage the form which the summing-up would take in trying to guide the jury as to how they should exercise their judgment to resolve any conflict of evidence. It would, in my judgement, result in a travesty of a trial and it is not surprising that it has never happened before, certainly in my experience or in any instance to which counsel could possibly refer me. Those are all matters which would make, at the very least, a trial conducted in this way unfair to the defendant.

[29] [1988] 3 All E.R. 431; *R. v. Blithing* (1983) 77 Cr.App.R. 86.
[30] Where the application is made under the Criminal Justice Act 1988, s.23(3) considerations of fairness must still be taken into account under sections 25 and 26.

This is a balancing exercise, and I must take account in exercising my discretion also of the interests of the Crown, or, put another way, I must take account, in measuring any unfairness to O'Loughlin, of O'Loughlin's own activities, or if not his own activities, the activities of others acting on his behalf. Into that balance would go the proof that the witnesses were being kept away not as a result of the direct intervention of the defendant but by others seeking to act in his interest. In those circumstances I see immediately that, of course, it can be said that it lies ill in his mouth to complain of unfairness. Also into this balance must go the fact that what I am being asked to admit here in relation to those two women are depositions, that is evidence which has been given on oath and which has been subjected to some cross-examination at least. As I say, those are matters which I acknowledge must weigh heavily against the defendants. Nevertheless, doing the best I can I have come to the conclusion here that to allow this trial to proceed, when the only evidence against O'Loughlin would be the depositions of these two women, would be to produce a trial which could be regarded as an unfair trial, and even that I would be allowing proceedings to take place which actually were not a trial at all but a travesty of a trial.

O'Loughlin is interpreting section 13 but the comments have relevance both to the 1996 provisions and to section 23(3) since, as is discussed below, the provisions of sections 25 and 26 mean that these considerations of fairness also apply to admissibility under sections 23 and 24 and that the leave of the court must be sought before such statements are introduced.

In one respect the new legislation is wider than section 23(3) because the judge is entitled to consider *any* reason for the witness' absence as a basis for allowing the committal statement to be read as evidence. Section 23 is restricted to situations where the maker is in fear or being kept out of the way. But generally, section 23(3) has the broader scope because it applies to *any* statement in a document which has been made in the course of a criminal investigation and not merely depositions before examining magistrates. There is no requirement that the accused has caused the fear or is keeping the witness out of the way and those elements of "fear" and "being kept out of the way" are read disjunctively so that the subsection would apply even where the witness attended court but was too fearful to testify or to continue testifying.[31] The "fear" is not necessarily objective and based on reasonable grounds as long as it is genuine.[32] A witness's statement that he or she was afraid, although hearsay, would be admissible to prove his or her state of mind.[33] The section is not limited to the prosecution but can also apply to defence witnesses.

Although section 23(3) has attracted criticism,[34] it has also been seen as protection for the vulnerable witness, especially victims of domestic violence:

[31] *R. v. Ashford Magistrates' Court ex p Hilden* [1993] 2 All E.R. 154.
[32] *R. v. Acton Justices ex p McMullen* (1990) 92 Cr.App.R. 98.
[33] *Neil v. North Antrim Magistrates' Court* [1992] 4 All E.R. 846.
[34] Wolchover D.' "Keeping Witnesses Out of the Way" 138 New L.J. 461 (1988).

Edwards S., "What Shall We do with a Frightened Witness?" 139 New L.J. 1740 at 1759 (1989)

. . . The court has the discretion to decide what constitutes fear and when a claim of 'fear' is legitimate.

How the courts will interpret the fear component in section 23 is yet to be tested. I would hope that the courts would consider seriously the vulnerable witness and in their definition of fear include a consideration of the victim's/witness's state of mind. Fear must be seen to be beyond mere fear of an appearance in court; it must relate to anticipation of subsequent action by or on behalf of the defendant following on from the giving of prejudicial evidence. Prosecution witnesses to particular offences may be more susceptible to this kind of direct intimidation or state of mind presupposing subsequent action, *i.e.* large scale fraud, terrorism, gang crimes, syndicate crimes, and crimes involving intimate victim/offender 'relationships'. Whilst it is true that section 23(3)(b) could be open to abuse by 'grasses' whose evidence then could not be tested, each case has to be examined in appreciating the particular pressures that are brought to bear. In domestic assault cases, allegations of previous violence in a witness statement, including previous convictions against the offender or injunctions served, and any indication of interference in the pre-trial stage could be put before the judge in helping him/her to assess the reasonableness of the alleged fear.

The standard of fear should be assessed in accordance not with the reasonable man standard but rather the battered woman's perception of fear standard. This latter concept has a specific meaning and this specific meaning has been accepted in the U.S. in cases where women pled self defence to killing violent husbands in accordance with the battered woman's perception of 'imminent danger' rather than the reasonable man standards. Many battered women live in fear and cannot make decisions in their own interests or those of their children because of fear. The meaning of fear must therefore be open to accommodate the vulnerable person and in this case the battered woman's perception of fear, even in the absence of proof of direct threats.[35]

A notorious example of these problems occurred in *R. v. Renshaw*[36] where the victim refused to testify against her cohabitee because of the threats that he had made against her and her child. She was jailed for contempt. Section 23 came into effect only weeks later, at which time her statement to the police could have been accepted as evidence. Witness intimidation obviously occurs. In such cases where the testimony is crucial to the prosecution case and admissibility of the statement would mean that the primary witness is not available for cross-examination, section 23 is rarely used[37] as the defendant might be seen as having been prejudiced by the admission of such evidence. But where the defendant's own activities can be demonstrated to be the cause of witnesses being unwilling to testify, can he or she complain that the trial was not fair, if written statements are used as evidence in place of oral testimony?

[35] The comments on fear must be read alongside the Divisional Court decision in *Acton Justices*; McEwan J. "Documentary Hearsay Evidence — Refuge for the Vulnerable Witness" [1989] Crim.L.R. 629.

[36] [1989] Crim.L.R. 811; *R. v. Holt*, *The Times Law Reports*, October 31, 1996.

[37] Royal Commission on Criminal Justice, *Report* (Cm. 2263 1993) para. 8.44; see discussion on sections 25 and 26 below.

Criminal Justice Act 1988, s.24 — Second-hand Documentary Hearsay

Section 24 is the successor to the reforms introduced following the decision in *Myers*, namely the 1965 Criminal Evidence Act and section 68 of the Police and Criminal Evidence Act 1984. As with its predecessors, section 24 is not limited to first-hand hearsay but applies where the hearsay is indirect. The motivation behind all this legislation was the need to admit business records into evidence but section 24 extends the scope of this exception:[38]

24.—(1) Subject —

a) to subsections (3) and (4) below;

b) to paragraph 1A of Schedule 2 to the Criminal Appeal Act 1968; and

c) to section 69 of the Police and Criminal Evidence Act 1984,

a statement in a document shall be admissible in criminal proceedings as evidence of any fact of which direct oral evidence would be admissible, if the following conditions are satisfied —

i) the document was created or received by a person in the course of a trade, business, profession or other occupation, or as a holder of a paid or unpaid office; and
ii) the information contained in the document was supplied by a person (whether or not the maker of the statement) who had, or may reasonably be supposed to have had, personal knowledge of the matters dealt with.

(2) Subsection (1) above applies whether the information contained in the document was supplied directly or indirectly but, if it was supplied indirectly, only if each person through whom it was supplied received it —

a) in the course of a trade, business profession or other occupation; or

b) as the holder of a paid or unpaid office.

(3) Subsection (1) does not render admissible a confession made by an accused person that would not be admissible under section 76 of the Police and Criminal Evidence Act 1984.

(4) A statement prepared otherwise than in accordance with section 3 of the Criminal Justice (international Co-Operation) Act 1990 or an order under paragraph 6 of Schedule 13 to this Act or under section 30 or 31 below for the purposes —

a) of pending or contemplated criminal proceedings; or

b) of a criminal investigation,

[38] McEvoy D., "Police Documents as Admissible Hearsay" [1993] Crim.L.R. 480; Smith J., "Sections 23 and 24 of the Criminal Justice Act 1988: Some Problems" [1994] Crim.L.R. 426.

shall not be admissible by virtue of subsection (1) above unless —

i) the requirements of one of the paragraphs of subsection (2) of section 23 above are satisfied; or
ii) the requirements of subsection (3) of that section are satisfied; or
iii) the person who made the statement cannot reasonably be expected (having regard to the time which has elapsed since he made the statement and to all the circumstances) to have any recollection of the matters dealt with in the statement.

The following points should be noted:

(1) section 24(2) allows documents which are the consequence of *multiple hearsay* (*i.e.* where the information is transferred at least twice) to be admitted. There is no limit to the length of the chain through which the information passes but:

- at some point, a person (usually the initial supplier of the information) would have been able to give direct oral information of the fact
- the supplier of the information would have had personal knowledge of the facts
- at each stage when the information was passed on (this can be done orally and not necessarily through intermediate documents), it must be received in the course of trade, business, etc. However this is not required of the initial supplier of the information.

(2) these are *simpler provisions* than section 68 of the Police and Criminal Evidence Act 1984:

- "record"[39] has been replaced by "statement in a document";
- the document no longer needs to have been "supplied or made in the course of business" but merely that it was "created or received".
- admissibility is governed by the reference to trade or business rather than the notion of "duty".

(3) these provisions greatly *extend the admissibility of documentary hearsay*. Whereas section 23 was meant to be restrictive in the sense that the party relying on the document had to prove that the witness

[39] See *R. v. Iqbal* [1990] 3 All E.R. 787 for the restrictions on admissibility created by this term.

was not available, there was no such restriction for "business records" envisaged under section 24. But it has been argued that the wording of section 24(1)(i) makes section 23 practically redundant. This allows for a document to be admissible where it is "created or received" within a business setting. "Created" provides few problems as the routine nature of the business world is some guarantee of accuracy. However, the term "received" poses difficulties: an everyday document such as a diary can become admissible under section 24 if it is handed over to the police who "receive" it in the course of their business.[40] If such an interpretation were correct, the writer of the diary need no longer to be proved to be unavailable.[41] This would give too wide a meaning to "receive". Obviously, if a letter is handed to a postman who receives it in the course of his or her employment, such a transaction should not bypass the requirements of section 23. Others[42] have argued that received must mean received "*qua* hearsay and not merely *qua* physical object". A sealed letter sent to your solicitor for safekeeping must remain a section 23 document whereas a letter outlining the provisions of your will and which becomes part of your file is admissible under section 24, although even in this scenario, it is difficult to understand why mere receipt should have any bearing on admissibility.

This drafting provides particular problems with regard to police documents. For example, an officer might well record in a notebook speculative information supplied to him or her by an informant but unseen by that informant and as such not a section 23 document. By the time of trial, the informant has died but the notebook could be admissible evidence under section 24(1)(i) which talks of "trade, business, profession or other occupation, or as the holder of a paid or unpaid office". This embraces not merely private business but the public sector, charities, private associations, the officers of sports clubs and so on. On any reading, police officers and their notebooks come within this. The courts would need to use their exclusionary discretion to ensure against a new form of "verbals". The old form were unverified police accounts of what the accused said on arrest, a practice which has to some extent been reduced through procedures under the Police and Criminal Evidence Act 1984. But the very breadth of section 24 holds the danger of "documentary verbals', not of the accused's statements but of statements by third parties implicating the accused and recorded in the officer's notebook.

[40] Ockelton M., "Documentary Hearsay in Criminal Cases" [1992] Crim.L.R. 15; Keane A., The Modern Law of Evidence (4th ed., 1996) 292–293.

[41] Although the court possesses an exclusionary discretionary discretion under section 25 as well as under the Police and Criminal Evidence Act 1984, s.78.

[42] McEvoy D., "Police Documents as Admissible Hearsay" [1993] Crim.L.R. 480; Smith J., "Sections 23 and 24 of the Criminal Justice Act 1988: Some Problems" [1994] Crim.L.R. 426 at 429.

(4) Unlike section 23, there is *no requirement that the witness be incapable of testifying*. However, under section 24(4) where the statement was made for the specific purpose of a criminal investigation or criminal proceedings, then it is only admissible if the witness is incapable of testifying and the requirements of section 23(2) or section 23(3) met. Section 24(4) creates an additional possibility, namely that the person who made the statement cannot reasonably be expected to have any recollection of the matters dealt with in the statement. This requirement under section 24(4)(iii) is wholly separate from those under section 24(4)(i) and (ii). In *Farrand v. Galland*[43] the accused was charged with supplying a car with a false odometer reading. The evidence was the record cards of a previous owner, a car hire firm. The person who had compiled the record was available but not called and the justices threw out the case. But the provisions have to be read disjunctively so that as long as one condition applies, that is sufficient. Here it would be unreasonable to expect the person who filled out the card to have any recollection of the mileage.

(5) *the terminology of section 24 is more complex than section 23* which, in providing for the admission of first-hand documentary hearsay, merely envisages one person who is the maker of the statement. Section 24 uses multiple terms, possibly storing up problems:

Smith J., "Sections 23 and 24 of the Criminal Justice Act 1988: Some Problems" [1994] Crim.L.R. 426 at 427–428

Section 24(1)(ii) distinguishes between 'the maker of the statement' and the supplier of the information. Following a curious drafting device used by the draftsman of PACE (section 68 and Sched. 3, para. 1), if the only person involved is the person with personal knowledge he is treated in this section (unlike s.23) as a person supplying information (presumably, to the paper he is writing on!). The Act goes on to make provisions concerning the maker of the statement.

(1) Where the statement has been prepared for the purposes of pending or contemplated criminal proceedings or of a criminal investigation, section 24(4) provides that it is not admissible unless the maker is unavailable for one of the reasons specified in section 23(2) or (3) or section 24(4)(iii).

(2) Schedule 2, para. 1, provides that the credit of the maker of the statement may be impeached by:

a) evidence which could have been called if the maker had been called as a witness (para. 1(a)), *e.g.* that he was mentally unstable or physically incapable of seeing what he states he saw: *Toohey*[44]; or that he had been convicted of, *e.g.* perjury or an offence involving dishonesty: Criminal Procedure Act 1865, s.6.

[43] [1989] Crim.L.R. 573 (relevant to section 24 although decided under Police and Criminal Evidence Act 1984, s.68).

[44] [1965] A.C. 595.

b) with the leave of the court, evidence of a matter which could have been put to him in cross-examination and as to which his answer would have been final (para. 1(b)), *e.g.* that he was expelled from university for cheating in examinations.
c) evidence of an earlier or later inconsistent statement made by him (para. 1 (c)).

(3) Schedule 2, para. 2 provides that a statement given in evidence by virtue of Part II (including sections 23 and 24) shall not be capable of corroborating evidence given by the person making it.

These provisions all re-enact provisions in PACE, but, in PACE, they applied not to the maker of the statement, but to the supplier of the information. They are apt provisions in relation to the supplier, but are quite inapt in relation to the maker. It is difficult to suppose that this change was intended. It looks like a gross drafting error. I suspect that the draftsman may have substituted 'maker' for 'supplier' to fit section 23 (which, as noted above, very sensibly does not refer to 'supplier') and failed to notice the dire effect on section 24. In *Bedi*[45] it was not necessary to decide the point, and the court did not purport to do so, because, though the judge ought to have considered whether the document was caught by section 24(4), there was no evidence on which he could have found that it did.

Consider the following example. An informer gives information to a police officer who writes it down. The informer does not authenticate the writing. Section 24(4) applies. The statement looks like 'a statement made to a police officer' but, within the literal meaning of the Act, it is not because it is a statement made, not to, but by a *police officer*. The informer is not the maker of the statement envisaged by section 24(1)(ii) but a supplier of information.

If the Act is applied literally it is necessary, in order to have the document admitted, to prove that the *policeman* is dead, or unfit, etc. It is the mental instability or incapacity to observe and recollect of the policeman, not that of the person who actually witnessed the relevant events, which the Act allows to be proved. The statement cannot corroborate any evidence which the policeman may give; but he has no personal knowledge of the matters in issue and is extremely unlikely to give evidence requiring corroboration. It is the informer who is likely to require corroboration; but there is no provision regarding him.

The literal meaning of the Act makes nonsense of these provisions. The source of the difficulty lies in the words in parentheses in section 24(1)(ii), '(whether or not the maker of the statement . . .)'. It is submitted that what the draftsman meant and what he ought to have written is '(whether or not the creator of the document . . .)'. We would then no longer have to distinguish the person supplying the information from the person making the statement. They must be the same person, if the Act is to make sense, but the creator of the document may be someone else.

The cases cited in *Craies on Statute Law*[46] show that, where the language of a statute is clear, the courts are generally unwilling to modify it even to avoid absurdity. Unfortunately the language of section 24 is clear . . .

[45] (1992) 95 Cr.App.R. 21 at 26–27.
[46] 7th ed., 86–91.

The problems are shown in *R. v. Bedi and Bedi*[47] where the defendants were shopkeepers accused of obtaining payments from a credit card company by submitting false sales vouchers, having used lost or stolen cards. The prosecution relied on documents to prove the cards were lost or stolen, the documents in question being either reports signed by the loser of the card or *pro formas* completed by an employee of the credit card company. Such documents satisfy the requirements of section 24(1)(i) and (ii) and the Court of Appeal held that they were not documents prepared for investigation under section 24(4) — such "lost and stolen" reports are designed to facilitate business and not to support prosecutions. However if (contrary to these facts) we assume that these documents were prepared with criminal investigation in mind, the case raises the issue as to whom the requirements of section 24(4) apply, in other words, who is the maker of the statement? The original holder of the card is the supplier of the information and, if he or she signs a form notifying the company of the loss or verifies such a form completed by an employee of the company, he or she is also the maker of the statement. This means that the requirements of section 24(4) must be satisfied with regard to him or her. But if the employee takes details over the phone and fills out a "lost or stolen" form, the Court of Appeal in *Bedi* considered that he or she was the "maker of the statement" with the result that it is the employee's absence from court that must be accounted for. Yet this is absurd since it is the person who supplied the information, the cardholder, who is in the position to account for the history of the card, whose hearsay statement is being admitted and who is, in truth, the absent witness.

In *R. v. Carrington*[48] the accused attempted to pay for goods in a supermarket using a stolen Switch card but made off when suspected. The cashier alerted the supervisors, one of whom spotted the accused driving out of the car park and noted the registration number of the car which was reported via the telephone to a second supervisor who wrote it down on a memo pad. Was the memo pad admissible? Here the information is noted with a view to criminal prosecution and section 24 (4) applies. The first supervisor is the supplier of the information and the "absent witness" but the Court of Appeal held that the second supervisor who wrote down the number was the "maker of the statement" whose absence had to be justified. They also held that the supervisor could not "reasonably be expected to have any recollection of the matters dealt with in the statement" so that the statement was admitted under section 24(4)(iii).

[47] (1991) 95 Cr.App.R. 21.
[48] (1993) 99 Cr.App.R. 376.

Safeguards under sections 25 and 26 — Discretion to Exclude and Leave to Admit

Whenever a document is admissible under sections 23 or 24, under section 25, the court has the power to exclude evidence, if in the interests of justice, it ought not to be admitted. Section 25(2), while not detracting from the generality of that discretion, directs the court to look particularly at several elements: at the nature and source of the document, to the extent to which other evidence on the issue is available, to the relevance of the evidence or to the risk of unfairness. It would appear that the burden of persuading the court that the document should be excluded, rests on the party objecting to admission.

But if a document is admissible under sections 23 or 24 but it is one prepared for the purposes of criminal investigation, leave from the court is required under section 26 before the evidence is admitted. In this situation, section 25 has no part to play.[49] The provisions of section 26 are less generous to the party tendering the statement who bears the burden of persuading the court that the admission of the statement is in the interests of justice:

25.—(1) If, having regard to all the circumstances (a court of trial or an appeal court) is of the opinion that in the interests of justice a statement which is admissible by virtue of section 23 or 24 above nevertheless ought not to be admitted, it may direct that the statement shall not be admitted.

(2) Without prejudice to the generality of subsection (1) above, it shall be the duty of the court to have regard -

a) to the nature and source of the document containing the statement and to whether or not, having regard to its nature and source and to any other circumstances that appear to the court to be relevant, it is likely that the document is authentic;
b) to the extent to which the statement appears to supply evidence which would otherwise not be readily available;
c) to the relevance of the evidence that it appears to supply to any issue which is likely to have to be determined in the proceedings; and
d) to any risk, having regard in particular to whether it is likely to be possible to controvert the statement if the person making it does not attend to give oral evidence in the proceedings, that its admission or exclusion will result in unfairness to the accused or, if there is more than one, to any of them.

26.—Where a statement which is admissible in criminal proceedings by virtue of section 23 or 24 above appears to the court to have been prepared . . . for the purposes —

a) of pending or contemplated criminal proceedings; or
b) of a criminal investigation,

the statement shall not be given in evidence in any criminal proceedings without the leave of the court, and the court shall not give leave unless it is of the opinion that

[49] This is not always recognised by the courts — *R. v. Jennings and Miles* [1995] Crim.L.R. 810.

the statement ought to be admitted in the interests of justice; and in considering whether its admission would be in the interests of justice, it shall be the duty of the court to have regard —

i) to the contents of the statements;
ii) to any risk, having regard in particular to whether it is likely to be possible to controvert the statement of the person making it does not attend to give oral evidence in the proceedings, that its admission or exclusion will result in unfairness to the accused or, if there is more than one, to any one of them; and
iii) to any other circumstances that appear to the court to be relevant.

These provisions are closely linked but perform different functions. These are explained in *R. v. Cole*,[50] a case of assault in which the prosecution sought to introduce the statement of an eyewitness who had subsequently died. Leave was required under section 26 and the appellant argued that this should have been refused as the only way of controverting the statement under section 26(ii) would be for the defendant to testify or to call witnesses and this amounted to putting improper pressure on the defendant:

R. v. Cole [1990] 2 All E.R. 108 at 115–117, *per* Ralph Gibson L.J.

The overall purpose of the provisions was to widen the power of the court to admit documentary hearsay while ensuring that the accused received a fair trial. In judging how to achieve the fairness of the trial a balance must on occasions be struck between the interests of the public in enabling the prosecution case to be properly presented and the interest of a particular defendant in not being put in a disadvantageous position, for example by the death or illness of a witness. The public of course also has a direct interest in the proper protection of the individual accused. The point of balance, as directed by Parliament, is set out in the sections.

It is not of course the case that these provisions are available only to enable the prosecution to put evidence before the court. A defendant also may wish to make use of the provisions in order to get before the jury documentary evidence which would not otherwise be admissible.

Next, some comment on the structure of these sections is necessary. By s.25, if, having regard to all the circumstances, the court is of the opinion that a statement , admissible by virtue of section 23 or s.24, 'in the interests of justice ought not to be admitted', it may direct that it be not admitted. The court is then, in considering that question, directed to have regard to the list of matters set out in section 25(2). They include 'any risk' of unfairness caused by the admission or exclusion of the statement 'having regard in particular to whether it is likely to be possible to controvert the statement if the person making it does not attend'. In short the court must be made to hold the opinion that the statement ought not to be admitted.

By contrast under s.26, which deals with documents prepared for purpose of criminal proceedings or investigations, when a statement is admissible in criminal proceedings by virtue of section 23 or s.24, and was prepared for the purposes of criminal proceedings, the statement shall not be given in evidence unless the court is of the opinion that the statement 'ought to be admitted in the interests of justice'.

[50] [1990] 2 All E.R. 108; see also *R. v. Price* [1991] Crim.L.R. 707 on the similar requirement in section 25(2)(d).

The matters to which the court must have regard have been set out above and they include, again, 'any risk' of unfairness caused by the admission or exclusion having regard to the possibility of controverting the statement. Again, in short, the court is not to admit the statement unless made to hold the opinion that in the interests of justice it 'ought to be admitted'. The emphasis is the other way round.

The first submission of counsel for the appellant was that the words 'whether it is likely to be possible to controvert the statement if the person making it does not attend' contemplate only, and should be restricted to, the possibility of controverting the statement by cross-examination directed to witnesses to be called for the prosecution.

We reject that submission. We see no reason to imply any such restriction on the plain meaning of the words. The meaning of 'controvert' includes that of 'dispute' or 'contradict'. The court is entitled, in our judgment, to have regard to such information as it has at the time that the application is made which shows 'whether it is likely to be possible to controvert the statement' in the absence of the ability to cross-examine the maker. The court cannot require to be told whether the accused intends to give evidence or to call witnesses, but the court is not required, in our judgment, to asses the possibility of controverting the statement upon the basis that the accused will not give evidence or call witnesses known to be available to him. The decision by an accused whether or not to give evidence or to call witnesses is to be made by him by reference to the admissible evidence put before the court; and the accused has no right, as we think, for the purposes of this provision, to be treated as having no possibility of controverting the statement because of his right not to give evidence or call witnesses. If Parliament had intended the question to be considered on that basis, express words would, we think, have been used to make that intention clear.

This question, however, is only one part of a complex balancing exercise which the court must perform. For example, the fact that the court concludes that it is likely to be possible for the accused to controvert the statement if the person making it cannot be cross-examined does not mean that the court will therefore necessarily be of opinion that admission of the statement will not result in unfairness to the accused or that the statement ought not to be admitted in the interests of justice.

The court must consider the contents of the statement, as explained in *R. v. Blithing*,[51] where the court was concerned with section 13(3) of the 1925 Act; the statement may leave relevant questions unanswered and appear to provide evidence of greater certainty than is warranted having regard to the absence of those answers. As Lord Griffiths observed in *Scott v. R*,[52] after reference to a need for proper warnings when a statement is admitted:

> It is the quality of the evidence in the deposition that is the crucial factor that should determine the exercise of the discretion. By way of example, if the deposition contains evidence of identification that is so weak that a judge in the absence of corroborative evidence would withdraw the case from the jury, then, if there is no corroborative evidence, the judge should exercise his discretion to refuse to admit the deposition for it would be unsafe to allow the jury to convict on it.

Thus the weight to be attached to the inability to cross-examine and the magnitude of any consequential risk that admission of the statement will result in unfairness to the accused, will depend in part on the court's assessment of the

[51] (1983) 77 Cr.App.R. 86.
[52] [1989] A.C. 1242 at 1529.

quality of the evidence shown by the contents of the statement. Each case, as is obvious, must turn on its own facts. The court should, we accept, consider whether, as was the court's view in *R. v. Blithing*, the inability to probe a statement by cross-examination of the maker of it must be regarded as having such consequences, having regard to the terms and substance of the statement in the light of the issues in the cases, that for that reason the statement should be excluded.

In considering a submission to that effect the court is entitled, and in our view required, to consider how far any potential unfairness, arising from the inability to cross-examine on the particular statement, may be effectively counter-balanced by the sort of warning and explanation in the summing up described by Lord Griffiths and in fact given by the judge in this case. The court will also, for example, consider whether, having regard to other evidence available to the prosecution, the interests of justice will be properly served by excluding the statement.

Little assistance is found in judgments about the details of "fairness" or "the interests of justice" that are involved in this "complex balancing act". It must be remembered that the central element of fairness in this context is the right to confront the evidence against you. Sections 23 and 24 remove that right and to that extent the statute creates an inherent unfairness which must be regulated:

(1) simple loss of the right to cross-examine is not *per se* unfair. To hold otherwise would be to nullify these provisions
(2) it is not unfair to pressure the accused into testifying or to call witnesses in order to controvert the statement. The authority for this is *Cole* but again to hold otherwise would limit the sections' effectiveness
(3) nor is it unfair if the defendant's actions can be demonstrated to have intimidated the witness[53]
(4) if there is other evidence, it is easier to conclude that admission of the statement is not unfair. In *Cole*, the deceased witness had the best view of the assault but was not the only witness. Equally it is not unfair where the absent witness is required only to be cross-examined about some collateral matter.[54]

But what about the situation where the disputed evidence forms the hub of the prosecution case? The potential for unfairness is much greater, even where the evidence is reliable and from an unimpeachable source. In *R. v. French*[55] the Court of Appeal ruled that leave should not be given in such a case but in *R. v. Grafton*,[56] the accused and his accountant, now deceased, were the only substantial witnesses. The accused had himself referred the investigators from Customs and Excise to the accountant for information about his business affairs.[57] The accountant had made a statement to

[53] *R. v. Fairfax* [1995] Crim.L.R. 949.

[54] *R. v. Holman* [1995] Crim.L.R. 80 where the written evidence of Irish bank employees was accepted.

[55] (1993) 97 Cr.App.R. 421.

[56] [1995] Crim.L.R. 61.

[57] At common law, such a vicarious admission where there is express authority might well be admissible — *Williams v. Innes* (1808) 1 Camp. 364.

them which was significantly adverse to the accused. In such circumstances, the statement was admitted.

(5) the balance between the parties is central to the idea of fairness in an adversarial setting. This means that the prosecution must not abuse the dominant position they hold in terms of resources or access to information.

(6) parties should not be permitted to use these provisions to avoid the consequences of their own incompetence.[58]

(7) reliability must not be equated with fairness. The quality and reliability of the maker of the statement and of the information do not make it necessarily fair to admit it. This was perhaps overlooked by Lord Griffiths in *Scott v. R.*,[59] when he commented,

> It is the quality of the evidence in the deposition that is the crucial factor that should determine the exercise of the discretion.

The converse is true as fairness is not served by the admission of unreliable written statements. In *R. v. Patel*,[60] the accused produced an alibi statement from a witness abroad, alleging that the accused was with him at the relevant time. The Recorder termed this 'very bald' and rejected the statement, although considering that the position might have been different had the prosecution had an opportunity to interview the witness. A similar approach can be seen in *R. v. Irish*.[61]

(8) the court must take into account the effect on all the defendants. In *R. v. Gregory and Mott*[62] the statement of a deceased witness would marginally have assisted one of the defendants but seriously harmed the case of the other. It was excluded and the balancing act envisaged in *Cole* here became a balance between the "degrees of unfairness" to the two defendants.

Finally, fairness is to be sought through the direction to the jury. The judge must stress that the evidence has not been tested by cross-examination and should point out any weaknesses or inconsistencies in the statement. In *R. v. Kennedy*,[63] the accused was a police officer accused of assaulting an alcoholic. The victim died before trial but his statements were admitted under section 23. Although the trial judge acted properly in admitting the statement and in warning the jury about the lack of cross-examination, he failed to mention how drunk the victim had been at the time of the incident and the inconsistencies between the statement and the testimony of other witnesses.

[58] *R. v. Bray* (1988) 88 Cr.App.R. 354.
[59] [1989] A.C. 1242 at 1529.
[60] [1993] Crim.L.R. 291.
[61] [1994] Crim.L.R. 922.
[62] [1995] Crim.L.R. 507.
[63] [1994] Crim.L.R. 50.

In directing the jury as to the weight to be attached to the document, the court must have regard to paragraph 3 of Schedule 2 of the 1988 Act which instructs the court that "... regard shall be had to all the circumstances from which any inference can reasonably be drawn as to its accuracy or otherwise". The sobriety of the witness was an obvious, if overlooked, factor in *Kennedy*. The speed with which the statement is made after the event or whether the supplier of the information or the creator of the document had any reason to distort the facts may be others.

This latter point raises a further issue. Although the jury are unable to see the demeanour of the witness or assess their credibility under cross-examination, the party affected by the admission of the document can still attack the credibility of the maker of the statement under paragraph 1 of Schedule 2 of the 1988 Act:

> Where a statement is admitted as evidence in criminal proceedings by virtue of Part II of this Act —
>
> a) any evidence which, if the person making the statement has been called as a witness, would have been admissible as relevant to his credibility as a witness shall be admissible for that purpose in those proceedings;
> b) evidence may, with the leave of the court, be given of any matter which, if that person had been called as a witness, could have been put to him in cross-examination as relevant to his credibility as a witness but of which evidence could not have been adduced by the cross-examining party; and
> c) evidence tending to prove that the person, whether before or after making the statement, made (whether orally or not) some other statement which is inconsistent with it shall be admissible for the purpose of showing that he has contradicted himself.

Generally a witness giving oral testimony can be cross-examined on collateral issues going to his or her credibility as a witness.[64] However, in cross-examination, there is the rule of finality of answers on collateral issues. Having received an answer on a matter of credibility, a party is, with some exceptions, not entitled to pursue the matter further or adduce independent evidence to contradict the witness. Subparagraph a) deals with those situations where the rule on finality does not apply and a party could adduce evidence in rebuttal:

(1) a party is allowed to adduce evidence attacking the absent witness's credibility which would have been permitted under those exceptions,[65] namely that the witness was biased,[66] suffered from a

[64] Such an attack usually opens up the accused who testifies to questioning about his or her own character — Criminal Evidence Act 1898, s.1(f)(ii). However that provision talks of "imputations on the character of the prosecutor or prosecution witnesses". The "maker of the statement" is not a witness and the accused will not become liable to such cross-examination.
[65] Generally see 367, *et seq.*
[66] *e.g. R. v. Mendy* (1976) 64 Cr.App.R. 4.

physical or mental disability,[67] had previous convictions[68] or was reputed to be untruthful.[69]

(2) the party introducing the statement is allowed to adduce evidence supporting the absent witness's credibility where that would have been admissible had the witness been in court. For example, if the document is alleged to be a recent fabrication, a prior statement, consistent with the contents of the document, would be admissible.[70]

There are questions which could have been put to the witness, had he or she been present in court, but which do not come under these exceptions and evidence in rebuttal could not have been given. Subparagraph b) deals with those situations where the rule of finality would have applied. The party adversely affected by the document is placed in a marginally improved position since, with the leave of the court, evidence can be adduced that the absent witness had behaved discreditably and in a way which renders that witness's statement in the document less credible.

Subparagraph c) allows a party to prove statements by the absent witness which are inconsistent with the contents of the document. Such statements are a further exception to the rule on finality of answers to collateral issues and may be proved under sections 4 or 5 of the Criminal Procedure Act 1865. They are referred to as "prior" inconsistent statements since in the normal situation, they are prior to the witness's oral testimony. The admission of a document under sections 23 or 24 makes "prior" or "previous" ambiguous because the maker of the statement may have made other statements, inconsistent with those in the document, both before or after the creation of the document. Subparagraph c) allows such statements to be proved in either situation.

These provisions under paragraph 1 of Schedule 2 also permit a party to attack the credibility of the "maker of the statement". This poses no problems for section 23 statements where the supplier of the information and maker of the statement are one and the same. This is not the case with section 24 and in cases such as *R. v. Carrington*[71] the Court of Appeal has suggested that the creator of the document is the maker of the statement. In that case the accused attempted to pay for goods in a supermarket using a stolen Switch card, the cashier alerted the supervisors, one of whom spotted the accused driving out of the car park and noted the registration number of the car which was reported via the telephone to a second supervisor who wrote it down. Under a literal reading of the paragraph, it is the credibility of the latter which can be attacked. But the accused might well have wished to question the first supervisor's eyesight and the second supervisor's hearing!

[67] *Toohey v. Metropolitan Police Commissioner* [1965] A.C. 595.

[68] These can be proved under the Criminal Procedure Act 1865, s.6.

[69] *R. v. Richardson* [1969] 1 Q.B. 299.

[70] *R. v. Oyesiku* (1971) 56 Cr.App.R. 240 — generally see 335, *et seq.*

[71] (1993) 99 Cr.App.R. 376.

Other Statutes Admitting Documentary Hearsay

The most significant of such exceptions is the provision in the Police and Criminal Evidence Act 1984 for the admission of confessions. This is discussed earlier in the context of police investigative procedures.[72] But there are many statutes admitting documentary hearsay as evidence. These can be found in the context of committal proceedings, summary proceedings in magistrates' courts, children's evidence and the use of depositions from committal proceedings in trials on indictment.

Committal proceedings

These are preliminary proceedings before the magistrates' court to decide whether there are grounds to commit the accused for trial at Crown Court.[73] To expedite matters, written statements are admissible evidence under section 5B of the Magistrates' Courts Act 1980.[74]

> 5B.—(1) For the purposes of section 5A above a written statement complies with this section if —
>
> a) the conditions falling within subsection (2) below are met, and
>
> b) such of the conditions falling within subsection (3) below as apply are met.
>
> (2) The conditions falling within this subsection are that —
>
> a) the statement purports to be signed by the person who made it;
>
> b) the statement contains a declaration by that person to the effect that it is true to the best of his knowledge and belief and that he made the statement knowing that, if it were tendered in evidence, he would be liable to prosecution if he wilfully stated in it anything which he knew to be false or did not believe to be true;
>
> c) before the statement is tendered in evidence, a copy of the statement is given, by or on behalf of the prosecutor, to each of the other parties to the proceedings; and

Prior to 1996, there was the opportunity for the defendant to object to the statement being tendered in written form[75] but the new legislation seeks to streamline both full committal hearings as well as short form committals.[76] Much of the evidence will now be given in this form

[72] Chap. 4.

[73] Committal proceedings were to be abolished under the Criminal Justice and Public Order Act 1994 but have been reinstated by the Criminal Procedure and Investigations Act 1996, s.47 and Sched 1.

[74] This section replaces the Magistrates' Court Act 1980, s.102 as a result of the Criminal Procedure and Investigations Act 1996, Sched. 1.

[75] Magistrates' Court Act 1980, s.102((2)(d).

[76] Magistrates' Courts Act 1980, s.6(2).

regardless of the the consent of the defence. Under section 5B(4), in full committals, such statements will normally be read out in open court.

Section 9 statements

A significant amount of evidence, especially in magistrates' courts, will be through the medium of agreed statements under section 9 of the Criminal Justice Act 1967:

9.—(1) In any criminal proceedings, other than committal proceedings, a written statement by any person shall, if such of the conditions mentioned in the next following subsection as are applicable are satisfied, be admissible evidence to the like extent as oral evidence to the like effect by that person.

(2) The said conditions are —

a) the statement purports to be signed by the person who made it;

b) the statement contains a declaration by that person to the effect that it is true to the best of his knowledge and belief and that he made the statement knowing that, if it were tendered in evidence, he would be liable to prosecution if he wilfully stated in it anything which he knew to be false or did not believe to be true;

c) before the hearing at which the statement is tendered in evidence, a copy of the statement is served, by or on behalf of the party proposing to tender it, to each of the other parties to the proceedings; and

d) none of the other parties or their solicitors, within seven days from the service of the copy of the statement, serves a notice on the party so proposing objecting to the statement being tendered in evidence under the section:

Provided that the conditions mentioned in c) and d) of this subsection shall not apply if the parties agree before or during the hearing the statement shall be so tendered.

(3) The following provisions shall also have effect in relation to any written statement tendered in evidence under this section, that is to say —

a) if the statement is made by a person under the age of 18,[77] it shall give his age;

b) if it is made by a person who cannot read it, it shall be read to him before he signs it and shall be accompanied by a declaration by the person who so read the statement to the effect that it was so read; and

c) if it refers to any other document as an exhibit, the copy served on any other party to the proceedings under paragraph c) of the last foregoing subsection shall be accompanied by a copy of that document or by such information as may be necessary in order to enable the party on whom it is served to inspect that document or a copy thereof.

(3A) In the case of a statement which indicates in pursuance of subsection (3)(a) of this section that the person making it has not attained the age of 14, subsection

[77] As amended by the Criminal Procedure and Investigations Act 1996, s.69.

(2)(b) of this section shall have effect as if for the words from 'made' onwards there were substituted the words 'understands the importance of telling the truth in it'.

(4) Notwithstanding that a written statement made by any person may be admissible as evidence by virtue of this section —

a) the party by whom or on whose behalf a copy of the statement was served may call that person to give evidence; and

b) the court may, of its own motion or on the application of any party to the proceedings, require that person to attend before the court and give evidence . . .

The section should be read in the light of the practice direction[78] regarding the editing of such statements. Statements under section 5B (the replacement for section 102) and under section 9 are frequently edited for the court to ensure orderly presentation and the exclusion of irrelevant or prejudicial information.[79] This should be done by a Crown Prosecutor. Although section 9 statements are ones which are agreed by the parties,[80] agreeing (or not objecting) to the admission of the statement does not mean that the statement is accepted as conclusive evidence and the contents of the statement may still be disputed at trial. In *Lister v. Quaife*[81] the defendant was accused of stealing a dress from Marks and Spencer. She testified that she had bought the dress from another branch on an earlier date and was seeking to exchange it. There were section 9 statements from the M&S head office to the effect that the particular dress could not have been bought at the time and in the shop as suggested by the defendant. The defendant was acquitted and the prosecution argued that, having not objected to the statements, it was not open to the accused to give evidence contradicting those statements and that the magistrates' decision was perverse. The Divisional Court upheld the magistrates' actions:

Lister v. Quaife [1983] 2 All E.R. 29 at 32–33, _per_ May L.J.

. . . we have come to the clear conclusion that the answer really lies in a proper appreciation of what section 9 in fact achieves. As I have already said, this is that the contents of the statements read are evidence in the case just as if, and only to the extent as if, the makers of those statements had been called as witnesses in the trial and given the evidence contained in the statements. If that had happened at the hearing before the King's Lynn justices in this case, and there had been no cross-examination about the possibility of mistake, or their evidence had not been challenged in any way, then when the respondent went into the witness box no doubt strong comment could have been made that nothing had been put to the witnesses about the possibility that the respondent might indeed have been able to and did buy the dress somewhere else . . .

[78] [1986] 2 All E.R. 511.

[79] The weaknesses in the process of recording witness statements are discussed in Heaton-Armstrong A. And Wolchover D. "Recording Witness Statements" [1992] Crim.L.R. 160.

[80] A failure to object within the time limit is not fatal as a party can ask the court to call the witness under section 9(4)(b) of the Act.

[81] [1983] 2 All E.R. 29.

Although any such comment by those representing the Crown would have had substantial force and might well have led the justices to view the respondent's evidence with a degree of scepticism, the position remains that the burden throughout was on the prosecution and although the proper procedure of putting a defence case to prosecution witnesses had not been followed, it would have been open to the justices, having heard all three witnesses, to have said: 'Well, it may be that that procedure laid down by Marks and Spencer was what should have happened, and it may have happened in at least the majority, if not in every other case concerning a dress of this nature, but we have also seen the respondent. She has given evidence. We cannot say that her evidence cannot be true, and in those circumstances there must be a doubt in our minds and accordingly we must acquit'.

If one realises that that is all that is achieved by a section 9 statement, then notwithstanding that criticism may be made of the fact that the respondent's legal advisers did not give any appropriate notice requiring the makers of the statements to attend at the trial, we do not think that in the end it is right to say that the two halves of that opinion of the justices are necessarily inconsistent and their decision perverse.

. . . We take the view that legal representatives of the defendants in criminal cases . . . should observe the well-known practice that you do put your case to witnesses for the prosecution, and failure to give a notice under section 9(2)(d) is not to be used as any sort of device whereby you can have the defendant present, giving evidence in person, and avoid the presence of witnesses whose statements under section 9 have been served and merely hear those statements read out in court. Everyone knows that there is a natural tendency for evidence given in person by a witness to have more impact than statements read out . . . We would deprecate any deliberate reluctance to give a notice under section 9(2)(d) of the 1967 Act in order to gain such an advantage.

In theory the statement has the same weight as oral evidence in the trial and jurors cannot be directed to prefer the oral testimony if it conflicts with the written statement.[82] This is in contrast to statements admitted under sections 23 and 24 of the Criminal Justice Act 1988 which require a judicial warning to the jury.

Children's evidence and section 32A of the Criminal Justice Act 1988

The adversarial system can be damaging to vulnerable witnesses, especially children, and there have been modifications of the system to avoid the worst effects.[83] The system of committal for trial originally meant that in serious cases, a child would have to give evidence not once but twice. The introduction of short-form committals reduced that possibility and the streamlined arrangements under the Criminal Procedure and Investigations Act 1996 will reduce it still further. However there will still be instances where oral evidence will be called for at a committal hearing. From 1963 it has been possible to replace a child's oral testimony with a written statement. These provisions are now consolidated under section 103 of the Magistrates' Court Act 1980:

[82] *R. v. Mitchell* [1995] Crim.L.R. 146; *R. v. Millen* [1995] Crim.L.R. 568.
[83] See 391, *et seq.*

103.—(1) In any proceedings before a magistrates' court inquiring as examining justices into an offence to which this section applies, a statement made in writing by or taken in writing from a child shall be admissible in evidence of any matter.[84]

(2) This section applies —

a) to an offence which involves an assault, or injury or a threat of injury, to a person;

b) to an offence under section 1 of the Children and Young Persons Act 1933 (cruelty to persons under 16);

c) to an offence under the Sexual Offences Act 1956, the Indecency with Children Act 1960, the Sexual offences Act 1967, section 54 of the Criminal Law Act 1977 or the Protection of Children Act 1978; and

d) to an offence which consists of attempting or conspiring to commit, or of aiding, abetting, counselling, procuring or inciting the commission of, an offence falling within paragraph a), b) or c) above.

(3) and (4) . . .[85]

(5) In this section 'child' has the same meaning as in section 53 of the Criminal Justice Act 1991.[86]

The result of section 103 is that, for a wide range of violent and sexual offences, there is no need for a child to testify twice and their evidence can be given in written or videotaped form, even in the face of defence objections.

Taking the evidence of children in advance of the trial itself has been another objective of reformers. The stress experienced by all witnesses is particularly acute for children, remembering the often lengthy periods between committal and trial, the strain of re-living the events, confrontation with the defendant and the ordeal of cross-examination:

Spencer J. and Flin J., *The Evidence of Children* (2nd ed., 1993), 82 (quoted)

However, this experience [indecent assault in a cinema] was not as frightening or as upsetting as the time I had giving evidence in the magistrates' court. I was accused of lying, fabrication and made to feel as though I was the accused and not an innocent nine-year-old victim . . . The defence lawyer treated me roughly as though I was 19 instead of nine-years-old, shouting at me, muddling me, confusing me. I hated him and still do for the way he treated me. The trouble is that after 23 years I still have horrible dreams now and then — not about the incident at the cinema, but of the court experience I made.

Pressure bought to bear by the NSPCC[87] led to provisions in the Prevention of Cruelty to Children (Amendment) Act 1894. These allowed

[84] As amended by the Criminal Procedure and Investigations Act 1996, Sched 1, para. 10.

[85] These subsections have been repealed by the Criminal Justice Act 1991, s.55(1) and the Criminal Procedure and Investigations Act 1996, Sched. 5.

[86] *i.e.* 14.

[87] *ibid.* 83ff.

the child to swear a deposition before a justice of the peace where there was serious danger to the life or health of the child. This deposition could then be admitted into evidence. These provisions were incorporated in sections 42 and 43 of the Children and Young Persons Act 1933 and these are still operative today. However, despite the broad potential of such provisions, they have been little used, probably because of the strictness of the "serious danger to health" criterion. However there is also a requirement that the defence must have notice of the taking of the deposition and have the opportunity to cross-examine the child. These provisions will be rendered obsolete by the provisions of section 32 of the Criminal Justice Act 1988 which allow a child witness to testify through a live television link and, more relevantly, by section 32A[88] of the 1988 Act which permits a further exception to hearsay, namely video recordings of testimony from child witnesses:

32A.—(1) This section applies in relation to the following proceedings, namely —

a) trials on indictment for any offence to which section 32(2) above applies[89]

b) appeals to the criminal division of the Court of Appeal and hearings of references under section 17 of the Criminal Appeal Act 1968 in respect of any such offence; and

c) proceedings in youth courts for any such offence and appeals to the Crown Court arising out of such proceedings.

(2) In any such proceedings a video recording of an interview which —

a) is conducted between an adult and a child who is not the accused or one of the accused ('the child witness'); and

b) relates to any matter in issue in the proceedings,

may, with the leave of the court, be given in evidence in so far as it is not excluded by the court under subsection (3) below.

(3) Where a video recording is tendered in evidence under this section, the court shall (subject to the exercise of any power of the court to exclude evidence which is otherwise admissible) give leave under subsection (2) unless —

a) it appears that the child witness will not be available for cross-examination;

b) any rules of court requiring disclosure of the circumstances in which the recording was made have not been complied with to the satisfaction of the court; or

c) the court is of the opinion, having regard to all the circumstances of the case, that in the interests of justice the recording ought not to be admitted;

and where the court gives such leave it may, if it is of the opinion that in the interests of justice any part of the recording ought not to be admitted, direct that that part shall be excluded.

[88] Inserted by the Criminal Justice Act 1991, s.54.
[89] This is an identical provision to the Magistrates' Court Act 1980, s.103(2), *supra*.

(4) In considering whether any part of a recording ought to be excluded under subsection (3) above, the court shall consider whether any prejudice to the accused, or one of the accused, which might result from the admission of that part is outweighed by the desirability of showing the whole, or substantially the whole, of the recorded interview.

(5) Where a video recording is admitted under this section —

a) the child witness shall be called by the party who tendered it in evidence;

b) that witness shall not be examined in chief on any matter which, in the opinion of the court, has been dealt with [adequately][90] in his recorded testimony.

(6) Where a video recording is given in evidence under this section, any statement made by the child witness which is disclosed by the recording shall be treated as if given by that witness in direct oral testimony; and accordingly —

a) any such statement shall be admissible evidence of any fact of which such testimony from him would be admissible;

b) no such statement shall be capable of corroborating any other evidence given by him;

and in estimating the weight, if any, to be attached to such a statement, regard shall be had to all the circumstances from which any inference can reasonably be drawn (as to its accuracy or otherwise.)

(7) In this section 'child' means a person who —

a) in the case of an offence falling within section 32(2) a) or b) above,[91] is under fourteen years of age or, if he was under that age when the video recording was made, is under fifteen years of age; or

b) in the case of an offence falling within section 32(2) c) above,[92] is under seventeen years of age or, if he was under that age when the video recording was made, is under eighteen years of age.

The court will not give leave to use a video recording if the child witness is not available for cross-examination. Thus these provisions merely remove the need for the examination-in-chief of a child. Such a witness is still open to cross-examination. However, if the child becomes so distressed as to be unable to testify at all, the recording might still be admissible under section 23 of the 1988 Act.

Depositions

Depositions are the written record of a witness's sworn statement.

(1) under section 105 of the Magistrates' Courts Act 1980, if a potential witness was dangerously ill and unlikely to recover, a

[90] Inserted by the Criminal Justice and Public Order Act 1994, s.50.
[91] That is, an offence of violence or child cruelty.
[92] That is, a sexual offence of various kinds.

justice of the peace was able to take a deposition from him or her which could be given in evidence in committal proceedings. This provision was repealed in 1996[93] and replaced by s.5C of the Magistrates' Court Act 1980 which provides for much more general use of depositions as evidence in committal proceedings.

(2) under section 6 of the Criminal Law Amendment Act 1867, depositions under section 105 were admissible at any trial on indictment. This provision was repealed in 1996[94] and replaced as a consequence of section 68 and Schedule 2 of the Criminal Procedure and Investigations Act 1996 which allows for the use of depositions as evidence at trial without the limitations of the 1867 Act.

(3) depositions taken at the committal were also able to be read as evidence at the trial on indictment under section 13(3) of the Criminal Justice Act 1925. As discussed earlier, where the witness was intimidated and unable to testify, the deposition could be used in place of oral evidence. This provision was also repealed in 1996[95] and replaced as a consequence of section 68 and Schedule 2 of the Criminal Procedure and Investigations Act 1996 which, as already mentioned, allows for more general use of depositions as evidence at trial.

The 1996 provisions must be read alongside section 23 of the Criminal Justice Act 1988. The importance of the change can be seen in *R. v. James*[96] where the eyewitness to a murder was the girlfriend of one of the accused. She failed to turn up at the trial to testify for the Crown. The prosecution made applications under section 13(3) of the 1925 Act and later under section 23(2)(c) of the 1988. It was this latter application that was accepted. The appeal was dismissed. As the judge had decided that there were suspicions but no proof that the witness was being kept out of the way by one of the accused, section 13(3) could not apply. Having decided this, the judge was justified in considering whether the provisions of section 23 applied. The language of section 23 is less restrictive than section 13(3) as it is no need to prove that the accused "caused" the fear or is instrumental in keeping the witness "out of the way". It remains to be seen whether this will cause a flood of "intimidated" witnesses or whether the courts will rigorously police this through the "leave to admit" provisions of section 26.

[93] Criminal Procedure and Investigations Act 1996, Sched. 1, para. 11.
[94] Criminal Procedure and Investigations Act 1996, Sched. 5.
[95] Criminal Procedure and Investigations Act 1996, Sched. 2, para. 6.
[96] [1995] Crim.L.R. 812.

19

STATUTORY EXCEPTIONS TO HEARSAY IN CIVIL PROCEEDINGS: CIVIL EVIDENCE ACT 1995

The Earlier Legislation

The rule against hearsay was never absolute. Not only was it affected by the exceptions developed at common law but also by statutory provisions allowing for the admission of hearsay statements. Many of these are concerned with specific cases such as Bankers' Books Evidence Act 1879 or, more recently, section 96 of the Children Act 1989 which sought to apply the more liberal practice of the wardship jurisdiction of the High Court to all courts dealing with matters affecting children.[1] A broader approach was evident in the Evidence Act 1938 which permitted the introduction of certain documentary hearsay into civil proceedings. This statute continued to govern civil proceedings in magistrates' courts until 1995.[2] A more thoroughgoing reform was introduced in the Civil Evidence Act 1968. As a result of this Act, certain hearsay statements became admissible evidence of the facts or opinions[3] contained in them. But the Act in no sense abolished the rule against hearsay, instead creating broad but still limited statutory exceptions. By section 1 hearsay statements became admissible:

- under the provisions of the Act
- under any other statutory provision
- with the consent of the parties.

Section 1 continued ". . . but not otherwise" and as a result, it was no longer possible to adduce any statement admissible under a common law

[1] Others include Births and Deaths Registration Acts 1836 to 1953; Marriage Act 1949; Army Act 1955, s.198(5); Solicitors Act 1974, s.18; Inheritance (Provision for Family and Dependants) Act 1975, s.21.

[2] This caused problems in poll tax cases: *R. v. Coventry Justices, ex parte Bullard*, *The Times*, February 24, 1992; Murdie A., "Hearsay Evidence in Poll Tax Cases" (1992) New L.J. 1551.

[3] The Civil Evidence Act 1972 extended the definition of "statement" to include "representation of opinion" as well as "representation of fact".

exception unless that exception had been specifically retained under section 9 of the Act. These preserved exceptions included informal admissions or the public records exception. Other statements, formerly admissible as common law exceptions such as *res gestae*, would only be admissible if they conformed to the general conditions for admissibility in section 2 or section 4 of the Act.

The objectives of the 1968 legislation were:

(1) to render first-hand hearsay admissible. By this is meant those situations where the witness directly heard the statement being made or where the document was made by the maker of the statement. This was achieved by section 2(1):

> 2.—(1) . . . a statement made, whether orally or in a document or otherwise, by any person, whether called as a witness in those proceedings or not, shall . . . be admissible as evidence of any fact stated [or opinion expressed] therein of which direct oral evidence by him would be admissible.

This established a general principle that hearsay statements, however made, were admissible in any case where direct oral evidence by the maker of the statement would have been admissible. The use of the phrase, ". . . a statement made . . ." suggests that the draftsmen were conceding Cross's argument that implied assertions are not hearsay. It would be legitimate to suggest that any words or conduct which are not intended to assert a fact are not "a statement made" and thus are not hearsay but admissible as original evidence for the finder of fact to draw inferences by the normal process of common sense and logic. But the breadth of the 1968 statutory exceptions meant that this argument was of little practical importance and indeed was never argued. In theory anyway, if it is accepted that implied assertions were not hearsay, the consequence would have been that in such cases, the conditions for admissibility laid down in the 1968 Act did not have to be complied with.[4]

The major limitation of s.2 was that it was intended only to apply to first-hand hearsay, *i.e.* where the statement adduced was one ". . . of which direct oral evidence by (the maker) would be admissible". This restriction was reinforced by section 2(3):

> 2.—(3) Where a statement . . . is admissible by virtue of this section, no evidence other than direct oral evidence by the person who made the statement or any person who heard it or otherwise perceived it being made shall be admissible for the purpose of proving it.

This excluded second-hand and other multiple hearsay — for example, those situations where the testifying witness has heard A

[4] This argument may also be made with regard to the procedural safeguards provided in the 1995 legislation.

repeat B's statement or where the court is presented with a document in which A has written down what he or she has been told by others (unless, of course, that other person has verified the document).

Section 2 of the Act only cured the vice of hearsay and, if the maker of the statement was not legally permitted to testify for some reason unconnected to the hearsay, this could not be evaded by adducing that testimony in hearsay form.[5]

(2) to make multiple hearsay admissible but only where the statements were contained in a documentary record. This was achieved by section 4:

> 4.—. . . a statement contained in a document shall . . . be admissible as evidence of any fact stated therein of which direct oral evidence would be admissible, if the document is . . . a record compiled by a person acting under a duty from information which was supplied by a person (whether acting under a duty or not) who had . . . personal knowledge of the matters dealt with and which, if not supplied . . . to the compiler of the record directly, . . . was supplied . . . indirectly through . . . intermediaries each acting under a duty.

Section 4 only applied only to documents and its purpose was to permit multiple hearsay which was contained in business records. There was considerable overlap with section 2 because much first-hand hearsay was also contained in such records. The situation envisaged in section 4 was that the original, non-testifying, witness had personal knowledge of the facts[6] which were communicated either directly or indirectly to someone whose duty it was to keep a record in a documentary form. That document was evidence of the facts contained, although, if what was relied on was an opinion, that was only admissible insofar as that opinion evidence would have been admissible by the original maker of the opinion.[7]

(3) to provide procedural safeguards to prevent the other party being taken by surprise by the production of such evidence.

(4) to put the common law exceptions on a statutory footing. The rules regarding informal admissions, public documents, reputation and pedigree were contained in section 9. Because hearsay was only admissible under the provisions of the Act,[8] it did not preserve those

[5] For example, if the statement involved public interest immunity or where the maker of the statement was an incompetent child witness as in *H. v. H.* [1989] 3 All E.R. 740.

[6] The provider of the information must have personal knowledge or ". . . may reasonably be supposed to have had . . ." such knowledge. In *Knight v. David* [1971] 3 All E.R. 1066, the party sought to rely on a map drawn up under the 1836 Tithes Act — the court were willing to infer personal knowledge on the part of the person who supplied the information and held the map admissible as a record.

[7] Civil Evidence Act 1972, s.1(2).

[8] Except in cases of other express statutory exceptions or where there was consent by the opposing party — s.1.

common law exceptions not expressly mentioned in section 9. In other words statements by deceased persons or *res gestae* statements were only admissible, if at all, under the provisions of section 2 of the Act.

(5) where previous inconsistent statements were proved against a witness by virtue of sections 3, 4 and 5 of the Criminal Procedure Act 1865, by section 3(1)(a) of the 1968 Act, these became admissible of the facts they contained and not merely evidence going to the credibility of the witness.

(6) where prior consistent statements made by a witness were proved to rebut any suggestion of recent fabrication, by section 3(1)(b) of the 1968 Act, these became admissible of the facts they contained and not merely evidence going to the credibility of the witness.

(7) where a witness was cross-examined on a document which was previously used to refresh that witness's memory, the document becomes evidence and, under section 3(2) was admissible as proof of any fact of which direct oral evidence would have been admissible.

(8) documents produced by a computer were to be admissible but only under further complex procedural safeguards laid down in section 5(2) of the Act, relating to regularity of use and proper operation of the computer.

The New Approach

The Civil Evidence Act 1995[9] implements the recommendations of the Law Commission Report.[10] The principle in 1968 was to maintain the exclusionary rule against hearsay but establish a broad statutory exception. But at the same time the reforms were hedged about with a range of restrictions (such as the level of hearsay admissible) and complex procedural safeguards. As a result the 1995 legislation adopts a more radical approach: principally section 1 abolishes the rule against the admission of hearsay evidence in all civil proceedings. Evidence cannot now be excluded on the ground that it is hearsay. The section also defines the concept of hearsay.[11]

> 1.—(1) In civil proceedings evidence shall not be excluded on the ground that it is hearsay.

[9] The Act was brought into force on January 31, 1997 — see S.I. (1996) Nos. 3217; 3219; 3218.

[10] "The Hearsay Rule in Civil Proceedings" (1993) (Law Comm. No. 216) Cm. 2321 — it follows a Consultation Paper, "The Hearsay Rule in Civil Proceedings" (1991) Law Comm. No. 117.

[11] This is in terms similar to those used by Cross's formulation which was approved by the House of Lords in *R. v. Sharp* [1988] 1 All E.R. 65 at 68c.

(2) In this Act —

a) 'hearsay' means a statement otherwise than by a person while giving oral evidence in the proceedings which is tendered as evidence of the matters stated; and
b) references to hearsay include hearsay of whatever degree.

(3) Nothing in this Act affects the admissibility of evidence admissible apart from this section.

(4) The provisions of sections 2 to 6 (safeguards and supplementary provisions relating to hearsay evidence) do not apply in relation to hearsay evidence admissible apart from this section, notwithstanding that it may also be admissible by virtue of this section.

Whilst the Act abolishes the rule against admitting hearsay evidence, the category of hearsay evidence still remains. There are safeguards in sections 2–6 which apply to hearsay evidence and to this limited extent it remains necessary to distinguish between hearsay and non-hearsay evidence:

(1) section 2 provides for notice to be given to the other party of any intention to adduce hearsay evidence.
(2) section 3 allows the other party to call the maker of the hearsay statement and to cross-examine him or her on that statement.
(3) section 4 provides a statutory checklist for the court in assessing the weight to be given to hearsay evidence.
(4) section 5 ensures that an incompetent witness shall not be made competent through the medium of a hearsay statement. It also allows the opposing party to adduce evidence that would cast doubt on the credibility of the maker of the statement.
(5) section 6 lays down the conditions for the admissibility of prior consistent statements.

As section 1(4) makes clear, these safeguards do not apply to hearsay evidence which is admissible independent of section 1(1). This was designed to preserve the effect of other statutory provisions which rendered hearsay admissible as evidence. The Law Commission stated:

> . . . It is not our policy to affect the operation of the existing statutory provisions rendering hearsay admissible, whether for particular purposes or in particular circumstances, or to add procedural burdens where none exist at present, particularly in the case of a statutory code as recent as the Children Act.

The status of the common law exceptions

The 1995 legislation does leave open one intriguing question: are hearsay statements in civil proceedings only admissible either under section 1(1) (and therefore affected by the limited safeguards) or under some other statutory provision (and therefore unaffected by such safeguards)? What is the place of the old common law exceptions to hearsay, especially statements by deceased persons and *res gestae*?

Under the 1968 Civil Evidence Act, the common law exceptions were either expressly retained by section 9 or otherwise had to conform to the conditions of admissibility laid down in sections 2 and 4. Thus the rules regarding statements by deceased persons and *res gestae* were effectively abolished. Neither were mentioned in section 9 and, if they were to be admissible, such statements had to be introduced under section 2 or section 4. But in the 1995 Act, section 1(3) states:

1.—(3) Nothing in this Act affects the admissibility of evidence admissible apart from this section

This does not include the phrase "by virtue of any statutory provision" and so it is necessary to consider whether hearsay statements can be admissible in other, non-statutory, ways. The answer is obvious: hearsay statements for centuries were admissible at common law through a range of exceptions and which are still applicable in criminal proceedings. It can be argued that the rules regarding statements by deceased persons and *res gestae* were not abolished in 1968 so much as put into abeyance. With the repeal of Part I of the Civil Evidence Act 1968, like a phoenix from the ashes, such statements become admissible again and the safeguards of the legislation do not apply. Not only would a party not have to give notice under section 2 but as well the opposing party would not have the benefit of section 3 because, although they could call the maker of the statement as a witness, they would not be permitted to treat the maker as a witness called by the other party and thereby cross-examine him or her.

An extension to this argument might be made out with regard to informal admissions. These were specifically provided for in section (9)(1) and section 9(2)(a) of the 1968 Act. The 1995 legislation regards such statements as coming naturally under section 1 and thus section 7(1) states:

7.—(1) The common law rule effectively preserved by section 9(1) and (2)(a) of the Civil Evidence Act 1968 (admissibility of admissions adverse to a party) is superseded by the provisions of this Act

Obviously the draftsmen considered that the rule as contained in section 9 of the 1968 Act was superseded by section 1(1). But the repeal of section 9 of the 1968 Act leaves the common law exception on informal admissions alive and kicking and therefore admissible under section 1(3). In such a case, a party relying on an informal admission would not need to give notice of the hearsay statement.

Thus hearsay statements are now admissible in civil proceedings:

- under section 1 of the Civil Evidence Act 1995
- under other statutory provisions
- where common law exceptions to hearsay apply.

Old Problems and New Solutions

The Law Commission identified a range of problems with the 1968 legislation:

Proceedings

Civil proceedings are defined by the 1995 Act:

> 11.—In this Act 'civil proceedings' means civil proceedings, before any tribunal, in relation to which the strict rules of evidence apply, whether as a matter of law or by agreement of the parties.

This provision retains the distinction in section 18(1) of the 1968 Act between those proceedings where the strict rules of evidence apply[12] and those tribunals which use more informal, less court-like procedures. As has been noted, the 1995 Act abolishes the exclusionary rule but retains the category of hearsay evidence to which certain procedural safeguards apply. Whereas tribunals applying "strict rules of evidence" will be bound to apply these procedural safeguards, other, less formal, tribunals will not be affected by the Act.

Prior to the 1995 Act, different rules of evidence applied in magistrates' courts depending on whether the proceedings were licensing applications, family, civil or criminal.[13] The same rules of evidence will now apply in all civil proceedings in magistrates' courts.

The notice provisions

Under the 1968 law, the major safeguard was the requirement to give notice of the intention to adduce hearsay evidence under sections 2, 4 or 5. Such notice was provided for in the rules of the County Court and of the High Court made under the provisions of section 8 of the 1968 Act. The notice had to specify how and by whom the statement was made. It also had to explain why the maker of the statement was not going to be called. The conditions were:

> . . . that the person in question is dead, or beyond the seas, or unfit by reason of his bodily or mental condition to attend as a witness or that despite the exercise of due diligence it has not been possible to identify or find him or that he cannot reasonably be expected to have any recollection of matters relevant to the accuracy or otherwise of the statement . . . [14]

[12] These include the Lands Tribunal, the Solicitors Disciplinary Tribunal and the Commissioners of Income Tax. For the position on arbitrations, see Law Commission, *op. cit.* para. 4.44.

[13] Law Commission, *op. cit.* paras. 3.22–3.31.

[14] R.S.C., Ord. 38, r.25.

The party relying on one of these conditions would have to establish that condition on the balance of probabilities.[15] The opposing party was permitted to serve a counter-notice requiring that the maker of the statement be called as witness.

Ultimately the court had an overriding discretion under section 8(3)(a) so that the court could admit (but not exclude) evidence despite the failure to comply with the necessary conditions.[16] If the party intending to rely on the hearsay statement were also intending to call the maker of the statement to testify, then leave of the court was also required under section 2(3):

Law Commission Report: *The Hearsay Rule in Civil Proceedings* (1993 Law Comm. No. 216)

There was general agreement by consultees with the view that the current regime is too elaborate and places unrealistic burdens on parties . . . The Law Society, for example, commented that the rules are rarely relied on, save where a witness has died, disappeared, or moved overseas. There has also been considerable criticism of the 'beyond the seas' rule which allows, for example, the admission of a statement by a person in Jersey and excludes a statement from a person in Newcastle. There was unanimity that the prescribed time limits were not complied with . . . we were told that this was a matter that was usually left until the pre-trial conferences with counsel, which could be so close to the beginning of the trial that compliance with the set time limits was extremely difficult, if not impossible.[17]

. . . the response on consultation has led us to conclude that there is widespread dissatisfaction with the complexity of the current rules, so much so that compliance with them may have become the exception rather than the rule, with the parties relying on the discretion of the court to admit the hearsay evidence notwithstanding non-compliance with the notice procedure or on agreements at trial to admit. It may, however, be true that the system, by and large, works after a fashion. The Supreme Court Procedure Committee, for example, considered that non-observance of the rules did not cause much practical difficulty and that their chief function was to exist as an early warning system and a reminder to parties of the need to give notice . . .[18]

We intend that a major safeguard against abuse of the freedom to adduce hearsay evidence should be found in a new, simplified notice provision . . . We intend our notice provision to be a departure from the complexity of the current notice rules which require a considerable amount of detail about the statement maker and the circumstances in which the statement was made. We endorse the objectives of the current system which are (a) that all issues arising out of the adduction of hearsay evidence should be dealt with before trial and (b) that there should be no surprises at trial . . .[19]

If a party does not give notice, where it would have been reasonable and practicable in all the circumstances for him to do so, we have decided not to recommend that the courts be allowed to refuse to admit the evidence. We consider

[15] *Rasool v. West Midlands Passenger Transport Executive* [1974] 3 All E.R. 638.

[16] *Ford v. Lewis* [1971] 1 W.L.R. 623; *Morris v. Stratford-on-Avon RDC* [1973] 3 All E.R. 263; *Rover International v. Cannon Films* [1987] 3 All E.R. 986.

[17] Paras. 3.2–3.3.

[18] *ibid.* para. 3.7.

[19] *ibid.* para. 4.9.

that a failure to comply with this safeguard is a matter which should be treated as an abuse of the court's process and not as one which should go to admissibility. In reaching this conclusion we have been influenced by arguments put during the passage through Parliament of the Bill that became the Civil Evidence (Scotland) Act 1988 . . . It was thought that this sanction could have the effect of simply re-introducing the rule against hearsay, which the Bill aimed to abolish completely . . . . . . We believe that the courts' inherent powers to control the conduct of proceedings include the power to rectify prejudice to parties adversely affected by a failure to comply. In these circumstances the relevant powers would be likely to include granting an adjournment to allow the recipient time to deal with the effect of late notification, or to compel the opposing party to perfect an inadequate notice. In extreme cases, it might involve ordering the trial to start again . . .[20]

Under section 2 of the Civil Evidence Act 1995, these concerns are addressed. Notice is regarded as important and rules of court will prescribe the manner of that notice. But a failure to comply with the provisions does not affect admissibility or lead to the evidence being excluded. The sanctions for failure to give notice are levied through allocating the costs of the action and, more importantly, by permitting the judge to give less weight to such a statement than to other hearsay statements where the proper procedures have been followed:

2.—(1) A party proposing to adduce hearsay evidence in civil proceedings shall, subject to the following provisions of this section, give to the other party or parties to the proceedings —

a) such notice (if any) of that fact, and
b) on request, such particulars of or relating to the evidence,

as is reasonable and practicable in the circumstances for the purpose of enabling him or them to deal with any matters arising from its being hearsay.

(2) Provision may be made by rules of court -

a) specifying classes of proceedings or evidence in relation to which subsection (1) does not apply, and
b) as to the manner in which (including the time within which) the duties imposed by that subsection are to be complied with in the cases where it does apply.

(3) Subsection (1) may also be excluded by agreement of the parties; and compliance with the duty to give notice may in any case be waived by the person to whom the notice is required to be given.

(4) A failure to comply with subsection (1), or with the rules under subsection (2)(b), does not affect the admissibility of the evidence but may be taken into account by the court —

a) in considering the exercise of its powers with respect to the course of proceedings and costs, and
b) as a matter adversely affecting the weight to be given to the evidence in accordance with section 4.

[20] *ibid.* paras. 4.11–4.12.

The timing of the notice is laid down by rules of court made under section 2(2) and this complies with the Law Commission's intention that notice should be given at the same time as witness statements are exchanged. Less importance is paid to the content of that notice. Previously a party had to specify how and by whom the statement was made as well as giving the reason why the maker of the statement was not going to be called. Under the 1995 Act, section 2(1), the recipient may request such particulars of the hearsay evidence "as is reasonable and practicable in the circumstances for the purpose of enabling him or them to deal with any matters arising from its being hearsay".

But the most significant change is that a failure to give notice does not affect admissibility but instead will be penalised, if at all, through costs, delay of trial or by the failure being ". . . a matter adversely affecting the weight to be given to the evidence . . ." under section 4.

Available witnesses — the power to call and to cross-examine

Under section 2 of the 1968 Act (but not under the provisions of section 4), a party had to prove the non-availability of the maker of the statement before the hearsay statement was admissible.[21] In drafting the 1995 legislation, the Law Commission considered whether hearsay statements ought to be excluded whenever it was reasonable and practicable to call the maker of the statement as a witness. This would have made a broad exception to the principle of general admissibility of hearsay statements, even were it restricted to those situations where there was a failure to give notice. As a result, hearsay statements have become admissible under section 1 regardless of the availability of the maker of the statement.

The safeguard that has been introduced by section 3 is to allow the opposing party to call the maker of the statement as a witness. Of course, where a party objects to the use of a hearsay statement, there is nothing, in theory, to prevent him or her from calling the maker of the statement (if available) as a witness. But the party would then be restricted in asking questions since it would not be possible to cross-examine the witness on the contents of the hearsay statement or to call into question his or her credibility as a witness, unless the witness were, in the opinion of the judge, to prove "adverse".[22] Section 3 addresses this problem:

> 3.—Rules of court may provide that where a party to civil proceedings adduces hearsay evidence of a statement made by a person and does not call that person as a witness, any other party to the proceedings may, with the leave of the court, call that person as a witness and cross-examine him on the statements as if he had been called by the first-mentioned party and as if the hearsay statement were his evidence in chief.

[21] The reasons were specified in the Civil Evidence Act 1968, s.8 and R.S.C., Ord. 38, r.25.
[22] Criminal Procedure Act 1865, s.3.

Again the general principle of the admissibility of hearsay evidence is underlined since the availability of a witness does not lead to the exclusion of the hearsay statement. In non-controversial matters, parties will no longer need the consent of the opposing parties as was needed under the 1968 Act. In controversial matters, there is a safeguard but even here the onus is shifted onto the party adversely affected by the statement who must obtain the leave of the court for permission to call and cross-examine the maker of the statement. The Law Commission considered it unlikely that this power would be often invoked since parties would wish to rely on "best evidence" and because relying on a hearsay statement of a witness who could have been called to testify will be another factor to be taken account of in evaluating the weight of the evidence under section 4.[23]

Weighing the evidence

The policy of the 1968 Civil Evidence Act was to exclude those "doubtful" hearsay statements such as

- multiple hearsay not contained in business records
- hearsay statements where the maker of the statement was available
- where there was a failure to give notice.

Under the 1995 legislation, exclusion is not an option. Instead the evidence is admitted and the defect is addressed through procedural devices such as delay of trial, through the mechanism of costs and through providing statutory guidelines by which the court is able to assess the weight to give to the hearsay statement:

Law Commission, *op. cit.* para. 4.18

The concept of providing guides as to weight is not novel: section 6(3) of the 1968 Act contains guidelines . . . We favour developing the use of guidelines for the following reasons. First, having abolished the exclusionary rule, we wish to place extra emphasis on the need for courts to be vigilant in testing the reliability of such evidence. Secondly, we think it important that parties are deterred from abusing the abolition of the rule, for example by deliberately failing to give notice, by giving late and inadequate notice, by relying on hearsay evidence in preference to calling a dubious witness to give direct evidence of a fact, or by attempting to conceal an essential weakness in a case by amassing hearsay statements on a point. As we have mentioned above, the draft Bill also gives an express indication that failure to comply with the duty to give notice may be taken into account at this stage as affecting the weight to be given to hearsay evidence, for instance, where the circumstances in which the evidence is adduced as hearsay are such as to suggest an attempt to prevent a proper evaluation of its weight.

[23] Law Commission, *op. cit.* para 4.16.

Some of the considerations relevant to weighing of hearsay evidence are specified in section 4:

4.—(1) In estimating the weight (if any) to be given to hearsay evidence in civil proceedings the court shall have regard to any circumstances from which any inference can reasonably be drawn as to the reliability or otherwise of the evidence.

(2) Regard may be had, in particular, to the following —

(a) whether it would have been reasonable and practicable for the party by whom the evidence was adduced to have produced the maker of the original statement as a witness;
(b) whether the original statement was made contemporaneously with the occurrence or existence of the matters stated;
(c) whether the evidence involves multiple hearsay;
(d) whether any person involved had any motive to conceal or misrepresent matters;
(e) whether the original statement was an edited account, or was made in collaboration with another or for a particular purpose;
(f) whether the circumstances in which the evidence is adduced as hearsay are such as to suggest an attempt to prevent proper evaluation of its weight.

It is a checklist of matters of which any court should take account as part of the normal process of assessing the weight of hearsay evidence. To the criticism that the section is self-evident, Lord Donaldson has commented that, as the guidelines became generally known and applied, a climate would continue to be fostered where practitioners would produce the best evidence available. Furthermore the section should concentrate the judicial mind on the issue of weight and, as the Lord Chancellor, Lord Mackay, has pointed out, the provision is especially useful for magistrates' courts which have not admitted hearsay evidence to the same extent as the higher civil courts.[24]

Competence

Under the 1968 Civil Evidence Act, the admissibility of all categories of hearsay depended on the capacity of the maker of the statement as a competent witness. There was a requirement that ". . . direct oral evidence by [the maker of the statement] would be admissible."[25] This position is not altered by the 1995 Act except that the requirement is spelt out expressly:

5.—(1) Hearsay evidence shall not be admitted in civil proceedings if or to the extent that it is shown to consist of, or to be proved by means of, a statement made by a person who at the time he made the statement was not competent as a witness.

For this purpose 'not competent as a witness' means suffering from such mental or physical infirmity, or lack of understanding as would render a person incompetent as a witness in civil proceedings; but a child shall be treated as competent as a

[24] 564 H.L. Official Reports (5th Series), col. 1051, May 25, 1995.
[25] Civil Evidence Act 1968, ss.2(1), 3(1) and 4(1).

witness if he satisfies the requirements of section 96(2)(a) and (b) of the Children Act 1989 (conditions for reception of unsworn evidence of child[26]).

To avoid doubt on the issue of the date on which the witness has to be competent,[27] the section states expressly that for a hearsay statement to be admissible, the maker of the statement had to be a competent witness on the date that the statement was made.

Credibility

Where the maker of the statement is absent from court and his or her testimony is instead represented by a document or another person who heard the statement, one of the major safeguards of adversarial trial, the right to impeach the credibility of the witness, would be denied to the party adversely affected by the admission of the hearsay statement. The Civil Evidence Act 1968 provided some protection through section 7(1)(a) which enabled a party adversely affected to adduce evidence which attacked the credibility of the maker of the statement. It also provided that the party relying on the statement could adduce evidence supporting the maker's credibility. The Law Commission did not seek to change that position.[28]

5.—(2) Where in civil proceedings hearsay evidence is adduced and the maker of the original statement, or of any statement relied upon to prove another statement, is not called as a witness —

(a) evidence which if he had been so called would be admissible for the purpose of attacking or supporting his credibility as a witness is admissible for that purpose in the proceedings; and
(b) evidence tending to prove that, whether before or after he made the statement, he made any other statement inconsistent with it is admissible for the purpose of showing that he had contradicted himself.

Provided that evidence may not be given of any matter of which, if he had been called as a witness and had denied that matter in cross-examination, evidence could not have been adduced by the cross-examining party.

Section 5(2) reflects the distinction between cross-examining on the issues and cross-examining as to credit. When the witness is present in

[26] These conditions are that a child must understand the duty to speak the truth and that he or she has sufficient understanding to justify the evidence being heard — this replicated the position in criminal proceedings under the Children and Young Persons Act 1933, 38(1) before that was repealed by the Criminal Justice Act 1991, s.52(2) which provides that children under 14 testify unsworn and that the power of the court to determine competence shall apply to children of tender years as it applies to other persons. A child's competence in criminal proceedings is governed by the Criminal Justice Act 1988, s.33A.
[27] Such a doubt arose in Scotland — *F. v. Kennedy* (1992) S.C.L.R. 139; *M and Another v. Kennedy* (1993) S.C.L.R. 69.
[28] Law Commission, *op. cit.* para. 4.29 — however it has simplified the language of the section.

court, this becomes important when counsel wants to introduce evidence in rebuttal of a witness's testimony. If this concerns the issues which the court has to decide, this is possible. But if it concerns a collateral issue, such as the credit of a witness, counsel is bound by the answer given by the witness and cannot call independent evidence in rebuttal.[29] Different scenarios are envisaged:

(1) the proviso to the subsection deals with the situation where, in normal cross-examination, a witness might be asked a question which impeaches his or her credit. He or she denies the matter. That is final since counsel cannot introduce evidence to rebut that denial. Where the testimony has been given by means of a hearsay statement, counsel is not permitted to adduce evidence which tends to substantiate the question that counsel has been unable to ask.

(2) paragraphs (a) and (b) allow counsel to adduce evidence in those situations where, even had the witness being normally cross-examined had denied the matter, counsel would have been able to rebut that denial. These are the situations which are exceptions to the rule of finality to answers on collateral issues. There are perhaps five exceptions to this rule:

   i) Where the witness is present and denies making prior inconsistent statements, these can be proved under sections 3, 4 or 5 Criminal Procedure Act 1865. If the testimony has been given by way of hearsay, such statements are admissible by virtue of section 5(2)(b), whether the inconsistent statements were made before or after the statement given in evidence.

   ii) Where a witness is present and denies previous convictions, these can be proved under section 6 of the Criminal Procedure Act 1865. If the testimony has been given by way of hearsay, such convictions are able to be proved by virtue of section 5(2)(a).

   iii) Where a witness is present and denies bias, evidence rebutting this is admissible.[30] If the testimony has been given by way of hearsay, such bias may be proved by virtue of section 5(2)(a).

   iv) Where a witness is present and denies any mental or physical disability, evidence rebutting this is admissible.[31] If the testimony has been given by way of hearsay, such disabilities may be proved by virtue of section 5(2)(a).

   v) Where a witness is present and denies having a reputation for untruthfulness, evidence rebutting this is admissible.[32] If the testimony has been given by way of hearsay, such a reputation may be proved by virtue of section 5(2)(a).

[29] *Attorney-General v. Hitchcock*, (1847) 1 Exch. 91.

[30] *R. v. Mendy* (1976) 64 Cr.App.R. 4; *R. v. Busby* (1981) 75 Cr.App.R. 79 ; *R. v. Edwards* [1991]) 2 All E.R. 266.

[31] *Toohey v. Met. Police Comm'r* [1965] A.C. 595.

[32] *R. v. Richardson* [1969] 1 Q.B. 299 .

Corroboration

Under section 6(4) of the 1968 Act, hearsay statements admissible under the Act were not admissible to corroborate the evidence of the maker of the statement. Whether such a provision was ever necessary is doubtful since, at common law, corroborative evidence must arise from a source independent of the witness needing to be corroborated. Furthermore it is doubtful whether a requirement for corroboration still exists in any area of civil litigation. As a result, the 1995 legislation does not include a similar provision.

Previous statements of witnesses

At common law previous statements of witnesses were inadmissible, both because they were hearsay (if a party sought to rely upon the facts they contained) but also because of the rule against narrative which excluded such statements if they were introduced merely as evidence of a witness's consistency and reliability. Under section 2 of the 1968 Civil Evidence Act, all previous statements of witnesses were admissible as evidence of the facts they contained. Unregulated, such a provision would encourage adducing superfluous evidence and section 2(2) required that, where a person was called as a witness, no previous statement could be adduced without notifying the opposing party and obtaining the leave of the court. In addition the maker of the statement had to testify before the previous statement could be given in evidence.[33] Section 2(2) also operated to restore aspects of adversarial trial in civil proceedings that were being circumvented:

> . . . to prevent a party from calling a witness simply to adduce evidence of his out-of-court written statement, without taking him through a proper examination-in-chief. It corrected a practice that had grown up under section 1 of the Evidence Act 1938, which allowed for the admission of an out-of-court statement simply by calling the maker to confirm the contents.[34]

The Law Commission's recommendations to maintain this position are included in section 6 of the Civil Evidence Act 1995:

> 6.—(1) Subject as follows, the provisions of this Act as to hearsay evidence in civil proceedings apply equally (but with any necessary modifications) in relation to a previous statement made by a person called as a witness in the proceedings.
>
> (2) A party who has called or intends to call a person as a witness in civil proceedings may not in those proceedings adduce evidence of a previous statement made by that person, except —

[33] There were some limited exceptions under Civil Evidence Act 1968, s.2(2)(b).

[34] Law Commission *op. cit.* para. 2.17; *Hilton v. The Lancashire Dynamo Nevelin Ltd* [1964] 1 W.L.R. 952.

(a) with the leave of the court, or
(b) for the purpose of rebutting a suggestion that his evidence has been fabricated.

This shall not be construed as preventing a witness statement (that is, a written statement of oral evidence which a party to the proceedings intends to lead) from being adopted by a witness in giving evidence or treated as his evidence.

(3) Where in the case of civil proceedings section 3, 4 or 5 of the Criminal Procedure Act 1865 applies, which makes provision as to —

(a) how far a witness may be discredited by the party producing him,
(b) the proof of contradictory statements made by a witness, and
(c) cross-examination as to previous statements in writing,

this Act does not authorise the adducing of evidence of a previous inconsistent or contradictory statement otherwise than in accordance with those sections.

(4) Nothing in this Act affects any of the rules of law as to the circumstances in which, where a person is called as a witness in civil proceedings is cross-examined on a document used by him to refresh his memory, that document may be made evidence in the proceedings.

(5) Nothing in this section shall be construed as preventing a statement of any description referred to above from being admissible by virtue of section 1 as evidence of the matters stated

The following points should be noted:

(1) a previous statement of a witness is only admissible as of right to rebut the suggestion that the witness's testimony has been fabricated: section 6(2)(b).
(2) in all other cases, the leave of the court must be obtained before a previous statement is advanced in evidence.
(3) the 1968 provisions (under section 2(2)(b)) regarding the course of evidence have been abandoned. The practice of judges varies and the Law Commission considered it inappropriate for this to be dealt with in primary legislation.[35]
(4) the proviso to section 6(2) of the 1995 Act recognises that where witness statements have been exchanged, under R.S.C., Ord. 38, r.2A the court may direct that the statement shall stand as the evidence-in-chief of the witness. Many witnesses as a result do not give evidence-in-chief.
(5) the section does not affect the rules contained in the Criminal Procedure Act 1865 concerning the treatment of adverse witnesses or the handling of inconsistent statements. Nor does the Act affect the rules whereby a document used to "refresh the memory"' can be made evidence in the proceedings.

[35] Law Commission, *op. cit.* para. 4.31.

Repetitious evidence

One argument against the relaxation of the hearsay rule was that it would lead to a proliferation of unnecessary evidence. Under the U.S. Federal Rules of Evidence, there is a power to exclude evidence if:

403.—. . . its probative value is substantially outweighed by . . . considerations of undue delay, waste of time, or needless presentation of cumulative evidence.[36]

The Law Commission decided that a similar provision was not needed,[37] concluding that there were sufficient existing powers of the court to exercise control over evidence adduced by the parties.

(1) at common law, the courts have power to rule evidence that is insufficiently relevant inadmissible. It has also been suggested that "needlessly prolix" evidence can be excluded where its production would cause needless vexation, expense or delay.[38]
(2) the court has inherent powers in order to be able to "act effectively within its jurisdiction".[39] The High Court and the County Court,[40] but not the magistrates' court, is able to prevent abuse of its own proceedings. Such powers have been rarely invoked but may be changing as the concept of the adversarial trial changes:

Law Commission, *op. cit.* paras. 4.56

We believe that the main reason why judicial powers to exclude repetitious and superfluous evidence have remained unfamiliar and obscure is the view that the judge's function is to be a 'passive umpire'. This militated against judicial intervention in the course of proceedings. There is good reason to think that this view of the judge as merely 'holding the ring' has recently undergone a reappraisal.

In *Mercer v. Chief Constable of the Lancashire Constabulary*[41] Lord Donaldson MR said that,

> Over the last quarter of a century there has been a sea change in legislative and judicial attitudes towards the conduct of litigation, taking the form of increased positive case management by the judiciary and the adoption of procedures designed (a) to identify the real issues in dispute and (b) to enable each party to assess the relative strengths and weaknesses of his own and his opponent's case at the earliest possible moment and well before any trial.

More recently in *A.B. v. John Wyeth and Brother Ltd*, Steyn L.J., in the context of a group action, said that,

[36] Federal Rules of Evidence, r.403.
[37] Law Commission, *op. cit.* paras. 4.20–4.24, 4.49–4.63.
[38] *Best on Evidence* (12th ed., 1922), para. 47.
[39] *per* Lord Morris of Borth-y-Gest in *Connelly v. DPP* [1964] A.C. 1255 at 1301 cited in Law Commission, *op. cit.* para. 4.53.
[40] County Courts Act 1984, s.76.
[41] [1991] 1 W.L.R. 367 at 373c.

> Inevitably, High Court judges assigned to the control of such litigation must depart from transitional procedures and adopt interventionist case management techniques.[42]

Steyn L.J. founded this proposition on the inherent jurisdiction of the court and, if this is so, it is difficult to see how, as a matter of logic, the power to adopt such techniques can be restricted to group actions.

Not only the Law Commission but also Lord Woolf[43] have argued that civil proceedings require greater pre-trial case management but also increased involvement in the adduction of evidence:

> The present practice is to allow every litigant unlimited time and unlimited scope so that the litigant and his advisors are able to conduct their case in all respects in the way which seems best to them. The results not infrequently are torrents of words, written and oral, which are oppressive and which the judge must examine in an attempt to eliminate everything which is not relevant, helpful and persuasive. The remedy lies in the judge taking time to read in advance pleadings, documents certified by counsel to be necessary, and short skeleton arguments of counsel.[44]

The Law Commission's conclusion was that the court should be more proactive in preventing the adduction of superfluous evidence but decided that, if such powers were to be made more explicit, this should be done by Rules of Court rather than by primary legislation.

Business records

Under section 4 of the 1968 Act, the problem elements were the references to "record" and "duty". "Record" was not defined but "a person acting under a duty" is defined under section 4(3) to include:

> . . . a person acting in the course of any trade, business, profession or other occupation in which he is engaged or employed or for the purpose of any paid or unpaid office held by him.

The difficulties in what constituted a record were shown in cases such as *H. v. Schering Chemicals*,[45] in which the plaintiffs sought to admit a file of information about a drug, Primodos. The file contained letters and articles published in *The Lancet* which were summaries of original research reports. Bingham J. held that the purpose of the 1968 Act was to admit evidence that a historian would see as "original or primary sources", including documents which gave effect to the transaction itself or were a

[42] [1993] 4 Med. L.R. 1 at 6.
[43] Lord Woolf, *Access to Justice* (1996).
[44] *per* Lord Templeman in *Banque Keyser Ullman S.A. v. Skandia (UK) Insurance Co. Ltd* [1991] 2 A.C. 249 at 280, cited by Law Commission, *op. cit.* para. 4.57.
[45] [1983] 1 All E.R. 849.

contemporaneous register of information supplied by those with direct knowledge of the facts. A digest of other people's research did not come within this. A similar narrow approach can be seen in *Savings and Investment Bank v. Gasco Investment*[46] where the court treated a report by Board of Trade inspectors appointed under the Companies Acts as a mere selection of material gathered together from other sources. *Re D.*[47] involved wardship proceedings. The maternal grandparents claimed custody of the child on the grounds that the father and his family had physically abused both mother (now dead) and daughter. Before her death, the mother had had an interview with her solicitor and her allegations were contained in the notes made by him. These were excluded because such notes were neither a statement approved by the mother under section 2 nor were they a record under section 4:

Law Commission, *op. cit.* para. 3.12

So far as records generally are concerned, consultees commented that the current rules are based on an old fashioned view of business methods and office procedure, where records were largely kept manually and where overall responsibility could be attributed to individual record keepers. Nowadays record keeping is less likely to be a separate function within an organisation and has been largely taken over by technology. The requirement to identify a person with a duty to compile the core information is often unrealistic. Whilst various categories of officialdom may have no difficulty in complying, for example tax inspectors, policemen and people carrying out duties imposed by statute, the rules are increasingly difficult to apply to commerce and industry, where procedures are likely to be less rigid . . .

The abolition of the exclusionary rule by section 1 of the 1995 Act means that business records are generally admissible and subject to the normal notice and weighing procedures. No longer is it necessary to prove a chain of duty linking the suppliers of information to the record in question and requiring personal knowledge by the compiler of the matters recorded. However the Law Commission considered that there should be a simpler regime to make the manner by which such documents are admitted into evidence easier:

Law Commission, *op. cit.* para. 4.39

. . . we consider that steps should be taken to make it easier to get such records admitted in evidence. Once it is accepted that there is often unlikely to be a witness who can give relevant and direct evidence of all or any of the aspects of the compilation of a record, it becomes artificial to require the record to be produced by a witness. We therefore propose that documents certified by an officer of a business or public authority should be capable of being received into evidence without further proof. . . . For the purposes of this section we propose that

[46] [1984] 1 All E.R. 296 .
[47] (1976) 2 F.L.R. 189.

'business' be defined widely so as to include 'any activity regularly carried out over a period of time, whether for profit or not, by any body (whether corporate or not) or by an individual'. This is to reflect our view that it is the quality of regularity that lends a business record its reliability, not the existence of a profit motive or the juridical nature of the person carrying on the activity.

This is provided for under the Act:

9.—(1) A document which is shown to form part of the records of a business or public authority may be received in evidence in civil proceedings without further proof.

(2) A document shall be taken to form part of the records of a business or public authority if there is produced to the court a certificate to that effect signed by an officer of the business or authority to which the records belong . . . .

(3) The absence of an entry in the records of a business or public authority may be proved in civil proceedings by affidavit of an officer of the business or authority to which the records belong.

(4) In this section —

'records' mean records in whatever form;

'business' includes any activity regularly carried on over a period of time, whether for profit or not, by any body (whether corporate or not) or by an individual;

'officer' includes any person occupying a responsible position in relation to the relevant activities of the business or public authority or in relation to its records; and

'public authority' includes any public or statutory undertaking, any government department and any person holding office under Her Majesty.

(5) The court may, having regard to the circumstances of the case, direct that all or any of the above provisions of this section do not apply in relation to a particular document or record, or description of documents or records.

Four points need emphasising:

(1) section 9 only provides for the manner by which business or public authority records are to be proved. Such documents are now generally admissible under section 1 and even if the records fail to come within the extended definitions in this section, this does not mean that they are not admissible, simply that they must be proved under the normal section 1 process.

(2) under subsection (2) a party needs only to produce the document and a statement signed by an officer of the business or authority stating that the document is part of the records of that business or authority.

(3) "record" is a wider concept than under the previous legislation:

We have sought to define the term 'records' in a manner which concentrates on the form in which they are kept[48] and which allows for the widest

[48] Presumably in contrast to the manner in which they are compiled?

possible admission. We have not sought to define the type of record which is capable of being admitted. However our proposals do not resolve the question . . . of whether a report by a DTI inspector constitutes a record . . .[49]

It is difficult to see that the material in *Savings and Investment Bank v. Gasco Investment*[50] or that in *H. v. Schering Chemicals*[51] comes within section 9. But this issue is less important since it only goes to the manner of admission and not to general admissibility. In both cases the material should be admissible under section 1.

(4) there is some controversy as to whether the absence of an entry in a record constitutes hearsay.[52] In civil proceedings, however, evidence to prove a negative is admissible even if drawing inferences from such evidence is fraught with difficulty. Section 9(3) allows the absence of such a record to be proved by the affidavit of an officer of the business or authority.

Computer records

The 1968 legislation revealed a fundamental mistrust of records held on computer. It was remarkable that at that date this novel form of evidence was considered at all.[53] The safeguards incorporated into section 5 were complex and inappropriate for the proliferation of desk-top computers in the 1990s. The section only applied to hearsay evidence and "real" evidence, such as that produced in the *Statue of Liberty*,[54] was not affected by the provisions of section 5.[55] The Law Commission found little disagreement with the position that the section 5 provisions were outdated and, more significantly, there was no good reason for distinguishing between different forms of record keeping or for maintaining a different regime for the admissibility of computer-generated documents.[56] As a result the Civil Evidence Act 1995 contains no special provisions in respect of computerised records which are treated similarly to other records, although the Law Commission Report considered that parties should be encouraged to provide information on the security of their systems.[57] "Document" is thus broadly defined:

[49] Law Commission, *op. cit.* para. 4.41.
[50] [1984] 1 All E.R. 296.
[51] [1983] 1 All E.R. 849.
[52] *R. v. Shone* [1983] 76 Cr.App.R. 72; *R. v. Shepherd* [1993] 3 All E.R. 225.
[53] Law Reform Committee, *13th Report Hearsay Evidence in Civil Proceedings* (1966) Cmnd. 2964, para. 10.
[54] [1968] 2 All E.R. 195.
[55] This is unlike the situation in criminal proceedings where all computer-generated evidence is subject to the provisions of s.69 of the Police and Criminal Evidence Act 1984.
[56] Law Commission, *op. cit.* para. 3.20.
[57] *ibid.*, para. 4.43.

13.—In this Act —

> . . . 'document' means anything in which information of any description is recorded and 'copy', in relation to a document, means anything onto which information recorded in the document has been copied, by whatever means and whether directly or indirectly . . .[58]

Common law exceptions

It was argued earlier that certain of the old common law exceptions to hearsay were put into abeyance under the 1968 Civil Evidence Act whereby the common law exceptions were either expressly retained by section 9 or otherwise had to conform to the conditions of admissibility laid down in sections 2 and 4.

This period of abeyance has been ended by the 1995 Act, section 1(3) states:

> 1.—(3) Nothing in this Act affects the admissibility of evidence admissible apart from this section

and by not limiting this to other statutory exceptions, it must mean that the common law exceptions to hearsay, such as statements by deceased persons, *res gestae* and (perhaps) informal admissions, are now again admissible in their own right and not subject to the safeguards in the 1995 legislation. But it is now necessary to distinguish between the common law exceptions admissible in their own right and those admissible under section 7 of the Civil Evidence Act 1995:

> 7.—(1) The common law rule effectively preserved by section 9(1) and (2)(a) of the Civil Evidence Act 1968 (admissibility of admissions adverse to a party) is superseded by the provisions of this Act.
>
> (2) The common law rules effectively preserved by section 9(1) and (2)(b) to (d) of the Civil Evidence Act 1968, that is, any rule of law whereby in civil proceedings —
>
> (a) published works dealing with matters of a public nature (for example, histories, scientific works, dictionaries and maps) are admissible as evidence of facts of a public nature stated in them,
> (b) public documents (for example, public registrers, and returns made under public authority with respect to matters of public interest) are admissible as evidence of the facts stated in them, or
> (c) records (for example, the records of certain courts, treaties, Crown grants, pardons and commissions) are admissible as evidence of facts stated in them,
>
> shall continue to have effect.

[58] This simple definition should be compared to the tortuous approach in the (now repealed) Civil Evidence Act 1968, s.10(1). Sched.1 of the 1995 Act applies this new definition to a number of other enactments.

(3) The common law rules effectively preserved by section 9(3) and (4) of the Civil Evidence Act 1968, that is, any rule of law whereby in civil proceedings —

(a) evidence of a person's reputation is admissible for the purpose of proving his good or bad character, or
(b) evidence of reputation or family tradition is admissible —
  (i) for the purpose of proving or disproving pedigree or the existence of a marriage, or
  (ii) for the purpose of proving or disproving the existence of any public or general right or of identifying any person or thing,

shall continue to have effect in so far as they authorise the court to treat such evidence as proving or disproving that matter.

Where any such rule applies, reputation or family tradition shall be treated for the purpose of this Act as a fact and not as a statement or multiplicity of statements about the matter in question.

(4) The words in which a rule of law mentioned in this section is described are intended only to identify the rule and shall not be construed as altering it in any way.

These have been discussed earlier.[59]

[59] Chap. 17.

20

OPINIONS AND THE EVIDENCE OF EXPERTS

Introduction

Witnesses give evidence of what they have seen, heard, smelt, felt or touched — direct evidence of their own perceptions. A witness's opinions, beliefs or inferences are not their perceptions but conclusions or opinions drawn from those perceptions. One of the central exclusionary rules is that opinions are not admissible to prove the truth of what is believed or inferred. The rationale for the rule has been put in different ways:

(1) opinions are seen as having little probative weight. In *R. v. Kearley*[1] the accused was charged with possession of drugs with intent to supply. Telephone callers and visitors to the house obviously believed that the accused was a supplier.

> What was said — in each case a request for drugs — is, of course, probative of the state of mind of the caller. But the state of mind of the caller is not the fact in issue and is, in itself, irrelevant, for it is not probative of anything other than its own existence. It becomes relevant only if and so far as the existence of other facts can be inferred from it. . . . if, at the trial, the prosecution had sought to adduce evidence from a witness not that drugs had been supplied but that it was his opinion or belief that drugs had been or would be supplied, that evidence would be inadmissible as amounting to no more than a statement of belief or opinion unsupported by facts upon which the belief was grounded.[2]

A bare opinion, by itself, has little, if any, probative weight. But an opinion can acquire weight: firstly, by the witness testifying as to the facts on which he or she bases that opinion; secondly from the very status of the witness. But is an opinion more worthy of belief simply because of the weight of numbers? An opinion held by one person has little weight — does such probative weight increase if there are a dozen witnesses who all share the same opinion?

It is a justifiable rationale to exclude opinion evidence on the basis of the lack of probative weight, but should such a principle be

[1] [1992] 2 All E.R. 345.
[2] *ibid.*, *per* Lord Oliver at 370j–371f.

expressed as a *rule* of exclusion? Any court has the discretionary power to reject irrelevant and worthless evidence, a power which would suffice to exclude unfounded opinion evidence.

(2) another reason for excluding a witness's opinion is that this usurps the function of the finder of fact whose task it is to draw the necessary inferences from the evidence. Although the trier of fact is free to reject an opinion, the policy behind the rule is to ensure that the trier of fact is not seduced into an easy acceptance of a convincingly-presented opinion. However desirable such a policy may be, it has now been largely abrogated in civil proceedings.[3] In criminal cases, there is a danger is that the operation of the rule can lead to the exclusion of potentially useful material.

(3) a third reason for exclusion is that a witness's opinion can often be based on evidence which, if stated expressly, would be inadmissible for one reason or another. This is illustrated in *Kearley* in which Lord Oliver suggested that a witness, present in court, who had previously been supplied with drugs by the accused, could give relevant and admissible evidence. But if the witness sought to support any opinion on Kearley's intent to supply by mentioning past drug dealing, this immediately infringes the rule against adducing evidence of bad character and raises difficult problems of similar fact evidence. The rule against the reception of a witness's opinion guards against the evasion of other exclusionary rules.

There are two major exceptions to the rule excluding opinion evidence:

(1) where the perceptions and statements of "fact" are conclusions in themselves or mixtures of inference and facts. This highlights the point that a strict distinction between perception and inference is not possible. When a witness identifies the accused, "That is the woman", this is as much an opinion as it is a reflection of the witness's perceptions on the offender's height, age, weight or colour of hair. Much testimony necessarily involves such a mixture.

    Non-expert witnesses are allowed to express their opinion on issues which do not call for specialist knowledge and where it would be impossible to separate observed fact from inference, such as identification or the speed of a car. It is impossible to be exact but generally the non-witness can give an opinion when the opinion is necessary for the coherence and comprehensibility of the testimony and when the opinion involves a everyday matter calling for no special expertise. Even in such cases, the non-expert is not permitted to testify as to the ultimate issue that has to be decided or as to those issues which are within the competence of the trier of fact.

(2) where the matter calls for special skill or knowledge which a judge or jury does not possess. In such a case an expert witness will be

[3] Civil Evidence Act 1972, s.3.

allowed to express an opinion. For example, in *R. v. Mason*,[4] the defence to a charge of murder was that the victim had committed suicide and the issue was whether the doctor could be asked whether the injuries could have been self-inflicted. The Court of Appeal held the answer admissible. In criminal proceedings, even experts are not permitted to give their opinion on the ultimate issue or on issues that are within the competence of the ordinary juror.

Expert Evidence

The common law always has accepted expert evidence. In *Folkes v. Chadd*[5] the opinion of an engineer was admitted on the issue of whether an embankment had caused the silting up of a harbour.

Folkes v. Chadd (1782) 3 Doug K.B. 157 at 158, *per* Lord Mansfield

The question is, to what has this decay been owing . . . That is a matter of opinion; the whole case is a question of opinion, from facts agreed upon. Nobody can swear that it was the cause; nobody thought that it would produce this mischief when the bank was erected . . . Mr Smeaton is called . . . It is objected that Mr Smeaton is going to speak, not as to facts, but as to opinion. That opinion, however, is deduced from facts which are not disputed — the situation of banks, the course of tides and of winds, and the shifting of sands. His opinion deduced from all these facts is that, mathematically speaking, the bank may contribute to the mischief but not sensibly. Mr Smeaton understands the construction of harbours, the causes of their destruction, and how remedied. In matters of science no other witnesses can be called. . . . I cannot believe that where the question is, whether a defect arises from a natural or an artificial cause, the opinions of men of science are not to be received. Handwriting is proved every day by opinion; and for false evidence on such questions a man may be indicted for perjury . . .

In the U.S.A., the Federal Rules of Evidence state:

702.—If scientific, technical, or other specialised knowledge will assist the trier of fact to understand the evidence or to determine a fact in issue, a witness qualified as an expert by knowledge, skill, experience, training, or education, may testify in the form of an opinion or otherwise.[6]

Expert testimony is not restricted to voicing opinions as to the effect of real or assumed facts. Expert witnesses may testify to their own findings or to the scientific or other principles relevant to the case as well as drawing inferences from such findings. But their opinions must be restricted to their field of expertise. If the issue does not require specialised knowledge and is within the competence of the trier of fact, the witness's opinion is inadmissible. In *R. v. Mackenney*[7] a psychologist watched the chief

[4] (1911) 7 Cr.App.R. 67.
[5] (1782) 3 Doug K.B. 157.
[6] Federal Rules of Evidence, r.702.
[7] (1981) 76 Cr.App.R. 271.

prosecution witness, Childs, testify and the defence sought to adduce his testimony that Childs was suffering from some mental disorder which would affect the reliability of his evidence. The trial judge rejected this evidence and this was upheld on appeal. One basis was the expert's credentials because he had no medical qualifications or diagnostic experience and his expertise was based on an extensive examination of the literature on psychopathy. In a proper case, medical testimony could be received to show that a witness was *incapable* of telling the truth.[8] Parties cannot adduce such testimony merely to cast doubt on the reliability of their opponent's witnesses or to suggest that a capable witness was in fact lying. That decision is the jury's.

The Scope for Expert Testimony

It would be idle to list areas of knowledge in expert testimony may be received,[9] encompassing matters scientific and medical, architectural and engineering. Bullets, blood and tachographs may all be the subject of expert analysis. Movements in the stock market or market values might all need exposition to the jury. In assessing whether expert evidence is admissible, one test may be that of assisting the trier of fact:

> There is no more certain test for determining when experts may be used than the common sense inquiry whether the untrained layman would be qualified to determine intelligently and to the best possible degree the particular issue without enlightenment from those having a specialised understanding of the subject involved in the dispute.[10]

Situations change and in some fields, expert testimony may become unnecessary and judicial knowledge be a more appropriate approach. The matter might be treated as coming within the ordinary competence of the juror, as with the question whether a computer has been operated properly:

> Documents produced by computers are an increasingly common feature of all business and more and more people are becoming familiar with their uses and operation. Computers vary immensely in their complexity and in the operations they perform. The nature of the evidence to discharge the burden of showing that there has been no improper use of the computer and that it was operating properly will inevitably vary from case to case. The evidence must be tailored to suit the needs of the case. I suspect that it will very rarely be necessary to call an expert and that in the vast majority of cases it will be possible to discharge the burden by calling a witness who is familiar with the operation of the computer in the sense of knowing what the computer is required to do and who can say that it is doing it properly.[11]

[8] *Toohey v. Metropolitan Police Commissioner* [1965] A.C. 595.
[9] There is a useful list of examples in Keane A., *The Modern Law of Evidence* (4th ed., 1996) 454.
[10] Ladd, "Expert Testimony" 5 Vand. L.R. 414 at 418 (1952).
[11] *R. v. Shepherd* [1993] 1 All E.R. 225 at 231b, *per* Lord Griffiths.

New forensic techniques and fields of knowledge emerge and the court must be satisfied, not only that the witness is qualified, but whether such evidence should be given. In their time, courts have looked with suspicion at both fingerprints and DNA testing.[12] New forensic techniques, such as ESDA,[13] have been vital element in uncovering miscarriages of justice. In contrast, psychological profiling has yet to be accepted as valid evidence.[14] The position in English law is that a field need not be generally accepted before expert testimony is admissible but it must be sufficiently established to be reliable. Techniques of voice identification were in issue in *R. v. Robb*[15] where the evidence consisted of recordings of ransom demands and control recordings of the accused's voice. The witness concluded that there was no distinction between the two voices. The court accepted that voice identification itself was a field calling for expert testimony. However the witness's techniques (which involved listening carefully to the tape recordings) were ones which were not scientific nor generally respected in the field of phonetics. The court took a pragmatic approach, accepting the evidence and treating any doubts about the accuracy of the techniques as a question of weight for the jury. The witness had described the features that he paid attention to and it was for the jury to assess the value to give to his opinion.

In the U.S.A., the decision in *Daubert v. Merrell Dow Pharmaceuticals*[16] takes a different line, requiring the judge to play a more pro-active role as gatekeeper in relation to scientific testimony and retreating from the principle that expert testimony was admissible where the approach had obtained widespread acceptance in the relevant discipline. The case concerned the drug Bendectin, approved by the federal Food and Drugs Administration. The drug was taken to relieve symptoms of nausea during pregnancy and was alleged to have caused birth defects. The plaintiffs employed expert witnesses whose testimony had never been subjected to peer review. The judgment draws on the theories of Karl Popper and in particular, his principle that the criterion on scientific status of a theory is its falsifiability, or refutability, or testability.[17] The Supreme Court considered this principle to be an appropriate approach for assessing the scope for expert evidence. This approach appears to place a heavier burden on the trial judge to determine whether the reasoning or methodology underlying the testimony is scientifically valid, taking into account the known or potential error rate and whether it has been subjected to peer review and publication. Trial judges would appear to have to distinguish good science from bad.

[12] Farington D., "Unacceptable Evidence" New L.J. (1993) 806 and 857.
[13] *R. v. Wellington* [1991] Crim.L.R. 543.
[14] The refusal of the court to accept such testimony led to the collapse of the case against Colin Stagg for the murder of Rachel Nickell — *The Guardian*, September 15, 1994. See Ormerod D., "Evidential Implications of Psychological Profiling", [1996] Crim.L.R. 863.
[15] (1991) 93 Cr.App.R. 161.
[16] 113 S.Ct. 2786 (1993).
[17] Popper K., *Conjectures and Refutations* (4th ed., 1972), 36–37.

To assess the admissibility of expert testimony in this way would appear a tall order for the judge faced with the complexities of phonetics and voice identification in *Robb* or the techniques of facial mapping.[18] Such difficulties would multiply in the context of expert psychiatric or psychological evidence where controversy surrounds the very existence of certain syndromes and disorders such as recovered memory syndrome, rape trauma syndrome, battered wife or child syndrome, post-traumatic stress disorder or multiple personality disorder, some of which have achieved strong empirical support whereas others have not. For example, expert evidence on "battered wife syndrome" was considered admissible in *R. v. Ahluwalia*.[19] The introduction of a *Daubert* approach in England and Wales might well lead to reconsideration of this position and it has been argued that such concepts might have therapeutic value but are scientifically unproved and unsuitable for courtroom presentation.

Credentials

The expert witness must establish his or her credentials in the topic requiring expertise. This may consist of practical experience or professional qualification. The opposing party is entitled to inquire into these. The question of whether a witness is an expert is a matter of fact for the judge. If there are some credentials, the evidence is likely to be admitted and the rest would be a matter of weight.[20] But if the witness is not qualified, the evidence will be excluded — in *R. v. Loake*[21] the accused was not permitted to call a magistrate who had visited him in his cell to testify as to his sanity.

Many cases have considered the qualifications of witnesses called to testify on a point of foreign law which needs establishing as a matter of fact.

> "The judge has not organs to know and to deal with the text of the foreign law, and therefore requires the assistance of a lawyer who knows how to interpret it."[22]

An English court should not conduct its own researches into foreign law[23] and if expert witnesses agree as to the interpretation of the foreign law, the judge is not entitled to reject that evidence.[24] However if the expert witnesses conflict as to the effect of foreign sources, the court is entitled to

[18] *R. v. Stockwell* (1993) 97 Cr.App.R. 260.
[19] [1992] 4 All E.R. 889.
[20] *R. v. Silverlock* (1894) 2 Q.B. 766 (in which a solicitor was accepted as an expert on handwriting though his experience had been picked up as an amateur); *R. v. Robb supra*; *R. v. Clare* [1995] Crim.L.R. 947 and comment Munday R., "Videotape Evidence and the Advent of the Expert Ad Hoc" (1995) 159 J.P. 547.
[21] (1911) 7 Cr.App.R. 71.
[22] *Sussex Peerage Case* (1844) 11 Cl & Fin 85 at 115, *per* Lord Brougham.
[23] *Duchess Di Sora v. Phillipps* (1863) 10 H.L. Cas. 624 at 640.
[24] *Bumper Development v. Metropolitan Police Commissioner* [1991] 4 All E.R. 638 at 646.

look at those sources to resolve the conflict.[25] Furthermore the Court of Appeal regards a trial judge's conclusion on a point of foreign law, although a finding of fact, as "a question of fact of a peculiar kind"[26] which may be re-examined on appeal.

At common law the credentials of an expert on foreign law were carefully scrutinised and only a judge or legal practitioner was properly qualified. This exclusive approach was demonstrated in decisions such as *Bristow v. Sequeville*[27] although other cases allowed witnesses whose expertise had been gathered in different ways (as an embassy official[28] or through business[29] or banking). Even academics were acceptable.[30] The common law has been consolidated in the Civil Evidence Act 1972.

4.—(1) It is hereby declared that in civil proceedings a person who is suitably qualified to do so on account of his knowledge or experience is competent to give expert evidence as to the law of any country or territory outside the United Kingdsom, or of any part of the United Kingdom other than England and Wales, irrespective of whether he has acted or is entitled to act as a legal practitioner there.

Expert opinion and hearsay

The facts on which an expert may form an opinion should be proved by admissible evidence.[31] Different situations may be envisaged:

(1) the facts on which any opinion is based may well be based on the witness's own perceptions: the pathologist who performs a post-mortem may testify as to his or her findings and give an opinion as to the cause of death.
(2) the opinion might also be on the basis of assumed facts: the witness might be asked what, given certain marks on the body, might be the likely cause of death. In *R. v. Mason*[32] a surgeon who had not seen the body was asked whether, given the nature of the wounds, these could have been self-inflicted. In such cases the expert should state the assumed facts on which the opinion is based so that the trier of fact can assess the weight of the opinion. The opinion is valueless unless the facts themselves are proved.
(3) an opinion can also be on the basis of facts supplied by others: the pathologist might well be relying on analyses of stomach contents or body tissues carried out by others.

[25] *Earl Nelson v. Lord Bridport* (1845) 8 Beav. 527 at 537.
[26] *Parkasho v. Singh* [1967] 1 All E.R. 737 at 746.
[27] (1850) 5 Exch. 275.
[28] *Re Dost Aly Khan's Goods* (1880) 6 P.D. 65.
[29] *Vander Donckt v. Thellusson* (1849) 8 C.B. 812.
[30] *Brailey v. Rhodesia Consolidated Ltd* [1910] 2 Ch. 95 but see *Bristow v. Sequeville supra.*
[31] Pattenden R., "Expert Opinion Based on Hearsay" [1982] Crim.L.R. 85.
[32] (1911) 7 Cr.App.R. 67.

In this latter case, the expert witness may rely on facts of which he or she has no first-hand knowledge and which, if retailed to the court, would be hearsay. In *R. v. Abadom*[33] the charge was robbery and the prosecution case rested on evidence that a window had been broken during the robbery and that fragments of glass were found in the accused's shoe. Did the splinters come from the scene of the robbery? The expert witness measured the refractive index of the glass from the window and that found in the shoe. He referred to Home Office statistics as to how common this kind of glass was. It occurred in only four per cent of glass samples investigated and consequently there was a very strong likelihood that the glass in the shoe originated from the window. The expert witness at that time[34] was relying on inadmissible hearsay contained in the Home Office statistics. On appeal it was submitted that he was not entitled to rely on such material and that the case was indistinguishable from *Myers v. DPP.*[35] The Court of Appeal disagreed:

R. v. Abadom [1983] 1 All E.R. 364 at 368e–j, *per* Kerr L.J.

First, where an expert relies on the existence or non-existence of some fact which is basic to the question on which he is asked to express his opinion, that fact must be proved by admissible evidence: see *English Exporters (London) Ltd v. Eldonwall Ltd.*[36] Thus, it would no doubt have been inadmissible if [the witness] had said in the present case that he had been told by somebody else that the refractive index of the fragments of glass and of the control sample was identical, and any opinion expressed by him on this basis would have been based on hearsay. If he had not himself determined the refractive index, it would have been necessary to call the person who had done so before [the witness] could have expressed an opinion based on this determination . . . Second, where the existence or non-existence of some fact is in issue, a report made by an expert who is not called as a witness is not admissible as evidence of that fact merely by production of the report, even though it was made by an expert: see eg *R. v. Crayden.*[37]

These, however, are in our judgment the limits of the hearsay rule in relation to evidence of opinion given by experts, both in principle and on the authorities. In other respects their evidence is not subject to the rule against hearsay in the same way as that of witnesses of fact . . . Once the primary facts on which their opinion have been proved by admissible evidence, they are entitled to draw on the work of others as part of the process of arriving at their conclusion. However, where they have done so, they should refer to this material in their evidence so that the cogency and probative value of their conclusion can be tested and evaluated by reference to it.

This process can also be seen in *R. v. Bradshaw.*[38] The accused was charged with murder and the only issue was diminished responsibility. The

[33] [1983] 1 All E.R. 364.
[34] Nowadays the tables would be admissible under the Criminal Justice Act 1988, ss.24 and 30.
[35] [1964] 2 All E.R. 881.
[36] [1973] 1 All E.R. 726 at 731.
[37] [1978] 2 All E.R. 700 at 702.
[38] (1985) 82 Cr.App.R. 79.

defence produced medical experts whose opinions were based in part that the defendant had told them that he was "in a state of unreality and confusion". Such statements were hearsay and, while the doctors could not testify to them as proof of their truth, they could testify to them to explain the basis on which they arrived at their conclusions about the defendant's mental condition. This is in contrast to *Abadom* where the primary facts (the refractive index of the of pieces of glass) were proved by direct evidence and it was only the secondary information (the statistical tables) that was hearsay. Where the primary information consists mainly or entirely of hearsay, the judge would be justified in warning the jury about the flimsiness of any foundation for that opinion. To some extent this was the situation in *Bradshaw* and the judge was justified in warning the defence of his intentions to warn the jury. As a result the accused unwillingly testified.

The English position by and large represents the U.S. position in the Federal Rules of Evidence:

> 703.—The facts or data in the particular case upon which an expert bases an opinion or inference may be those perceived by or made known to the expert at or before the hearing. If of a type reasonably relied upon by experts in the particular field in forming opinions or inferences upon the subject, the facts or data need not be admissible in evidence.[39]

English courts have not expressly stated that the hearsay information which is the foundation of an expert's opinion must be of a type reasonably relied on by experts in the field, although the field itself must be well-established so as to pass the tests of relevance and reliability. However, even if there is general acceptance by experts of the legitimacy of using hearsay evidence as the basis of their opinion, there is still a residual power in the court to exclude evidence which would have an unduly prejudicial effect. For example, in an American case involving an aeroplane crash, the court refused to allow expert testimony about another accident which involved an identical aeroplane, since the other accident did not occur under conditions substantially similar to the accident at issue. The introduction of the evidence was seen as likely to have a prejudicial effect on the jury.[40]

In civil proceedings prior to 1995, expert testimony was a legitimate technique to outflank the hearsay rule. In *H. v. Schering Chemicals*,[41] the plaintiffs sought to admit a file of information about a drug, Primodos. The file contained letters and articles published in *The Lancet* which were summaries of original research reports. This was not admissible under section 4 of the Civil Evidence Act 1968 but could have been relied upon by any expert witness as the basis for an opinion. However under section 1

[39] Federal Rules of Evidence, r.703.
[40] *Machtshien v. Beech Aircraft Corp* 847 F. 2d 1261 (7th Cir 1988).
[41] [1983] 1 All E.R. 849.

of the Civil Evidence Act 1995, no evidence can be excluded on the ground that it is hearsay, of whatever level.

Matters within the competence of the jury

In criminal cases,[42] one major limitation on the testimony of expert witnesses is that they should not express opinions on those matters which are within the competence of the jury. We will refer to this as the *Turner* rule.[43] For example, juries are daily asked to decide whether a defendant intended or foresaw a particular consequence or believed or knew a particular fact. They are expected to reach these conclusions from the accused's behaviour, his or her statements or the surrounding circumstances, almost certainly testing their conclusions from what they, the jurors, might have known, intended or foreseen in a like situation. The jurors are representatives of the community and are expected to understand how "normal" people behave and react. Expert evidence by psychologists is not admissible on such issues. Such evidence is only admissible in dealing with the "abnormal" defendant whose actions are assumed to be outside the experience of the jury.

This causes problems, especially in the area of psychiatric and psychological testimony. Such testimony might be introduced not merely with specific defences such as insanity, diminished responsibility and provocation but generally with *mens rea* issues. In *Turner*, the accused killed his girlfriend by battering her over the head with a hammer. His defence was provocation and that he had lost his self-control when she told him that she had been having affairs with other men while he had been in prison. The judge refused the defence leave to call a psychiatrist who would have testified that the accused was not suffering from mental illness but was likely to have killed her in an "explosive release of blind rage" at hearing her confession. On appeal, it was submitted that the witness's opinion as to Turner's personality and mental make-up was relevant as it showed that he was likely to be easily provoked and that his account of the killing was likely to be true.

R. v. Turner [1975] 1 All E.R. 70 at 74b-e, *per* Lawton L.J.

Opinions from knowledgeable persons about a man's personality and mental make-up play a part in many human judgments. In our judgment the psychiatrist's opinion was relevant. Relevance, however, does not result in evidence being admissible: it is a condition precedent to admissibility. Our law excludes evidence of many matters which in life outside the courts sensible people take into consideration when making decisions. Two broad heads of exclusion are hearsay and opinion . . .

[42] This does not apply in civil proceedings since under the Civil Evidence Act 1972, s.3(1), ". . . where a person is called as a witness . . . his opinion on any relevant matter on which he is qualified to give expert evidence shall be admissible in evidence."
[43] [1975] 1 All E.R. 70.

The foundation of these rules was laid down by Lord Mansfield CJ in *Folkes v. Chadd*[44] and was well laid: 'The opinion of scientific men upon proven facts', he said, 'may be given by men of science within their own science.' An expert's opinion is admissible to furnish the court with scientific information which is likely to be outside the experience and knowledge of a judge or jury. If on the proven facts a judge or jury can form their own conclusions without help then the opinion of an expert is unnecessary. In such a case if it is given dressed up in scientific jargon it may make judgment more difficult. The fact that an expert witness has impressive scientific qualifications does not by that fact alone make his opinion on matters of human nature and behaviour within the limits of normality any more helpful than that of the jurors themselves; but there is a danger that they may think it does.

The Court of Appeal upheld the conviction, arguing that, although mental illness was within the expert witness's province, Turner's emotional attachment to the victim and his outburst of rage was within ordinary human experience and the jury did not require the assistance of an expert for them to assess the defendant's account. The *Turner* rule says that expert evidence is not admissible:

- when it concerns an issue within the knowledge and experience of the jury
- when it concerns an issue of human nature and behaviour within the bounds of normality.

In *R. v. Chard*,[45] the defendant was accused of murder. The defence was neither diminished responsibility nor insanity but the defendant sought to introduce the testimony of a psychiatrist as to his mental state at the time of the killing — that is, whether he was likely to have possessed the intent to kill or to cause grievous bodily harm. The Court of Appeal upheld the trial judge's rejection of such evidence:

R. v. Chard (1971) 56 Cr.App.R. 268 at 270–271, _per_ Roskill L.J.

. . . one purpose of jury trials is to bring into the jury box a body of men and women who are able to judge ordinary day-to-day questions by their own standards, that is, the standards in the eyes of the law of theoretically ordinary reasonable men and women. That is something which they are well able by their ordinary experience to judge for themselves. Where the matters in issue go outside that experience and they are invited to deal with someone supposedly abnormal, for example, supposedly suffering from insanity or diminished responsibility, then plainly in such a case they are entitled to the benefit of expert evidence. But where, as in the present case, they are dealing with someone who by concession was on the medical evidence entirely normal, it seems to this Court abundantly plain on first principles of the admissibility of expert evidence, that it is not permissible to call a witness, whatever his personal experience, merely to tell the jury how he thinks an

[44] (1782) 3 Doug K.B. 157 at 159.
[45] (1971) 56 Cr.App.R. 268.

accused man's mind — assumedly a normal mind — operated at the time of the alleged crime with reference to the crucial question of what that man's intention was.

In *R. v. Masih*[46] the accused, who was charged with rape, had an I.Q. of 72. Expert evidence was inadmissible on the issue of whether he realised that the victim was not consenting. The borderline between the normal and abnormal was seen as the arbitrary line of an I.Q. of 69, below which the defendant would have been a mental defective and expert evidence would have been admissible, "in order to enlighten the jury upon a matter which is abnormal and therefore, ex hypothesi, presumably outside their experience".[47] Similarly in *R. v. Weightman*[48] a mother killed her child and the appellate court upheld the trial judge's refusal to admit expert evidence of her abnormal and histrionic personality which, however, did not amount to mental illness. In *R. v. Reynolds*[49] evidence was excluded that the defendant was emotionally disturbed and living in a fantasy world and thus did not form the *mens rea* for murder.

There has been one exception to the *Turner* rule: in *R. v. Lowery*[50] the two defendants were charged with a sadistic murder of a young girl. Both accused sought to lay the blame on the other. A clinical psychologist examined both accused and testified on behalf of Lowery's co-defendant, King. He testified that King was immature and emotionally shallow and was likely to be dominated by a more aggressive man. He also testified that Lowery had a strong aggressive drive with weak controls. Such evidence is, on its face, evidence of Lowery's predisposition to the crime and normally inadmissible. But Lowery had testified on his own behalf and had already mentioned his own good character. The psychologist's evidence is admissible in rebuttal. However, even had the defence case not raised the issue of character, the Privy Council held that the evidence would have been admissible:

R. v. Lowery [1973] 3 All E.R. 662 at 671b–e, *per* Lord Morris

If in imaginary circumstances similar to those of this case, it was apparent that one of the accused was a man of great physical strength whereas the other was a weakling it could hardly be doubted that in forming an opinion as to the probabilities it would be relevant to have the disparity between the two in mind. Physical characteristics may often be of considerable relevance: see *Toohey v. Metropolitan Police Commissioner*.[51] The evidence of Professor Cox was not related to crime or criminal tendencies: it was scientific evidence as to the respective personalities of the two accused as, and to the extent, revealed by certain well-

[46] [1986] Crim.L.R. 395.
[47] *per* Lane L.C.J.
[48] [1991] Crim.L.R. 204.
[49] [1989] Crim.L.R. 220; *R. v. Wood* [1990] Crim.L.R. 264; *R. v. Toner* [1991] 93 Cr.App.R. 382.
[50] [1973] 3 All E.R. 662.
[51] [1965] 1 All E.R. 506.

known tests. Whether it assisted the jury is not a matter that can be known. All that is known is that the jury convicted both the accused. But insofar as it might help in considering the probabilities as to what happened at the spot to which the girl was taken it was not only relevant to and necessary for the case advanced by King but it was made relevant and admissible in view of the case advanced by Lowery and in view of Lowery's assertions against King.

The case put forward by counsel on behalf of King involved posing to the jury the question 'which of these two men is the more likely to have killed this girl?' and inviting the jury to come to the conclusion that it was Lowery. If the crime was one which was committed apparently without any kind of motive unless it was for the sensation experienced in the killing then unless both men acted in concert the deed was that of one of them. It would be unjust to prevent either of them from calling any evidence of probative value which could point to the probability that the perpetrator was the one rather than the other.

Turner can be reconciled with this decision since, in the circumstances of *Lowery*, the jury needed expert assistance in relation to the relative aggression of the two accused. Recently in some areas of criminal law, *Turner* has appeared of less importance. In the defence of provocation, the jury must consider the effect of the provoking words or acts on a person with reasonable self-control but otherwise possessing the characteristics of the accused.[52] The personality of the accused is one of those characteristics. In *R. v. Humphreys*[53] a young prostitute killed her pimp with whom she had a tempestuous and abusive relationship. A consultant psychiatrist testified that she was of abnormal mentality, with immature, explosive and attention-seeking traits, the last referring to her tendency to slash her wrists:

R. v. Humphreys [1995] 4 All E.R. 1008 at 1014g–1015s, _per_ Hirst L.J.

The criticism raised in the first ground of appeal focuses upon the subsequent direction to the jury as to the way they should treat Dr Tarsh's evidence in relation to the concept of the reasonable man. This crucial direction . . . ..was as follows:

> It is for you to decide, taking into account all the evidence, as to what effect that jeering at her over not having made a good job of cutting her wrists might have had on a young woman who had got herself into that situation ***but did not have a distorted and explosive personality*** (Our emphasis).

It is common ground that the judge was in this passage and, in particular, in the use of the word 'distorted' in the words to which we have added emphasis, explicitly directing the jury as a matter of law not to attribute to the reasonable young woman, in her situation, any of the seriously abnormal characteristics described by Dr Tarsh, including her attention-seeking trait through her tendency to wrist-cutting.

The crux of [the appellant's] submission is that this direction was erroneous in principle, and that it was obligatory on the judge that the first and third traits

[52] *DPP v. Camplin* [1978] 2 All E.R. 168.
[53] [1995] 4 All E.R. 1008.

described by Dr Tarsh (immaturity and most particularly attention-seeking) were matters which they were entitled to take into account as eligible for atttribution to the reasonable man, it being, of course, for the jury to decide what weight, if any, to give to them.[54]

Decisions[55] such as *Humphreys* opens the door to a more liberal approach to the admissibility of expert testimony on such characteristics in provocation, moving away from decisions such as *R. v. Roberts*[56] where the defendant was profoundly and pre-lingually deaf. The court refused to permit psychiatric evidence as to the likely effect of physical abuse by the father of the accused.

A similar approach would be expected in pleas of duress where the substantive law, as laid down in *R. v. Graham*,[57] is analogous as it requires the court to consider the effect that the threats might have on a person of reasonable firmness but one who otherwise shared the defendant's characteristics. Indeed the approach was copied in *R. v. Emery*[58] when a unmarried mother of a young child was convicted of failing to protect her child from its father. She was permitted to call expert testimony to the effect that she had been reduced to a state of dependent helplessness, unable to protect her child. The Court of Appeal accepted the trial judge's decision to admit the evidence:

> There is potential expert evidence to the effect that if she is right, her will could have been crushed. That would afford her a good defence . . . Therefore, without further explanation or understanding, the jury's lack of understanding might lead to a guilty verdict, whereas if they were to consider the expert evidence which seeks to explain her conduct, they [might] find her not guilty. It follows from that that in my judgment the effects of abuse of the scale and persistence she describes might well not be within the capacity of a jury to understand unassisted by expert evidence.[59]

However in *R. v. Hegarty*,[60] evidence that the accused was emotionally unstable and especially vulnerable to threats was not accepted. The Court of Appeal considered that to allow such evidence would be to circumvent the objective test of "a person of reasonable firmness". But an identical argument might be made in relation to provocation where the test is one of "a person of reasonable self-control". The common law's reluctance to admit psychological and psychiatric evidence may create divergence in the substantive rules in this area.

Zuckerman has defended this overall reluctance:

[54] The appellant's submission was accepted by the court at 1022j.
[55] *R. v. Morhall* [1995] 3 All E.R. 659 but also *Luc Thien Thuan v. R* [1996] 2 All E.R. 1033.
[56] [1990] Crim.L.R. 122.
[57] (1982) 74 Cr.App.R. 235, approved by the House of Lords in *R. v. Howe* [1987] A.C. 417.
[58] (1993) 14 Cr.App.R.(S) 394.
[59] *ibid.* at 397.
[60] [1994] Crim.L.R. 353; see also *R. v. Horne* [1994] Crim.L.R. 584.

Zuckerman A., *The Principles of Criminal Evidence* (1989), 67

A judge deciding whether expert opinion should be accepted as an arbiter of a certain matter has to consider the state of public opinion on the point. If the community has come to defer to professional standards on the matters in question, the courts will normally follow suit. Medical evidence is admissible on matters of health because we accept the authority of the medical profession in this regard. Psychiatry has not yet obtained a like acceptance. Psychiatric evidence is admissible on the issue of insanity but not . . . on the mental state of a normal person. It is argued that the distinction is irrational; for to understand abnormality psychiatry has first to master the normal mental processes. However, as long as the community does not defer to psychiatry on matters such as intention and credibility, the scope for expert evidence on such matters must remain limited . . . Only when public opinion is clear one way or another can we demand consistency from the courts.

Others have echoed the need to restrict the role of psychological and psychiatric expert witnesses in court:

> Studies show that professionals often fail to reach reliable or valid conclusions and that the accuracy of their judgements does not necessarily surpass that of laypersons, thus raising substantial doubt that psychologists or psychiatrists meet the legal standards for expertise.[61]

Others are less sceptical. Are such restrictions on the accused's ability to mount a full defence justified? If there is professional opinion to go before a jury, there is little reason to reject it. Pattenden[62] has suggested that the *Turner* rule rests on three fallacies: that there is a clear demarcation between the normal and the abnormal;[63] that the 'common sense' of the jury is a good basis on which to assess the behaviour of a person who is not mentally disordered; and finally that experts only concern themselves with abnormal people. People's reactions and behaviour are often counter-intuitive, for example, in response to outside pressures. While we recognise external situational causes as contributing to our own actions, we tend to underestimate these factors in the actions of others and to overestimate the importance of internal, dispositional factors.[64]

Mackay R. D. and Colman A., "Excluding Expert Evidence; A Tale of Ordinary Folk and Common Experience" [1991] Crim.L.R. 800 at 809

What might be a reasonable approach to the admissibility of expert psychological and psychiatric evidence? One recent commentator has suggested that, since no

[61] Faust D. and Ziskin J., "The expert witness in psychology and psychiatry" *Science*, July 24, 1988 1.31–35.

[62] Pattenden R., "Conflicting Approaches to Psychiatric Evidence" [1986] Crim.L.R. 92 at 100.

[63] Mackay R. D. and Colman A., "Excluding Expert Evidence; A Tale of Ordinary Folk and Common Experience" [1991] Crim.L.R. 800; Mackay R. D. and Colman A., "Equivocal Rulings on Expert Psychological and Psychiatric Evidence; Turning a Muddle into a Nonsense" [1991] Crim.L.R. 800; Sheldon D. and MacLeod M., "From Normative to Positive Data: Expert Psychological Evidence Re-examined" [1991] Crim.L.R. 811.

[64] Mackay R. D. and Colman A. [1991] *op. cit.* at 807–808.

clear line can be drawn between the normal and the abnormal, 'all expert evidence as to personality should be admitted subject to its relevance.'[65] We do not advocate such a radical solution, partly because it is the task of the jury to try the facts of a case and it is therefore right that expert testimony should be excluded on matters that are well understood by ordinary people, and partly because we recognise that such a solution would in any event be unacceptable to the judiciary. We advocate instead that expert psychological and psychiatric testimony should be limited but that the range of admissible evidence be extended beyond its present bounds.

It is clear that the *Turner* rule has already been breached by a number of exceptions, but in our view it is still being interpreted too narrowly. The fundamental purpose of the rule is to exclude expert evidence that. in the court's opinion, will not help the jury to understand the accused's state of mind; its reference to 'human nature and behaviour within the limits of normality' is subservient to this purpose. In decisions regarding admissibility, the crucial question ought to be whether or not the expert evidence could make a significant contribution to the jury's understanding of the accused's state of mind. This must depend, of course, on the judge's assessment of the probative value of the evidence. If the expert evidence points to an abnormal state of mind or personality of any degree on the defendant's part at the time of the alleged offence, then we submit that the court ought to exercise its discretion in favour of admitting the evidence. There are many abnormal states of mind brought about by situational forces . . . which, although they do not involve mental disorders in any medical sense, none the less lie demonstrably beyond the undertanding of ordinary people, and in relation to which expert evidence could therefore contribute significantly to a jury's understanding. In the spirit of the *Turner* rule, evidence on such matters ought in our view to be admitted, for to exclude it might deprive the jury of evidence that could help them understand the defendant's state of mind at the material time.

The narrow interpretation of *Turner* encourages a futile attempt to divide mental abnormalities into forms that require elucidation by an expert witness and those that do not. In contrast, in a French criminal investigation supervised by a *juge d'instruction*, psychological examination of specific witnesses can be ordered so that the quality of their testimony can be objectively appraised.[66]

The ultimate issue rule

This rule has traditionally prevented an expert or non-expert witness from expressing an opinion on the very point that the trier of fact has to decide, namely, the ultimate issue. The rule may usefully be linked:

(1) to the rule that limits the admission of expert opinion on matters within the competence of the trier of fact. It is the function of the judge or jury to decide upon the existence of the facts in issue in the case.

(2) to the rule that the construction of an ordinary word of the English language is a matter of fact for the jury[67]

[65] D. Ormerod commenting on *Weightman* [1991] Crim.L.R. 204 at 205.
[66] Cooper J., "Criminal Investigations in France" New L.J. (1991) 381.
[67] *Brutus v. Cozens* [1973] A.C. 854.

For example, at common law it would be impermissible to ask a doctor, as a medical expert in a medical malpractice case, whether the defendant's actions measured up to the standard of the reasonable professional doctor or to ask an eyewitness in a dangerous driving case whether he or she considered the driving to be dangerous. The rationale is that the finder of fact might be unduly influenced by an experts but in many trials, especially civil, any expert evidence for one party is likely to be countered by expert evidence from the other side, not surprisingly coming to diametrically opposed conclusions favouring the party by whom they are retained. In civil cases the rule was often evaded so that the expert witness was allowed to express an opinion on the final issue so long as he or she used different language to that employed by the court[68] and was finally overturned by the Civil Evidence Act 1972[69]:

> 3.—(1) Subject to any rules of court made in pursuance of this Act, where a person is called as a witness in any civil proceedings, his opinion on any relevant matter on which he is qualified to give expert evidence shall be admissible in evidence.
>
> (2) It is hereby declared that where a person is called as a witness in any civil proceedings, a statement of opinion by him on any relevant matter on which he is not qualified to give expert evidence, if made as a way of conveying relevant facts personally perceived by him, is admissible as evidence of what he perceived.
>
> (3) In this section 'relevant matter' includes an issue in the proceedings in question.

As a result of subsection (3), witnesses, whether expert or not, are able to express an opinion on the facts in issue in the case, although for the non-expert, this is only where the expression of such an opinion is a natural way of expressing what he or she has seen or heard. A similar reformulation has been advocated for criminal trials as well[70] although the Court of Appeal has recently described the existing rule as "more a matter of form than of substance" and that an expert should be entitled to give an opinion on an issue in the case, although the jury should be warned that such an opinion was not in itself decisive.[71]

In *DPP v. ABC Chewing Gum*[72] the issue was whether the "battle cards" sold with the chewing gum might deprave and corrupt children contrary to the Obscene Publications Act 1959. The prosecution sought to introduce experts in child psychiatry to testify as to the likely effects on children. The magistrates refused to hear the evidence. The prosecution appeal was upheld by the Divisional Court.

[68] In *Rich v. Pierpoint* (1862) 3 F&F 35, the issue was medical negligence — a doctor who had been present in court throughout the proceedings could not be asked whether the defendant was guilty of any want of skill but might be asked whether anything he heard suggested improper conduct on the defendant's part.

[69] As amended by the Civil Evidence Act 1995, Sched. 2.

[70] Criminal Law Revision Committee, *11th Report* (Cmnd. 4991) para. 268; Smith J.C., *Criminal Evidence* (1995), 116 recommended the abolition of the rule to the Royal Commission on Criminal Justice in 1993 but their final report ignores the issue.

[71] *R. v. Stockwell* (1993) 97 Cr.App.R. 260 at 265.

[72] [1968] 1 Q.B. 159.

DPP v. ABC Chewing Gum [1968] 1 Q.B. 159 at 164, *per* Parker L.C.J.

Now what was submitted to the justices and has been submitted to this court is that, as a general rule, a long-standing rule of common law, evidence is inadmissible if it is on the very issue the court has to determine. For my part, and I am only dealing with this case, I cannot think that the evidence tendered was on that very issue. There were two matters really for consideration. What sort of effect would these cards singly or together have upon children, and no doubt children of different ages; what would it lead them to do? Secondly, was what they were led to do a sign of corruption or depravity? As it seems to me, it would be perfectly proper to call a psychiatrist and to ask him in the first instance what his experience, if any, with children was, and to say what the effect on the minds of children of different groups would be if certain types of photographs or pictures were put before them, and indeed, having got his general evidence, to put one or more of the cards in question to him and say what would their effect be upon the child. For myself, I think it would be wrong to ask the direct question as to whether any particular cards tended to corrupt and deprave, because that final stage was a matter which was entirely for the justices. No doubt, however, in such a case the defence might well put it to the witness that a particular card or cards could not corrupt, and no doubt, whatever the strict position may be, that question coming from the defence would be allowed, if only to give the defence an opportunity of getting an answer 'No' from the expert.

On that ground alone, as it seems to me, the evidence in the present case was admissible.

I myself would go a little further in that I cannot help feeling that with the advance of science more and more inroads have been made into the old common law principles. Those who practice in the criminal courts see every day cases of experts being called on the question of diminished responsibility, and although technically the final question 'Do you think he was suffering from diminished responsibilty?' is strictly inadmissible, it is allowed time and again without objection. No doubt when dealing with the effect of certain things on the mind science may still be less exact thán evidence as to what effects some particular thing will have on the body, but that, as it seems to me, is purely a question of weight . . .

The court drew a fine distinction between the admissible (expert testimony as to the observable effects of the cards on children) and the inadmissible (whether those effects amounted to corruption and depravity). At the same time Lord Parker doubted the value of such distinctions. This approach was not followed in *R. v. Stamford*[73] where the issue was whether an indecent or obscene article had been sent through the post. The Court of Appeal held that this was a matter for the judge and jury and that the judge was right in preventing the accused from calling evidence on current moral standards.

In the speech of Lord Morris of Borth-y-Gest [in *Shaw v. DPP*[74]] the following appears, 'Even if accepted public standards may to some extent vary from generation to generation, current standards are in the keeping of juries, who can be trusted to maintain the corporate good sense of the community and to discern attacks upon values that must be preserved', That says in a sentence all

[73] [1972] 2 All E.R. 427.
[74] [1962] A.C. 220 at 292.

that needs to be said upon the task which is entrusted to juries and their competence to discharge their duty. They do not need assistance: they are themselves, so to speak, the custodians of the standards for the time being.[75]

General acceptance of expert testimony would lengthen trials but criminal trials frequently have significance beyond the immediate parties, especially where the prosecution involves social conflict (such as industrial disputes) or unusual charges, especially those of a moral character such as conspiring to outrage public decency:

> . . . 'outrage', like 'corrupt' is a very strong word. 'Outraging public decency' goes considerably beyond offending the susceptibilities of, or even shocking, reasonable people . . . The offence is concerned with the recognised minimum standards of decency, which are likely to vary from time to time . . . Notwithstanding that 'public' in the offence is used in a locative sense, public decency must be viewed as a whole; and . . . the jury should be invited, where appropriate, to remember that they live in a plural society, with a tradition of tolerance towards minorities, and that this atmosphere of tolerance is itself part of public decency.[76]

Such charges frequently bring in their wake issues of literary merit[77] or contemporary standards of artistic expression: in *R. v. Gibson*[78] the accused exhibited earrings made from freeze-dried human foetuses of three or four months gestation and was charged with outraging public decency. Should expert testimony be permitted in such cases or, tempting as it is, should the issue of the minimum standards of public decency be left to justices of the peace or to a jury? One argument for the former may be that the form of the adversarial trial itself allied to a liberal approach to expert evidence provides a forum for informed debate on such standards.

Weight accorded to expert testimony

It is the jury who must decide what weight is to be given to the evidence of an expert witness, making their own independent judgment from the facts and principles proved in evidence. This is obviously the case where there is conflicting expert evidence but also the case where there is no conflict:

(1) juries should not be directed to accept inevitably the evidence of an expert witness, even where uncontradicted[79]

(2) nor should juries be invited to disregard it in favour of their own unaided lay opinion. In a notorious obscenity trial, the accused published a "School Kids Issue" of their magazine, *Oz*, and were

[75] *Stamford supra* at 432c–e, *per* Ashworth J.
[76] *Knuller v. DPP* [1972] 3 All E.R. 898 at 936, *per* Lord Simon.
[77] Obscene Publications Act 1959, s.4.
[78] (1991) 91 Cr.App.R. 341.
[79] *Davie v. Edinburgh Magistrates* 1953 S.C. 34.

> charged with a conspiracy to corrupt public morals. The judge was criticised by the appeal court when he invited the jury to disregard expert testimony, referring in his summing up to "so-called experts".[80]

In *R. v. Sanders*[81] the accused relied on the defence of diminished responsibility to a charge of murder. The defence medical experts were uncontested but the Crown contended that, although the defendant had some abnormality of mind, it had not diminished his responsibility and that he had killed his victim in a premeditated fashion, overwhelmed by feelings of bitterness and jealousy. It was clear that, if there were no other circumstances to consider, the uncontradicted medical evidence should be accepted. However those other circumstances need not be medical ones. In *Sanders*, the medical evidence had to be considered in the light of circumstances which had been introduced into evidence by the prosecution.

Disclosure of expert testimony

In civil proceedings, a party must obtain the leave of the court to adduce expert testimony.[82] The application must be made in good time and in the cases where the expert is to give oral evidence, the court will direct that the substance of the evidence is disclosed to the opposing party in the absence of special reasons to the contrary.[83] But the effect of the Civil Evidence Act 1995 will be to allow a party to rely upon the written statement of an expert witness and not to call that witness in uncontroversial cases. Under the Act, there are rules for giving notice of such evidence and the opposing party may still call the witness for cross-examination.[84] Failure to call an expert witness in a controversial case would be a factor for the judge in assessing the weight to be given to that evidence.[85]

In criminal proceedings, the defendant, in any trial on indictment,[86] is entitled to advance notice, not only of any expert testimony the prosecution intend to rely upon but of all the prosecution evidence and also of "unused material". There was never any such common law obligation on the defence, although statutory exceptions had been introduced in the case

[80] *Anderson v. R* [1972] A.C. 100.
[81] [1991] Crim.L.R. 781.
[82] R.S.C., Ord. 38, r.36.
[83] *ibid.* r.37(1); *Derby & Co Ltd v. Weldon (No 9)* [1991] 2 All E.R. 901 (where report needs not to be disclosed); *Naylor v. Preston Area Health Authority* [1987] 2 All E.R. 353 (decision to disclose in medical negligence cases).
[84] Civil Evidence Act 1995, s.3.
[85] Civil Evidence Act 1995, s.4.
[86] In summary trials, there is no obligation on the prosecution to disclose in summary offences but there is a statutory obligation in the case of triable-either-way offences being tried summarily — Criminal Law Act 1977, s.48 and Magistrates Courts (Advance Information) Rules 1985 (S.I. 1985, No. 601).

of alibi evidence,[87] and preparatory hearings in serious fraud cases.[88] There is now a statutory requirement for the defence to disclose the likely line of the defence.[89]

Disclosure of expert evidence relied on by the defence has been required for many years. The Royal Commission on Criminal Procedure[90] considered that the delay and inconvenience brought about by the surprise production of expert evidence on behalf of the defence justified placing an obligation on the defence to disclose proposed expert evidence and this was done by section 81 of the Police and Criminal Evidence Act 1984 and and the rules of court made under that section.[91] Although these rules provide for the mutual disclosure of expert evidence, they do not restrict the prosecution's common law obligations:

R. v. Ward [1993] 2 All E.R. 577 at 628f–j, _per_ Glidewell L.J.

. . . we believe that the surest way of preventing the misuse of scientific evidence is by ensuring that there is a proper understanding of the nature and scope of the prosecution's duty of disclosure. In our view there was an imperfect understanding of that position in 1974. [The Crown] suggested to us that the problem was solved by the Crown Court (Advance Notice of Expert Evidence) Rules . . . Those rules enable the legal representatives of a defendant in a Crown Court criminal case to require the prosecution by writing to provide in respect of scientific evidence a copy of (or an opportunity to inspect) 'the record of any observation, test, calculation or other procedure on which [any] finding or opinion is based' (r.3(1)(b) The new rules are helpful. But it is a misconception to regard them as exhaustive: they do not in any way supplant or detract from the prosecution's general duty of disclosure in respect of scientific evidence. That duty exists irrespective of any request by the defence. It is also not limited to documentation on which the opinion or findings of an expert is based. It extends to anything which may arguably assist the defence. It is therefore wider in scope than the rule. Moreover it is a positive duty, which in the context of scientific evidence obliges the prosecution to make full and proper inquiries from forensic scientists in order to ascertain whether there is discoverable material. Given the undoubted inequality as between prosecution and defence in access to forensic scientists, we regard it as of paramount importance that the common law of disclosure, as we have explained it, should be appreciated by those who prosecute and defend in criminal cases . . .

Such principles apply to prosecution and defence:

. . . What the rules do not say in terms is that if an expert witness has carried out experiments or tests which tend to disprove or cast doubt upon the opinion he is expressing, or if such experiments or tests have been carried out in his laboratory and are known to him, the party calling him must also disclose the record of such experiments or tests. In our view the rules do not state this in terms because they can only be read as requiring the record of all relevant

[87] Criminal Justice Act 1967, s.11.
[88] Criminal Justice Act 1987, s.9.
[89] Criminal Procedure and Investigations Act 1996: see 321, *et seq*.
[90] *Report* (1981) Cmnd. 8092, para. 8.22.
[91] Crown Court (Advance Notice of Expert Evidence) Rules 1987 (S.I. 1987, No. 716).

experiments or tests to be disclosed. It follows that an expert witness who ahs carried out or knows of experiments or tests which tend to cast doubt on the opinions he is expressing is in our view under a clear obligation to bring the records of such experiments or tests to the attention of the solicitor who is instructing him so that it may be disclosed to the other party.[92]

The role of the expert witness

In Glidewell L.J.'s observations on the prosecution's duties to disclose in *Ward*, he said:

> . . . we have identified the cause of the injustice done to the appellant on the scientific side of this case as stemming from the fact that three senior forensic scientists at RARDE[93] regarded their task as to help the police. They became partisan. It is the clear duty of government forensic scientists to assist in a neutral and impartial way in criminal investigations. They must act in the cause of justice. That duty should be spelt out to all engaged or to be engaged in forensic services in the clearest terms.[94]

Such an ideal contrasts with the realities of criminal investigation or of civil proceedings. In the former, there are public sector agencies such as the Forensic Science Service which is an executive agency of the Home Office, the Metropolitan Police Forensic Science Laboratory, the Ministry of Defence's Research Defence Agency or the Department of Trade's Laboratory of the Government Chemist.[95] The problems of laboratories responsible directly to a government department or to the police are immediately apparent and the Royal Commission recommended the establishment of a new forensic science advisory council which would oversee the effectiveness of the public sector laboratories, developing a code of practice covering professional ethics and duties of disclosure and keeping under review the extent to which the interests of the defence are being properly looked after by the various providers of forensic science services.

Many of the problems for the expert witness flow from the adversarial nature of trial. For the scientist the courtroom is not the place nor cross-examination the technique to settle scientific disputes. Although the Royal Commission recommended compulsory use of informal pre-trial hearings,[96] no formal changes have been introduced. The preparatory hearings introduced by Part 3 of the Criminal Procedure and Investigations Act 1996 are not empowered to settle such issues.

[92] Ward at 632 e–g.
[93] Royal Armaments Research and Development Establishment at Woolwich.
[94] *Ward supra*, at 628d–f; see Cresswell J. in *National Justice Cia Naviera SA v. Prudential Assurance Co Ltd* [1993] 2 Lloyd's Rep. 68 at 81, where he said "An expert witness should provide independent assistance to the Court by way of objective unbiased opinion in relation to matters within his expertise . . . [He] should never assume the role of an advocate."
[95] These are discussed further in Royal Commission on Criminal Justice: *Report* (1993) Cm. 2263 Chap. 9; it is based on Roberts P. and Willmore C., *The Role of Forensic Science Evidence in Criminal Proceedings* (Royal Commission on Criminal Justice Research Study No. 11) (1993).
[96] *ibid.* para. 9.68.

Where the expert evidence is not controversial, section 30 of the Criminal Justice Act 1988 does permit the report to be introduced without the expert testifying orally:

30.—(1) An expert report shall be admissible as evidence in criminal proceedings, whether or not the person making it attends to give oral evidence in those proceedings.

(2) If it is proposed that the person making the report shall not give oral evidence, the report shall only be admissible with the leave of the court.

(3) For the purpose of determining whether to give leave the court shall have regard —

- (a) to the contents of the report;
- (b) to the reasons why it is proposed that the person making the report shall not give oral evidence;
- (c) to any risk, having regard in particular to whether it is likely to be possible to controvert statements in the report of the person making it does not attend to give oral evidence in the proceedings, that its admission or exclusion will result in unfairness to the accused or, if there is more than one, to any of them; and
- (d) to any other circumstances that appear to the court to be relevant.

The Royal Commission felt that this provision was underused and that greater use should be made of summaries of expert testimony.[97] Expert witnesses should also be protected to some extent from cross-examination:

Royal Commission on Criminal Justice: *Report* (1993) Cm. 2263 para. 9.73

. . . many experts feel that they are not always given a proper opportuinty to explain what the scientific evidence really means. This may be because counsel stop short of asking vital questions from lack of scientific knowledge or inadequate briefing or because they make inadequate use of the the opportunity to re-examine after cross-examination or because they do not want the answer to be heard. We recommend that trial judges, where the evidence is disputed, ask expert witnesses before they leave the witness box whether there is anything else that they wish to say. To avoid inadmissible evidence being heard, the judge should put this question in the absence of the jury and, if the expert witness does indicate a wish to clarify the evidence, it should be heard before the jury returns. If the judge is satisfied that there can be no objection to the evidence, it should be put before the jury . . .

However a more controversial issue was the suggestion that independent court experts should be appointed. The Royal Commission was not in favour:

Royal Commission, *op. cit.* para 9.74

Some of our witnesses would go further . . . In their view expert evidence should be given by a court expert, either instead of or in addition to the experts who appear

[97] *ibid.* para. 9.71.

for the prosecution and the defence. Alternatively, some would recommend that judges should sit in the relevant cases with an expert assessor or assessors. We have considered these suggestions but are not in favour of them. A court expert, even if subject to examination and cross-examination, would by implication carry more weight than an expert for the prosecution or the defence. There would, however, be no guarantee that he or she was any nearer to the truth of the matter than the expert witnesses for the parties. A court expert should not in our view be the only expert, since that would deprive the parties of the opportunity of leading their own expert evidence. But to have a court expert in addition to the experts for the parties would greatly extend the amount of time spent in examination and cross-examination of all three experts without making discovery of the truth any more certain. The worse solution of all, in our view, would be to have the expert sitting with the judge as an assessor, since his or her evidence would not be susceptible to examination or cross-examination by either side.[98]

A court-appointed, independent, expert witness is an option in civil proceedings at the application of either party.[99] Either party can cross-examine the witness on his or her report and adduce their own expert testimony on the same issue. In the U.S.A., both civil and criminal courts have such a power[1] and the trend is increasingly to provide for their use. However in England, such an appointment is not a possibility in criminal proceedings. John Spencer has argued against the current system and for such impartial experts:

Spencer J. R., "The Neutral Expert: an implausible bogey" [1991] Crim.L.R. 106

[The attack upon the idea of neutral experts makes three general assertions . . .]

Things are not as bad as the critics say

(a) . . . experts are already subject to an efficient system of quality control.

I disagree. It is true, of course that questioning by the judge and by the opposing party prevents a party putting forward as an expert witness someone who has neither practical experience nor theoretical qualifications. What it does not prevent, however is either or both of the parties palming off upon the court someone who, though not bogus in this sense, is cranky, senile or generally ill-respected . . . Matters are made worse in this respect by two particular features of our version of the accusatorial system. Firstly, there is the fact that the defence (although not the prosecution) is free to shop around, tearing up one 'unhelpful' expert report after another, until at last it finds the man or woman who is ready to say what it wants the court to hear. And secondly, there is the fact that the expert must undergo an adversarial cross-examination . . . which discourages many of the best but least flamboyant experts from acting as witnesses . . .

[98] A fuller argument is put by Howard M., "The Neutral Expert: a plausible threat to justice" [1991] Crim.L.R. 98.
[99] R.S.C., Ord. 40, r.1.
[1] Federal Rules Of Evidence, r.706.

(b) . . . it is a myth that the adversarial system . . . distorts the evidence of experts.

I beg to differ . . . A number of experts have said so in public.[2] So have at least some lawyers.[3] Much of what is written in the way of guidance for potential expert wtinesses assumes that it does . . .

(c) . . . it does not undermine the quality of an expert's evidence that he is appearing on behalf of one of the parties. In fact an expert actually gives superior evidence if his research was 'goal directed' . . .

Whether this is so depends, of course on what is meant by evidence of superior quality. For counsel in an adversarial trial, 'goal directed' expert evidence is obviously superior in the sense that it fits his case . . . But it does not follow that such evidence is superior in the sense that it is the kind of evidence most likely to be true. An expert who follows this method is working contrary to the most basic principle of scientific research, which is that a scientist must search for the truth, however inconvenient the truth may be.

Anyone who really believes that 'goal directed' scientists are more likely to get to the truth than neutral experts should read the Interim Report of the May Committee on the Maguire Case.[4] There, the fact that their work was 'goal directed' and 'produced under the dual pressure of expectations and the threat of attack by the opposition' actually seem to have led a group of scientists employed by the prosecutions to suppress information which showed the defence case could be true . . .

The real reason experts dislike the adversarial system is that it forces them to undergo an adversarial cross-examination; but this inconvenience is inevitable if their evidence is to be tested and justice is to be done.

. . . It is false to say that the traditional in-court cross-examination is the only — or even the best — way of testing their conclusions. Under the French Code of Criminal Procedure, for example, the report of the court expert . . . is circulated to the parties and they then discuss it at a special hearing before the *juge d'instruction* which takes place in private and well-ahead of the final trial. The experts can be questioned about their reports and if the parties are not satisfied by the answers they can ask the *juge d'instruction* to appoint a further expert . . . French writers explain the philosophy behind this as follows:

The Code of Criminal Procedure has tried to avoid inadequacies in the expert opinion being discussed before the court of trial, at a public hearing, and in conditions harmful to the good name of science — eminent workers being called on to expose in the witness box differences that may arise from a simple misunderstanding — and also harmful to the good name of justice. It takes the position that attacks upon the work of experts should be presented more discreetly, and also while there is still time for gaps or imperfections to be put right.[5]

[2] Gee D.J., "The Expert Witness in the Criminal Trial" [1987] Crim.L.R. 307.
[3] Carson D., *Professionals and the Courts — A Handbook for Expert Witnesses* (1990).
[4] House of Commons Papers 1990/556.
[5] Stefani, Levasseur and Bouloc, *Precis Dalloz de Procedure Penale* (14th ed., 1990), para. 602.

A system of court-appointed experts would produce a set of different problems worse than any we have under the present system . . .

(a) Because court experts would necessarily be of poor quality.

Wrong. In France, at least the system furnishes the courts with experts of high quality. There the Court of Appeal for each area maintains a standing list of experts of all kinds, admission to which is strictly controlled by a committee. There is competition among experts to be included, and broadly speaking it seems to be only those who are most highly regarded by their colleagues whose names are added to it . . .

(b) The defence would lose their existing right to challenge the opinion of the court expert, either by cross-examining him, or by calling evidence to rebut it, and so would be gravely prejudicied.

Wrong! Because there is a neutral court-appointed expert, of course it does not follow that the defence must lose the right to use their own expert, and call him or her as a witness. In both France and Germany, where court experts are used, the defence are entitled to call their own experts as witnesses if they wish. In fact they rarely do so, however. The usual method of challenging the court expert's opinion is by asking the court to appoint a further expert to give a second opinion . . .

(c) If the parties were allowed to challenge the court expert by using their own expert witness, the system would be even more cumbersome and expensive than the present system, because instead of two sets of experts we should have three.

Not necessarily . . . It does not happen in France, although the parties have the right to call their own expert witnesses, because both prosecution and defence make use of their right to ask the juge d'instruction to appoint a supplementary expert — or in a really difficult case, to summon a 'college of experts'. Under this system it seems that the views of a number of experts can be put before the court more cheaply and conveniently than under the English system . . .[6]

NON-EXPERT OPINION

The non-expert witness can give an opinion in relation to those matters where it is almost impossible to separate out the inferences from the perceived facts on which the inferences were based: age[7], weather, handwriting, the identification of people or objects might all be given as examples. In *Fryer v. Gathercole*[8] a witness testified that she had received a libellous pamphlet from the defendant. She had lent it to other people and gave evidence that that the pamphlet in front of the court was the same one that she had received from the defendant although there were no obvious identifying marks. It was objected that this was mere opinion:

[6] Spencer's arguments are carried further in Spencer J.R. and Flin R., *The Evidence of Children — the Law and the Psychology* (2nd ed., 1993) Chap. 9.
[7] *R. v. Cox* [1898] 1 Q.B. 179.
[8] (1849) 4 Ex. 262.

***Fryer v. Gathercole* (1849) 4 Ex. 262 at 265, *per* Pollock C.B.**

. . . the question resolved itself into one question of degree only. The witness could say no more than this: 'I believe the copy of the pamphlet produced to be the same with that which I received from the defendant, because when I lent that copy to other persons it was returned to me, and I had no reason to believe it otherwise when I got it back. I then for certainty put my name on it.' If the name had been written in the first instance no doubt could have arisen . . . As has been truly argued, there are many cases of identification where the law would be rendered ridiculous if positive certainty were required from witnesses . . . The evidence in this case was therefore properly received; any objection to it goes merely to its value.

One obvious example is a witness's estimation of the speed of a car: legislation provides that a witness can testify as to the speed (although this opinion requires corroboration). Under the Road Traffic Regulation Act 1984:

89.—(2) A person prosecuted for such an offence shall not be liable to be convicted solely on the evidence of one witness to the effect that, in the opinion of the witness, the person prosecuted was driving the vehicle at a speed exceeding a specified limit.

The condition of objects or their general value[9] might also be a suitable subject for a witness's comment. Even an opinion as to the sanity of a person can, in some circumstances, be admissible. In *Wright v. Tatham*[10] the sanity of a deceased testator was in issue and it was sought to introduce letters written by acquaintances of the deceased on business matters which implicitly showed the writers' opinion that the testator was sane:

Each of the three letters, no doubt, indicates that in the opinion of the writer the testator was a rational person. He is spoken of in respectful terms in all. Mr Ellershaw describes him as possessing hospitality and benevolent politeness; and Mr Marton addresses him as competent to do business to the limited extent to which his letter calls on him to act; and there is no question but that, if any one of those writers had been living, his evidence, founded on personal observation, that the testator possessed the qualities which justified the opinion expressed or implied in his letters, would be admissible on this issue.[11]

However in a criminal case, untutored opinion is insufficient for a jury to base a special verdict of not guilty through reason of insanity — the testimony of two medical practitioners is required.[12] There is no similar provision in the legislation providing for the defence of diminished responsibility although non-expert testimony is likely to be given little weight. As with experts, opinion evidence is only admissible when based on

[9] *R. v. Beckett* (1913) 8 Cr.App.R. 204.
[10] (1838) 4 Bing. N.C. 489.
[11] *ibid.* at 543–544, *per* Parke B.
[12] Criminal Procedure (Insanity and Unfitness to Plead) Act 1991, s.1(1).

facts which are themselves proved by admissible evidence. The statement of opinion is a convenient method of conveying personal observations. As a result opinions based on hearsay evidence, although admissible where an expert relies on third party information,[13] are inadmissible.

In *R. v. Davies*[14] the charge at a court martial was driving a vehicle while unfit through drink. The witness testified that the accused had been drinking and was in no condition to handle the car. On appeal, Lord Parker C.J. said:

R. v. Davies [1962] 3 All E.R. 97 at 1112–1113, _per_ Parker C.J.

The defence had strongly taken the stand that the witness should be allowed to speak only as to facts he had seen, because it was for the court to say what was the appellant's condition. Apparently the judge advocate advised the court that the witness could state the impression he formed as to the appellant's condition at the time if he was a witness who knew what was entailed in the driving of a car. It is to observed that the witness was allowed to speak about two matters which are quite distinct; one is what his impression was as to whether drink had been taken by the appellant, and the second was his opinion as to whether as the result of that drink he was fit or unfit to drive a car. The court has come clearly to the conclusion that a witness can quite properly give his general impression as to whether a driver had taken drink. He must describe of course the facts upon which he relies, but it seems to this court that he is perfectly entitled to give his impression as to whether drink had been taken or not. On the other hand, as regards the second matter, it cannot be said, as it seems to this court, that a witness, merely because he is a driver himself, is in the expert witness category so that it is proper to ask him his opinion as to fitness or unfitness to drive. That is the very matter which the court itself has to determine . . .

A non-expert witness can testify as to whether somebody has been drinking but only an expert witness could testify as to whether the accused was fit to drive — and even then might fall foul of the "ultimate issue" rule. At common law a witness could not give an opinion as to any matter within the competence of the trier of fact or as to any fact in issue. But in civil proceedings, the role of the non-expert witness is laid down in the Civil Evidence Act 1972 which also amends the "ultimate issue" restraint by section 3(3)[15]:

3.—(2) It is hereby declared that where a person is called as a witness in any civil proceedings, a statement of opinion by him on any relevant matter on which he is not qualified to give expert evidence, if made as a way of conveying relevant facts personally perceived by him, is admissible as evidence of what he perceived.

(3) In this section 'relevant matter' includes an issue in the proceedings in question.

[13] Homicide Act 1957, s.2.
[14] *English Exporters (London) Ltd v. Eldonwall Ltd* [1973] 1 All E.R. 726.
[15] As amended by the Civil Evidence Act 1995, Sched. 2.

It has been recommended that a similar provision be enacted for criminal trials.[16] This still awaits legislation and in theory, an eyewitness in a dangerous driving case should not be asked whether the driving was dangerous, even where the opinion is rationally based on the speed of the car, the road conditions and the driver's control. In the U.S.A., the rule is put more liberally. Under the Federal Rules of Evidence:

701.—If the witness is not testifying as an expert, the witness's testimony in the form of opinions or inferences is limited to those opinions or inferences which are (a) rationally based on the perception of the witness and (b) helpful to a clear understanding of the witness's testimony or the determination of a fact in issue.[17]

[16] 11th Report, Criminal Law Revision Committee (Cmnd. 4991), para. 270.
[17] Federal Rules of Evidence, r.701.

21

MATTERS NOT REQUIRING FULL PROOF

INTRODUCTION

One of the key characteristics of adversarial trial is the "day in court" at which point all the evidence is put in front of the trier of fact who makes the necessary decisions based on that evidence alone. However:

> In conducting a process of judicial reasoning, as of other reasoning, not a step can be taken without assuming something which has not been proved; and the capacity to do this with competent judgment and efficiency, is imputed to judges and juries as part of their necessary mental outfit.[1]

In everyday life we constantly make assumptions and use generalisations. We employ such "non-evidence" facts to assess other information that is given to us more directly. This of necessity occurs in court:

Heydon J. D., *Evidence* (3rd ed., 1991) 503–504

In general all material facts — whether facts in issue or subordinate facts — must be proved by evidence. In consequence the Court cannot act on material which the parties have not had the opportunity of rebutting or qualifying.

But the world of trials is not a Cartesian one. The mind of the trier of fact is not a complete blank waiting only for the parties to write . . .

First, the trier of fact may take for granted the English language so far as the ordinary meaning of generally used words is concerned[2] but not technical ones. Thus when a witness uses the word 'car' in a case about a car accident, his hearers, at least until corrected by evidence, think about an automobile, not any other vehicle, they assume it to have an engine, probably an internal combustion engine, and four wheels with rubber tyres. Secondly, the trier of fact may take into account the ordinary data of day to day living and his own experience of the ordinary progress of affairs and the habits of mankind. He cannot and ought not to ignore it. He cannot begin to reason without drawing on some store of accepted knowledge. This is particularly so in relation to estimating the relevance and weight of evidence. A multitude of facts are thus relied on without being proved, for example, that it is common for the possessor of housebreaking implements to use them for

[1] Thayer, *Preliminary Treatise on Evidence* (1898), 279–280.
[2] *Chapman v. Kirke* [1948] 2 All E.R. 556.

criminal purposes. If a witness talks of a 'car', his hearers apply their basic knowledge of how cars work and how their drivers normally behave . . . A jury can infer substantial intoxication from the accused's having two and a half times the legal blood alcohol limit.[3] This type of knowledge can be difficult to distinguish from those facts..which are judicially noticed without inquiry.

Thirdly, the trier of fact may assume the ordinary processes of simple mathematical and syllogistic reasoning and may draw inferences as to the causes and effects of established facts. If a witness says 'It was wet and dark, we had no lights, and our car was doing 100 miles, *per* hour', his hearers will subject to evidence, draw some conclusions as to the cause of an accident.

Obviously there is no need for parties to adduce evidence to prove matters within people's common experience or to tell the trier of fact how to carry out everyday logical operations. But a trier of fact may well have relevant personal knowledge which is peculiar to him or her. Knowledge of the immediate facts of the case should disqualify the trier from hearing the case nor should he or she seek to acquire such knowledge away from the courtroom.[4] However the trier may possess knowledge or expertise which is of value in assessing the evidence. In *Wetherall v. Harrison*[5] the accused driver was charged with failing to provide a urine or blood sample without reasonable excuse. He had been taken to a police station where he had apparently had a fit. At the court hearing, one of the magistrates was a doctor who, in the retiring room, gave his views on whether the fit was genuine or simulated:

Wetherall v. Hanson [1976] 1 All E.R. 241 at 243h–244d, _per_ Lord Widgery C.J.

For my part, I do not think that the position of a justice of the peace is the same, in this regard, as the position of a trained judge. If you have a judge sitting alone, trying a civil case it is perfectly feasible and sensible that he should be instructed and trained to exclude certain factors from his consideration of the problem. Justices are not so trained. They are much more like jurymen in this respect. I think it would be wrong to start with the proposition that justices' use of their own local or personal knowledge is governed by exactly the same rule as is laid down in the case of trained judges. I do not believe that a serious restriction on a magistrate's use of his own knowledge or the knowledge of his colleagues can really be enforced. Laymen (by which I mean non-lawyers) sitting as justices considering a case which has just been heard before them lack the ability to put out of their minds certain features of the case. In particular, if the magistrate is a specialist, be he a doctor or an engineer or an accountant, or what you will, it is not possible for him to approach the decision in the case as though he had not got that training, and indeed I think it would be a very bad thing if he had to. In a sense, the bench of justices is like a jury, it is a cross-section of people, and one of the advantages which they have is that they bring a lot of varied experience into the courtroom and use it.

So I start with the proposition that it is not improper for a magistrate who has special knowledge of the circumstances forming the background to a particular case

[3] *R. v. Hunt* [1980] R.T.R. 29.
[4] Wasik M., "Knowledge of Previous Convictions" [1996] Crim.L.R. 851.
[5] [1976] 1 All E.R. 241.

to draw on that special knowledge in interpretation of the evidence which he has heard. I stress that last sentence, because it would be quite wrong if the magistrate went on, as it were, to give evidence to himself in contradiction of that which has been heard in court. He is not there to give evidence to himself, still more is he not there to give evidence to the other justices; but that he can employ his basic knowledge in considering, weighing up and assessing the evidence given before the court is I think beyond doubt.

Furthermore, I do not see why he should not, certainly if requested by his fellow justices to, tell his fellow justices the way in which his specialised knowledge has caused him to look at the evidence . . .

But beyond common experience and personal knowledge, there are other circumstances where there is no need to adduce evidence. In some, more technical, situations, full presentation of the evidence necessary to prove a fact is dispensed with. The four situations discussed here where this occurs are: where judicial notice is taken of a fact; where there is an estoppel; where there is a previous judicial finding; or where there is the operation of a presumption.

Judicial Notice

There is no need to adduce evidence where the fact is generally known or is capable of accurate determination so that it is beyond dispute:

. . . whenever a fact is so generally known that every ordinary person may be reasonably presumed to be aware of it, the court 'notices' it, either simpliciter or if it is at once satisfied of the fact without more, or after such information and investigation as it considers reliable and necessary in order to eliminate any reasonable doubt.[6]

In the U.S.A., under the Federal Rules of Evidence:

201(6).—A judicially noticed fact must be one not subject to reasonable dispute in that it is either (1) generally known within the territorial jurisdiction of the trial court or (2) capable of accurate and ready determination by resort to sources whose accuracy cannot reasonably be questioned.[7]

There are different forms of judicial notice:

(1) *without any inquiry:* these are facts which are so commonly known that there existence is not in dispute. For example, a court will take note of the fact that nine months is the normal term for a pregnancy,[8] that cats are kept for domestic purposes[9] and that universities are established for the advancement of learning.[10] The

[6] *Holland v. Jones* (1917) 23 C.L.R. 149 at 153, *per* Isaacs J.
[7] Federal Rules of Evidence, r.201(b).
[8] *Preston-Jones v. Preston-Jones* [1951] A.C. 391.
[9] *Nye v. Niblett* [1918] 1 K.B. 23.
[10] *Re Oxford Poor Rate Case* (1857) 8 E&B 184.

fact can be generally known but to a small number of people or in a local area — in *Paul v. DPP*[11] the justices were entitled to use their local knowledge of an area (which was a frequent haunt of prostitutes) to infer that the appellant's conduct in "kerb-crawling" was likely to cause a nuisance to others. However some assumptions made by a court can be problematic. An illustration is *Hawkins v. United States*[12] in which the Supreme Court refused to discard the common law rule that one spouse could not testify against the other, saying, "Adverse testimony given in criminal proceedings would, we think, be likely to destroy almost any marriage." This conclusion has a large intermixture of fact, but the factual aspect is scarcely indisputable.[13]

(2) *with inquiry:* a court can take account of facts after investigation even though such facts are not generally known as long as they can readily be ascertained from authoritative sources. For example, firstly a court will take judicial notice of certain political facts such as the status of a foreign government[14] or the existence of a state of war.[15] Courts normally act on the certificate of the relevant minister of state. Secondly a court may refer to authoritative works to ascertain historical or other readily identifiable facts — in *Read v. The Bishop of Lincoln*[16] the court investigated whether the practice of mixing communion wine with water was contrary to church law. Thirdly judicial notice will be taken of general customs which have been proved with some frequency in other cases[17] and of professional practices.[18]

(3) *by statute:* there are many statutes permitting or compelling judicial notice to be taken of certain facts. Evidence is not required to prove the contents of a statute. The Interpretation Act 1978 provides that:

> 3.—Every Act is a public Act to be judicially noticed as such unless the contrary is expressly provided by the Act[19]

But private Acts (passed before 1851) and foreign law cannot be the subject of judicial notice and must be proved by evidence.

[11] [1989] Crim.L.R. 660.

[12] 358 U.S. 74, 79 S.Ct. 136, 3 L.Ed.2d 125 (1958).

[13] The Supreme Court permits parties to introduce material on the social and economic background to the case (a "Brandeis brief") — *Miller v. Oregon* 208 U.S. 412 (1908).

[14] *Carl Zeiss Stiftung v. Rayner & Keeler Ltd (No. 2)* [1967] 1 A.C. 853; *Duff Development Co v. Government of Kelantan* [1924] A.C. 797.

[15] *R. v. Bottrill ex parte Kuechenmeister* [1946] 2 All E.R. 434.

[16] [1892] A.C. 644.

[17] *Brandao v. Barnett* (1846) 12 Cl. & Fin. 787 where the House of Lords took notice of the custom of bankers' lien which had been judicially ascertained in earlier cases.

[18] *Davey v. Harrow Corpn* [1958] 1 Q.B. 60.

[19] There is a similar provision for the judicial notice of European law under section 3(2) of the European Communities Act 1972.

The process of judicial notice can appear close to a usurpation of the function of the trier of fact. In *McQuaker v. Goddard*[20] the trial judge consulted books and experts on whether camels were wild by nature and held that they were domestic animals. There was some dispute over that conclusion but the Court of Appeal held that judicial notice could be taken of the matter and that the issue would then be withdrawn from the jury. In his consultations the judge was not taking evidence in the ordinary sense but conducting an inquiry prior to taking judicial notice of the fact. Where a judge takes judicial notice of a fact, there should be no evidence given in disproof. In the U.S.A.[21] a judicially noticed fact is conclusive in a civil case but in a criminal trial the jury is not required to accept it as conclusive.

A final question is whether taking judicial notice of a fact constitutes a precedent for inferior courts, a theory which would mean that there could no longer be any dispute about the domestic nature of the camel. An alternative view would be that judicial notice was a substitute for proof and could no more be a precedent than any other finding of fact by a court. Best practice might be found in *Thomas v. Thomas*[22] where it was suggested that a judge should give notice of an intent to take judicial notice of certain facts, subject to anything the parties might urge to the contrary. Despite the convenience of the doctrine of judicial notice, it needs to be subject to the requirements of procedural fairness.

Estoppel

> . . . an excellent and curious kinde of learning . . . [I]t is called an estoppel . . . because a man's owne act or acceptance stoppeth or closeth up his mouth to alleadge or plead the truth (Lord Coke C.J.).

People act in certain ways or say particular things so that others believe their assertions and perhaps act in reliance on them. The principle of estoppel, in certain circumstances, prevents such people, when they are parties to litigation, from contradicting those assertions. Estoppel arises with respect to court judgments when the facts are treated as a matter of *record*; when the facts are stated in a *deed*; or when a clear representation of fact arises as a result of the party's *conduct*. The party relying on the estoppel need only adduce limited proof of the facts whereas the other party is prohibited from leading evidence in disproof.

Whether estoppel is a rule of substantive law or a rule of evidence is debateable. In *Mills v. Cooper*[23] Diplock L.J. said:

[20] [1940] 1 K.B. 687.
[21] Federal Rules of Evidence, r.201(g).
[22] [1961] 1 All E.R. 19.
[23] [1967] 2 All E.R. 100.

Mills v. Cooper [1967] 2 All E.R. 100 at 104i–105a, _per_ Diplock L.J.

Whatever may be said of other rules of law to which the label of 'estoppel' is attached, 'issue estoppel' is not a rule of evidence. True, subject to the qualifications I have stated, it has the effect of preventing the party 'estopped' from calling evidence to show that the assertion which is the subject of the 'issue estoppel' is incorrect, but that is because the existence of the 'issue estoppel' results in there being no issue in the subsequent civil proceedings to which such evidence would be relevant. Issue estoppel is a particular application of the general rule of public policy that there should be finality in litigation.

It matters little whether we term estoppel a rule of "evidence" or of "law". But estoppel is an example of a technique of proof, analogous to presumptions, by which if a party can prove Fact A (in essence a secondary fact), Fact B (the primary fact) is taken to exist. Thus if you can prove that your opponent executed a deed (Fact A) asserting a state of affairs, the court will presume that that state of affairs (Fact B) in fact exists and will not permit evidence to be given in rebuttal.

This is an evidentiary process, a process which tells us how facts are to be established. Substantive rules of law tell us what the rights and duties of parties are, given certain facts. Such rules specify what facts in issue need to be proved. But estoppel does not mean that a fact in issue is no longer an issue; it means that such an issue is taken to be proved irrebuttably by adducing evidence of a court judgment, of a deed or of relevant conduct:

> Estoppel is only a rule of evidence; you cannot found an action upon estoppel. Estoppel is only important as being one step in the progress towards relief on the hypothesis that the defendant is estopped from denying the truth of something he has said.[24]

This is supported by Brandon L.J. who suggested:

> . . . the true proposition of law, that, while a party cannot in terms found a cause of action on an estoppel, he may, as a result of being able to rely on an estoppel, succeed on a cause of action on which, without being able to rely on that estoppel, he would necessarily have failed.[25]

It is often said that estoppels cannot override the general law of the land. In *R. Leslie Ltd v. Shiell*,[26] a child's misrepresentation as to his age did not estop him from pleading contractual incapacity. In *Re Exchange Securities and Commodities Ltd*[27] a liquidator was under a statutory duty to distribute the assets of a company amongst its creditors. The court held that estoppel was only a rule of evidence and was not conclusive in liquidations or

[24] *Low v. Bouverie* [1891] 3 Ch. 82 at 105, *per* Bowen L.J.

[25] *Amalgamated Investment and Property Co Ltd v. Texas Commerce International Bank Ltd* [1981] 3 All E.R. 577 at 591h.

[26] [1914] 3 K.B. 607.

[27] [1987] 2 All E.R. 272.

bankruptcies when considering the distribution of the statutory estate. Such decisions recall Lord Diplock's comment in *Mills v. Cooper* when he said that issue estoppel was only an application of the public policy of finality to litigation. It may be that, although estoppel operates against individual litigants, its boundaries are delimited generally by consideration of the public interest.

Estoppel by record

Such estoppels exist where there is a judgment of a court.[28] This is conclusive in that, when there is subsequent litigation, it stops the parties from denying the facts on which the judgment was based. However the effect of such an estoppel can be avoided where the initial judgment was obtained by fraud or collusion. In addition, it is only the parties (and their privies[29]) to the judgment who are estopped. This was shown in *The Duchess of Kingston's Case*[30] where the Duchess was indicted for bigamy and tried in the House of Lords. Her defence was that the Consistory Court of the Bishop of London had already considered the question of her alleged first marriage to the Earl of Bristol. That court had admonished the Earl for wickedly and maliciously boasting and publicly asserting that there was such a marriage. In the House of Lords, de Grey C.J. held that, although a person who was a party to legal proceedings in which a judgment was given is estopped from denying the facts on which the judgment was based, the judgment was not binding on any third party. The Crown was not a party to the proceedings in the Consistory Court and was not prevented from contradicting the facts on which the judgment was based. Furthermore, if it could be shown that the original judgment was based on fraud, this vitiated all judicial acts.

The principles on which such estoppel is based are:

- that there is a public interest, namely that there should be a finality to litigation
- that nobody should be sued twice on the same grounds.

There are two facets of a judgment that must be distinguished:

(1) judgments are conclusive against all persons as to the legal state of affairs. If, for example, there has been a divorce decree, a finding of bankruptcy or a conviction, the whole world is estopped from adducing evidence to deny that legal result.

[28] The only other situation where estoppel by record might arise is where there is a grant of letters patent by the Crown.

[29] By "privies" is meant those parties who derive title from the earlier party or who share a common interest in blood, estate or law.

[30] (1776) 20 St. Tr. 355.

However such judgments are not conclusive as to the factual state of affairs, at least in respect of those who were not parties to the action. If an accused has been acquitted and chooses to bring an action for malicious prosecution against the police, they would not be estopped from adducing evidence that the plaintiff had in fact committed the offence. The record is conclusive as to A's conviction, if that is in issue, but not as to whether he committed the offence. A similar case would be where a third party sued for and won damages from a master for the injuries caused by the negligence of the defendant's servant. Were the master to sue the employee for recovery of those damages, the employee could not contest the amount of damages which had been awarded but could contest his or her own negligence.[31]

(2) judgments can be conclusive of the facts on which they are based but only in certain circumstances, namely where the same parties or their privies are concerned. In subsequent proceedings, those parties are estopped from adducing evidence to contradict the grounds on which the previous judgement was based.

This distinction requires us to split the discussion of estoppel by record into two: cause of action estoppel and issue estoppel.

Cause of action estoppel

Parties are expected to bring forward their whole case at the original hearing. If they bring an action and there is a judgment, they are not permitted to open the same matter against the same party in subsequent litigation.[32]

***Henderson v. Henderson* (1843) 3 Hare 100 at 114, *per* Wigram V.C.**

. . . where a given matter becomes the subject of litigation in, and of adjudication by, a court of competent jurisdiction, the court requires the parties to that litigation to bring forward their whole case, and will not (except under special circumstances) permit the same parties to open the same subject of litigation in respect of matter which might have been brought forward as part of the subject in contest, but which was not brought forward, only because they have, from negligence, inadvertence, or even accident, omitted part of their case. The plea of res judicata applies, except in special cases, not only to points upon which the court was actually required by the parties to form an opinion and pronounce a judgment, but to every point which properly belonged to the subject of litigation, and which the parties, exercising reasonable diligence, might have brought forward at the time.

This dicta in *Henderson* was approved in the House of Lords in *Arnold v. National Westminster Bank plc*[33] which suggested that the bar is absolute in

[31] *Green v. New River Co* (1792) 4 Term. Rep. 589.

[32] *Conquer v. Boot* [1928] 2 K.B. 336; however cause of action estoppel does not apply in cases of default judgments or similar situations — *New Brunswick Rail Co v. British and French Trust Corporation Ltd* [1938] 4 All E.R. 747.

[33] [1991] 3 All E.R. 41.

relation to cause of action estoppel unless fraud or collusion was alleged. However, as is shown below, there is greater flexibility in respect of issue estoppel. An issue may be re-opened where further relevant material emerges which could not have been discovered by the parties exercising due diligence at the time of the original litigation. *Henderson* was also applied in *Talbot v. Berkshire County Council*,[34] a personal injury case where the passenger in a car sued the driver for negligent driving and sued the local authority for nuisance on the highway. The driver also had a potential claim against the authority arising from the same nuisance but failed to pursue it at that time. The passenger succeeded in both claims. When the driver later issued a writ against the highway authority claiming a contribution, the Court of Appeal held that he was barred by cause of action estoppel since it was a claim which could have been litigated at the earlier time. This seems a harsh application of the rule.

In an Australian case[35] there was a similar situation to *Talbot*. In an original action for negligence, the first defendant, the port authority, had to pay 90 per cent of the damages awarded with the co-defendants paying only 10 per cent. The authority failed at the time of the original hearing to claim an indemnity to which they were entitled. They later sought to recover their share of the damages from their co-defendants but were held to be estopped. The High Court of Australia put it:

Port of Melbourne Authority v. Anshun Pty Ltd (No. 2) (1981) 147 C.L.R. 589 at 602–604

In this situation we would prefer to say that there will be no estoppel unless it appears that the matter relied upon as a defence in the second action was so relevant to the subject matter of the first action that it would have been unreasonable not to rely on it. Generally speaking, it would be unreasonable not to plead a defence if, having regard to the nature of the plaintiff's claim, and its subject matter, it would be expected that the defendant would raise the defence and thereby enable the relevant issues to be determined in the one proceeding. In this respect, we need to recall that there are a variety of circumstances, some referred to in the earlier cases, why a party may justifiably refrain from litigating an issue in one proceeding yet wish to litigate the issue in other proceedings, for example, expense, importance of the particular issue, motives extraneous to the actual litigation, to mention but a few . . .

It has generally been accepted that a party will be estopped from bringing an action which, if it succeeds, will result in a judgment which conflicts with an earlier judgment. In this respect the discussion in *Brewer v. Brewer*[36] is illuminating. There it was held that the wife's omission to plead matters which would have constituted a discretionary bar to her husband's suit for dissolution of marriage on the ground of adultery did not estop her from raising those matters in subsequent proceedings for maintenance. Fullager J. said,

[34] [1993] 4 All E.R. 9.
[35] *Port of Melbourne Authority v. Anshun Pty Ltd (No. 2)* (1981) 147 C.L.R. 589.
[36] (1953) 88 C.L.R. 1.

In Hoystead's case[37] the Commissioner was not merely seeking to raise on the second appeal a point which he might have raised but had omitted to raise on the first appeal. He was seeking to raise a point which could not be decided in his favour consistently with the decision on the first appeal. The point had not been argued on the first appeal, and there was therefore no express decision on the point. But the Commissioner had allowed it to be assumed against him, and the assumption was fundamental to the decision in the sense that, if the assumption had not been made, the decision must have been different. As Somervell L.J. said: 'He was therefore seeking to obtain an order which was on the face of it and in form in direct conflict with the order which had been made previously' The point in question had been 'the groundwork of the decision itself, though not then directly the point at issue' . . .

The likelihood that the omission to plead a defence will contribute to the existence of conflicting judgments is obviously an important factor to be taken into account in deciding whether the omission to plead can found an estoppel against the assertion of the same matter as a foundation for a cause of action in a second proceeding. By 'conflicting' judgments we include judgments which are contradictory, though they may not be pronounced on the same cause of action. It is enough that they appear to declare rights which are inconsistent in respect of the same transaction.

It is for this reason that we regard the judgment that the Authority seeks to obtain as one which would conflict with the existing judgment, though the new judgment would be based on a different cause of action, a contractual indemnity.

Taking into consideration the relevant factors we conclude that the Full Court was right in holding that there was an estoppel. The matter now sought to be raised by the Authority was a defence . . . in the first action. It was so closely connected with the subject matter of that action that it was expected that it would be relied upon as a defence to that claim and as a basis of recovery by the Authority . . .

Issue estoppel

Within an action, once an issue has been raised and distinctly determined between parties, neither party can be allowed to fight that issue all over again. It was put by Diplock L.J. in *Mills v. Cooper*,[38]

Mills v. Cooper [1967] 2 All E.R. 100 at 104g–105c, *per* Diplock L.J.

The doctrine of issue estoppel in civil proceedings is of fairly recent and sporadic development, though none the worse for that. Although *Hoystead v. Taxation Commissioner*[39] did not purport to break new ground, it can be regarded as the starting point of the modern common law doctrine, the application of which to different kinds of civil actions is currently being worked out in the courts. That doctrine: so far as it affects civil proceedings, may be stated thus: a party to civil proceedings is not entitled to make, as against the other party, an assertion, whether of fact or of the legal consequences of facts, the correctness of which is an essential element in his cause of action or defence, if the same assertion was an essential element in his previous cause of action or defence in previous civil proceedings between the same parties or their predecessors in title, and was found by a court of competent jurisdiction in such previous civil proceedings to be

[37] *Hoystead v. Taxation Commissioner* [1926] A.C. 155.
[38] [1967] 2 All E.R. 100.
[39] [1926] A.C. 155.

incorrect, unless further material which is relevant to the correctness or incorrectness of the assertion and could not by reasonable diligence have been adduced by that party in the previous proceedings has since become available to him.

. . . That general rule applies also to criminal proceedings, but in a form modified by the distinctive character of criminal as compared with civil litigation. Here it takes the form of the rule against double jeopardy, of which the simplest application is to be found in the pleas of *autrefois* convict and *autrefois acquit*; but the rule against double jeopardy also applies in circumstances in which those ancient pleas are not strictly available; and it is in connection with the wider application that the High Court of Australia in particular in the cases cited[40] has used the same expression as is used in civil proceedings: 'issue estoppel'. I think with great respect that the use of that expression in criminal and civil proceedings alike may lead to confusion, for there are obvious differences — lack of mutuality is but one — between the application of the rule against double jeopardy in criminal cases, and the rule that there should be finality in civil litigation.

Issue estoppel is less strict than cause of action estoppel:

(1) it is only those issues that are in fact raised in the previous proceedings that are subject to an estoppel: the *Henderson* principles relating to cause of action estoppel do not apply to issue estoppel which therefore does not extend to those issues which a party exercising due diligence could have raised.

(2) issue estoppel does not apply where significant fresh evidence is available or where the justice of the case requires re-litigation. The test is that the new evidence must be such as "entirely changes the aspect of the case . . . and was not and could not by reasonable diligence have been ascertained before".[41]

In *Arnold v. National Westminster Bank plc*[42] a lease contained a clause for rent review every five years, that rent to be decided on the basis of a fair market rent for a hypothetical lease for the residue of the term. In 1983 there was a dispute as to whether that hypothetical lease should or should not contain a clause for rent review. It was decided by arbitration and appeal that it should not. However by 1988 subsequent decisions made it clear that this interpretation was wrong. Were the lessees estopped from relitigating the issue? The landlords appealed to the House of Lords:

Arnold v. National Westminster Bank plc [1991] 3 All E.R. 41 at 50b–52d, _per_ Lord Keith

It was argued that there was no logical distinction between cause of action estoppel and issue estoppel and that, if the rule was absolute in the one case as regards points actually decided, so it should be in the other case. But

[40] *R. v. Wilkes* (1948) 77 C.L.R. 511; *Mraz v. R (No. 2)* (1956) 96 C.L.R. 62.

[41] *Phosphate Sewage Co v. Molleson* (1879) 4 App. Cas. 801 at 814, *per* Earl Cairns L.C. This was approved by Lord Diplock in *Hunter v. Chief Constable of West Midlands* [1981] 3 All E.R. 727 at 736c.

[42] [1991] 3 All E.R. 41.

there is room for the view that the underlying principles upon which estoppel is based, public policy and justice, have greater force in cause of action estoppel, the subject matter of the two proceedings being identical, than they do in issue estoppel, where the subject matter is different. Once it is accepted that different considerations apply to issue estoppel, it is hard to perceive any logical distinction between a point which was previously raised and decided and one which might have been but was not. Given that the further material which would have put an entirely different complexion on the point was at the earlier stage unknown to the party and could not by reasonable diligence have been discovered by him, it is hard to see why there should be a different result according to whether he decided not to take the point, thinking it hopeless, or argue it faintly without any real hope of success. In my opinion your Lordships should affirm it to be the law that there may be an exception to issue estoppel in the special circumstance that there has become available to a party further material relevant to the correct determination of a point involved in the earlier proceedings, whether or not that point was specifically raised and decided, being material which could not by reasonable diligence have been adduced in those proceedings. . . .

It is next for consideration whether the further relevant material which a party may be permitted to bring forward in the later proceedings is confined to matters of fact, or whether what may not entirely inappropriately described as a change in the law may result in or be an element in special circumstances enabling an issue to be reopened . . .

. . . I find myself in respectful agreement with the passage in the judgment of Sir Nicholas Browne-Wilkinson V-C where he said[43]

> In my judgment a change in the law subsequent to the first decision is capable of bringing the case within the exception to issue estoppel. If, as I think, the yardstick of whether issue estoppel should be held to apply is the justice to the parties, injustice can flow as much from a subsequent change in the law as from the subsequent discovery of new facts. In both case the injustice lies in a successful party to the first action being held to have rights which in fact he does not possess. I can, therefore, see no reason for holding that a subsequent change in the law can never be sufficient to bring the case within the exception . . .

There are five basic conditions necessary for issue estoppel to be invoked. These are firstly that a court of competent jurisdiction must have made a final judgement on the merits of the case; secondly that the parties to the initial proceedings must be the same as the parties to the subsequent proceedings; thirdly that the parties to the initial proceedings must be acting in the same capacity; fourthly that the same issues must be involved and fifthly that the estoppel must be specifically pleaded.

(a) A court of competent jurisdiction must have made a final judgement on the merits of the case.

The tribunal can be a foreign court[44] under the Civil Jurisdiction and Judgments Act 1982:

[43] [1988] 3 All E.R. 977 at 983.
[44] *Carl Zeiss Stiftung v. Rayner & Keeler Ltd (No. 2)* [1967] 1 A.C. 853.

> 34.—No proceedings may be brought by a person in England and Wales or Northern Ireland on a cause of action in respect of which a judgment has been given in his favour on proceedings between the same parties, or their privies, in a court in another part of the United Kingdom or in a court of an overseas country, unless that judgment is not enforceable or entitled to recognition in England and Wales or, as the case may be, Northern Ireland[45]

The question of whether a tribunal is one of competent jurisdiction can be troublesome. In *The Speedlink Vanguard and the European Gateway*[46] an investigation into a collision at sea had been held under the Merchant Shipping Act 1894. Were the owners of the two ships involved bound by the findings of the court of formal investigation which operated with all the powers of a magistrates' court? The Court of Appeal held that it was necessary to look at the function of the court (here the role was investigatory with its primary aim the safety of life and property at sea) and whether in the proceedings there was a defined issue, a *lis*, between the contending shipowners. As there had been no adjudication of the legal rights of the parties, issue estoppel did not arise. But there is no reason why the decision of an inferior tribunal with a limited jurisdiction and a limited function should not be capable of creating an issue estoppel. In *Crown Estate Commissioners v. Dorset County Council*[47] the court considered the role of the commons commissioner who had a statutory jurisdiction which, *inter alia*, included the power to decide whether or not road verges should be registered as common land. As part of this function, there was a ruling whether the verges formed part of the highway or not. The Crown Estate was estopped in subsequent litigation from challenging this finding.

The judgment must be final:

> What it means in the context of judgments delivered by courts of justice is that the court has held that it has jurisdiction to adjudicate on an issue raised in the cause of action to which the particular set of facts give rise, and that its judgment on that cause of action is one that cannot be varied, reopened or set aside by the court that delivered it or any other court of co-ordinate jurisdiction although it may be subject to appeal to a court of higher jurisdiction.[48]

In addition the judgment must be on the merits of the action. No estoppel can arise if the action has been withdrawn, dismissed or terminated for some reason. The rules will be strictly interpreted if there has been a default judgment.[49] However a decision at *voire dire* on the admissibility of evidence will estop a party in any subsequent civil case. In the Court of Appeal in *Hunter v. Chief Constable of West Midlands*[50] Lord

[45] *The Indian Endurance* [1993] 1 All E.R. 998.
[46] [1986] 3 All E.R. 554.
[47] [1990] 1 All E.R. 19.
[48] *DSV Silo und Verwaltungsgesellschaft mbH v. Owners of the Sennar* [1985] 2 All E.R. 104 at 106g–h, *per* Lord Diplock.
[49] *New Brunswick Rail Co v. British and French Trust Corporation Ltd* [1938] 4 All E.R. 747.
[50] [1980] 2 All E.R. 227 — the case also is known as *McIlkenny v. Chief Constable of West Midlands*.

Denning held that the Birmingham Six were estopped from raising the issue of the admissibility of their confession, a matter which had been determined against them at their original trial:

> . . . when an issue has been decided by a competent court against a party in an earlier proceeding, it should only be regarded as final if he has had a full and fair opportunity of defending himself therein and the circumstances are such that it would not be fair or just to allow him to re-open it in subsequent proceedings.[51]

(b) The parties to the initial proceedings must be the same as the parties to the subsequent proceedings.

In *Townsend v. Bishop*,[52] a father had allowed his son to drive the car. The car was hit by the defendant who was sued by the father for damages to the car. The defendant won on the grounds of contributory negligence by the son, which at that time was a complete defence. Subsequently the son sued the defendant for damages for personal injury and the court held that the son was not a party to the initial action and was thus not estopped from denying his contributory negligence.

This shows a narrow approach to the specific identities of the parties concerned which can have absurd results. In *Petrie v. Nuttall*[53] a person initiated (but was not himself the prosecutor) a successful prosecution against a landowner for obstructing the highway. In subsequent proceedings, he was himself sued by the landowner for trespass on the same land on the ground that it was not a highway. The landowner was not estopped from arguing that it was private land because the defendant, although he had initiated the proceedings, was not a party to the original prosecution. This state of affairs was considered in *Hunter v. Chief Constable of West Midlands*[54] which concerned the six men were convicted of causing the Birmingham pub bombings. At their criminal trial, the men's confessions were proffered as evidence by the prosecution. The men argued that they had confessed as a result of police violence. After a *voire dire* hearing, the trial judge admitted the confessions into evidence. The men later sued the police in a civil action for the alleged assaults, using new medical evidence as well as statements from prison officers that they had been assaulted before arriving at prison. The police applied to strike out the action arguing that the plaintiffs were estopped from raising the question of assault since that issue had been determined by the original criminal court. In the Court of Appeal, Lord Denning and Sir George Baker held that the police and the Crown (technically the party in the original criminal trial), although not identical, were in privity, preferring the broader reasoning adopted by the American courts in cases such as *Eagle, Star and British Dominions Insurance Co. v. Heller*.[55]

[51] *ibid.* at 238j.
[52] [1939] 1 All E.R. 805.
[53] (1856) 11 Exch. 569.
[54] [1981] 3 All E.R. 727; the Court of Appeal judgment is at [1980] 2 All E.R. 227.
[55] (1927) 140 S.E. 314.

Lord Denning said:

> Our friends in the United States have been just as scathing as Jeremy Bentham. They have rejected the doctrine of mutuality altogether, and they have limited the doctrine of privity. They take a distinction between a decision in favour of a man and a decision against him. If a decision has been given against a man on the identical issue arising in the previous proceedings and he had a full and fair opportunity of defending himself in it, then he is estopped from contesting it again in subsequent proceedings. Not only is he estopped but so are those in privity with him. But there is no corresponding estoppel on the person in whose favour it operates.[56]

Thus the plaintiffs were estopped from arguing that they been assaulted by the police. Goff L.J., dissenting on this point, rejected the argument about identity of parties and issue estoppel, feeling the court was bound by dicta in *Mills v. Cooper* and in *Carl-Zeiss-Stiftung*. In the latter case Lord Upjohn said:

> It is clear that a party relying on such a plea must at least prove that the earlier proceedings were determinative of the issues arising in the second proceedings; that the same parties or their privies are common to both proceedings and that the earlier proceedings were within the jurisdiction of the court and were final and conclusive of the relevant issues.[57]

The Crown as state prosecutors and the Chief Constable as a tortfeasor by statute could not be in privity. Instead Goff L.J. struck out the claim on the grounds of abuse of process. Lord Diplock in the House of Lords agreed with the approach of Goff L.J. and, although he found it unnecessary to discuss estoppel at length, did approve the comments on the characteristics of issue estoppel.[58] It would appear that a litigant is not estopped from raising an issue, decided in earlier proceedings, when he or she (or the opponent) was not a party or privy to those proceedings.

(c) The parties to the initial proceedings must be acting in the same capacity

In *Marginson v. Blackburn Borough Council*[59] Marginson was in his car being driven by his wife. There was an accident with a bus belonging to the council and being driven by one of their workers. Mrs Marginson was killed and he was injured. Some adjoining houses were damaged. The owners of the houses sued Marginson and the council who were held to be vicariously and equally liable. Marginson then sued the council, both personally for injuries he himself suffered and as personal representative of his wife's estate. In a personal capacity, he was estopped from denying his

[56] *Hunter* (Court of Appeal) *supra* at 235j, *per* Lord Denning.
[57] *Carl-Zeiss-Stiftung v. Rayner and Keeler Ltd (No. 2)* [1966] 2 All E.R. 536 at 570.
[58] *Hunter* (House of Lords) at 733a–b.
[59] [1939] 1 All E.R. 273.

wife's contributory negligence (a complete defence at that time) as this issue had been decided at the original hearing where he and the council were parties. But in his role as representative of his wife's estate, he was acting in a different capacity, had not been a party to the original decision and was not therefore estopped.

(d) The same issues must be involved.

Usually this does not mean a narrow approach of whether the issues are formally legally identical but whether they are substantially the same with regard to the issues of fact, the evidence to support them and the legal arguments. In *Marginson*, the action by the householders involved proof of the wife's negligent driving whereas in the second case the defendant council raised her contributory negligence as a defence. Formally these are different issues but in substance they are the same. The husband in his personal capacity was estopped from denying that contributory negligence. Similarly in *Bell v. Holmes*[60] where two drivers were involved in an accident. Both were sued by a passenger in one of the cars and both were held liable, although damages were apportioned unequally between them. In subsequent proceedings between the two drivers, the plaintiff was estopped from denying the apportionment.

But there is a diversity of approach apparent in the cases. The argument that there is a difference (in such road accidents) between the duty of care owed to other drivers and the duty owed to passengers found favour in *Randolph v. Tuck.*[61] But in *Wall v. Radford*[62] there was a collision between a Volkswagen and a BMW. A passenger in the VW sued both drivers and damages were apportioned equally. The VW driver subsequently brought an action against the BMW driver for personal injuries arising out of the collision. She argued that the duties owed to the passenger by the drivers were not the same as they owed to each other and to themselves. Consequently there was no room for issue estoppel:

Wall v. Radford [1991] 2 All E.R. 741 at 750j–751b, _per_ Popplewell J.

It is, I think, very important to recognise that although a separate duty is owed to another driver from that owed to a passenger, that does not mean in the instant case that the duty is in any way different. The facts giving rise to a breach of that duty are identical and liability for that breach of duty is identical. If two drivers collide in the middle of a wide road, it is quite impossible to see why they should not be found 50 per cent responsible inter se for injury to a passenger, 50 per cent for injury to the other driver and 50 per cent contributorily negligent in respect of their own claim. The duty is to take reasonable care. It is in the absence of special circumstances (which do not apply in the instant case) the same care which has to be taken in respect of the passenger, another driver and the driver himself. In the

[60] [1956] 3 All E.R. 449.
[61] [1961] 1 All E.R. 814.
[62] [1991] 2 All E.R. 741.

instant case if he fails to take that reasonable care he will be liable to his passenger, to the other driver and for his own contributory negligence in identical proportions. It is not a different duty. It is the same duty owed to a different person.

I am therefore wholly unpersuaded that the alleged difference in duty owed to the third party and that owed to the other driver or to himself plays any part in this case. I prefer the decisions in *Bell v. Holmes* and *Wood v. Luscombe*[63] to that of *Randolph v. Tuck*.

A similar issue arose in *North West Water v. Binnie & Partners*[64] when an explosion occurred in a valve house attached to an underground tunnel link for water distribution. A group of local residents were being shown round at the time and several were killed or injured. The victims sued both the water authority, the contractors and the consultant engineers. The Court of Appeal held the latter, Binnies, wholly to blame for the disaster. The water authority then sued the engineers for the damage to tunnelling. The narrow approach would suggest that there is a difference between the duty owed to the original victims and that owed to the authority. The broader approach was again preferred:

> I find it unreal to hold that the issues raised in the two actions arising from identical facts are different solely because the parties are different or because the duty of care owed to different persons is in law different. However, I must at once stress my use of the word "solely". I think great caution must be exercised before shutting out a party from putting forward his case on the grounds of issue estoppel or abuse of process. Before doing so the court should be quite satisfied that there is no real or practical difference between the issues to be litigated and that already decided, and the evidence which may properly be called on those issues in the new action.[65]

(e) an estoppel has to be specifically pleaded.

In *Vooght v. Winch*[66] the defendant in an action for diverting water from a stream proffered in evidence a judgment in an earlier action between the same parties for the same cause of action. The judge refused to accept that it acted as an estoppel and this decision was upheld:

Vooght v. Winch (1819) 2 B. & Old. 662 at 668, _per_ Abbott C.J.

I am of the opinion that the verdict and judgment obtained for the defendant in the former action was not conclusive evidence against the plaintiff upon the plea of not guilty. It would indeed have been conclusive if pleaded in bar to the action by way of estoppel. In that case the plaintiff would not be allowed to discuss the case with the defendant, and for the second time to disturb and vex him by the agitation of the same question. But the defendant has pleaded not guilty, and has thereby elected to submit his case to a jurisdiction. Now if the former verdict was proper to

[63] [1964] 3 All E.R. 972.
[64] [1990] 3 All E.R. 547.
[65] *ibid.* at 561c–d, *per* Drake J.
[66] (1819) 2 B. & Ald. 662.

be received in evidence by the learned judge, its effect must be left to the jury. If it were conclusive indeed, the learned judge ought immediately to have nonsuited the plaintiff, or to have told the jury that they were bound, in point of law, to find a verdict for the defendant. It appears to me, however, that the party, by not pleading the former judgment in bar, consents that the whole matter shall go to the jury, and leaves it open to them to inquire into the same upon evidence, and they are to give their verdict upon the whole evidence then submitted to them.[67]

Issue estoppel in matrimonial causes

It is important to bear in mind that in matrimonial matters the court has a duty to inquire into the facts under section 1(3) of the Matrimonial Causes Act 1973. This means that the ordinary principles of estoppel must be modified. It is said that estoppel binds the parties who have no right to reopen issues but does not bind the court which can, if it sees fit, inquire into the facts.

In *Thompson v. Thompson*[68] the wife applied to the court for an order for maintenance against her husband on the grounds of his wilful neglect to maintain her after she had left him, allegedly because of his cruelty. The husband made a similar charge of cruelty against the wife. The application was dismissed. Subsequently the husband petitioned for divorce, again on the grounds of cruelty. The wife denied this and prayed for judicial separation because of her husband's cruelty. He sought to have this struck out on the grounds that the issue of his cruelty had already been determined in the maintenance proceedings and she was estopped from raising them again:

Thompson v. Thompson [1957] 1 All E.R. 161 at 165d–g, _per_ Lord Denning

The situation has been neatly summarised by saying that in the divorce court 'estoppels bind the parties but do not bind the court'; but this is perhaps a little too abbreviated. The full proposition is that, once an issue of a matrimonial offence has been litigated between the parties and decided by a competent court, neither party can claim as of right to reopen the issue and litigate it all over again if the other party objects (that is what is meant by saying that estoppels bind the parties): but the divorce court has the right, and indeed the duty in a proper case, to reopen the issue, or to allow either party to reopen it, despite the objection of the other party (that is what is meant by saying that estoppels do not bind the court). Whether the divorce court should reopen the issue depends on the circumstances. If the court is satisfied that there has already been a full and proper inquiry in the previous litigation, it will often hold that it is not necessary to hold another inquiry all over again: but if the court is not so satisfied it has a right and a duty to inquire into it afresh. If the court does decide to reopen the matter, then there is no longer any estoppel on either party. Each can go into the matter afresh . . .

[67] Interestingly the court were happy for the trial judge to admit the former judgment as evidence of the facts on which it was based, apparently in contradiction to the rule in *Hollington v. Hewthorn* which is discussed later in this chapter.
[68] [1957] 1 All E.R. 161.

Problems arise in divorce largely because inferior tribunals, especially the magistrates' court, can be involved in granting some preliminary relief to the parties. In *Hayward v. Hayward*[69] a husband and wife suspected that their marriage was bigamous and therefore void. The husband still admitted liability in maintenance proceedings in a magistrates' court. Subsequent proceedings alleged that the marriage was void on grounds of bigamy. It was held that estoppel did not prevent this from being asserted:

Hayward v. Hayward [1961] P. 152 at 158–159, *per* Phillimore J.

It would surely be remarkable as a proposition of law if this court were to be prevented from declaring the truth, namely that a marriage is bigamous and so correcting the status of the parties to it and of their dependants merely because one or both of them had chosen to assert its validity or because one of them failed to dispute or had concurred in the assertion of its validity by the other. This court deals not merely with disputes between parties but with status. Marriage is not an ordinary contract — it is an institution which confers status on the parties to it and upon the children that issue from it . . . It is an old maxim that estoppels are odious because they tend to shut out the truth . . . and it is well settled that they cannot override the law of the land . . . If the law declares a bigamous marriage void and criminal, is this court nevertheless to treat it as valid and refuse to declare the truth by reason of the conduct, however unmeritorious, of one or both of the parties to it? The consequences to which this doctrine might lead are surely remarkable.[70]

Spouses are able to go to the magistrates' court for judicial separation orders, for maintenance orders[71] or indeed personal protection orders.[72] Divorce proceedings themselves come under the Matrimonial Causes Act 1973 which lays down the single ground for divorce, namely, "irretrievable breakdown". The conduct on which a spouse may rely for preliminary relief might of course be the same conduct relied on later in a divorce action. Under section 4 of the 1973 Act the jurisdiction of the court in divorce is not precluded by reason only that one of the parties has on the same (or substantially similar) facts obtained preliminary relief. However the court may treat such an earlier decree or order as sufficient proof of the adultery, desertion or other ground on which it was granted. The court must not grant a divorce without receiving evidence from the petitioner.

Section 4 only applies to petitions for divorce where preliminary relief has been granted. In cases not coming within this, it would appear that a magistrates' court is bound by findings of the divorce court[73] or of another magistrates' court[74] and that the divorce court is bound by its own previous findings[75] but not by those of a magistrates' court.[76] Finally estoppel does

[69] [1961] P. 152.
[70] See also *Harriman v. Harriman* [1909] P. 123.
[71] Matrimonial Proceedings (Magistrates' Courts) Act 1960.
[72] Domestic Proceedings and Magistrates' Courts Act 1978.
[73] *James v. James* [1948] 1 All E.R. 214.
[74] *Stokes v. Stokes* [1911] P. 195.
[75] *Finney v. Finney* (1868) L.R. 1 P&D 483.
[76] *Winnan v. Winnan* [1949] P. 174.

not operate in the fullest sense even in ancillary proceedings after a divorce decree. In *Porter v. Porter*[77] the husband petitioned for divorce alleging desertion. The wife initially denied this and alleged cruelty and adultery. In the event, she allowed the petition to proceed undefended. Subsequently she sought maintenance and sought to advance evidence of her husband's cruelty:

Porter v. Porter [1971] 2 All E.R. 1037 at 1039a–1040c, _per_ Ormrod J.

This then is yet another case on the much argued problems of estoppel in matrimonial causes . . . It arises from a conflict between two issues of public policy: on the one hand the desirability of finality in litigation . . . and on the other hand, the importance in the interests of justice to the individuals concerned, that the discretionary powers of the court in ancillary matters should be exercised with a full knowledge of all the relevant facts rather than on a basis, partly of fact, and partly of assumptions, arising from such rules as estoppel. It is particularly difficult to do justice in so personal a field as matrimonial cases if the realities of the situation are allowed to be obscured by the application of rules or principles which in other situations assist the cause of justice . . .

The answer to this question is to be found in the valuable judgment of Sachs J. in *Hull v. Hull*,[78] the effect of which may be summarised in this way. Estoppel operates to prevent a party in ancillary proceedings from challenging the ground on which the decree was pronounced in the suit, and from attacking the express findings of fact of the trial judge. Thus a respondent against whom a decree has been pronounced on the ground of adultery cannot be heard in ancillary proceedings to deny such adultery or to set up an absolute bar to a decree on this ground, *e.g.* connivance or condonation . . . Alternatively, where a wife has denied her adultery on oath and the trial judge has pronounced a decree on the basis that such a denial was accepted, the husband is estopped from alleging such adultery in ancillary proceedings . . . Similarly where the trial judge has made specific findings, *e.g.* that the husband did not strike the wife as alleged . . . that finding is conclusive. Apart from these two categories there is no estoppel. (Whether in custody proceedings estoppel operates at all may be a matter of doubt . . .)

Applying these conclusions to the present appeal, it follows that the wife cannot be heard to deny that she deserted the husband as found by the trial judge. To allow her to do so would be to allow her to attempt to destroy the very basis on which the jurisdiction of the court to award maintenance depends. Accordingly, she cannot set up just cause for leaving her husband, nor can she assert that he has treated her with cruelty within the meaning of the Matrimonial Causes Act 1965, because this would be equivalent to asserting just cause. On the other hand, I see no reason why she should not raise any matters of complaint against the husband by way of mitigation of her desertion. If she is prevented from doing so the court, in the exercise of its discretionary jurisdiction, will be failing to carry out its statutory duty to consider 'conduct of the parties' which is not the same as asking who obtained the decree and on what ground . . .

Issue estoppel in criminal cases

There are the special pleas of *autrefois acquit* and *autrefois convict* which act in a similar fashion to cause of action estoppel. They are based on the

[77] [1971] 2 All E.R. 1037.
[78] [1960] 1 All E.R. 378.

double jeopardy rule and enable a defendant in subsequent criminal proceedings to argue that he or she has been acquitted or convicted of the same offence at an earlier proceeding. The same offence means one for which the defendant could have lawfully been convicted at the original hearing.[79] Thus if the defendant is convicted of causing grievous bodily harm contrary to section 18 of the Offences Against the Person Act 186, there would be a bar to a subsequent charge of malicious wounding under section 20 of that Act but no bar to a homicide prosecution if the victim died subsequent to the GBH conviction.

In *Sambasivam v. Malaya Federation Public Prosecutor*[80] at the original trial, the defendant was charged with both possession of ammunition and with carrying firearms. He was acquitted on the first charge and a new trial was ordered on the second charge. At the subsequent trial, the prosecution relied on a statement by the accused in which he admitted carrying a firearm but also admitted being in possession of ammunition. The conviction was quashed since the court failed to direct the two assessors that the prosecution were bound by the acquittal and thus that part of the confession must be regarded as untrue:

Sambasivam v. Malaya Federation Public Prosecutor [1950] A.C. 458 at 479, _per_ Lord MacDermott

The effect of a verdict of acquittal pronounced by a competent court on a lawful charge and after a lawful trial is not completely stated by saying that the person acquitted cannot be tried again for the same offence. To that it must be added that the verdict is binding and conclusive in all subsequent proceedings between the parties to the adjudication. The maxim *res iudicata pro veritate accipitur* is no less applicable to criminal than to civil proceedings. Here, the appellant having been acquitted at the first trial on a charge of having ammunition in his possession, the prosecution was bound to accept the correctness of that verdict and was precluded from taking any step to challenge it at the second trial. And the appellant was no less entitled to rely on his acquittal so far as it might be relevant in his defence.

This Privy Council decision was supported by the Court of Appeal in *R. v. Hay*.[81] The accused made a statement confessing to two offences, arson and burglary, which were tried separately. He was acquitted of arson and in his burglary trial asked for the whole of the statement to be put to the jury. However the trial judge refused an application to adduce evidence of the acquittal on the arson charge in order to show that confession to burglary made on the same occasion was also likely to be unreliable. The jury should have been directed that, in considering the truth of the burglary confession, they should bear in mind the fact that the arson confession was untrue. The accused was entitled to have any independent evidence put before the jury which, if believed, might show a material part of the statement to be false.

[79] Criminal Law Act 1967, s.6(3).
[80] [1950] A.C. 458.
[81] [1983] Crim.L.R. 390.

In *G. v. Coltart*[82] G, a domestic servant, was charged with two counts of theft, one from her mistress and the other from a guest in the house. No evidence was offered on the latter charge and there was a directed acquittal. But on the first charge the prosecution sought to rebut G's line of defence which was that she had taken the property but intended to return it. They adduced evidence that she had also taken the guest's property and had not returned that. G's conviction was quashed as the prosecution were estopped from arguing that G was guilty of another offence of which she had been acquitted. The Divisional Court distinguished *R. v. Ollis*[83] where the defendant was acquitted of an offence involving passing a dud cheque to one, Ramsey, on July 5. He was later charged with similar offences on June 24 and 26 and July 6. The prosecution called Ramsey to give the same evidence as he had at the original trial, arguing that it did not reopen that issue but that it showed the accused's knowledge about the state of his bank account. The principle is clear and probably correct but does the fact that Ollis passed a dud cheque on July 6 show guilty knowledge on the June 24? The chronology leads one to doubt that the testimony logically leads to that particular inference.[84]

Such decisions do not support an argument that issue estoppel has a place in criminal proceedings. In *DPP v. Humphrys*,[85] the defendant was initially acquitted of driving while disqualified on July 18, 1972. Although a police officer gave evidence of identification, the defendant testified that he had not driven any vehicle in 1972. He was later charged with perjury in relation to that statement. The prosecution had other witnesses as to his driving during the relevant period but also were allowed to re-introduce the evidence of the police officer. The House of Lords upheld the conviction, affirming that there is no such thing as issue estoppel in criminal law:

DPP v. Humphrys [1976] 2 All E.R. 497 at 523d–524b, _per_ Lord Hailsham

Since this opinion is already long, I venture to summarise it as follows. (1) The doctrine of issue estoppel as it has been developed in civil proceedings is not applicable to criminal proceedings. It follows that the decision in *R. v. Hogan*[86] was wrong and should not be followed . . . (2) Although the civil doctrine of issue estoppel as it has been developed in civil proceedings is not applicable to criminal proceedings, there is a doctrine applicable to criminal proceedings which is in some ways analogous to issue estoppel, and has sometimes been described by that name. However, (3) the civil doctrine is based on the necessity for finality between private litigants, whereas the doctrine in criminal proceedings is based on the prohibition

[82] [1967] 1 All E.R. 271.
[83] [1900] 2 Q.B. 758.
[84] Indeed it appears to be more prejudicial than probative. However *Ollis* is applied in *R. v. Caceres-Moreira* [1995] Crim.L.R. 489.
[85] [1976] 2 All E.R. 497.
[86] [1974] 2 All E.R. 142 where the accused was convicted of GBH and held to be estopped from denying *mens rea* at a subsequent murder trial after the victim had died.

of double jeopardy, *i.e.* the maxim nemo debet bis vexari pro una et eadam causa. It follows (4) that whereas the civil doctrine is equally applicable to either of the two civil parties, the criminal doctrine is available to the accused but not to the Crown. (5) Whereas the civil doctrine applies to all cases where an individual issue can be isolated and identified as determined, the criminal doctrine is not so limited but is primarily concerned with verdicts, and applies to verdicts which are either in form or in substance inconsistent. (6) In general, the doctrine in criminal law precludes the Crown from adducing evidence or making suggestions which are inconsistent with a previous verdict of acquittal when its real effect is determined. The doctrine is one of substance rather than form. The court will inquire into realities and not mere technicalities. (7) Where a second charge is brought which is different both in substance and in form from an earlier charge, the mere fact that some of the evidence adduced in support of the second charge is inconsistent with innocence on the earlier charge does not preclude the Crown from adducing that evidence in asserting the truth when considering a verdict on the second charge. (8) Where the second charge consists in an allegation that the accused in the first charge has committed perjury in his evidence given on his own behalf in his defence on the former charge, the mere fact that some of the evidence brought in support of the charge of perjury is identical with evidence given in the first charge and inconsistent with innocence on that charge does not preclude the Crown from adducing that evidence or asserting its truth where it is accompanied by other evidence in support of the charge of perjury, nut (9) where the evidence is substantially identical with the evidence given at the first trial without any addition and the Crown is in substance simply seeking to get behind a verdict of acquittal, the second charge is inadmissible both on the ground that it infringes the rule against double jeopardy and on the ground that it is an abuse of the process of the court whether or not the charge is in form a charge of perjury at the first trial. (10) Except where the formal pleas of autrefois acquit or convict are admissible, when it is the practice to empanel a jury, it is the duty of the court to examine facts of the first trial in case of any dispute, and in any case it is the duty of the court to rule as a matter of law on the legal consequences deriving from such facts. In any case it is, therefore for the court to determine whether on the facts found there is as a matter of law a double jeopardy involved in the later proceedings and to direct a jury accordingly.

The net result in the present case is that the appeal of the Director of Public Prosecutions succeeds . . .[87]

There are many reasons[88] canvassed for this rejection of issue estoppel:

(1) the difficulty of defining the issues in criminal cases would be too great in the absence of pleadings and a reasoned decision, although this would appear to vary from case to case. It does not appear to have been a difficulty in either *Hogan* or *Humphrys*.

(2) the standard of proof might mean that estoppel would operate unfairly in the defendant's favour. If Hogan had been acquitted of GBH, perhaps because the jury found that there was a reasonable doubt that he possessed the necessary mens rea, should that bar any further prosecution for murder if the victim dies because the Crown would be unable to re-open the issue of intent?

[87] *Humphrys supra* at 523d–524b, *per* Lord Hailsham.

[88] Others are canvassed in Mirfield P., "Shedding a Tear for Issue Estoppel" [1980] Crim.L.R. 336.

(3) such a doctrine might be equally unfair on the defendant:

> On a charge of murder the onus lies on the prosecution to prove their case, not by technical doctrine but by evidence, and the jury's duty is to decide the case on the evidence called before them, which might be quite different from the evidence adduced in the previous trial.[89]

(4) the doctrines of *autrefois acquit* and *autrefois convict* adequately protect the accused.

But is *Humphrys* reconcilable with the extension of the *autrefois acquit* rule as laid down in *Sambasivam*?

Hirst M., "Contradicting Previous Acquittals" [1991] Crim.L.R. 510 at 516–518

A serious potential challenge to the *Sambasivam* rule arose in *DPP v. Humphrys*. It is submitted that, but for the way in which *Humphrys* was argued, the *Sambasivam* rule might well have been repudiated by the House of Lords in that case, and even though this did not happen, the two cases remain most difficult to reconcile with each other . . .

The resounding rejection of issue estoppel [in *Humphrys*] was not, however matched by any rejection of the *Sambasivam* rule. On the contrary, this rule was approved, on the ground that it was 'concerned with the binding nature of a previous verdict of acquittal rather than with the determination of any particular issue at the previous trial.' With respect, however, this approval is irreconcilable with the cogent reasons given for the rejection of issue estoppel. The *Sambasivam* rule can and does produce the very kind of 'artificial and unfair' results to which Lord Salmon referred . . .

A further difficulty with *Humphrys* is that nobody seems to have recognised that D could equally have argued his case on the basis of the *Sambasivam* rule. Their Lordships seem to have taken the view that the prosecution did not infringe that rule, because they did not seek to prove that D rode his machine *whilst disqualified*. [The police officer's] evidence merely referred to D's use of the machine on the day in question.

The attempt to limit the scope of the *Sambasivam* rule is, however, inconsistent with *Sambasivam* itself. The prosecution will rarely seek to prove that D was wrongly acquitted on the previous occasion. What they may seek to do is to adduce evidence which happens to be inconsistent with his innocence on that occasion, having regard to the case as a whole and to the lack of alternative explanations for that acquittal. This is what happened in *Sambasivam* and in those cases which have followed it; and this is what the defence complained of in *Humphrys*.

. . . One can only speculate as to how the House of Lords might have ruled if *Humphrys* had been argued on the basis of the *Sambasivam* rule. It seems clear that their Lordships were determined to ensure that an acquittal procured by perjury should not give the perjurer any immunity from prosecution; but this could have been avoided in either of two ways. They could have repudiated *Sambasivam* as they repudiated issue estoppel, or they could have restricted the scope of the rule so that it could not apply in cases where there is evidence of perjury at the first trial . . .

[89] *Humphrys supra* at 529d–e, *per* Lord Salmon.

The difficulties and artificialities created by the *Sambasivam* rule and preventing evidence from being adduced at a later trial which is inconsistent with an earlier acquittal sits uneasily alongside the rejection of issue estoppel. However that rejection was confirmed by the House of Lords in *Hunter*.

Estoppel by deed

If a person is a party to a deed which asserts a particular fact, that person and those in privity with him or her are estopped from denying the truth of that fact. This common law rule was put forward in *Bowman v. Taylor*,[90] a case in which the plaintiff sought royalties from the defendant. He had granted the defendant, by deed, a licence to use looms. That deed stated that the plaintiff was the inventor of certain improvements to the looms, had obtained letters patent and caused a specification to be enrolled. It was held that the defendant was estopped from denying these matters:

> An estoppel operates because it concludeth a man to allege the truth by reason of the assertion of the party that that fact is true . . . If a party has by his deed directly asserted a specific fact, it is impossible to say that he shall not be precluded from disputing that fact, thus solemnly admitted by him on the face of his deed . . .[91]

But whether both parties are so bound depends on the intentions of the parties,[92] an issue discussed in *Greer v. Kettle*.[93] A company had guaranteed under seal a loan from one company to another. In the guarantee document, the lender had recited that the load had been advanced on the security of certain shares but in fact the shares had not been validly issued. Was the guarantor estopped by this?

Greer v. Kettle [1937] 4 All E.R. 396 at 404a–f, *per* Lord Maugham

Estoppel by deed is a rule of evidence founded on the principle that a solemn and unambiguous statement or engagement in a deed must be taken as binding between parties and privies and therefore as not admitting any contradictory proof. It is important to observe that this is a rule of common law, though it may be noted that an exception arises when the deed is fraudulent or illegal. The position in equity is and was always different in this respect, that where there are proper grounds for rectifying a deed, *e.g.* because it is based upon a common mistake of fact, then to the extent of the rectification there can plainly be no estoppel based on the original form of the instrument. It is at least equally clear that in equity a party to a deed could not set up an estoppel in reliance on a deed in relation to which there is an equitable right to rescission or in reliance on an untrue statement or an untrue recital induced by his own representation, whether innocent or otherwise, to the

[90] (1834) 4 L.J.K.B. 58.
[91] *ibid.* at 61, *per* Lord Denman.
[92] *Stroughill v. Buck* (1850) 14 Q.B. 781.
[93] [1937] 4 All E.R. 396.

other party. Authority is scarcely needed for so clear a consequence of a rectification order or an admitted or proved right to such an order. The well-known rule of the Chancery courts in regard to a receipt clause in a deed not effecting an estoppel if the money has not in fact been paid is a good illustration of the equity view . . . The decision of Lord Romilly in *Brooke v. Haymes*[94] is even more closely in point, and it may be added that the statement of the law in that case appears never to have been doubted. The headnote being as follows: 'A party to a deed is not estopped in equity from averring against or offering evidence to controvert a recital therein contrary to the fact, which has been introduced into the deed by mistake of fact, and not through fraud or deception on his part'.

Estoppel by conduct

In *Freeman v. Cooke*[95] the sheriff had seized goods under a writ of execution which belonged to Benjamin Broadbent. His brother, William, expecting execution against himself, had removed some of his own property to Benjamin's house. When the officers arrived, William assumed the writ was against himself and told them that the goods were Benjamin's, whereupon the officers produced their writ against Benjamin. William then claimed the goods belonged to another brother and finally admitted they were his. But the officers still removed the goods. William became bankrupt and his assignees sought to recover the goods. The sheriff as defendant to the action argued that the assignees were estopped by William's statements from denying that the property was Benjamin's:

Freeman v. Cooke (1848) 18 L.J. Ex. 114 at 119, *per* Parke B.

The only question is whether it be an estoppel. It is contended that it was, upon the authority of the rule laid down in *Pickard v. Sears*.[96] That rule is that 'where one by his words or conduct wilfully causes another to believe in the existence of a certain state of things, and induces him to act on that behalf, or to alter his own previous position, the former is concluded from averring against the latter a different state of things as existing at the time' . . . By the term 'wilfully', however, in that rule, we must understand, if not that the party represents that to be true which he knows to be untrue, at least that he means his representation to be acted upon, and that it is acted upon accordingly; and if, whatever a man's meaning may be, he so conducts himself that a reasonable man would take the representation to be true, and believe that it was meant he should act upon it, and did act upon it as true, the party making the representation would be equally precluded from contesting its truth; and conduct by negligence or omission, when there is a duty cast upon a person by usage of trade, or otherwise, to disclose the truth, may often have the same effect . . .

Estoppel by conduct comes about when a person by words or conduct causes another to believe in a state of affairs and induces him or her to act on that belief. That person is estopped from denying that state of affairs.

[94] (1868) L.R. 6 Eq. 25.
[95] (1848) 18 L.J. Ex. 114.
[96] (1837) 6 A.&E. 469.

As no reasonable person could have had any faith in any of William Broadbent's statements, there was no basis for any estoppel.

There are three[97] forms of such estoppel by conduct:

(a) estoppel by representation: where a person makes a representation of existing fact, by words or conduct, with the intention, actual or presumed, of inducing another to act on the faith of that representation and alter his or her position to his or her detriment, the representor is estopped from denying the facts as represented. In *Greenwood v. Martins Bank Ltd*[98] the plaintiff's wife forged his signature to cheques drawn on the defendant bank. The husband discovered the forgeries but did not tell the bank. Eventually he confronted his wife, threatening to disclose them. The wife killed herself. The plaintiff sought to recover from the bank the amounts paid out on the forged cheques:

Greenwood v. Martins Bank Ltd [1933] A.C. 51 at 57–58, _per_ Lord Tomlin

Mere silence cannot amount to a representation, but when there is a duty to disclose, deliberate silence may become significant and amount to a representation. The existence of a duty on the part of the customer of a bank to disclose his knowledge of such a forgery as the one in question in this case is rightly admitted . . . The appellant's silence, therefore, was deliberate and intended to produce the effect which it in fact produced — namely the leaving of the respondents in ignorance of the true facts so that no action might be taken by them against the appellant's wife. The deliberate abstention from speaking in those circumstances seems to me to amount to a representation to the respondents that the forged cheques were in fact in order, and assuming that detriment to the respondents followed, there were, it seems to me, present all the elements essential to estoppel.

In *Greenwood* the husband clearly owed the bank a duty to disclose his wife's misfeasance. A broader approach is apparent in *Taylor Fashions Ltd v. Liverpool Victoria Trustees Co Ltd*[99] the defendant landlords and the plaintiff lessees all acquiesced in the assumption that there was a valid option to renew the leases when the original term finished. That option was void for lack of registration but the lessees had altered the frontage and internal layout of the properties in reliance on extending the term of the leases. The plaintiffs sought specific performance of the lease and argued that the defendants were estopped from relying on the invalidity of the option clause:

[97] This text will not cover *High Trees* promissory estoppel: *Central London Property Trust Ltd v. High Trees House Ltd* [1947] K.B. 130.
[98] [1933] A.C. 51.
[99] [1981] 1 All E.R. 897.

Taylor Fashions Ltd v. Liverpool Victoria Trustees Co. Ltd [1981] 1 All E.R. 897 at 915j–916a, _per_ Oliver J.

. . . the more recent cases indicate, in my judgment, that the application of the . . . principle (whether you call it proprietary estoppel, estoppel by acquiescence or estoppel by encouragement is really immaterial) requires a very much broader approach which is directed to ascertaining whether, in particular individual circumstances, it would be unconscionable for a party to be permitted to deny that which, knowingly or unknowingly, he has allowed or encouraged another to assume to his detriment rather than to inquiring whether the circumstances can be fitted within the confines of some preconceived formula serving as a universal yardstick for every form of unconscionable behaviour.

So regarded, knowledge of the true position by the party alleged to be estopped becomes merely one of the relevant factors (it might even be a determining factor in certain cases) in the overall inquiry . . .

The doctrine of estoppel by acquiescence is not restricted to cases where the representor is aware of his or her strict rights and where the representee is led to believe that those rights will not be enforced against him or her. The test is one of unconscionability: here there was a mistake of law common to all the parties and whether the landlords were aware of the true position was just one of the factors to be taken into account in assessing unconscionability.

(b) estoppel by agreement: where the parties have agreed together to base their relationship on an accepted state of affairs, neither party can be allowed to deny that state of affairs. In *Cooke v. Loxley*[1] a landlord sued his tenant for use and occupation of the land. The defendant argued that the plaintiff had no title to the land but this evidence was rejected:

Cooke v. Loxley (1792) 5 T.R. 4 at 5, _per_ Lord Kenyon C.J.

. . . in an action for use and occupation it ought not to be permitted to a tenant, who occupies land by the licence of another, to call upon that other to show the title under which he let the land. This is not a mere technical rule but is founded in public convenience and policy . . . Here the defendant, who occupied the land, did so by the permission of the plaintiff, and then refused to pay his rent under an idea that he might contest the plaintiff's right; but the plaintiff could not be supposed to come to trial prepared to meet such a defence and to make out his title; such an action as the present does not involve the question of title.

Similarly an agent or bailee could not deny the title of the principal or bailor. This is an analogous situation to estoppel by representation or acquiescence and the test of unconscionability in *Taylor Fashions Ltd v. Liverpool Victoria Trustees Co Ltd*,[2] discussed above, must be relevant.

[1] (1792) 5 T.R. 4.
[2] [1981] 1 All E.R. 897.

(c) estoppel by negligence: in *Coventry, Sheppard & Co v. Great Eastern Railway,*[3] a railway company negligently issued two delivery orders in respect of only one consignment of wheat. As a result a fraudulent individual was enabled to obtain two advances from the plaintiff company. Were GER estopped from denying that there were two consignments?

> The negligence of the defendants was to the prejudice of the plaintiffs and allowed the fraud to be perpetrated upon them. It seems to me, therefore, that the defendants are estopped as against the plaintiffs, their negligence having been the immediate cause of the advance . . .[4]

Where the negligence leads to a state of affairs being incorrectly represented as true and enabling a fraud to be perpetrated, the party responsible is estopped from denying the truth of that state of affairs. Such circumstances can also be seen in *Moorgate Mercantile Co Ltd v. Twitchings*[5] where the plaintiffs were a finance company, the owners of a car that they let on hire purchase to a third party. That third party purported to sell it to the defendant who, before completing the purchase, checked with an organisation, Hire Purchase Information (HPI), that the vehicle was not subject to an HP agreement. HPI had been set up by finance companies to prevent fraud and both the plaintiffs and defendant were members but by oversight the plaintiffs had failed to register their interest in the vehicle. They sought to recover damages from the defendant for conversion as the car had now been sold on to a private person. The defendants argued that the plaintiffs were estopped from asserting their title to the car. The House of Lords held by a majority that there was no duty of care existing:

Moorgate Mercantile Co. Ltd v. Twitchings [1976] 2 All E.R. 641 at 659a–c, _per_ Lord Edmund-Davies

It is, of course, desirable that finance companies who are members of HPI should promptly and accurately notify HPI of any new agreement entered into, and this both in their own interest and in that of dealer-members of that organisation. But they are, I think, under no sort of obligation to join it at all, though Lord Denning M.R.[6] went so far as to say that they abstain at their peril, for even non-members may find themselves estopped by their failure to join from asserting title against an innocent buyer or seller. I have to say respectfully that such an approach illustrates the risk of creating legal duties where none was ever contemplated. In most situations it is better to be careful than careless, but it is quite another thing to elevate carelessness into a tort. Liability has to be based on a legal duty not to be careless, and I can find none in this case.

Dissenting, Lord Wilberforce concluded:

> . . . that a finance company belonging to the HPI scheme is under a duty towards dealers, members of HPI, to take reasonable care to register any hire-

[3] (1883) 11 Q.B.D. 776.
[4] *ibid.* at 780, *per* Brett M.R.
[5] [1976] 2 All E.R. 641.
[6] In the Court of Appeal — [1975] 3 All E.R. 314 at 325.

> purchase agreements to which it is a party so that if in reliance on the absence of any such registration a dealer acts to his prejudice the finance company is estopped from asserting his title against that dealer. In saying this I should make it clear that it does not follow that the finance company is under a similar duty to any other persons, *e.g.* non-member dealers or members of the public. These are separate categories as to which different considerations may apply . . .[7]

Estoppel by negligence does require a breach of duty to the victim and might well be seen simply as part of the substantive law of negligence. It has been argued that this form of estoppel could and perhaps should be subsumed within the category of estoppel by representation. All that is necessary is proof of intentional words, acts or conduct which can be reasonably construed as a representation by the representor to the representee who need not be in a direct relationship.[8] In *Moorgate Mercantile* this approach was considered and was rejected on the facts:

> To constitute an estoppel a representation must be clear and must unequivocally state the fact which, ultimately, the maker is to be prevented from denying. The answer given by HPI to the defendant's enquiry cannot in my opinion bear the meaning for which the defendant must contend. It was simply and carefully drafted . . . It is quite clear that the answer given by HPI, both intrinsically and as it was understood by this particular motor dealer, conveyed nothing more than information as to the state of the records of HPI; it did not profess to and did not say anything as to the ownership or lack of ownership of any finance house members of HPI . . .[9]

Judgments as Evidence of the Facts upon which they were Based

Under the doctrine of estoppel by record, judgments can be conclusive:

- against the world as to the legal state of affairs or
- against the parties and their privies as to the facts on which a judgment was based.

But those who were not parties to an earlier case, although they are unable to dispute the legal state of affairs that case brings about, are not bound by the facts on which any earlier judgment was based. At common law, this doctrine is taken further: not only are the parties in subsequent litigation not bound by the facts as found in the previous judgment, they are unable to use that judgment even as evidence of the facts.

This is illustrated by *Hollington v. F. Hewthorn & Co Ltd.*[10] There was a collision between two cars in which the plaintiff's car was damaged. The drivers were the only eyewitnesses. The driver of the defendant's car was

[7] *ibid.* at 648b–c, *per* Lord Wilberforce.
[8] Tapper C., *Cross and Tapper on Evidence* (8th ed., 1995), p. 105.
[9] *Moorgate Mercantile supra* at 644g–645b, *per* Lord Wilberforce.
[10] [1943] 2 All E.R. 35.

convicted of careless driving. The plaintiff, who had not been involved in the accident, brought an action against the defendant and the convicted driver. Before the case came to court, the person driving the plaintiff's car died, depriving the plaintiff of his only witness. He sought to rely on the conviction to prove his case. The Court of Appeal held that the plaintiff was not entitled to use the conviction of the defendant driver as evidence of the latter's negligence. The rationale in part was founded on the principle that a later court should not be bound by the earlier court's opinion as to the facts.

It was a rule that also applied in criminal proceedings: in *R. v. Spinks*[11] a third party, F, had stabbed the victim and had been convicted under section 18 of the Offences Against the Person Act 1861. Spinks, who had played no part in the assault but had hidden the knife, was tried under section 4 Criminal Law Act 1967 with doing an act intended to impede the prosecution of a person, knowing or believing that person to be guilty of an arrestable offence. The defendants were tried together but the Court of Appeal were of the opinion that, had F been tried and convicted prior to Spinks, his conviction would not have been admissible evidence that F had committed an arrestable offence:

***R. v. Spinks* [1982] 1 All E.R. 587 at 589b–e, *per* Russell J.**

. . . the only evidence that Fairey had stabbed anyone came from his own admissions to the police, made in the absence of the appellant . . . The short point that is taken, therefore, is that the Crown had no admissible evidence as against the appellant to prove the first ingredient of the offence with which he was charged, namely as alleged in the particulars of offence, that Fairey had committed the arrestable offence of wounding. The only evidence of that fact came from an out of court admission of a co-defendant which was not admissible against the appellant.

For the Crown, it was argued that in some way the admission of Fairey was 'evidence in the case', and that the jury could act on it when considering the case of the appellant. But, as it seems to this court, the fallacy of that argument can be demonstrated in a number of ways. If Fairey had pleaded guilty and had not given evidence against the appellant, or if the appellant had been indicted and tried separately, could the Crown have relied on Fairey's conviction to prove the first ingredient of the offence? The answer must be in the negative. The appellant can be in no worse position because he was being tried alongside Fairey . . .

This absurd position has now been altered as a result of sections 11–13 of the Civil Evidence Act 1968 and section 74 of the Police and Criminal Evidence Act 1984.

Civil proceedings — convictions

The narrow ratio of *Hollington* was that in civil proceedings a conviction was not admissible evidence of the fact that the person concerned committed the offence in question. Under the Civil Evidence Act 1968:

11 [1982] 1 All E.R. 587.

11.—(1) In any civil proceedings the fact that a person has been convicted of an offence by or before any court in the United Kingdom or by a court-martial there or elsewhere shall (subject to subsection (3) below) be admissible in evidence for the purpose of proving, where to do so is relevant to any issue in those proceedings, that he committed that offence, whether he was so convicted upon plea of guilty or otherwise and whether or not he is a party to the civil proceedings; but no conviction other than a subsisting one shall be admissible in evidence by virtue of this section.

(2) In any civil proceedings in which by virtue of this section a person is proved to have been convicted of an offence by or before any court in the United Kingdom or by a court-martial there or elsewhere —

(a) he shall be taken to have committed that offence unless the contrary is proved; and
(b) without prejudice to the reception of any other admissible evidence for the purpose of identifying the facts on which the conviction was based, the contents of any document which is admissible as evidence of the conviction, and the contents of the information, complaint, indictment or charge-sheet on which the person in question was convicted, shall be admissible in evidence for that purpose.

Any party seeking to rely on a previous conviction under the section must, in the pleadings, give particulars of that conviction as well as indicating the issue in the case to which the conviction is relevant.[12]

This section overturns *Hollington*. It applies only to subsisting convictions. "Subsisting" excludes those which have been quashed on appeal but not those pending appeal,[13] nor those which are spent under the Rehabilitation of Offenders Act 1974.[14] "Convictions" do not include convictions in foreign courts or any findings of police disciplinary tribunals.[15]

It is clear that, where a conviction is proved, section 11(2) puts the legal burden of disproof onto the party denying the facts on which the conviction was based. This appears to be proof on the balance of probabilities.[16] In *Taylor v. Taylor*[17] Davies L.J. said:

> [s.11] . . . means that the onus of proof of upsetting the previous conviction is on the person who seems to do so. It is probable . . . that that is an onus of proof on the balance of probabilities. But, having said that, it nevertheless is obvious that, when a man has been convicted by 12 of his fellow countrymen and countrywomen at a criminal trial, the verdict of the jury is a matter which is entitled to very great weight when the convicted person is seeking, in the words of the statute, to prove the contrary[18]

[12] R.S.C., Ord. 18, r.17A.
[13] *Re Raphael Raphael v. D'Antin* [1973] 3 All E.R. 19.
[14] s.4.
[15] *Thorpe v. Chief Constable of the Greater Manchester Police* [1989] 2 All E.R. 827.
[16] *Sutton v. Sutton* [1969] 3 All E.R. 1348.
[17] [1970] 2 All E.R. 609.
[18] *ibid.* at 613.

In *Stupple v. Royal Insurance Co Ltd*[19] the plaintiff had been convicted of robbing a bank. During a police search, a sum of money had been found in the plaintiff's possession which had been paid over to the defendants who had indemnified the bank. The plaintiff now sought the recovery of that money:

Stupple v. Royal Insurance Co. Ltd [1970] 3 All E.R. 230 at 239b–j, _per_ Buckley L.J.

The effect of the bare proof of conviction is, I think, spent in bringing section 11(2)(a) into play. But very much weight may have to be given to such circumstances of the criminal proceedings as are brought out in the evidence in the civil action. Witnesses may be called in the civil proceedings who might have been but were not called in the criminal proceedings, or vice versa. The judge may feel that he should take account of the fact that the judge or jury in the criminal proceedings disbelieved a witness who is called in the civil proceedings or that the defendant pleaded guilty or not guilty, as the case may be. Many examples could be suggested of ways in which what occurred or did not occur in the criminal proceedings may have a bearing on the judge's decision in the civil proceedings: but the judge's duty in the civil proceedings is still to decide that case on the evidence adduced to him. He is not concerned with the evidence in the criminal proceedings except so far as it is reproduced in the evidence called before him, or is made evidence in the civil proceedings under the Civil Evidence Act 1968, s.2, or is established before him in cross-examination. He is not concerned with the propriety of the conviction except so far as his view of the evidence before him may lead him incidentally to the conclusion that the conviction was justified or open to criticism: but even if it does so, this must be a consequence of his decision and cannot be a reason for it. The propriety or otherwise of the conviction is irrelevant to the steps leading to his decision.

It was suggested in argument that so to view section 11 would result in the issues in the criminal proceedings being retried in the civil proceedings, and that this would be contrary to an intention of the part of the legislature to avoid this sort of duplication.

I do not myself think that this would be the result in most cases, and I do not discern any such general intention in the section. If the fact of conviction were meant to carry some weight in determining whether the convicted man has successfully discharged the onus under section 11(2)(a) of proving that he did not commit the offence, what weight should it carry? I cannot accept that this should depend on such considerations as, for instance, the status of the court which convicted, or whether the decision was unanimous or a majority verdict of a jury. I cannot discover any measure of the weight which the unexplored fact of conviction should carry. Although the section has made proof of conviction admissible and has given proof of conviction a particular statutory effect under section 11(2)(a), it remains, I think, as true today as before the Act that mere proof of conviction proves nothing relevant to the plaintiff's claim, and it clearly cannot be intended to shut out or, I think, to mitigate the effect of any evidence tending to show that the convicted person did not commit the offence. In my judgment, proof of conviction under this section gives rise to the statutory presumption laid down in section 11(2)(a), which, like any other statutory presumption, will give way to evidence establishing the contrary on the balance of probability, without itself affording any evidential weight to be taken into account in determining whether that onus has been discharged.

[19] [1970] 3 All E.R. 230.

In *Hunter v. Chief Constable of West Midlands Police*[20] Lord Denning suggested that the weight given to proof of conviction was much greater, requiring the convicted person to show that the conviction was obtained by fraud or collusion or by adducing fresh and conclusive evidence. In the House of Lords, Lord Diplock disapproved of this, reiterating that the standard of proof was on the balance of probabilities, although after a conviction, that would be an uphill task.[21]

Civil proceedings — findings of paternity or adultery

12.—(1) In any civil proceedings—

(a) the fact that a person has been found guilty of adultery in any matrimonial proceedings; and
(b) the fact that a person has been found to be the father of a child in relevant proceedings before any court in England and Wales or has been adjudged to be the father of a child in affiliation proceedings before any court in the United Kingdom,

shall (subject to subsection (3) below) be admissible in evidence for the purpose of proving, where to do so is relevant to any issue in those civil proceedings, that he committed the adultery to which the finding relates or, as the case may be, is (or was) the father of that child, whether or not he offered any defence to the allegation of adultery or paternity and whether or not he is a party to the civil proceedings; but no finding or adjudication other than a subsisting one shall be admissible in evidence by virtue of this section.

(2) In any civil proceedings in which by virtue of this section a person is proved to have been found guilty of adultery as mentioned in subsection (1)(a) above or to have been found or adjudged to be the father of a child as mentioned in subsection (1)(b) above —

(a) he shall be taken to have committed the adultery to which the finding relates or, as the case may be, to be (or have been) the father of that child, unless the contrary is proved; and
(b) without prejudice to the reception of any other admissible evidence for the purpose of identifying the facts on which the finding or adjudication was based, the contents of any document which was before the court, or which contains any pronouncement of the court, in the other proceedings in question shall be admissible in evidence for that purpose.[22]

This makes provisions, parallel to those relating to convictions, for findings of adultery or paternity in previous proceedings. Again the effect is to shift the burden of proof onto the party seeking to deny such findings.

Civil proceedings — defamation actions

Under section 13, a conviction is conclusive in a defamation action. As a matter of public policy, a person should not incur liability for stating that a

[20] [1980] 2 All E.R. 227.
[21] [1981] 3 All E.R. 727 at 735–6.
[22] As amended by the Family Law Reform Act 1987, s.29.

person is guilty of an offence for which he or she has been convicted. A convicted person cannot use the libel laws to re-open a conviction, even where there is considerable evidence of innocence which is well known to the defendant:

> 13.—(1) In an action for libel or slander in which the question whether the plaintiff did or did not commit a criminal offence is relevant to an issue arising in the action, proof that, at the time when that issue falls to be determined, he stands convicted of that offence shall be conclusive evidence that he committed that offence; and his conviction thereof shall be admissible in evidence accordingly.
>
> (2) In any such action as aforesaid in which by virtue of this section the plaintiff is proved to have been convicted of an offence, the contents of any document which is admissible as evidence of the conviction, and the contents of the information, complaint, indictment or charge-sheet on which he was convicted, shall, without prejudice to the reception of any other admissible evidence for the purpose of identifying the facts on which the conviction was based, be admissible in evidence for the purpose of identifying those facts.
>
> (2A) In the case of an action for libel or slander in which there is more than one plaintiff —
>
> (a) the references in subsections (1) and (2) above to the plaintiff shall be construed as references to any of the plaintiffs, and
> (b) proof that any of the plaintiffs stands convicted of an offence shall be conclusive evidence that he committed that offence so far as that fact is relevant to any issue arising in relation to his cause of action or that of any other plaintiff.[23]

In contrast, proof of an acquittal is not admissible evidence.

Civil proceedings — acquittals and other judicial findings

The general rule is that acquittals are not conclusive evidence of innocence. In *Loughans v. Odhams Press*[24] the plaintiff brought a libel action against the defendants for publishing a statement that suggested that he had in fact committed a murder twenty years previously although he had been acquitted of that murder. The defendants pleaded justification and proved on the balance of probabilities that the plaintiff was guilty, a finding which is not inconsistent with the result of the original trial where the prosecution failed to prove the defendant guilty beyond reasonable doubt. Public policy considerations might suggest that a person acquitted of a crime should be immune from further allegations that he or she committed the offence:

> . . . in defamation actions, where the statement complained of alleges that the plaintiff had been guilty of a criminal offence, proof that he has been convicted of that offence and that the conviction has not been set aside should be conclusive evidence of his guilt, and proof that he was acquitted of that offence should be conclusive evidence of his innocence.[25]

[23] As amended by the Defamation Act 1996, s.12.
[24] [1963] 1 Q.B. 299.
[25] Law Reform Committee: *15th Report* (1967) Cmnd. 3391, para. 41.

But the question remains as to whether an acquittal is admissible evidence at all? A broad reading of *Hollington* would exclude not merely convictions but judicial findings generally as evidence of the facts on which they are based. *Hollington* might thus be held to apply to all other judicial findings which do not come within the scope of sections 11–13 of the Act, including acquittals and findings in a civil court. For example, a driver, D, is involved in an accident with another car injuring another driver, A, and a passenger, B. Were A to sue D successfully for damages on the basis of the defendant's negligence, B may well not be able to rely on that finding of negligence if he or she brought a later action against the defendant. The only exceptions to such an argument are findings of adultery or paternity which are covered by section 12 of the Act.

Lord Denning's approach to this problem in *Hunter v. Chief Constable of West Midlands Police Force*[26] is much more robust,

> "Beyond doubt, Hollington v. Hewthorn was wrongly decided. It was done in ignorance of previous authorities. It was done, *per* incuriam."[27]

Denning goes beyond the question of using a previous judgment simply as evidence of its underlying facts and states that, in civil or criminal proceedings, where there is a judicial finding *against* a party, that person is estopped from disputing that issue in later actions unless it can be shown that there was collusion or fraud or that there was new evidence. This ratio applied not merely to judgments themselves but to findings such as a holding at *voire dire* that a confession was admissible evidence:

Hunter v. Chief Constable of West Midlands Police Force [1980] 2 All E.R. 227 at 238a–d, _per_ Lord Denning

To illustrate my view of the present law, I would take this example. Suppose there is a road accident in which a lorry driver runs down a group of people on the pavement waiting for a bus. One of the injured persons sues the lorry driver for negligence and succeeds. Suppose now that another of the injured persons sues the lorry driver for damages also. Has he to prove the negligence all over again? Can the lorry driver (*against* whom the previous decision went) dispute his liability to the other injured person? It seems to me that if the lorry driver (with the backing of his employer) has had a full and fair opportunity of contesting the issue of negligence in the first action, he should be estopped from disputing it in the second action. He was a party to the first action and should be bound by the result of it. Not only the lorry driver, but also his employer should be estopped from disputing the issue of negligence in a second action on the ground that the employer was in privity with the lorry driver.

Such a radical approach to issue estoppel would make the debate about the scope of the *Hollington* rule redundant. However Lord Denning's view

[26] [1980] 2 All E.R. 227, reported as *McIlkenny v. Chief Constable of West Midlands Police Force*. The House of Lords judgment is at [1981] 3 All E.R. 727.
[27] *ibid.* at 237a.

did not attract the support of the House of Lords although they avoided a direct decision on this point.

Civil proceedings — non-judicial findings

Many tribunals, formal and informal, hear evidence and come to findings of fact. For example, a rugby player punches another player, injuring him. The assailant is sent off by the referee for violent conduct. The player's county association have formal disciplinary proceedings to determine the punishment, usually a period of suspension from playing the game. But the victim also starts an action for damages for battery. Can either party use the findings of the disciplinary board as evidence in such proceedings? The introduction of such findings might be attacked on the grounds that they are hearsay (although now admissible under the Civil Evidence Act 1995). But should they be excluded under the *Hollington* rule? The broad rationale of that case, however ill-founded, was that a later court should not receive as evidence an earlier court's opinion as to the facts and, right or wrong, that should be the common law position. There is no obvious reason to restrict this to judicial findings. But, were this to be taken to extremes, this would exclude the findings of any sort of inquiry or indeed the conclusions of an expert investigator. Perhaps this reveals the weakness in the *Hollington* decision. Certainly a preferable approach is taken in *Hill v. Clifford*[28] where the plaintiff was seeking dissolution of a dentists' practice on the grounds that his partners had been guilty of professional misconduct. There had been a hearing in front of the General Medical Council, operating in accordance with duty of inquiry under the Dentists Act 1878, who had ordered that the partners should be struck off the Register of Dentists. The Court of Appeal accepted that the order was admissible evidence of the fact that the Cliffords had been guilty of such misconduct.

Criminal proceedings — convictions

The Criminal Law Revision Committee considered that *Hollington v. Hewthorn* applied in criminal proceedings, giving as an example *R. v. Turner*[29] where it was suggested that in a case of receiving stolen property, the conviction of the thief would not have been admissible evidence that the goods had been stolen, a fact in issue which would have to be proved by other means.[30] More recently, in *R. v. Shepherd*,[31] landlords were charged with harassment of certain tenants. The landlords had been tried and convicted at an earlier hearing of the harassment of the same tenants in

[28] [1907] 2 Ch. 236.
[29] (1832) 1 Mood C.C. 347.
[30] *11th Report* (Cmnd. 4991) para. 218.
[31] [1980] Crim.L.R. 428.

the same building. Although the previous convictions of a defendant are normally inadmissible, the prosecution were allowed to adduce evidence of that conviction. The Court of Appeal quashed the conviction on the grounds that the previous conduct did not come within the similar fact rules[32] and was likely to unduly prejudice the jury.[33] The rejection of the conviction as evidence is some authority that the *Hollington* rule applied in criminal cases: the reasoning in *Shepherd* was that the prior conviction was the magistrates' court's opinion as to the landlord's intention and this is reminiscent of the rationale in *Hollington* that the opinion of the previous court is irrelevant on the trial of the issue in the present case. *Spinks*[34] and *R. v. Hassan*[35] provide additional support. In the latter case, the defendant was charged with living off immoral earnings of a prostitute. Her prior conviction for prostitution was deemed not to be admissible at the defendant's trial. These decisions have now been overturned by section 74 of the Police and Criminal Evidence Act 1984:

74.—(1) In any proceedings the fact that a person other than the accused has been convicted of an offence by or before any court in the United Kingdom or by a Service court outside the United Kingdom shall be admissible in evidence for the purpose of proving where to do so is relevant to any issue in those proceedings, that the person committed that offence, whether or not any other evidence of his having committed that offence is given.

(2) In any proceedings in which by virtue of this section a person other than the accused is proved to have been convicted of an offence by or before any court in the United Kingdom or by a Service court outside the United Kingdom, he shall be taken to have committed that offence unless the contrary is proved.

(3) In any proceedings where evidence is admissible of the fact that the accused has committed an offence in so far as that evidence is relevant to any matter in issue in the proceedings for a reason other than a tendency to show in the accused a disposition to commit the kind of offence with which he is charged, if the accused is proved to have been convicted of the offence —

(a) by or before any court in the United Kingdom; or
(b) by a Service court outside the United Kingdom,

he shall be taken to have committed that offence unless the contrary is proved.[36]

75.—Where evidence that a person has been convicted of an offence is admissible by virtue of section 74 above, then without prejudice to the reception of any other admissible evidence for the purpose of identifying the facts on which the conviction was based —

[32] See Chap. 14.
[33] But it may be argued that the previous conviction may well have been relevant to rebut a defence of accident or mistake, showing animosity to the tenants, and should have been admitted on analogy with the acquittal which was proved in *R. v. Ollis* [1900] 2 Q.B. 758.
[34] *supra.*
[35] [1970] 1 Q.B. 423.
[36] This subsection ensures that, if prior convictions are proved against an accused under Criminal Evidence Act 1898, s.1(f)(ii) or under Theft Act 1968, s.27(3), he or she is not estopped from denying them although he or she has the burden of disproof.

(a) the contents of any document which is admissible as evidence of the conviction, and
(b) the contents of the information, complaint, indictment or charge-sheet on which the person in question was convicted,

shall be admissible in evidence for that purpose.

These sections deal with convictions of persons other than the accused. These are admissible where proof of that conviction would be relevant to an issue in the case. Obviously the earlier convictions for wounding and for prostitution were directly relevant to the charges faced by the accused in both *Spinks* and *Hassan* but it is not always as clear. In *R. v. Robertson*; *R. v. Golder*[37] Robertson was charged with conspiracy to commit burglary and the Crown were permitted to adduce evidence of convictions for burglaries carried out by his alleged co-conspirators. These convictions showed that there was such a conspiracy although not that the defendant was a party to it:

R. v. Robertson [1987] 3 All E.R. 231 at 236a–237c, _per_ Lord Lane C.J.

The matter has already been considered by this court in . . . *R. v. O'Connor.*[38] O'Connor was charged with conspiring with a man named Beck to obtain property by deception. He pleaded not guilty and was tried. Beck pleaded guilty and evidence of that plea was admitted at O'Connor's trial . . . The following is an extract from the judgment in that case.

> The terms of section 74 clearly were designed, in the judgment of this court, to deal with the situation where it was necessary as a preliminary matter for it to be proved that a person other than the accused had been convicted of an offence. The object, it would seem, of the section is to avoid that matter having to be proved twice where the other person had already pleaded guilty to the offence it was necessary to prove. In effect therefore the object of the section, in our view, was to deal with cases where it was necessary to prove the conviction of another as a condition precedent to the conviction of the defendant of the charge laid against him. The most obvious example would be a case where it is necessary to prove against another that he was guilty of theft before the person before the court could be convicted of handling or harbouring.

Counsel for the appellant's case is that this view of the restricted application of section 74(1) is in accordance with the Criminal Law Revision Committee . . .

The heart of the problem is the correct interpretation of the expression 'issue in the proceedings'. Only when that is determined can the court decide what in the particular circumstances is relevant and thus admissible. . . . We think the time has come to attempt to provide some guidance for courts who have the task of applying s.74. The word 'issue' in relation to a trial is apt to cover not only an issue which is an essential ingredient in the offence charged, for instance in a handling case the fact that the goods were stolen (that is the restricted meaning), but also less fundamental issues, for instance evidential issues arising during the course of the

[37] [1987] 3 All E.R. 231.
[38] [1987] Crim.L.R. 260.

proceedings (that is the extended meaning). Section 74 by using the words 'any issue in those proceedings' does not seek to limit the word 'issue' to the restricted meaning indicated above. Although the Report of the Criminal Law Revision Committee is an indication that the committee may have been regarding the matter at least primarily in the restricted sense, it seems to us that we are not entitled to use that possibility as showing that the words of the section mean other than what they plainly state . . .

So far as the present case is concerned, there was certainly an issue. Indeed it was probably an issue in the restricted sense, namely the issue of whether there was a conspiracy between Poole and Long (of which their joint conviction of burglary was the clearest evidence). It was that conspiracy to which the prosecution sought to prove the appellant was a party . . .

Golder was charged with robbery at a garage. The prosecution produced a confession which the defendant contested. Two of the co-accused pleaded guilty to that offence and to a previous robbery. The Crown was also permitted to adduce evidence of these pleas:

> The prosecution contended that in the particular circumstances of this case those convictions were relevant. The admissions which he has according to the police made to them were contested. It was suggested to the officers that they had fabricated their story and that no such admission had been made. The prosecution's desire to put the convictions of Moran and Eley in was in order to show that the contents of the alleged confessions by the appellant were in accordance with the facts as they were known and the confessions were therefore more likely to be true.[39]

In *Golder*, the key issue was the weight to be accorded to the confession. The accused's statements in that confession provided details about the previous robbery by his co-accused. Proof that the robbery in fact took place went to the issue of the probative weight to be accorded to that confession. However in *R. v. Pigram*[40] two men were arrested transferring video recorders from a car into a lorry. On a joint charge of handling, one pleaded guilty and the other was convicted after the trial judge admitted the plea of guilty for the purpose of proving that the recorders were stolen goods. But does it? It proves that the co-accused believed the goods to be stolen but as he was not the thief, it seems an insubstantial basis for establishing that fact as against the defendant who, under section 74(2), now has to prove the contrary. The case also raises another point:

R. v. Pigram [1995] Crim.L.R. 808 at 809 — commentary by Prof. John Smith

Arguably, section 74 should have been limited by Parliament to convictions upon a plea of not guilty where the matter in question has been contested and decided by the court in the earlier case. The conviction upon a plea of guilty has more weight than the mere admission because of the solemnity of the occasion on which it is

[39] *ibid.* at 240c–e, *per* Lord Lane C.J.
[40] [1995] Crim.L.R. 808.

made and the consequences for the person pleading guilty; but there may be more than one motive for pleading guilty and the assumptions on which the plea is made may not be well founded.[41]

The key problem is fairness.[42] A co-accused's out-of-court statements are inadmissible evidence as against another accused for that reason and yet a defendant might find himself or herself being contaminated by a co-accused's guilty plea being admitted into evidence. In *R. v. Skinner*[43] one of the accused was charged with aiding and abetting rape. The actual rapist pleaded guilty and the Crown were permitted to introduce evidence of this, as it was relevant to the issue of the accomplice's liability. That aiding and abetting charge foundered at the close of the prosecution case when the judge ruled that there was no case to answer. But the trial continued since there were several defendants charged with rape and indecent assault on the same victim. The men were all convicted and argued that the admission into evidence of the guilty plea was not relevant to any issue affecting their guilt and was prejudicial as the jury might well have concluded that, if one of the men had realised that the victim was incapable of consenting, why should not the other accused have the same knowledge? The Court of Appeal held that under section 78 Police and Criminal Evidence Act 1984 the admission of the guilty plea would have had an adverse effect on the fairness of the proceedings and ordered a new trial.

The courts have remained concerned about the impact of section 74:

R. v. Robertson [1987] 3 All E.R. 231 at 237h–j, _per_ Lord Lane C.J.

Section 74 is a provision which should be sparingly used. There will be occasions where, although the evidence may be technically admissible, its effect is likely to be so slight that it will be wiser not to adduce it. This is particularly so where there is any danger of a contravention of s.78. There is nothing to be gained by adducing evidence of doubtful value at the risk of having the conviction quashed because the admission of that evidence rendered the conviction unsafe or unsatisfactory. Secondly, where the evidence is admitted, the judge should be careful, as the judge was here, to explain to the jury the effect of the evidence and its limitations.

In *O'Connor*, two men were charged with conspiracy to obtain property by deception. Beck pleaded guilty. At O'Connor's trial, the guilty plea was admitted but Beck was not called to testify for either the prosecution or the defence. The burden of proof was placed on the accused with no opportunity to cross-examine the main witness. The court excluded the evidence under section 78. Similarly in *R. v. Mattison*[44] two males were

[41] *Golder* decided that a guilty plea is a conviction within the meaning of section 74 — *supra* at 240a.
[42] Munday R., "Guilt by Association under Section 74 of Police and Criminal Evidence Act 1984" [1990] Crim.L.R. 236.
[43] [1995] Crim.L.R. 805.
[44] [1990] Crim.L.R. 117.

charged with gross indecency. One pleaded guilty while the other denied the offence. Although the plea was obviously relevant evidence, at the same time it was deeply prejudicial and was excluded on that basis.[45]

Presumptions

At trial, facts in issue or other relevant facts are only established by some form of judicial evidence. By this is meant witness testimony, documentary evidence or real evidence. As we have seen, the doctrine of judicial notice, estoppels and the use of previous judgments provide shortcuts to full proof. The last of these are presumptions. Presumptions operate where certain facts may be presumed to exist even in the absence of complete proof. For example, there is a presumption that a person is dead if that person has not been heard from for over seven years. As a result, a litigant who needs to prove that the person is dead, need not show that the person is in fact dead but merely that, during seven years, nobody who could be expected to have heard from them has in fact heard from them. An older example would be where a plaintiff's claim rested on his or her legitimacy: there is no need to have blood and DNA tests to show that you are the child of your lawfully married parents. If it is proved that you were born while your parents were still married to each other, you are presumed to be legitimate.

To put it in general terms, where a party is seeking to establish a relevant fact, he or she may be unable to do so but will be permitted to prove another fact from which that relevant fact will be presumed. There is a *basic* fact (the seven year absence, the birth during wedlock) and a *presumed* fact (the person's death, the plaintiff's legitimacy). When we use the word "presumption" in an evidentiary sense, this is what is meant.

The effect of applying a presumption is to change the allocation of risk of losing in relation to a particular issue. In the examples above, it would be for the party adversely affected to satisfy the court on the balance of probabilities that the person was still alive or that the plaintiff was not the biological offspring of his lawfully married parents. The discussion of presumptions is directly bound up with questions of the burden of proof. But the relationship between burden of proof and presumptions is complex as there can be differences in the nature of the burden which is allocated. It is necessary to distinguish between different categories of presumption, although many of these categories are not "true" presumptions and merely reflect the different senses in which the word is used.

As a way of stating the burden of proof

The first "category" of presumptions does not reflect "presumption" in the sense being employed here since the allocation of risk is not altered. If we

[45] See also *R. v. Curry* [1991] Crim.L.R. 274; *R. v. Hillier and Farrar* (1993) 97 Cr.App.R. 349; *R. v. Kempster* (1990) 90 Cr.App.R. 14.

take the example of the presumption of innocence, there is no requirement that a basic fact is proved before the presumption is raised. It is an alternative method of stating that the burden of proof in a criminal trial rests on the prosecution.[46] Where the Crown fails to satisfy the trier of fact of guilt, the accused must be acquitted. Similarly judges talk (loosely?) of the presumption of sanity:

Bratty v. Att.-Gen. for Northern Ireland **[1961] 3 All E.R. 523 at 535a–e, *per* Lord Denning**

[W]hilst the ultimate burden rests on the Crown of proving every element essential in the crime, nevertheless in order to prove that the act was a voluntary act, the Crown is entitled to rely on the presumption that every man has sufficient mental capacity to be responsible for his crimes; and that if the defence wish to displace the presumption they must give some evidence from which the contrary may reasonably be inferred. Thus a drunken man is presumed to have the capacity to form the specific intent necessary to constitute the crime, unless evidence is given from which it can be reasonably be inferred that he was incapable of forming it . . . So it also seems to me that a man's act is presumed to be a voluntary act unless there is evidence from which it can be reasonably be inferred that it was involuntary. To use the words of Devlin J. the defence of automatism 'ought not to be considered at all until the defence has produced at least prima facie evidence,' see *Hill v. Baxter*;[47] and the words of North J. in New Zealand 'unless a proper foundation is laid,' see *R. v. Cottle*.[48] The necessity of laying the proper foundation is on the defence: and if it is not so laid, the defence of automatism need not be left to the jury . . .

What, then, is a proper foundation? The presumption of mental capacity of which I have spoken is a provisional presumption only. It does not put the legal burden on the defence in the same way as the presumption of sanity does. It leaves the legal burden on the prosecution, but nevertheless, until it is displaced it enables the prosecution to discharge the ultimate burden of proving that the act was voluntary. Not because the presumption is evidence itself, but because it takes the place of evidence. In order to displace the presumption of mental capacity, the defence must give sufficient evidence from which it may reasonably be inferred that the act was involuntary . . .

The language of presumptions in this context is not helpful since the questions before the court are "To whom does the law allocate the evidential burden of raising particular defences?" and "To whom does the law allocate the legal burden of proving or disproving those defences?" As we have seen, the defendant has the responsibility of raising particular defences, whether provocation, self-defence or insane or non-insane automatism. Normally he or she merely bears the evidential burden of proof, namely to adduce sufficient evidence that a reasonable jury properly directed might conclude that there was a reasonable doubt. The legal burden remains on the prosecution although with insanity, the accused bears not only this evidential burden but also the legal burden and must

[46] *Woolmington v. DPP* [1935] A.C. 462.
[47] [1958] 1 All E.R. 193 at 196.
[48] [1958] N.Z.L.R. 999 at 1025.

satisfy the jury that he or she is not sane on the balance of probabilities. Presumptions in the technical sense may be said to have nothing to do with it.

As conclusive proof of a fact

A second "category" of presumptions is that of irrebuttable or conclusive presumptions. Again it can be argued that these are not "true" presumptions but are rules of substantive law which provide that once the basic fact has been proved, the presumed fact is taken as established and no evidence to the contrary is admissible to rebut that conclusion. For example, at common law, boys under the age of 14 were conclusively presumed to be incapable of sexual intercourse and therefore could not be convicted of rape or other sexual offences of that nature.[49]

This form of "constructive" thought can be a tempting solution for judges and can emerge in unlikely places. In the common law, the doctrine of constructive malice in murder was an example of a conclusive presumption. It existed in two situations: killing an officer while resisting arrest and killing in the course of a felony where the intent to kill was presumed from either the intent to resist arrest or to commit the felony itself. The doctrine was abolished in 1957[50] but judges have long memories! In *DPP v. Smith*[51] the accused was stopped by a police officer who wished to examine his van in which there was stolen property. The accused drove off, seeking to avoid arrest, and the officer jumped on the bonnet, only to be thrown off and killed. Prior to 1957, this would have been murder. It was argued for the appellant that he lacked malice aforethought, in particular that he did not foresee serious harm coming to the officer:

DPP v. Smith [1960] 3 All E.R. 161 at 167a–d, _per_ Viscount Kilmuir

> The jury must, of course, in such a case as the present make up their minds on the evidence whether the accused was unlawfully and voluntarily doing something to someone. The unlawful and voluntary act must clearly be aimed at someone . . . Once, however, the jury are satisfied as to that, it matters not what the accused in fact contemplated as the probable result or whether he ever contemplated at all, provided he was in law responsible and accountable for his actions, that is, was a man capable of forming an intent, not insane within the M'Naghten Rules and not suffering from diminished responsibility. On the assumption that he is so accountable for his actions, the sole question is whether the unlawful and voluntary act was of such a kind that grievous bodily harm was the natural and probable result. The only test available for this is what the ordinary responsible man would, in all the circumstances of the case, have contemplated as the natural and probable result . . .

Lord Kilmuir came to the unfortunate conclusion that, if a reasonable person would have foreseen serious harm, the accused must be presumed

[49] *R. v. Groombridge* (1836) 7 C&P 582 — the common law presumption was overturned by s.1 of the Sexual Offences Act 1993.
[50] Homicide Act 1957, s.1.
[51] [1960] 3 All E.R. 161.

to have foreseen the same result, regardless of any evidence to the contrary, an irrebuttable evidential presumption of intention for murder.[52]

Many such conclusive presumptions are the creatures of statute. Under section 50 of the Children and Young Persons Act 1933:

> 50.—It shall be conclusively presumed that no child under the age of ten[53] can be guilty of any offence

and under section 13 of the Civil Evidence Act 1968:

> 13.—(1) In an action for libel or slander in which the question whether the plaintiff did or did not commit a criminal offence is relevant to an issue arising in the action, proof that, at the time when that issue falls to be determined, he stands convicted of that offence shall be conclusive evidence that he committed that offence; and his conviction thereof shall be admissible in evidence accordingly . . .

As a factual inference

These again are not presumptions in the technical sense but we use the language of presumptions to describe the processes of inferential thought. When an accused is shown to have stabbed, shot, raped or stolen, common sense logic leads to the conclusion that he or she intended those actions. A person is taken to intend the natural consequences of his or her acts.[54] That conclusion remains provisional and there is no rule of law that the jury must draw that conclusion. In the Court of Appeal decision in *DPP v. Smith*[55] Byrne L.J. put it clearly:

> Although . . . that is an inference which may be drawn, and on the facts in certain circumstances, must inevitably be drawn, yet if on all the facts of a particular case it is not the correct inference, then it should not be drawn.[56]

If a reasonable person would have appreciated the risk and thus intended the consequences, the jury was entitled to infer that the defendant did likewise. But in all the circumstances of the case, if that was not the correct inference, (*i.e.* if there was evidence that the accused did not intend those consequences), that inference should not be drawn. In other words, the fact in issue was the subjective state of mind of the accused. One could draw inferences about that by using common sense objective standards but such inferences were always rebuttable by evidence that the defendant was not, for example, a reasonable person!

[52] This result was overturned by Criminal Justice Act 1967, s.8. It is arguable that irrebuttable presumptions still infect malice aforethought since intent to cause serious harm is still regarded as sufficient mens rea for murder — *R. v. Cunningham* [1981] 2 All E.R. 863. Is this a hidden evidential presumption with the intent to cause GBH being the basic fact and the intent to kill being the presumed fact?.

[53] Substituted by the Children and Young Persons Act 1963, 16(1).

[54] *R. v. Steane* [1947] 1 All E.R. 813.

[55] [1960] 2 All E.R. 450.

[56] *ibid.* at 453.

Presumptions of fact are provisional inferences that we are willing to make unless and until there is further evidence which makes it necessary to reassess. Again these are not presumptions in the strict sense since this is the normal rational process by which inferences are drawn from evidence. The allocation of risk is not formally changed in any way. Thus, where the accused is provisionally assumed to have intended the offence, he or she is under neither a legal nor evidential burden to adduce evidence that there was no such intention. He or she would be entitled to a direction from the judge that the legal burden of proof lay on the Crown who must prove intent beyond reasonable doubt. Of course, informally, once the accused has been proved to have committed the act, he or she is at increased risk that the jury will find against them unless they adduce some evidence of lack of intent. But this is merely a shift in the tactical balance of the trial.

Other areas of such factual inferences are the continuance of life. In *R. v. Lumley*[57] a woman married her first husband in 1836, left him in 1843 and remarried in 1847. The trial judge held there to be a presumption of law that the first husband was alive at the date of the second marriage. The conviction was quashed:

***R. v. Lumley* (1869) L.R. 1 C.C.R. 196 at 198, *per* Lush J.**

. . . it is incumbent on the prosecution to prove to the satisfaction of the jury that the husband or wife, as the case may be, was alive at the date of the second marriage. This is purely a question of fact. The existence of the party at an antecedent date may, or may not, afford a reasonable inference that he is living at the subsequent date. If, for example, it was proved that he was in good health on the day preceding the marriage, the inference would be strong, almost irresistible, that he was living on the latter day, and the jury would in all probability find that he was so. If, on the other hand, it were proved that he was then in a dying condition, and nothing further was proved, they would probably decline to draw that inference. Thus, the question is entirely for the jury. The law makes no presumption either way.

Another example is proof of guilty knowledge, a necessary element before any conviction on charges of handling stolen property. The jury should be directed that where the accused is found in possession of recently stolen goods, that possession calls for an explanation and, if none is given, they are entitled to infer, according to the circumstances, that the defendant is the handler or the thief.[58] But the burden of proof remains on the prosecution and if the explanation given by the accused leaves the jury in doubt, then the Crown has not proved its case.[59] The judge is now able to direct the jury that they may draw inferences, probably adverse to the defence, in certain circumstances:

(1) under sections 34–37 of the Criminal Justice and Public Order Act 1994 where the accused has failed to mention a fact to the police

[57] (1869) L.R. 1 C.C.R. 196.
[58] *R. v. Schama* (1914) 11 Cr.App.R. 45; *R. v. Garth* [1949] 1 All E.R. 773.
[59] *R. v. Hepworth* [1955] 2 All E.R. 918.

which has later been relied on in the defence; where the accused has failed to testify; where the accused has failed to account for marks or possession of objects which suggests participation in the offence; where the accused has to account for his or her presence at a particular place which again would suggest participation in the offence.

(2) under section 11(3) of the Criminal Procedure and Investigations Act 1996. The statute requires a defendant to disclose the nature of the defence and where that statement of defence is flawed, inferences can be drawn. For example, the statement of defence may be non-existent or late, reveal inconsistent defences or be different from the defence put forward at trial.

The jury is entitled to draw such inferences as appear proper in the circumstances. Such inferences may well be about the *weight* that the jury are willing to give to evidence, for example, to a defence which has been advanced for the first time at trial. But the jury can also make *inferences* of fact, such as guilty knowledge from a failure to account to the police or the court for the possession of prohibited articles. Neither statute alters the formal position regarding the burden of proof but informally and tactically the prosecution's position is inevitably strengthened.

As rebuttable proof of a fact

This may be described as the true presumption, not as evidence but as a way of dealing with evidence. On the proof of a basic fact, a further fact is presumed to exist in the absence of evidence to the contrary. The allocation of risk shifts so that the party adversely affected by the presumption bears the burden of disproving it. This burden of disproof can be either a legal burden or an evidential burden.

(1) if a party proves that he or she was born while the mother and father were married, the legal burden of satisfying the court that he or she is illegitimate rests on the other party who must satisfy the court on the balance of probabilities and might, for example, bring in evidence to show that the alleged father was impotent or absent from the country at the relevant time

(2) the presumption of death arises where there is no affirmative evidence by people who are likely to have heard that the person has been alive during a continuous period of seven years. Once this has been demonstrated to the court, this casts a burden on the party seeking to show that that person was or is alive at the relevant time. In this case it is only an evidential burden and not a persuasive one. As long as some evidence to the contrary has been adduced, the persuasive burden still rests on the party who asserts that the person is dead.

In the U.S.A., presumptions are simply evidence. Under the Federal Rules of Evidence:

301.—In all civil actions and proceedings not otherwise provided for by Acts of Congress or by those rules, a presumption imposes on the party against whom it is directed the burden of going forward with evidence to rebut or meet the presumption, but does not shift to such party the burden of proof in the sense of the risk of nonpersuasion, which remains throughout the trial upon the party on whom it was originally cast.[60]

In outline, here are some of the commoner presumptions.

Doli Incapax

Under the common law, a child under the age of 14[61] is presumed to have insufficient understanding to distinguish between right and wrong and is therefore incapable of committing a crime. This presumption can only be rebutted by evidence that the child knew that what he or she was doing was wrong.[62] This rule has attracted judicial and academic criticism.[63] One reform which was mooted was the reversal of the presumption so that a child under 14 would be presumed to be capable of crime unless it was shown by the defence that he or she lacked the ability to distinguish between right and wrong:

Commentary by Birch D. on *JBH and JH (minors) v. O'Connell* [1981] Crim.L.R. 632 at 633

Evidence that any normal child of the accused's age would inevitably realise his act was so wrong might be thought to be sufficient to rebut the presumption in the absence of some evidence of abnormality. To place an evidential burden on the defence in such circumstances is consistent with the rules concerning proof of abnormality generally, but may overlook the degree of preoccupation with the state of mind of the individual which the courts exhibit in this area, often drawing their inferences from evidence of the upbringing, background and personal characteristics of the child in a way reminiscent of the inquiries conducted to decide whether a child can be sworn. Nevertheless it is submitted that the imposition of such a burden would be justified, and that the criticism voiced by Forbes J. that 'in these days of universal education from the age of five it seems ridiculous that evidence of some mischievous discretion should be required if a case of malicious damage is committed as it was in this case' cannot be said to be without foundation.

In *C. v. DPP*[64] the House of Lords reviewed the Divisional Court's ruling that the presumption was no longer good law. Lord Lowery recognised that there was a case for change but:

[60] Federal Rules of Evidence, r.301.
[61] A child under the age of 10 is presumed conclusively to be incapable of crime.
[62] *J.M. v. Runeckles* (1984) 79 Cr.App.R. 225; evidence of background and character, including previous convictions, is admissible for this purpose: *R. v. B* [1979] 3 All E.R. 460.
[63] There is a review by Lord Lowry in *C. v. DPP* [1995] 2 All E.R. 43.
[64] *supra.*

> The distinction between the treatment and the punishment of child 'offenders' has popular and political overtones, a fact which shows that we have been discussing not so much a legal as a social problem, with a dash of politics thrown in, and emphasises that it should be within the exclusive remit of Parliament.[65]

In the light of a long and uncontradicted line of authority, the House declined to abolish the presumption or to tailor it to modern needs, feeling that the imposition of full criminal responsibility from the age of ten was a matter best left to the legislature.

Presumption of Marriage

There are three presumptions linked to the fact of marriage itself: these are the presumptions of formal validity, essential validity and of marriage through cohabitation.

(1) *presumption of formal validity:* a marriage may be void because of a failure to observe some formality such as the reading of the banns or obtaining a licence. This presumption places the burden of proving such failures onto the person seeking to disprove the validity of the marriage. If two people, who intend to get married, go through a ceremony of marriage, there is a presumption that the marriage is formally valid and the burden of proving its invalidity is cast onto the other party. This is a legal burden. A leading case here is *Piers v. Piers*[66] in which a marriage was celebrated in a private house. There was no evidence that a special licence had been obtained but the House of Lords upheld the validity of the marriage. Once there was proof of the ceremony, the marriage was presumed to be valid unless the party contesting that validity can prove that it was not. This also applies to foreign ceremonies of marriage — *Mahadervan v. Mahadervan*[67] and this case also suggests that the standard of proof on the contesting party would be that of beyond reasonable doubt. But since that time, section 26 of the Family Law Reform Act 1969 has laid down a lower standard on the balance of probabilities for the presumption of legitimacy and it is difficult to think that different standards could rationally apply.

This presumption might be compared to another regarding the rightness of official acts, according to the maxim, *omnia praesumuntur rite esse acta*. Where a public official is shown to have acted as such, it is presumed that the act has been properly performed in the absence of evidence to the contrary. For example, *Berryman v. Wise*[68] concerned an action by an attorney for words spoken of him

[65] *C. v. DPP supra* at 64c.
[66] (1849) 2 H.L. Cas. 331.
[67] [1964] P. 233.
[68] (1791) 4 T.R. 366.

in the way of his profession and it was held that it was not necessary to prove that he was an attorney by production of his certificate or the roll of attorneys. In the case of peace officers, justices of the peace, constables and other such, it was sufficient to show that they acted in those characters without proving their appointment. In *R. v. Roberts*[69] the rule was applied to a county court judge. The burden appears to be only an evidential burden for the other party to produce some evidence that everything was not as it should be. The prosecution in criminal cases cannot rely on this to establish essential element of an offence. In *Dillon v. R.*,[70] a police officer was charged with allowing prisoners lawfully in custody to escape. Could the prosecution rely on the presumption to avoid adducing evidence as to the lawfulness of the custody?

Dillon v. R. [1982] 1 All E.R. 1017 at 1019h–1020b, _per_ Lord Fraser

Their Lordships are of opinion that it was essential for the Crown to establish that the arrest and detention were lawful and that the omission to do so was fatal to the conviction of the appellant . . . The lawfulness of the detention was a necessary precondition for the offence of permitting escape, and it is well established that the courts will not presume the existence of facts which are central to an offence (see *R. v. Willis*[71] and *Scott v. Baker*[72]).

Moreover this particular offence is one which touches the liberty of the subject, and on which there is, for that reason also, no room for presumptions in favour of the Crown. If there were to be a presumption that any person de facto in custody was there lawfully, the scales would be tipped in favour of the fait accompli in a way that might constitute a serious threat to liberty. It has to be remembered that, in every case where a police officer commits the offence of negligently permitting a prisoner to escape from lawful custody, the prisoner himself commits an offence by escaping, and it would be contrary to fundamental principles of law that the onus should be on a prisoner to rebut a presumption that he was being lawfully detained, which he could only do by the (notoriously difficult) process of proving a negative.

On the other hand, there is not likely to be any difficulty for the Crown in proving the lawfulness of the detention, when it exists. Production of the warrant for arrest, or of a magistrate's order for detention, or of a suitably certified copy, is normally all that is required . . .

(2) *presumption of essential validity:* a marriage is void if the parties lack the capacity to marry, for example, because of lack of age, of being too closely related, or of being already married to another person. The basic fact that there was, on its face, a proper ceremony of marriage raises the presumption that the parties had the capacity

[69] (1878) 14 Cox C.C. 101.
[70] [1982] 1 All E.R. 1017.
[71] (1872) 12 Cox C.C. 164.
[72] [1968] 2 All E.R. 993.

to marry. This is a rebuttable presumption with the legal burden on the party who seeks to invalidate the marriage. The standard is the ordinary civil standard of proof. In *Re Peete*[73] a woman claimed as the testator's widow under the Inheritance Act 1938. There was evidence that she had gone through a ceremony of marriage with the testator in 1919 but also evidence that she had been previously married although she testified that her first husband had been killed in 1916. The presumption of the validity of the 1919 marriage was rebutted by the evidence of the first marriage and the woman's testimony was insufficient to satisfy the burden of proof resting on her.

In *Monckton v. Tarr*,[74] H1 married W1 in 1882 only to desert her in 1887. W1 married H2 in 1895, at which time there was no evidence that H1 was still alive. However H2 left W1 and married W2 in 1913, knowing that W1 was still alive. W2 now claimed workmen's compensation as H2's widow. While the plaintiff can initially rely on the presumption in favour of the 1913 ceremony, this is rebutted by proof of the 1895 marriage and that W1 was still alive in 1913. This puts the burden of proof back onto the plaintiff who can only succeed by showing that the 1895 ceremony was a nullity and therefore that H2 was free to marry in 1913. In 1895 the first husband had been absent for seven years without contacting his wife and was thus presumed dead. W2 can only succeed by showing some evidence that H1 was alive at that time and this she is unable to do.

Such cases raise issues of conflicting presumptions:

Heydon J.D., *Evidence* (3rd ed., 1991) 64–65

Presumptions may conflict, but this is not typical of, nor limited to, presumptions of the same kind. But even two presumptions of the same kind need not conflict, because a presumption merely directs that a conclusion should or may be drawn in the absence of a certain amount of contrary evidence. How much contrary evidence depends on the degree of probability associated with the presumption and the circumstances of the case. A conflict between two presumptions of the validity of marriage is almost always illusory, because one in fact will be more probable than the other, and the general facts of the case will resolve any conflict between them, or at least will cause the case to be decided in accordance with the burden of proof. Further, presumptions of different kinds — a persuasive presumption and a provisional presumption — may or may not conflict; but this will not depend on the formal hierarchy but on the intrinsic weight of the presumptions on the facts. The persuasive presumption of innocence in theory outweighs the provisional or evidential presumption of theft based on the possession of stolen property; but if the accused does not testify he may very well be convicted. If H marries W1 (aged 70) in 1900, W2 (aged

[73] *Re Peete Peete v. Crompton* [1952] 2 All E.R. 599.
[74] (1930) 23 B.W.C.C. 504.

> 20) in 1930, and W3 in 1931, the persuasive presumption of the validity of the 1900 marriage does not conflict with the provisional presumption of the continuance of W1's life because the latter is so weak. On the other hand, the presumption of validity of the third marriage is much weaker than the presumption of the continuance of W2's life . . .

(3) *presumption of marriage from cohabitation:* there is a presumption that, if a couple are shown to have been living together, in the absence of contrary evidence, they are lawfully married. In *Re Taplin*,[75] the plaintiffs sought a declaration that their children were legitimate. The parents alleged that they had been married in Victoria in 1860 where registration was compulsory but there was no record in the Victoria archives. Despite this, the children were still declared legitimate. Similarly in *Re Taylor*[76] the presumption was held to apply although the period of cohabitation was short.

Presumption of Legitimacy

If a child is born or conceived during marriage, in the absence of sufficient evidence to the contrary, the child is presumed to be the legitimate offspring of the partners in that marriage. This presumption is made even where the parties are living apart or divorce proceedings have been started: although in such cases, evidence of rebuttal might be easier to obtain. The presumption puts a persuasive legal burden on the party seeking to disprove legitimacy. At common law the standard was beyond reasonable doubt but is now on the balance of probabilities as a result of section 26 of the Family Law Reform Act 1969:

> Any presumption of law as to the legitimacy or illegitimacy of any person may in any civil proceedings be rebutted by evidence which shows that it is more probable than not that the person is illegitimate or legitimate as the case may be and it shall not be necessary to prove that fact beyond reasonable doubt in order to rebut the presumption.

Although simple evidence of adultery is probably insufficient to rebut the presumption, lack of access of husband to wife at the time of conception, impotence or infertility, cohabitation of wife with another, blood groups, admission by another of paternity may be evidence in rebuttal. There is less significance for this presumption nowadays as reforms in the area of family law have made the distinction between legitimate and illegitimate offspring less important, in addition to which DNA testing can provide conclusive proof of paternity.

Presumption of Death

Any party wishing to rely on the presumption of death must show that there is no affirmative evidence that the person has been alive during a continuous period of seven years and:

[75] [1937] 3 All E.R. 105.
[76] [1961] 1 All E.R. 55.

(1) that there were persons who would have been likely to have heard from that person. In *Chard v. Chard*[77] the husband married his first wife in 1909 and his second wife in 1933. He had last heard from his first wife in 1917 but he had been in prison during the period and was therefore not someone who was likely to have heard:

Chard v. Chard [1956] P. 259 at 269–273, _per_ Sachs J.

On the basis, which I have adopted, that any presumption of continuance of life is simply one of fact, the various decisions cited to me and the dicta therein become reconciled. Further, due weight can thus be given in each case to the different circumstances of any given individual, *e.g.* whether a friendless orphan or a gregarious man in public life, whether in good or bad health, and whether following a quiet or a dangerous occupation.

Turning next to the question as to presumptions of death (whether before or after a lapse of seven years) the same reasoning to my mind generally applies — save in one set of circumstances to which I will refer later. I respectfully agree with Harman J.'s conclusion in *Re Watkins*[78] that, where no statute applies, there is no 'magic' in the mere fact of a period of seven years elapsing without there being positive evidence if a person being alive. It is, generally speaking, a matter in each case of taking the facts as a whole and of balancing, as a jury would, the respective probabilities of life continuing and having ceased . . .

My view is thus that in matters where no statute lays down an applicable rule, the issue of whether a person is, or is not to be presumed dead, is generally speaking one of fact and not subject to a presumption of law.

To that there is an exception which can be assumed without affecting the present case. By virtue of a long sequence of judicial statements, which either assert or assume such a rule, it appears accepted that there is a convenient presumption of law applicable to certain cases of seven years' absence where no statute applies. That presumption in its modern shape takes effect . . . substantially as follows. Where as regards 'AB' there is no acceptable affirmative evidence that he was alive at some time during a continuous period of seven years or more, then if it can be proved first, that there are persons who would be likely to have heard of him over that period, secondly that those persons have not heard of him, and thirdly that all due inquiries have been made appropriate to the circumstances, 'AB' will be presumed to have died at some time within that period . . .

The present case is thus one where there is no suggestion that in 1917 the 1909 wife was other than a woman of normal health, nor any evidence of any fact by reason of which her expectation of life could be regarded as greatly sub-normal. There are many factors which, as previously mentioned, might have led her not to wish to be heard of by the [petitioner] or his family, that there is no one known who would naturally have heard of her, and there is no registration of a relevant death . . .

As a result the court held that there was no presumption of law in the case either of continuance of life or as to death and that the correct inference was that the first wife was still living at the time of the marriage ceremony in 1933.

[77] [1956] P. 259.
[78] [1953] 2 All E.R. 1113.

(2) that those persons have not heard. In *Prudential Assurance Co v. Edmonds*[79] there was a claim on a life insurance policy. Was Robert Nutt dead? He had not been heard of by the family but there was a niece who testified that she had seen him in Melbourne, but did not speak to him as she lost him in the crowd.

Prudential Assurance Co. v. Edmunds [1877] 2 A.C. 487 at 511, _per_ Lord Blackburn

Supposing the jurymen had found as a fact that they thought she was mistaken, would or would not the grounds have existed upon which the presumption from a seven years' absence would arise that the man not heard of was dead? I think certainly they would. It seems to me that when she said, 'I have seen the man in the streets of Melbourne,' it upset the presumption arising from the relatives, including herself, never having seen or heard of him, and it turned the onus the other way. It was possible, however, that it might have been proved that the man she saw was not Robert Nutt, but somebody else. If that had been proved, it would have left the matter just as if she had never made the statement. When she said she thought she had seen him, and all the others had heard it from her, although that unexplained and uncontradicted statement affected the onus, yet, as soon as it was made out by satisfactory evidence that she was mistaken, the hearing from her was gone, and the presumption would remain as it was before . . .

Seven years absence creates a presumption of death and there is an evidential burden on the party seeking to show that the person is still alive. The niece's evidence, if believed by the jury, satisfies that and the onus reverts to the party seeking to show that the person is not dead who must persuade the jury of this fact on the balance of probabilities.

(3) that the appropriate inquiries have been made although whether this needs to be proved depends on the circumstances.[80] Failure to make inquiries may be justified but conversely proof of proper investigation may render proof of the other basic facts unnecessary.

Where these conditions are satisfied and death is presumed, the problem arises as to the moment of that death. Is the person presumed to have died seven years before the court hearing or seven years after disappearance? The strict view is that the subject is only dead at the date of the proceedings. In *Chipchase v. Chipchase*,[81] Sir Boyd Merriman said:

That presumption — I am taking the statement of it from the judgment of Giffard L.J. in *Re Phene's Trusts*,[82] — is that 'the law presumes a person who has

[79] [1877] 2 A.C. 487.
[80] *Bullock v. Bullock* [1960] 2 All E.R. 307.
[81] [1939] P. 391.
[82] (1870) 5 Ch. 139.

not been heard of for over seven years to be dead, but in the absence of special circumstances draws no presumption from the fact as to the particular period at which he died.[83]

In *Phene's Trusts* the testator died in January 1861, leaving his estate to his nieces and nephews. One nephew had not been heard of since 1860 when he deserted from the U.S. Navy. A claim was made for his share of the estate but the court would not presume that he had survived the testator. The court did not apparently consider the strong factual inference that might have been drawn that the nephew continued to live from 1860 to 1861. In *Chipchase* the wife's complaint in front of the magistrates was of her husband's adultery, desertion and failure to maintain. She had gone through a ceremony of marriage with him in 1928, having gone through a previous ceremony with another man in 1915. She testified that she had not heard from her first husband for seven years before the second ceremony. The magistrates dismissed the complaint as there was no evidence that the first husband was dead. The Divisional Court remitted the case to the magistrates to consider whether there was any evidence to rebut the presumption of death which implies a more liberal view that the subject is presumed to have died at a date seven years after the disappearance.

There are various statutory provisions. By section 184 of the Law of Property Act 1925:

184.—In all cases where, after the commencement of this Act, two or more persons have died in circumstances rendering it uncertain which of them survived the other or others, such deaths shall (subject to any order of the court), for all purposes affecting the title of property, be presumed to have occurred in order of seniority, and accordingly the younger shall be deemed to have survived the elder.

By section 19 of the Matrimonial Causes Act 1973:

19.—(1) Any married person who alleges that reasonable grounds exist for supposing that the other party to the marriage is dead may . . . present a petition to the court to have it presumed that the other party is dead and to have the marriage dissolved, and the court may, if satisfied that such reasonable grounds exist, grant a decree of presumption of death and dissolution of the marriage.

(2) . . .

(3) In any proceedings under this section the fact that for a period of seven years or more the other party to the marriage has been continuously absent from the petitioner and the petitioner has no reason to believe that the other party has been living within that time shall be evidence that the other party is dead until the contrary be proved.

By the proviso to section 57 of the Offences Against the Person Act 1861 which defines the offence of bigamy:

[83] *Chipchase supra* at 393–394.

Provided that nothing in this section contained shall extend . . . to any person marrying a second time whose husband or wife shall have been continually absent from such person for the space of seven years then last past, and shall not have been known by such person to be living within that time.

Res Ipsa Loquitur

Where a swab is left in a patient after surgery, a sack of sugar falls from a warehouse crane or a car crosses the central reservation of a dual carriageway and collides with vehicles travelling in the opposite direction, the incident is such that observers assume that the accident has occurred because of the negligence of the surgeon, the warehouse keeper or the driver and will stick to that conclusion in the absence of any contradictory information. The plaintiff, normally suing for personal injuries, still is under the obligation to prove negligence which can be onerous since the true cause of the accident is often only known to the defendant. However the law adopts a common sense inference: where some thing is shown to have been under the management of the defendant or his or her servants and the accident which occurred was such that in the ordinary course would not have happened, there is a presumption that *res ipsa loquitur*, the thing speaks for itself, and that the accident was the result of negligence:

> But where the thing is shown to be under the management of the defendant or his servants, and the accident is such as in the ordinary course of things does not happen if those who have the management use proper care, it affords reasonable evidence, in the absence of explanation by the defendants, that the accident arose from want of care.[84]

The problem is the impact of this maxim. It can be treated in three ways:

(1) *as an inference of fact:* were the defendant to adduce no evidence of reasonable care, although tactically unwise, the trier of fact would not be bound to find in the plaintiff's favour. In some circumstances, the facts raising the presumption may be weaker than in others and even if the defendant produced no evidence, he or she may still win

(2) *as a persuasive presumption:* the presumption would alter the burden of proof so that the defendant would need to show on the balance of probabilities that he or she was not negligent. In *Barkway v. South Wales Transport*[85] the defendant's bus had fallen down an embankment. The defendant adduced evidence that it had left the road because of a burst tyre:

[84] *Scott v. London and St Katherine Docks Co* (1865) 3 H&C 596 at 601, *per* Erle C.J.
[85] [1948] 2 All E.R. 460; see also *Woods v. Duncan* [1946] A.C. 401.

Barkway v. South Wales Transport [1948] 2 All E.R. 460 at 471, _per_ Asquith L.J.

. . . (i) If the defendant's omnibus leaves the road and falls down an embankment, and this without more is proved, then res ipsa loquitur, there is a presumption that the event is caused by negligence on the part of the defendants, and the plaintiff succeeds unless the defendants can rebut this presumption. (ii) It is no rebuttal for the defendants to show, again without more, that the immediate cause of the omnibus leaving the road is a tyre-burst, since a tyre-burst *per se* is a neutral event consistent, and equally consistent, with negligence or due diligence on the part of the defendants. When a balance has been tilted one way, you cannot redress it by adding an equal weight to each scale. The depressed scale will remain down . . . (iii) To displace the presumption, the defendants must go further and prove (or it must emerge from the evidence as a whole) either (a) that the burst itself was due to a specific cause which does not connote negligence on their part but points to its absence as more probable, or (b), if they can point to no more such specific cause, that they used all reasonable care in and about the management of their tyres.

(3) *as an evidential presumption:* the presumption would not alter the legal burden of proof but merely the evidential burden so that the defendant must adduce some evidence of reasonable diligence. In such circumstances, the legal burden remains on the plaintiff so that were the probabilities to remain balanced, the plaintiff would lose. In *Ng Chun Pui v. Lee Chuen Tat*[86] a coach owned by the defendants left the carriageway, crossed the central reservation and collided with a bus being driven in the opposite direction. The plaintiffs relied on the fact of the accident as evidence of negligence under the doctrine of *res ipsa loquitur*:

Ng Chun Pui v. Lee Chuen Tat [1988] R.T.R. 298, _per_ Lord Griffiths (delivering the judgment of the Privy Council)

. . . There can be no doubt that the plaintiffs were justified in taking this course. In ordinary circumstances if a well-maintained coach is being properly driven it will not cross the central reservation of a dual carriageway and collide with on-coming traffic in the other carriageway. In the absence of any explanation of the behaviour of the coach the proper inference to draw is that it was not being driven with the standard of care required by the law and that the driver was therefore negligent. If the defendants had called no evidence the plaintiffs would undoubtedly have been entitled to judgment . . . [The judge] made the following findings of fact:

'The evidence led by the defendants shows clearly that the coach was proceeding along a straight stretch of the road . . . The coach was travelling in the fast or outer lane and in that lane there was other traffic about two coach lengths ahead of it. In the inner lane there was a vehicle about 10 to 20 feet ahead and between that vehicle and the coach there was a blue car

[86] [1988] R.T.R. 298.

travelling a little faster than the coach. Suddenly that blue car, which did not subsequently stop and has not been traced, cut into the fast lane some six to eight feet ahead of the coach. That was clearly a very dangerous manoeouvre and the first defendant reacted to it by braking and swerving a little to his right. The coach then skidded across the central reservation . . .'

The judge however was of the view that, despite those findings of fact, because the plaintiffs had originally relied upon the doctrine of *res ipsa loquitur*, the burden of disproving negligence remained upon the defendants and they had failed to discharge it. In their Lordships' opinion this shows a misunderstanding of the so-called doctrine of res ipsa loquitur, which is no more than the use of a Latin maxim to describe a state of the evidence from which it is proper to draw an inference of negligence. Although it had been said in a number of cases, it is misleading to talk of the burden of proof shifting to the defendant in a *res ipsa loquitur* situation. The burden of proving negligence rests throughout the case on the plaintiff. Where the plaintiff has suffered injuries as a result of an accident which ought not to have happened if the defendant had taken due care, it will often be possible for the plaintiff to discharge the burden of proof by inviting the court to draw the inference that on the balance of probabilities the defendant must have failed to exercise due care, even though the plaintiff does not know in what particular respects the failure occurred . . .

So in an appropriate case the plaintiff establishes a prima facie case by relying upon the fact of the accident. If the defendant adduces no evidence there is nothing to rebut the inference of negligence and the plaintiff will have proved his case. But if the defendant does adduce evidence that evidence must be evaluated to see if it is still reasonable to draw the inference of negligence from the mere fact of the accident. Loosely speaking this may be referred to as a burden on the defendant to show that he was not negligent, but that only means that faced with a prima facie case of negligence the defendant will be found negligent unless he produces evidence that is capable of rebutting the prima facie case. Resort to the burden of proof is a poor way to decide a case; it is the duty of the judge to examine all the evidence at the end of the case and decide whether on the facts he finds to have been proved and on the inferences he is prepared to draw he is satisfied that negligence has been established. In so far as resort is had to the burden of proof the burden remains at the end of the case as it was at the beginning upon the plaintiff to prove that his injury was caused by the negligence of the defendants . . .

The English authorities show divergent approaches to the problem, some suggesting that the presumption shifts the legal burden of proof, others that it merely casts an evidential burden on the defendant. However the strength of the presumption necessarily varies with the basic facts which bring it into play and the cases suggest that it has no artificial weight superior to its natural weight. Is it appropriate to label it persuasive, evidential or provisional?[87]

[87] Heydon, *op. cit.* at 60.

INDEX